D1367589

COMMON
ENGLISH
BIBLE

a translation to touch the heart and mind

COMMON ENGLISH BIBLE

a translation to touch the heart and mind

New Testament, Psalms, and Proverbs

978-1-60926-212-9 Flexcover Pocket Thinline New Testament, Psalms, and Proverbs
978-1-60926-164-8 Deluxe Baby New Testament, Psalms, and Proverbs

www.CommonEnglishBible.com

To His Glory
Printed in China

978-1-60926-212-9	CEB Pocket New Testament with Psalms and Proverbs
978-1-60926-194-8	CEB Baby New Testament with Psalms and Proverbs

17 18 19 20 21 22 23 24—10 9 8 7 6 5 4 3
Printed in China

CONTENTS

CONTENTS

CONTENTS
ALPHABETICAL

CONTENTS
ALPHABETICAL

ABBREVIATIONS

Aram Aramaic
Gk Greek
Gk uncertain the meaning of the Greek text is uncertain
Heb Hebrew
Heb uncertain the meaning of the Hebrew text is uncertain
Lat Latin
LXX Septuagint (Greek translation of Hebrew Bible)
OL Old Latin (manuscripts in Latin prior to the Vulgate)
Syr Syriac (a translation known as the Peshitta in a dialect of the Aramaic language)
Tg Targum (Aramaic translation of Hebrew Bible)
Vulg Vulgate (standardized Latin version of the Bible)

WEIGHTS AND MEASURES

denarion, denaria (pl) *a coin equivalent in value to one day's work*
drachme, drachmen (pl) *a silver coin equivalent in value to a denarion; also possibly a daric*
kodrantes *a coin equivalent to two lepta*
lepto, lepta (pl) *a coin equivalent to 1/128 of a denarion*
litra *a Roman pound equal to approximately twelve ounces dry*
maneh, manehs (pl) *in Hebrew possibly fifty or sixty sanctuary shekels, in Greek a monetary unit equivalent to one hundred denaria*
pechon *traditionally a cubit, equal to approximately eighteen inches*
stadion, stades (pl) *a Roman linear measurement of approximately 607 feet*
talanta, talantas (pl) *a coin equivalent to six thousand denaria; traditionally a talent. In the Greek period, one talent is approximately 57 pounds of weight.*

We encourage you to carry this pocket New Testament with you wherever you go. It's small enough to fit inside a purse or back pocket. When you have a few extra minutes during the day, take it out and read it. If you meet someone who needs it, give it to them and pick up another.

Tips for Reading the Bible with Understanding

Often when people begin reading the Bible they find it frustrating and difficult to understand. Here are a few tips you may find helpful:

1. Begin with prayer. Here's a simple one: *Lord, as I open the Bible to read, please speak to me. Open my heart and mind and allow me to hear your word for my life. Amen.*

2. Begin with the Gospel of Matthew. Read no more than one chapter.

3. Don't feel that you must understand everything. Find one or two verses that seem to speak to you.

4. Have a notepad handy to write down your insights and how the passage or verse speaks to you.

5. Ask these questions: *What does this passage teach me about God? About Jesus? About human beings? About God's will?*

6. Read the verses that spoke to you again, aloud this time. Then do it once more. What additional insights do you see?

7. Try praying the scripture. Read the scripture and turn it into a prayer. *Lord, help me to be more like . . .*

8. Don't give up. If a chapter doesn't yield any verses that speak to you, move on to the next chapter.

May this book be a lamp before your feet and a light for your journey
(Psalm 119:105)

Pastor Adam Hamilton
The United Methodist Church of the Resurrection

NEW TESTAMENT NINETY-DAY READING PLAN

If you've always wanted to read through the Bible but never found an entry point to get started, the New Testament is a great place to begin. With this Bible reading plan, you will typically read two or three chapters each day for ninety days.

1. Matthew 1–2
2. Matthew 3–4
3. Matthew 5–7
4. Matthew 8–9
5. Matthew 10–11
6. Matthew 12–13
7. Matthew 14–16
8. Matthew 17–18
9. Matthew 19–20
10. Matthew 21–23
11. Matthew 24–25
12. Matthew 26–28
13. Mark 1–2
14. Mark 3–4
15. Mark 5–6
16. Mark 7–8
17. Mark 9–10
18. Mark 11–12
19. Mark 13–14
20. Mark 15–16
21. Luke 1–3
22. Luke 4–5
23. Luke 6–7
24. Luke 8–9
25. Luke 10–11
26. Luke 12–14
27. Luke 15–17
28. Luke 18–19
29. Luke 20–22
30. Luke 23–24

31. John 1–3
32. John 4–5
33. John 6–7
34. John 8–9
35. John 10–11
36. John 12–14
37. John 15–17
38. John 18–19
39. John 20–21
40. Acts 1–2
41. Acts 3–4
42. Acts 5–7
43. Acts 8–10
44. Acts 11–13
45. Acts 14–16
46. Acts 17–18
47. Acts 19–20
48. Acts 21–22
49. Acts 23–24
50. Acts 25–26
51. Acts 27–28
52. Romans 1–3
53. Romans 4–5
54. Romans 6–8
55. Romans 9–10
56. Romans 11–13
57. Romans 14–16
58. 1 Corinthians 1–3
59. 1 Corinthians 4–6
60. 1 Corinthians 7–8

61. 1 Corinthians 9–11
62. 1 Corinthians 12–14
63. 1 Corinthians 15–16
64. 2 Corinthians 1–3
65. 2 Corinthians 4–6
66. 2 Corinthians 7–9
67. 2 Corinthians 10–11
68. 2 Corinthians 12–13
69. Galatians
70. Ephesians
71. Philippians, Colossians
72. 1 Thessalonians
73. 2 Thessalonians
74. 1 Timothy
75. 2 Timothy
76. Titus, Philemon
77. Hebrews 1–5
78. Hebrews 6–9
79. Hebrews 10–13
80. James
81. 1 Peter, 2 Peter
82. 1–3 John, Jude
83. Revelation 1–3
84. Revelation 4–6
85. Revelation 7–9
86. Revelation 10–12
87. Revelation 13–15
88. Revelation 16–18
89. Revelation 19–20
90. Revelation 21–22

PREFACE

The King James Version of the Bible was published in 1611. For two centuries the KJV competed for readership with the Geneva Bible. However, by the nineteenth century in America, the KJV would be described as the "common English Bible," because it was the most widely used translation of Christian scripture. Numerous translations have appeared since that time. However, it has proved difficult to combine concern for accuracy and accessibility in one translation that the typical reader or worshipper would be able to understand. Therefore, readers in the twenty-first century, four hundred years after the creation of the KJV, need and deserve a new translation that is suitable for personal devotion, for communal worship, and for classroom study.

The Common English Bible (CEB), completed in 2011, is a fresh translation of the Bible. Some editions include the books of the Apocrypha that are used in Anglican, Orthodox, and Catholic congregations. The translation is sponsored by the Common English Bible Committee, which is an alliance of denominational publishers, including Presbyterian (USA), Episcopalian, United Methodist, Disciples of Christ, and United Church of Christ representatives.

One hundred twenty biblical scholars from twenty-two faith traditions worked as translators for the CEB. In addition, members of seventy-seven reading groups from congregations throughout North America reviewed and responded to early drafts of the translation. As a result, more than five hundred individuals were integrally involved in the preparation of the CEB. These individuals represent the sorts of diversity that permit this new translation to speak to people of various religious convictions and different social locations.

The translators, reviewers, and editors represent the following faith communities: African Methodist Episcopal Church, American Baptist, Anglican, Baptist, Baptist General Conference, Church of the Nazarene, Disciples of Christ, Episcopal Church, Evangelical Free Church, Evangelical Lutheran Church, Free Methodist, Mennonite, Moravian, National Baptist, Presbyterian (USA), Progressive National Baptist, Quaker, Reformed Church in America, Reform Judaism, Roman Catholic Church, Seventh-day Adventist, United Churches of Christ, and United Methodist. The CEB is truly a Bible created by churches and for the Church.

Accuracy and clarity. The CEB translators balance rigorous accuracy in the rendition of ancient texts with an equally passionate commitment to clarity of expression in the target language. Translators create sentences and choose vocabulary that will be readily understood when the biblical text is read aloud. Two examples illustrate this concern for accuracy and clarity.

First, *ben 'adam* (Hebrew) and *huios tou anthrōpou* (Greek) are best translated as "human being" (rather than "son of man") except in cases of direct address, where CEB renders "human one" (instead of "son of man" or "mortal"; e.g., Ezek 2:1). When *ho huios tou anthropou* is used as a title for Jesus, the CEB refers to Jesus as "the Human One." People who have grown accustomed to hearing Jesus refer to himself in the Gospels as "the Son of Man" may find this jarring. Why "Human One"? Jesus's primary language would have been Aramaic, so he would have used the Aramaic phrase *bar enosha*. This phrase has the sense of "a human" or "a human such as I." This phrase was taken over into Greek in a phrase that might be translated woodenly as "son of humanity." However, Greek usage often refers to "a son of x" in the sense of "one who has the character of x." For example, Luke 10:6 refers in Greek to "a son of peace," a phrase that has the sense of "one who shares in peace." In the Greek of Acts 13:10 Paul calls a sorcerer "a son of the devil." This is not a reference to the sorcerer's actual ancestry, but it serves to identify his character. He is devilish—or more simply in English "a devil." Human or human one represents accurately the Aramaic and Greek idioms and reflects common English usage. Finally, many references to Jesus as "the Human One" refer back to Daniel 7:13, where Daniel "saw one like a human being" (Greek *huios anthropou*). By using the title Human One in the Gospels and Acts, the CEB preserves this connection to Daniel's vision.

Second, the phrase "Lord of hosts" (*Yahweh sebaoth* in Hebrew; *Kyrios sabaoth* in Greek) appears hundreds of times in older Bibles and persists as an idiom in translations that preserve King James usage. This archaic translation is no longer meaningful to most English speakers. The CEB renders *Yahweh sebaoth* and *Kyrios sabaoth* as "Lord of heavenly forces," which conveys accurately the meaning of the Hebrew and Greek phrases by using contemporary English language.

English speakers, especially when telling a story, writing a letter, or engaging in conversation, make frequent use of contractions. As a result, translators have often used contractions, particularly in direct speech, in the CEB. However, formal genres of literature typically do not include contractions. As a result, translators did not include contractions in contexts such as (a) formal trials or royal interviews (socially formal situations), (b) much divine discourse (e.g., Hos 11:9; Exod 24:12), and (c) poetic and/or liturgical discourse (several types of psalms).

Texts. Translators of the Old Testament used as their base text the Masoretic Text (MT) as found in Biblia Hebraica Stuttgartensia and the published fascicles of Biblia Hebraica Quinta. For some books the Hebrew University Bible Project was consulted. Judicious departures from the Masoretic Text, based on ancient manuscript (e.g., reading with the Dead Sea Scrolls in 1 Sam 10:27b or Deut 32:8) and versional evidence (e.g., reading with the Septuagint in Gen 4:8), were sometimes necessary. In those situations, in which one may postulate two literary editions of a biblical book, or in which there are major or lengthy differences between the Masoretic Text and other texts or versions (e.g., 1 Sam 17), the CEB translated the edition that became canon in the Masoretic Text.

Translators of the New Testament used as their base text the eclectic Greek text known as Nestle Aland, the twenty-seventh edition, which was published in 1993.

Translators of the Apocrypha faced a more complicated set of choices. Translators generally used the base text presented in the Göttingen Septuagint. For those books not yet published in the fascicles of the Göttingen Septuagint, translators used the 2006 revised edition of Rahlfs' Septuaginta, edited by Robert Hanhart. However, in those instances in which Hebrew texts have survived and offer a better reading (e.g., in Sirach and Tobit), the translator noted alternative readings to the Greek Septuagint. Second Esdras presents a special problem, explained in a footnote about the Latin text.

Footnotes. Translators decided, in certain instances, that they should explain their translations or textual decisions. However, notes are kept to a minimum and are rendered with utmost concision. Such notes when present offer: (a) evidence from ancient texts and versions (e.g., LXX; MT *men of*); (b) brief philological comment (e.g., Heb uncertain); (c) explanations of anomalies in versification (e.g., Acts 8:37: *Critical editions of the Gk New Testament do not include 8:37 Philip said to him, "If you believe with your whole heart, you can be." The eunuch answered, "I believe that Jesus Christ is God's Son"*); (d) citations of the Old Testament in the New Testament; and rarely (e) alternative translations (e.g., Or *everyone*). In those instances in which the Old Testament is cited in the New Testament, the quoted text is set in italic font.

Measurements. When possible, the CEB converts linear and spatial dimensions to feet and inches. Thus archaic terms such as rods, cubits, spans, handbreadths, and fingerbreadths are replaced with feet and inches. For example, Genesis 6:15 gives the dimensions of Noah's ark in *'ammah* or "forearms." Most translations since the KJV use the archaic English cubit to translate *'ammah*: "the length of the ark three hundred cubits, its width fifty cubits, and its height thirty cubits." The CEB translates the dimensions of the ark as "four hundred fifty feet long, seventy-five feet wide, and forty-five feet high."

The CEB prefers to transliterate (rather than translate) measurements of capacity, both wet (e.g., bath) and dry (e.g., homer), as well as measurements of weight (e.g., kikkar). When feasible, a footnote is allowed to calculate the rough equivalent in a U.S. English measurement, such as quarts.

Monetary values are inherently relative, and prices are constantly changing. Therefore, the CEB prefers to transliterate (rather than translate) monetary weights (e.g., shekel) and coins (e.g., denarion).

Months in the biblical lunar calendar are transliterated, with a footnote to indicate the approximate month or months in the Gregorian solar calendar (e.g., Nisan is March–April).

Hebrew and Greek a pronoun is often bound with the verb. If the translator is too literal, the English reader loses the antecedent of the pronoun so that one cannot tell who is speaking or acting in the sentence or paragraph. This problem occurs throughout much biblical literature. The CEB addresses this issue by substituting a noun for a pronoun, but only when the antecedent is clear. Because this problem and its resolution are so common, the CEB usually does not offer footnotes to identify these substitutions. CEB translators also use gender-inclusive or neutral syntax for translating pronouns that refer to humans, unless context requires otherwise.

Consistency. Although translators often try to use the same English word for a Hebrew or Greek word, many words in any language offer a breadth of meanings that do not readily correlate with a single word in the target language. For example, the Hebrew word *torah*, which has often been translated as Law, is often better translated as Instruction. The same could be said for Sheol (Hebrew) and Hades (Greek). The CEB translates these two terms as "grave" or "death" and "underworld" or "hell," respectively depending on context. A mechanical selection of any one term for words that involve semantic breadth would preclude a translation sensitive to the originating literary context.

The women and men who participated in the creation of the CEB hope that those who read and study it will find the translation to be an accurate, clear, and inspiring version of Christian scripture.

The Editorial Board of the Common English Bible
www.CommonEnglishBible.com

New Testament

MATTHEW

Genealogy of Jesus

A record of the ancestors of Jesus Christ, son of David, son of Abraham:

[2] Abraham was the father of Isaac.

Isaac was the father of Jacob.

Jacob was the father of Judah and his brothers.

[3] Judah was the father of Perez and Zerah,

whose mother was Tamar.

Perez was the father of Hezron.

Hezron was the father of Aram.

[4] Aram was the father of Amminadab.

Amminadab was the father of Nahshon.

Nahshon was the father of Salmon.

[5] Salmon was the father of Boaz, whose mother was Rahab.

Boaz was the father of Obed, whose mother was Ruth.

Obed was the father of Jesse.

[6] Jesse was the father of David the king.

David was the father of Solomon,

whose mother had been the wife of Uriah.

[7] Solomon was the father of Rehoboam.

Rehoboam was the father of Abijah.

Abijah was the father of Asaph.

[8] Asaph was the father of Jehoshaphat.

Jehoshaphat was the father of Joram.

Joram was the father of Uzziah.

[9] Uzziah was the father of Jotham.

Jotham was the father of Ahaz.

Ahaz was the father of Hezekiah.

[10] Hezekiah was the father of Manasseh.

Manasseh was the father of Amos.

Amos was the father of Josiah.

[11] Josiah was the father of Jechoniah and his brothers.

This was at the time of the exile to Babylon.

[12] After the exile to Babylon: Jechoniah was the father of Shealtiel.

Shealtiel was the father of Zerubbabel.

[13] Zerubbabel was the father of Abiud.

Abiud was the father of Eliakim.

Eliakim was the father of Azor.

[14] Azor was the father of Zadok.

Zadok was the father of Achim.

Achim was the father of Eliud.

[15] Eliud was the father of Eleazar.

Eleazar was the father of Matthan.

Matthan was the father of Jacob.

[16] Jacob was the father of Joseph, the husband of Mary—of whom Jesus was born, who is called the Christ.

[17] So there were fourteen generations from Abraham to David, fourteen generations from David to the exile to Babylon, and fourteen generations from the exile to Babylon to the Christ.

Birth of Jesus

[18] This is how the birth of Jesus Christ took place. When Mary his mother was engaged to Joseph, before they were married, she became pregnant by the Holy Spirit. [19] Joseph her

husband was a righteous man. Because he didn't want to humiliate her, he decided to call off their engagement quietly. [20]As he was thinking about this, an angel from the Lord appeared to him in a dream and said, "Joseph son of David, don't be afraid to take Mary as your wife, because the child she carries was conceived by the Holy Spirit. [21]She will give birth to a son, and you will call him Jesus, because he will save his people from their sins." [22]Now all of this took place so that what the Lord had spoken through the prophet would be fulfilled:

[23] Look! A virgin will become pregnant
    and give birth to a son,
    And they will call him,
      Emmanuel.[a]

    (*Emmanuel* means "God with us.")

[24]When Joseph woke up, he did just as an angel from God commanded and took Mary as his wife. [25]But he didn't have sexual relations with her until she gave birth to a son. Joseph called him Jesus.

Coming of the magi

2 After Jesus was born in Bethlehem in the territory of Judea during the rule of King Herod, magi came from the east to Jerusalem. [2]They asked, "Where is the newborn king of the Jews? We've seen his star in the east, and we've come to honor him."

[3]When King Herod heard this, he was troubled, and everyone in Jerusalem was troubled with him. [4]He gathered all the chief priests and the legal experts and asked them where the Christ was to be born. [5]They said, "In Bethlehem of Judea, for this is what the prophet wrote:

[6] *You, Bethlehem, land of Judah,*
    by no means are you least
    among the rulers of Judah,
    because from you will come
      one who governs,
    who will shepherd
      my people Israel."[b]

[7]Then Herod secretly called for the magi and found out from them the time when the star had first appeared. [8]He sent them to Bethlehem, saying, "Go and search carefully for the child. When you've found him, report to me so that I too may go and honor him." [9]When they heard the king, they went; and look, the star they had seen in the east went ahead of them until it stood over the place where the child was. [10]When they saw the star, they were filled with joy. [11]They entered the house and saw the child with Mary his mother. Falling to their knees, they honored him. Then they opened their treasure chests and presented him with gifts of gold, frankincense, and myrrh. [12]Because they were warned in a dream not to return to Herod, they went back to their own country by another route.

Escape to Egypt

[13]When the magi had departed, an angel from the Lord appeared to Joseph in a dream and said, "Get up. Take the child and his mother and escape to Egypt. Stay there until I tell you, for Herod will soon search for the child in order to kill him." [14]Joseph got up and, during the night, took the child and his mother to Egypt. [15]He stayed there until Herod died. This fulfilled what the

---

[a]Isa 7:14   [b]Mic 5:2; 2 Sam 5:2

Lord had spoken through the prophet: *I have called my son out of Egypt.*[c]

Murder of the Bethlehem children

[16]When Herod the magi had fooled him, he grew very angry. He sent soldiers to kill all the children in Bethlehem and in all the surrounding territory who were two years old and younger, according to the time that he had learned from the magi. [17]This fulfilled the word spoken through Jeremiah the prophet:

[18] *A voice was heard in Ramah,*
　　weeping and much grieving.
　　　Rachel weeping for her children,
　　　and she did not want
　　　to be comforted,
　　　because they were no more.[d]

Return from Egypt

[19]After King Herod died, an angel from the Lord appeared in a dream to Joseph in Egypt. [20]"Get up," the angel said, "and take the child and his mother and go to the land of Israel. Those who were trying to kill the child are dead." [21]Joseph got up, took the child and his mother, and went to the land of Israel. [22]But when he heard that Archelaus ruled over Judea in place of his father Herod, Joseph was afraid to go there. Having been warned in a dream, he went to the area of Galilee. [23]He settled in a city called Nazareth so that what was spoken through the prophets might be fulfilled: He will be called a Nazarene.

Ministry of John the Baptist

3 In those days John the Baptist appeared in the desert of Judea announcing, [2]"Change your hearts and lives! Here comes the kingdom of heaven!" [3]He was the one of whom Isaiah the prophet spoke when he said:

The voice of one shouting
　　in the wilderness,
"Prepare the way for the Lord;
　　make his paths straight."[e]

[4]John wore clothes made of camel's hair, with a leather belt around his waist. He ate locusts and wild honey. [5]People from Jerusalem, throughout Judea, and all around the Jordan River came to him. [6]As they confessed their sins, he baptized them in the Jordan River. [7]Many Pharisees and Sadducees came to be baptized by John. He said to them, "You children of snakes! Who warned you to escape from the angry judgment that is coming soon? [8]Produce fruit that shows you have changed your hearts and lives. [9]And don't even think about saying to yourselves, Abraham is our father. I tell you that God is able to raise up Abraham's children from these stones. [10]The ax is already at the root of the trees. Therefore, every tree that doesn't produce good fruit will be chopped down and tossed into the fire. [11]I baptize with water those of you who have changed your hearts and lives. The one who is coming after me is stronger than I am. I'm not worthy to carry his sandals. He will baptize you with the Holy Spirit and with fire. [12]The shovel he uses to sift the wheat from the husks is in his hands. He will clean out his threshing area and bring the wheat into his barn. But he will burn the husks with a fire that can't be put out."

[c]Hos 11:1　[d]Jer 31:15　[e]Isa 40:3

Baptism of Jesus

[13] At that time Jesus came from Galilee to the Jordan River so that John would baptize him. [14] John tried to stop him and said, "I need to be baptized by you; yet you come to me?"

[15] Jesus answered, "Allow me to be baptized now. This is necessary to fulfill all righteousness."

So John agreed to baptize Jesus. [16] When Jesus was baptized, he immediately came up out of the water. Heaven had opened to him, and he saw the Spirit of God coming down like a dove and resting on him. [17] A voice from heaven said, "This is my Son whom I dearly love; I find happiness in him."

Temptation of Jesus

4 Then the Spirit led Jesus up into the wilderness so that the devil might tempt him. [2] After Jesus had fasted for forty days and forty nights, he was starving. [3] The tempter came to him and said, "Since you are God's Son, command these stones to become bread."

[4] Jesus replied, "It's written, *People won't live only by bread, but by every word spoken by God.*"[f]

[5] After that the devil brought him into the holy city and stood him at the highest point of the temple. He said to him, [6] "Since you are God's Son, throw yourself down; for it is written, *I will command my angels concerning you, and they will take you up in their hands so that you won't hit your foot on a stone.*"[g]

[7] Jesus replied, "Again it's written, *Don't test the Lord your God.*"[h]

[8] Then the devil brought him to a very high mountain and showed him all the kingdoms of the world and their glory.

[9] He said, "I'll give you all these if you bow down and worship me."

[10] Jesus responded, "Go away, Satan, because it's written, *You will worship the Lord your God and serve only him.*"[i] [11] The devil left him, and angels came and took care of him.

Move to Galilee

[12] Now when Jesus heard that John was arrested, he went to Galilee. [13] He left Nazareth and settled in Capernaum, which lies alongside the sea in the area of Zebulun and Naphtali. [14] This fulfilled what Isaiah the prophet said:

[15] *Land of Zebulun and land of Naphtali,*
　　alongside the sea, across the Jordan,
　　Galilee of the Gentiles,
[16] *the people who lived in the dark*
　　have seen a great light,
　and a light has come upon
　　those who lived in the region
　　and in shadow of death.[j]

[17] From that time Jesus began to announce, "Change your hearts and lives! Here comes the kingdom of heaven!"

Calling of the first disciples

[18] As Jesus walked alongside the Galilee Sea, he saw two brothers, Simon, who is called Peter, and Andrew, throwing fishing nets into the sea, because they were fishermen. [19] "Come, follow me," he said, "and I'll show you how to fish for people." [20] Right away, they left their nets and followed him. [21] Continuing on, he saw another set of brothers, James the son of Zebedee and his brother John. They were in a boat with Zebedee their father repairing their nets. Jesus called them and

[f] Deut 8:3　[g] Ps 91:11-12　[h] Deut 6:16　[i] Deut 6:13　[j] Isa 9:1-2

²²immediately they left the boat and their father and followed him.

Ministry to the crowds

²³Jesus traveled throughout Galilee, teaching in their synagogues. He announced the good news of the kingdom and healed every disease and sickness among the people. ²⁴News about him spread throughout Syria. People brought to him all those who had various kinds of diseases, those in pain, those possessed by demons, those with epilepsy, and those who were paralyzed, and he healed them. ²⁵Large crowds followed him from Galilee, the Decapolis, Jerusalem, Judea, and from the areas beyond the Jordan River.

5 Now when Jesus saw the crowds, he went up a mountain. He sat down and his disciples came to him. ²He taught them, saying:

Happy people

³"Happy are people who are hopeless, because the kingdom of heaven is theirs.

⁴"Happy are people who grieve, because they will be made glad.

⁵"Happy are people who are humble, because they will inherit the earth.

⁶"Happy are people who are hungry and thirsty for righteousness, because they will be fed until they are full.

⁷"Happy are people who show mercy, because they will receive mercy.

⁸"Happy are people who have pure hearts, because they will see God.

⁹"Happy are people who make peace, because they will be called God's children.

¹⁰"Happy are people whose lives are harassed because they are righteous, because the kingdom of heaven is theirs.

¹¹"Happy are you when people insult you and harass you and speak all kinds of bad and false things about you, all because of me. ¹²Be full of joy and be glad, because you have a great reward in heaven. In the same way, people harassed the prophets who came before you.

Salt and light

¹³"You are the salt of the earth. But if salt loses its saltiness, how will it become salty again? It's good for nothing except to be thrown away and trampled under people's feet. ¹⁴You are the light of the world. A city on top of a hill can't be hidden. ¹⁵Neither do people light a lamp and put it under a basket. Instead, they put it on top of a lampstand, and it shines on all who are in the house. ¹⁶In the same way, let your light shine before people, so they can see the good things you do and praise your Father who is in heaven.

Jesus and the Law

¹⁷"Don't even begin to think that I have come to do away with the Law and the Prophets. I haven't come to do away with them but to fulfill them. ¹⁸I say to you very seriously that as long as heaven and earth exist, neither the smallest letter nor even the smallest stroke of a pen will be erased from the Law until everything there becomes a reality. ¹⁹Therefore, whoever ignores one of the least of these commands and teaches others to do the same will be called the lowest in the kingdom of heaven. But whoever keeps these commands and teaches people to keep them will be called great in the kingdom of

heaven. ²⁰I say to you that unless your righteousness is greater than the righteousness of the legal experts and the Pharisees, you will never enter the kingdom of heaven.

Law of murder

²¹"You have heard that it was said to those who lived long ago, *Don't commit murder,*[k] and all who commit murder will be in danger of judgment. ²²But I say to you that everyone who is angry with their brother or sister will be in danger of judgment. If they say to their brother or sister, 'You idiot,' they will be in danger of being condemned by the governing council. And if they say, 'You fool,' they will be in danger of fiery hell. ²³Therefore, if you bring your gift to the altar and there remember that your brother or sister has something against you, ²⁴leave your gift at the altar and go. First make things right with your brother or sister and then come back and offer your gift. ²⁵Be sure to make friends quickly with your opponents while you are with them on the way to court. Otherwise, they will haul you before the judge, the judge will turn you over to the officer of the court, and you will be thrown into prison. ²⁶I say to you in all seriousness that you won't get out of there until you've paid the very last penny.

Law of adultery

²⁷"You have heard that it was said, *Don't commit adultery.*[l] ²⁸But I say to you that every man who looks at a woman lustfully has already committed adultery in his heart. ²⁹And if your right eye causes you to fall into sin, tear it out and throw it away. It's better that you lose a part of your body than that your whole body be thrown into hell. ³⁰And if your right hand causes you to fall into sin, chop it off and throw it away. It's better that you lose a part of your body than that your whole body go into hell.

Law of divorce

³¹"It was said, 'Whoever divorces his wife must *give her a divorce certificate.*'[m] ³²But I say to you that whoever divorces his wife except for sexual unfaithfulness forces her to commit adultery. And whoever marries a divorced woman commits adultery.

Making solemn pledges

³³"Again you have heard that it was said to those who lived long ago: *Don't make a false solemn pledge, but you should follow through on what you have pledged to the Lord.*[n] ³⁴But I say to you that you must not pledge at all. You must not pledge by heaven, because it's God's throne. ³⁵You must not pledge by the earth, because it's God's footstool. You must not pledge by Jerusalem, because it's the city of the great king. ³⁶And you must not pledge by your head, because you can't turn one hair white or black. ³⁷Let your *yes* mean yes, and your *no* mean no. Anything more than this comes from the evil one.

Law of retaliation

³⁸"You have heard that it was said, *An eye for an eye and a tooth for a tooth.*[o] ³⁹But I say to you that you must not

[k]Exod 20:13 [l]Exod 20:14; Deut 5:18 [m]Deut 24:1 [n]Lev 19:12; Num 30:2; Deut 23:21
[o]Exod 21:24; Lev 24:20; Deut 19:21

oppose those who want to hurt you. If people slap you on your right cheek, you must turn the left cheek to them as well. [40]When they wish to haul you to court and take your shirt, let them have your coat too. [41]When they force you to go one mile, go with them two. [42]Give to those who ask, and don't refuse those who wish to borrow from you.

Law of love

[43]"You have heard that it was said, *You must love your neighbor*[p] and hate your enemy. [44]But I say to you, love your enemies and pray for those who harass you [45]so that you may be acting as children of your Father who is in heaven. He makes the sun rise on both the evil and the good and sends rain on both the righteous and the unrighteous. [46]If you love only those who love you, what reward do you have? Don't even the tax collectors do the same? [47]And if you greet only your brothers and sisters, what more are you doing? Don't even the Gentiles do the same? [48]Therefore, just as your heavenly Father is complete in showing love to everyone, so also you must be complete.

Showy religion

6 "Be careful that you don't practice your religion in front of people to draw their attention. If you do, you will have no reward from your Father who is in heaven.

[2]"Whenever you give to the poor, don't blow your trumpet as the hypocrites do in the synagogues and in the streets so that they may get praise from people. I assure you, that's the only

reward they'll get. [3]But when you give to the poor, don't let your left hand know what your right hand is doing [4]so that you may give to the poor in secret. Your Father who sees what you do in secret will reward you.

Showy prayer

[5]"When you pray, don't be like hypocrites. They love to pray standing in the synagogues and on the street corners so that people will see them. I assure you, that's the only reward they'll get. [6]But when you pray, go to your room, shut the door, and pray to your Father who is present in that secret place. Your Father who sees what you do in secret will reward you.

Proper prayer

[7]"When you pray, don't pour out a flood of empty words, as the Gentiles do. They think that by saying many words they'll be heard. [8]Don't be like them, because your Father knows what you need before you ask. [9]Pray like this:
> Our Father who is in heaven,
>   uphold the holiness of your name.
> [10]Bring in your kingdom
>   so that your will be done on earth
>   as it's done in heaven.
> [11]Give us the bread we need for today.
> [12]Forgive us for the ways we have
>   wronged you,
>   just as we also forgive those who
>   have wronged us.
> [13]And don't lead us into temptation,
>   but rescue us from the evil one.

[14]"If you forgive others their sins, your heavenly Father will also forgive you. [15]But if you don't forgive others, neither will your Father forgive your sins.

[p]Lev 19:18

Showy fasting

[16] "And when you fast, don't put on a sad face like the hypocrites. They distort their faces so people will know they are fasting. I assure you that they have their reward. [17] When you fast, brush your hair and wash your face. [18] Then you won't look like you are fasting to people, but only to your Father who is present in that secret place. Your Father who sees in secret will reward you.

Earthly and heavenly treasures

[19] "Stop collecting treasures for your own benefit on earth, where moth and rust eat them and where thieves break in and steal them. [20] Instead, collect treasures for yourselves in heaven, where moth and rust don't eat them and where thieves don't break in and steal them. [21] Where your treasure is, there your heart will be also.

Seeing and serving

[22] "The eye is the lamp of the body. Therefore, if your eye is healthy, your whole body will be full of light. [23] But if your eye is bad, your whole body will be full of darkness. If then the light in you is darkness, how terrible that darkness will be! [24] No one can serve two masters. Either you will hate the one and love the other, or you will be loyal to the one and have contempt for the other. You cannot serve God and wealth.

Worry about necessities

[25] "Therefore, I say to you, don't worry about your life, what you'll eat or what you'll drink, or about your body, what you'll wear. Isn't life more than food and the body more than clothes? [26] Look at the birds in the sky. They don't sow seed or harvest grain or gather crops into barns. Yet your heavenly Father feeds them. Aren't you worth much more than they are? [27] Who among you by worrying can add a single moment to your life? [28] And why do you worry about clothes? Notice how the lilies in the field grow. They don't wear themselves out with work, and they don't spin cloth. [29] But I say to you that even Solomon in all of his splendor wasn't dressed like one of these. [30] If God dresses grass in the field so beautifully, even though it's alive today and tomorrow it's thrown into the furnace, won't God do much more for you, you people of weak faith? [31] Therefore, don't worry and say, 'What are we going to eat?' or 'What are we going to drink?' or 'What are we going to wear?' [32] Gentiles long for all these things. Your heavenly Father knows that you need them. [33] Instead, desire first and foremost God's kingdom and God's righteousness, and all these things will be given to you as well. [34] Therefore, stop worrying about tomorrow, because tomorrow will worry about itself. Each day has enough trouble of its own.

Judging

7 "Don't judge, so that you won't be judged. [2] You'll receive the same judgment you give. Whatever you deal out will be dealt out to you. [3] Why do you see the splinter that's in your brother's or sister's eye, but don't notice the log in your own eye? [4] How can you say to your brother or sister, 'Let me take the splinter out of your eye,' when there's a log in your eye? [5] You deceive yourself! First take the log out of your eye, and then you'll see clearly to take the splinter out of your brother's or sister's eye. [6] Don't give holy things to dogs, and don't throw your pearls in front of pigs. They will stomp on the pearls, then turn around and attack you.

Asking, seeking, knocking

⁷"Ask, and you will receive. Search, and you will find. Knock, and the door will be opened to you. ⁸For everyone who asks, receives. Whoever seeks, finds. And to everyone who knocks, the door is opened. ⁹Who among you will give your children a stone when they ask for bread? ¹⁰Or give them a snake when they ask for fish? ¹¹If you who are evil know how to give good gifts to your children, how much more will your heavenly Father give good things to those who ask him. ¹²Therefore, you should treat people in the same way that you want people to treat you; this is the Law and the Prophets.

Narrow gate

¹³"Go in through the narrow gate. The gate that leads to destruction is broad and the road wide, so many people enter through it. ¹⁴But the gate that leads to life is narrow and the road difficult, so few people find it.

Tree and fruit

¹⁵"Watch out for false prophets. They come to you dressed like sheep, but inside they are vicious wolves. ¹⁶You will know them by their fruit. Do people get bunches of grapes from thorny weeds, or do they get figs from thistles? ¹⁷In the same way, every good tree produces good fruit, and every rotten tree produces bad fruit. ¹⁸A good tree can't produce bad fruit. And a rotten tree can't produce good fruit. ¹⁹Every tree that doesn't produce good fruit is chopped down and thrown into the fire. ²⁰Therefore, you will know them by their fruit.

Entrance requirements

²¹"Not everybody who says to me, 'Lord, Lord,' will get into the kingdom of heaven. Only those who do the will of my Father who is in heaven will enter. ²²On the Judgment Day, many people will say to me, 'Lord, Lord, didn't we prophesy in your name and expel demons in your name and do lots of miracles in your name?' ²³Then I'll tell them, 'I've never known you. Get away from me, you people who do wrong.'

Two foundations

²⁴"Everybody who hears these words of mine and puts them into practice is like a wise builder who built a house on bedrock. ²⁵The rain fell, the floods came, and the wind blew and beat against that house. It didn't fall because it was firmly set on bedrock. ²⁶But everybody who hears these words of mine and doesn't put them into practice will be like a fool who built a house on sand. ²⁷The rain fell, the floods came, and the wind blew and beat against that house. It fell and was completely destroyed."

Crowd's response

²⁸When Jesus finished these words, the crowds were amazed at his teaching ²⁹because he was teaching them like someone with authority and not like their legal experts.

A man with a skin disease

8 Now when Jesus had come down from the mountain, large crowds followed him. ²A man with a skin disease came, kneeled before him, and said, "Lord, if you want, you can make me clean."

³Jesus reached out his hand and touched him, saying, "I do want to. Become clean." Instantly his skin disease was cleansed. ⁴Jesus said to him, "Don't say anything to anyone. Instead, go and show yourself to the priest and offer the gift that Moses commanded. This will be a testimony to them."

Healing of the centurion's servant

⁵When Jesus went to Capernaum, a centurion approached, ⁶pleading with him, "Lord, my servant is flat on his back at home, paralyzed, and his suffering is awful."

⁷Jesus responded, "I'll come and heal him."

⁸But the centurion replied, "Lord, I don't deserve to have you come under my roof. Just say the word and my servant will be healed. ⁹I'm a man under authority, with soldiers under me. I say to one, 'Go,' and he goes, and to another, 'Come,' and he comes. I say to my servant, 'Do this,' and the servant does it."

¹⁰When Jesus heard this, he was impressed and said to the people following him, "I say to you with all seriousness that even in Israel I haven't found faith like this. ¹¹I say to you that there are many who will come from east and west and sit down to eat with Abraham and Isaac and Jacob in the kingdom of heaven. ¹²But the children of the kingdom will be thrown outside into the darkness. People there will be weeping and grinding their teeth." ¹³Jesus said to the centurion, "Go; it will be done for you just as you have believed." And his servant was healed that very moment.

Healing of many people

¹⁴Jesus went home with Peter and saw Peter's mother-in-law lying in bed with a fever. ¹⁵He touched her hand, and the fever left her. Then she got up and served them. ¹⁶That evening people brought to Jesus many who were demon-possessed. He threw the spirits out with just a word. He healed everyone who was sick. ¹⁷This happened so that what Isaiah the prophet said would be fulfilled: *He is the one who took our illnesses and carried away our diseases.*�q

Discussions about following

¹⁸Now when Jesus saw the crowd, he ordered his disciples to go over to the other side of the lake. ¹⁹A legal expert came and said to him, "Teacher, I'll follow you wherever you go."

²⁰Jesus replied, "Foxes have dens, and the birds in the sky have nests, but the Human Oneʳ has no place to lay his head."

²¹Another man, one of his disciples, said to him, "Lord, first let me go and bury my father."

²²But Jesus said to him, "Follow me, and let the dead bury their own dead."

Calming a storm

²³When Jesus got into a boat, his disciples followed him. ²⁴A huge storm arose on the lake so that waves were sloshing over the boat. But Jesus was asleep. ²⁵They came and woke him, saying, "Lord, rescue us! We're going to drown!"

²⁶He said to them, "Why are you afraid, you people of weak faith?" Then he got up and gave orders to the winds and the lake, and there was a great calm.

�q Isa 53:4   ʳ Or *Son of Man*

[27]The people were amazed and said, "What kind of person is this? Even the winds and the lake obey him!"

Jesus frees demon-possessed men

[28]When Jesus arrived on the other side of the lake in the country of the Gadarenes, two men who were demon-possessed came from among the tombs to meet him. They were so violent that nobody could travel on that road. [29]They cried out, "What are you going to do with us, Son of God? Have you come to torture us before the time of judgment?" [30]Far off in the distance a large herd of pigs was feeding. [31]The demons pleaded with him, "If you throw us out, send us into the herd of pigs."

[32]Then he said to the demons, "Go away," and they came out and went into the pigs. The whole herd rushed down the cliff into the lake and drowned. [33]Those who tended the pigs ran into the city and told everything that had happened to the demon-possessed men. [34]Then the whole city came out and met Jesus. When they saw him, they pleaded with him to leave their region.

Healing of a man who was paralyzed

9 Boarding a boat, Jesus crossed to the other side of the lake and went to his own city. [2]People brought to him a man who was paralyzed, lying on a cot. When Jesus saw their faith, he said to the man who was paralyzed, "Be encouraged, my child, your sins are forgiven."

[3]Some legal experts said among themselves, "This man is insulting God." [4]But Jesus knew what they were thinking and said, "Why do you fill your minds with evil things? [5]Which is easier—to say, 'Your sins are forgiven,' or to say, 'Get up and walk'? [6]But so you will know that the Human One[s] has authority on the earth to forgive sins"—he said to the man who was paralyzed—"Get up, take your cot, and go home." [7]The man got up and went home. [8]When the crowds saw what had happened, they were afraid and praised God, who had given such authority to human beings.

Calling of Matthew

[9]As Jesus continued on from there, he saw a man named Matthew sitting at a kiosk for collecting taxes. He said to him, "Follow me," and he got up and followed him. [10]As Jesus sat down to eat in Matthew's house, many tax collectors and sinners joined Jesus and his disciples at the table.

[11]But when the Pharisees saw this, they said to his disciples, "Why does your teacher eat with tax collectors and sinners?"

[12]When Jesus heard it, he said, "Healthy people don't need a doctor, but sick people do. [13]Go and learn what this means: *I want mercy and not sacrifice.*[t] I didn't come to call righteous people, but sinners."

Question about fasting

[14]At that time John's disciples came and asked Jesus, "Why do we and the Pharisees frequently fast, but your disciples never fast?"

[15]Jesus responded, "The wedding guests can't mourn while the groom is still with them, can they? But the days

[s]Or *Son of Man*   [t]Hos 6:6

will come when the groom will be taken away from them, and then they'll fast. ¹⁶"No one sews a piece of new, unshrunk cloth on old clothes because the patch tears away the cloth and makes a worse tear. ¹⁷No one pours new wine into old wineskins. If they did, the wineskins would burst, the wine would spill, and the wineskins would be ruined. Instead, people pour new wine into new wineskins so that both are kept safe."

A ruler's daughter and the woman who touched Jesus' clothes

¹⁸While Jesus was speaking to them, a ruler came and knelt in front of him, saying, "My daughter has just died. But come and place your hand on her, and she'll live." ¹⁹So Jesus and his disciples got up and went with him. ²⁰Then a woman who had been bleeding for twelve years came up behind Jesus and touched the hem of his clothes. ²¹She thought, If I only touch his robe I'll be healed.

²²When Jesus turned and saw her, he said, "Be encouraged, daughter. Your faith has healed you." And the woman was healed from that time on.

²³When Jesus went into the ruler's house, he saw the flute players and the distressed crowd. ²⁴He said, "Go away, because the little girl isn't dead but is asleep"; but they laughed at him. ²⁵After he had sent the crowd away, Jesus went in and touched her hand, and the little girl rose up. ²⁶News about this spread throughout that whole region.

Healing of two blind men

²⁷As Jesus departed, two blind men followed him, crying out, "Show us mercy, Son of David."
²⁸When he came into the house, the blind men approached him. Jesus said to them, "Do you believe I can do this?"

"Yes, Lord," they replied.

²⁹Then Jesus touched their eyes and said, "It will happen for you just as you have believed." ³⁰Their eyes were opened. Then Jesus sternly warned them, "Make sure nobody knows about this." ³¹But they went out and spread the word about him throughout that whole region.

Healing of a man unable to speak

³²As they were leaving, people brought to him a man who was demon-possessed and unable to speak. ³³When Jesus had thrown out the demon, the man who couldn't speak began to talk. The crowds were amazed and said, "Nothing like this has ever been seen in Israel."

³⁴But the Pharisees said, "He throws out demons with the authority of the ruler of demons."

Compassion

³⁵Jesus traveled among all the cities and villages, teaching in their synagogues, announcing the good news of the kingdom, and healing every disease and every sickness. ³⁶Now when Jesus saw the crowds, he had compassion for them because they were troubled and helpless, like sheep without a shepherd. ³⁷Then he said to his disciples, "The size of the harvest is bigger than you can imagine, but there are few workers. ³⁸Therefore, plead with the Lord of the harvest to send out workers for his harvest."

Mission of the Twelve

10 He called his twelve disciples and gave them authority over unclean spirits to throw them out and to heal every disease and every sickness. ²Here are the names of the twelve apostles: first, Simon, who is called Peter; and Andrew his brother; James the son of Zebedee; and John his brother; ³Philip; and Bartholomew; Thomas; and Matthew the tax collector; James the son of Alphaeus; and Thaddaeus; ⁴Simon the Cananaean;ᵘ and Judas, who betrayed Jesus.

Commissioning of the Twelve

⁵Jesus sent these twelve out and commanded them, "Don't go among the Gentiles or into a Samaritan city. ⁶Go instead to the lost sheep, the people of Israel. ⁷As you go, make this announcement: 'The kingdom of heaven has come near.' ⁸Heal the sick, raise the dead, cleanse those with skin diseases, and throw out demons. You received without having to pay. Therefore, give without demanding payment. ⁹Workers deserve to be fed, so don't gather gold or silver or copper coins for your money belts to take on your trips. ¹⁰Don't take a backpack for the road or two shirts or sandals or a walking stick. ¹¹Whatever city or village you go into, find somebody in it who is worthy and stay there until you go on your way. ¹²When you go into a house, say, 'Peace!' ¹³If the house is worthy, give it your blessing of peace. But if the house isn't worthy, take back your blessing. ¹⁴If anyone refuses to welcome you or listen to your words, shake the dust off your feet as you leave that house or city. ¹⁵I assure you that it will be more bearable for the land of Sodom and Gomorrah on Judgment Day than it will be for that city.

Response to harassment

¹⁶"Look, I'm sending you as sheep among wolves. Therefore, be wise as snakes and innocent as doves. ¹⁷Watch out for people—because they will hand you over to councils and they will beat you in their synagogues. ¹⁸They will haul you in front of governors and even kings because of me so that you may give your testimony to them and to the Gentiles. ¹⁹Whenever they hand you over, don't worry about how to speak or what you will say, because what you can say will be given to you at that moment. ²⁰You aren't doing the talking, but the Spirit of my Father is doing the talking through you. ²¹Brothers and sisters will hand each other over to be executed. A father will turn his child in. Children will defy their parents and have them executed. ²²Everyone will hate you on account of my name. But whoever stands firm until the end will be saved. ²³Whenever they harass you in one city, escape to the next, because I assure that you will not go through all the cities of Israel before the Human Oneᵛ comes.

²⁴"Disciples aren't greater than their teacher, and slaves aren't greater than their master. ²⁵It's enough for disciples to be like their teacher and slaves like their master. If they have called the head of the house Beelzebul, it's certain that they will call the members of his household by even worse names.

Whom to fear

²⁶"Therefore, don't be afraid of those people because nothing is hidden that won't be revealed, and nothing secret that won't be brought out into the open. ²⁷What I say to you in the darkness, tell

---

ᵘOr zealot ᵛOr Son of Man

in the light; and what you hear whispered, announce from the rooftops. ²⁸Don't be afraid of those who kill the body but can't kill the soul. Instead, be afraid of the one who can destroy both body and soul in hell. ²⁹Aren't two sparrows sold for a small coin? But not one of them will fall to the ground without your Father knowing about it already. ³⁰Even the hairs of your head are all counted. ³¹Don't be afraid. You are worth more than many sparrows.

Confessing Christ to people

³²"Therefore, everyone who acknowledges me before people, I also will acknowledge before my Father who is in heaven. ³³But everyone who denies me before people, I also will deny before my Father who is in heaven.

Trouble in the family

³⁴"Don't think that I've come to bring peace to the earth. I haven't come to bring peace but a sword. ³⁵I've come to turn a man *against his father, a daughter against her mother, and a daughter-in-law against her mother-in-law. ³⁶People's enemies are members of their own households.*ᵂ

³⁷"Those who love father or mother more than me aren't worthy of me. Those who love son or daughter more than me aren't worthy of me. ³⁸Those who don't pick up their crosses and follow me aren't worthy of me. ³⁹Those who find their lives will lose them, and those who lose their lives because of me will find them.

Rewards

⁴⁰"Those who receive you are also receiving me, and those who receive me are receiving the one who sent me. ⁴¹Those who receive a prophet as a prophet will receive a prophet's reward. Those who receive a righteous person as a righteous person will receive a righteous person's reward. ⁴²I assure you that everybody who gives even a cup of cold water to these little ones because they are my disciples will certainly be rewarded."

Ministry to the people

11When Jesus finished teaching his twelve disciples, he went on from there to teach and preach in their cities.

Question from John the Baptist

²Now when John heard in prison about the things the Christ was doing, he sent word by his disciples to Jesus, asking, ³"Are you the one who is to come, or should we look for another?"

⁴Jesus responded, "Go, report to John what you hear and see. ⁵*Those who were blind are able to see.* Those who were crippled are walking. People with skin diseases are cleansed. Those *who were deaf now hear.* Those who were dead are raised up. *The poor have good news proclaimed to them.*ˣ ⁶Happy are those who don't stumble and fall because of me."

Appeal of John's ministry

⁷When John's disciples had gone, Jesus spoke to the crowds about John: "What did you go out to the wilderness to see? A stalk blowing in the wind? ⁸What did you go out to see? A man dressed up in refined clothes? Look, those who wear refined clothes are in royal palaces. ⁹What did you go out to see? A prophet? Yes, I tell you, and

ᵂMic 7:6 ˣIsa 35:5-6; 61:1

more than a prophet. [10]He is the one of whom it is written: *Look, I'm sending my messenger before you, who will prepare your way before you.*[y]

Significance of John's ministry

[11]"I assure you that no one who has ever been born is greater than John the Baptist. Yet whoever is least in the kingdom of heaven is greater than he. [12]From the days of John the Baptist until now the kingdom of heaven is violently attacked as violent people seize it. [13]All the Prophets and the Law prophesied until John came. [14]If you are willing to accept it, he is Elijah who is to come. [15]Let the person who has ears, hear.

This generation

[16]"To what will I compare this generation? It is like a child sitting in the marketplaces calling out to others, [17]'We played the flute for you and you didn't dance. We sang a funeral song and you didn't mourn.' [18]For John came neither eating nor drinking, and they say, 'He has a demon.' [19]Yet the Human One[z] came eating and drinking, and they say, 'Look, a glutton and a drunk, a friend of tax collectors and sinners.' But wisdom is proved to be right by her works."

Condemnation of Bethsaida and Capernaum

[20]Then he began to scold the cities where he had done his greatest miracles because they didn't change their hearts and lives. [21]"How terrible it will be for you, Chorazin! How terrible it will be for you, Bethsaida! For if the miracles done among you had been done in Tyre and Sidon, they would have changed their hearts and lives and put on funeral clothes and ashes a long time ago. [22]But I say to you that Tyre and Sidon will be better off on Judgment Day than you. [23]And you, Capernaum, will you be honored by being raised up to heaven? No, you will be thrown down to the place of the dead. After all, if the miracles that were done among you had been done in Sodom, it would still be here today. [24]But I say to you that it will be better for the land of Sodom on the Judgment Day than it will be for you."

The Father and the Son

[25]At that time Jesus said, "I praise you, Father, Lord of heaven and earth, because you've hidden these things from the wise and intelligent and have shown them to babies. [26]Indeed, Father, this brings you happiness.

[27]"My Father has handed all things over to me. No one knows the Son except the Father. And nobody knows the Father except the Son and anyone to whom the Son wants to reveal him.

[28]"Come to me, all you who are struggling hard and carrying heavy loads, and I will give you rest. [29]Put on my yoke, and learn from me. I'm gentle and humble. And you will find rest for yourselves. [30]My yoke is easy to bear, and my burden is light."

Working on the Sabbath

12At that time Jesus went through the wheat fields on the Sabbath. His disciples were hungry so they were picking heads of wheat and eating them. [2]When the Pharisees saw this, they said to him, "Look, your disciples are breaking the Sabbath law."

---

[y]Mal 3:1   [z]Or Son of Man

³But he said to them, "Haven't you read what David did when he and those with him were hungry? ⁴He went into God's house and broke the law by eating the bread of the presence, which only the priests were allowed to eat. ⁵Or haven't you read in the Law that on the Sabbath the priests in the temple treat the Sabbath as any other day and are still innocent? ⁶But I tell you that something greater than the temple is here. ⁷If you had known what this means, *I want mercy and not sacrifice*,ᵃ you wouldn't have condemned the innocent. ⁸The Human Oneᵇ is Lord of the Sabbath."

Healing on the Sabbath

⁹Jesus left that place and went into their synagogue. ¹⁰A man with a withered hand was there. Wanting to bring charges against Jesus, they asked, "Does the Law allow a person to heal on the Sabbath?"

¹¹Jesus replied, "Who among you has a sheep that falls into a pit on the Sabbath and will not take hold of it and pull it out? ¹²How much more valuable is a person than a sheep! So the Law allows a person to do what is good on the Sabbath." ¹³Then Jesus said to the man, "Stretch out your hand." So he did and it was made healthy, just like the other one. ¹⁴The Pharisees went out and met in order to find a way to destroy Jesus.

Healing the crowd

¹⁵Jesus knew what they intended to do, so he went away from there. Large crowds followed him, and he healed them all. ¹⁶But he ordered them not to spread the word about him, ¹⁷so that what was spoken through Isaiah the prophet might be fulfilled:

¹⁸ *Look, my Servant whom I chose,*
   the one I love,
      in whom I find great pleasure.
   I'll put my Spirit upon him,
      and he'll announce judgment
         to the Gentiles.
¹⁹ *He won't argue or shout,*
      and nobody will hear his voice
         in the streets.
²⁰ *He won't break a bent stalk,*
      and he won't snuff out
         a smoldering wick,
      until he makes justice win.
²¹ *And the Gentiles will put their hope*
      *in his name.*ᶜ

²²They brought to Jesus a demon-possessed man who was blind and unable to speak. Jesus healed him so that he could both speak and see. ²³All the crowds were amazed and said, "This man couldn't be the Son of David, could he?"

²⁴When the Pharisees heard, they said, "This man throws out demons only by the authority of Beelzebul, the ruler of the demons."

²⁵Because Jesus knew what they were thinking, he replied, "Every kingdom involved in civil war becomes a wasteland. Every city or house torn apart by divisions will collapse. ²⁶If Satan throws out Satan, he is at war with himself. How then can his kingdom endure? ²⁷And if I throw out demons by the authority of Beelzebul, then by whose authority do your followers throw them out? Therefore, they will be your judges. ²⁸But if I throw out demons by the power of God's Spirit, then God's kingdom has already

ᵃHos 6:6 ᵇOr Son of Man ᶜIsa 42:1-4

overtaken you. [29]Can people go into a house that belongs to a strong man and steal his possessions, unless they first tie up the strong man? Then they can rob his house. [30]Whoever isn't with me is against me, and whoever doesn't gather with me scatters.

Insulting the Holy Spirit

[31]"Therefore, I tell you that people will be forgiven for every sin and insult to God. But insulting the Holy Spirit won't be forgiven. [32]And whoever speaks a word against the Human One[d] will be forgiven. But whoever speaks against the Holy Spirit won't be forgiven, not in this age or in the age that is coming.

Trees and fruits

[33]"Either consider the tree good and its fruit good, or consider the tree rotten and its fruit rotten. A tree is known by its fruit. [34]Children of snakes! How can you speak good things while you are evil? What fills the heart comes out of the mouth. [35]Good people bring out good things from their good treasure. But evil people bring out evil things from their evil treasure. [36]I tell you that people will have to answer on Judgment Day for every useless word they speak. [37]By your words you will be either judged innocent or condemned as guilty."

Request for a sign

[38]At that time some of the legal experts and the Pharisees requested of Jesus, "Teacher, we would like to see a sign from you."

[39]But he replied, "An evil and unfaithful generation searches for a sign, but it won't receive any sign except Jonah's sign. [40]Just as *Jonah was in the whale's belly for three days and three nights,*[e] so the Human One[f] will be in the heart of the earth for three days and three nights. [41]The citizens of Nineveh will stand up at the judgment with this generation and condemn it as guilty, because they changed their hearts and lives in response to Jonah's preaching. And look, someone greater than Jonah is here. [42]The queen of the South will be raised up by God at the judgment with this generation and condemn it because she came from a distant land to hear Solomon's wisdom. And look, someone greater than Solomon is here.

Unclean spirit seeking a home

[43]"When an unclean spirit leaves a person, it wanders through dry places looking for a place to rest. But it doesn't find any. [44]Then it says, 'I'll go back to the house I left.' When it arrives, it finds the place vacant, cleaned up, and decorated. [45]Then it goes and brings with it seven other spirits more evil than itself. They go in and make their home there. That person is worse off at the end than at the beginning. This is the way it will be also for this evil generation."

Jesus' family

[46]While Jesus was speaking to the crowds, his mother and brothers stood outside trying to speak with him. [47]Someone said to him, "Look, your mother and brothers are outside wanting to speak with you."

[48]Jesus replied, "Who is my mother?

---

[d]Or *Son of Man*   [e]Jonah 1:17   [f]Or *Son of Man*

Who are my brothers?" ⁴⁹He stretched out his hand toward his disciples and said, "Look, here are my mother and my brothers. ⁵⁰Whoever does the will of my Father who is in heaven is my brother, sister, and mother."

Setting for the parables

13 That day Jesus went out of the house and sat down beside the lake. ²Such large crowds gathered around him that he climbed into a boat and sat down. The whole crowd was standing on the shore.

Parable of the soils

³He said many things to them in parables: "A farmer went out to scatter seed. ⁴As he was scattering seed, some fell on the path, and birds came and ate it. ⁵Other seed fell on rocky ground where the soil was shallow. They sprouted immediately because the soil wasn't deep. ⁶But when the sun came up, it scorched the plants, and they dried up because they had no roots. ⁷Other seed fell among thorny plants. The thorny plants grew and choked them. ⁸Other seed fell on good soil and bore fruit, in one case a yield of one hundred to one, in another case a yield of sixty to one, and in another case a yield of thirty to one. ⁹Everyone who has ears should pay attention."

Why Jesus speaks in parables

¹⁰Jesus' disciples came and said to him, "Why do you use parables when you speak to the crowds?"

¹¹Jesus replied, "Because they haven't received the secrets of the kingdom of heaven, but you have. ¹²For those

who have will receive more and they will have more than enough. But as for those who don't have, even the little they have will be taken away from them. ¹³This is why I speak to the crowds in parables: although they see, they don't really see; and although they hear, they don't really hear or understand. ¹⁴What Isaiah prophesied has become completely true for them:

You will hear, to be sure,
  but never understand;
    and you will certainly see
    but never recognize
      what you are seeing.
¹⁵ *For this people's senses*
  have become calloused,
    and they've become hard of hearing,
    and they've shut their eyes
      so that they won't see
        with their eyes
      or hear with their ears
      or understand with their minds,
        and change their hearts and lives
          *that I may heal them.*ᵍ

¹⁶"Happy are your eyes because they see. Happy are your ears because they hear. ¹⁷I assure you that many prophets and righteous people wanted to see what you see and hear what you hear, but they didn't.

Explanation of the parable of the farmer

¹⁸"Consider then the parable of the farmer. ¹⁹Whenever people hear the word about the kingdom and don't understand it, the evil one comes and carries off what was planted in their hearts. This is the seed that was sown on the path. ²⁰As for the seed that was spread on rocky ground, this refers to

---

ᵍIsa 6:9-10

people who hear the word and immediately receive it joyfully. ²¹Because they have no roots, they last for only a little while. When they experience distress or abuse because of the word, they immediately fall away. ²²As for the seed that was spread among thorny plants, this refers to those who hear the word, but the worries of this life and the false appeal of wealth choke the word, and it bears no fruit.²³As for what was planted on good soil, this refers to those who hear and understand, and bear fruit and produce—in one case a yield of one hundred to one, in another case a yield of sixty to one, and in another case a yield of thirty to one."

Parable of the weeds

²⁴Jesus told them another parable: "The kingdom of heaven is like someone who planted good seed in his field. ²⁵While people were sleeping, an enemy came and planted weeds among the wheat and went away. ²⁶When the stalks sprouted and bore grain, then the weeds also appeared.

²⁷"The servants of the landowner came and said to him, 'Master, didn't you plant good seed in your field? Then how is it that it has weeds?'

²⁸"'An enemy has done this,' he answered.

"The servants said to him, 'Do you want us to go and gather them?'

²⁹"But the landowner said, 'No, because if you gather the weeds, you'll pull up the wheat along with them. ³⁰Let both grow side by side until the harvest. And at harvesttime I'll say to the harvesters, "First gather the weeds and tie them together in bundles to be burned. But bring the wheat into my barn."'"

Parable of the mustard seed

³¹He told another parable to them: "The kingdom of heaven is like a mustard seed that someone took and planted in his field. ³²It's the smallest of all seeds. But when it's grown, it's the largest of all vegetable plants. It becomes a tree so that the birds in the sky come and nest in its branches."

Parable of the yeast

³³He told them another parable: "The kingdom of heaven is like yeast, which a woman took and hid in a bushel of wheat flour until the yeast had worked its way through all the dough."

Purpose of parables to the crowds

³⁴Jesus said all these things to the crowds in parables, and he spoke to them only in parables. ³⁵This was to fulfill what the prophet spoke:

I'll speak in parables;
I'll declare what has been hidden
since the beginning of the world.ʰ

Explanation of the parable of the weeds

³⁶Jesus left the crowds and went into the house. His disciples came to him and said, "Explain to us the parable of the weeds in the field."

³⁷Jesus replied, "The one who plants the good seed is the Human One.ⁱ ³⁸The field is the world. And the good seeds are the followers of the kingdom. But the weeds are the followers of the evil one. ³⁹The enemy who planted them is the devil. The harvest is the end of the

---

ʰPs 78:2 ⁱOr Son of Man

present age. The harvesters are the angels. ⁴⁰Just as people gather weeds and burn them in the fire, so it will be at the end of the present age. ⁴¹The Human One^j will send his angels, and they will gather out of his kingdom all things that cause people to fall away and all people who sin. ⁴²He will throw them into a burning furnace. People there will be weeping and grinding their teeth. ⁴³Then the righteous will shine like the sun in their Father's kingdom. Those who have ears should hear."

Parable of the treasure

⁴⁴"The kingdom of heaven is like a treasure that somebody hid in a field, which someone else found and covered up. Full of joy, the finder sold everything and bought that field.

Parable of the merchant

⁴⁵"Again, the kingdom of heaven is like a merchant in search of fine pearls. ⁴⁶When he found one very precious pearl, he went and sold all that he owned and bought it.

Parable of the net

⁴⁷"Again, the kingdom of heaven is like a net that people threw into the lake and gathered all kinds of fish. ⁴⁸When it was full, they pulled it to the shore, where they sat down and put the good fish together into containers. But the bad fish they threw away. ⁴⁹That's the way it will be at the end of the present age. The angels will go out and separate the evil people from the righteous people, ⁵⁰ and will throw the evil ones into a burning furnace. People there will be weeping and grinding their teeth.

Treasures new and old

⁵¹"Have you understood all these things?" Jesus asked.

They said to him, "Yes."

⁵²Then he said to them, "Therefore, every legal expert who has been trained as a disciple for the kingdom of heaven is like the head of a household who brings old and new things out of their treasure chest."

Jesus in his hometown

⁵³When Jesus finished these parables, he departed. ⁵⁴When he came to his hometown, he taught the people in their synagogue. They were surprised and said, "Where did he get this wisdom? Where did he get the power to work miracles? ⁵⁵Isn't he the carpenter's son? Isn't his mother named Mary? Aren't James, Joseph, Simon, and Judas his brothers? ⁵⁶And his sisters, aren't they here with us? Where did this man get all this?" ⁵⁷They were repulsed by him and fell into sin.

But Jesus said to them, "Prophets are honored everywhere except in their own hometowns and in their own households." ⁵⁸He was unable to do many miracles there because of their disbelief.

Death of John the Baptist

14 At that time Herod the ruler^k heard the news about Jesus. ²He said to his servants, "This is John the Baptist. He's been raised from the dead. This is why these miraculous powers are at work through him." ³Herod had arrested John, bound him, and put him in prison because of Herodias, the wife of Herod's brother Philip.

⁴That's because John told Herod, "It's against the law for you to marry her."

---

^j Or *Son of Man*　^k Or *tetrarch*, which refers to a prince over a small region

⁵Although Herod wanted to kill him, he feared the crowd because they thought John was a prophet. ⁶But at Herod's birthday party Herodias' daughter danced in front of the guests and thrilled Herod. ⁷Then he swore to give her anything she asked.

⁸At her mother's urging, the girl said, "Give me the head of John the Baptist here on a plate." ⁹Although the king was upset, because of his solemn pledge and his guests he commanded that they give it to her. ¹⁰Then he had John beheaded in prison. ¹¹They brought his head on a plate and gave it to the young woman, and she brought it to her mother. ¹²But John's disciples came and took his body and buried it. Then they went and told Jesus what had happened.

Feeding the five thousand

¹³When Jesus heard about John, he withdrew in a boat to a deserted place by himself. When the crowds learned this, they followed him on foot from the cities. ¹⁴When Jesus arrived and saw a large crowd, he had compassion for them and healed those who were sick.¹⁵That evening his disciples came and said to him, "This is an isolated place and it's getting late. Send the crowds away so they can go into the villages and buy food for themselves."

¹⁶But Jesus said to them, "There's no need to send them away. You give them something to eat."

¹⁷They replied, "We have nothing here except five loaves of bread and two fish."

¹⁸He said, "Bring them here to me." ¹⁹He ordered the crowds to sit down on the grass. He took the five loaves of bread and the two fish, looked up to heaven, blessed them and broke the loaves apart and gave them to his disciples. Then the disciples gave them to the crowds. ²⁰Everyone ate until they were full, and they filled twelve baskets with the leftovers. ²¹About five thousand men plus women and children had eaten.

Walking on the water

²²Right then, Jesus made the disciples get into the boat and go ahead to the other side of the lake while he dismissed the crowds. ²³When he sent them away, he went up onto a mountain by himself to pray. Evening came and he was alone. ²⁴Meanwhile, the boat, fighting a strong headwind, was being battered by the waves and was already far away from land. ²⁵Very early in the morning he came to his disciples, walking on the lake. ²⁶When the disciples saw him walking on the lake, they were terrified and said, "It's a ghost!" They were so frightened they screamed.

²⁷Just then Jesus spoke to them, "Be encouraged! It's me. Don't be afraid."

²⁸Peter replied, "Lord, if it's you, order me to come to you on the water."

²⁹And Jesus said, "Come."

Then Peter got out of the boat and was walking on the water toward Jesus. ³⁰But when Peter saw the strong wind, he became frightened. As he began to sink, he shouted, "Lord, rescue me!"

³¹Jesus immediately reached out and grabbed him, saying, "You man of weak faith! Why did you begin to have doubts?" ³²When they got into the boat, the wind settled down.

³³Then those in the boat worshipped Jesus and said, "You must be God's Son!"

Healing the sick

³⁴When they had crossed the lake, they landed at Gennesaret. ³⁵When the

people who lived in that place recognized him, they sent word throughout that whole region, and they brought to him everyone who was sick. 36 Then they begged him that they might just touch the edge of his clothes. Everyone who touched him was cured.

Rules from the elders

15 Then Pharisees and legal experts came to Jesus from Jerusalem and said, 2 "Why are your disciples breaking the elders' rules handed down to us? They don't ritually purify their hands by washing before they eat."

3 Jesus replied, "Why do you break the command of God by keeping the rules handed down to you? 4 For God said, *Honor your father and your mother,*[1] and *The person who speaks against father or mother will certainly be put to death.*[m] 5 But you say, 'If you tell your father or mother, "Everything I'm expected to contribute to you I'm giving to God as a gift," then you don't have to honor your father.' 6 So you do away with God's Law for the sake of the rules that have been handed down to you. 7 Hypocrites! Isaiah really knew what he was talking about when he prophesied about you, 8 *This people honors me with their lips, but their hearts are far away from me.* 9 *Their worship of me is empty since they teach instructions that are human rules.*"[n]

10 Jesus called the crowd near and said to them, "Listen and understand. 11 It's not what goes into the mouth that contaminates a person in God's sight. It's what comes out of the mouth that contaminates the person."

12 Then the disciples came and said to him, "Do you know that the Pharisees were offended by what you just said?"

13 Jesus replied, "Every plant that my heavenly Father didn't plant will be pulled up. 14 Leave the Pharisees alone. They are blind people who are guides to blind people. But if a blind person leads another blind person, they will both fall into a ditch."

15 Then Peter spoke up, "Explain this riddle to us."

16 Jesus said, "Don't you understand yet? 17 Don't you know that everything that goes into the mouth enters the stomach and goes out into the sewer? 18 But what goes out of the mouth comes from the heart. And that's what contaminates a person in God's sight. 19 Out of the heart come evil thoughts, murders, adultery, sexual sins, thefts, false testimonies, and insults. 20 These contaminate a person in God's sight. But eating without washing hands doesn't contaminate in God's sight."

Canaanite woman

21 From there, Jesus went to the regions of Tyre and Sidon. 22 A Canaanite woman from those territories came out and shouted, "Show me mercy, Son of David. My daughter is suffering terribly from demon possession." 23 But he didn't respond to her at all.

His disciples came and urged him, "Send her away; she keeps shouting out after us."

24 Jesus replied, "I've been sent only to the lost sheep, the people of Israel."

25 But she knelt before him and said, "Lord, help me."

26 He replied, "It is not good to take the children's bread and toss it to dogs.

[1] Exod 20:12; Deut 5:16 [m] Exod 21:17; Lev 20:9 [n] Isa 29:13

²⁷She said, "Yes, Lord. But even the dogs eat the crumbs that fall off their masters' table."

²⁸Jesus answered, "Woman, you have great faith. It will be just as you wish." And right then her daughter was healed.

Healing of many people

²⁹Jesus moved on from there along the shore of the Galilee Sea. He went up a mountain and sat down. ³⁰Large crowds came to him, including those who were paralyzed, blind, injured, and unable to speak, and many others. They laid them at his feet, and he healed them. ³¹So the crowd was amazed when they saw those who had been unable to speak talking, and the paralyzed cured, and the injured walking, and the blind seeing. And they praised the God of Israel.

Feeding of the four thousand

³²Now Jesus called his disciples and said, "I feel sorry for the crowd because they have been with me for three days and have nothing to eat. I don't want to send them away hungry for fear they won't have enough strength to travel."

³³His disciples replied, "Where are we going to get enough food in this wilderness to satisfy such a big crowd?"

³⁴Jesus said, "How much bread do you have?"

They responded, "Seven loaves and a few fish."

³⁵He told the crowd to sit on the ground. ³⁶He took the seven loaves of bread and the fish. After he gave thanks, he broke them into pieces and gave them to the disciples, and the disciples gave them to the crowds. ³⁷Everyone ate until they were full. The disciples collected seven baskets full of leftovers. ³⁸Four thousand men ate, plus women

and children. ³⁹After dismissing the crowds, Jesus got into the boat and came to the region of Magadan.

Demand for a sign

16 The Pharisees and Sadducees came to Jesus. In order to test him they asked him to show them a sign from heaven.

²But he replied, "At evening you say, 'It will be nice weather because the sky is bright red.' ³And in the morning you say, 'There will be bad weather today because the sky is cloudy.' You know how to make sense of the sky's appearance. But you are unable to recognize the signs that point to what the time is. ⁴An evil and unfaithful generation searches for a sign. But it won't receive any sign except Jonah's sign." Then he left them and went away.

Yeast of the Pharisees and Sadducees

⁵When the disciples arrived on the other side of the lake, they had forgotten to bring bread. ⁶Jesus said to them, "Watch out and be on your guard for the yeast of the Pharisees and Sadducees."

⁷They discussed this among themselves and said, "We didn't bring any bread."

⁸Jesus knew what they were discussing and said, "You people of weak faith! Why are you discussing among yourselves the fact that you don't have any bread? ⁹Don't you understand yet? Don't you remember the five loaves that fed the five thousand and how many baskets of leftovers you gathered? ¹⁰And the seven loaves that fed the four thousand and how many large baskets of leftovers you gathered? ¹¹Don't you know that I wasn't talking

about bread? But be on your guard for the yeast of the Pharisees and Sadducees." ¹²Then they understood that he wasn't telling them to be on their guard for yeast used in making bread. No, he was telling them to watch out for the teaching of the Pharisees and Sadducees.

Peter's declaration about Jesus

¹³Now when Jesus came to the area of Caesarea Philippi, he asked his disciples, "Who do people say the Human Oneº is?"

¹⁴They replied, "Some say John the Baptist, others Elijah, and still others Jeremiah or one of the other prophets."

¹⁵He said, "And what about you? Who do you say that I am?"

¹⁶Simon Peter said, "You are the Christ, the Son of the living God."

¹⁷Then Jesus replied, "Happy are you, Simon son of Jonah, because no human has shown this to you. Rather my Father who is in heaven has shown you. ¹⁸I tell you that you are Peter.ᴾ And I'll build my church on this rock. The gates of the underworld won't be able to stand against it. ¹⁹I'll give you the keys of the kingdom of heaven. Anything you fasten on earth will be fastened in heaven. Anything you loosen on earth will be loosened in heaven." ²⁰Then he ordered the disciples not to tell anybody that he was the Christ.

First prediction of Jesus' death and resurrection

²¹From that time Jesus began to show his disciples that he had to go to Jerusalem and suffer many things from the elders, chief priests, and legal experts, and that he had to be killed and raised on the third day. ²²Then Peter took hold of Jesus and, scolding him, began to correct him: "God forbid, Lord! This won't happen to you." ²³But he turned to Peter and said, "Get behind me, Satan. You are a stone that could make me stumble, for you are not thinking God's thoughts but human thoughts."

Saving and losing life

²⁴Then Jesus said to his disciples, "All who want to come after me must say no to themselves, take up their cross, and follow me. ²⁵All who want to save their lives will lose them. But all who lose their lives because of me will find them. ²⁶Why would people gain the whole world but lose their lives? What will people give in exchange for their lives? ²⁷For the Human One�q is about to come with the majesty of his Father with his angels. And then he will repay each one for what that person has done. ²⁸I assure you that some standing here won't die before they see the Human Oneʳ coming in his kingdom."

Jesus' transformation

17 Six days later Jesus took Peter, James, and John his brother, and brought them to the top of a very high mountain. ²He was transformed in front of them. His face shone like the sun, and his clothes became as white as light.

³Moses and Elijah appeared to them, talking with Jesus. ⁴Peter reacted to all of this by saying to Jesus, "Lord, it's good that we're here. If you want, I'll make three shrines: one for you, one for Moses, and one for Elijah.

ºOr *Son of Man* ᴾPeter means *rock.* qOr *Son of Man* ʳOr *Son of Man*

⁵While he was still speaking, look, a bright cloud overshadowed them. A voice from the cloud said, "This is my Son whom I dearly love. I am very pleased with him. Listen to him!" ⁶Hearing this, the disciples fell on their faces, filled with awe.

⁷But Jesus came and touched them. "Get up," he said. "Don't be afraid." ⁸When they looked up, they saw no one except Jesus.

⁹As they were coming down the mountain, Jesus commanded them, "Don't tell anybody about the vision until the Human One* is raised from the dead."

¹⁰The disciples asked, "Then why do the legal experts say that Elijah must first come?"

¹¹Jesus responded, "Elijah does come first and will restore all things. ¹²In fact, I tell you that Elijah has already come, and they didn't know him. But they did to him whatever they wanted. In the same way the Human One† is also going to suffer at their hands." ¹³Then the disciples realized he was telling them about John the Baptist.

Healing of a boy who was demon-possessed

¹⁴When they came to the crowd, a man met Jesus. He knelt before him, ¹⁵saying, "Lord, show mercy to my son. He is epileptic and suffers terribly, for he often falls into the fire or the water. ¹⁶I brought him to your disciples, but they couldn't heal him."

¹⁷Jesus answered, "You faithless and crooked generation, how long will I be with you? How long will I put up with you? Bring the boy here to me." ¹⁸Then

Jesus spoke harshly to the demon. And it came out of the child, who was healed from that time on.

¹⁹Then the disciples came to Jesus in private and said, "Why couldn't we throw the demon out?"

²⁰"Because you have little faith," he said. "I assure you that if you have faith the size of a mustard seed, you could say to this mountain, 'Go from here to there,' and it will go. There will be nothing that you can't do."ᵘ

Second prediction of Jesus' death and resurrection

²²When the disciples came together in Galilee, Jesus said to them, "The Human One* is about to be delivered over into human hands. ²³They will kill him. But he will be raised on the third day." And they were heartbroken.

Paying the temple tax

²⁴When they came to Capernaum, the people who collected the half-shekel temple tax came to Peter and said, "Doesn't your teacher pay the temple tax?"

²⁵"Yes," he said.

But when they came into the house, Jesus spoke to Peter first. "What do you think, Simon? From whom do earthly kings collect taxes, from their children or from strangers?"

²⁶"From strangers," he said.

Jesus said to him, "Then the children don't have to pay. ²⁷But just so we don't offend them, go to the lake, throw out a fishing line and hook, and take the first fish you catch. When you open its mouth, you will find a shekel coin. Take it and pay the tax for both of us."

ˢOr *Son of Man* ᵗOr *Son of Man* ᵘ17:21 is omitted in most critical editions of the Gk New Testament *This kind doesn't come out except through prayer and fasting.* ᵛOr *Son of Man*

Greatest in the kingdom

18 At that time the disciples came to Jesus and asked, "Who is the greatest in the kingdom of heaven?"

[2] Then he called a little child over to sit among the disciples, [3] and said, "I assure you that if you don't turn your lives around and become like this little child, you will definitely not enter the kingdom of heaven. [4] Those who humble themselves like this little child will be the greatest in the kingdom of heaven. [5] Whoever welcomes one such child in my name welcomes me.

Falling into sin

[6] "As for whoever causes these little ones who believe in me to trip and fall into sin, it would be better for them to have a huge stone hung around their necks and be drowned in the bottom of the lake. [7] How terrible it is for the world because of the things that cause people to trip and fall into sin! Such things have to happen, but how terrible it is for the person who causes those things to happen! [8] If your hand or your foot causes you to fall into sin, chop it off and throw it away. It's better to enter into life crippled or lame than to be thrown into the eternal fire with two hands or two feet. [9] If your eye causes you to fall into sin, tear it out and throw it away. It's better to enter into life with one eye than to be cast into a burning hell with two eyes.

Parable of the lost sheep

[10] "Be careful that you don't look down on one of these little ones. I say to you that their angels in heaven are always looking into the face of my Father who is in heaven.[w] [12] What do you think? If someone had one hundred sheep and one of them wandered off, wouldn't he leave the ninety-nine on the hillsides and go in search for the one that wandered off? [13] If he finds it, I assure you that he is happier about having that one sheep than about the ninety-nine who didn't wander off. [14] In the same way, my Father who is in heaven doesn't want to lose one of these little ones.

Sinning brother or sister

[15] "If your brother or sister sins against you, go and correct them when you are alone together. If they listen to you, then you've won over your brother or sister. [16] But if they won't listen, take with you one or two others so that *every word may be established by the mouth of two or three witnesses.*[x] [17] But if they still won't pay attention, report it to the church. If they won't pay attention even to the church, treat them as you would a Gentile and tax collector. [18] I assure you that whatever you fasten on earth will be fastened in heaven. And whatever you loosen on earth will be loosened in heaven. [19] Again I assure you that if two of you agree on earth about anything you ask, then my Father who is in heaven will do it for you. [20] For where two or three are gathered in my name, I'm there with them."

Parable of the unforgiving servant

[21] Then Peter said to Jesus, "Lord, how many times should I forgive my brother or sister who sins against me? Should I forgive as many as seven times?"

[w]18:11 is omitted in most critical editions of the Gk New Testament *For the Human One has come to save the lost.* [x]Deut 19:15

²²Jesus said, "Not just seven times, but rather as many as seventy-seven times.ʸ ²³Therefore, the kingdom of heaven is like a king who wanted to settle accounts with his servants. ²⁴When he began to settle accounts, they brought to him a servant who owed him ten thousand bags of gold.ᶻ ²⁵Because the servant didn't have enough to pay it back, the master ordered that he should be sold, along with his wife and children and everything he had, and that the proceeds should be used as payment. ²⁶But the servant fell down, kneeled before him, and said, 'Please, be patient with me, and I'll pay you back.' ²⁷The master had compassion on that servant, released him, and forgave the loan.

²⁸"When that servant went out, he found one of his fellow servants who owed him one hundred coins.ᵃ He grabbed him around the throat and said, 'Pay me back what you owe me.'

²⁹"Then his fellow servant fell down and begged him, 'Be patient with me, and I'll pay you back.' ³⁰But he refused. Instead, he threw him into prison until he paid back his debt.

³¹"When his fellow servants saw what happened, they were deeply offended. They came and told their master all that happened. ³²His master called the first servant and said, 'You wicked servant! I forgave you all that debt because you appealed to me. ³³Shouldn't you also have mercy on your fellow servant, just as I had mercy on you?' ³⁴His master was furious and handed him over to the guard

responsible for punishing prisoners, until he had paid the whole debt.

³⁵"My heavenly Father will also do the same to you if you don't forgive your brother or sister from your heart."

Teaching about divorce

19 When Jesus finished saying these things, he left Galilee and came to the area of Judea on the east side of the Jordan. ²Large crowds followed him, and he healed them. ³Some Pharisees came to him. In order to test him, they said, "Does the Law allow a man to divorce his wife for just any reason?"

⁴Jesus answered, "Haven't you read that at the beginning the creator *made them male and female?*ᵇ ⁵And God said, *'Because of this a man should leave his father and mother and be joined together with his wife, and the two will be one flesh.'*ᶜ ⁶So they are no longer two but one flesh. Therefore, humans must not pull apart what God has put together."

⁷The Pharisees said to him, "Then why did Moses command us to *give a divorce certificate and divorce her?*ᵈ"

⁸Jesus replied, "Moses allowed you to divorce your wives because your hearts are unyielding. But it wasn't that way from the beginning. ⁹I say to you that whoever divorces his wife, except for sexual unfaithfulness, and marries another woman commits adultery."

¹⁰His disciples said to him, "If that's the way things are between a man and his wife, then it's better not to marry."

¹¹He replied, "Not everybody can accept this teaching, but only those who have received the ability to accept it.

ʸOr *seventy times seven*   ᶻOr *ten thousand talanta*, an amount equal to the wages for sixty million days   ᵃOr *one hundred denaria*, an amount equal to the wages for one hundred days   ᵇGen 1:27; 5:2   ᶜGen 2:24   ᵈDeut 24:1

¹²For there are eunuchs who have been eunuchs from birth. And there are eunuchs who have been made eunuchs by other people. And there are eunuchs who have made themselves eunuchs because of the kingdom of heaven. Those who can accept it should accept it."

Jesus blesses children

¹³Some people brought children to Jesus so that he would place his hands on them and pray. But the disciples scolded them. ¹⁴"Allow the children to come to me," Jesus said. "Don't forbid them, because the kingdom of heaven belongs to people like these children." ¹⁵Then he blessed the children and went away from there.

A rich man's question

¹⁶A man approached him and said, "Teacher, what good thing must I do to have eternal life?"

¹⁷Jesus said, "Why do you ask me about what is good? There's only one who is good. If you want to enter eternal life, keep the commandments."

¹⁸The man said, "Which ones?"

Then Jesus said, "*Don't commit murder. Don't commit adultery. Don't steal. Don't give false testimony.* ¹⁹*Honor your father and mother,*ᵉ and *love your neighbor as you love yourself.*"ᶠ

²⁰The young man replied, "I've kept all these. What am I still missing?"

²¹Jesus said, "If you want to be complete, go, sell what you own, and give the money to the poor. Then you will have treasure in heaven. And come follow me."

²²But when the young man heard this, he went away saddened, because he had many possessions.

Teaching about giving up things

²³Then Jesus said to his disciples, "I assure you that it will be very hard for a rich person to enter the kingdom of heaven. ²⁴In fact, it's easier for a camel to squeeze through the eye of a needle than for a rich person to enter God's kingdom."

²⁵When his disciples heard this, they were stunned. "Then who can be saved?" they asked.

²⁶Jesus looked at them carefully and said, "It's impossible for human beings. But all things are possible for God."

²⁷Then Peter replied, "Look, we've left everything and followed you. What will we have?"

²⁸Jesus said to them, "I assure you who have followed me that, when everything is made new, when the Human Oneᵍ sits on his magnificent throne, you also will sit on twelve thrones overseeing the twelve tribes of Israel. ²⁹And all who have left houses, brothers, sisters, father, mother, children, or farms because of my name will receive one hundred times more and will inherit eternal life. ³⁰But many who are first will be last. And many who are last will be first.

Workers in the vineyard

20 "The kingdom of heaven is like a landowner who went out early in the morning to hire workers for his vineyard. ²After he agreed with the workers to pay them a denarion,ʰ he sent them into his vineyard.

ᵉExod 20:12-16; Deut 5:16-20   ᶠLev 19:18   ᵍOr *Son of Man*   ʰA denarion was a typical day's wage.

³"Then he went out around nine in the morning and saw others standing around the marketplace doing nothing. ⁴He said to them, 'You also go into the vineyard, and I'll pay you whatever is right.' ⁵And they went.

"Again around noon and then at three in the afternoon, he did the same thing. ⁶Around five in the afternoon he went and found others standing around, and he said to them, 'Why are you just standing around here doing nothing all day long?'

⁷"'Because nobody has hired us,' they replied.

"He responded, 'You also go into the vineyard.'

⁸"When evening came, the owner of the vineyard said to his manager, 'Call the workers and give them their wages, beginning with the last ones hired and moving on finally to the first.' ⁹When those who were hired at five in the afternoon came, each one received a denarion. ¹⁰Now when those hired first came, they thought they would receive more. But each of them also received a denarion. ¹¹When they received it, they grumbled against the landowner, ¹²'These who were hired last worked one hour, and they received the same pay as we did even though we had to work the whole day in the hot sun.'

¹³"But he replied to one of them, 'Friend, I did you no wrong. Didn't I agree to pay you a denarion? ¹⁴Take what belongs to you and go. I want to give to this one who was hired last the same as I give to you. ¹⁵Don't I have the right to do what I want with what belongs to me? Or are you resentful because I'm generous?' ¹⁶So those who are

last will be first. And those who are first will be last."

Jesus predicts his death and resurrection

¹⁷As Jesus was going up to Jerusalem, he took the Twelve aside by themselves on the road. He told them, ¹⁸"Look, we are going up to Jerusalem. The Human One[i] will be handed over to the chief priests and legal experts. They will condemn him to death. ¹⁹They will hand him over to the Gentiles to be ridiculed, tortured, and crucified. But he will be raised on the third day."

Request from James and John's mother

²⁰Then the mother of Zebedee's sons came to Jesus along with her sons. Bowing before him, she asked a favor of him.

²¹"What do you want?" he asked.

She responded, "Say that these two sons of mine will sit, one on your right hand and one on your left, in your kingdom."

²²Jesus replied, "You don't know what you're asking! Can you drink from the cup that I'm about to drink from?"

They said to him, "We can."

²³He said to them, "You will drink from my cup, but to sit at my right or left hand isn't mine to give. It belongs to those for whom my Father prepared it."

²⁴Now when the other ten disciples heard about this, they became angry with the two brothers. ²⁵But Jesus called them over and said, "You know that those who rule the Gentiles show off their authority over them and their high-ranking officials order them around. ²⁶But that's not

[i] Or Son of Man

the way it will be with you. Whoever wants to be great among you will be your servant. ²⁷Whoever wants to be first among you will be your slave— ²⁸just as the Human One^j didn't come to be served but rather to serve and to give his life to liberate many people."

Healing of two blind men

²⁹As Jesus and his disciples were going out of Jericho a large crowd followed him. ³⁰When two blind men sitting along the road heard that Jesus was passing by, they shouted, "Show us mercy, Lord, Son of David!"

³¹Now the crowd scolded them and told them to be quiet. But they shouted even louder, "Show us mercy, Lord, Son of David!"

³²Jesus stopped in his tracks and called to them. "What do you want me to do for you?" he asked.

³³"Lord, we want to see," they replied. ³⁴Jesus had compassion on them and touched their eyes. Immediately they were able to see, and they followed him.

Entry into Jerusalem

21 When they approached Jerusalem and came to Bethphage on the Mount of Olives, Jesus gave two disciples a task. ²He said to them, "Go into the village over there. As soon as you enter, you will find a donkey tied up and a colt with it. Untie them and bring them to me. ³If anyone says anything to you, say that their master needs them." He sent them off right away. ⁴Now this happened to fulfill what the prophet said, ⁵*Say to Daughter Zion, "Look, your king is coming to you, humble and riding on a donkey, and on a colt the donkey's*

offspring."^k ⁶The disciples went and did just as Jesus had ordered them. ⁷They brought the donkey and the colt and laid their clothes on them. Then he sat on them.

⁸Now a large crowd spread their clothes on the road. Others cut palm branches off the trees and spread them on the road. ⁹The crowds in front of him and behind him shouted, *"Hosanna to the Son of David! Blessings on the one who comes in the name of the Lord!*^l *Hosanna in the highest!"* ¹⁰And when Jesus entered Jerusalem, the whole city was stirred up. "Who is this?" they asked. ¹¹The crowds answered, "It's the prophet Jesus from Nazareth in Galilee."

Cleansing the temple

¹²Then Jesus went into the temple and threw out all those who were selling and buying there. He pushed over the tables used for currency exchange and the chairs of those who sold doves. ¹³He said to them, "It's written, *My house will be called a house of prayer.*^m But you've made it a hideout for crooks."

¹⁴People who were blind and lame came to Jesus in the temple, and he healed them. ¹⁵But when the chief priests and legal experts saw the amazing things he was doing and the children shouting in the temple, *"Hosanna to the Son of David!"* they were angry. ¹⁶They said to Jesus, "Do you hear what these children are saying?"

"Yes," he answered. "Haven't you ever read, *From the mouths of babies and infants you've arranged praise for yourself?"*ⁿ ¹⁷Then he left them and went

---

^jOr *Son of Man* ^kIsa 62:11; Zech 9:9 ^lPs. 118:26 ^mIsa 56:7; Jer 7:11 ⁿPs 8:3 LXX

out of the city to Bethany and spent the night there.

Cursing the fig tree

¹⁸Early in the morning as Jesus was returning to the city, he was hungry. ¹⁹He saw a fig tree along the road, but when he came to it, he found nothing except leaves. Then he said to it, "You'll never again bear fruit!" The fig tree dried up at once.

²⁰When the disciples saw it, they were amazed. "How did the fig tree dry up so fast?" they asked.

²¹Jesus responded, "I assure you that if you have faith and don't doubt, you will not only do what was done to the fig tree. You will even say to this mountain, 'Be lifted up and thrown into the lake.' And it will happen. ²²If you have faith, you will receive whatever you pray for."

Jesus' authority questioned

²³When Jesus entered the temple, the chief priests and elders of the people came to him as he was teaching. They asked, "What kind of authority do you have for doing these things? Who gave you this authority?"

²⁴Jesus replied, "I have a question for you. If you tell me the answer, I'll tell you what kind of authority I have to do these things. ²⁵Where did John get his authority to baptize? Did he get it from heaven or from humans?"

They argued among themselves, "If we say 'from heaven,' he'll say to us, 'Then why didn't you believe him?' ²⁶But we can't say 'from humans' because we're afraid of the crowd, since everyone thinks John was a prophet." ²⁷Then they replied, "We don't know."

Jesus also said to them, "Neither will I tell you what kind of authority I have to do these things.

Parable of two sons

²⁸"What do you think? A man had two sons. Now he came to the first and said, 'Son, go and work in the vineyard today.'

²⁹"'No, I don't want to,' he replied. But later he changed his mind and went.

³⁰"The father said the same thing to the other son, who replied, 'Yes, sir.' But he didn't go.

³¹"Which one of these two did his father's will?"

They said, "The first one."

Jesus said to them, "I assure you that tax collectors and prostitutes are entering God's kingdom ahead of you. ³²For John came to you on the righteous road, and you didn't believe him. But tax collectors and prostitutes believed him. Yet even after you saw this, you didn't change your hearts and lives and you didn't believe him.

Parable of the tenant farmers

³³"Listen to another parable. There was a landowner who planted a vineyard. He put a fence around it, dug a winepress in it, and built a tower. Then he rented it to tenant farmers and took a trip. ³⁴When it was time for harvest, he sent his servants to the tenant farmers to collect his fruit. ³⁵But the tenant farmers grabbed his servants. They beat some of them, and some of them they killed. Some of them they stoned to death.

³⁶"Again he sent other servants, more than the first group. They treated them in the same way. ³⁷Finally he sent his son to them. 'They will respect my son,' he said.

38"But when the tenant farmers saw the son, they said to each other, 'This is the heir. Come on, let's kill him and we'll have his inheritance.' 39They grabbed him, threw him out of the vineyard, and killed him.

40"When the owner of the vineyard comes, what will he do to those tenant farmers?"

41They said, "He will totally destroy those wicked farmers and rent the vineyard to other tenant farmers who will give him the fruit when it's ready."

42Jesus said to them, "Haven't you ever read in the scriptures, *The stone that the builders rejected has become the cornerstone. The Lord has done this, and it's amazing in our eyes?*o 43Therefore, I tell you that God's kingdom will be taken away from you and will be given to a people who produce its fruit. 44Whoever falls on this stone will be crushed. And the stone will crush the person it falls on."

45Now when the chief priests and the Pharisees heard the parable, they knew Jesus was talking about them. 46They were trying to arrest him, but they feared the crowds, who thought he was a prophet.

Parable of the wedding party

22 Jesus responded by speaking again in parables: 2"The kingdom of heaven is like a king who prepared a wedding party for his son. 3He sent his servants to call those invited to the wedding party. But they didn't want to come. 4Again he sent other servants and said to them, 'Tell those who have been invited, "Look, the meal is all prepared. I've butchered the oxen and

oPs 118:22-23

the fattened cattle. Now everything's ready. Come to the wedding party!"' 5But they paid no attention and went away—some to their fields, others to their businesses. 6The rest of them grabbed his servants, abused them, and killed them.

7"The king was angry. He sent his soldiers to destroy those murderers and set their city on fire. 8Then he said to his servants, 'The wedding party is prepared, but those who were invited weren't worthy. 9Therefore, go to the roads on the edge of town and invite everyone you find to the wedding party.'

10"Then those servants went to the roads and gathered everyone they found, both evil and good. The wedding party was full of guests. 11Now when the king came in and saw the guests, he spotted a man who wasn't wearing wedding clothes. 12He said to him, 'Friend, how did you get in here without wedding clothes?' But he was speechless. 13Then the king said to his servants, 'Tie his hands and feet and throw him out into the farthest darkness. People there will be weeping and grinding their teeth.'

14"Many people are invited, but few people are chosen."

Question about taxes

15Then the Pharisees met together to find a way to trap Jesus in his words. 16They sent their disciples, along with the supporters of Herod, to him. "Teacher," they said, "we know that you are genuine and that you teach God's way as it really is. We know that you are not swayed by people's opinions, because you don't show favoritism.

¹⁷So tell us what you think: Does the Law allow people to pay taxes to Caesar or not?"

¹⁸Knowing their evil motives, Jesus replied, "Why do you test me, you hypocrites? ¹⁹Show me the coin used to pay the tax." And they brought him a denarion. ²⁰"Whose image and inscription is this?" he asked.

²¹"Caesar's," they replied.

Then he said, "Give to Caesar what belongs to Caesar and to God what belongs to God." ²²When they heard this they were astonished, and they departed.

Question about resurrection

²³That same day Sadducees, who deny that there is a resurrection, came to Jesus. ²⁴They asked, "Teacher, Moses said, *If a man who doesn't have children dies, his brother must marry his wife and produce children for his brother.*ᵖ ²⁵Now there were seven brothers among us. The first one married, then died. Because he had no children he left his widow to his brother. ²⁶The same thing happened with the second brother and the third, and in fact with all seven brothers. ²⁷Finally, the woman died. ²⁸At the resurrection, which of the seven brothers will be her husband? They were all married to her."

²⁹Jesus responded, "You are wrong because you don't know either the scriptures or God's power. ³⁰At the resurrection people won't marry nor will they be given in marriage. Instead, they will be like angels from God. ³¹As for the resurrection of the dead, haven't you read what God told you, ³²*I'm the God of Abraham, the God of Isaac, and the God of Jacob?*�q He isn't the God of the dead but of the living." ³³Now when the crowd heard this, they were astonished at his teaching.

Great commandment

³⁴When the Pharisees heard that Jesus had left the Sadducees speechless, they met together. ³⁵One of them, a legal expert, tested him. ³⁶"Teacher, what is the greatest commandment in the Law?"

³⁷He replied, *"You must love the Lord your God with all your heart, with all your being,*ʳ *and with all your mind.* ³⁸This is the first and greatest commandment. ³⁹And the second is like it: *You must love your neighbor as you love yourself.*ˢ ⁴⁰All the Law and the Prophets depend on these two commands."

Question about David's son

⁴¹Now as the Pharisees were gathering, Jesus asked them, ⁴²"What do you think about the Christ? Whose son is he?"

"David's son," they replied.

⁴³He said, "Then how is it that David, inspired by the Holy Spirit, called him Lord when he said, ⁴⁴*The Lord said to my lord, 'Sit at my right side until I turn your enemies into your footstool'?*ᵗ ⁴⁵If David calls him Lord, how can he be David's son?" ⁴⁶Nobody was able to answer him. And from that day forward nobody dared to ask him anything.

Ways of the legal experts and the Pharisees

23 Then Jesus spoke to the crowds and his disciples, ²"The legal experts and the Pharisees sit on Moses' seat. ³Therefore, you must take care

ᵖDeut 25:5   qExod 3:6, 15-16   ʳDeut 6:5   ˢLev 19:18   ᵗPs 110:1

to do everything they say. But don't do what they do. ⁴For they tie together heavy packs that are impossible to carry. They put them on the shoulders of others, but are unwilling to lift a finger to move them. ⁵Everything they do, they do to be noticed by others. They make extra-wide prayer bands for their arms and long tassels for their clothes. ⁶They love to sit in places of honor at banquets and in the synagogues. ⁷They love to be greeted with honor in the markets and to be addressed as 'Rabbi.'

⁸"But you shouldn't be called *Rabbi*, because you have one teacher, and all of you are brothers and sisters. ⁹Don't call anybody on earth your father, because you have one Father, who is heavenly. ¹⁰Don't be called *teacher*, because Christ is your one teacher. ¹¹But the one who is greatest among you will be your servant. ¹²All who lift themselves up will be brought low. But all who make themselves low will be lifted up.

Condemnation of the legal experts and the Pharisees

¹³"How terrible it will be for you legal experts and Pharisees! Hypocrites! You shut people out of the kingdom of heaven. You don't enter yourselves, and you won't allow those who want to enter to do so.ᵘ

¹⁵"How terrible it will be for you, legal experts and Pharisees! Hypocrites! You travel over sea and land to make one convert. But when they've been converted, they become twice the child of hell you are.

¹⁶"How terrible it will be for you

blind guides who say, 'If people swear by the temple, it's nothing. But if people swear by the gold in the temple, they are obligated to do what they swore.' ¹⁷You foolish and blind people! Which is greater, the gold or the temple that makes the gold holy? ¹⁸You say, 'If people swear by the altar, it's nothing. But if they swear by the gift on the altar, they are obligated to do what they swore.' ¹⁹You blind people! Which is greater, the gift or the altar that makes the gift holy? ²⁰Therefore, those who swear by the altar swear by it and by everything that's on it. ²¹Those who swear by the temple swear by it and by everything that's part of it. ²²Those who swear by heaven swear by God's throne and by the one who sits on it.

²³"How terrible it will be for you legal experts and Pharisees! Hypocrites! You give to God a tenth of mint, dill, and cumin, but you forget about the more important matters of the Law: justice, peace, and faith. You ought to give a tenth but without forgetting about those more important matters. ²⁴You blind guides! You filter out an ant but swallow a camel.

²⁵"How terrible it will be for you legal experts and Pharisees! Hypocrites! You clean the outside of the cup and plate, but inside they are full of violence and pleasure seeking. ²⁶Blind Pharisee! First clean the inside of the cup so that the outside of the cup will be clean too.

²⁷"How terrible it will be for you legal experts and Pharisees! Hypocrites! You are like whitewashed tombs. They look beautiful on the outside. But inside

---

ᵘMost critical editions of the Gk New Testament omit 23:14 *How terrible it will be for you legal experts and Pharisees! Hypocrites! You eat up widows' houses and make a show of praying long prayers. Therefore, you will receive greater judgment.*

they are full of dead bones and all kinds of filth. ²⁸ In the same way you look righteous to people. But inside you are full of pretense and rebellion.

²⁹ "How terrible it will be for you legal experts and Pharisees! Hypocrites! You build tombs for the prophets and decorate the graves of the righteous. ³⁰ You say, 'If we had lived in our ancestors' days, we wouldn't have joined them in killing the prophets.' ³¹ You testify against yourselves that you are children of those who murdered the prophets. ³² Go ahead, complete what your ancestors did. ³³ You snakes! You children of snakes! How will you be able to escape the judgment of hell? ³⁴ Therefore, look, I'm sending you prophets, wise people, and legal experts. Some of them you will kill and crucify. And some you will beat in your synagogues and chase from city to city. ³⁵ Therefore, upon you will come all the righteous blood that has been poured out on the earth, from the blood of that righteous man Abel to the blood of Zechariah the son of Barachiah, whom you killed between the temple and the altar. ³⁶ I assure you that all these things will come upon this generation.

Crying over Jerusalem

³⁷ "Jerusalem, Jerusalem! You who kill the prophets and stone those who were sent to you. How often I wanted to gather your people together, just as a hen gathers her chicks under her wings. But you didn't want that. ³⁸ Look, your house is left to you deserted. ³⁹ I tell you, you won't see me until you say, *Blessings on the one who comes in the Lord's name.*"^v

^v Ps 118:26

The temple's fate

24 Now Jesus left the temple and was going away. His disciples came to point out to him the temple buildings. ² He responded, "Do you see all these things? I assure you that no stone will be left on another. Everything will be demolished."

Beginning of troubles

³ Now while Jesus was sitting on the Mount of Olives, the disciples came to him privately and said, "Tell us, when will these things happen? What will be the sign of your coming and the end of the age?"

⁴ Jesus replied, "Watch out that no one deceives you. ⁵ Many will come in my name, saying, 'I'm the Christ.' They will deceive many people. ⁶ You will hear about wars and reports of wars. Don't be alarmed. These things must happen, but this isn't the end yet. ⁷ Nations and kingdoms will fight against each other, and there will be famines and earthquakes in all sorts of places. ⁸ But all these things are just the beginning of the sufferings associated with the end. ⁹ They will arrest you, abuse you, and they will kill you. All nations will hate you on account of my name. ¹⁰ At that time many will fall away. They will betray each other and hate each other. ¹¹ Many false prophets will appear and deceive many people. ¹² Because disobedience will expand, the love of many will grow cold. ¹³ But the one who endures to the end will be delivered. ¹⁴ This gospel of the kingdom will be proclaimed throughout the world as a testimony to all the nations. Then the end will come.

The great suffering

15 "When you see the disgusting and destructive thing that Daniel talked about standing in the holy place (the reader should understand this), 16 then those in Judea must escape to the mountains. 17 Those on the roof shouldn't come down to grab things from their houses. 18 Those in the field shouldn't come back to grab their clothes. 19 How terrible it will be at that time for women who are pregnant and for women who are nursing their children. 20 Pray that it doesn't happen in winter or on the Sabbath day. 21 There will be great suffering such as the world has never before seen and will never again see. 22 If that time weren't shortened, nobody would be rescued. But for the sake of the ones whom God chose, that time will be cut short.

23 "Then if somebody says to you, 'Look, here's the Christ,' or 'He's over here,' don't believe it. 24 False christs and false prophets will appear, and they will offer great signs and wonders in order to deceive, if possible, even those whom God has chosen. 25 Look, I've told you ahead of time. 26 So if they say to you, 'Look, he's in the desert,' don't go out. And if they say, 'Look, he's in the rooms deep inside the house,' don't believe it. 27 Just as the lightning flashes from the east to the west, so it will be with the coming of the Human One.w 28 The vultures gather wherever there's a dead body.

Coming of the Human One

29 "Now immediately after the suffering of that time the sun will become dark, and the moon won't give its light. The stars will fall from the sky and the planets and other heavenly bodies will be shaken. 30 Then the sign of the Human Onex will appear in the sky. At that time all the tribes of the earth will be full of sadness, and they will see the Human Oney coming in the heavenly cloudsz with power and great splendor. 31 He will send his angels with the sound of a great trumpet, and they will gather his chosen ones from the four corners of the earth, from one end of the sky to the other.

A lesson from the fig tree

32 "Learn this parable from the fig tree. After its branch becomes tender and it sprouts new leaves, you know that summer is near. 33 In the same way, when you see all these things, you know that the Human Onea is near, at the door. 34 I assure you that this generation won't pass away until all these things happen. 35 Heaven and earth will pass away, but my words will certainly not pass away.

Day and hour

36 "But nobody knows when that day or hour will come, not the heavenly angels and not the Son. Only the Father knows. 37 As it was in the time of Noah, so it will be at the coming of the Human One.b 38 In those days before the flood, people were eating and drinking, marrying and giving in marriage, until the day Noah entered the ark. 39 They didn't know what was happening until the flood came and swept them all away. The coming of

---

wOr Son of Man   xOr Son of Man   yOr Son of Man   zDan 7:13 I suddenly saw one like a human being (Aram kebar enash) coming with the heavenly clouds.   aOr Son of Man   bOr Son of Man the Human One^c will be like that. ⁴⁰At that time there will be two men in the field. One will be taken and the other left. ⁴¹Two women will be grinding at the mill. One will be taken and the other left. ⁴²Therefore, stay alert! You don't know what day the Lord is coming. ⁴³But you understand that if the head of the house knew at what time the thief would come, he would keep alert and wouldn't allow the thief to break into his house. ⁴⁴Therefore, you also should be prepared, because the Human One^d will come at a time you don't know.

Faithful and unfaithful servants

⁴⁵"Who then are the faithful and wise servants whom their master puts in charge of giving food at the right time to those who live in his house? ⁴⁶Happy are those servants whom the master finds fulfilling their responsibilities when he comes. ⁴⁷I assure you that he will put them in charge of all his possessions. ⁴⁸But suppose those bad servants should say to themselves, My master won't come until later. ⁴⁹And suppose they began to beat their fellow servants and to eat and drink with the drunks? ⁵⁰The master of those servants will come on a day when they are not expecting him, at a time they couldn't predict. ⁵¹He will cut them in pieces and put them in a place with the hypocrites. People there will be weeping and grinding their teeth.

Parable of the ten young bridesmaids

25 "At that time the kingdom of heaven will be like ten young bridesmaids who took their lamps and went out to meet the groom. ²Now five of them were wise, and the other five were foolish. ³The foolish ones took their lamps but didn't bring oil for them. ⁴But the wise ones took their lamps and also brought containers of oil.

⁵"When the groom was late in coming, they all became drowsy and went to sleep. ⁶But at midnight there was a cry, 'Look, the groom! Come out to meet him.'

⁷"Then all those bridesmaids got up and prepared their lamps. ⁸But the foolish bridesmaids said to the wise ones, 'Give us some of your oil, because our lamps have gone out.'

⁹"But the wise bridesmaids replied, 'No, because if we share with you, there won't be enough for our lamps and yours. We have a better idea. You go to those who sell oil and buy some for yourselves.' ¹⁰But while they were gone to buy oil, the groom came. Those who were ready went with him into the wedding. Then the door was shut.

¹¹"Later the other bridesmaids came and said, 'Lord, lord, open the door for us.'

¹²"But he replied, 'I tell you the truth, I don't know you.'

¹³"Therefore, keep alert, because you don't know the day or the hour.

Parable of the valuable coins

¹⁴"The kingdom of heaven is like a man who was leaving on a trip. He called his servants and handed his possessions over to them. ¹⁵To one he gave five valuable coins,^e and to another he gave two, and to another he gave one.

---

^c Or Son of Man   ^d Or Son of Man   ^e Or *talantas* (talents)

He gave to each servant according to that servant's ability. Then he left on his journey.

¹⁶"After the man left, the servant who had five valuable coins took them and went to work doing business with them. He gained five more. ¹⁷In the same way, the one who had two valuable coins gained two more. ¹⁸But the servant who had received the one valuable coin dug a hole in the ground and buried his master's money.

¹⁹"Now after a long time the master of those servants returned and settled accounts with them. ²⁰The one who had received five valuable coins came forward with five additional coins. He said, 'Master, you gave me five valuable coins. Look, I've gained five more.'

²¹"His master replied, 'Excellent! You are a good and faithful servant! You've been faithful over a little. I'll put you in charge of much. Come, celebrate with me.'

²²"The second servant also came forward and said, 'Master, you gave me two valuable coins. Look, I've gained two more.'

²³"His master replied, 'Well done! You are a good and faithful servant. You've been faithful over a little. I'll put you in charge of much. Come, celebrate with me.'

²⁴"Now the one who had received one valuable coin came and said, 'Master, I knew that you are a hard man. You harvest grain where you haven't sown. You gather crops where you haven't spread seed. ²⁵So I was afraid. And I hid my valuable coin in the ground. Here, you have what's yours.'

²⁶"His master replied, 'You evil and lazy servant! You knew that I harvest grain where I haven't sown and that I gather crops where I haven't spread seed? ²⁷In that case, you should have turned my money over to the bankers so that when I returned, you could give me what belonged to me with interest. ²⁸Therefore, take from him the valuable coin and give it to the one who has ten coins. ²⁹Those who have much will receive more, and they will have more than they need. But as for those who don't have much, even the little bit they have will be taken away from them. ³⁰Now take the worthless servant and throw him outside into the darkness.'

"People there will be weeping and grinding their teeth.

Judgment of the nations

³¹"Now when the Human One[f] comes in his majesty and all his angels are with him, he will sit on his majestic throne. ³²All the nations will be gathered in front of him. He will separate them from each other, just as a shepherd separates the sheep from the goats. ³³He will put the sheep on his right side. But the goats he will put on his left.

³⁴"Then the king will say to those on his right, 'Come, you who will receive good things from my Father. Inherit the kingdom that was prepared for you before the world began. ³⁵I was hungry and you gave me food to eat. I was thirsty and you gave me a drink. I was a stranger and you welcomed me. ³⁶I was naked and you gave me clothes to wear. I was sick and you took care of me. I was in prison and you visited me.'

³⁷"Then those who are righteous will reply to him, 'Lord, when did we see you

[f] Or Son of Man

hungry and feed you, or thirsty and give you a drink? ³⁸When did we see you as a stranger and welcome you, or naked and give you clothes to wear? ³⁹When did we see you sick or in prison and visit you?'

⁴⁰"Then the king will reply to them, 'I assure you that when you have done it for one of the least of these brothers and sisters of mine, you have done it for me.'

⁴¹"Then he will say to those on his left, 'Get away from me, you who will receive terrible things. Go into the unending fire that has been prepared for the devil and his angels. ⁴²I was hungry and you didn't give me food to eat. I was thirsty and you didn't give me anything to drink. ⁴³I was a stranger and you didn't welcome me. I was naked and you didn't give me clothes to wear. I was sick and in prison, and you didn't visit me.'

⁴⁴"Then they will reply, 'Lord, when did we see you hungry or thirsty or a stranger or naked or sick or in prison and didn't do anything to help you?' ⁴⁵Then he will answer, 'I assure you that when you haven't done it for one of the least of these, you haven't done it for me.' ⁴⁶And they will go away into eternal punishment. But the righteous ones will go into eternal life."

Plot to kill Jesus

26 When Jesus finished speaking all these words, he said to his disciples, ²"You know that the Passover is two days from now. And the Human One^g will be handed over to be crucified."

³Then the chief priests and elders of the people gathered in the courtyard of Caiaphas the high priest. ⁴They were plotting to arrest Jesus by cunning tricks and to kill him. ⁵But they agreed that it shouldn't happen during the feast so there wouldn't be an uproar among the people.

A woman pouring perfume on Jesus

⁶When Jesus was at Bethany visiting the house of Simon, who had a skin disease, ⁷a woman came to him with a vase made of alabaster containing very expensive perfume. She poured it on Jesus' head while he was sitting at dinner. ⁸Now when the disciples saw it they were angry and said, "Why this waste? ⁹This perfume could have been sold for a lot of money and given to the poor."

¹⁰But Jesus knew what they were thinking. He said, "Why do you make trouble for the woman? She's done a good thing for me. ¹¹You always have the poor with you, but you won't always have me. ¹²By pouring this perfume over my body she's prepared me to be buried. ¹³I tell you the truth that wherever in the whole world this good news is announced, what she's done will also be told in memory of her."

Judas betrays Jesus

¹⁴Then one of the Twelve, who was called Judas Iscariot, went to the chief priests ¹⁵and said, "What will you give me if I turn Jesus over to you?" They paid him thirty pieces of silver. ¹⁶From that time on he was looking for an opportunity to turn him in.

Passover with the disciples

¹⁷On the first day of the Festival of Unleavened Bread, the disciples came to

^g Or *Son of Man*

Jesus and said, "Where do you want us to prepare for you to eat the Passover meal?"

¹⁸He replied, "Go into the city, to a certain man, and say, 'The teacher says, "My time is near. I'm going to celebrate the Passover with my disciples at your house."'" ¹⁹The disciples did just as Jesus instructed them. They prepared the Passover.

²⁰That evening he took his place at the table with the twelve disciples. ²¹As they were eating he said, "I assure you that one of you will betray me."

²²Deeply saddened, each one said to him, "I'm not the one, am I, Lord?"

²³He replied, "The one who will betray me is the one who dips his hand with me into this bowl. ²⁴The Human One[h] goes to his death just as it is written about him. But how terrible it is for that person who betrays the Human One![i] It would have been better for him if he had never been born."

²⁵Now Judas, who would betray him, replied, "It's not me, is it, Rabbi?"

Jesus answered, "You said it."

Last supper

²⁶While they were eating, Jesus took bread, blessed it, broke it, and gave it to the disciples and said, "Take and eat. This is my body." ²⁷He took a cup, gave thanks, and gave it to them, saying, "Drink from this, all of you. ²⁸This is my blood of the covenant, which is poured out for many so that their sins may be forgiven. ²⁹I tell you, I won't drink wine again until that day when I drink it in a new way with you in my Father's kingdom." ³⁰Then, after singing songs of praise, they went to the Mount of Olives.

Predictions about disciples leaving Jesus

³¹Then Jesus said to his disciples, "Tonight you will all fall away because of me. This is because it is written, *I will hit the shepherd, and the sheep of the flock will go off in all directions.*[j] ³²But after I'm raised up, I'll go before you to Galilee."

³³Peter replied, "If everyone else stumbles because of you, I'll never stumble."

³⁴Jesus said to him, "I assure you that, before the rooster crows tonight, you will deny me three times."

³⁵Peter said, "Even if I must die alongside you, I won't deny you." All the disciples said the same thing.

Jesus in prayer

³⁶Then Jesus went with his disciples to a place called Gethsemane. He said to the disciples, "Stay here while I go and pray over there." ³⁷When he took Peter and Zebedee's two sons, he began to feel sad and anxious. ³⁸Then he said to them, "I'm very sad. It's as if I'm dying. Stay here and keep alert with me." ³⁹Then he went a short distance farther and fell on his face and prayed, "My Father, if it's possible, take this cup of suffering away from me. However—not what I want but what you want."

⁴⁰He came back to the disciples and found them sleeping. He said to Peter, "Couldn't you stay alert one hour with me? ⁴¹Stay alert and pray so that you won't give in to temptation. The spirit is eager, but the flesh is weak." ⁴²A second time he went away and prayed, "My Father, if it's not possible that this cup be taken away unless I drink it, then let it be what you want."

[h]Or Son of Man [i]Or Son of Man [j]Zech 13:7

[43] Again he came and found them sleeping. Their eyes were heavy with sleep. [44] But he left them and again went and prayed the same words for the third time. [45] Then he came to his disciples and said to them, "Will you sleep and rest all night? Look, the time has come for the Human One[k] to be betrayed into the hands of sinners. [46] Get up. Let's go. Look, here comes my betrayer."

Arrest

[47] While Jesus was still speaking, Judas, one of the Twelve, came. With him was a large crowd carrying swords and clubs. They had been sent by the chief priests and elders of the people. [48] His betrayer had given them a sign: "Arrest the man I kiss." [49] Just then he came to Jesus and said, "Hello, Rabbi." Then he kissed him.

[50] But Jesus said to him, "Friend, do what you came to do." Then they came and grabbed Jesus and arrested him. [51] One of those with Jesus reached for his sword. Striking the high priest's slave, he cut off his ear. [52] Then Jesus said to him, "Put the sword back into its place. All those who use the sword will die by the sword. [53] Or do you think that I'm not able to ask my Father and he will send to me more than twelve battle groups[l] of angels right away? [54] But if I did that, how would the scriptures be fulfilled that say this must happen?" [55] Then Jesus said to the crowds, "Have you come with swords and clubs to arrest me, like a thief? Day after day, I sat in the temple teaching, but you didn't arrest me. [56] But all this has happened so that what the prophets said in the scriptures might be fulfilled." Then all the disciples left Jesus and ran away.

Jesus before the council

[57] Those who arrested Jesus led him to Caiaphas the high priest. The legal experts and the elders had gathered there. [58] Peter followed him from a distance until he came to the high priest's courtyard. He entered that area and sat outside with the officers to see how it would turn out.

[59] The chief priests and the whole council were looking for false testimony against Jesus so that they could put him to death. [60] They didn't find anything they could use from the many false witnesses who were willing to come forward. But finally they found two [61] who said, "This man said, 'I can destroy God's temple and rebuild it in three days.'"

[62] Then the high priest stood and said to Jesus, "Aren't you going to respond to the testimony these people have brought against you?"

[63] But Jesus was silent.

The high priest said, "By the living God, I demand that you tell us whether you are the Christ, God's Son."

[64] "You said it," Jesus replied. "But I say to you that from now on you'll see *the Human One[m] sitting on the right side of the Almighty[n] and coming on the heavenly clouds.*"[o]

[65] Then the high priest tore his clothes and said, "He's insulting God! Why do we need any more witnesses? Look, you've heard his insult against God. [66] What do you think?"

[k] Or Son of Man   [l] Or legions (of the Roman army, about five thousand soldiers each)   [m] Or Son of Man   [n] Or the Power   [o] Dan 7:13

And they answered, "He deserves to die!" [67]Then they spit in his face and beat him. They hit him [68]and said, "Prophesy for us, Christ! Who hit you?"

Peter's denial

[69]Meanwhile, Peter was sitting outside in the courtyard. A servant woman came and said to him, "You were also with Jesus the Galilean."

[70]But he denied it in front of all of them, saying, "I don't know what you are talking about."

[71]When he went over to the gate, another woman saw him and said to those who were there, "This man was with Jesus, the man from Nazareth."

[72]With a solemn pledge, he denied it again, saying, "I don't know the man."

[73]A short time later those standing there came and said to Peter, "You must be one of them. The way you talk gives you away."

[74]Then he cursed and swore, "I don't know the man!" At that very moment the rooster crowed. [75]Peter remembered Jesus' words, "Before the rooster crows you will deny me three times." And Peter went out and cried uncontrollably.

Jesus before Pilate

27 Early in the morning all the chief priests and the elders of the people reached the decision to have Jesus put to death. [2]They bound him, led him away, and turned him over to Pilate the governor.

Judas' death

[3]When Judas, who betrayed Jesus, saw that Jesus was condemned to die,

he felt deep regret. He returned the thirty pieces of silver to the chief priests and elders, and [4]said, "I did wrong because I betrayed an innocent man."

But they said, "What is that to us? That's your problem." [5]Judas threw the silver pieces into the temple and left. Then he went and hanged himself.

[6]The chief priests picked up the silver pieces and said, "According to the Law it's not right to put this money in the treasury. Since it was used to pay for someone's life, it's unclean." [7]So they decided to use it to buy the potter's field where strangers could be buried. [8]That's why that field is called "Field of Blood" to this very day. [9]This fulfilled the words of Jeremiah the prophet: *And I took the thirty pieces of silver, the price for the one whose price had been set by some of the Israelites,* [10]*and I gave them for the potter's field, as the Lord commanded me.*[p]

Questioned by Pilate

[11]Jesus was brought before the governor. The governor said, "Are you the king of the Jews?"

Jesus replied, "That's what you say." [12]But he didn't answer when the chief priests and elders accused him.

[13]Then Pilate said, "Don't you hear the testimony they bring against you?" [14]But he didn't answer, not even a single word. So the governor was greatly amazed.

Death sentence

[15]It was customary during the festival for the governor to release to the crowd one prisoner, whomever they might choose. [16]At that time there was

a well-known prisoner named Jesus Barabbas. [17] When the crowd had come together, Pilate asked them, "Whom would you like me to release to you, Jesus Barabbas or Jesus who is called Christ?" [18] He knew that the leaders of the people had handed him over because of jealousy.

[19] While he was serving as judge, his wife sent this message to him, "Leave that righteous man alone. I've suffered much today in a dream because of him."

[20] But the chief priests and the elders persuaded the crowds to ask for Barabbas and kill Jesus. [21] The governor said, "Which of the two do you want me to release to you?"

"Barabbas," they replied.

[22] Pilate said, "Then what should I do with Jesus who is called Christ?"

They all said, "Crucify him!"

[23] But he said, "Why? What wrong has he done?"

They shouted even louder, "Crucify him!"

[24] Pilate saw that he was getting nowhere and that a riot was starting. So he took water and washed his hands in front of the crowd. "I'm innocent of this man's blood," he said. "It's your problem."

[25] All the people replied, "Let his blood be on us and on our children." [26] Then he released Barabbas to them. He had Jesus whipped, then handed him over to be crucified.

Soldiers mocking Jesus

[27] The governor's soldiers took Jesus into the governor's house, and they gathered the whole company[q] of soldiers around him. [28] They stripped him and put a red military coat on him.

[29] They twisted together a crown of thorns and put it on his head. They put a stick in his right hand. Then they bowed down in front of him and mocked him, saying, "Hey! King of the Jews!" [30] After they spit on him, they took the stick and struck his head again and again. [31] When they finished mocking him, they stripped him of the military coat and put his own clothes back on him. They led him away to crucify him.

Crucifixion

[32] As they were going out, they found Simon, a man from Cyrene. They forced him to carry his cross. [33] When they came to a place called Golgotha, which means Skull Place, [34] they gave Jesus wine mixed with vinegar to drink. But after tasting it, he didn't want to drink it. [35] After they crucified him, they divided up his clothes among them by drawing lots. [36] They sat there, guarding him. [37] They placed above his head the charge against him. It read, "This is Jesus, the king of the Jews." [38] They crucified with him two outlaws, one on his right side and one on his left.

[39] Those who were walking by insulted Jesus, shaking their heads [40] and saying, "So you were going to destroy the temple and rebuild it in three days, were you? Save yourself! If you are God's Son, come down from the cross."

[41] In the same way, the chief priests, along with the legal experts and the elders, were making fun of him, saying, [42] "He saved others, but he can't save himself. He's the king of Israel, so let him come down from the cross now. Then we'll believe in him. [43] He trusts in God, so let God deliver him now if

[q] Or *cohort* (approximately six hundred soldiers)

he wants to. He said, 'I'm God's Son.'"
[44] The outlaws who were crucified with
him insulted him in the same way.

Death

[45] From noon until three in the afternoon the whole earth was dark. [46] At
about three Jesus cried out with a loud
shout, *"Eli, Eli, lama sabachthani,"* which
means, "My God, my God, why have
you left me?"[r]

[47] After hearing him, some standing
there said, "He's calling Elijah." [48] One
of them ran over, took a sponge full of
vinegar, and put it on a pole. He offered
it to Jesus to drink.

[49] But the rest of them said, "Let's see
if Elijah will come and save him."

[50] Again Jesus cried out with a loud
shout. Then he died.

[51] Look, the curtain of the sanctuary
was torn in two from top to bottom.
The earth shook, the rocks split, [52] and
the bodies of many holy people who
had died were raised. [53] After Jesus' resurrection they came out of their graves
and went into the holy city where they
appeared to many people. [54] When the
centurion and those with him who were
guarding Jesus saw the earthquake and
what had just happened, they were
filled with awe and said, "This was certainly God's Son."

[55] Many women were watching from
a distance. They had followed Jesus
from Galilee to serve him. [56] Among
them were Mary Magdalene, Mary the
mother of James and Joseph, and the
mother of Zebedee's sons.

Burial

[57] That evening a man named Joseph came. He was a rich man from
Arimathea who had become a disciple
of Jesus. [58] He came to Pilate and asked
for Jesus' body. Pilate gave him permission to take it. [59] Joseph took the body,
wrapped it in a clean linen cloth, [60] and
laid it in his own new tomb, which he
had carved out of the rock. After he
rolled a large stone at the door of the
tomb, he went away. [61] Mary Magdalene
and the other Mary were there, sitting
in front of the tomb.

Guard at the tomb

[62] The next day, which was the day
after Preparation Day, the chief priests
and the Pharisees gathered before Pilate. [63] They said, "Sir, we remember
that while that deceiver was still alive
he said, 'After three days I will arise.'
[64] Therefore, order the grave to be
sealed until the third day. Otherwise,
his disciples may come and steal the
body and tell the people, 'He's been
raised from the dead.' This last deception will be worse than the first."

[65] Pilate replied, "You have soldiers
for guard duty. Go and make it as secure as you know how." [66] Then they
went and secured the tomb by sealing
the stone and posting the guard.

Resurrection

28
After the Sabbath, at dawn on
the first day of the week, Mary
Magdalene and the other Mary came
to look at the tomb. [2] Look, there was a
great earthquake, for an angel from the
Lord came down from heaven. Coming
to the stone, he rolled it away and sat
on it. [3] Now his face was like lightning
and his clothes as white as snow. [4] The
guards were so terrified of him that

[r] Ps 22:1

they shook with fear and became like dead men. [5]But the angel said to the women, "Don't be afraid. I know that you are looking for Jesus who was crucified. [6]He isn't here, because he's been raised from the dead, just as he said. Come, see the place where they laid him. [7]Now hurry, go and tell his disciples, 'He's been raised from the dead. He's going on ahead of you to Galilee. You will see him there.' I've given the message to you."

[8]With great fear and excitement, they hurried away from the tomb and ran to tell his disciples. [9]But Jesus met them and greeted them. They came and grabbed his feet and worshipped him. [10]Then Jesus said to them, "Don't be afraid. Go and tell my brothers that I am going into Galilee. They will see me there."

Guards' report

[11]Now as the women were on their way, some of the guards came into the city and told the chief priests everything that had happened. [12]They met with the elders and decided to give a large sum of money to the soldiers. [13]They told them, "Say that Jesus' disciples came at night and stole his body while you were sleeping. [14]And if the governor hears about this, we will take care of it with him so you will have nothing to worry about." [15]So the soldiers took the money and did as they were told. And this report has spread throughout all Judea to this very day.

Commissioning of the disciples

[16]Now the eleven disciples went to Galilee, to the mountain where Jesus told them to go. [17]When they saw him, they worshipped him, but some doubted. [18]Jesus came near and spoke to them, "I've received all authority in heaven and on earth. [19]Therefore, go and make disciples of all nations, baptizing them in the name of the Father and of the Son and of the Holy Spirit, [20]teaching them to obey everything that I've commanded you. Look, I myself will be with you every day until the end of this present age."

MARK

Beginning of good news

1 The beginning of the good news about Jesus Christ, God's Son, [2]happened just as it was written about in the prophecy of Isaiah:

Look, I am sending my messenger
    before you.
He will prepare your way,
[3] a voice shouting in the wilderness:
    "Prepare the way for the Lord;
    make his paths straight."[a]

John's preaching

[4]John the Baptist was in the wilderness calling for people to be baptized to show that they were changing their hearts and lives and wanted God to forgive their sins. [5]Everyone in Judea and all the people of Jerusalem went out to the Jordan River and were being baptized by John as they confessed their sins. [6]John wore clothes made of camel's hair, with a leather belt around his

[a]Isa 40:3; Mal 3:1; Exod 23:20

waist. He ate locusts and wild honey. [7]He announced, "One stronger than I am is coming after me. I'm not even worthy to bend over and loosen the strap of his sandals. [8]I baptize you with water, but he will baptize you with the Holy Spirit."

Jesus is baptized and tempted

[9]About that time, Jesus came from Nazareth of Galilee, and John baptized him in the Jordan River. [10]While he was coming up out of the water, Jesus saw heaven splitting open and the Spirit, like a dove, coming down on him. [11]And there was a voice from heaven: "You are my Son, whom I dearly love; in you I find happiness."

[12]At once the Spirit forced Jesus out into the wilderness. [13]He was in the wilderness for forty days, tempted by Satan. He was among the wild animals, and the angels took care of him.

Jesus' message

[14]After John was arrested, Jesus came into Galilee announcing God's good news, [15]saying, "Now is the time! Here comes God's kingdom! Change your hearts and lives, and trust this good news!"

Jesus calls disciples

[16]As Jesus passed alongside the Galilee Sea, he saw two brothers, Simon and Andrew, throwing fishing nets into the sea, for they were fishermen. [17]"Come, follow me," he said, "and I'll show you how to fish for people." [18]Right away, they left their nets and followed him. [19]After going a little farther, he saw James and John, Zebedee's sons, in their boat repairing the fishing nets. [20]At that very moment he called them. They followed him, leaving their father Zebedee in the boat with the hired workers.

Jesus throws a demon out

[21]Jesus and his followers went into Capernaum. Immediately on the Sabbath Jesus entered the synagogue and started teaching. [22]The people were amazed by his teaching, for he was teaching them with authority, not like the legal experts. [23]Suddenly, there in the synagogue, a person with an evil spirit screamed, [24]"What have you to do with us, Jesus of Nazareth? Have you come to destroy us? I know who you are. You are the holy one from God."

[25]"Silence!" Jesus said, speaking harshly to the demon. "Come out of him!" [26]The unclean spirit shook him and screamed, then it came out.

[27]Everyone was shaken and questioned among themselves, "What's this? A new teaching with authority! He even commands unclean spirits and they obey him!" [28]Right away the news about him spread throughout the entire region of Galilee.

Jesus heals Simon's mother-in-law

[29]After leaving the synagogue, Jesus, James, and John went home with Simon and Andrew. [30]Simon's mother-in-law was in bed, sick with a fever, and they told Jesus about her at once. [31]He went to her, took her by the hand, and raised her up. The fever left her, and she served them.

Jesus' ministry spreads

[32]That evening, at sunset, people brought to Jesus those who were sick or demon-possessed. [33]The whole town gathered near the door. [34]He healed

many who were sick with all kinds of diseases, and he threw out many demons. But he didn't let the demons speak, because they recognized him.

³⁵ Early in the morning, well before sunrise, Jesus rose and went to a deserted place where he could be alone in prayer. ³⁶ Simon and those with him tracked him down. ³⁷ When they found him, they told him, "Everyone's looking for you!"

³⁸ He replied, "Let's head in the other direction, to the nearby villages, so that I can preach there too. That's why I've come." ³⁹ He traveled throughout Galilee, preaching in their synagogues and throwing out demons.

A man with a skin disease

⁴⁰ A man with a skin disease approached Jesus, fell to his knees, and begged, "If you want, you can make me clean."

⁴¹ Incensed,[b] Jesus reached out his hand, touched him, and said, "I do want to. Be clean." ⁴² Instantly, the skin disease left him, and he was clean. ⁴³ Sternly, Jesus sent him away, ⁴⁴ saying, "Don't say anything to anyone. Instead, go and show yourself to the priest and offer the sacrifice for your cleansing that Moses commanded. This will be a testimony to them." ⁴⁵ Instead, he went out and started talking freely and spreading the news so that Jesus wasn't able to enter a town openly. He remained outside in deserted places, but people came to him from everywhere.

Healing and forgiveness

2 After a few days, Jesus went back to Capernaum, and people heard that

he was at home. ² So many gathered that there was no longer space, not even near the door. Jesus was speaking the word to them. ³ Some people arrived, and four of them were bringing to him a man who was paralyzed. ⁴ They couldn't carry him through the crowd, so they tore off part of the roof above where Jesus was. When they had made an opening, they lowered the mat on which the paralyzed man was lying. ⁵ When Jesus saw their faith, he said to the paralytic, "Child, your sins are forgiven!"

⁶ Some legal experts were sitting there, muttering among themselves, ⁷ "Why does he speak this way? He's insulting God. Only the one God can forgive sins."

⁸ Jesus immediately recognized what they were discussing, and he said to them, "Why do you fill your minds with these questions? ⁹ Which is easier—to say to a paralyzed person, 'Your sins are forgiven,' or to say, 'Get up, take up your bed, and walk'? ¹⁰ But so you will know that the Human One[c] has authority on the earth to forgive sins"— he said to the man who was paralyzed, ¹¹ "Get up, take your mat, and go home."

¹² Jesus raised him up, and right away he picked up his mat and walked out in front of everybody. They were all amazed and praised God, saying, "We've never seen anything like this!"

Eating with sinners

¹³ Jesus went out beside the lake again. The whole crowd came to him, and he began to teach them. ¹⁴ As he continued along, he saw Levi, Alphaeus' son, sitting at a kiosk for collecting

---

[b]Most critical editions of the Gk New Testament read *filled with compassion.*　　[c]Or *Son of Man*

taxes. Jesus said to him, "Follow me." Levi got up and followed him.

¹⁵Jesus sat down to eat at Levi's house. Many tax collectors and sinners were eating with Jesus and his disciples. Indeed, many of them had become his followers. ¹⁶When some of the legal experts from among the Pharisees saw that he was eating with sinners and tax collectors, they asked his disciples, "Why is he eating with sinners and tax collectors?"

¹⁷When Jesus heard it, he said to them, "Healthy people don't need a doctor, but sick people do. I didn't come to call righteous people, but sinners."

When to fast

¹⁸John's disciples and the Pharisees had a habit of fasting. Some people asked Jesus, "Why do John's disciples and the Pharisees' disciples fast, but yours don't?"

¹⁹Jesus said, "The wedding guests can't fast while the groom is with them, can they? As long as they have the groom with them, they can't fast. ²⁰But the days will come when the groom will be taken away from them, and then they will fast.

²¹"No one sews a piece of new, unshrunk cloth on old clothes; otherwise, the patch tears away from it, the new from the old, and makes a worse tear. ²²No one pours new wine into old leather wineskins; otherwise, the wine would burst the wineskins and the wine would be lost and the wineskins destroyed. But new wine is for new wineskins."

Scripture and the Sabbath

²³Jesus went through the wheat fields on the Sabbath. As the disciples made their way, they were picking the heads of wheat. ²⁴The Pharisees said to Jesus, "Look! Why are they breaking the Sabbath law?"

²⁵He said to them, "Haven't you ever read what David did when he was in need, when he and those with him were hungry? ²⁶During the time when Abiathar was high priest, David went into God's house and ate the bread of the presence, which only the priests were allowed to eat. He also gave bread to those who were with him." ²⁷Then he said, "The Sabbath was created for humans; humans weren't created for the Sabbath. ²⁸This is why the Human One[d] is Lord even over the Sabbath."

Healing on the Sabbath

3 Jesus returned to the synagogue. A man with a withered hand was there. ²Wanting to bring charges against Jesus, they were watching him closely to see if he would heal on the Sabbath. ³He said to the man with the withered hand, "Step up where people can see you." ⁴Then he said to them, "Is it legal on the Sabbath to do good or to do evil, to save life or to kill?" But they said nothing. ⁵Looking around at them with anger, deeply grieved at their unyielding hearts, he said to the man, "Stretch out your hand." So he did, and his hand was made healthy. ⁶At that, the Pharisees got together with the supporters of Herod to plan how to destroy Jesus.

Healing and throwing demons out

⁷Jesus left with his disciples and went to the lake. A large crowd followed him because they had heard what

[d] Or Son of Man

he was doing. They were from Galilee, ³Judea, Jerusalem, Idumea, beyond the Jordan, and the area surrounding Tyre and Sidon. ⁹Jesus told his disciples to get a small boat ready for him so the crowd wouldn't crush him. ¹⁰He had healed so many people that everyone who was sick pushed forward so that they could touch him. ¹¹Whenever the evil spirits saw him, they fell down at his feet and shouted, "You are God's Son!" ¹²But he strictly ordered them not to reveal who he was.

Jesus appoints twelve apostles

¹³Jesus went up on a mountain and called those he wanted, and they came to him. ¹⁴He appointed twelve and called them apostles. He appointed them to be with him, to be sent out to preach, ¹⁵and to have authority to throw out demons. ¹⁶He appointed twelve: Peter, a name he gave Simon; ¹⁷James and John, Zebedee's sons, whom he nicknamed Boanerges, which means "sons of Thunder"; ¹⁸Andrew; Philip; Bartholomew; Matthew; Thomas; James, Alphaeus' son; Thaddaeus; Simon the Cananaean;ᵉ ¹⁹and Judas Iscariot, who betrayed Jesus.

Misunderstandings about Jesus

²⁰Jesus entered a house. A crowd gathered again so that it was impossible for him and his followers even to eat. ²¹When his family heard what was happening, they came to take control of him. They were saying, "He's out of his mind!"

²²The legal experts came down from Jerusalem. Over and over they charged, "He's possessed by Beelzebul. He throws

out demons with the authority of the ruler of demons."

²³When Jesus called them together he spoke to them in a parable: "How can Satan throw Satan out? ²⁴A kingdom involved in civil war will collapse. ²⁵And a house torn apart by divisions will collapse. ²⁶If Satan rebels against himself and is divided, then he can't endure. He's done for. ²⁷No one gets into the house of a strong person and steals anything without first tying up the strong person. Only then can the house be burglarized. ²⁸I assure you that human beings will be forgiven for everything, for all sins and insults of every kind. ²⁹But whoever insults the Holy Spirit will never be forgiven. That person is guilty of a sin with consequences that last forever." ³⁰He said this because the legal experts were saying, "He's possessed by an evil spirit."

³¹His mother and brothers arrived. They stood outside and sent word to him, calling for him. ³²A crowd was seated around him, and those sent to him said, "Look, your mother, brothers, and sisters are outside looking for you."

³³He replied, "Who is my mother? Who are my brothers?" ³⁴Looking around at those seated around him in a circle, he said, "Look, here are my mother and my brothers. ³⁵Whoever does God's will is my brother, sister, and mother."

Parable of the soils

4 Jesus began to teach beside the lake again. Such a large crowd gathered that he climbed into a boat there on the lake. He sat in the boat while the whole crowd was nearby on the shore. ²He said

ᵉOr zealot

many things to them in parables. While teaching them, he said, ³"Listen to this! A farmer went out to scatter seed. ⁴As he was scattering seed, some fell on the path; and the birds came and ate it. ⁵Other seed fell on rocky ground where the soil was shallow. They sprouted immediately because the soil wasn't deep. ⁶When the sun came up, it scorched the plants; and they dried up because they had no roots. ⁷Other seed fell among thorny plants. The thorny plants grew and choked the seeds, and they produced nothing. ⁸Other seed fell into good soil and bore fruit. Upon growing and increasing, the seed produced in one case a yield of thirty to one, in another case a yield of sixty to one, and in another case a yield of one hundred to one." ⁹He said, "Whoever has ears to listen should pay attention!"

Jesus explains his parable

¹⁰When they were alone, the people around Jesus, along with the Twelve, asked him about the parables. ¹¹He said to them, "The secret of God's kingdom has been given to you, but to those who are outside everything comes in parables. ¹²This is so that they can look and see but have no insight, and they can hear but not understand. Otherwise, they might turn their lives around and be forgiven.

¹³"Don't you understand this parable? Then how will you understand all the parables? ¹⁴The farmer scatters the word. ¹⁵This is the meaning of the seed that fell on the path: When the word is scattered and people hear it, right away Satan comes and steals the word that was planted in them. ¹⁶Here's the meaning of the seed that fell on rocky ground: When people hear the word,

they immediately receive it joyfully. ¹⁷Because they have no roots, they last for only a little while. When they experience distress or abuse because of the word, they immediately fall away. ¹⁸Others are like the seed scattered among the thorny plants. These are the ones who have heard the word; ¹⁹but the worries of this life, the false appeal of wealth, and the desire for more things break in and choke the word, and it bears no fruit. ²⁰The seed scattered on good soil are those who hear the word and embrace it. They bear fruit, in one case a yield of thirty to one, in another case sixty to one, and in another case one hundred to one."

Parables about lamps and measures

²¹Jesus said to them, "Does anyone bring in a lamp in order to put it under a basket or a bed? Shouldn't it be placed on a lampstand? ²²Everything hidden will be revealed, and everything secret will come out into the open. ²³Whoever has ears to listen should pay attention!"

²⁴He said to them, "Listen carefully! God will evaluate you with the same standard you use to evaluate others. Indeed, you will receive even more. ²⁵Those who have will receive more, but as for those who don't have, even what they don't have will be taken away from them."

More parables about God's kingdom

²⁶Then Jesus said, "This is what God's kingdom is like. It's as though someone scatters seed on the ground ²⁷then sleeps and wakes night and day. The seed sprouts and grows, but the farmer doesn't know how. ²⁸The earth

produces crops all by itself, first the stalk, then the head, then the full head of grain. [29]Whenever the crop is ready, the farmer goes out to cut the grain because it's harvestime."

[30]He continued, "What's a good image for God's kingdom? What parable can I use to explain it? [31]Consider a mustard seed. When scattered on the ground, it's the smallest of all the seeds on the earth; [32]but when it's planted, it grows and becomes the largest of all vegetable plants. It produces such large branches that the birds in the sky are able to nest in its shade."

[33]With many such parables he continued to give them the word, as much as they were able to hear. [34]He spoke to them only in parables, then explained everything to his disciples when he was alone with them.

Jesus stops a storm

[35]Later that day, when evening came, Jesus said to them, "Let's cross over to the other side of the lake." [36]They left the crowd and took him in the boat just as he was. Other boats followed along.

[37]Gale-force winds arose, and waves crashed against the boat so that the boat was swamped. [38]But Jesus was in the rear of the boat, sleeping on a pillow. They woke him up and said, "Teacher, don't you care that we're drowning?"

[39]He got up and gave orders to the wind, and he said to the lake, "Silence! Be still!" The wind settled down and there was a great calm. [40]Jesus asked them, "Why are you frightened? Don't you have faith yet?"

[41]Overcome with awe, they said to each other, "Who then is this? Even the wind and the sea obey him!"

Jesus frees a demon-possessed man

5 Jesus and his disciples came to the other side of the lake, to the region of the Gerasenes. [2]As soon as Jesus got out of the boat, a man possessed by an evil spirit came out of the tombs. [3]This man lived among the tombs, and no one was ever strong enough to restrain him, even with a chain. [4]He had been secured many times with leg irons and chains, but he broke the chains and smashed the leg irons. No one was tough enough to control him. [5]Night and day in the tombs and the hills, he would howl and cut himself with stones. [6]When he saw Jesus from far away, he ran and knelt before him, [7]shouting, "What have you to do with me, Jesus, Son of the Most High God? Swear to God that you won't torture me!"

[8]He said this because Jesus had already commanded him, "Unclean spirit, come out of the man!"

[9]Jesus asked him, "What is your name?"

He responded, "Legion is my name, because we are many." [10]They pleaded with Jesus not to send them out of that region.

[11]A large herd of pigs was feeding on the hillside. [12]"Send us into the pigs!" they begged. "Let us go into the pigs!" [13]Jesus gave them permission, so the unclean spirits left the man and went into the pigs. Then the herd of about two thousand pigs rushed down the cliff into the lake and drowned.

[14]Those who tended the pigs ran away and told the story in the city and in the countryside. People came to see what had happened. [15]They came to Jesus and saw the man who used to be demon-possessed. They saw the very

man who had been filled with many demons sitting there fully dressed and completely sane, and they were filled with awe. [16] Those who had actually seen what had happened to the demon-possessed man told the others about the pigs. [17] Then they pleaded with Jesus to leave their region.

[18] While he was climbing into the boat, the one who had been demon-possessed pleaded with Jesus to let him come along as one of his disciples. [19] But Jesus wouldn't allow it. "Go home to your own people," Jesus said, "and tell them what the Lord has done for you and how he has shown you mercy." [20] The man went away and began to proclaim in the Ten Cities all that Jesus had done for him, and everyone was amazed.

Jesus heals two people

[21] Jesus crossed the lake again, and on the other side a large crowd gathered around him on the shore. [22] Jairus, one of the synagogue leaders, came forward. When he saw Jesus, he fell at his feet [23] and pleaded with him, "My daughter is about to die. Please, come and place your hands on her so that she can be healed and live." [24] So Jesus went with him.

A swarm of people were following Jesus, crowding in on him. [25] A woman was there who had been bleeding for twelve years. [26] She had suffered a lot under the care of many doctors, and had spent everything she had without getting any better. In fact, she had gotten worse. [27] Because she had heard about Jesus, she came up behind him in the crowd and touched his clothes. [28] She was thinking, If I can just touch his clothes, I'll be healed. [29] Her

bleeding stopped immediately, and she sensed in her body that her illness had been healed.

[30] At that very moment, Jesus recognized that power had gone out from him. He turned around in the crowd and said, "Who touched my clothes?"

[31] His disciples said to him, "Don't you see the crowd pressing against you? Yet you ask, 'Who touched me?'" [32] But Jesus looked around carefully to see who had done it.

[33] The woman, full of fear and trembling, came forward. Knowing what had happened to her, she fell down in front of Jesus and told him the whole truth. [34] He responded, "Daughter, your faith has healed you; go in peace, healed from your disease."

[35] While Jesus was still speaking with her, messengers came from the synagogue leader's house, saying to Jairus, "Your daughter has died. Why bother the teacher any longer?"

[36] But Jesus overheard their report and said to the synagogue leader, "Don't be afraid; just keep trusting." [37] He didn't allow anyone to follow him except Peter, James, and John, James' brother. [38] They came to the synagogue leader's house, and he saw a commotion, with people crying and wailing loudly. [39] He went in and said to them, "What's all this commotion and crying about? The child isn't dead. She's only sleeping." [40] They laughed at him, but he threw them all out. Then, taking the child's parents and his disciples with him, he went to the room where the child was. [41] Taking her hand, he said to her, "*Talitha koum*," which means, "Young woman, get up." [42] Suddenly the young woman got up and began to walk around. She was 12 years old. They were

shocked! ⁴³He gave them strict orders that no one should know what happened. Then he told them to give her something to eat.

Jesus in his hometown

6 Jesus left that place and came to his hometown. His disciples followed him. ²On the Sabbath, he began to teach in the synagogue. Many who heard him were surprised. "Where did this man get all this? What's this wisdom he's been given? What about the powerful acts accomplished through him? ³Isn't this the carpenter? Isn't he Mary's son and the brother of James, Joses, Judas, and Simon? Aren't his sisters here with us?" They were repulsed by him and fell into sin.

⁴Jesus said to them, "Prophets are honored everywhere except in their own hometowns, among their relatives, and in their own households." ⁵He was unable to do any miracles there, except that he placed his hands on a few sick people and healed them. ⁶He was appalled by their disbelief.

Sending out the disciples

Then Jesus traveled through the surrounding villages teaching.

⁷He called for the Twelve and sent them out in pairs. He gave them authority over unclean spirits. ⁸He instructed them to take nothing for the journey except a walking stick—no bread, no bags, and no money in their belts. ⁹He told them to wear sandals but not to put on two shirts. ¹⁰He said, "Whatever house you enter, remain there until you leave that place. ¹¹If a place doesn't welcome you or listen to

you, as you leave, shake the dust off your feet as a witness against them." ¹²So they went out and proclaimed that people should change their hearts and lives. ¹³They cast out many demons, and they anointed many sick people with olive oil and healed them.

Death of John the Baptist

¹⁴Herod the king heard about these things, because the name of Jesus had become well-known. Some were saying, "John the Baptist has been raised from the dead, and this is why miraculous powers are at work through him." ¹⁵Others were saying, "He is Elijah." Still others were saying, "He is a prophet like one of the ancient prophets." ¹⁶But when Herod heard these rumors, he said, "John, whom I beheaded, has been raised to life."

¹⁷He said this because Herod himself had arranged to have John arrested and put in prison because of Herodias, the wife of Herod's brother Philip. Herod had married her, ¹⁸but John told Herod, "It's against the law for you to marry your brother's wife!" ¹⁹So Herodias had it in for John. She wanted to kill him, but she couldn't. ²⁰This was because Herod respected John. He regarded him as a righteous and holy person, so he protected him. John's words greatly confused Herod, yet he enjoyed listening to him.

²¹Finally, the time was right. It was on one of Herod's birthdays, when he had prepared a feast for his high-ranking officials and military officers and Galilee's leading residents. ²²Herod's daughter Herodias^f came in and danced, thrilling Herod and his dinner guests.

^fOr *the daughter of Herodias herself*; Gk uncertain

The king said to the young woman, "Ask me whatever you wish, and I will give it to you." [23] Then he swore to her, "Whatever you ask I will give to you, even as much as half of my kingdom."

[24] She left the banquet hall and said to her mother, "What should I ask for?"

"John the Baptist's head," Herodias replied.

[25] Hurrying back to the ruler, she made her request: "I want you to give me John the Baptist's head on a plate, right this minute." [26] Although the king was upset, because of his solemn pledge and his guests, he didn't want to refuse her. [27] So he ordered a guard to bring John's head. The guard went to the prison, cut off John's head, [28] brought his head on a plate, and gave it to the young woman, and she gave it to her mother. [29] When John's disciples heard what had happened, they came and took his dead body and laid it in a tomb.

Jesus feeds five thousand people

[30] The apostles returned to Jesus and told him everything they had done and taught. [31] Many people were coming and going, so there was no time to eat. He said to the apostles, "Come by yourselves to a secluded place and rest for a while." [32] They departed in a boat by themselves for a deserted place.

[33] Many people saw them leaving and recognized them, so they ran ahead from all the cities and arrived before them. [34] When Jesus arrived and saw a large crowd, he had compassion on them because they were like sheep without a shepherd. Then he began to teach them many things.

[35] Late in the day, his disciples came to him and said, "This is an isolated place, and it's already late in the day. [36] Send them away so that they can go to the surrounding countryside and villages and buy something to eat for themselves."

[37] He replied, "You give them something to eat."

But they said to him, "Should we go off and buy bread worth almost eight months' pay[g] and give it to them to eat?"

[38] He said to them, "How much bread do you have? Take a look."

After checking, they said, "Five loaves of bread and two fish."

[39] He directed the disciples to seat all the people in groups as though they were having a banquet on the green grass. [40] They sat down in groups of hundreds and fifties. [41] He took the five loaves and the two fish, looked up to heaven, blessed them, broke the loaves into pieces, and gave them to his disciples to set before the people. He also divided the two fish among them all. [42] Everyone ate until they were full. [43] They filled twelve baskets with the leftover pieces of bread and fish. [44] About five thousand had eaten.

Jesus walks on water

[45] Right then, Jesus made his disciples get into a boat and go ahead to the other side of the lake, toward Bethsaida, while he dismissed the crowd. [46] After saying good-bye to them, Jesus went up onto a mountain to pray. [47] Evening came and the boat was in the middle of the lake, but he was alone on the land. [48] He saw his disciples struggling. They were trying to row forward, but the wind was blowing against them.

[g] Or *two hundred denarii*; a denarion was a typical day's wage.

Very early in the morning, he came to them, walking on the lake. He intended to pass by them. ⁴⁹When they saw him walking on the lake, they thought he was a ghost and they screamed. ⁵⁰Seeing him was terrifying to all of them. Just then he spoke to them, "Be encouraged! It's me. Don't be afraid." ⁵¹He got into the boat, and the wind settled down. His disciples were so baffled they were beside themselves. ⁵²That's because they hadn't understood about the loaves. Their minds had been closed so that they resisted God's ways.

Healings at Gennesaret

⁵³When Jesus and his disciples had crossed the lake, they landed at Gennesaret, anchored the boat, ⁵⁴and came ashore. People immediately recognized Jesus ⁵⁵and ran around that whole region bringing sick people on their mats to wherever they heard he was. ⁵⁶Wherever he went—villages, cities, or farming communities—they would place the sick in the marketplaces and beg him to allow them to touch even the hem of his clothing. Everyone who touched him was healed.

What contaminates a life?

7 The Pharisees and some legal experts from Jerusalem gathered around Jesus. ²They saw some of his disciples eating food with unclean hands. (They were eating without first ritually purifying their hands through washing. ³The Pharisees and all the Jews don't eat without first washing their hands carefully. This is a way of observing the rules handed down by the elders. ⁴Upon returning from the marketplace, they don't eat without first immersing themselves. They observe many other rules that have been handed down, such as the washing of cups, jugs, pans, and sleeping mats.) ⁵So the Pharisees and legal experts asked Jesus, "Why are your disciples not living according to the rules handed down by the elders but instead eat food with ritually unclean hands?"

⁶He replied, "Isaiah really knew what he was talking about when he prophesied about you hypocrites. He wrote,

This people honors me with their lips,
 but their hearts are far away
  from me.
⁷ *Their worship of me is empty*
  since they teach instructions
   *that are human words.*ʰ

⁸You ignore God's commandment while holding on to rules created by humans and handed down to you." ⁹Jesus continued, "Clearly, you are experts at rejecting God's commandment in order to establish these rules. ¹⁰Moses said, *Honor your father and your mother*,ⁱ and *The person who speaks against father or mother will certainly be put to death.*ʲ ¹¹But you say, 'If you tell your father or mother, "Everything I'm expected to contribute to you is *corban* (that is, a gift I'm giving to God)," ¹²then you are no longer required to care for your father or mother.' ¹³In this way you do away with God's word in favor of the rules handed down to others. And you do a lot of other things just like that."

¹⁴Then Jesus called the crowd again and said, "Listen to me, all of you, and understand. ¹⁵Nothing outside of a person can enter and contaminate a

---

ʰIsa 29:13 ⁱExod 20:12; Deut 5:16 ʲExod 21:17; Lev 20:9

person in God's sight; rather, the things that come out of a person contaminate the person."^k

¹⁷After leaving the crowd, he entered a house where his disciples asked him about that riddle. ¹⁸He said to them, "Don't you understand either? Don't you know that nothing from the outside that enters a person has the power to contaminate? ¹⁹That's because it doesn't enter into the heart but into the stomach, and it goes out into the sewer." By saying this, Jesus declared that no food could contaminate a person in God's sight. ²⁰"It's what comes out of a person that contaminates someone in God's sight," he said. ²¹"It's from the inside, from the human heart, that evil thoughts come: sexual sins, thefts, murders, ²²adultery, greed, evil actions, deceit, unrestrained immorality, envy, insults, arrogance, and foolishness. ²³All these evil things come from the inside and contaminate a person in God's sight."

An immigrant's daughter is delivered

²⁴Jesus left that place and went into the region of Tyre. He didn't want anyone to know that he had entered a house, but he couldn't hide. ²⁵In fact, a woman whose young daughter was possessed by an unclean spirit heard about him right away. She came and fell at his feet. ²⁶The woman was Greek, Syrophoenician by birth. She begged Jesus to throw the demon out of her daughter. ²⁷He responded, "The children have to be fed first. It isn't right to take the children's bread and toss it to the dogs."

²⁸But she answered, "Lord, even the dogs under the table eat the children's crumbs."

²⁹"Good answer!" he said. "Go on home. The demon has already left your daughter." ³⁰When she returned to her house, she found the child lying on the bed and the demon gone.

A deaf man is healed

³¹After leaving the region of Tyre, Jesus went through Sidon toward the Galilee Sea through the region of the Ten Cities. ³²Some people brought to him a man who was deaf and could hardly speak, and they begged him to place his hand on the man for healing. ³³Jesus took him away from the crowd by himself and put his fingers in the man's ears. Then he spit and touched the man's tongue. ³⁴Looking into heaven, Jesus sighed deeply and said, "*Ephphatha*," which means, "Open up." ³⁵At once, his ears opened, his twisted tongue was released, and he began to speak clearly.

³⁶Jesus gave the people strict orders not to tell anyone. But the more he tried to silence them, the more eagerly they shared the news. ³⁷People were overcome with wonder, saying, "He does everything well! He even makes the deaf to hear and gives speech to those who can't speak."

Jesus feeds four thousand people

8 In those days there was another large crowd with nothing to eat. Jesus called his disciples and told them, ²"I feel sorry for the crowd because they have been with me for three days and

---

^k7:16 is omitted in most critical editions of the Gk New Testament *Whoever has ears to listen should pay attention!*

have nothing to eat. ³If I send them away hungry to their homes, they won't have enough strength to travel, for some have come a long distance."

⁴His disciples responded, "How can anyone get enough food in this wilderness to satisfy these people?"

⁵Jesus asked, "How much bread do you have?"

They said, "Seven loaves."

⁶He told the crowd to sit on the ground. He took the seven loaves, gave thanks, broke them apart, and gave them to his disciples to distribute; and they gave the bread to the crowd. ⁷They also had a few fish. He said a blessing over them, then gave them to the disciples to hand out also. ⁸They ate until they were full. They collected seven baskets full of leftovers. ⁹This was a crowd of about four thousand people! Jesus sent them away, ¹⁰then got into a boat with his disciples and went over to the region of Dalmanutha.

Looking for proof

¹¹The Pharisees showed up and began to argue with Jesus. To test him, they asked for a sign from heaven. ¹²With an impatient sigh, Jesus said, "Why does this generation look for a sign? I assure you that no sign will be given to it." ¹³Leaving them, he got back in the boat and crossed to the other side of the lake.

Understanding about the bread

¹⁴Jesus' disciples had forgotten to bring any bread, so they had only one loaf with them in the boat. ¹⁵He gave them strict orders: "Watch out and be on your guard for the yeast of the Pharisees as well as the yeast of Herod."

¹⁶The disciples discussed this among themselves, "He said this because we have no bread."

¹⁷Jesus knew what they were discussing and said, "Why are you talking about the fact that you don't have any bread? Don't you grasp what has happened? Don't you understand? Are your hearts so resistant to what God is doing? ¹⁸Don't you have eyes? Why can't you see? Don't you have ears? Why can't you hear? Don't you remember? ¹⁹When I broke five loaves of bread for those five thousand people, how many baskets full of leftovers did you gather?"

They answered, "Twelve."

²⁰"And when I broke seven loaves of bread for those four thousand people, how many baskets full of leftovers did you gather?"

They answered, "Seven."

²¹Jesus said to them, "And you still don't understand?"

A blind man is healed

²²Jesus and his disciples came to Bethsaida. Some people brought a blind man to Jesus and begged him to touch and heal him. ²³Taking the blind man's hand, Jesus led him out of the village. After spitting on his eyes and laying his hands on the man, he asked him, "Do you see anything?"

²⁴The man looked up and said, "I see people. They look like trees, only they are walking around."

²⁵Then Jesus placed his hands on the man's eyes again. He looked with his eyes wide open, his sight was restored, and he could see everything clearly. ²⁶Then Jesus sent him home, saying, "Don't go into the village!"

Jesus predicts his death

²⁷Jesus and his disciples went into the villages near Caesarea Philippi. On the way he asked his disciples, "Who do people say that I am?"

²⁸They told him, "Some say John the Baptist, others Elijah, and still others one of the prophets."

²⁹He asked them, "And what about you? Who do you say that I am?"

Peter answered, "You are the Christ."

³⁰Jesus ordered them not to tell anyone about him.

³¹Then Jesus began to teach his disciples: "The Human One[l] must suffer many things and be rejected by the elders, chief priests, and the legal experts, and be killed, and then, after three days, rise from the dead." ³²He said this plainly. But Peter took hold of Jesus and, scolding him, began to correct him. ³³Jesus turned and looked at his disciples, then sternly corrected Peter: "Get behind me, Satan. You are not thinking God's thoughts but human thoughts."

³⁴After calling the crowd together with his disciples, Jesus said to them, "All who want to come after me must say no to themselves, take up their cross, and follow me. ³⁵All who want to save their lives will lose them. But all who lose their lives because of me and because of the good news will save them. ³⁶Why would people gain the whole world but lose their lives? ³⁷What will people give in exchange for their lives? ³⁸Whoever is ashamed of me and my words in this unfaithful and sinful generation, the Human One[m] will be ashamed of that person when he comes in the Father's glory with the holy angels."

9Jesus continued, "I assure you that some standing here won't be before they see God's kingdom arrive in power."

Jesus transformed

²Six days later Jesus took Peter, James, and John, and brought them to the top of a very high mountain where they were alone. He was transformed in front of them, ³and his clothes were amazingly bright, brighter than if they had been bleached white. ⁴Elijah and Moses appeared and were talking with Jesus. ⁵Peter reacted to all of this by saying to Jesus, "Rabbi, it's good that we're here. Let's make three shrines—one for you, one for Moses, and one for Elijah." ⁶He said this because he didn't know how to respond, for the three of them were terrified.

⁷Then a cloud overshadowed them, and a voice spoke from the cloud, "This is my Son, whom I dearly love. Listen to him!" ⁸Suddenly, looking around, they no longer saw anyone with them except Jesus.

⁹As they were coming down the mountain, he ordered them not to tell anyone what they had seen until after the Human One[n] had risen from the dead. ¹⁰So they kept it to themselves, wondering, "What's this 'rising from the dead'?" ¹¹They asked Jesus, "Why do the legal experts say that Elijah must come first?"

¹²He answered, "Elijah does come first to restore all things. Why was it written that the Human One[o] would suffer many things and be rejected? ¹³In fact, I tell you that Elijah has come, but they did to him whatever they wanted, just as it was written about him."

[l]Or Son of Man [m]Or Son of Man [n]Or Son of Man [o]Or Son of Man

A demon-possessed boy

[14]When Jesus, Peter, James, and John approached the other disciples, they saw a large crowd surrounding them and legal experts arguing with them. [15]Suddenly the whole crowd caught sight of Jesus. They ran to greet him, overcome with excitement. [16]Jesus asked them, "What are you arguing about?"

[17]Someone from the crowd responded, "Teacher, I brought my son to you, since he has a spirit that doesn't allow him to speak. [18]Wherever it overpowers him, it throws him into a fit. He foams at the mouth, grinds his teeth, and stiffens up. So I spoke to your disciples to see if they could throw it out, but they couldn't."

[19]Jesus answered them, "You faithless generation, how long will I be with you? How long will I put up with you? Bring him to me."

[20]They brought him. When the spirit saw Jesus, it immediately threw the boy into a fit. He fell on the ground and rolled around, foaming at the mouth. [21]Jesus asked his father, "How long has this been going on?"

He said, "Since he was a child. [22]It has often thrown him into a fire or into water trying to kill him. If you can do anything, help us! Show us compassion!"

[23]Jesus said to him, "If you can do anything'? All things are possible for the one who has faith."

[24]At that the boy's father cried out, "I have faith; help my lack of faith!"

[25]Noticing that the crowd had surged together, Jesus spoke harshly to the unclean spirit, "Mute and deaf spirit, I command you to come out of him and never enter him again." [26]After screaming and shaking the boy horribly, the spirit came out. The boy seemed to be dead; in fact, several people said that he had died. [27]But Jesus took his hand, lifted him up, and he arose.

[28]After Jesus went into a house, his disciples asked him privately, "Why couldn't we throw this spirit out?"

[29]Jesus answered, "Throwing this kind of spirit out requires prayer."

Jesus predicts his death

[30]From there Jesus and his followers went through Galilee, but he didn't want anyone to know it. [31]This was because he was teaching his disciples, "The Human One[p] will be delivered into human hands. They will kill him. Three days after he is killed he will rise up." [32]But they didn't understand this kind of talk, and they were afraid to ask him.

[33]They entered Capernaum. When they had come into a house, he asked them, "What were you arguing about during the journey?" [34]They didn't respond, since on the way they had been debating with each other about who was the greatest. [35]He sat down, called the Twelve, and said to them, "Whoever wants to be first must be least of all and the servant of all." [36]Jesus reached for a little child, placed him among the Twelve, and embraced him. Then he said, [37]"Whoever welcomes one of these children in my name welcomes me; and whoever welcomes me isn't actually welcoming me but rather the one who sent me."

Recognize your allies

[38]John said to Jesus, "Teacher, we saw someone throwing demons out in

[p]Or *Son of Man*

your name, and we tried to stop him because he wasn't following us."

³⁹Jesus replied, "Don't stop him. No one who does powerful acts in my name can quickly turn around and curse me. ⁴⁰Whoever isn't against us is for us. ⁴¹I assure you that whoever gives you a cup of water to drink because you belong to Christ will certainly be rewarded.

⁴²"As for whoever causes these little ones who believe in me to trip and fall into sin, it would be better for them to have a huge stone hung around their necks and to be thrown into the lake. ⁴³If your hand causes you to fall into sin, chop it off. It's better for you to enter into life crippled than to go away with two hands into the fire of hell, which can't be put out.�q ⁴⁵If your foot causes you to fall into sin, chop it off. It's better for you to enter life lame than to be thrown into hell with two feet.ʳ ⁴⁷If your eye causes you to fall into sin, tear it out. It's better for you to enter God's kingdom with one eye than to be thrown into hell with two. ⁴⁸That's a place where worms don't die and the fire never goes out.ˢ ⁴⁹Everyone will be salted with fire. ⁵⁰Salt is good; but if salt loses its saltiness, how will it become salty again? Maintain salt among yourselves and keep peace with each other."

Divorce and remarriage

10 Jesus left that place and went beyond the Jordan and into the region of Judea. Crowds gathered around him again and, as usual, he taught them. ²Some Pharisees came

and, trying to test him, they asked, "Does the Law allow a man to divorce his wife?"

³Jesus answered, "What did Moses command you?"

⁴They said, "Moses allowed a man to write a divorce certificate and to divorce his wife."

⁵Jesus said to them, "He wrote this commandment for you because of your unyielding hearts. ⁶At the beginning of creation, God made them male and female.ᵗ ⁷Because of this, a man should leave his father and mother and be joined together with his wife, ⁸and the two will be one flesh.ᵘ So they are no longer two but one flesh. ⁹Therefore, humans must not pull apart what God has put together."

¹⁰Inside the house, the disciples asked him again about this. ¹¹He said to them, "Whoever divorces his wife and marries another commits adultery against her; ¹²and if a wife divorces her husband and marries another, she commits adultery."

Jesus blesses children

¹³ People were bringing children to Jesus so that he would bless them. But the disciples scolded them. ¹⁴When Jesus saw this, he grew angry and said to them, "Allow the children to come to me. Don't forbid them, because God's kingdom belongs to people like these children. ¹⁵ I assure you that whoever doesn't welcome God's kingdom like a child will never enter it." ¹⁶Then he hugged the children and blessed them.

�q9:44 is omitted in most critical editions of the Gk New Testament *where worms don't die and the fire never goes out.* ʳ9:46 is omitted in most critical editions of the Gk New Testament *where worms don't die and the fire never goes out.* ˢIsa 66:24 ᵗGen 1:27 ᵘGen 2:24

A rich man's question

¹⁷As Jesus continued down the road, a man ran up, knelt before him, and asked, "Good Teacher, what must I do to obtain eternal life?"

¹⁸Jesus replied, "Why do you call me good? No one is good except the one God. ¹⁹You know the commandments: *Don't commit murder. Don't commit adultery. Don't steal. Don't give false testimony. Don't cheat. Honor your father and mother.*^v

²⁰"Teacher," he responded, "I've kept all of these things since I was a boy."

²¹Jesus looked at him carefully and loved him. He said, "You are lacking one thing. Go, sell what you own, and give the money to the poor. Then you will have treasure in heaven. And come, follow me." ²²But the man was dismayed at this statement and went away saddened, because he had many possessions.

²³Looking around, Jesus said to his disciples, "It will be very hard for the wealthy to enter God's kingdom!" ²⁴His words startled the disciples, so Jesus told them again, "Children, it's difficult to enter God's kingdom! ²⁵It's easier for a camel to squeeze through the eye of a needle than for a rich person to enter God's kingdom."

²⁶They were shocked even more and said to each other, "Then who can be saved?"

²⁷Jesus looked at them carefully and said, "It's impossible with human beings, but not with God. All things are possible for God."

²⁸Peter said to him, "Look, we've left everything and followed you."

²⁹Jesus said, "I assure you that anyone who has left house, brothers, sisters, mother, father, children, or farms because of me and because of the good news ³⁰will receive one hundred times as much now in this life—houses, brothers, sisters, mothers, children, and farms (with harassment)—and in the coming age, eternal life. ³¹But many who are first will be last. And many who are last will be first."

Jesus predicts his death and resurrection

³²Jesus and his disciples were on the road, going up to Jerusalem, with Jesus in the lead. The disciples were amazed while the others following behind were afraid. Taking the Twelve aside again, he told them what was about to happen to him. ³³"Look!" he said. "We're going up to Jerusalem. The Human One^w will be handed over to the chief priests and the legal experts. They will condemn him to death and hand him over to the Gentiles. ³⁴They will ridicule him, spit on him, torture him, and kill him. After three days, he will rise up."

A request from James and John

³⁵James and John, Zebedee's sons, came to Jesus and said, "Teacher, we want you to do for us whatever we ask."

³⁶"What do you want me to do for you?" he asked.

³⁷They said, "Allow one of us to sit on your right and the other on your left when you enter your glory."

³⁸Jesus replied, "You don't know what you're asking! Can you drink the cup I drink or receive the baptism I receive?"

³⁹"We can," they answered.

---

^vExod 12:16; Deut 16:20   ^wOr *Son of Man*

Jesus said, "You will drink the cup I drink and receive the baptism I receive, [40] but to sit at my right or left hand isn't mine to give. It belongs to those for whom it has been prepared."

[41] Now when the other ten disciples heard about this, they became angry with James and John. [42] Jesus called them over and said, "You know that the ones who are considered the rulers by the Gentiles show off their authority over them and their high-ranking officials order them around. [43] But that's not the way it will be with you. Whoever wants to be great among you will be your servant. [44] Whoever wants to be first among you will be the slave of all, [45] for the Human One[x] didn't come to be served but rather to serve and to give his life to liberate many people."

Healing of blind Bartimaeus

[46] Jesus and his followers came into Jericho. As Jesus was leaving Jericho, together with his disciples and a sizable crowd, a blind beggar named Bartimaeus, Timaeus' son, was sitting beside the road. [47] When he heard that Jesus of Nazareth was there, he began to shout, "Jesus, Son of David, show me mercy!" [48] Many scolded him, telling him to be quiet, but he shouted even louder, "Son of David, show me mercy!"

[49] Jesus stopped and said, "Call him forward."

They called the blind man, "Be encouraged! Get up! He's calling you." [50] Throwing his coat to the side, he jumped up and came to Jesus.

[51] Jesus asked him, "What do you want me to do for you?"

The blind man said, "Teacher, I want to see."

[52] Jesus said, "Go, your faith has healed you." At once he was able to see, and he began to follow Jesus on the way.

Jesus enters Jerusalem

11 When Jesus and his followers approached Jerusalem, they came to Bethphage and Bethany at the Mount of Olives. Jesus gave two disciples a task, [2] saying to them, "Go into the village over there. As soon as you enter it, you will find tied up there a colt that no one has ridden. Untie it and bring it here. [3] If anyone says to you, 'Why are you doing this?' say, 'Its master needs it, and he will send it back right away.'"

[4] They went and found a colt tied to a gate outside on the street, and they untied it. [5] Some people standing around said to them, "What are you doing, untying the colt?" [6] They told them just what Jesus said, and they left them alone. [7] They brought the colt to Jesus and threw their clothes upon it, and he sat on it. [8] Many people spread out their clothes on the road while others spread branches cut from the fields. [9] Those in front of him and those following were shouting, "*Hosanna! Blessings on the one who comes in the name of the Lord*[y] [10] Blessings on the coming kingdom of our ancestor David! Hosanna in the highest!" [11] Jesus entered Jerusalem and went into the temple. After he looked around at everything, because it was already late in the evening, he returned to Bethany with the Twelve.

Fig tree and the temple

[12] The next day, after leaving Bethany, Jesus was hungry. [13] From far away, he noticed a fig tree in leaf, so he went

---

[x] Or *Son of Man*   [y] Ps 118:26

to see if he could find anything on it. When he came to it, he found nothing except leaves, since it wasn't the season for figs. ¹⁴So he said to it, "No one will ever again eat your fruit!" His disciples heard this.

¹⁵They came into Jerusalem. After entering the temple, he threw out those who were selling and buying there. He pushed over the tables used for currency exchange and the chairs of those who sold doves. ¹⁶He didn't allow anyone to carry anything through the temple. ¹⁷He taught them, "Hasn't it been written, *My house will be called a house of prayer for all nations?*ᵃ But you've turned it into *a hideout for crooks.*"ᵃ ¹⁸The chief priests and legal experts heard this and tried to find a way to destroy him. They regarded him as dangerous because the whole crowd was enthralled at his teaching. ¹⁹When it was evening, Jesus and his disciples went outside the city.

Power, prayer, and forgiveness

²⁰Early in the morning, as Jesus and his disciples were walking along, they saw the fig tree withered from the root up. ²¹Peter remembered and said to Jesus, "Rabbi, look how the fig tree you cursed has dried up."

²²Jesus responded to them, "Have faith in God! ²³I assure you that whoever says to this mountain, 'Be lifted up and thrown into the sea'—and doesn't waver but believes that what is said will really happen—it will happen. ²⁴Therefore I say to you, whatever you pray and ask for, believe that you will receive it, and it will be so for you. ²⁵And whenever you stand up to pray, if you have

something against anyone, forgive so that your Father in heaven may forgive you your wrongdoings."ᵇ

Controversy over authority

²⁷Jesus and his disciples entered Jerusalem again. As Jesus was walking around the temple, the chief priests, legal experts, and elders came to him. ²⁸They asked, "What kind of authority do you have for doing these things? Who gave you this authority to do them?"

²⁹Jesus said to them, "I have a question for you. Give me an answer, then I'll tell you what kind of authority I have to do these things. ³⁰Was John's baptism of heavenly or of human origin? Answer me."

³¹They argued among themselves, "If we say, 'It's of heavenly origin,' he'll say, 'Then why didn't you believe him?' ³²But we can't say, 'It's of earthly origin.'" They said this because they were afraid of the crowd, because they all thought John was a prophet. ³³They answered Jesus, "We don't know."

Jesus replied, "Neither will I tell you what kind of authority I have to do these things."

Parable of the tenant farmers

12Jesus spoke to them in parables. "A man planted a vineyard, put a fence around it, dug a pit for the winepress, and built a tower. Then he rented it to tenant farmers and took a trip. ²When it was time, he sent a servant to collect from the tenants his share of the fruit of the vineyard. ³But they grabbed the servant, beat him, and sent him away empty-handed. ⁴Again the landowner

ᵃIsa 56:7 ᵃJer 7:11 ᵇ11:26 is omitted in most critical editions of the Gk New Testament *And if you don't forgive, neither will your Father in heaven forgive you your wrongdoings.*

sent another servant to them, but they struck him on the head and treated him disgracefully. [5]He sent another one; that one they killed. The landlord sent many other servants, but the tenants beat some and killed others. [6]Now the landowner had one son whom he loved dearly. He sent him last, thinking, They will respect my son. [7]But those tenant farmers said to each other, 'This is the heir. Let's kill him, and the inheritance will be ours.' [8]They grabbed him, killed him, and threw him out of the vineyard.

[9]"So what will the owner of the vineyard do? He will come and destroy those tenants and give the vineyard to others. [10]Haven't you read this scripture, *The stone that the builders rejected has become the cornerstone.* [11]*The Lord has done this, and it's amazing in our eyes?*"[c]

[12]They wanted to arrest Jesus because they knew that he had told the parable against them. But they were afraid of the crowd, so they left him and went away.

A question about taxes

[13]They sent some of the Pharisees and supporters of Herod to trap him in his words. [14]They came to him and said, "Teacher, we know that you're genuine and you don't worry about what people think. You don't show favoritism but teach God's way as it really is. Does the Law allow people to pay taxes to Caesar or not? Should we pay taxes or not?"

[15]Since Jesus recognized their deceit, he said to them, "Why are you testing me? Bring me a coin. Show it to me." [16]And they brought one. He said to them, "Whose image and inscription is this?"

"Caesar's," they replied.

[17]Jesus said to them, "Give to Caesar what belongs to Caesar and to God what belongs to God." His reply left them overcome with wonder.

A question about the resurrection

[18]Sadducees, who deny that there is a resurrection, came to Jesus and asked, [19]"Teacher, Moses wrote for us that *if a man's brother dies, leaving a widow but no children, the brother must marry the widow and raise up children for his brother.*[d] [20]Now there were seven brothers. The first one married a woman; when he died, he left no children. [21]The second married her and died without leaving any children. The third did the same. [22]None of the seven left any children. Finally, the woman died. [23]At the resurrection, when they all rise up, whose wife will she be? All seven were married to her."

[24]Jesus said to them, "Isn't this the reason you are wrong, because you don't know either the scriptures or God's power? [25]When people rise from the dead, they won't marry nor will they be given in marriage. Instead, they will be like God's angels. [26]As for the resurrection from the dead, haven't you read in the scroll from Moses, in the passage about the burning bush, how God said to Moses, *I am the God of Abraham, the God of Isaac, and the God of Jacob?*[e] [27]He isn't the God of the dead but of the living. You are seriously mistaken."

God's most important command

[28]One of the legal experts heard their dispute and saw how well Jesus answered them. He came over and

---

[c]Ps 118:22-23   [d]Deut 25:5; Gen 38:8   [e]Exod 3:6, 15-16

asked him, "Which commandment is the most important of all?"

²⁹Jesus replied, "The most important one is *Israel, listen! Our God is the one Lord,* ³⁰ *and you must love the Lord your God with all your heart, with all your being, with all your mind, and with all your strength.*ᶠ ³¹The second is this, *You will love your neighbor as yourself.*ᵍ No other commandment is greater than these."

³²The legal expert said to him, "Well said, Teacher. You have truthfully said that God is one and there is no other besides him. ³³And to love God with all of the heart, a full understanding, and all of one's strength, and to love one's neighbor as oneself is much more important than all kinds of entirely burned offerings and sacrifices."

³⁴When Jesus saw that he had answered with wisdom, he said to him, "You aren't far from God's kingdom." After that, no one dared to ask him any more questions.

Jesus corrects the legal experts

³⁵While Jesus was teaching in the temple, he said, "Why do the legal experts say that the Christ is David's son? ³⁶David himself, inspired by the Holy Spirit, said, *The Lord said to my lord, 'Sit at my right side until I turn your enemies into your footstool.'*ʰ ³⁷David himself calls him 'Lord,' so how can he be David's son?" The large crowd listened to him with delight.

³⁸As he was teaching, he said, "Watch out for the legal experts. They like to walk around in long robes. They want to be greeted with honor in the markets.

³⁹They long for places of honor in the synagogues and at banquets. ⁴⁰They are the ones who cheat widows out of their homes, and to show off they say long prayers. They will be judged most harshly."

A poor widow's contribution

⁴¹Jesus sat across from the collection box for the temple treasury and observed how the crowd gave their money. Many rich people were throwing in lots of money. ⁴²One poor widow came forward and put in two small copper coins worth a penny.ⁱ ⁴³Jesus called his disciples to him and said, "I assure you that this poor widow has put in more than everyone who's been putting money in the treasury. ⁴⁴All of them are giving out of their spare change. But she from her hopeless poverty has given everything she had, even what she needed to live on."

The temple's fate

13 As Jesus left the temple, one of his disciples said to him, "Teacher, look! What awesome stones and buildings!"

²Jesus responded, "Do you see these enormous buildings? Not even one stone will be left upon another. All will be demolished."

³Jesus was sitting on the Mount of Olives across from the temple. Peter, James, John, and Andrew asked him privately, ⁴"Tell us, when will these things happen? What sign will show that all these things are about to come to an end?"

ᶠDeut 6:4-5 ᵍLev 19:18 ʰPs 110:1 ⁱOr two *lepta* (the smallest Greek copper coin, each worth 1/128 of a single day's pay), that is, a *kodrantes* (the smallest Roman coin, equal in value to two *lepta*)

Keep watch!

5 Jesus said, "Watch out that no one deceives you. 6 Many people will come in my name, saying, 'I'm the one!' They will deceive many people. 7 When you hear of wars and reports of wars, don't be alarmed. These things must happen, but this isn't the end yet. 8 Nations and kingdoms will fight against each other, and there will be earthquakes and famines in all sorts of places. These things are just the beginning of the sufferings associated with the end.

9 "Watch out for yourselves. People will hand you over to the councils. You will be beaten in the synagogues. You will stand before governors and kings because of me so that you can testify before them. 10 First, the good news must be proclaimed to all the nations. 11 When they haul you in and hand you over, don't worry ahead of time about what to answer or say. Instead, say whatever is given to you at that moment, for you aren't doing the speaking but the Holy Spirit is. 12 Brothers and sisters will hand each other over to death. A father will turn in his children. Children will rise up against their parents and have them executed. 13 Everyone will hate you because of my name. But whoever stands firm until the end will be saved.

14 "When you see the disgusting and destructive thing standing where it shouldn't be (the reader should understand this), then those in Judea must escape to the mountains. 15 Those on the roof shouldn't come down or enter their houses to grab anything. 16 Those in the field shouldn't come back to grab their clothes. 17 How terrible it will be at that time for women who are pregnant and for women who are nursing their children. 18 Pray that it doesn't happen in winter. 19 In those days there will be great suffering such as the world has never before seen and will never again see. 20 If the Lord hadn't shortened that time, no one would be rescued. But for the sake of the chosen ones, the ones whom God chose, he has cut short the time.

21 "Then if someone says to you, 'Look, here's the Christ,' or 'There he is,' don't believe it. 22 False christs and false prophets will appear, and they will offer signs and wonders in order to deceive, if possible, those whom God has chosen. 23 But you, watch out! I've told you everything ahead of time.

24 "In those days, after the suffering of that time, the sun will become dark, and the moon won't give its light. 25 The stars will fall from the sky, and the planets and other heavenly bodies will be shaken. 26 Then they will see the Human One[j] coming in the clouds with great power and splendor. 27 Then he will send the angels and gather together his chosen people from the four corners of the earth, from the end of the earth to the end of heaven.

A lesson from the fig tree

28 "Learn this parable from the fig tree. After its branch becomes tender and it sprouts new leaves, you know that summer is near. 29 In the same way, when you see these things happening, you know that he's near, at the door. 30 I assure you that this generation won't pass away until all these things happen. 31 Heaven and earth will

[j]Or Son of Man

pass away, but my words will certainly not pass away.

³²"But nobody knows when that day or hour will come, not the angels in heaven and not the Son. Only the Father knows. ³³Watch out! Stay alert! You don't know when the time is coming. ³⁴It is as if someone took a trip, left the household behind, and put the servants in charge, giving each one a job to do, and told the doorkeeper to stay alert. ³⁵Therefore, stay alert! You don't know when the head of the household will come, whether in the evening or at midnight, or when the rooster crows in the early morning or at daybreak. ³⁶Don't let him show up when you weren't expecting and find you sleeping. ³⁷What I say to you, I say to all: Stay alert!"

Preparation for burial

14 It was two days before Passover and the Festival of Unleavened Bread. The chief priests and legal experts through cunning tricks were searching for a way to arrest Jesus and kill him. ²But they agreed that it shouldn't happen during the festival; otherwise, there would be an uproar among the people.

³Jesus was at Bethany visiting the house of Simon, who had a skin disease. During dinner, a woman came in with a vase made of alabaster and containing very expensive perfume of pure nard. She broke open the vase and poured the perfume on his head. ⁴Some grew angry. They said to each other, "Why waste the perfume? ⁵This perfume could have been sold for almost a year's pay[k] and the money given to the poor." And they scolded her.

⁶Jesus said, "Leave her alone. Why do you make trouble for her? She has done a good thing for me. ⁷You always have the poor with you; and whenever you want, you can do something good for them. But you won't always have me. ⁸She has done what she could. She has anointed my body ahead of time for burial. ⁹I tell you the truth, that, wherever in the whole world the good news is announced, what she's done will also be told in memory of her."

Passover meal

¹⁰Judas Iscariot, one of the Twelve, went to the chief priests to give Jesus up to them. ¹¹When they heard it, they were delighted and promised to give him money. So he started looking for an opportunity to turn him in.

¹²On the first day of the Festival of Unleavened Bread, when the Passover lamb was sacrificed, the disciples said to Jesus, "Where do you want us to prepare for you to eat the Passover meal?"

¹³He sent two of his disciples and said to them, "Go into the city. A man carrying a water jar will meet you. Follow him. ¹⁴Wherever he enters, say to the owner of the house, 'The teacher asks, "Where is my guest room where I can eat the Passover meal with my disciples?" ' ¹⁵He will show you a large room upstairs already furnished. Prepare for us there." ¹⁶The disciples left, came into the city, found everything just as he had told them, and they prepared the Passover meal.

¹⁷That evening, Jesus arrived with the Twelve. ¹⁸During the meal, Jesus said, "I assure you that one of you will betray me—someone eating with me."

[k]Or *three hundred denaria*; a denarion was equivalent to a day's pay.

[19] Deeply saddened, they asked him, one by one, "It's not me, is it?"

[20] Jesus answered, "It's one of the Twelve, one who is dipping bread with me into this bowl. [21] The Human One[l] goes to his death just as it is written about him. But how terrible it is for that person who betrays the Human One![m] It would have been better for him if he had never been born."

[22] While they were eating, Jesus took bread, blessed it, broke it, and gave it to them, and said, "Take; this is my body." [23] He took a cup, gave thanks, and gave it to them, and they all drank from it. [24] He said to them, "This is my blood of the covenant, which is poured out for many. [25] I assure you that I won't drink wine again until that day when I drink it in a new way in God's kingdom." [26] After singing songs of praise, they went out to the Mount of Olives.

Predictions about disciples leaving Jesus

[27] Jesus said to them, "You will all falter in your faithfulness to me. It is written, *I will hit the shepherd, and the sheep will go off in all directions.*[n] [28] But after I'm raised up, I will go before you to Galilee."

[29] Peter said to him, "Even if everyone else stumbles, I won't."

[30] But Jesus said to him, "I assure you that on this very night, before the rooster crows twice, you will deny me three times."

[31] But Peter insisted, "If I must die alongside you, I won't deny you." And they all said the same thing.

Jesus in prayer

[32] Jesus and his disciples came to a place called Gethsemane. Jesus said to them, "Sit here while I pray." [33] He took Peter, James, and John along with him. He began to feel despair and was anxious. [34] He said to them, "I'm very sad. It's as if I'm dying. Stay here and keep alert." [35] Then he went a short distance farther and fell to the ground. He prayed that, if possible, he might be spared the time of suffering. [36] He said, "Abba, Father, for you all things are possible. Take this cup of suffering away from me. However—not what I want but what you want."

[37] He came and found them sleeping. He said to Peter, "Simon, are you asleep? Couldn't you stay alert for one hour? [38] Stay alert and pray so that you won't give in to temptation. The spirit is eager, but the flesh is weak."

[39] Again, he left them and prayed, repeating the same words. [40] And, again, when he came back, he found them sleeping, for they couldn't keep their eyes open, and they didn't know how to respond to him. [41] He came a third time and said to them, "Will you sleep and rest all night? That's enough! The time has come for the Human One[o] to be betrayed into the hands of sinners. [42] Get up! Let's go! Look, here comes my betrayer."

Arrest

[43] Suddenly, while Jesus was still speaking, Judas, one of the Twelve, came with a mob carrying swords and clubs. They had been sent by the chief priests, legal experts, and elders. [44] His betrayer had given them a sign: "Arrest the man I kiss, and take him away under guard." [45] As soon as he got there, Judas said

[l]Or *Son of Man*   [m]Or *Son of Man*   [n]Zech 13:7   [o]Or *Son of Man*

to Jesus, "Rabbi!" Then he kissed him. [46]Then they came and grabbed Jesus and arrested him.

[47]One of the bystanders drew a sword and struck the high priest's slave and cut off his ear. [48]Jesus responded, "Have you come with swords and clubs to arrest me, like an outlaw? [49]Day after day, I was with you, teaching in the temple, but you didn't arrest me. But let the scriptures be fulfilled." [50]And all his disciples left him and ran away. [51]One young man, a disciple, was wearing nothing but a linen cloth. They grabbed him, [52]but he left the linen cloth behind and ran away naked.

A hearing before the Sanhedrin

[53]They led Jesus away to the high priest, and all the chief priests, elders, and legal experts gathered. [54]Peter followed him from a distance, right into the high priest's courtyard. He was sitting with the guards, warming himself by the fire. [55]The chief priests and the whole Sanhedrin were looking for testimony against Jesus in order to put him to death, but they couldn't find any. [56]Many brought false testimony against him, but they contradicted each other. [57]Some stood to offer false witness against him, saying, [58]"We heard him saying, 'I will destroy this temple, constructed by humans, and within three days I will build another, one not made by humans.'" [59]But their testimonies didn't agree even on this point.

[60]Then the high priest stood up in the middle of the gathering and examined Jesus. "Aren't you going to respond to the testimony these people have brought against you?" [61]But Jesus was silent and didn't answer. Again, the high priest asked, "Are you the Christ, the Son of the blessed one?"

[62]Jesus said, "I am. And you will see the Human One[p] sitting on the right side of the Almighty[q] and coming on the heavenly clouds."

[63]Then the high priest tore his clothes and said, "Why do we need any more witnesses? [64]You've heard his insult against God. What do you think?"

They all condemned him. "He deserves to die!"

[65]Some began to spit on him. Some covered his face and hit him, saying, "Prophesy!" Then the guards took him and beat him.

Peter denies Jesus

[66]Meanwhile, Peter was below in the courtyard. A woman, one of the high priest's servants, approached [67]and saw Peter warming himself by the fire. She stared at him and said, "You were also with the Nazarene, Jesus."

[68]But he denied it, saying, "I don't know what you're talking about. I don't understand what you're saying." And he went outside into the outer courtyard. A rooster crowed.

[69]The female servant saw him and began a second time to say to those standing around, "This man is one of them." [70]But he denied it again.

A short time later, those standing around again said to Peter, "You must be one of them, because you are also a Galilean."

[71]But he cursed and swore, "I don't know this man you're talking about." [72]At that very moment, a rooster crowed a second time. Peter remembered what

---

[p]Or Son of Man   [q]Or the Power

Jesus told him, "Before a rooster crows twice, you will deny me three times." And he broke down, sobbing.

Trial before Pilate

15 At daybreak, the chief priests—with the elders, legal experts, and the whole Sanhedrin—formed a plan. They bound Jesus, led him away, and turned him over to Pilate. ²Pilate questioned him, "Are you the king of the Jews?"

Jesus replied, "That's what you say." ³The chief priests were accusing him of many things.

⁴Pilate asked him again, "Aren't you going to answer? What about all these accusations?" ⁵But Jesus gave no more answers, so that Pilate marveled.

⁶During the festival, Pilate released one prisoner to them, whomever they requested. ⁷A man named Barabbas was locked up with the rebels who had committed murder during an uprising. ⁸The crowd pushed forward and asked Pilate to release someone, as he regularly did. ⁹Pilate answered them, "Do you want me to release to you the king of the Jews?" ¹⁰He knew that the chief priests had handed him over because of jealousy. ¹¹But the chief priests stirred up the crowd to have him release Barabbas to them instead. ¹²Pilate replied, "Then what do you want me to do with the one you call king of the Jews?"

¹³They shouted back, "Crucify him!"

¹⁴Pilate said to them, "Why? What wrong has he done?"

They shouted even louder, "Crucify him!"

¹⁵Pilate wanted to satisfy the crowd, so he released Barabbas to them. He had Jesus whipped, then handed him over to be crucified.

Jesus is tortured and killed

¹⁶The soldiers led Jesus away into the courtyard of the palace known as the governor's headquarters,ʳ and they called together the whole company of soldiers.ˢ ¹⁷They dressed him up in a purple robe and twisted together a crown of thorns and put it on him. ¹⁸They saluted him, "Hey! King of the Jews!" ¹⁹Again and again, they struck his head with a stick. They spit on him and knelt before him to honor him. ²⁰When they finished mocking him, they stripped him of the purple robe and put his own clothes back on him. Then they led him out to crucify him.

²¹Simon, a man from Cyrene, Alexander and Rufus' father, was coming in from the countryside. They forced him to carry his cross.

²²They brought Jesus to the place called Golgotha, which means Skull Place. ²³They tried to give him wine mixed with myrrh, but he didn't take it. ²⁴They crucified him. They divided up his clothes, drawing lots for them to determine who would take what. ²⁵It was nine in the morning when they crucified him. ²⁶The notice of the formal charge against him was written, "The king of the Jews." ²⁷They crucified two outlaws with him, one on his right and one on his left.ᵗ

²⁹People walking by insulted him, shaking their heads and saying, "Ha! So

---

ʳOr *praetorium*   ˢOr *cohort* (approximately six hundred soldiers)   ᵗ15:28 is omitted in most critical editions of the Gk New Testament *The scripture was fulfilled, which says, He was numbered among criminals.*

you were going to destroy the temple and rebuild it in three days, were you? ³⁰Save yourself and come down from that cross!"

³¹In the same way, the chief priests were making fun of him among themselves, together with the legal experts. "He saved others," they said, "but he can't save himself. ³²Let the Christ, the king of Israel, come down from the cross. Then we'll see and believe." Even those who had been crucified with Jesus insulted him.

³³From noon until three in the afternoon the whole earth was dark. ³⁴At three, Jesus cried out with a loud shout, "*Eloi, eloi, lama sabachthani,*" which means, "My God, my God, why have you left me?"

³⁵After hearing him, some standing there said, "Look! He's calling Elijah!" ³⁶Someone ran, filled a sponge with sour wine, and put it on a pole. He offered it to Jesus to drink, saying, "Let's see if Elijah will come to take him down." ³⁷But Jesus let out a loud cry and died.

³⁸The curtain of the sanctuary was torn in two from top to bottom. ³⁹When the centurion, who stood facing Jesus, saw how he died, he said, "This man was certainly God's Son."

⁴⁰Some women were watching from a distance, including Mary Magdalene and Mary the mother of James (the younger one) and Joses, and Salome. ⁴¹When Jesus was in Galilee, these women had followed and supported him, along with many other women who had come to Jerusalem with him.

Jesus' burial

⁴²Since it was late in the afternoon on Preparation Day, just before the

Sabbath, ⁴³Joseph from Arimathea dared to approach Pilate and ask for Jesus' body. (Joseph was a prominent council member who also eagerly anticipated the coming of God's kingdom.) ⁴⁴Pilate wondered if Jesus was already dead. He called the centurion and asked him whether Jesus had already died. ⁴⁵When he learned from the centurion that Jesus was dead, Pilate gave the dead body to Joseph. ⁴⁶He bought a linen cloth, took Jesus down from the cross, wrapped him in the cloth, and laid him in a tomb that had been carved out of rock. He rolled a stone against the entrance to the tomb. ⁴⁷Mary Magdalene and Mary the mother of Joses saw where he was buried.

Empty tomb

16 When the Sabbath was over, Mary Magdalene, Mary the mother of James, and Salome bought spices so that they could go and anoint Jesus' dead body. ²Very early on the first day of the week, just after sunrise, they came to the tomb. ³They were saying to each other, "Who's going to roll the stone away from the entrance for us?" ⁴When they looked up, they saw that the stone had been rolled away. (And it was a very large stone!) ⁵Going into the tomb, they saw a young man in a white robe seated on the right side; and they were startled. ⁶But he said to them, "Don't be alarmed! You are looking for Jesus of Nazareth, who was crucified.ᵘ He has been raised. He isn't here. Look, here's the place where they laid him. ⁷Go, tell his disciples, especially Peter, that he is going ahead of you into Galilee. You will see him there, just as he

ᵘOr *the Crucified One*

told you." ⁸Overcome with terror and dread, they fled from the tomb. They said nothing to anyone, because they were afraid.^v

Endings Added Later O········

[⁹They promptly reported all of the young man's instructions to those who were with Peter. Afterward, through the work of his disciples, Jesus sent out, from the east to the west, the sacred and undying message of eternal salvation. Amen.]

[[⁹After Jesus rose up early on the first day of the week, he appeared first to Mary Magdalene, from whom he had cast out seven demons. ¹⁰She went and reported to the ones who had been with him, who were mourning and weeping. ¹¹But even after they heard the news, they didn't believe that Jesus was alive and that Mary had seen him.

¹²After that he appeared in a different form to two of them who were walking along in the countryside. ¹³When they returned, they reported it to the others, but they didn't believe them.

¹⁴Finally he appeared to the eleven while they were eating. Jesus criticized their unbelief and stubbornness because they didn't believe those who saw him after he was raised up. ¹⁵He said to them, "Go into the whole world and proclaim the good news to every creature. ¹⁶Whoever believes and is baptized will be saved, but whoever doesn't believe will be condemned. ¹⁷These signs will be associated with those who believe: they will throw out demons in my name. They will speak in new languages. ¹⁸They will pick up snakes with their hands. If they drink anything poisonous, it will not hurt them. They will place their hands on the sick, and they will get well."

¹⁹After the Lord Jesus spoke to them, he was lifted up into heaven and sat down on the right side of God. ²⁰But they went out and proclaimed the message everywhere. The Lord worked with them, confirming the word by the signs associated with them.]]

LUKE

Luke's purpose

1 Many people have already applied themselves to the task of compiling an account of the events that have been fulfilled among us. ²They used what the original eyewitnesses and servants of the word handed down to us. ³Now, after having investigated everything carefully from the beginning, I have also decided to write a carefully ordered account for you, most honorable Theophilus. ⁴I want you to have

^vIn most critical editions of the Gk New Testament, the Gospel of Mark ends at 16:8.

confidence in the soundness of the instruction you have received.

John the Baptist's birth foretold

5During the rule of King Herod of Judea there was a priest named Zechariah who belonged to the priestly division of Abijah. His wife Elizabeth was a descendant of Aaron. 6They were both righteous before God, blameless in their observance of all the Lord's commandments and regulations. 7They had no children because Elizabeth was unable to become pregnant and they both were very old. 8One day Zechariah was serving as a priest before God because his priestly division was on duty. 9Following the customs of priestly service, he was chosen by lottery to go into the Lord's sanctuary and burn incense. 10All the people who gathered to worship were praying outside during this hour of incense offering. 11An angel from the Lord appeared to him, standing to the right of the altar of incense. 12When Zechariah saw the angel, he was startled and overcome with fear.

13The angel said, "Don't be afraid, Zechariah. Your prayers have been heard. Your wife Elizabeth will give birth to your son and you must name him John. 14He will be a joy and delight to you, and many people will rejoice at his birth, 15for he will be great in the Lord's eyes. He must not drink wine and liquor. He will be filled with the Holy Spirit even before his birth. 16He will bring many Israelites back to the Lord their God. 17He will go forth before the Lord, equipped with the spirit and power of Elijah. He will turn the hearts of fathersa back to their children,

and he will turn the disobedient to righteous patterns of thinking. He will make ready a people prepared for the Lord."

18Zechariah said to the angel, "How can I be sure of this? My wife and I are very old."

19The angel replied, "I am Gabriel. I stand in God's presence. I was sent to speak to you and to bring this good news to you. 20Know this: What I have spoken will come true at the proper time. But because you didn't believe, you will remain silent, unable to speak until the day when these things happen."

21Meanwhile, the people were waiting for Zechariah, and they wondered why he was in the sanctuary for such a long time. 22When he came out, he was unable to speak to them. They realized he had seen a vision in the temple, for he gestured to them and couldn't speak. 23When he completed the days of his priestly service, he returned home. 24Afterward, his wife Elizabeth became pregnant. She kept to herself for five months, saying, 25"This is the Lord's doing. He has shown his favor to me by removing my disgrace among other people."

Jesus' birth foretold

26When Elizabeth was six months pregnant, God sent the angel Gabriel to Nazareth, a city in Galilee, 27to a virgin who was engaged to a man named Joseph, a descendant of David's house. The virgin's name was Mary. 28When the angel came to her, he said, "Rejoice, favored one! The Lord is with you!" 29She was confused by these words

aOr parents

and wondered what kind of greeting this might be. ³⁰The angel said, "Don't be afraid, Mary. God is honoring you. ³¹Look! You will conceive and give birth to a son, and you will name him Jesus. ³²He will be great and he will be called the Son of the Most High. The Lord God will give him the throne of David his father. ³³He will rule over Jacob's house forever, and there will be no end to his kingdom."

³⁴Then Mary said to the angel, "How will this happen since I haven't had sexual relations with a man?"

³⁵The angel replied, "The Holy Spirit will come over you and the power of the Most High will overshadow you. Therefore, the one who is to be born will be holy. He will be called God's Son. ³⁶Look, even in her old age, your relative Elizabeth has conceived a son. This woman who was labeled 'unable to conceive' is now six months pregnant. ³⁷Nothing is impossible for God."

³⁸Then Mary said, "I am the Lord's servant. Let it be with me just as you have said." Then the angel left her.

Mary visits Elizabeth

³⁹Mary got up and hurried to a city in the Judean highlands. ⁴⁰She entered Zechariah's home and greeted Elizabeth. ⁴¹When Elizabeth heard Mary's greeting, the child leaped in her womb, and Elizabeth was filled with the Holy Spirit. ⁴²With a loud voice she blurted out, "God has blessed you above all women, and he has blessed the child you carry. ⁴³Why do I have this honor, that the mother of my Lord should come to me? ⁴⁴As soon as I heard your greeting, the baby in my womb jumped for joy. ⁴⁵Happy is she who believed that the Lord would fulfill the promises he made to her."

Mary praises God

⁴⁶Mary said,
"With all my heart I glorify the Lord!
⁴⁷In the depths of who I am I rejoice
    in God my savior.
⁴⁸ He has looked with favor
    on the low status of his servant.
    Look! From now on,
    everyone will consider me
    highly favored
⁴⁹ because the mighty one
    has done great things for me.
Holy is his name.
⁵⁰ He shows mercy to everyone,
    from one generation to the next,
    who honors him as God.
⁵¹ He has shown strength with his arm.
    He has scattered those
    with arrogant thoughts
    and proud inclinations.
⁵² He has pulled the powerful down
    from their thrones
    and lifted up the lowly.
⁵³ He has filled the hungry
    with good things
    and sent the rich away
    empty-handed.
⁵⁴ He has come to the aid
    of his servant Israel,
    remembering his mercy,
⁵⁵ just as he promised
    to our ancestors,
    to Abraham and to Abraham's
    descendants forever."

⁵⁶Mary stayed with Elizabeth about three months, and then returned to her home.

⁵⁷When the time came for Elizabeth to have her child, she gave birth to a boy. ⁵⁸Her neighbors and relatives celebrated with her because they had heard that the Lord had shown her great mercy. ⁵⁹On the eighth day, it came time to circumcise the child. They

wanted to name him Zechariah because that was his father's name. [60]But his mother replied, "No, his name will be John."

[61]They said to her, "None of your relatives have that name." [62]Then they began gesturing to his father to see what he wanted to call him.

[63]After asking for a tablet, he surprised everyone by writing, "His name is John." [64]At that moment, Zechariah was able to speak again, and he began praising God.

[65]All their neighbors were filled with awe, and everyone throughout the Judean highlands talked about what had happened. [66]All who heard about this considered it carefully. They said, "What then will this child be?" Indeed, the Lord's power was with him.

Zechariah's prophecy

[67]John's father Zechariah was filled with the Holy Spirit and prophesied,

[68]"Bless the Lord God of Israel
   because he has come to help
      and has delivered his people.
[69]He has raised up a mighty savior
   for us in his servant David's house,
[70]just as he said through the mouths
      of his holy prophets long ago.
[71]He has brought salvation
      from our enemies
   and from the power of all those
      who hate us.
[72]He has shown the mercy promised
      to our ancestors,
   and remembered
      his holy covenant,
[73]the solemn pledge he made
      to our ancestor Abraham.
He has granted [74]that we would
   be rescued
      from the power of our enemies

so that we could serve him
      without fear,
[75]in holiness and righteousness
   in God's eyes,
      for as long as we live.
[76]You, child, will be called a prophet
   of the Most High,
      for you will go before the Lord
         to prepare his way.
[77]You will tell his people
   how to be saved
      through the forgiveness
         of their sins.
[78]Because of our God's deep compassion,
   the dawn from heaven
      will break upon us,
[79]to give light to those
   who are sitting in darkness
      and in the shadow of death,
         to guide us on the path of peace."

[80]The child grew up, becoming strong in character. He was in the wilderness until he began his public ministry to Israel.

Jesus' birth

2 In those days Caesar Augustus declared that everyone throughout the empire should be enrolled in the tax lists. [2]This first enrollment occurred when Quirinius governed Syria. [3]Everyone went to their own cities to be enrolled. [4]Since Joseph belonged to David's house and family line, he went up from the city of Nazareth in Galilee to David's city, called Bethlehem, in Judea. [5]He went to be enrolled together with Mary, who was promised to him in marriage and who was pregnant. [6]While they were there, the time came for Mary to have her baby. [7]She gave birth to her firstborn child, a son, wrapped him snugly, and laid him in a manger, because there was no place for them in the guestroom.

Announcement to shepherds

[8]Nearby shepherds were living in the fields, guarding their sheep at night. [9]The Lord's angel stood before them, the Lord's glory shone around them, and they were terrified.

[10]The angel said, "Don't be afraid! Look! I bring good news to you—wonderful, joyous news for all people. [11]Your savior is born today in David's city. He is Christ the Lord. [12]This is a sign for you: you will find a newborn baby wrapped snugly and lying in a manger." [13]Suddenly a great assembly of the heavenly forces was with the angel praising God. They said, [14]"Glory to God in heaven, and on earth peace among those whom he favors."

[15]When the angels returned to heaven, the shepherds said to each other, "Let's go right now to Bethlehem and see what's happened. Let's confirm what the Lord has revealed to us." [16]They went quickly and found Mary and Joseph, and the baby lying in the manger. [17]When they saw this, they reported what they had been told about this child. [18]Everyone who heard it was amazed at what the shepherds told them. [19]Mary committed these things to memory and considered them carefully. [20]The shepherds returned home, glorifying and praising God for all they had heard and seen. Everything happened just as they had been told.

Jesus' circumcision, naming, and temple presentation

[21]When eight days had passed, Jesus' parents circumcised him and gave him the name Jesus. This was the name given to him by the angel before he was conceived. [22]When the time came for their ritual cleansing, in accordance with the Law from Moses, they brought Jesus up to Jerusalem to present him to the Lord. ([23]It's written in the Law of the Lord, "Every firstborn male will be dedicated to the Lord.") [24]They offered a sacrifice in keeping with what's stated in the Law of the Lord, *A pair of turtledoves or two young pigeons.*[b]

Simeon's response to Jesus

[25]A man named Simeon was in Jerusalem. He was righteous and devout. He eagerly anticipated the restoration of Israel, and the Holy Spirit rested on him. [26]The Holy Spirit revealed to him that he wouldn't die before he had seen the Lord's Christ. [27]Led by the Spirit, he went into the temple area. Meanwhile, Jesus' parents brought the child to the temple so that they could do what was customary under the Law. [28]Simeon took Jesus in his arms and praised God. He said,

[29] "Now, master, let your servant
    go in peace according to your word,
[30]because my eyes have seen
    your salvation.
[31] You prepared this salvation
    in the presence of all peoples.
[32] It's a light for revelation
    to the Gentiles
    and a glory for your people Israel."

[33]His father and mother were amazed by what was said about him. [34]Simeon blessed them and said to Mary his mother, "This boy is assigned to be the cause of the falling and rising of many in Israel and to be a sign that generates opposition [35]so that the inner thoughts of many will be

[b]Lev 12:8; 5:11 LXX

revealed. And a sword will pierce your innermost being too."

Anna's response to Jesus

³⁶There was also a prophet, Anna the daughter of Phanuel, who belonged to the tribe of Asher. She was very old. After she married, she lived with her husband for seven years. ³⁷She was now an 84-year-old widow. She never left the temple area but worshipped God with fasting and prayer night and day. ³⁸She approached at that very moment and began to praise God and to speak about Jesus to everyone who was looking forward to the redemption of Jerusalem.

Jesus as a child in Nazareth

³⁹When Mary and Joseph had completed everything required by the Law of the Lord, they returned to their hometown, Nazareth in Galilee. ⁴⁰The child grew up and became strong. He was filled with wisdom, and God's favor was on him.

Jesus in the temple at Passover

⁴¹Each year his parents went to Jerusalem for the Passover Festival. ⁴²When he was 12 years old, they went up to Jerusalem according to their custom. ⁴³After the festival was over, they were returning home, but the boy Jesus stayed behind in Jerusalem. His parents didn't know it. ⁴⁴Supposing that he was among their band of travelers, they journeyed on for a full day while looking for him among their family and friends. ⁴⁵When they didn't find Jesus, they returned to Jerusalem to look for him. ⁴⁶After three days they found him

in the temple. He was sitting among the teachers, listening to them and putting questions to them. ⁴⁷Everyone who heard him was amazed by his understanding and his answers. ⁴⁸When his parents saw him, they were shocked.

His mother said, "Child, why have you treated us like this? Listen! Your father and I have been worried. We've been looking for you!"

⁴⁹Jesus replied, "Why were you looking for me? Didn't you know that it was necessary for me to be in my Father's house?" ⁵⁰But they didn't understand what he said to them.

⁵¹Jesus went down to Nazareth with them and was obedient to them. His mother cherished every word in her heart. ⁵²Jesus matured in wisdom and years, and in favor with God and with people.

John the Baptist's message

3In the fifteenth year of the rule of the emperor Tiberius—when Pontius Pilate was governor over Judea and Herod was ruler[c] over Galilee, his brother Philip was ruler[d] over Ituraea and Trachonitis, and Lysanias was ruler[e] over Abilene, ²during the high priesthood of Annas and Caiaphas—God's word came to John son of Zechariah in the wilderness. ³John went throughout the region of the Jordan River, calling for people to be baptized to show that they were changing their hearts and lives and wanted God to forgive their sins. ⁴This is just as it was written in the scroll of the words of Isaiah the prophet,

A voice crying out in the wilderness:
"Prepare the way for the Lord;
make his paths straight.

---

[c]Or tetrarch   [d]Or tetrarch   [e]Or tetrarch

⁵ Every valley will be filled,
    and every mountain
    and hill will be leveled.
  The crooked will be made straight
    and the rough places made smooth.
⁶ All humanity will see God's salvation."ᶠ

⁷Then John said to the crowds who came to be baptized by him, "You children of snakes! Who warned you to escape from the angry judgment that is coming soon? ⁸Produce fruit that shows you have changed your hearts and lives. And don't even think about saying to yourselves, Abraham is our father. I tell you that God is able to raise up Abraham's children from these stones. ⁹The ax is already at the root of the trees. Therefore, every tree that doesn't produce good fruit will be chopped down and tossed into the fire."

¹⁰The crowds asked him, "What then should we do?"

¹¹He answered, "Whoever has two shirts must share with the one who has none, and whoever has food must do the same."

¹²Even tax collectors came to be baptized. They said to him, "Teacher, what should we do?"

¹³He replied, "Collect no more than you are authorized to collect."

¹⁴Soldiers asked, "What about us? What should we do?"

He answered, "Don't cheat or harass anyone, and be satisfied with your pay."

Responses to John

¹⁵The people were filled with expectation, and everyone wondered whether John might be the Christ. ¹⁶John replied to them all, "I baptize you with water, but the one who is more powerful than me is coming. I'm not worthy to loosen the strap of his sandals. He will baptize you with the Holy Spirit and fire. ¹⁷The shovel he uses to sift the wheat from the husks is in his hands. He will clean out his threshing area and bring the wheat into his barn. But he will burn the husks with a fire that can't be put out." ¹⁸With many other words John appealed to them, proclaiming good news to the people.

¹⁹But Herod the ruler had been criticized harshly by John because of Herodias, Herod's brother's wife, and because of all the evil he had done. ²⁰He added this to the list of his evil deeds: he locked John up in prison.

Jesus' baptism

²¹When everyone was being baptized, Jesus also was baptized. While he was praying, heaven was opened ²²and the Holy Spirit came down on him in bodily form like a dove. And there was a voice from heaven: "You are my Son, whom I dearly love; in you I find happiness."

Jesus' genealogy

²³Jesus was about 30 years old when he began his ministry. People supposed that he was the son of Joseph son of Heli ²⁴son of Matthat son of Levi son of Melchi son of Jannai son of Joseph ²⁵son of Mattathias son of Amos son of Nahum son of Esli son of Naggai ²⁶son of Maath son of Mattathias son of Semein son of Josech son of Joda ²⁷son of Joanan son of Rhesa son of Zerubbabel son of Shealtiel son of Neri ²⁸son of Melchi son of Addi son of Cosam son of Elmadam son of Er ²⁹son of Joshua son of Eliezer son of Jorim

---

ᶠIsa 40:3-5

son of Matthat son of Levi ³⁰son of Simeon son of Judah son of Joseph son of Jonam son of Eliakim ³¹son of Melea son of Menna son of Mattatha son of Nathan son of David ³²son of Jesse son of Obed son of Boaz son of Sala son of Nahshon ³³son of Amminadab son of Admin son of Arni son of Hezron son of Perez son of Judah ³⁴son of Jacob son of Isaac son of Abraham son of Terah son of Nahor ³⁵son of Serug son of Reu son of Peleg son of Eber son of Shelah ³⁶son of Cainan son of Arphaxad son of Shem son of Noah son of Lamech ³⁷son of Methuselah son of Enoch son of Jared son of Mahalalel son of Cainan ³⁸son of Enos son of Seth son of Adam son of God.

Jesus' temptation

4 Jesus returned from the Jordan River full of the Holy Spirit, and was led by the Spirit into the wilderness. ²There he was tempted for forty days by the devil. He ate nothing during those days and afterward Jesus was starving. ³The devil said to him, "Since you are God's Son, command this stone to become a loaf of bread."

⁴Jesus replied, "It's written, *People won't live only by bread.*"g

⁵Next the devil led him to a high place and showed him in a single instant all the kingdoms in the world. ⁶The devil said, "I will give you this whole domain and the glory of all these kingdoms. It's been entrusted to me and I can give it to anyone I want. ⁷Therefore, if you will worship me, it will all be yours."

⁸Jesus answered, "It's written, *You will worship the Lord your God and serve only him.*"h

⁹The devil brought him into Jerusalem and stood him at the highest point of the temple. He said to him, "Since you are God's Son, throw yourself down from here; ¹⁰for it's written: *He will command his angels concerning you, to protect you* ¹¹and *they will take you up in their hands so that you won't hit your foot on a stone.*"i

¹²Jesus answered, "It's been said, *Don't test the Lord your God.*"j ¹³After finishing every temptation, the devil departed from him until the next opportunity.

Jesus announces good news to the poor

¹⁴Jesus returned in the power of the Spirit to Galilee, and news about him spread throughout the whole countryside. ¹⁵He taught in their synagogues and was praised by everyone.

¹⁶Jesus went to Nazareth, where he had been raised. On the Sabbath he went to the synagogue as he normally did and stood up to read. ¹⁷The synagogue assistant gave him the scroll from the prophet Isaiah. He unrolled the scroll and found the place where it was written:

¹⁸ *The Spirit of the Lord is upon me,*
      because the Lord has anointed me.
   He has sent me to preach good news
      to the poor,
   to proclaim release to the prisoners
      and recovery of sight to the blind,
      to liberate the oppressed,
¹⁹ *and to proclaim the year*
      *of the Lord's favor.*k

²⁰He rolled up the scroll, gave it back to the synagogue assistant, and sat down. Every eye in the synagogue was fixed on him. ²¹He began to explain to

gDeut 8:3   hDeut 6:13   iPs 91:11-12   jDeut 6:16   kIsa 61:1-2; 58:6

them, "Today, this scripture has been fulfilled just as you heard it."

²²Everyone was raving about Jesus, so impressed were they by the gracious words flowing from his lips. They said, "This is Joseph's son, isn't it?"

²³Then Jesus said to them, "Undoubtedly, you will quote this saying to me: 'Doctor, heal yourself. Do here in your hometown what we've heard you did in Capernaum.'" ²⁴He said, "I assure you that no prophet is welcome in the prophet's hometown. ²⁵And I can assure you that there were many widows in Israel during Elijah's time, when it didn't rain for three and a half years and there was a great food shortage in the land. ²⁶Yet Elijah was sent to none of them but only to a widow in the city of Zarephath in the region of Sidon. ²⁷There were also many persons with skin diseases in Israel during the time of the prophet Elisha, but none of them were cleansed. Instead, Naaman the Syrian was cleansed."

²⁸When they heard this, everyone in the synagogue was filled with anger. ²⁹They rose up and ran him out of town. They led him to the crest of the hill on which their town had been built so that they could throw him off the cliff. ³⁰But he passed through the crowd and went on his way.

Jesus in Capernaum

³¹Jesus went down to the city of Capernaum in Galilee and taught the people each Sabbath. ³²They were amazed by his teaching because he delivered his message with authority.

³³A man in the synagogue had the spirit of an unclean demon. He screamed, ³⁴"Hey! What have you to do with us, Jesus of Nazareth? Have you

come to destroy us? I know who you are. You are the holy one from God."

³⁵"Silence!" Jesus said, speaking harshly to the demon. "Come out of him!" The demon threw the man down before them, then came out of him without harming him.

³⁶They were all shaken and said to each other, "What kind of word is this, that he can command unclean spirits with authority and power, and they leave?" ³⁷Reports about him spread everywhere in the surrounding region.

³⁸After leaving the synagogue, Jesus went home with Simon. Simon's mother-in-law was sick with a high fever, and the family asked Jesus to help her. ³⁹He bent over her and spoke harshly to the fever, and it left her. She got up at once and served them.

⁴⁰When the sun was setting, everyone brought to Jesus relatives and acquaintances with all kinds of diseases. Placing his hands on each of them, he healed them. ⁴¹Demons also came out of many people. They screamed, "You are God's Son." But he spoke harshly to them and wouldn't allow them to speak because they recognized that he was the Christ. ⁴²When daybreak arrived, Jesus went to a deserted place. The crowds were looking for him. When they found him, they tried to keep him from leaving them. ⁴³But he said to them, "I must preach the good news of God's kingdom in other cities too, for this is why I was sent." ⁴⁴So he continued preaching in the Judean synagogues.

Jesus calls disciples

5 One day Jesus was standing beside Lake Gennesaret when the crowd pressed in around him to hear God's

word. [2]Jesus saw two boats sitting by the lake. The fishermen had gone ashore and were washing their nets. [3]Jesus boarded one of the boats, the one that belonged to Simon, then asked him to row out a little distance from the shore. Jesus sat down and taught the crowds from the boat. [4]When he finished speaking to the crowds, he said to Simon, "Row out farther, into the deep water, and drop your nets for a catch."

[5]Simon replied, "Master, we've worked hard all night and caught nothing. But because you say so, I'll drop the nets."

[6]So they dropped the nets and their catch was so huge that their nets were splitting. [7]They signaled for their partners in the other boat to come and help them. They filled both boats so full that they were about to sink. [8]When Simon Peter saw the catch, he fell at Jesus' knees and said, "Leave me, Lord, for I'm a sinner!" [9]Peter and those with him were overcome with amazement because of the number of fish they caught. [10]James and John, Zebedee's sons, were Simon's partners and they were amazed too.

Jesus said to Simon, "Don't be afraid. From now on, you will be fishing for people." [11]As soon as they brought the boats to the shore, they left everything and followed Jesus.

A man with a skin disease

[12]Jesus was in one of the towns where there was also a man covered with a skin disease. When he saw Jesus, he fell on his face and begged, "Lord, if you want, you can make me clean."

[13]Jesus reached out his hand, touched him, and said, "I do want to. Be clean."

Instantly, the skin disease left him. [14]Jesus ordered him not to tell anyone. "Instead," Jesus said, "go and show yourself to the priest and make an offering for your cleansing, as Moses instructed. This will be a testimony to them." [15]News of him spread even more and huge crowds gathered to listen and to be healed from their illnesses. [16]But Jesus would withdraw to deserted places for prayer.

Jesus heals a paralyzed man

[17]One day when Jesus was teaching, Pharisees and legal experts were sitting nearby. They had come from every village in Galilee and Judea, and from Jerusalem. Now the power of the Lord was with Jesus to heal. [18]Some men were bringing a man who was paralyzed, lying on a cot. They wanted to carry him in and place him before Jesus, [19]but they couldn't reach him because of the crowd. So they took him up on the roof and lowered him—cot and all—through the roof tiles into the crowded room in front of Jesus. [20]When Jesus saw their faith, he said, "Friend, your sins are forgiven."

[21]The legal experts and Pharisees began to mutter among themselves, "Who is this who insults God? Only God can forgive sins!"

[22]Jesus recognized what they were discussing and responded, "Why do you fill your minds with these questions? [23]Which is easier—to say, 'Your sins are forgiven,' or to say, 'Get up and walk'? [24]But so that you will know that the Human One[l] has authority on the earth to forgive sins"—Jesus now spoke to the man who was paralyzed,

[l]Or *Son of Man*

"I say to you, get up, take your cot, and go home." [25] Right away, the man stood before them, picked up his cot, and went home, praising God.

[26] All the people were beside themselves with wonder. Filled with awe, they glorified God, saying, "We've seen unimaginable things today."

Jesus calls a tax collector

[27] Afterward, Jesus went out and saw a tax collector named Levi sitting at a kiosk for collecting taxes. Jesus said to him, "Follow me."

[28] Levi got up, left everything behind, and followed him. [29] Then Levi threw a great banquet for Jesus in his home. A large number of tax collectors and others sat down to eat with them. [30] The Pharisees and their legal experts grumbled against his disciples. They said, "Why do you eat and drink with tax collectors and sinners?"

[31] Jesus answered, "Healthy people don't need a doctor, but sick people do. [32] I didn't come to call righteous people but sinners to change their hearts and lives."

The old and the new

[33] Some people said to Jesus, "The disciples of John fast often and pray frequently. The disciples of the Pharisees do the same, but your disciples are always eating and drinking."

[34] Jesus replied, "You can't make the wedding guests fast while the groom is with them, can you? [35] The days will come when the groom will be taken from them, and then they will fast."

[36] Then he told them a parable. "No one tears a patch from a new garment to patch an old garment. Otherwise, the new garment would be ruined, and the new patch wouldn't match the old garment. [37] Nobody pours new wine into old wineskins. If they did, the new wine would burst the wineskins, the wine would spill, and the wineskins would be ruined. [38] Instead, new wine must be put into new wineskins. [39] No one who drinks a well-aged wine wants new wine, but says, 'The well-aged wine is better.'"

Activities on the Sabbath

6 One Sabbath, as Jesus was going through the wheat fields, his disciples were picking the heads of wheat, rubbing them in their hands, and eating them. [2] Some Pharisees said, "Why are you breaking the Sabbath law?"

[3] Jesus replied, "Haven't you read what David and his companions did when they were hungry? [4] He broke the Law by going into God's house and eating the bread of the presence, which only the priests can eat. He also gave some of the bread to his companions." [5] Then he said to them, "The Human One[m] is Lord of the Sabbath."

[6] On another Sabbath, Jesus entered a synagogue to teach. A man was there whose right hand was withered. [7] The legal experts and the Pharisees were watching him closely to see if he would heal on the Sabbath. They were looking for a reason to bring charges against him. [8] Jesus knew their thoughts, so he said to the man with the withered hand, "Get up and stand in front of everyone." He got up and stood there. [9] Jesus said to the legal experts and Pharisees, "Here's a question for you: Is it legal on the Sabbath to do good or to do evil,

[m] Or Son of Man

to save life or to destroy it?" [10]Looking around at them all, he said to the man, "Stretch out your hand." So he did and his hand was made healthy. [11]They were furious and began talking with each other about what to do to Jesus.

Jesus chooses apostles

[12]During that time, Jesus went out to the mountain to pray, and he prayed to God all night long. [13]At daybreak, he called together his disciples. He chose twelve of them whom he called apostles: [14]Simon, whom he named Peter; his brother Andrew; James; John; Philip; Bartholomew; [15]Matthew; Thomas; James the son of Alphaeus; Simon, who was called a zealot; [16]Judas the son of James; and Judas Iscariot, who became a traitor.

Jesus' popularity increases

[17]Jesus came down from the mountain with them and stood on a large area of level ground. A great company of his disciples and a huge crowd of people from all around Judea and Jerusalem and the area around Tyre and Sidon joined him there. [18]They came to hear him and to be healed from their diseases, and those bothered by unclean spirits were healed. [19]The whole crowd wanted to touch him, because power was going out from him and he was healing everyone.

Happy people and doomed people

[20]Jesus raised his eyes to his disciples and said:

"Happy are you who are poor,
    because God's kingdom is yours.
[21] Happy are you who hunger now,

because you will be satisfied.
Happy are you who weep now,
    because you will laugh.
[22]Happy are you when people hate you, reject you, insult you, and condemn your name as evil because of the Human One.[n] [23]Rejoice when that happens! Leap for joy because you have a great reward in heaven. Their ancestors did the same things to the prophets.
[24] But how terrible for you
    who are rich,
    because you have already received
        your comfort.
[25] How terrible for you
    who have plenty now,
    because you will be hungry.
    How terrible for you who laugh now,
        because you will mourn and weep.
[26] How terrible for you when all
    speak well of you.
    Their ancestors did the same things
        to the false prophets.

Behaving as God's children

[27]"But I say to you who are willing to hear: Love your enemies. Do good to those who hate you. [28]Bless those who curse you. Pray for those who mistreat you. [29]If someone slaps you on the cheek, offer the other one as well. If someone takes your coat, don't withhold your shirt either. [30]Give to everyone who asks and don't demand your things back from those who take them. [31]Treat people in the same way that you want them to treat you.

[32]"If you love those who love you, why should you be commended? Even sinners love those who love them. [33]If you do good to those who do good to you, why should you be commended?

[n]Or Son of Man

Even sinners do that. ³⁴If you lend to those from whom you expect repayment, why should you be commended? Even sinners lend to sinners expecting to be paid back in full. ³⁵Instead, love your enemies, do good, and lend expecting nothing in return. If you do, you will have a great reward. You will be acting the way children of the Most High act, for he is kind to ungrateful and wicked people. ³⁶Be compassionate just as your Father is compassionate.

³⁷"Don't judge, and you won't be judged. Don't condemn, and you won't be condemned. Forgive, and you will be forgiven. ³⁸Give, and it will be given to you. A good portion—packed down, firmly shaken, and overflowing—will fall into your lap. The portion you give will determine the portion you receive in return."

Avoiding self-deception

³⁹Jesus also told them a riddle. "A blind person can't lead another blind person, right? Won't they both fall into a ditch? ⁴⁰Disciples aren't greater than their teacher, but whoever is fully prepared will be like their teacher. ⁴¹Why do you see the splinter in your brother's or sister's eye but don't notice the log in your own eye? ⁴²How can you say to your brother or sister, 'Brother, Sister, let me take the splinter out of your eye,' when you don't see the log in your own eye? You deceive yourselves! First take the log out of your eye, and then you will see clearly to take the splinter out of your brother's or sister's eye.

⁴³"A good tree doesn't produce bad fruit, nor does a bad tree produce good fruit. ⁴⁴Each tree is known by its own fruit. People don't gather figs from thorny plants, nor do they pick grapes

from prickly bushes. ⁴⁵A good person produces good from the good treasury of the inner self, while an evil person produces evil from the evil treasury of the inner self. The inner self overflows with words that are spoken.

⁴⁶"Why do you call me 'Lord, Lord' and don't do what I say? ⁴⁷I'll show what it's like when someone comes to me, hears my words, and puts them into practice. ⁴⁸It's like a person building a house by digging deep and laying the foundation on bedrock. When the flood came, the rising water smashed against that house, but the water couldn't shake the house because it was well built. ⁴⁹But those who don't put into practice what they hear are like a person who built a house without a foundation. The floodwater smashed against it and it collapsed instantly. It was completely destroyed."

A servant is healed

7After Jesus finished presenting all his words among the people, he entered Capernaum. ²A centurion had a servant who was very important to him, but the servant was ill and about to die. ³When the centurion heard about Jesus, he sent some Jewish elders to Jesus to ask him to come and heal his servant. ⁴When they came to Jesus, they earnestly pleaded with Jesus. "He deserves to have you do this for him," they said. ⁵"He loves our people and he built our synagogue for us."

⁶Jesus went with them. He had almost reached the house when the centurion sent friends to say to Jesus, "Lord, don't be bothered. In fact, I didn't even consider myself worthy to come to you. Just say the

word and my servant will be healed.
⁸I'm also a man appointed under authority, with soldiers under me. I say to one, 'Go,' and he goes, and to another, 'Come,' and he comes. I say to my servant, 'Do this,' and the servant does it."

⁹When Jesus heard these words, he was impressed with the centurion. He turned to the crowd following him and said, "I tell you, even in Israel I haven't found faith like this." ¹⁰When the centurion's friends returned to his house, they found the servant restored to health.

Jesus raises a widow's son

¹¹A little later Jesus went to a city called Nain. His disciples and a great crowd traveled with him. ¹²As he approached the city gate, a dead man was being carried out. He was his mother's only son, and she was a widow. A large crowd from the city was with her. ¹³When he saw her, the Lord had compassion for her and said, "Don't cry." ¹⁴He stepped forward and touched the stretcher on which the dead man was being carried. Those carrying him stood still. Jesus said, "Young man, I say to you, get up." ¹⁵The dead man sat up and began to speak, and Jesus gave him to his mother.

¹⁶Awestruck, everyone praised God. "A great prophet has appeared among us," they said. "God has come to help his people." ¹⁷This news about Jesus spread throughout Judea and the surrounding region.

John the Baptist and Jesus

¹⁸John's disciples informed him about all these things. John called two

of his disciples ¹⁹and sent them to the Lord. They were to ask him, "Are you the one who is coming, or should we look for someone else?"

²⁰When they reached Jesus, they said, "John the Baptist sent us to you. He asks, 'Are you the one who is coming, or should we look for someone else?'"

²¹Right then, Jesus healed many of their diseases, illnesses, and evil spirits, and he gave sight to a number of blind people. ²²Then he replied to John's disciples, "Go, report to John what you have seen and heard. *Those who were blind are able to see.* People who were crippled now walk. People with skin diseases are cleansed. *Those who were deaf now hear. Those who were dead are raised up. And good news is preached to the poor.*ᵒ ²³Happy is anyone who doesn't stumble along the way because of me."

²⁴After John's messengers were gone, Jesus spoke to the crowds about John. "What did you go out into the wilderness to see? A stalk blowing in the wind? ²⁵What did you go out to see? A man dressed up in refined clothes? Look, those who dress in fashionable clothes and live in luxury are in royal palaces. ²⁶What did you go out to see? A prophet? Yes, I tell you, and more than a prophet. ²⁷He is the one of whom it's written: *Look, I'm sending my messenger before you, who will prepare your way before you.*ᴾ ²⁸I tell you that no greater human being has ever been born than John. Yet whoever is least in God's kingdom is greater than he."

²⁹Everyone who heard this, including the tax collectors, acknowledged God's justice because they had been baptized

---

ᵒIsa 35:5-6; 61:1 ᴾMal 3:1

by John. ³⁰But the Pharisees and legal experts rejected God's will for themselves because they hadn't been baptized by John.

³¹"To what will I compare the people of this generation?" Jesus asked. "What are they like? ³²They are like children sitting in the marketplace calling out to each other, 'We played the flute for you and you didn't dance. We sang a funeral song and you didn't cry.' ³³John the Baptist came neither eating bread nor drinking wine, and you say, 'He has a demon.' ³⁴Yet the Human One[q] came eating and drinking, and you say, 'Look, a glutton and a drunk, a friend of tax collectors and sinners.' ³⁵But wisdom is proved to be right by all her descendants."

Forgiveness and gratitude

³⁶One of the Pharisees invited Jesus to eat with him. After he entered the Pharisee's home, he took his place at the table. ³⁷Meanwhile, a woman from the city, a sinner, discovered that Jesus was dining in the Pharisee's house. She brought perfumed oil in a vase made of alabaster. ³⁸Standing behind him at his feet and crying, she began to wet his feet with her tears. She wiped them with her hair, kissed them, and poured the oil on them. ³⁹When the Pharisee who had invited Jesus saw what was happening, he said to himself, If this man were a prophet, he would know what kind of woman is touching him. He would know that she is a sinner.

⁴⁰Jesus replied, "Simon, I have something to say to you."

"Teacher, speak," he said.

⁴¹"A certain lender had two debtors. One owed enough money to pay five hundred people for a day's work.[r] The other owed enough money for fifty. ⁴²When they couldn't pay, the lender forgave the debts of them both. Which of them will love him more?"

⁴³Simon replied, "I suppose the one who had the largest debt canceled."

Jesus said, "You have judged correctly."

⁴⁴Jesus turned to the woman and said to Simon, "Do you see this woman? When I entered your home, you didn't give me water for my feet, but she wet my feet with tears and wiped them with her hair. ⁴⁵You didn't greet me with a kiss, but she hasn't stopped kissing my feet since I came in. ⁴⁶You didn't anoint my head with oil, but she has poured perfumed oil on my feet. ⁴⁷This is why I tell you that her many sins have been forgiven; so she has shown great love. The one who is forgiven little loves little."

⁴⁸Then Jesus said to her, "Your sins are forgiven."

⁴⁹The other table guests began to say among themselves, "Who is this person that even forgives sins?"

⁵⁰Jesus said to the woman, "Your faith has saved you. Go in peace."

Women who followed Jesus

8 Soon afterward, Jesus traveled through the cities and villages, preaching and proclaiming the good news of God's kingdom. The Twelve were with him, ²along with some women who had been healed of evil spirits and sicknesses. Among them were Mary Magdalene (from whom seven demons had been thrown out), ³Joanna (the wife of Herod's servant Chuza), Susanna, and many others

[q]Or Son of Man [r]Or five hundred denaria

who provided for them out of their resources.

Parable of the soils

⁴"When a great crowd was gathering and people were coming to Jesus from one city after another, he spoke to them in a parable: ⁵"A farmer went out to scatter his seed. As he was scattering it, some fell on the path where it was crushed, and the birds in the sky came and ate it. ⁶Other seed fell on rock. As it grew, it dried up because it had no moisture. ⁷Other seed fell among thorny plants. The thorns grew with the plants and choked them. ⁸Still other seed landed on good soil. When it grew, it produced one hundred times more grain than was scattered." As he said this, he called out, "Everyone who has ears should pay attention."

⁹His disciples asked him what this parable meant. ¹⁰He said, "You have been given the mysteries of God's kingdom, but these mysteries come to everyone else in parables so that *when they see, they can't see, and when they hear, they can't understand.*[s]

¹¹"The parable means this: The seed is God's word. ¹²The seed on the path are those who hear, but then the devil comes and steals the word from their hearts so that they won't believe and be saved. ¹³The seed on the rock are those who receive the word joyfully when they hear it, but they have no root. They believe for a while but fall away when they are tempted. ¹⁴As for the seed that fell among thorny plants, these are the ones who, as they go about their lives, are choked by the concerns, riches, and pleasures of life, and their fruit never

matures. ¹⁵The seed that fell on good soil are those who hear the word and commit themselves to it with a good and upright heart. Through their resolve, they bear fruit.

Sharing the light

¹⁶"No one lights a lamp and then covers it with a bowl or puts it under a bed. Instead, they put it on top of a lampstand so that those who enter can see the light. ¹⁷Nothing is hidden that won't be exposed. Nor is anything concealed that won't be made known and brought to the light. ¹⁸Therefore, listen carefully. Those who have will receive more, but as for those who don't have, even what they seem to have will be taken away from them."

Jesus' family

¹⁹Jesus' mother and brothers came to him but were unable to reach him because of the crowd. ²⁰Someone told him, "Your mother and brothers are standing outside, wanting to see you."

²¹He replied, "My mother and brothers are those who listen to God's word and do it."

Jesus calms the sea

²²One day Jesus and his disciples boarded a boat. He said to them, "Let's cross over to the other side of the lake." So they set sail. ²³While they were sailing, he fell asleep. Gale-force winds swept down on the lake. The boat was filling up with water and they were in danger. ²⁴So they went and woke Jesus, shouting, "Master, Master, we're going to drown!" But he got up and gave orders to the

[s]Isa 6:9

wind and the violent waves. The storm died down and it was calm.

²⁵He said to his disciples, "Where is your faith?"

Filled with awe and wonder, they said to each other, "Who is this? He commands even the winds and the water, and they obey him!"

Jesus frees a demon-possessed man

²⁶Jesus and his disciples sailed to the Gerasenes' land, which is across the lake from Galilee. ²⁷As soon as Jesus got out of the boat, a certain man met him. The man was from the city and was possessed by demons. For a long time, he had lived among the tombs, naked and homeless. ²⁸When he saw Jesus, he shrieked and fell down before him. Then he shouted, "What have you to do with me, Jesus, Son of the Most High God? I beg you, don't torture me!" ²⁹He said this because Jesus had already commanded the unclean spirit to come out of the man. Many times it had taken possession of him, so he would be bound with leg irons and chains and placed under guard. But he would break his restraints, and the demon would force him into the wilderness.

³⁰Jesus asked him, "What is your name?"

"Legion," he replied, because many demons had entered him. ³¹They pleaded with him not to order them to go back into the abyss.ᵗ ³²A large herd of pigs was feeding on the hillside. The demons begged Jesus to let them go into the pigs. Jesus gave them permission, ³³and the demons left the man and entered the pigs. The herd

rushed down the cliff into the lake and drowned.

³⁴When those who tended the pigs saw what happened, they ran away and told the story in the city and in the countryside. ³⁵People came to see what had happened. They came to Jesus and found the man from whom the demons had gone. He was sitting at Jesus' feet, fully dressed and completely sane. They were filled with awe. ³⁶Those people who had actually seen what had happened told them how the demon-possessed man had been delivered. ³⁷Then everyone gathered from the region of the Gerasenes asked Jesus to leave their area because they were overcome with fear. So he got into the boat and returned across the lake. ³⁸The man from whom the demons had gone begged to come along with Jesus as one of his disciples. Jesus sent him away, saying, ³⁹"Return home and tell the story of what God has done for you." So he went throughout the city proclaiming what Jesus had done for him.

Jesus heals two women

⁴⁰When Jesus returned, the crowd welcomed him, for they had been waiting for him. ⁴¹A man named Jairus, who was a synagogue leader, came and fell at Jesus' feet. He pleaded with Jesus to come to his house ⁴²because his only daughter, a twelve-year-old, was dying.

As Jesus moved forward, he faced smothering crowds. ⁴³A woman was there who had been bleeding for twelve years. She had spent her entire livelihood on doctors, but no one could heal her. ⁴⁴She came up behind him and touched the hem of his clothes, and at once her bleeding stopped.

ᵗOr *underworld*

⁴⁵"Who touched me?" Jesus asked.

When everyone denied it, Peter said, "Master, the crowds are surrounding you and pressing in on you!"

⁴⁶But Jesus said, "Someone touched me. I know that power has gone out from me."

⁴⁷When the woman saw that she couldn't escape notice, she came trembling and fell before Jesus. In front of everyone, she explained why she had touched him and how she had been immediately healed.

⁴⁸"Daughter, your faith has healed you," Jesus said. "Go in peace."

⁴⁹While Jesus was still speaking, someone came from the synagogue leader's house, saying to Jairus, "Your daughter has died. Don't bother the teacher any longer."

⁵⁰When Jesus heard this, he responded, "Don't be afraid; just keep trusting, and she will be healed."

⁵¹When he came to the house, he didn't allow anyone to enter with him except Peter, John, and James, and the child's father and mother. ⁵²They were all crying and mourning for her, but Jesus said, "Don't cry. She isn't dead. She's only sleeping."

⁵³They laughed at him because they knew she was dead.

⁵⁴Taking her hand, Jesus called out, "Child, get up." ⁵⁵Her life returned and she got up at once. He directed them to give her something to eat. ⁵⁶Her parents were beside themselves with joy, but he ordered them to tell no one what had happened.

The Twelve sent out

9 Jesus called the Twelve together and he gave them power and authority over all demons and to heal sicknesses. ²He sent them out to proclaim God's kingdom and to heal the sick. ³He told them, "Take nothing for the journey—no walking stick, no bag, no bread, no money, not even an extra shirt. ⁴Whatever house you enter, remain there until you leave that place. ⁵Wherever they don't welcome you, as you leave that city, shake the dust off your feet as a witness against them." ⁶They departed and went through the villages proclaiming the good news and healing people everywhere.

Herod's confusion

⁷Herod the ruler[u] heard about everything that was happening. He was confused because some people were saying that John had been raised from the dead, ⁸others that Elijah had appeared, and still others that one of the ancient prophets had come back to life. ⁹Herod said, "I beheaded John, so now who am I hearing about?" Herod wanted to see him.

Jesus feeds the five thousand

¹⁰When the apostles returned, they described for Jesus what they had done. Taking them with him, Jesus withdrew privately to a city called Bethsaida. ¹¹When the crowds figured it out, they followed him. He welcomed them, spoke to them about God's kingdom, and healed those who were sick.

¹²When the day was almost over, the Twelve came to him and said, "Send the crowd away so that they can go to the nearby villages and countryside and find lodging and food, because we are in a deserted place."

[u]Or tetrarch

¹³He replied, "You give them something to eat."

But they said, "We have no more than five loaves of bread and two fish—unless we go and buy food for all these people." ¹⁴(They said this because about five thousand men were present.)

Jesus said to his disciples, "Seat them in groups of about fifty." They did so, and everyone was seated. ¹⁶He took the five loaves and the two fish, looked up to heaven, blessed them, and broke them and gave them to the disciples to set before the crowd. ¹⁷Everyone ate until they were full, and the disciples filled twelve baskets with the leftovers.

Following Christ

¹⁸Once when Jesus was praying by himself, the disciples joined him, and he asked them, "Who do the crowds say that I am?"

¹⁹They answered, "John the Baptist, others Elijah, and still others that one of the ancient prophets has come back to life."

²⁰He asked them, "And what about you? Who do you say that I am?"

Peter answered, "The Christ sent from God."

²¹Jesus gave them strict orders not to tell this to anyone. ²²He said, "The Human One*ᵛ* must suffer many things and be rejected—by the elders, chief priests, and the legal experts—and be killed and be raised on the third day."

²³Jesus said to everyone, "All who want to come after me must say no to themselves, take up their cross daily, and follow me. ²⁴All who want to save their lives will lose them. But all who lose their lives because of me will save

them. ²⁵What advantage do people have if they gain the whole world for themselves yet perish or lose their lives? ²⁶Whoever is ashamed of me and my words, the Human One*ʷ* will be ashamed of that person when he comes in his glory and in the glory of the Father and of the holy angels. ²⁷I assure you that some standing here won't die before they see God's kingdom."

Jesus transformed

²⁸About eight days after Jesus said these things, he took Peter, John, and James, and went up on a mountain to pray. ²⁹As he was praying, the appearance of his face changed and his clothes flashed white like lightning. ³⁰Two men, Moses and Elijah, were talking with him. ³¹They were clothed with heavenly splendor and spoke about Jesus' departure, which he would achieve in Jerusalem. ³²Peter and those with him were almost overcome by sleep, but they managed to stay awake and saw his glory as well as the two men with him.

³³As the two men were about to leave Jesus, Peter said to him, "Master, it's good that we're here. We should construct three shrines: one for you, one for Moses, and one for Elijah"—but he didn't know what he was saying. ³⁴Peter was still speaking when a cloud overshadowed them. As they entered the cloud, they were overcome with awe. ³⁵Then a voice from the cloud said, "This is my Son, my chosen one. Listen to him!" ³⁶Even as the voice spoke, Jesus was found alone. They were speechless and at the time told no one what they had seen.

ᵛOr *Son of Man*   ʷOr *Son of Man*

Jesus heals a boy

37The next day, when Jesus, Peter, John, and James had come down from the mountain, a large crowd met Jesus. 38A man from the crowd shouted, "Teacher, I beg you to take a look at my son, my only child. 39Look, a spirit seizes him and, without any warning, he screams. It shakes him and causes him to foam at the mouth. It tortures him and rarely leaves him alone. 40I begged your disciples to throw it out, but they couldn't."

41Jesus answered, "You faithless and crooked generation, how long will I be with you and put up with you? Bring your son here." 42While he was coming, the demon threw him down and shook him violently. Jesus spoke harshly to the unclean spirit, healed the child, and gave him back to his father. 43Everyone was overwhelmed by God's greatness.

Jesus warns about his arrest

While everyone was marveling at everything he was doing, Jesus said to his disciples, 44"Take these words to heart: the Human One[x] is about to be delivered into human hands." 45They didn't understand this statement. Its meaning was hidden from them so they couldn't grasp it. And they were afraid to ask him about it.

Jesus corrects the disciples

46An argument arose among the disciples about which of them was the greatest. 47Aware of their deepest thoughts, Jesus took a little child and had the child stand beside him. 48Jesus said to his disciples, "Whoever welcomes this child in my name welcomes me. Whoever welcomes me, welcomes the one who sent me. Whoever is least among you all is the greatest."

49John replied, "Master, we saw someone throwing demons out in your name, and we tried to stop him because he isn't in our group of followers."

50But Jesus replied, "Don't stop him, because whoever isn't against you is for you."

Jesus sets out for Jerusalem

51As the time approached when Jesus was to be taken up into heaven, he determined to go to Jerusalem. 52He sent messengers on ahead of him. Along the way, they entered a Samaritan village to prepare for his arrival, 53but the Samaritan villagers refused to welcome him because he was determined to go to Jerusalem. 54When the disciples James and John saw this, they said, "Lord, do you want us to call fire down from heaven to consume them?" 55But Jesus turned and spoke sternly to them, 56and they went on to another village.

Following Jesus

57As Jesus and his disciples traveled along the road, someone said to him, "I will follow you wherever you go."

58Jesus replied, "Foxes have dens and the birds in the sky have nests, but the Human One[y] has no place to lay his head."

59Then Jesus said to someone else, "Follow me."

He replied, "Lord, first let me go and bury my father."

60Jesus said to him, "Let the dead bury their own dead. But you go and spread the news of God's kingdom."

61Someone else said to Jesus, "I will follow you, Lord, but first let me say good-bye to those in my house."

xOr Son of Man yOr Son of Man

⁶²Jesus said to him, "No one who puts a hand on the plow and looks back is fit for God's kingdom."

Seventy-two sent out

10After these things, the Lord commissioned seventy-two others and sent them on ahead in pairs to every city and place he was about to go. ²He said to them, "The harvest is bigger than you can imagine, but there are few workers. Therefore, plead with the Lord of the harvest to send out workers for his harvest. ³Go! Be warned, though, that I'm sending you out as lambs among wolves. ⁴Carry no wallet, no bag, and no sandals. Don't even greet anyone along the way. ⁵Whenever you enter a house, first say, 'May peace be on this house.' ⁶If anyone there shares God's peace, then your peace will rest on that person. If not, your blessing will return to you. ⁷Remain in this house, eating and drinking whatever they set before you, for workers deserve their pay. Don't move from house to house. ⁸Whenever you enter a city and its people welcome you, eat what they set before you. ⁹Heal the sick who are there, and say to them, 'God's kingdom has come upon you.' ¹⁰Whenever you enter a city and the people don't welcome you, go out into the streets and say, ¹¹'As a complaint against you, we brush off the dust of your city that has collected on our feet. But know this: God's kingdom has come to you.' ¹²I assure you that Sodom will be better off on Judgment Day than that city.

Judgment against cities that reject Jesus

¹³"How terrible it will be for you, Chorazin. How terrible it will be for you, Bethsaida. If the miracles done among you had been done in Tyre and Sidon, they would have changed their hearts and lives long ago. They would have sat around in funeral clothes and ashes. ¹⁴But Tyre and Sidon will be better off at the judgment than you. ¹⁵And you, Capernaum, will you be honored by being raised up to heaven? No, you will be cast down to the place of the dead. ¹⁶Whoever listens to you listens to me. Whoever rejects you rejects me. Whoever rejects me rejects the one who sent me."

The seventy-two return

¹⁷The seventy-two returned joyously, saying, "Lord, even the demons submit themselves to us in your name."

¹⁸Jesus replied, "I saw Satan fall from heaven like lightning. ¹⁹Look, I have given you authority to crush snakes and scorpions underfoot. I have given you authority over all the power of the enemy. Nothing will harm you. ²⁰Nevertheless, don't rejoice because the spirits submit to you. Rejoice instead that your names are written in heaven."

²¹At that very moment, Jesus overflowed with joy from the Holy Spirit and said, "I praise you, Father, Lord of heaven and earth, because you've hidden these things from the wise and intelligent and shown them to babies. Indeed, Father, this brings you happiness. ²²My Father has handed all things over to me. No one knows who the Son is except the Father, or who the Father is except the Son and anyone to whom the Son wants to reveal him." ²³Turning to the disciples, he said privately, "Happy are the eyes that see what you see. ²⁴I assure you that many prophets and kings wanted to see what you see and hear what you hear, but they didn't."

Loving your neighbor

²⁵A legal expert stood up to test Jesus. "Teacher," he said, "what must I do to gain eternal life?"

²⁶Jesus replied, "What is written in the Law? How do you interpret it?"

²⁷He responded, *"You must love the Lord your God with all your heart, with all your being, with all your strength, and with all your mind, and love your neighbor as yourself."*ᶻ

²⁸Jesus said to him, "You have answered correctly. Do this and you will live."

²⁹But the legal expert wanted to prove that he was right, so he said to Jesus, "And who is my neighbor?"

³⁰Jesus replied, "A man went down from Jerusalem to Jericho. He encountered thieves, who stripped him naked, beat him up, and left him near death. ³¹Now it just so happened that a priest was also going down the same road. When he saw the injured man, he crossed over to the other side of the road and went on his way. ³²Likewise, a Levite came by that spot, saw the injured man, and crossed over to the other side of the road and went on his way. ³³A Samaritan, who was on a journey, came to where the man was. But when he saw him, he was moved with compassion. ³⁴The Samaritan went to him and bandaged his wounds, tending them with oil and wine. Then he placed the wounded man on his own donkey, took him to an inn, and took care of him. ³⁵The next day, he took two full days' worth of wages and gave them to the innkeeper. He said, 'Take care of him, and when I return, I will pay you back for any additional costs.' ³⁶What do you think? Which one of these three was a neighbor to the man who encountered thieves?"

³⁷Then the legal expert said, "The one who demonstrated mercy toward him."

Jesus told him, "Go and do likewise."

Jesus visits Martha and Mary

³⁸While Jesus and his disciples were traveling, Jesus entered a village where a woman named Martha welcomed him as a guest. ³⁹She had a sister named Mary, who sat at the Lord's feet and listened to his message. ⁴⁰By contrast, Martha was preoccupied with getting everything ready for their meal. So Martha came to him and said, "Lord, don't you care that my sister has left me to prepare the table all by myself? Tell her to help me."

⁴¹The Lord answered, "Martha, Martha, you are worried and distracted by many things. ⁴²One thing is necessary. Mary has chosen the better part. It won't be taken away from her."

Teaching the disciples to pray

11 Jesus was praying in a certain place. When he finished, one of his disciples said, "Lord, teach us to pray, just as John taught his disciples."

²Jesus told them, "When you pray, say:
'Father, uphold the holiness
    of your name.
Bring in your kingdom.
³Give us the bread we need for today.
⁴Forgive us our sins,
    for we also forgive everyone
        who has wronged us.
And don't lead us into temptation.'"

⁵He also said to them, "Imagine that one of you has a friend and you go to

---

ᶻDeut 6:5; Lev 19:18

that friend in the middle of the night. Imagine saying, 'Friend, loan me three loaves of bread [6]because a friend of mine on a journey has arrived and I have nothing to set before him.' [7]Imagine further that he answers from within the house, 'Don't bother me. The door is already locked, and my children and I are in bed. I can't get up to give you anything.' [8]I assure you, even if he wouldn't get up and help because of his friendship, he will get up and give his friend whatever he needs because of his friend's brashness. [9]And I tell you: Ask and you will receive. Seek and you will find. Knock and the door will be opened to you. [10]Everyone who asks, receives. Whoever seeks, finds. To everyone who knocks, the door is opened.

[11]"Which father among you would give a snake to your child if the child asked for a fish? [12]If a child asked for an egg, what father would give the child a scorpion? [13]If you who are evil know how to give good gifts to your children, how much more will the heavenly Father give the Holy Spirit to those who ask him?"

Controversy over Beelzebul

[14]Jesus was throwing out a demon that causes muteness. When the demon was gone, the man who couldn't speak began to talk. The crowds were amazed. [15]But some of them said, "He throws out demons with the authority of Beelzebul, the ruler of demons." [16]Others were testing him, seeking a sign from heaven.

[17]Because Jesus knew what they were thinking, he said to them, "Every kingdom involved in civil war becomes a wasteland, and a house torn apart by divisions will collapse. [18]If Satan is at war with himself, how will his kingdom endure? I ask this because you say that I throw out demons by the authority of Beelzebul. [19]If I throw out demons by the authority of Beelzebul, then by whose authority do your followers throw them out? Therefore, they will be your judges. [20]But if I throw out demons by the power[a] of God, then God's kingdom has already overtaken you. [21]When a strong man, fully armed, guards his own palace, his possessions are secure. [22]But as soon as a stronger one attacks and overpowers him, the stronger one takes away the armor he had trusted and divides the stolen goods.

[23]"Whoever isn't with me is against me, and whoever doesn't gather with me, scatters. [24]When an unclean spirit leaves a person, it wanders through dry places looking for a place to rest. But it doesn't find any. Then it says, 'I'll go back to the house I left.' [25]When it arrives, it finds the house cleaned up and decorated. [26]Then it goes and brings with it seven other spirits more evil than itself. They go in and make their home there. That person is worse off at the end than at the beginning."

On seeking signs

[27]While Jesus was saying these things, a certain woman in the crowd spoke up: "Happy is the mother who gave birth to you and who nursed you."

[28]But he said, "Happy rather are those who hear God's word and put it into practice."

[29]When the crowds grew, Jesus said,

[a]Or *finger*

"This generation is an evil generation. It looks for a sign, but no sign will be given to it except Jonah's sign. ³⁰Just as Jonah became a sign to the people of Nineveh, so the Human One[b] will be a sign to this generation. ³¹The queen of the South will rise up at the judgment with the people of this generation and condemn them, because she came from a distant land to hear Solomon's wisdom. And look, someone greater than Solomon is here. ³²The people of Nineveh will rise up at the judgment with this generation and condemn it, because they changed their hearts and lives in response to Jonah's preaching—and one greater than Jonah is here.

³³"People don't light a lamp and then put it in a closet or under a basket. Rather, they place the lamp on a lampstand so that those who enter the house can see the light. ³⁴Your eye is the lamp of your body. When your eye is healthy, your whole body is full of light. But when your eye is bad, your whole body is full of darkness. ³⁵Therefore, see to it that the light in you isn't darkness. ³⁶If your whole body is full of light—with no part darkened—then it will be as full of light as when a lamp shines brightly on you."

Jesus condemns Pharisees and legal experts

³⁷While Jesus was speaking, a Pharisee invited him to share a meal with him, so Jesus went and took his place at the table. ³⁸When the Pharisee saw that Jesus didn't ritually purify his hands by washing before the meal, he was astonished.

³⁹The Lord said to him, "Now, you Pharisees clean the outside of the cup and platter, but your insides are stuffed with greed and wickedness. ⁴⁰Foolish people! Didn't the one who made the outside also make the inside? ⁴¹Therefore, give to those in need from the core of who you are and you will be clean all over.

⁴²"How terrible for you Pharisees! You give a tenth of your mint, rue, and garden herbs of all kinds, while neglecting justice and love for God. These you ought to have done without neglecting the others.

⁴³"How terrible for you Pharisees! You love the most prominent seats in the synagogues and respectful greetings in the marketplaces.

⁴⁴"How terrible for you! You are like unmarked graves, and people walk on them without recognizing it."

⁴⁵One of the legal experts responded, "Teacher, when you say these things, you are insulting us too."

⁴⁶Jesus said, "How terrible for you legal experts too! You load people down with impossible burdens and you refuse to lift a single finger to help them.

⁴⁷"How terrible for you! You built memorials to the prophets, whom your ancestors killed. ⁴⁸In this way, you testify that you approve of your ancestors' deeds. They killed the prophets, and you build memorials! ⁴⁹Therefore, God's wisdom has said, 'I will send prophets and apostles to them and they will harass and kill some of them.' ⁵⁰As a result, this generation will be charged with the murder of all the prophets since the beginning of time. ⁵¹This includes the murder of every

[b]Or Son of Man

prophet—from Abel to Zechariah—who was killed between the altar and the holy place. Yes, I'm telling you, this generation will be charged with it.

⁵²"How terrible for you legal experts! You snatched away the key of knowledge. You didn't enter yourselves, and you stood in the way of those who were entering."

⁵³As he left there, the legal experts and Pharisees began to resent him deeply and to ask him pointed questions about many things. ⁵⁴They plotted against him, trying to trap him in his words.

Warnings to Jesus' friends

12 When a crowd of thousands upon thousands had gathered so that they were crushing each other, Jesus began to speak first to his disciples: "Watch out for the yeast of the Pharisees—I mean, the mismatch between their hearts and lives. ²Nothing is hidden that won't be revealed, and nothing is secret that won't be brought out into the open. ³Therefore, whatever you have said in the darkness will be heard in the light, and whatever you have whispered in the rooms deep inside the house will be announced from the rooftops.

⁴"I tell you, my friends, don't be terrified by those who can kill the body but after that can do nothing more. ⁵I'll show you whom you should fear: fear the one who, after you have been killed, has the authority to throw you into hell. Indeed, I tell you, that's the one you should fear. ⁶Aren't five sparrows sold for two small coins?ᶜ Yet not one of them is overlooked by God. ⁷Even

the hairs on your head are all counted. Don't be afraid. You are worth more than many sparrows.

Acknowledging the Human One

⁸"I tell you, everyone who acknowledges me before humans, the Human Oneᵈ will acknowledge before God's angels. ⁹But the one who rejects me before others will be rejected before God's angels. ¹⁰Anyone who speaks a word against the Human Oneᵉ will be forgiven, but whoever insults the Holy Spirit won't be forgiven. ¹¹When they bring you before the synagogues, rulers, and authorities, don't worry about how to defend yourself or what you should say. ¹²The Holy Spirit will tell you at that very moment what you must say."

Warning against greed

¹³Someone from the crowd said to him, "Teacher, tell my brother to divide the inheritance with me."

¹⁴Jesus said to him, "Man, who appointed me as judge or referee between you and your brother?"

¹⁵Then Jesus said to them, "Watch out! Guard yourself against all kinds of greed. After all, one's life isn't determined by one's possessions, even when someone is very wealthy." ¹⁶Then he told them a parable: "A certain rich man's land produced a bountiful crop. ¹⁷He said to himself, What will I do? I have no place to store my harvest! ¹⁸Then he thought, Here's what I'll do. I'll tear down my barns and build bigger ones. That's where I'll store all my grain and goods. ¹⁹I'll say to myself, You have stored up plenty of goods, enough for

---

ᶜOr two assaria—that is, 1/8 of a day's wage ᵈOr Son of Man ᵉOr Son of Man several years. Take it easy! Eat, drink, and enjoy yourself. [20]But God said to him, 'Fool, tonight you will die. Now who will get the things you have prepared for yourself?' [21]This is the way it will be for those who hoard things for themselves and aren't rich toward God."

Warning about worry

[22]Then Jesus said to his disciples, "Therefore, I say to you, don't worry about your life, what you will eat, or about your body, what you will wear. [23]There is more to life than food and more to the body than clothing. [24]Consider the ravens: they neither plant nor harvest, they have no silo or barn, yet God feeds them. You are worth so much more than birds! [25]Who among you by worrying can add a single moment to your life?[f] [26]If you can't do such a small thing, why worry about the rest? [27]Notice how the lilies grow. They don't wear themselves out with work, and they don't spin cloth. But I say to you that even Solomon in all his splendor wasn't dressed like one of these. [28]If God dresses grass in the field so beautifully, even though it's alive today and tomorrow it's thrown into the furnace, how much more will God do for you, you people of weak faith! [29]Don't chase after what you will eat and what you will drink. Stop worrying. [30]All the nations of the world long for these things. Your Father knows that you need them. [31]Instead, desire his kingdom and these things will be given to you as well.

[32]"Don't be afraid, little flock, because your Father delights in giving you the kingdom. [33]Sell your possessions and give to those in need. Make for yourselves wallets that don't wear out—a treasure in heaven that never runs out. No thief comes near there, and no moth destroys. [34]Where your treasure is, there your heart will be too.

Warning about being prepared

[35]"Be dressed for service and keep your lamps lit. [36]Be like people waiting for their master to come home from a wedding celebration, who can immediately open the door for him when he arrives and knocks on the door. [37]Happy are those servants whom the master finds waiting up when he arrives. I assure you that, when he arrives, he will dress himself to serve, seat them at the table as honored guests, and wait on them. [38]Happy are those whom he finds alert, even if he comes at midnight or just before dawn.[g] [39]But know this, if the homeowner had known what time the thief was coming, he wouldn't have allowed his home to be broken into. [40]You also must be ready, because the Human One[h] is coming at a time when you don't expect him."

[41]Peter said, "Lord, are you telling this parable for us or for everyone?"

[42]The Lord replied, "Who are the faithful and wise managers whom the master will put in charge of his household servants, to give them their food at the proper time? [43]Happy are the servants whom the master finds fulfilling their responsibilities when he comes. [44]I assure you that the master will put them in charge of all his possessions.

[45]"But suppose that these servants should say to themselves, My master is taking his time about coming. And

---

[f]Or eighteen inches to your height   [g]Or in the second or third watch   [h]Or Son of Man

suppose they began to beat the servants, both men and women, and to eat, drink, and get drunk. ⁴⁶The master of those servants would come on a day when they weren't expecting him, at a time they couldn't predict. The master will cut them into pieces and assign them a place with the unfaithful. ⁴⁷That servant who knew his master's will but didn't prepare for it or act on it will be beaten severely. ⁴⁸The one who didn't know the master's will but who did things deserving punishment will be beaten only a little. Much will be demanded from everyone who has been given much, and from the one who has been entrusted with much, even more will be asked.

Conflicts brought by Jesus

⁴⁹"I came to cast fire upon the earth. How I wish that it was already ablaze! ⁵⁰I have a baptism I must experience. How I am distressed until it's completed! ⁵¹Do you think that I have come to bring peace to the earth? No, I tell you, I have come instead to bring division. ⁵²From now on, a household of five will be divided—three against two and two against three. ⁵³Father will square off against son and son against father; mother against daughter and daughter against mother; and mother-in-law against daughter-in-law and daughter-in-law against mother-in-law."

Learning and practicing good judgment

⁵⁴Jesus also said to the crowds, "When you see a cloud forming in the west, you immediately say, 'It's going to rain.' And indeed it does. ⁵⁵And when a

south wind blows, you say, 'A heat wave is coming.' And it does. ⁵⁶Hypocrites! You know how to interpret conditions on earth and in the sky. How is it that you don't know how to interpret the present time? ⁵⁷And why don't you judge for yourselves what is right? ⁵⁸As you are going to court with your accuser, make your best effort to reach a settlement along the way. Otherwise, your accuser may bring you before the judge, and the judge hand you over to the officer, and the officer throw you into prison. ⁵⁹I tell you, you won't get out of there until you have paid the very last cent."ⁱ

Demand for genuine change

13 Some who were present on that occasion told Jesus about the Galileans whom Pilate had killed while they were offering sacrifices. ²He replied, "Do you think the suffering of these Galileans proves that they were more sinful than all the other Galileans? ³No, I tell you, but unless you change your hearts and lives, you will die just as they did. ⁴What about those eighteen people who were killed when the tower of Siloam fell on them? Do you think that they were more guilty of wrongdoing than everyone else who lives in Jerusalem? ⁵No, I tell you, but unless you change your hearts and lives, you will die just as they did."

⁶Jesus told this parable: "A man owned a fig tree planted in his vineyard. He came looking for fruit on it and found none. ⁷He said to his gardener, 'Look, I've come looking for fruit on this fig tree for the past three years, and I've never found any. Cut it down! Why

---

ⁱOr *leptos* (1/128 of a day's wages)

should it continue depleting the soil's nutrients?' [8]The gardener responded, 'Lord, give it one more year, and I will dig around it and give it fertilizer. [9]Maybe it will produce fruit next year; if not, then you can cut it down.'"

Healing on a Sabbath

[10]Jesus was teaching in one of the synagogues on the Sabbath. [11]A woman was there who had been disabled by a spirit for eighteen years. She was bent over and couldn't stand up straight. [12]When he saw her, Jesus called her to him and said, "Woman, you are set free from your sickness." [13]He placed his hands on her and she straightened up at once and praised God.

[14]The synagogue leader, incensed that Jesus had healed on the Sabbath, responded, "There are six days during which work is permitted. Come and be healed on those days, not on the Sabbath day."

[15]The Lord replied, "Hypocrites! Don't each of you on the Sabbath untie your ox or donkey from its stall and lead it out to get a drink? [16]Then isn't it necessary that this woman, a daughter of Abraham, bound by Satan for eighteen long years, be set free from her bondage on the Sabbath day?" [17]When he said these things, all his opponents were put to shame, but all those in the crowd rejoiced at all the extraordinary things he was doing.

Growth of God's kingdom

[18]Jesus asked, "What is God's kingdom like? To what can I compare it? [19]It's like a mustard seed that someone took and planted in a garden. It grew and developed into a tree and the birds in the sky nested in its branches."

[20]Again he said, "To what can I compare God's kingdom? [21]It's like yeast, which a woman took and hid in a bushel of wheat flour until the yeast had worked its way through the whole."

Who will be saved?

[22]Jesus traveled through cities and villages, teaching and making his way to Jerusalem. [23]Someone said to him, "Lord, will only a few be saved?"

Jesus said to them, [24]"Make every effort to enter through the narrow gate. Many, I tell you, will try to enter and won't be able to. [25]Once the owner of the house gets up and shuts the door, then you will stand outside and knock on the door, saying, 'Lord, open the door for us.' He will reply, 'I don't know you or where you are from.' [26]Then you will begin to say, 'We ate and drank in your presence, and you taught in our streets.' [27]He will respond, 'I don't know you or where you are from. *Go away from me, all you evildoers!*[j] [28]There will be weeping and grinding of teeth when you see Abraham, Isaac, Jacob, and all the prophets in God's kingdom, but you yourselves will be thrown out. [29]People will come from east and west, north and south, and sit down to eat in God's kingdom. [30]Look! Those who are last will be first and those who are first will be last."

Sorrow for Jerusalem

[31]At that time, some Pharisees approached Jesus and said, "Go! Get away from here, because Herod wants to kill you."

[j]Ps 6:9 LXX

[32]Jesus said to them, "Go, tell that fox, 'Look, I'm throwing out demons and healing people today and tomorrow, and on the third day I will complete my work. [33]However, it's necessary for me to travel today, tomorrow, and the next day because it's impossible for a prophet to be killed outside of Jerusalem.'

[34]"Jerusalem, Jerusalem, you who kill the prophets and stone those who were sent to you! How often I have wanted to gather your people just as a hen gathers her chicks under her wings. But you didn't want that. [35]Look, your house is abandoned. I tell you, you won't see me until the time comes when you say, *Blessings on the one who comes in the Lord's name.*"[k]

Healing on the Sabbath

14 One Sabbath, when Jesus went to share a meal in the home of one of the leaders of the Pharisees, they were watching him closely. [2]A man suffering from an abnormal swelling of the body was there. [3]Jesus asked the lawyers and Pharisees, "Does the Law allow healing on the Sabbath or not?" [4]But they said nothing. Jesus took hold of the sick man, cured him, and then let him go. [5]He said to them, "Suppose your child or ox fell into a ditch on the Sabbath day. Wouldn't you immediately pull it out?" [6]But they had no response.

Lessons on humility and generosity

[7]When Jesus noticed how the guests sought out the best seats at the table, he told them a parable. [8]"When someone invites you to a wedding celebration, don't take your seat in the place of honor. Someone more highly regarded than you could have been invited by your host. [9]The host who invited both of you will come and say to you, 'Give your seat to this other person.' Embarrassed, you will take your seat in the least important place. [10]Instead, when you receive an invitation, go and sit in the least important place. When your host approaches you, he will say, 'Friend, move up here to a better seat.' Then you will be honored in the presence of all your fellow guests. [11]All who lift themselves up will be brought low, and those who make themselves low will be lifted up."

[12]Then Jesus said to the person who had invited him, "When you host a lunch or dinner, don't invite your friends, your brothers and sisters, your relatives, or rich neighbors. If you do, they will invite you in return and that will be your reward. [13]Instead, when you give a banquet, invite the poor, crippled, lame, and blind. [14]And you will be blessed because they can't repay you. Instead, you will be repaid when the just are resurrected."

[15]When one of the dinner guests heard Jesus' remarks, he said to Jesus, "Happy are those who will feast in God's kingdom."

[16]Jesus replied, "A certain man hosted a large dinner and invited many people. [17]When it was time for the dinner to begin, he sent his servant to tell the invited guests, 'Come! The dinner is now ready.' [18]One by one, they all began to make excuses. The first one told him, 'I bought a farm and must go and see it. Please excuse me.' [19]Another said, 'I bought five teams of oxen, and I'm

going to check on them. Please excuse me.' ²⁰Another said, 'I just got married, so I can't come.' ²¹When he returned, the servant reported these excuses to his master. The master of the house became angry and said to his servant, 'Go quickly to the city's streets, the busy ones and the side streets, and bring the poor, crippled, blind, and lame.' ²²The servant said, 'Master, your instructions have been followed and there is still room.' ²³The master said to the servant, 'Go to the highways and back alleys and urge people to come in so that my house will be filled. ²⁴I tell you, not one of those who were invited will taste my dinner.'"

Discipleship's demands

²⁵Large crowds were traveling with Jesus. Turning to them, he said, ²⁶"Whoever comes to me and doesn't hate father and mother, spouse and children, and brothers and sisters—yes, even one's own life—cannot be my disciple. ²⁷Whoever doesn't carry their own cross and follow me cannot be my disciple.

²⁸"If one of you wanted to build a tower, wouldn't you first sit down and calculate the cost, to determine whether you have enough money to complete it? ²⁹Otherwise, when you have laid the foundation but couldn't finish the tower, all who see it will begin to belittle you. ³⁰They will say, 'Here's the person who began construction and couldn't complete it!' ³¹Or what king would go to war against another king without first sitting down to consider whether his ten thousand soldiers could go up against the twenty thousand coming against him? ³²And if he didn't think he could win, he would send a representative to discuss terms

of peace while his enemy was still a long way off. ³³In the same way, none of you who are unwilling to give up all your possessions can be my disciple.

³⁴"Salt is good. But if salt loses its flavor, how will it become salty again? ³⁵It has no value, neither for the soil nor for the manure pile. People throw it away. Whoever has ears to hear should pay attention."

Occasions for celebration

15 All the tax collectors and sinners were gathering around Jesus to listen to him. ²The Pharisees and legal experts were grumbling, saying, "This man welcomes sinners and eats with them."

³Jesus told them this parable: ⁴"Suppose someone among you had one hundred sheep and lost one of them. Wouldn't he leave the other ninety-nine in the pasture and search for the lost one until he finds it? ⁵And when he finds it, he is thrilled and places it on his shoulders. ⁶When he arrives home, he calls together his friends and neighbors, saying to them, 'Celebrate with me because I've found my lost sheep.' ⁷In the same way, I tell you, there will be more joy in heaven over one sinner who changes both heart and life than over ninety-nine righteous people who have no need to change their hearts and lives.

⁸"Or what woman, if she owns ten silver coins and loses one of them, won't light a lamp and sweep the house, searching her home carefully until she finds it? ⁹When she finds it, she calls together her friends and neighbors, saying, 'Celebrate with me because I've found my lost coin.' ¹⁰In the same way, I tell you, joy breaks out in the presence of God's angels over one sinner who changes both heart and life."

[11] Jesus said, "A certain man had two sons. [12] The younger son said to his father, 'Father, give me my share of the inheritance.' Then the father divided his estate between them. [13] Soon afterward, the younger son gathered everything together and took a trip to a land far away. There, he wasted his wealth through extravagant living.

[14] "When he had used up his resources, a severe food shortage arose in that country and he began to be in need. [15] He hired himself out to one of the citizens of that country, who sent him into his fields to feed pigs. [16] He longed to eat his fill from what the pigs ate, but no one gave him anything. [17] When he came to his senses, he said, 'How many of my father's hired hands have more than enough food, but I'm starving to death! [18] I will get up and go to my father, and say to him, "Father, I have sinned against heaven and against you. [19] I no longer deserve to be called your son. Take me on as one of your hired hands." ' [20] So he got up and went to his father.

"While he was still a long way off, his father saw him and was moved with compassion. His father ran to him, hugged him, and kissed him. [21] Then his son said, 'Father, I have sinned against heaven and against you. I no longer deserve to be called your son.' [22] But the father said to his servants, 'Quickly, bring out the best robe and put it on him! Put a ring on his finger and sandals on his feet! [23] Fetch the fattened calf and slaughter it. We must celebrate with feasting [24] because this son of mine was dead and has come back to life! He was lost and is found!' And they began to celebrate.

[25] "Now his older son was in the field. Coming in from the field, he approached the house and heard music and dancing. [26] He called one of the servants and asked what was going on. [27] The servant replied, 'Your brother has arrived, and your father has slaughtered the fattened calf because he received his son back safe and sound.' [28] Then the older son was furious and didn't want to enter in, but his father came out and begged him. [29] He answered his father, 'Look, I've served you all these years, and I never disobeyed your instruction. Yet you've never given me as much as a young goat so I could celebrate with my friends. [30] But when this son of yours returned, after gobbling up your estate on prostitutes, you slaughtered the fattened calf for him.' [31] Then his father said, 'Son, you are always with me, and everything I have is yours. [32] But we had to celebrate and be glad because this brother of yours was dead and is alive. He was lost and is found.' "

Faithfulness with money

16 Jesus also said to the disciples, "A certain rich man heard that his household manager was wasting his estate. [2] He called the manager in and said to him, 'What is this I hear about you? Give me a report of your administration because you can no longer serve as my manager.'

[3] "The household manager said to himself, What will I do now that my master is firing me as his manager? I'm not strong enough to dig and too proud to beg. [4] I know what I'll do so that, when I am removed from my management position, people will welcome me into their houses. [5] "One by one, the manager sent for each person who owed his master

money. He said to the first, 'How much do you owe my master?' [6] He said, 'Nine hundred gallons of olive oil.'[l] The manager said to him, 'Take your contract, sit down quickly, and write four hundred fifty gallons.' [7] Then the manager said to another, 'How much do you owe?' He said, 'One thousand bushels of wheat.'[m] He said, 'Take your contract and write eight hundred.'

[8] "The master commended the dishonest manager because he acted cleverly. People who belong to this world are more clever in dealing with their peers than are people who belong to the light. [9] I tell you, use worldly wealth to make friends for yourselves so that when it's gone, you will be welcomed into the eternal homes.

[10] "Whoever is faithful with little is also faithful with much, and the one who is dishonest with little is also dishonest with much. [11] If you haven't been faithful with worldly wealth, who will trust you with true riches? [12] If you haven't been faithful with someone else's property, who will give you your own? [13] No household servant can serve two masters. Either you will hate the one and love the other, or you will be loyal to the one and have contempt for the other. You cannot serve God and wealth."

Jesus responds to Pharisees

[14] The Pharisees, who were money-lovers, heard all this and sneered at Jesus. [15] He said to them, "You are the ones who justify yourselves before other people, but God knows your hearts. What is highly valued by people is deeply offensive to God. [16] Until John, there was only the Law and the Prophets. Since then, the good news of God's kingdom is preached, and everyone is urged to enter it. [17] It's easier for heaven and earth to pass away than for the smallest stroke of a pen in the Law to drop out. [18] Any man who divorces his wife and marries another commits adultery, and a man who marries a woman divorced from her husband commits adultery.

[19] "There was a certain rich man who clothed himself in purple and fine linen, and who feasted luxuriously every day. [20] At his gate lay a certain poor man named Lazarus who was covered with sores. [21] Lazarus longed to eat the crumbs that fell from the rich man's table. Instead, dogs would come and lick his sores.

[22] "The poor man died and was carried by angels to Abraham's side. The rich man also died and was buried. [23] While being tormented in the place of the dead, he looked up and saw Abraham at a distance with Lazarus at his side. [24] He shouted, 'Father Abraham, have mercy on me. Send Lazarus to dip the tip of his finger in water and cool my tongue, because I'm suffering in this flame.' [25] But Abraham said, 'Child, remember that during your lifetime you received good things, whereas Lazarus received terrible things. Now Lazarus is being comforted and you are in great pain. [26] Moreover, a great crevasse has been fixed between us and you. Those who wish to cross over from here to you cannot. Neither can anyone cross from there to us.'

[l]Or one hundred jugs (approximately nine gallons each)   [m]Or eighty measures (ten to twelve bushels each)

²⁷"The rich man said, 'Then I beg you, Father, send Lazarus to my father's house. ²⁸I have five brothers. He needs to warn them so that they don't come to this place of agony.' ²⁹Abraham replied, 'They have Moses and the Prophets. They must listen to them.' ³⁰The rich man said, 'No, Father Abraham! But if someone from the dead goes to them, they will change their hearts and lives.' ³¹Abraham said, 'If they don't listen to Moses and the Prophets, then neither will they be persuaded if someone rises from the dead.'"

Faithful service

17 Jesus said to his disciples, "Things that cause people to trip and fall into sin must happen, but how terrible it is for the person through whom they happen. ²It would be better for them to be thrown into a lake with a large stone hung around their neck to cause one of these little ones to trip and fall into sin. ³Watch yourselves! If your brother or sister sins, warn them to stop. If they change their hearts and lives, forgive them. ⁴Even if someone sins against you seven times in one day and returns to you seven times and says, 'I am changing my ways,' you must forgive that person."

⁵The apostles said to the Lord, "Increase our faith!"

⁶The Lord replied, "If you had faith the size of a mustard seed, you could say to this mulberry tree, 'Be uprooted and planted in the sea,' and it would obey you.

⁷"Would any of you say to your servant, who had just come in from the field after plowing or tending sheep, 'Come! Sit down for dinner'? ⁸Wouldn't you say instead, 'Fix my dinner. Put on the clothes of a table servant and wait on me while I eat and drink. After that, you can eat and drink'? ⁹You won't thank the servant because the servant did what you asked, will you? ¹⁰In the same way, when you have done everything required of you, you should say, 'We servants deserve no special praise. We have only done our duty.'"

Jesus heals a Samaritan

¹¹On the way to Jerusalem, Jesus traveled along the border between Samaria and Galilee. ¹²As he entered a village, ten men with skin diseases approached him. Keeping their distance from him, ¹³they raised their voices and said, "Jesus, Master, show us mercy!"

¹⁴When Jesus saw them, he said, "Go, show yourselves to the priests." As they left, they were cleansed. ¹⁵One of them, when he saw that he had been healed, returned and praised God with a loud voice. ¹⁶He fell on his face at Jesus' feet and thanked him. He was a Samaritan. ¹⁷Jesus replied, "Weren't ten cleansed? Where are the other nine? ¹⁸No one returned to praise God except this foreigner?" ¹⁹Then Jesus said to him, "Get up and go. Your faith has healed you."

The kingdom is coming

²⁰Pharisees asked Jesus when God's kingdom was coming. He replied, "God's kingdom isn't coming with signs that are easily noticed. ²¹Nor will people say, 'Look, here it is!' or 'There it is!' Don't you see? God's kingdom is already among you."

²²Then Jesus said to the disciples, "The time will come when you will long to see one of the days of the Human

One,[n] and you won't see it. [23]People will say to you, 'Look there!' or 'Look here!' Don't leave or go chasing after them. [24]The Human One[o] will appear on his day in the same way that a flash of lightning lights up the sky from one end to the other. [25]However, first he must suffer many things and be rejected by this generation.

[26]"As it was in the days of Noah, so it will be during the days of the Human One.[p] [27]People were eating, drinking, marrying, and being given in marriage until the day Noah entered the ark and the flood came and destroyed them all. [28]Likewise in the days of Lot, people were eating, drinking, buying, selling, planting, and building. [29]But on the day Lot left Sodom, fire and sulfur rained down from heaven and destroyed them all. [30]That's the way it will be on the day the Human One[q] is revealed. [31]On that day, those on the roof, whose possessions are in the house, shouldn't come down to grab them. Likewise, those in the field shouldn't turn back. [32]Remember Lot's wife! [33]Whoever tries to preserve their life will lose it, but whoever loses their life will preserve it. [34]I tell you, on that night two people will be in the same bed: one will be taken and the other left. [35]Two women will be grinding grain together: one will be taken and the other left."[r]

[37]The disciples asked, "Where, Lord?"

Jesus said, "The vultures gather wherever there's a dead body."

Justice for the faithful

18 Jesus was telling them a parable about their need to pray continuously and not to be discouraged. [2]He said, "In a certain city there was a judge who neither feared God nor respected people. [3]In that city there was a widow who kept coming to him, asking, 'Give me justice in this case against my adversary.' [4]For a while he refused but finally said to himself, I don't fear God or respect people. [5]but I will give this widow justice because she keeps bothering me. Otherwise, there will be no end to her coming here and embarrassing me." [6]The Lord said, "Listen to what the unjust judge says. [7]Won't God provide justice to his chosen people who cry out to him day and night? Will he be slow to help them? [8]I tell you, he will give them justice quickly. But when the Human One[s] comes, will he find faithfulness on earth?"

The Pharisee and the tax collector

[9]Jesus told this parable to certain people who had convinced themselves that they were righteous and who looked on everyone else with disgust: [10]"Two people went up to the temple to pray. One was a Pharisee and the other a tax collector. [11]The Pharisee stood and prayed about himself with these words, 'God, I thank you that I'm not like everyone else—crooks, evildoers, adulterers—or even like this tax collector. [12]I fast twice a week. I give a tenth of everything I receive.' [13]But the tax collector stood at a distance. He wouldn't even lift his eyes to look toward heaven. Rather, he struck his chest and said, 'God, show mercy to me, a sinner.' [14]I tell you, this person went

---

[n]Or Son of Man [o]Or Son of Man [p]Or Son of Man [q]Or Son of Man [r]Critical editions of the Gk New Testament do not include 17:36 *Two will be in a field: one will be taken and the other left.* [s]Or Son of Man

down to his home justified rather than the Pharisee. All who lift themselves up will be brought low, and those who make themselves low will be lifted up."

Jesus blesses children

¹⁵People were bringing babies to Jesus so that he would bless them. When the disciples saw this, they scolded them. ¹⁶Then Jesus called them to him and said, "Allow the children to come to me. Don't forbid them, because God's kingdom belongs to people like these children. ¹⁷I assure you that whoever doesn't welcome God's kingdom like a child will never enter it."

A rich man's question

¹⁸A certain ruler asked Jesus, "Good Teacher, what must I do to obtain eternal life?"

¹⁹Jesus replied, "Why do you call me good? No one is good except the one God. ²⁰You know the commandments: *Don't commit adultery. Don't murder. Don't steal. Don't give false testimony. Honor your father and mother.*"[t]

²¹Then the ruler said, "I've kept all of these things since I was a boy."

²²When Jesus heard this, he said, "There's one more thing. Sell everything you own and distribute the money to the poor. Then you will have treasure in heaven. And come, follow me." ²³When he heard these words, the man became sad because he was extremely rich.

²⁴When Jesus saw this, he said, "It's very hard for the wealthy to enter God's kingdom! ²⁵It's easier for a camel to squeeze through the eye of a needle than for a rich person to enter God's kingdom."

²⁶Those who heard this said, "Then who can be saved?"

²⁷Jesus replied, "What is impossible for humans is possible for God."

²⁸Peter said, "Look, we left everything we own and followed you."

²⁹Jesus said to them, "I assure you that anyone who has left house, husband, wife, brothers, sisters, parents, or children because of God's kingdom ³⁰will receive many times more in this age and eternal life in the coming age."

Jesus predicts his death and resurrection

³¹Jesus took the Twelve aside and said, "Look, we're going up to Jerusalem, and everything written about the Human One[u] by the prophets will be accomplished. ³²He will be handed over to the Gentiles. He will be ridiculed, mistreated, and spit on. ³³After torturing him, they will kill him. On the third day, he will rise up." ³⁴But the Twelve understood none of these words. The meaning of this message was hidden from them and they didn't grasp what he was saying.

A blind man is healed

³⁵As Jesus came to Jericho, a certain blind man was sitting beside the road begging. ³⁶When the man heard the crowd passing by, he asked what was happening. ³⁷They told him, "Jesus the Nazarene is passing by."

³⁸The blind man shouted, "Jesus, Son of David, show me mercy." ³⁹Those leading the procession scolded him, telling him to be quiet, but he shouted even louder, "Son of David, show me mercy."

[t]Deut 5:16-20; Exod 20:12-16   [u]Or *Son of Man*

⁴⁰Jesus stopped and called for the man to be brought to him. When he was brought Jesus asked, ⁴¹"What do you want me to do for you?"

He said, "Lord, I want to see."

⁴²Jesus said to him, "Receive your sight! Your faith has healed you." ⁴³At once he was able to see, and he began to follow Jesus, praising God. When all the people saw it, they praised God too.

A rich tax collector

19 Jesus entered Jericho and was passing through town. ²A man there named Zacchaeus, a ruler among tax collectors, was rich. ³He was trying to see who Jesus was, but, being a short man, he couldn't because of the crowd. ⁴So he ran ahead and climbed up a sycamore tree so he could see Jesus, who was about to pass that way. ⁵When Jesus came to that spot, he looked up and said, "Zacchaeus, come down at once. I must stay in your home today." ⁶So Zacchaeus came down at once, happy to welcome Jesus.

⁷Everyone who saw this grumbled, saying, "He has gone to be the guest of a sinner."

⁸Zacchaeus stopped and said to the Lord, "Look, Lord, I give half of my possessions to the poor. And if I have cheated anyone, I repay them four times as much."

⁹Jesus said to him, "Today, salvation has come to this household because he too is a son of Abraham. ¹⁰The Human One^v came to seek and save the lost."

Faithful service

¹¹As they listened to this, Jesus told them another parable because he was near Jerusalem and they thought God's kingdom would appear right away. ¹²He said, "A certain man who was born into royalty went to a distant land to receive his kingdom and then return. ¹³He called together ten servants and gave each of them money worth four months' wages.^w He said, 'Do business with this until I return.' ¹⁴His citizens hated him, so they sent a representative after him who said, 'We don't want this man to be our king.' ¹⁵After receiving his kingdom, he returned and called the servants to whom he had given the money to find out how much they had earned. ¹⁶The first servant came forward and said, 'Your money has made a return of one thousand percent.' ¹⁷The king replied, 'Excellent! You are a good servant. Because you have been faithful in a small matter, you will have authority over ten cities.'

¹⁸"The second servant came and said, 'Master, your money has made a return of five hundred percent.' ¹⁹To this one, the king said, 'You will have authority over five cities.'

²⁰"Another servant came and said, 'Master, here is your money. I wrapped it up in a scarf for safekeeping. ²¹I was afraid of you because you are a stern man. You withdraw what you haven't deposited and you harvest what you haven't planted.' ²²The king replied, 'I will judge you by the words of your own mouth, you worthless servant! You knew, did you, that I'm a stern man, withdrawing what I didn't deposit, and harvesting what I didn't plant? ²³Why then didn't you put my money in the bank? Then when I arrived, at least I could have gotten it back with interest.'

^vOr *Son of Man*   ^wOr *he divided ten minas among them*

²⁴"He said to his attendants, 'Take his money and give it to the one who has ten times as much.' ²⁵'But Master,' they said, 'he already has ten times as much!' ²⁶He replied, 'I say to you that everyone who has will be given more, but from those who have nothing, even what they have will be taken away. ²⁷As for my enemies who don't want me as their king, bring them here and slaughter them before me.'"

²⁸After Jesus said this, he continued on ahead, going up to Jerusalem.

Procession into Jerusalem

²⁹As Jesus came to Bethphage and Bethany on the Mount of Olives, he gave two disciples a task. ³⁰He said, "Go into the village over there. When you enter it, you will find tied up there a colt that no one has ever ridden. Untie it and bring it here. ³¹If anyone asks, 'Why are you untying it?' just say, 'Its master needs it.'" ³²Those who had been sent found it exactly as he had said.

³³As they were untying the colt, its owners said to them, "Why are you untying the colt?"

³⁴They replied, "Its master needs it." ³⁵They brought it to Jesus, threw their clothes on the colt, and lifted Jesus onto it. ³⁶As Jesus rode along, they spread their clothes on the road.

³⁷As Jesus approached the road leading down from the Mount of Olives, the whole throng of his disciples began rejoicing. They praised God with a loud voice because of all the mighty things they had seen. ³⁸They said,

"Blessings on the king who comes in the name of the Lord.

　　Peace in heaven and glory in the highest heavens."

³⁹Some of the Pharisees from the crowd said to Jesus, "Teacher, scold your disciples! Tell them to stop!"

⁴⁰He answered, "I tell you, if they were silent, the stones would shout."

Jesus predicts Jerusalem's destruction

⁴¹As Jesus came to the city and observed it, he wept over it. ⁴²He said, "If only you knew on this of all days the things that lead to peace. But now they are hidden from your eyes. ⁴³The time will come when your enemies will build fortifications around you, encircle you, and attack you from all sides. ⁴⁴They will crush you completely, you and the people within you. They won't leave one stone on top of another within you, because you didn't recognize the time of your gracious visit from God."

Jesus clears the temple

⁴⁵When Jesus entered the temple, he threw out those who were selling things there. ⁴⁶He said to them, "It's written, *My house will be a house of prayer, but you have made it a hideout for crooks.*"ˣ

⁴⁷Jesus was teaching daily in the temple. The chief priests, the legal experts, and the foremost leaders among the people were seeking to kill him. ⁴⁸However, they couldn't find a way to do it because all the people were enthralled with what they heard.

Controversy over authority

20On one of the days when Jesus was teaching the people in the temple and proclaiming the good news,

ˣIsa 56:7; Jer 7:11

the chief priests, legal experts, and elders approached him. ²They said, "Tell us: What kind of authority do you have for doing these things? Who gave you this authority?"

³He replied, "I have a question for you. Tell me: ⁴Was John's baptism of heavenly or of human origin?"

⁵They discussed among themselves, "If we say, 'It's of heavenly origin,' he'll say, 'Why didn't you believe him?' ⁶But if we say, 'It's of human origin,' all the people will stone us to death because they are convinced that John was a prophet." ⁷They answered that they didn't know where it came from.

⁸Then Jesus replied, "Neither will I tell you what kind of authority I have to do these things."

Parable of the tenant farmers

⁹Jesus told the people this parable: "A certain man planted a vineyard, rented it to tenant farmers, and went on a trip for a long time. ¹⁰When it was time, he sent a servant to collect from the tenants his share of the fruit of the vineyard. But the tenants sent him away, beaten and empty-handed. ¹¹The man sent another servant. But they beat him, treated him disgracefully, and sent him away empty-handed as well. ¹²He sent a third servant. They wounded this servant and threw him out. ¹³The owner of the vineyard said, 'What should I do? I'll send my son, whom I love dearly. Perhaps they will respect him.' ¹⁴But when they saw him, they said to each other, 'This is the heir. Let's kill him so the inheritance will be ours.' ¹⁵They threw him out of the vineyard and killed him.

What will the owner of the vineyard do to them? ¹⁶He will come and destroy those tenants and give the vineyard to others."

When the people heard this, they said, "May this never happen!"

¹⁷Staring at them, Jesus said, "Then what is the meaning of this text of scripture: *The stone that the builders rejected has become the cornerstone?*ʸ ¹⁸Everyone who falls on that stone will be crushed. And the stone will crush the person it falls on." ¹⁹The legal experts and chief priests wanted to arrest him right then because they knew he had told this parable against them. But they feared the people.

An attempt to trap Jesus

²⁰The legal experts and chief priests were watching Jesus closely and sent spies who pretended to be sincere. They wanted to trap him in his words so they could hand him over to the jurisdiction and authority of the governor. ²¹They asked him, "Teacher, we know that you are correct in what you say and teach. You don't show favoritism but teach God's way as it really is. ²²Does the Law allow people to pay taxes to Caesar or not?"

²³Since Jesus recognized their deception, he said to them, ²⁴"Show me a coin.ᶻ Whose image and inscription does it have on it?"

"Caesar's," they replied.

²⁵He said to them, "Give to Caesar what belongs to Caesar and to God what belongs to God." ²⁶They couldn't trap him in his words in front of the people. Astonished by his answer, they were speechless.

ʸPs 118:22   ᶻOr denarion

Question about the resurrection

27Some Sadducees, who deny that there's a resurrection, came to Jesus and asked, 28"Teacher, Moses wrote for us that *if a man's brother dies leaving a widow but no children, the brother must marry the widow and raise up children for his brother.*[a] 29Now there were seven brothers. The first man married a woman and then died childless. 30The second 31and then the third brother married her. Eventually all seven married her, and they all died without leaving any children. 32Finally, the woman died too. 33In the resurrection, whose wife will she be? All seven were married to her."

34Jesus said to them, "People who belong to this age marry and are given in marriage. 35But those who are considered worthy to participate in that age, that is, in the age of the resurrection from the dead, won't marry nor will they be given in marriage. 36They can no longer die, because they are like angels and are God's children since they share in the resurrection. 37Even Moses demonstrated that the dead are raised—in the passage about the burning bush, when he speaks of the Lord as *the God of Abraham, the God of Isaac, and the God of Jacob.*[b] 38He isn't the God of the dead but of the living. To him they are all alive."

39Some of the legal experts responded, "Teacher, you have answered well." 40No one dared to ask him anything else.

41Jesus said to them, "Why do they say that the Christ is David's son? 42David himself says in the scroll of Psalms, *The Lord said to my lord, 'Sit at my right side* 43*until I make your enemies a footstool for your feet.'*[c] 44Since David calls him 'Lord,' how can he be David's son?"

Jesus condemns the legal experts

45In the presence of all the people, Jesus said to his disciples, 46"Watch out for the legal experts. They like to walk around in long robes. They love being greeted with honor in the markets. They long for the places of honor in the synagogues and at banquets. 47They are the ones who cheat widows out of their homes, and to show off they say long prayers. They will be judged most harshly."

A poor widow's offering

21 Looking up, Jesus saw rich people throwing their gifts into the collection box for the temple treasury. 2He also saw a poor widow throw in two small copper coins worth a penny.[d] 3He said, "I assure you that this poor widow has put in more than them all. 4All of them are giving out of their spare change. But she from her hopeless poverty has given everything she had to live on."

The temple's fate

5Some people were talking about the temple, how it was decorated with beautiful stones and ornaments dedicated to God. Jesus said, 6"As for the things you are admiring, the time is coming when not even one stone will be left upon another. All will be demolished."

7They asked him, "Teacher, when will these things happen? What sign will

[a]Deut 25:5; Gen 38:8   [b]Exod 3:6, 15-16   [c]Ps 110:1   [d]Or *two lepta*

show that these things are about to happen?"

⁸Jesus said, "Watch out that you aren't deceived. Many will come in my name, saying, 'I'm the one!' and 'It's time!' Don't follow them. ⁹When you hear of wars and rebellions, don't be alarmed. These things must happen first, but the end won't happen immediately."

¹⁰Then Jesus said to them, "Nations and kingdoms will fight against each other. ¹¹There will be great earthquakes and wide-scale food shortages and epidemics. There will also be terrifying sights and great signs in the sky. ¹²But before all this occurs, they will take you into custody and harass you because of your faith. They will hand you over to synagogues and prisons, and you will be brought before kings and governors because of my name. ¹³This will provide you with an opportunity to testify. ¹⁴Make up your minds not to prepare your defense in advance. ¹⁵I'll give you words and wisdom that none of your opponents will be able to counter or contradict. ¹⁶You will be betrayed by your parents, brothers and sisters, relatives, and friends. They will execute some of you. ¹⁷Everyone will hate you because of my name. ¹⁸Still, not a hair on your head will be lost. ¹⁹By holding fast, you will gain your lives.

²⁰"When you see Jerusalem surrounded by armies, then you will know that its destruction is close at hand. ²¹At that time, those in Judea must flee to the mountains, those in the city must escape, and those in the country-side must not enter the city. ²²These are the days of punishment, when everything written will find its fulfillment. ²³How terrible it will be at that time for women who are pregnant or for women who are nursing their children. There will be great agony on the earth and angry judgment on this people. ²⁴They will fall by the edge of the sword and be taken away as captives among all nations. Jerusalem will be plundered by Gentiles until the times of the Gentiles are concluded.

²⁵"There will be signs in the sun, moon, and stars. On the earth, there will be dismay among nations in their confusion over the roaring of the sea and surging waves. ²⁶The planets and other heavenly bodies will be shaken, causing people to faint from fear and foreboding of what is coming upon the world. ²⁷Then they will see the Human One[e] coming on a cloud with power and great splendor. ²⁸Now when these things begin to happen, stand up straight and raise your heads, because your redemption is near."

A lesson from the fig tree

²⁹Jesus told them a parable: "Look at the fig tree and all the trees. ³⁰When they sprout leaves, you can see for your-selves and know that summer is near. ³¹In the same way, when you see these things happening, you know that God's kingdom is near. ³²I assure you that this generation won't pass away until everything has happened. ³³Heaven and earth will pass away, but my words will certainly not pass away.

³⁴"Take care that your hearts aren't dulled by drinking parties, drunkenness, and the anxieties of day-to-day life. Don't let that day fall upon you

[e]Or Son of Man

unexpectedly, [35]like a trap. It will come upon everyone who lives on the face of the whole earth. [36]Stay alert at all times, praying that you are strong enough to escape everything that is about to happen and to stand before the Human One.[f]

[37]Every day Jesus was teaching in the temple, but he spent each night on the Mount of Olives. [38]All the people rose early in the morning to hear him in the temple area.

Plot to kill Jesus

22 The Festival of Unleavened Bread, which is called Passover, was approaching. [2]The chief priests and the legal experts were looking for a way to kill Jesus, because they were afraid of the people. [3]Then Satan entered Judas, called Iscariot, who was one of the Twelve. [4]He went out and discussed with the chief priests and the officers of the temple guard how he could hand Jesus over to them. [5]They were delighted and arranged payment for him. [6]He agreed and began looking for an opportunity to hand Jesus over to them—a time when the crowds would be absent.

Disciples prepare for the Passover

[7]The Day of Unleavened Bread arrived, when the Passover had to be sacrificed. [8]Jesus sent Peter and John with this task: "Go and prepare for us to eat the Passover meal."

[9]They said to him, "Where do you want us to prepare it?"

[10]Jesus replied, "When you go into the city, a man carrying a water jar will meet you. Follow him to the house he enters. [11]Say to the owner of the house, 'The teacher says to you, "Where is the guestroom where I can eat the Passover meal with my disciples?"' [12]He will show you a large upstairs room, already furnished. Make preparations there."

[13]They went and found everything just as he had told them, and they prepared the Passover meal.

The Passover meal

[14]When the time came, Jesus took his place at the table, and the apostles joined him. [15]He said to them, "I have earnestly desired to eat this Passover with you before I suffer. [16]I tell you, I won't eat it until it is fulfilled in God's kingdom." [17]After taking a cup and giving thanks, he said, "Take this and share it among yourselves. [18]I tell you that from now on I won't drink from the fruit of the vine until God's kingdom has come." [19]After taking the bread and giving thanks, he broke it and gave it to them, saying, "This is my body, which is given for you. Do this in remembrance of me." [20]In the same way, he took the cup after the meal and said, "This cup is the new covenant by my blood, which is poured out for you. [21]But look! My betrayer is with me; his hand is on this table. [22]The Human One[g] goes just as it has been determined. But how terrible it is for that person who betrays him." [23]They began to argue among themselves about which of them it could possibly be who would do this.

The disciples debate greatness

[24]An argument broke out among the disciples over which one of them should be regarded as the greatest.

[f]Or Son of Man   [g]Or Son of Man

²⁵But Jesus said to them, "The kings of the Gentiles rule over their subjects, and those in authority over them are called 'friends of the people.' ²⁶But that's not the way it will be with you. Instead, the greatest among you must become like a person of lower status and the leader like a servant. ²⁷So which one is greater, the one who is seated at the table or the one who serves at the table? Isn't it the one who is seated at the table? But I am among you as one who serves.

²⁸"You are the ones who have continued with me in my trials. ²⁹And I confer royal power on you just as my Father granted royal power to me. ³⁰Thus you will eat and drink at my table in my kingdom, and you will sit on thrones overseeing the twelve tribes of Israel.

Peter's denial predicted

³¹"Simon, Simon, look! Satan has asserted the right to sift you all like wheat. ³²However, I have prayed for you that your faith won't fail. When you have returned, strengthen your brothers and sisters."

³³Peter responded, "Lord, I'm ready to go with you, both to prison and to death!"

³⁴Jesus replied, "I tell you, Peter, the rooster won't crow today before you have denied three times that you know me."

Call for preparedness

³⁵Jesus said to them, "When I sent you out without a wallet, bag, or sandals, you didn't lack anything, did you?"

They said, "Nothing."

³⁶Then he said to them, "But now, whoever has a wallet must take it, and likewise a bag. And those who don't own a sword must sell their clothes and buy one. ³⁷I tell you that this scripture must be fulfilled in relation to me: *And he was counted among criminals.*[h] Indeed, what's written about me is nearing completion."

³⁸They said to him, "Lord, look, here are two swords."

He replied, "Enough of that!"

Jesus in prayer

³⁹Jesus left and made his way to the Mount of Olives, as was his custom, and the disciples followed him. ⁴⁰When he arrived, he said to them, "Pray that you won't give in to temptation." ⁴¹He withdrew from them about a stone's throw, knelt down, and prayed. ⁴²He said, "Father, if it's your will, take this cup of suffering away from me. However, not my will but your will must be done." ⁴³Then a heavenly angel appeared to him and strengthened him. ⁴⁴He was in anguish and prayed even more earnestly. His sweat became like drops of blood falling on the ground. ⁴⁵When he got up from praying, he went to the disciples. He found them asleep, overcome by grief. ⁴⁶He said to them, "Why are you sleeping? Get up and pray so that you won't give in to temptation."

Jesus' arrest

⁴⁷While Jesus was still speaking, a crowd appeared, and the one called Judas, one of the Twelve, was leading them. He approached Jesus to kiss him. ⁴⁸Jesus said to him, "Judas, would you betray the Human One[i] with a kiss?"

---

[h]Isa 53:12   [i]Or *Son of Man*

⁴⁹When those around him recognized what was about to happen, they said, "Lord, should we fight with our swords?" ⁵⁰One of them struck the high priest's servant, cutting off his right ear.

⁵¹Jesus responded, "Stop! No more of this!" He touched the slave's ear and healed him.

⁵²Then Jesus said to the chief priests, the officers of the temple guard, and the elders who had come to get him, "Have you come with swords and clubs to arrest me, as though I were a thief? ⁵³Day after day I was with you in the temple, but you didn't arrest me. But this is your time, when darkness rules."

Peter denies knowing Jesus

⁵⁴After they arrested Jesus, they led him away and brought him to the high priest's house. Peter followed from a distance. ⁵⁵When they lit a fire in the middle of the courtyard and sat down together, Peter sat among them.

⁵⁶Then a servant woman saw him sitting in the firelight. She stared at him and said, "This man was with him too."

⁵⁷But Peter denied it, saying, "Woman, I don't know him!"

⁵⁸A little while later, someone else saw him and said, "You are one of them too."

But Peter said, "Man, I'm not!"

⁵⁹An hour or so later, someone else insisted, "This man must have been with him, because he is a Galilean too."

⁶⁰Peter responded, "Man, I don't know what you are talking about!" At that very moment, while he was still speaking, a rooster crowed. ⁶¹The Lord turned and looked straight at Peter, and

Peter remembered the Lord's words: "Before a rooster crows today, you will deny me three times." ⁶²And Peter went out and cried uncontrollably.

Jesus taunted

⁶³The men who were holding Jesus in custody taunted him while they beat him. ⁶⁴They blindfolded him and asked him repeatedly, "Prophesy! Who hit you?" ⁶⁵Insulting him, they said many other horrible things against him.

Jesus before the Jerusalem leadership

⁶⁶As morning came, the elders of the people, both chief priests and legal experts, came together, and Jesus was brought before their council.

⁶⁷They said, "If you are the Christ, tell us!"

He answered, "If I tell you, you won't believe. ⁶⁸And if I ask you a question, you won't answer. ⁶⁹But from now on, *the Human One^j will be seated on the right side of the power of God.*"^{k}

⁷⁰They all said, "Are you God's Son, then?"

He replied, "You say that I am."

⁷¹Then they said, "Why do we need further testimony? We've heard it from his own lips."

Jesus before Pilate

23 The whole assembly got up and led Jesus to Pilate and ²began to accuse him. They said, "We have found this man misleading our people, opposing the payment of taxes to Caesar, and claiming that he is the Christ, a king."

³Pilate asked him, "Are you the king of the Jews?"

---

^{j}Or Son of Man ^{k}Ps 110:1

Jesus replied, "That's what you say."

[4] Then Pilate said to the chief priests and the crowds, "I find no legal basis for action against this man."

[5] But they objected strenuously, saying, "He agitates the people with his teaching throughout Judea—starting from Galilee all the way here."

Jesus before Herod

[6] Hearing this, Pilate asked if the man was a Galilean. [7] When he learned that Jesus was from Herod's district, Pilate sent him to Herod, who was also in Jerusalem at that time. [8] Herod was very glad to see Jesus, for he had heard about Jesus and had wanted to see him for quite some time. He was hoping to see Jesus perform some sign. [9] Herod questioned Jesus at length, but Jesus didn't respond to him. [10] The chief priests and the legal experts were there, fiercely accusing Jesus. [11] Herod and his soldiers treated Jesus with contempt. Herod mocked him by dressing Jesus in elegant clothes and sent him back to Pilate. [12] Pilate and Herod became friends with each other that day. Before this, they had been enemies.

Jesus and Barabbas

[13] Then Pilate called together the chief priests, the rulers, and the people. [14] He said to them, "You brought this man before me as one who was misleading the people. I have questioned him in your presence and found nothing in this man's conduct that provides a legal basis for the charges you have brought against him. [15] Neither did Herod, because Herod returned him to us. He's done nothing that deserves death. [16] Therefore, I'll have him whipped, then let him go."[1]

[18] But with one voice they shouted, "Away with this man! Release Barabbas to us." ([19] Barabbas had been thrown into prison because of a riot that had occurred in the city, and for murder.) [20] Pilate addressed them again because he wanted to release Jesus. [21] They kept shouting out, "Crucify him! Crucify him!"

[22] For the third time, Pilate said to them, "Why? What wrong has he done? I've found no legal basis for the death penalty in his case. Therefore, I will have him whipped, then let him go." [23] But they were adamant, shouting their demand that Jesus be crucified. Their voices won out. [24] Pilate issued his decision to grant their request. [25] He released the one they asked for, who had been thrown into prison because of a riot and murder. But he handed Jesus over to their will.

On the way to the cross

[26] As they led Jesus away, they grabbed Simon, a man from Cyrene, who was coming in from the countryside. They put the cross on his back and made him carry it behind Jesus. [27] A huge crowd of people followed Jesus, including women, who were mourning and wailing for him. [28] Jesus turned to the women and said, "Daughters of Jerusalem, don't cry for me. Rather, cry for yourselves and your children. [29] The time will come when they will say, 'Happy are those who are unable to become pregnant, the wombs that

---

[1] Critical editions of the Gk New Testament do not include 23:17 *He had to release one prisoner for them because of the festival.*

never gave birth, and the breasts that never nursed a child.' ³⁰Then *they will say to the mountains, 'Fall on us,' and to the hills, 'Cover us.'*[m] ³¹If they do these things when the tree is green, what will happen when it is dry?"

Jesus on the cross

³²They also led two other criminals to be executed with Jesus. ³³When they arrived at the place called The Skull, they crucified him, along with the criminals, one on his right and the other on his left. ³⁴Jesus said, "Father, forgive them, for they don't know what they're doing." They drew lots as a way of dividing up his clothing.

³⁵The people were standing around watching, but the leaders sneered at him, saying, "He saved others. Let him save himself if he really is the Christ sent from God, the chosen one."

³⁶The soldiers also mocked him. They came up to him, offering him sour wine ³⁷and saying, "If you really are the king of the Jews, save yourself." ³⁸Above his head was a notice of the formal charge against him. It read "This is the king of the Jews."

³⁹One of the criminals hanging next to Jesus insulted him: "Aren't you the Christ? Save yourself and us!"

⁴⁰Responding, the other criminal spoke harshly to him, "Don't you fear God, seeing that you're also been sentenced to die? ⁴¹We are rightly condemned, for we are receiving the appropriate sentence for what we did. But this man has done nothing wrong." ⁴²Then he said, "Jesus, remember me when you come into your kingdom."

⁴³Jesus replied, "I assure you that today you will be with me in paradise."

Jesus' death

⁴⁴It was now about noon, and darkness covered the whole earth until about three o'clock, ⁴⁵while the sun stopped shining. Then the curtain in the sanctuary tore down the middle. ⁴⁶Crying out in a loud voice, Jesus said, "Father, *into your hands I entrust my life.*"[n] After he said this, he breathed for the last time.

⁴⁷When the centurion saw what happened, he praised God, saying, "It's really true: this man was righteous." ⁴⁸All the crowds who had come together to see this event returned to their homes beating their chests after seeing what had happened. ⁴⁹And everyone who knew him, including the women who had followed him from Galilee, stood at a distance observing these things.

Jesus' burial

⁵⁰Now there was a man named Joseph who was a member of the council. He was a good and righteous man. ⁵¹He hadn't agreed with the plan and actions of the council. He was from the Jewish city of Arimathea and eagerly anticipated God's kingdom. ⁵²This man went to Pilate and asked for Jesus' body. ⁵³Taking it down, he wrapped it in a linen cloth and laid it in a tomb carved out of the rock, in which no one had ever been buried. ⁵⁴It was the Preparation Day for the Sabbath, and the Sabbath was quickly approaching. ⁵⁵The women who had come with Jesus from Galilee followed Joseph. They saw the tomb and how Jesus' body was laid in it, ⁵⁶then they went away and prepared fragrant spices and perfumed oils. They rested on the Sabbath, in keeping with the commandment.

[m]Hos 10:8 [n]Ps 31:5

The empty tomb

24 Very early in the morning on the first day of the week, the women went to the tomb, bringing the fragrant spices they had prepared. [2]They found the stone rolled away from the tomb, [3]but when they went in, they didn't find the body of the Lord Jesus. [4]They didn't know what to make of this. Suddenly, two men were standing beside them in gleaming bright clothing. [5]The women were frightened and bowed their faces toward the ground, but the men said to them, "Why do you look for the living among the dead? [6]He isn't here, but has been raised. Remember what he told you while he was still in Galilee, [7]that the Human One[o] must be handed over to sinners, be crucified, and on the third day rise again." [8]Then they remembered his words. [9]When they returned from the tomb, they reported all these things to the eleven and all the others. [10]It was Mary Magdalene, Joanna, Mary the mother of James, and the other women with them who told these things to the apostles. [11]Their words struck the apostles as nonsense, and they didn't believe the women. [12]But Peter ran to the tomb. When he bent over to look inside, he saw only the linen cloth. Then he returned home, wondering what had happened.

Encounter on the Emmaus road

[13]On that same day, two disciples were traveling to a village called Emmaus, about seven miles from Jerusalem. [14]They were talking to each other about everything that had happened. [15]While they were discussing these things, Jesus himself arrived and joined them on their journey. [16]They were prevented from recognizing him.

[17]He said to them, "What are you talking about as you walk along?" They stopped, their faces downcast.

[18]The one named Cleopas replied, "Are you the only visitor to Jerusalem who is unaware of the things that have taken place there over the last few days?"

[19]He said to them, "What things?"

They said to him, "The things about Jesus of Nazareth. Because of his powerful deeds and words, he was recognized by God and all the people as a prophet. [20]But our chief priests and our leaders handed him over to be sentenced to death, and they crucified him. [21]We had hoped he was the one who would redeem Israel. All these things happened three days ago. [22]But there's more: Some women from our group have left us stunned. They went to the tomb early this morning [23]and didn't find his body. They came to us saying that they had even seen a vision of angels who told them he is alive. [24]Some of those who were with us went to the tomb and found things just as the women said. They didn't see him."

[25]Then Jesus said to them, "You foolish people! Your dull minds keep you from believing all that the prophets talked about. [26]Wasn't it necessary for the Christ to suffer these things and then enter into his glory?" [27]Then he interpreted for them the things written about himself in all the scriptures, starting with Moses and going through all the Prophets.

[28]When they came to Emmaus, he acted as if he was going on ahead. [29]But they urged him, saying, "Stay with us.

[o]Or Son of Man

It's nearly evening, and the day is almost over." So he went in to stay with them. [30]After he took his seat at the table with them, he took the bread, blessed and broke it, and gave it to them. [31]Their eyes were opened and they recognized him, but he disappeared from their sight. [32]They said to each other, "Weren't our hearts on fire when he spoke to us along the road and when he explained the scriptures for us?"

[33]They got up right then and returned to Jerusalem. They found the eleven and their companions gathered together. [34]They were saying to each other, "The Lord really has risen! He appeared to Simon!" [35]Then the two disciples described what had happened along the road and how Jesus was made known to them as he broke the bread.

Jesus appears to the disciples

[36]While they were saying these things, Jesus himself stood among them and said, "Peace be with you!" [37]They were terrified and afraid. They thought they were seeing a ghost.

[38]He said to them, "Why are you startled? Why are doubts arising in your hearts? [39]Look at my hands and my feet. It's really me! Touch me and see, for a ghost doesn't have flesh and bones like you see I have." [40]As he said this, he showed them his hands and feet.

[41]Because they were wondering and questioning in the midst of their happiness, he said to them, "Do you have anything to eat?" [42]They gave him a piece of baked fish. [43]Taking it, he ate it in front of them.

[44]Jesus said to them, "These are my words that I spoke to you while I was still with you—that everything written about me in the Law from Moses, the Prophets, and the Psalms must be fulfilled." [45]Then he opened their minds to understand the scriptures. [46]He said to them, "This is what is written: the Christ will suffer and rise from the dead on the third day, [47]and a change of heart and life for the forgiveness of sins must be preached in his name to all nations, beginning from Jerusalem. [48]You are witnesses of these things. [49]Look, I'm sending to you what my Father promised, but you are to stay in the city until you have been furnished with heavenly power."

Ascension of Jesus

[50]He led them out as far as Bethany, where he lifted his hands and blessed them. [51]As he blessed them, he left them and was taken up to heaven. [52]They worshipped him and returned to Jerusalem overwhelmed with joy. [53]And they were continuously in the temple praising God.

JOHN

Story of the Word

1 In the beginning was the Word
   and the Word was with God
   and the Word was God.

2 The Word was with God
   in the beginning.

3 Everything came into being
   through the Word,
   and without the Word
   nothing came into being.

What came into being
4 through the Word was life,[a]
   and the life was the light
   for all people.

5 The light shines in the darkness,
   and the darkness
   doesn't extinguish the light.

6 A man named John was sent from God. 7 He came as a witness to testify concerning the light, so that through him everyone would believe in the light. 8 He himself wasn't the light, but his mission was to testify concerning the light.

9 The true light that shines
   on all people
   was coming into the world.

10 The light was in the world,
   and the world came into being
   through the light,
   but the world didn't recognize
   the light.

11 The light came to his own people,
   and his own people
   didn't welcome him.

12 But those who did welcome him,
   those who believed
   in his name,
   he authorized to become
   God's children,

13 born not from blood
   nor from human desire
   or passion,
   but born from God.

14 The Word became flesh
   and made his home among us.
   We have seen his glory,
   glory like that of a father's
   only son,
   full of grace and truth.

15 John testified about him, crying out, "This is the one of whom I said, 'He who comes after me is greater than me because he existed before me.'"

16 From his fullness we have
   all received grace upon grace;

17 as the Law was given
   through Moses,
   so grace and truth came into being
   through Jesus Christ.

18 No one has ever seen God.
   God the only Son,
   who is at the Father's side,
   has made God known.

John's witness

19 This is John's testimony when the Jewish leaders in Jerusalem sent priests and Levites to ask him, "Who are you?"

20 John confessed (he didn't deny but confessed), "I'm not the Christ."

21 They asked him, "Then who are you? Are you Elijah?"

John said, "I'm not."

"Are you the prophet?"

[a]Or *Everything came into being through the Word, /and without the Word / nothing came into being that came into being. In the Word was life*

John answered, "No."

²²They asked, "Who are you? We need to give an answer to those who sent us. What do you say about yourself?"

²³John replied,

*"I am a voice crying out in the
    wilderness,
Make the Lord's path straight,*[b]
    just as the prophet Isaiah said."

²⁴Those sent by the Pharisees ²⁵asked, "Why do you baptize if you aren't the Christ, nor Elijah, nor the prophet?"

²⁶John answered, "I baptize with water. Someone greater stands among you, whom you don't recognize. ²⁷He comes after me, but I'm not worthy to untie his sandal straps." ²⁸This encounter took place across the Jordan in Bethany where John was baptizing.

²⁹The next day John saw Jesus coming toward him and said, "Look! The Lamb of God who takes away the sin of the world! ³⁰This is the one about whom I said, 'He who comes after me is really greater than me because he existed before me.' ³¹Even I didn't recognize him, but I came baptizing with water so that he might be made known to Israel." ³²John testified, "I saw the Spirit coming down from heaven like a dove, and it rested on him. ³³Even I didn't recognize him, but the one who sent me to baptize with water said to me, 'The one on whom you see the Spirit coming down and resting is the one who baptizes with the Holy Spirit.' ³⁴I have seen and testified that this one is God's Son."

Jesus calls disciples

³⁵The next day John was standing again with two of his disciples. ³⁶When he saw Jesus walking along he said, "Look! The Lamb of God!" ³⁷The two disciples heard what he said, and they followed Jesus.

³⁸When Jesus turned and saw them following, he asked, "What are you looking for?"

They said, "Rabbi (which is translated *Teacher*), where are you staying?"

³⁹He replied, "Come and see." So they went and saw where he was staying, and they remained with him that day. It was about four o'clock in the afternoon.

⁴⁰One of the two disciples who heard what John said and followed Jesus was Andrew, the brother of Simon Peter. ⁴¹He first found his own brother Simon and said to him, "We have found the Messiah" (which is translated *Christ*[c]). ⁴²He led him to Jesus.

Jesus looked at him and said, "You are Simon, son of John. You will be called Cephas" (which is translated *Peter*).

⁴³The next day Jesus wanted to go into Galilee, and he found Philip. Jesus said to him, "Follow me." ⁴⁴Philip was from Bethsaida, the hometown of Andrew and Peter.

⁴⁵Philip found Nathanael and said to him, "We have found the one Moses wrote about in the Law and the Prophets: Jesus, Joseph's son, from Nazareth."

⁴⁶Nathanael responded, "Can anything from Nazareth be good?"

Philip said, "Come and see."

⁴⁷Jesus saw Nathanael coming toward him and said about him, "Here is a genuine Israelite in whom there is no deceit."

⁴⁸Nathanael asked him, "How do you know me?"

[b]Isa 40:3   [c]Or Anointed One

Jesus answered, "Before Philip called you, I saw you under the fig tree."

[49] Nathanael replied, "Rabbi, you are God's Son. You are the king of Israel."

[50] Jesus answered, "Do you believe because I told you that I saw you under the fig tree? You will see greater things than these! [51] I assure you that you will see heaven open and God's angels going up to heaven and down to earth on the Human One."[d]

Wedding at Cana

2 On the third day there was a wedding in Cana of Galilee. Jesus' mother was there, and [2] Jesus and his disciples were also invited to the celebration. [3] When the wine ran out, Jesus' mother said to him, "They don't have any wine."

[4] Jesus replied, "Woman, what does that have to do with me? My time hasn't come yet."

[5] His mother told the servants, "Do whatever he tells you." [6] Nearby were six stone water jars used for the Jewish cleansing ritual, each able to hold about twenty or thirty gallons.

[7] Jesus said to the servants, "Fill the jars with water," and they filled them to the brim. [8] Then he told them, "Now draw some from them and take it to the headwaiter," and they did. [9] The headwaiter tasted the water that had become wine. He didn't know where it came from, though the servants who had drawn the water knew.

The headwaiter called the groom [10] and said, "Everyone serves the good wine first. They bring out the second-rate wine only when the guests are drinking freely. You kept the good wine until now." [11] This was the first miraculous sign that Jesus did in Cana of Galilee. He revealed his glory, and his disciples believed in him.

[12] After this, Jesus and his mother, his brothers, and his disciples went down to Capernaum and stayed there for a few days.

Jesus in Jerusalem at Passover

[13] It was nearly time for the Jewish Passover, and Jesus went up to Jerusalem. [14] He found in the temple those who were selling cattle, sheep, and doves, as well as those involved in exchanging currency sitting there. [15] He made a whip from ropes and chased them all out of the temple, including the cattle and the sheep. He scattered the coins and overturned the tables of those who exchanged currency. [16] He said to the dove sellers, "Get these things out of here! Don't make my Father's house a place of business." [17] His disciples remembered that it is written, *Passion for your house consumes me.*[e]

[18] Then the Jewish leaders asked him, "By what authority are you doing these things? What miraculous sign will you show us?"

[19] Jesus answered, "Destroy this temple and in three days I'll raise it up."

[20] The Jewish leaders replied, "It took forty-six years to build this temple, and you will raise it up in three days?" [21] But the temple Jesus was talking about was his body. [22] After he was raised from the dead, his disciples remembered what he had said, and they believed the scripture and the word that Jesus had spoken.

[23] While Jesus was in Jerusalem for the Passover Festival, many believed

[d] Or Son of Man [e] Ps 69:9

in his name because they saw the miraculous signs that he did. ²⁴But Jesus didn't trust himself to them because he knew all people. ²⁵He didn't need anyone to tell him about human nature, for he knew what human nature was.

Jesus and Nicodemus

3 There was a Pharisee named Nicodemus, a Jewish leader. ²He came to Jesus at night and said to him, "Rabbi, we know that you are a teacher who has come from God, for no one could do these miraculous signs that you do unless God is with him."

³Jesus answered, "I assure you, unless someone is born anew,ᶠ it's not possible to see God's kingdom."

⁴Nicodemus asked, "How is it possible for an adult to be born? It's impossible to enter the mother's womb for a second time and be born, is it?"

⁵Jesus answered, "I assure you, unless someone is born of water and the Spirit, it's not possible to enter God's kingdom. ⁶Whatever is born of the flesh is flesh, and whatever is born of the Spirit is spirit. ⁷Don't be surprised that I said to you, 'You must be born anew.' ⁸God's Spiritᵍ blows wherever it wishes. You hear its sound, but you don't know where it comes from or where it is going. It's the same with everyone who is born of the Spirit."

⁹Nicodemus said, "How are these things possible?"

¹⁰"Jesus answered, "You are a teacher of Israel and you don't know these things? ¹¹I assure you that we speak about what we know and testify about what we have seen, but you don't receive our testimony. ¹²If I have

told you about earthly things and you don't believe, how will you believe if I tell you about heavenly things? ¹³No one has gone up to heaven except the one who came down from heaven, the Human One.ʰ ¹⁴Just as Moses lifted up the snake in the wilderness, so must the Human One be lifted up ¹⁵so that everyone who believes in him will have eternal life. ¹⁶God so loved the world that he gave his only Son, so that everyone who believes in him won't perish but will have eternal life. ¹⁷God didn't send his Son into the world to judge the world, but that the world might be saved through him. ¹⁸Whoever believes in him isn't judged; whoever doesn't believe in him is already judged, because they don't believe in the name of God's only Son.

¹⁹"This is the basis for judgment: The light came into the world, and people loved darkness more than the light, for their actions are evil. ²⁰All who do wicked things hate the light and don't come to the light for fear that their actions will be exposed to the light. ²¹Whoever does the truth comes to the light so that it can be seen that their actions were done in God."

John's final witness

²²After this Jesus and his disciples went into Judea, where he spent some time with them and was baptizing. ²³John was baptizing at Aenon near Salem because there was a lot of water there, and people were coming to him and being baptized. (²⁴John hadn't yet been thrown into prison.)

²⁵A debate started between John's disciples and a certain Jew about

ᶠOr *from above* ᵍOr *wind* ʰOr *Son of Man* ⁱOr *Son of Man* cleansing rituals. ²⁶They came to John and said, "Rabbi, look! The man who was with you across the Jordan, the one about whom you testified, is baptizing and everyone is flocking to him."

²⁷John replied, "No one can receive anything unless it is given from heaven. ²⁸You yourselves can testify that I said that I'm not the Christ but that I'm the one sent before him. ²⁹The groom is the one who is getting married. The friend of the groom stands close by and, when he hears him, is overjoyed at the groom's voice. Therefore, my joy is now complete. ³⁰He must increase and I must decrease. ³¹The one who comes from above is above all things. The one who is from the earth belongs to the earth and speaks as one from the earth. The one who comes from heaven is above all things. ³²He testifies to what he has seen and heard, but no one accepts his testimony. ³³Whoever accepts his testimony confirms that God is true. ³⁴The one whom God sent speaks God's words because God gives the Spirit generously. ³⁵The Father loves the Son and gives everything into his hands. ³⁶Whoever believes in the Son has eternal life. Whoever doesn't believe in the Son won't see life, but the angry judgment of God remains on them."

Jesus leaves Judea

4 Jesus learned that the Pharisees had heard that he was making more disciples and baptizing more than John (²although Jesus' disciples were baptizing, not Jesus himself). ³Therefore, he left Judea and went back to Galilee.

Jesus in Samaria

⁴Jesus had to go through Samaria. ⁵He came to a Samaritan city called Sychar, which was near the land Jacob had given to his son Joseph. ⁶Jacob's well was there. Jesus was tired from his journey, so he sat down at the well. It was about noon.

⁷A Samaritan woman came to the well to draw water. Jesus said to her, "Give me some water to drink." ⁸His disciples had gone into the city to buy him some food.

⁹The Samaritan woman asked, "Why do you, a Jewish man, ask for something to drink from me, a Samaritan woman?" (Jews and Samaritans didn't associate with each other.)

¹⁰Jesus responded, "If you recognized God's gift and who is saying to you, 'Give me some water to drink,' you would be asking him and he would give you living water."

¹¹The woman said to him, "Sir, you don't have a bucket and the well is deep. Where would you get this living water? ¹²You aren't greater than our father Jacob, are you? He gave this well to us, and he drank from it himself, as did his sons and his livestock."

¹³Jesus answered, "Everyone who drinks this water will be thirsty again, ¹⁴but whoever drinks from the water that I will give will never be thirsty again. The water that I give will become in those who drink it a spring of water that bubbles up into eternal life."

¹⁵The woman said to him, "Sir, give me this water, so that I will never be thirsty and will never need to come here to draw water!"

¹⁶Jesus said to her, "Go, get your husband, and come back here."

¹⁷The woman replied, "I don't have a husband."

"You are right to say, 'I don't have a husband,'" Jesus answered. ¹⁸"You've had five husbands, and the man you are with now isn't your husband. You've spoken the truth."

¹⁹The woman said, "Sir, I see that you are a prophet. ²⁰Our ancestors worshipped on this mountain, but you and your people say that it is necessary to worship in Jerusalem."

²¹Jesus said to her, "Believe me, woman, the time is coming when you and your people will worship the Father neither on this mountain nor in Jerusalem. ²²You and your people worship what you don't know; we worship what we know because salvation is from the Jews. ²³But the time is coming—and is here!—when true worshippers will worship in spirit and truth. The Father looks for those who worship him this way. ²⁴God is spirit, and it is necessary to worship God in spirit and truth."

²⁵The woman said, "I know that the Messiah is coming, the one who is called the Christ. When he comes, he will teach everything to us."

²⁶Jesus said to her, "I Am—the one who speaks with you."ʲ

²⁷Just then, Jesus' disciples arrived and were shocked that he was talking with a woman. But no one asked, "What do you want?" or "Why are you talking with her?" ²⁸The woman put down her water jar and went into the city. She said to the people, ²⁹"Come and see a man who has told me everything I've done! Could this man be the Christ?" ³⁰They left the city and were on their way to see Jesus.

³¹In the meantime the disciples spoke to Jesus, saying, "Rabbi, eat."

³²Jesus said to them, "I have food to eat that you don't know about."

³³The disciples asked each other, "Has someone brought him food?"

³⁴Jesus said to them, "I am fed by doing the will of the one who sent me and by completing his work. ³⁵Don't you have a saying, 'Four more months and then it's time for harvest'? Look, I tell you: open your eyes and notice that the fields are already ripe for the harvest. ³⁶Those who harvest are receiving their pay and gathering fruit for eternal life so that those who sow and those who harvest can celebrate together. ³⁷This is a true saying, that one sows and another harvests. ³⁸I have sent you to harvest what you didn't work hard for; others worked hard, and you will share in their hard work."

³⁹Many Samaritans in that city believed in Jesus because of the woman's word when she testified, "He told me everything I've ever done." ⁴⁰So when the Samaritans came to Jesus, they asked him to stay with them, and he stayed there two days. ⁴¹Many more believed because of his word, ⁴²and they said to the woman, "We no longer believe because of what you said, for we have heard for ourselves and know that this one is truly the savior of the world."

Jesus arrives in Galilee

⁴³After two days Jesus left for Galilee. (⁴⁴Jesus himself had testified that prophets have no honor in their own country.) ⁴⁵When he came to Galilee, the Galileans welcomed him because they had seen all the things he had done in Jerusalem during the festival, for they also had been at the festival.

ʲOr It is I, the one who speaks with you.

Jesus' second miraculous sign in Galilee

[46] He returned to Cana in Galilee where he had turned the water into wine. In Capernaum there was a certain royal official whose son was sick. [47] When he heard that Jesus was coming from Judea to Galilee, he went out to meet him and asked Jesus if he would come and heal his son, for his son was about to die. [48] Jesus said to him, "Unless you see miraculous signs and wonders, you won't believe."

[49] The royal official said to him, "Lord, come before my son dies."

[50] Jesus replied, "Go home. Your son lives." The man believed the word that Jesus spoke to him and set out for his home.

[51] While he was on his way, his servants were already coming to meet him. They said, "Your son lives!" [52] So he asked them at what time his son had started to get better. And they said, "The fever left him yesterday at about one o'clock in the afternoon." [53] Then the father realized that this was the hour when Jesus had said to him, "Your son lives." And he and his entire household believed in Jesus. [54] This was the second miraculous sign Jesus did while going from Judea to Galilee.

Sabbath healing

5 After this there was a Jewish festival, and Jesus went up to Jerusalem. [2] In Jerusalem near the Sheep Gate in the north city wall is a pool with the Aramaic name Bethsaida. It had five covered porches, [3] and a crowd of people who were sick, blind, lame, and paralyzed sat there.[k] [5] A certain man was there who had been sick for thirty-eight years. [6] When Jesus saw him lying there, knowing that he had already been there a long time, he asked him, "Do you want to get well?"

[7] The sick man answered him, "Sir,[l] I don't have anyone who can put me in the water when it is stirred up. When I'm trying to get to it, someone else has gotten in ahead of me."

[8] Jesus said to him, "Get up! Pick up your mat and walk." [9] Immediately the man was well, and he picked up his mat and walked. Now that day was the Sabbath.

[10] The Jewish leaders said to the man who had been healed, "It's the Sabbath; you aren't allowed to carry your mat."

[11] He answered, "The man who made me well said to me, 'Pick up your mat and walk.'"

[12] They inquired, "Who is this man who said to you, 'Pick it up and walk'?" [13] The man who had been cured didn't know who it was, because Jesus had slipped away from the crowd gathered there.

[14] Later Jesus found him in the temple and said, "See! You have been made well. Don't sin anymore in case something worse happens to you." [15] The man went and proclaimed to the Jewish leaders that Jesus was the man who had made him well.

[16] As a result, the Jewish leaders were harassing Jesus, since he had done these things on the Sabbath. [17] Jesus replied, "My Father is still working,

---

[k] Critical editions of the Gk New Testament do not include the following addition *waiting for the water to move.* [4] *Sometimes an angel would come down to the pool and stir up the water. Then the first one going into the water after it had been stirred up was cured of any sickness.* [l] Or *Lord*

and I am working too." [18]For this reason the Jewish leaders wanted even more to kill him—not only because he was doing away with the Sabbath but also because he called God his own Father, thereby making himself equal with God.

Work of the Father and the Son

[19]Jesus responded to the Jewish leaders, "I assure you that the Son can't do anything by himself except what he sees the Father doing. Whatever the Father does, the Son does likewise. [20]The Father loves the Son and shows him everything that he does. He will show him greater works than these so that you will marvel. [21]As the Father raises the dead and gives life, so too does the Son give life to whomever he wishes. [22]The Father doesn't judge anyone, but he has given all judgment to the Son [23]so that everyone will honor the Son just as they honor the Father. Whoever doesn't honor the Son doesn't honor the Father who sent him.

[24]"I assure you that whoever hears my word and believes in the one who sent me has eternal life and won't come under judgment but has passed from death into life.

[25]"I assure you that the time is coming—and is here!—when the dead will hear the voice of God's Son, and those who hear it will live. [26]Just as the Father has life in himself, so he has granted the Son to have life in himself. [27]He gives the Son authority to judge, because he is the Human One.[m] [28]Don't be surprised by this, because the time is coming when all who are in their graves will hear his voice. [29]Those who

did good things will come out into the resurrection of life, and those who did wicked things into the resurrection of judgment. [30]I can't do anything by myself. Whatever I hear, I judge, and my judgment is just. I don't seek my own will but the will of the one who sent me.

Witnesses to Jesus

[31]"If I testify about myself, my testimony isn't true. [32]There is someone else who testifies about me, and I know his testimony about me is true. [33]You sent a delegation to John, and he testified to the truth. [34]Although I don't accept human testimony, I say these things so that you can be saved. [35]John was a burning and shining lamp, and, at least for a while, you were willing to celebrate in his light.

[36]"I have a witness greater than John's testimony. The Father has given me works to do so that I might complete them. These works I do testify about me that the Father sent me. [37]And the Father who sent me testifies about me. You have never even heard his voice or seen his form, [38]and you don't have his word dwelling with you because you don't believe the one whom he has sent. [39]Examine the scriptures, since you think that in them you have eternal life. They also testify about me, [40]yet you don't want to come to me so that you can have life.

[41]"I don't accept praise from people, [42]but I know you, that you don't have God's love in you. [43]I have come in my Father's name, and you don't receive me. If others come in their own name, you receive them. [44]How can you believe when you receive praise from each

[m]Or Son of Man

other but don't seek the praise that comes from the only God?

⁴⁵"Don't think that I will accuse you before the Father. Your accuser is Moses, the one in whom your hope rests. ⁴⁶If you believed Moses, you would believe me, because Moses wrote about me. ⁴⁷If you don't believe the writings of Moses, how will you believe my words?"

Feeding of the five thousand

6 After this Jesus went across the Galilee Sea (that is, the Tiberias Sea). ²A large crowd followed him, because they had seen the miraculous signs he had done among the sick. ³Jesus went up a mountain and sat there with his disciples. ⁴It was nearly time for Passover, the Jewish festival.

⁵Jesus looked up and saw the large crowd coming toward him. He asked Philip, "Where will we buy food to feed these people?" ⁶Jesus said this to test him, for he already knew what he was going to do.

⁷Philip replied, "More than a half year's salary[n] worth of food wouldn't be enough for each person to have even a little bit."

⁸One of his disciples, Andrew, Simon Peter's brother, said, ⁹"A youth here has five barley loaves and two fish. But what good is that for a crowd like this?"

¹⁰Jesus said, "Have the people sit down." There was plenty of grass there. They sat down, about five thousand of them. ¹¹Then Jesus took the bread. When he had given thanks, he distributed it to those who were sitting there. He did the same with the fish, each getting as much as they wanted. ¹²When they had plenty to eat, he said to his disciples, "Gather up the leftover pieces, so that nothing will be wasted." ¹³So they gathered them and filled twelve baskets with the pieces of the five barley loaves that had been left over by those who had eaten.

¹⁴When the people saw that he had done a miraculous sign, they said, "This is truly the prophet who is coming into the world." ¹⁵Jesus understood that they were about to come and force him to be their king, so he took refuge again, alone on a mountain.

Jesus walks on water

¹⁶When evening came, Jesus' disciples went down to the lake. ¹⁷They got into a boat and were crossing the lake to Capernaum. It was already getting dark and Jesus hadn't come to them yet. ¹⁸The water was getting rough because a strong wind was blowing. ¹⁹When the wind had driven them out for about three or four miles, they saw Jesus walking on the water. He was approaching the boat and they were afraid. ²⁰He said to them, "I AM.[o] Don't be afraid." ²¹Then they wanted to take him into the boat, and just then the boat reached the land where they had been heading.

²²The next day the crowd that remained on the other side of the lake realized that only one boat had been there. They knew Jesus hadn't gone with his disciples, but that the disciples had gone alone. ²³Some boats came from Tiberias, near the place where they had eaten the bread over which the Lord had given thanks. ²⁴When the crowd saw that neither Jesus nor his disciples were there, they got into the

---

[n]Or two hundred denaria   [o]Or It is I.

boats and came to Capernaum looking for Jesus. ²⁵When they found him on the other side of the lake, they asked him, "Rabbi, when did you get here?"

Bread of life

²⁶Jesus replied, "I assure you that you are looking for me not because you saw miraculous signs but because you ate all the food you wanted. ²⁷Don't work for the food that doesn't last but for the food that endures for eternal life, which the Human One[p] will give you. God the Father has confirmed him as his agent to give life."

²⁸They asked, "What must we do in order to accomplish what God requires?"

²⁹Jesus replied, "This is what God requires, that you believe in him whom God sent."

³⁰They asked, "What miraculous sign will you do, that we can see and believe you? What will you do? ³¹Our ancestors ate manna in the wilderness, just as it is written, *He gave them bread from heaven to eat.*[q]

³²Jesus told them, "I assure you, it wasn't Moses who gave the bread from heaven to you, but my Father gives you the true bread from heaven. ³³The bread of God is the one who comes down from heaven and gives life to the world."

³⁴They said, "Sir,[r] give us this bread all the time!"

³⁵Jesus replied, "I am the bread of life. Whoever comes to me will never go hungry, and whoever believes in me will never be thirsty. ³⁶But I told you that you have seen me and still don't believe. ³⁷Everyone whom the Father gives to me will come to me, and I won't send away anyone who comes to me. ³⁸I have

come down from heaven not to do my will, but the will of him who sent me. ³⁹This is the will of the one who sent me, that I won't lose anything he has given me, but I will raise it up at the last day. ⁴⁰This is my Father's will: that all who see the Son and believe in him will have eternal life, and I will raise them up at the last day."

⁴¹The Jewish opposition grumbled about him because he said, "I am the bread that came down from heaven."

⁴²They asked, "Isn't this Jesus, Joseph's son, whose mother and father we know? How can he now say, 'I have come down from heaven'?"

⁴³Jesus responded, "Don't grumble among yourselves. ⁴⁴No one can come to me unless they are drawn to me by the Father who sent me, and I will raise them up at the last day. ⁴⁵It is written in the Prophets, And they *will all be taught by God.*[s] Everyone who has listened to the Father and learned from him comes to me. ⁴⁶No one has seen the Father except the one who is from God. He has seen the Father. ⁴⁷I assure you, whoever believes has eternal life. ⁴⁸I am the bread of life. ⁴⁹Your ancestors ate manna in the wilderness and they died. ⁵⁰This is the bread that comes down from heaven so that whoever eats from it will never die. ⁵¹I am the living bread that came down from heaven. Whoever eats this bread will live forever, and the bread that I will give for the life of the world is my flesh."

⁵²Then the Jews debated among themselves, asking, "How can this man give us his flesh to eat?"

⁵³Jesus said to them, "I assure you, unless you eat the flesh of the Human

---

ᴾOr *Son of Man* ��q Ps 78:24 ʳOr *Lord* ˢIsa 54:13

One[t] and drink his blood, you have no life in you. ⁵⁴Whoever eats my flesh and drinks my blood has eternal life, and I will raise them up at the last day. ⁵⁵My flesh is true food and my blood is true drink. ⁵⁶Whoever eats my flesh and drinks my blood remains in me and I in them. ⁵⁷As the living Father sent me, and I live because of the Father, so whoever eats me lives because of me. ⁵⁸This is the bread that came down from heaven. It isn't like the bread your ancestors ate, and then they died. Whoever eats this bread will live forever." ⁵⁹Jesus said these things while he was teaching in the synagogue in Capernaum.

⁶⁰Many of his disciples who heard this said, "This message is harsh. Who can hear it?"

⁶¹Jesus knew that the disciples were grumbling about this and he said to them, "Does this offend you? ⁶²What if you were to see the Human One[u] going up where he was before? ⁶³The Spirit is the one who gives life and the flesh doesn't help at all. The words I have spoken to you are spirit and life. ⁶⁴Yet some of you don't believe." Jesus knew from the beginning who wouldn't believe and the one who would betray him. ⁶⁵He said, "For this reason I said to you that none can come to me unless the Father enables them to do so." ⁶⁶At this, many of his disciples turned away and no longer accompanied him.

⁶⁷Jesus asked the Twelve, "Do you also want to leave?"

⁶⁸Simon Peter answered, "Lord, where would we go? You have the words of eternal life. ⁶⁹We believe and know that you are God's holy one."

⁷⁰Jesus replied, "Didn't I choose you twelve? Yet one of you is a devil." ⁷¹He was speaking of Judas, Simon Iscariot's son, for he, one of the Twelve, was going to betray him.

Jesus goes to Jerusalem

7After this Jesus traveled throughout Galilee. He didn't want to travel in Judea, because the Jewish authorities wanted to kill him. ²When it was almost time for the Jewish Festival of Booths, ³Jesus' brothers said to him, "Leave Galilee. Go to Judea so that your disciples can see the amazing works that you do. ⁴Those who want to be known publicly don't do things secretly. Since you can do these things, show yourself to the world." ⁵His brothers said this because even they didn't believe in him.

⁶Jesus replied, "For you, anytime is fine. But my time hasn't come yet. ⁷The world can't hate you. It hates me, though, because I testify that its works are evil. ⁸You go up to the festival. I'm not going to this one because my time hasn't yet come." ⁹Having said this, he stayed in Galilee. ¹⁰However, after his brothers left for the festival, he went too—not openly but in secret.

¹¹The Jewish leaders were looking for Jesus at the festival. They kept asking, "Where is he?" ¹²The crowds were murmuring about him. "He's a good man," some said, but others were saying, "No, he tricks the people." ¹³No one spoke about him publicly, though, for fear of the Jewish authorities.

Jesus teaches in the temple

¹⁴Halfway through the festival, Jesus went up to the temple and started to

---

⁴⁰When some in the crowd heard these words, they said, "This man is truly the prophet." ⁴¹Others said, "He's the Christ." But others said, "The Christ can't come from Galilee, can he? ⁴²Didn't the scripture say that the Christ comes from David's family and from Bethlehem, David's village?" ⁴³So the crowd was divided over Jesus. ⁴⁴Some wanted to arrest him, but no one grabbed him.

⁴⁵The guards returned to the chief priests and Pharisees, who asked, "Why didn't you bring him?"

⁴⁶The guards answered, "No one has ever spoken the way he does."

⁴⁷The Pharisees replied, "Have you too been deceived? ⁴⁸Have any of the leaders believed in him? Has any Pharisee? ⁴⁹No, only this crowd, which doesn't know the Law. And they are under God's curse!"

⁵⁰Nicodemus, who was one of them and had come to Jesus earlier, said, ⁵¹"Our Law doesn't judge someone without first hearing him and learning what he is doing, does it?"

⁵²They answered him, "You are not from Galilee too, are you? Look it up and you will see that the prophet doesn't come from Galilee."

Pharisees test Jesus

⁵³They each went to their own homes, ¹and Jesus went to the Mount of Olives. ²Early in the morning he returned to the temple. All the people gathered around him, and he sat down and taught them. ³The legal experts and Pharisees brought a woman caught in adultery. Placing her in the center of the group, ⁴they said to Jesus, "Teacher, this woman was caught in the act of committing adultery. ⁵In the Law, Moses commanded us to stone women like this. What do you say?" ⁶They said this to test him, because they wanted a reason to bring an accusation against him. Jesus bent down and wrote on the ground with his finger.

⁷They continued to question him, so he stood up and replied, "Whoever hasn't sinned should throw the first stone." ⁸Bending down again, he wrote on the ground. ⁹Those who heard him went away, one by one, beginning with the elders. Finally, only Jesus and the woman were left in the middle of the crowd. ¹⁰Jesus stood up and said to her, "Woman, where are they? Is there no one to condemn you?" ¹¹She said, "No one, sir."ʷ Jesus said, "Neither do I condemn you. Go, and from now on, don't sin anymore."ˣ

Jesus continues to teach in the temple

¹²Jesus spoke to the people again, saying, "I am the light of the world. Whoever follows me won't walk in darkness but will have the light of life."

¹³Then the Pharisees said to him, "Because you are testifying about yourself, your testimony isn't valid."

¹⁴Jesus replied, "Even if I testify

ʷOr *Lord* ˣCritical editions of the Gk New Testament do not contain 7:53–8:11.

about myself, my testimony is true, since I know where I came from and where I'm going. You don't know where I come from or where I'm going. [15]You judge according to human standards, but I judge no one. [16]Even if I do judge, my judgment is truthful, because I'm not alone. My judgments come from me and from the Father who sent me. [17]In your Law it is written that the witness of two people is true. [18]I am one witness concerning myself, and the Father who sent me is the other."

[19]They asked him, "Where is your Father?"

Jesus answered, "You don't know me and you don't know my Father. If you knew me, you would also know my Father." [20]He spoke these words while he was teaching in the temple area known as the treasury. No one arrested him, because his time hadn't yet come.

[21]Jesus continued, "I'm going away. You will look for me, and you will die in your sin. Where I'm going, you can't come."

[22]The Jewish leaders said, "He isn't going to kill himself, is he? Is that why he said, 'Where I'm going, you can't come'?"

[23]He said to them, "You are from below; I'm from above. You are from this world; I'm not from this world. [24]This is why I told you that you would die in your sins. If you don't believe that I Am, you will die in your sins."

[25]"Who are you?" they asked.

Jesus replied, "I'm exactly who I have claimed to be from the beginning. [26]I have many things to say in judgment concerning you. The one who sent me is true, and what I have heard from him

I tell the world." [27]They didn't know he was speaking about his Father. [28]So Jesus said to them, "When the Human One[y] is lifted up,[z] then you will know that I Am.[a] Then you will know that I do nothing on my own, but I say just what the Father has taught me. [29]He who sent me is with me. He doesn't leave me by myself, because I always do what makes him happy. [30]While Jesus was saying these things, many people came to believe in him.

Children of Abraham

[31]Jesus said to the Jews who believed in him, "You are truly my disciples if you remain faithful to my teaching. [32]Then you will know the truth, and the truth will set you free."

[33]They responded, "We are Abraham's children; we've never been anyone's slaves. How can you say that we will be set free?"

[34]Jesus answered, "I assure you that everyone who sins is a slave to sin. [35]A slave isn't a permanent member of the household, but a son is. [36]Therefore, if the Son makes you free, you really will be free. [37]I know that you are Abraham's children, yet you want to kill me because you don't welcome my teaching. [38]I'm telling you what I've seen when I am with the Father, but you are doing what you've heard from your father."

[39]They replied, "Our father is Abraham."

Jesus responded, "If you were Abraham's children, you would do Abraham's works. [40]Instead, you want to kill me, though I am the one who has spoken the truth I heard from God.

[y]Or Son of Man [z]Or exalted [a]Or that I am he

Abraham didn't do this. [41]You are doing your father's works."

They said, "Our ancestry isn't in question! The only Father we have is God!"

[42]Jesus replied, "If God were your Father, you would love me, for I came from God. Here I am. I haven't come on my own. God sent me. [43]Why don't you understand what I'm saying? It's because you can't really hear my words. [44]Your father is the devil. You are his children, and you want to do what your father wants. He was a murderer from the beginning. He has never stood for the truth, because there's no truth in him. Whenever that liar speaks, he speaks according to his own nature, because he's a liar and the father of liars. [45]Because I speak the truth, you don't believe me. [46]Who among you can show I'm guilty of sin? Since I speak the truth, why don't you believe me? [47]God's children listen to God's words. You don't listen to me because you aren't God's children."

[48]The Jewish opposition answered, "We were right to say that you are a Samaritan and have a demon, weren't we?"

[49]"I don't have a demon," Jesus replied. "But I honor my Father and you dishonor me. [50]I'm not trying to bring glory to myself. There's one who is seeking to glorify me, and he's the judge. [51]I assure you that whoever keeps my word will never die."

Abraham and Jesus

[52]The Jewish opposition said to Jesus, "Now we know that you have a demon. Abraham and the prophets died, yet you say, 'Whoever keeps my word will never die.' [53]Are you greater than our father Abraham? He died and the prophets died, so who do you make yourself out to be?"

[54]Jesus answered, "If I glorify myself, my glory is meaningless. My Father, who you say is your God, is the one who glorifies me. [55]You don't know him, but I do. If I said I didn't know him, I would be like you, a liar. But I do know him, and I keep his word. [56]Your father Abraham was overjoyed that he would see my day. He saw it and was happy."

[57]"You aren't even 50 years old!" the Jewish opposition replied. "How can you say that you have seen Abraham?"

[58]"I assure you," Jesus replied, "before Abraham was, I Am." [59]So they picked up stones to throw at him, but Jesus hid himself and left the temple.

Jesus heals a blind man

9 As Jesus walked along, he saw a man who was blind from birth. [2]Jesus' disciples asked, "Rabbi, who sinned so that he was born blind, this man or his parents?"

[3]Jesus answered, "Neither he nor his parents. This happened so that God's mighty works might be displayed in him. [4]While it's daytime, we must do the works of him who sent me. Night is coming when no one can work. [5]While I am in the world, I am the light of the world." [6]After he said this, he spit on the ground, made mud with the saliva, and smeared the mud on the man's eyes. [7]Jesus said to him, "Go, wash in the pool of Siloam" (this word means *sent*). So the man went away and washed. When he returned, he could see.

Disagreement about the healing

[8]The man's neighbors and those who used to see him when he was a beggar said, "Isn't this the man who used to sit and beg?"

⁹Some said, "It is," and others said, "No, it's someone who looks like him."

But the man said, "Yes, it's me!"

¹⁰So they asked him, "How are you now able to see?"

¹¹He answered, "The man they call Jesus made mud, smeared it on my eyes, and said, 'Go to the pool of Siloam and wash.' So I went and washed, and then I could see."

¹²They asked, "Where is this man?"

He replied, "I don't know."

¹³Then they led the man who had been born blind to the Pharisees. ¹⁴Now Jesus made the mud and smeared it on the man's eyes on a Sabbath day. ¹⁵So Pharisees also asked him how he was able to see.

The man told them, "He put mud on my eyes, I washed, and now I see."

¹⁶Some Pharisees said, "This man isn't from God, because he breaks the Sabbath law." Others said, "How can a sinner do miraculous signs like these?" So they were divided. ¹⁷Some of the Pharisees questioned the man who had been born blind again: "What do you have to say about him, since he healed your eyes?"

He replied, "He's a prophet."

Conflict over the healing

¹⁸The Jewish leaders didn't believe the man had been blind and received his sight until they called for his parents. ¹⁹The Jewish leaders asked them, "Is this your son? Are you saying he was born blind? How can he now see?"

²⁰His parents answered, "We know he is our son. We know he was born blind. ²¹But we don't know how he now sees, and we don't know who healed his eyes. Ask him. He's old enough to speak

for himself." ²²His parents said this because they feared the Jewish authorities. This is because the Jewish authorities had already decided that whoever confessed Jesus to be the Christ would be expelled from the synagogue. ²³That's why his parents said, "He's old enough. Ask him."

²⁴Therefore, they called a second time for the man who had been born blind and said to him, "Give glory to God. We know this man is a sinner."

²⁵The man answered, "I don't know whether he's a sinner. Here's what I do know: I was blind and now I see."

²⁶They questioned him: "What did he do to you? How did he heal your eyes?"

²⁷He replied, "I already told you, and you didn't listen. Why do you want to hear it again? Do you want to become his disciples too?"

²⁸They insulted him: "You are his disciple, but we are Moses' disciples. ²⁹We know that God spoke to Moses, but we don't know where this man is from."

³⁰The man answered, "This is incredible! You don't know where he is from, yet he healed my eyes! ³¹We know that God doesn't listen to sinners. God listens to anyone who is devout and does God's will. ³²No one has ever heard of a healing of the eyes of someone born blind. ³³If this man wasn't from God, he couldn't do this."

³⁴They responded, "You were born completely in sin! How is it that you dare to teach us?" Then they expelled him.

Jesus finds the man born blind

³⁵Jesus heard they had expelled the man born blind. Finding him, Jesus said, "Do you believe in the Human One?"[b]

ᵇOr *Son of Man*

³⁶He answered, "Who is he, sir?^c I want to believe in him."

³⁷Jesus said, "You have seen him. In fact, he is the one speaking with you."

³⁸The man said, "Lord,^d I believe." And he worshipped Jesus.

Jesus teaches the Pharisees

³⁹Jesus said, "I have come into the world to exercise judgment so that those who don't see can see and those who see will become blind."

⁴⁰Some Pharisees who were with him heard what he said and asked, "Surely we aren't blind, are we?"

⁴¹Jesus said to them, "If you were blind, you wouldn't have any sin, but now that you say, 'We see,' your sin remains.

10 I assure you that whoever doesn't enter into the sheep pen through the gate but climbs over the wall is a thief and an outlaw. ²The one who enters through the gate is the shepherd of the sheep. ³The guard at the gate opens the gate for him, and the sheep listen to his voice. He calls his own sheep by name and leads them out. ⁴Whenever he has gathered all of his sheep, he goes before them and they follow him, because they know his voice. ⁵They won't follow a stranger but will run away because they don't know the stranger's voice." ⁶Those who heard Jesus use this analogy didn't understand what he was saying.

I am the gate

⁷So Jesus spoke again, "I assure you that I am the gate of the sheep. ⁸All who came before me were thieves and outlaws, but the sheep didn't listen to them. ⁹I am the gate. Whoever enters through me will be saved. They will come in and go out and find pasture.

¹⁰The thief enters only to steal, kill, and destroy. I came so that they could have life—indeed, so that they could live life to the fullest.

I am the good shepherd

¹¹"I am the good shepherd. The good shepherd lays down his life for the sheep. ¹²When the hired hand sees the wolf coming, he leaves the sheep and runs away. That's because he isn't the shepherd; the sheep aren't really his. So the wolf attacks the sheep and scatters them. ¹³He's only a hired hand and the sheep don't matter to him.

¹⁴"I am the good shepherd. I know my own sheep and they know me, ¹⁵just as the Father knows me and I know the Father. I give up my life for the sheep. ¹⁶I have other sheep that don't belong to this sheep pen. I must lead them too. They will listen to my voice and there will be one flock, with one shepherd.

¹⁷"This is why the Father loves me: I give up my life so that I can take it up again. ¹⁸No one takes it from me, but I give it up because I want to. I have the right to give it up, and I have the right to take it up again. I received this commandment from my Father."

¹⁹There was another division among the Jews because of Jesus' words. ²⁰Many of them said, "He has a demon and has lost his mind. Why listen to him?" ²¹Others said, "These aren't the words of someone who has a demon. Can a demon heal the eyes of people who are blind?"

Jesus at the Festival of Dedication

²²The time came for the Festival of Dedication^e in Jerusalem. It was winter,

^cOr *Lord* ^dOr *Sir* ^eHanukkah

²³and Jesus was in the temple, walking in the covered porch named for Solomon. ²⁴The Jewish opposition circled around him and asked, "How long will you test our patience? If you are the Christ, tell us plainly."

²⁵Jesus answered, "I have told you, but you don't believe. The works I do in my Father's name testify about me, ²⁶but you don't believe because you don't belong to my sheep. ²⁷My sheep listen to my voice. I know them and they follow me. ²⁸I give them eternal life. They will never die, and no one will snatch them from my hand. ²⁹My Father, who has given them to me, is greater than all, and no one is able to snatch them from my Father's hand. ³⁰I and the Father are one,"

³¹Again the Jewish opposition picked up stones in order to stone him. ³²Jesus responded, "I have shown you many good works from the Father. For which of those works do you stone me?"

³³The Jewish opposition answered, "We don't stone you for a good work but for insulting God. You are human, yet you make yourself out to be God."

³⁴Jesus replied, "Isn't it written in your Law, *I have said, you are gods?*[f] ³⁵Scripture calls those to whom God's word came *gods*, and scripture can't be abolished. ³⁶So how can you say that the one whom the Father has made holy and sent into the world insults God because he said, 'I am God's Son'? ³⁷If I don't do the works of my Father, don't believe me. ³⁸But if I do them, and you don't believe me, believe the works so that you can know and recognize that the Father is in me and I am in the Father." ³⁹Again, they wanted to arrest him, but he escaped from them.

Jesus at the Jordan

⁴⁰Jesus went back across the Jordan to the place where John had baptized at first, and he stayed there. ⁴¹Many people came to him. "John didn't do any miraculous signs," they said, "but everything John said about this man was true." ⁴²Many believed in Jesus there.

Lazarus is ill

11 A certain man, Lazarus, was ill. He was from Bethany, the village of Mary and her sister Martha. (²This was the Mary who anointed the Lord with fragrant oil and wiped his feet with her hair. Her brother Lazarus was ill.) ³So the sisters sent word to Jesus, saying, "Lord, the one whom you love is ill."

⁴When he heard this, Jesus said, "This illness isn't fatal. It's for the glory of God so that God's Son can be glorified through it." ⁵Jesus loved Martha, her sister, and Lazarus. ⁶When he heard that Lazarus was ill, he stayed where he was. After two days, ⁷he said to his disciples, "Let's return to Judea again."

⁸The disciples replied, "Rabbi, the Jewish opposition wants to stone you, but you want to go back?"

⁹Jesus answered, "Aren't there twelve hours in the day? Whoever walks in the day doesn't stumble because they see the light of the world. ¹⁰But whoever walks in the night does stumble because the light isn't in them."

¹¹He continued, "Our friend Lazarus is sleeping, but I am going in order to wake him up."

¹²The disciples said, "Lord, if he's sleeping, he will get well." ¹³They thought Jesus meant that Lazarus was

---

fPs 82:6

in a deep sleep, but Jesus had spoken about Lazarus' death.

¹⁴ Jesus told them plainly, "Lazarus has died. ¹⁵ For your sakes, I'm glad I wasn't there so that you can believe. Let's go to him."

¹⁶ Then Thomas (the one called Didymus) said to the other disciples, "Let us go too so that we may die with Jesus."

Jesus with Martha and Mary

¹⁷ When Jesus arrived, he found that Lazarus had already been in the tomb for four days. ¹⁸ Bethany was a little less than two miles from Jerusalem. ¹⁹ Many Jews had come to comfort Martha and Mary after their brother's death. ²⁰ When Martha heard that Jesus was coming, she went to meet him, while Mary remained in the house. ²¹ Martha said to Jesus, "Lord, if you had been here, my brother wouldn't have died. ²² Even now I know that whatever you ask God, God will give you."

²³ Jesus told her, "Your brother will rise again."

²⁴ Martha replied, "I know that he will rise in the resurrection on the last day."

²⁵ Jesus said to her, "I am the resurrection and the life. Whoever believes in me will live, even though they die. ²⁶ Everyone who lives and believes in me will never die. Do you believe this?"

²⁷ She replied, "Yes, Lord, I believe that you are the Christ, God's Son, the one who is coming into the world."

²⁸ After she said this, she went and spoke privately to her sister Mary, "The teacher is here and he's calling for you." ²⁹ When Mary heard this, she got up quickly and went to Jesus. ³⁰ He hadn't entered the village but was still in the place where Martha had met him. ³¹ When the Jews who were comforting Mary in the house saw her get up quickly and leave, they followed her. They assumed she was going to mourn at the tomb.

³² When Mary arrived where Jesus was and saw him, she fell at his feet and said, "Lord, if you had been here, my brother wouldn't have died."

³³ When Jesus saw her crying and the Jews who had come with her crying also, he was deeply disturbed and troubled. ³⁴ He asked, "Where have you laid him?"

They replied, "Lord, come and see."

³⁵ Jesus began to cry. ³⁶ The Jews said, "See how much he loved him!" ³⁷ But some of them said, "He healed the eyes of the man born blind. Couldn't he have kept Lazarus from dying?"

Jesus at Lazarus' tomb

³⁸ Jesus was deeply disturbed again when he came to the tomb. It was a cave, and a stone covered the entrance. ³⁹ Jesus said, "Remove the stone."

Martha, the sister of the dead man, said, "Lord, the smell will be awful! He's been dead four days."

⁴⁰ Jesus replied, "Didn't I tell you that if you believe, you will see God's glory?" ⁴¹ So they removed the stone. Jesus looked up and said, "Father, thank you for hearing me. ⁴² I know you always hear me. I say this for the benefit of the crowd standing here so that they will believe that you sent me." ⁴³ Having said this, Jesus shouted with a loud voice, "Lazarus, come out!" ⁴⁴ The dead man came out, his feet bound and his hands tied, and his face covered with a cloth. Jesus said to them, "Untie him and let him go."

⁴⁵ Therefore, many of the Jews who came with Mary and saw what Jesus did

believed in him. ⁴⁶But some of them went to the Pharisees and told them what Jesus had done.

Caiaphas prophesies

⁴⁷Then the chief priests and Pharisees called together the council⁸ and said, "What are we going to do? This man is doing many miraculous signs! ⁴⁸If we let him go on like this, everyone will believe in him. Then the Romans will come and take away both our temple and our people."

⁴⁹One of them, Caiaphas, who was high priest that year, told them, "You don't know anything! ⁵⁰You don't see that it is better for you that one man die for the people rather than the whole nation be destroyed." ⁵¹He didn't say this on his own. As high priest that year, he prophesied that Jesus would soon die for the nation—⁵²and not only for the nation. Jesus would also die so that God's children scattered everywhere would be gathered together as one. ⁵³From that day on they plotted to kill him.

The Passover draws near

⁵⁴Therefore, Jesus was no longer active in public ministry among the Jewish leaders. Instead, he left Jerusalem and went to a place near the wilderness, to a city called Ephraim, where he stayed with his disciples.

⁵⁵It was almost time for the Jewish Passover, and many people went from the countryside up to Jerusalem to purify themselves through ritual washing before the Passover. ⁵⁶They were looking for Jesus. As they spoke to each other in the temple, they said, "What do you think? He won't come to the festival, will he?" ⁵⁷The chief priests and Pharisees had given orders that anyone who knew where he was should report it, so they could arrest him.

Mary anoints Jesus' feet

12 Six days before Passover, Jesus came to Bethany, home of Lazarus, whom Jesus had raised from the dead. ²Lazarus and his sisters hosted a dinner for him. Martha served and Lazarus was among those who joined him at the table. ³Then Mary took an extraordinary amount, almost three-quarters of a pound,ᵇ of very expensive perfume made of pure nard. She anointed Jesus' feet with it, then wiped his feet dry with her hair. The house was filled with the aroma of the perfume. ⁴Judas Iscariot, one of his disciples (the one who was about to betray him), complained, ⁵"This perfume was worth a year's wages!ⁱ Why wasn't it sold and the money given to the poor?" (⁶He said this not because he cared about the poor but because he was a thief. He carried the money bag and would take what was in it.)

⁷Then Jesus said, "Leave her alone. This perfume was to be used in preparation for my burial, and this is how she has used it. ⁸You will always have the poor among you, but you won't always have me."

⁹Many Jews learned that he was there. They came not only because of Jesus but also to see Lazarus, whom he had raised from the dead. ¹⁰The chief priests decided that they would kill

---

⁸Or *Sanhedrin* ᵇOr *a litra*, a Roman pound, approximately twelve ounces ⁱOr *three hundred denaria*

Lazarus too. [11]It was because of Lazarus that many of the Jews had deserted them and come to believe in Jesus.

Jesus enters Jerusalem

[12]The next day the great crowd that had come for the festival heard that Jesus was coming to Jerusalem. [13]They took palm branches and went out to meet him. They shouted,

"Hosanna!
Blessings on the one who comes
in the name of the Lord![j]
Blessings on the king of Israel!"

[14]Jesus found a young donkey and sat on it, just as it is written,

[15] *Don't be afraid, Daughter Zion.*
Look! Your king is coming,
sitting on a donkey's colt.[k]

[16]His disciples didn't understand these things at first. After he was glorified, they remembered that these things had been written about him and that they had done these things to him. [17]The crowd who had been with him when he called Lazarus out of the tomb and raised him from the dead were testifying about him. [18]That's why the crowd came to meet him, because they had heard about this miraculous sign that he had done. [19]Therefore, the Pharisees said to each other, "See! You've accomplished nothing! Look! The whole world is following him!"

Jesus teaches about his death

[20]Some Greeks were among those who had come up to worship at the festival. [21]They came to Philip, who was from Bethsaida in Galilee, and made a request: "Sir, we want to see Jesus." [22]Philip told Andrew, and Andrew and Philip told Jesus.

[23]Jesus replied, "The time has come for the Human One[l] to be glorified. [24]I assure you that unless a grain of wheat falls into the earth and dies, it can only be a single seed. But if it dies, it bears much fruit. [25]Those who love their lives will lose them, and those who hate their lives in this world will keep them forever. [26]Whoever serves me must follow me. Wherever I am, there my servant will also be. My Father will honor whoever serves me.

[27]"Now *I am deeply troubled.*[m] What should I say? 'Father, save me from this time'? No, for this is the reason I have come to this time. [28]Father, glorify your name!"

Then a voice came from heaven, "I have glorified it, and I will glorify it again."

[29]The crowd standing there heard and said, "It's thunder." Others said, "An angel spoke to him."

[30]Jesus replied, "This voice wasn't for my benefit but for yours. [31]Now is the time for judgment of this world. Now this world's ruler will be thrown out. [32]When I am lifted up[n] from the earth, I will draw everyone to me." ([33]He said this to show how he was going to die.)

[34]The crowd responded, "We have heard from the Law that the Christ remains forever. How can you say that the Human One[o] must be lifted up? Who is this Human One?"[p]

[35]Jesus replied, "The light is with you for only a little while. Walk while you have the light so that darkness doesn't overtake you. Those who walk in the darkness don't know where they are going. [36]As long as you have the light, believe in the light so that you might become people whose lives are

---

[j]Ps 118:26 [k]Zech 9:9 [l]*Or Son of Man* [m]Ps 6:2 [n]*Or exalted* [o]*Or Son of Man* [p]*Or Son of Man*

determined by the light." After Jesus said these things, he went away and hid from them.

Fulfillment of prophecy

[37]Jesus had done many miraculous signs before the people, but they didn't believe in him. [38]This was to fulfill the word of the prophet Isaiah:

> Lord, who has believed
> through our message?
> To whom is the arm of the Lord
> fully revealed?[q]

[39]Isaiah explains why they couldn't believe:

> [40] He made their eyes blind
> and closed their minds
> so that they might not see
> with their eyes,
> understand with their minds,
> and turn their lives around—
> and I would heal them.[r]

[41]Isaiah said these things because he saw Jesus' glory; he spoke about Jesus. [42]Even so, many leaders believed in him, but they wouldn't acknowledge their faith because they feared that the Pharisees would expel them from the synagogue. [43]They believed, but they loved human praise more than God's glory.

Summary of Jesus' teaching

[44]Jesus shouted, "Whoever believes in me doesn't believe in me but in the one who sent me. [45]Whoever sees me sees the one who sent me. [46]I have come as a light into the world so that everyone who believes in me won't live in darkness. [47]If people hear my words and don't keep them, I don't judge them. I didn't come to judge the world but to save it. [48]Whoever rejects me and doesn't receive my words will be judged at the last day by the word I have spoken. [49]I don't speak on my own, but the Father who sent me commanded me regarding what I should speak and say. [50]I know that his commandment is eternal life. Therefore, whatever I say is just as the Father has said to me."

Foot washing

13 Before the Festival of Passover, Jesus knew that his time had come to leave this world and go to the Father. Having loved his own who were in the world, he loved them fully.

[2]Jesus and his disciples were sharing the evening meal. The devil had already provoked Judas, Simon Iscariot's son, to betray Jesus. [3]Jesus knew the Father had given everything into his hands and that he had come from God and was returning to God. [4]So he got up from the table and took off his robes. Picking up a linen towel, he tied it around his waist. [5]Then he poured water into a washbasin and began to wash the disciples' feet, drying them with the towel he was wearing. [6]When Jesus came to Simon Peter, Peter said to him, "Lord, are you going to wash my feet?"

[7]Jesus replied, "You don't understand what I'm doing now, but you will understand later."

[8]"No!" Peter said. "You will never wash my feet!"

Jesus replied, "Unless I wash you, you won't have a place with me."

[9]Simon Peter said, "Lord, not only my feet but also my hands and my head!"

[10]Jesus responded, "Those who have bathed need only to have their feet

[q]Isa 53:1 [r]Isa 6:10

washed, because they are completely clean. You disciples are clean, but not every one of you." [11] He knew who would betray him. That's why he said, "Not every one of you is clean."

[12] After he washed the disciples' feet, he put on his robes and returned to his place at the table. He said to them, "Do you know what I've done for you? [13] You call me 'Teacher' and 'Lord,' and you speak correctly, because I am. [14] If I, your Lord and teacher, have washed your feet, you too must wash each other's feet. [15] I have given you an example: Just as I have done, you also must do. [16] I assure you, servants aren't greater than their master, nor are those who are sent greater than the one who sent them. [17] Since you know these things, you will be happy if you do them. [18] I'm not speaking about all of you. I know those whom I've chosen. But this is to fulfill the scripture, *The one who eats my bread has turned against me.*[s]

[19] "I'm telling you this now, before it happens, so that when it does happen you will believe that I Am. [20] I assure you that whoever receives someone I send receives me, and whoever receives me receives the one who sent me."

Announcement of the betrayal

[21] After he said these things, Jesus was deeply disturbed and testified, "I assure you, one of you will betray me."

[22] His disciples looked at each other, confused about which of them he was talking about. [23] One of the disciples, the one whom Jesus loved, was at Jesus' side. [24] Simon Peter nodded at him to get him to ask Jesus who he was talking about. [25] Leaning back toward Jesus, this disciple asked, "Lord, who is it?"

[26] Jesus answered, "It's the one to whom I will give this piece of bread once I have dipped into the bowl." Then he dipped the piece of bread and gave it to Judas, Simon Iscariot's son. [27] After Judas took the bread, Satan entered into him. Jesus told him, "What you are about to do, do quickly." [28] No one sitting at the table understood why Jesus said this to him. [29] Some thought that, since Judas kept the money bag, Jesus told him, "Go, buy what we need for the feast," or that he should give something to the poor. [30] So when Judas took the bread, he left immediately. And it was night.

Love commandment

[31] When Judas was gone, Jesus said, "Now the Human One[t] has been glorified, and God has been glorified in him. [32] If God has been glorified in him, God will also glorify the Human One[u] in himself and will glorify him immediately. [33] Little children, I'm with you for a little while longer. You will look for me—but, just as I told the Jewish leaders, I also tell you now—'Where I'm going, you can't come.'

[34] "I give you a new commandment: Love each other. Just as I have loved you, so you also must love each other. [35] This is how everyone will know that you are my disciples, when you love each other."

Announcement of Peter's denial

[36] Simon Peter said to Jesus, "Lord, where are you going?"

Jesus answered, "Where I am going,

---

[s] Ps 41:9   [t] Or *Son of Man*   [u] Or *Son of Man*

you can't follow me now, but you will follow later."

[37] Peter asked, "Lord, why can't I follow you now? I'll give up my life for you."

[38] Jesus replied, "Will you give up your life for me? I assure you that you will deny me three times before the rooster crows.

The way, the truth, and the life

14 "Don't be troubled. Trust in God. Trust also in me. [2] My Father's house has room to spare. If that weren't the case, would I have told you that I'm going to prepare a place for you? [3] When I go to prepare a place for you, I will return and take you to be with me so that where I am you will be too. [4] You know the way to the place I'm going."

[5] Thomas asked, "Lord, we don't know where you are going. How can we know the way?"

[6] Jesus answered, "I am the way, the truth, and the life. No one comes to the Father except through me. [7] If you have really known me, you will also know the Father. From now on you know him and have seen him."

[8] Philip said, "Lord, show us the Father; that will be enough for us."

[9] Jesus replied, "Don't you know me, Philip, even after I have been with you all this time? Whoever has seen me has seen the Father. How can you say, 'Show us the Father'? [10] Don't you believe that I am in the Father and the Father is in me? The words I have spoken to you I don't speak on my own. The Father who dwells in me does his works. [11] Trust me when I say that I am in the Father and the Father is in me, or at least believe on account of the works themselves. [12] I

assure you that whoever believes in me will do the works that I do. They will do even greater works than these because I am going to the Father. [13] I will do whatever you ask for in my name, so that the Father can be glorified in the Son. [14] When you ask me for anything in my name, I will do it.

I won't leave you as orphans

[15] "If you love me, you will keep my commandments. [16] I will ask the Father, and he will send another Companion,[v] who will be with you forever. [17] This Companion is the Spirit of Truth, whom the world can't receive because it neither sees him nor recognizes him. You know him, because he lives with you and will be with you.

[18] "I won't leave you as orphans. I will come to you. [19] Soon the world will no longer see me, but you will see me. Because I live, you will live too. [20] On that day you will know that I am in my Father, you are in me, and I am in you. [21] Whoever has my commandments and keeps them loves me. Whoever loves me will be loved by my Father, and I will love them and reveal myself to them."

[22] Judas (not Judas Iscariot) asked, "Lord, why are you about to reveal yourself to us and not to the world?"

[23] Jesus answered, "Whoever loves me will keep my word. My Father will love them, and we will come to them and make our home with them. [24] Whoever doesn't love me doesn't keep my words. The word that you hear isn't mine. It is the word of the Father who sent me.

[25] "I have spoken these things to you while I am with you. [26] The Companion,[w]

---

[v] Or Advocate   [w] Or Advocate

the Holy Spirit, whom the Father will send in my name, will teach you everything and will remind you of everything I told you.

²⁷"Peace I leave with you. My peace I give you. I give to you not as the world gives. Don't be troubled or afraid. ²⁸You have heard me tell you, 'I'm going away and returning to you.' If you loved me, you would be happy that I am going to the Father, because the Father is greater than me. ²⁹I have told you before it happens so that when it happens you will believe. ³⁰I won't say much more to you because this world's ruler is coming. He has nothing on me. ³¹Rather, he comes so that the world will know that I love the Father and do just as the Father has commanded me. Get up. We're leaving this place.

I am the true vine

15 "I am the true vine, and my Father is the vineyard keeper. ²He removes any of my branches that don't produce fruit, and he trims any branch that produces fruit so that it will produce even more fruit. ³You are already trimmed because of the word I have spoken to you. ⁴Remain in me, and I will remain in you. A branch can't produce fruit by itself, but must remain in the vine. Likewise, you can't produce fruit unless you remain in me. ⁵I am the vine; you are the branches. If you remain in me and I in you, then you will produce much fruit. Without me, you can't do anything. ⁶If you don't remain in me, you will be like a branch that is thrown out and dries up. Those branches are gathered up, thrown into a fire, and burned. ⁷If you remain in me and my words remain in you, ask for whatever you want and it will be done

for you. ⁸My Father is glorified when you produce much fruit and in this way prove that you are my disciples.

Love each other

⁹"As the Father loved me, I too have loved you. Remain in my love. ¹⁰If you keep my commandments, you will remain in my love, just as I kept my Father's commandments and remain in his love. ¹¹I have said these things to you so that my joy will be in you and your joy will be complete. ¹²This is my commandment: love each other just as I have loved you. ¹³No one has greater love than to give up one's life for one's friends. ¹⁴You are my friends if you do what I command you. ¹⁵I don't call you servants any longer, because servants don't know what their master is doing. Instead, I call you friends, because everything I heard from my Father I have made known to you. ¹⁶You didn't choose me, but I chose you and appointed you so that you could go and produce fruit and so that your fruit could last. As a result, whatever you ask the Father in my name, he will give you. ¹⁷I give you these commandments so that you can love each other.

If the world hates you

¹⁸"If the world hates you, know that it hated me first. ¹⁹If you belonged to the world, the world would love you as its own. However, I have chosen you out of the world, and you don't belong to the world. This is why the world hates you. ²⁰Remember what I told you, 'Servants aren't greater than their master.' If the world harassed me, it will harass you too. If it kept my word, it will also keep yours. ²¹The world will do all these things to you on account of

my name, because it doesn't know the one who sent me.

[22]"If I hadn't come and spoken to the people of this world, they wouldn't be sinners. But now they have no excuse for their sin. [23]Whoever hates me also hates the Father. [24]If I hadn't done works among them that no one else had done, they wouldn't be sinners. But now they have seen and hated both me and my Father. [25]This fulfills the word written in their Law, *They hated me without a reason.*[x]

[26]"When the Companion[y] comes, whom I will send from the Father—the Spirit of Truth who proceeds from the Father—he will testify about me. [27]You will testify too, because you have been with me from the beginning.

16 I have said these things to you so that you won't fall away. [2]They will expel you from the synagogue. The time is coming when those who kill you will think that they are doing a service to God. [3]They will do these things because they don't know the Father or me. [4]But I have said these things to you so that when their time comes, you will remember that I told you about them.

I go away

"I didn't say these things to you from the beginning, because I was with you. [5]But now I go away to the one who sent me. None of you ask me, 'Where are you going?' [6]Yet because I have said these things to you, you are filled with sorrow. [7]I assure you that it is better for you that I go away. If I don't go away, the Companion[z] won't come to you. But if I go, I will send him to you. [8]When he comes, he will show the world it was

wrong about sin, righteousness, and judgment. [9]He will show the world it was wrong about sin because they don't believe in me. [10]He will show the world it was wrong about righteousness because I'm going to the Father and you won't see me anymore. [11]He will show the world it was wrong about judgment because this world's ruler stands condemned.

I still have many things to say

[12]"I have much more to say to you, but you can't handle it now. [13]However, when the Spirit of Truth comes, he will guide you in all truth. He won't speak on his own, but will say whatever he hears and will proclaim to you what is to come. [14]He will glorify me, because he will take what is mine and proclaim it to you. [15]Everything that the Father has is mine. That's why I said that the Spirit takes what is mine and will proclaim it to you. [16]Soon you won't be able to see me; soon after that, you will see me."

I will see you again

[17]Some of Jesus' disciples said to each other, "What does he mean: 'Soon you won't see me, and soon after that you will see me' and 'Because I'm going to the Father'? [18]What does he mean by 'soon'? We don't understand what he's talking about."

[19]Jesus knew they wanted to ask him, so he said, "Are you trying to find out from each other what I meant when I said, 'Soon you won't see me, and soon after that you will see me'? [20]I assure you that you will cry and lament, and the world will be happy. You will be

---

[x]Pss 35:19; 69:4   [y]Or *Advocate*   [z]Or *Advocate*

sorrowful, but your sorrow will turn into joy. ²¹When a woman gives birth, she has pain because her time has come. But when the child is born, she no longer remembers her distress because of her joy that a child has been born into the world. ²²In the same way, you have sorrow now; but I will see you again, and you will be overjoyed. No one takes away your joy. ²³In that day, you won't ask me anything. I assure you that the Father will give you whatever you ask in my name. ²⁴Up to now, you have asked nothing in my name. Ask and you will receive so that your joy will be complete.

I have conquered the world

²⁵"I've been using figures of speech with you. The time is coming when I will no longer speak to you in such analogies. Instead, I will tell you plainly about the Father. ²⁶In that day you will ask in my name. I'm not saying that I will ask the Father on your behalf. ²⁷The Father himself loves you, because you have loved me and believed that I came from God. ²⁸I left the Father and came into the world. I tell you again: I am leaving the world and returning to the Father."

²⁹His disciples said, "See! Now you speak plainly; you aren't using figures of speech. ³⁰Now we know that you know everything and you don't need anyone to ask you. Because of this we believe you have come from God."

³¹Jesus replied, "Now you believe? ³²Look! A time is coming—and is here!—when each of you will be scattered to your own homes and you will leave me alone. I'm not really alone, for the Father is with me. ³³I've said these things to you so that you will

have peace in me. In the world you have distress. But be encouraged! I have conquered the world."

Jesus prays

17 When Jesus finished saying these things, he looked up to heaven and said, "Father, the time has come. Glorify your Son, so that the Son can glorify you. ²You gave him authority over everyone so that he could give eternal life to everyone you gave him. ³This is eternal life: to know you, the only true God, and Jesus Christ whom you sent. ⁴I have glorified you on earth by finishing the work you gave me to do. ⁵Now, Father, glorify me in your presence with the glory I shared with you before the world was created.

⁶"I have revealed your name to the people you gave me from this world. They were yours and you gave them to me, and they have kept your word. ⁷Now they know that everything you have given me comes from you. ⁸This is because I gave them the words that you gave me, and they received them. They truly understood that I came from you, and they believed that you sent me.

⁹"I'm praying for them. I'm not praying for the world but for those you gave me, because they are yours. ¹⁰Everything that is mine is yours and everything that is yours is mine; I have been glorified in them. ¹¹I'm no longer in the world, but they are in the world, even as I'm coming to you. Holy Father, watch over them in your name, the name you gave me, that they will be one just as we are one. ¹²When I was with them, I watched over them in your name, the name you gave me, and I kept them safe. None of them were lost, except the one who was destined for destruction,

so that scripture would be fulfilled. [13]Now I'm coming to you and I say these things while I'm in the world so that they can share completely in my joy. [14]I gave your word to them and the world hated them, because they don't belong to this world, just as I don't belong to this world. [15]I'm not asking that you take them out of this world but that you keep them safe from the evil one. [16]They don't belong to this world, just as I don't belong to the truth. [17]Make them holy in the truth; your word is truth. [18]As you sent me into the world, so I have sent them into the world. [19]I made myself holy on their behalf so that they also would be made holy in the truth.

[20]"I'm not praying only for them but also for those who believe in me because of their word. [21]I pray they will be one, Father, just as you are in me and I am in you. I pray that they also will be in us, so that the world will believe that you sent me. [22]I've given them the glory that you gave me so that they can be one just as we are one. [23]I'm in them and you are in me so that they will be made perfectly one. Then the world will know that you sent me and that you have loved them just as you loved me.

[24]"Father, I want those you gave me to be with me where I am. Then they can see my glory, which you gave me because you loved me before the creation of the world. [25]"Righteous Father, even the world didn't know you, but I've known you, and these believers know that you sent me. [26]I've made your name known to them and will continue to make it known so that your love for me will be in them, and I myself will be in them."

Arrest in the garden

18After he said these things, Jesus went out with his disciples and crossed over to the other side of the Kidron Valley. He and his disciples entered a garden there. [2]Judas, his betrayer, also knew the place because Jesus often gathered there with his disciples. [3]Judas brought a company of soldiers[a] and some guards from the chief priests and Pharisees. They came there carrying lanterns, torches, and weapons. [4]Jesus knew everything that was to happen to him, so he went out and asked, "Who are you looking for?"

[5]They answered, "Jesus the Nazarene."

He said to them, "I Am."[b] (Judas, his betrayer, was standing with them.) [6]When he said, "I Am," they shrank back and fell to the ground. [7]He asked them again, "Who are you looking for?"

They said, "Jesus the Nazarene."

[8]Jesus answered, "I told you, 'I Am.'[c] If you are looking for me, then let these people go." [9]This was so that the word he had spoken might be fulfilled: "I didn't lose anyone of those whom you gave me."

[10]Then Simon Peter, who had a sword, drew it and struck the high priest's servant, cutting off his right ear. (The servant's name was Malchus.) [11]Jesus told Peter, "Put your sword away! Am I not to drink the cup the Father has given me?" [12]Then the company of soldiers, the commander, and the guards from the Jewish leaders took Jesus into custody. They bound him [13]and led him first to Annas. He was the father-in-law of Caiaphas, the high priest that year. ([14]Caiaphas was the one who had advised the Jewish

[a]Or cohort (approximately six hundred soldiers) [b]Or It is I [c]Or It is I

leaders that it was better for one person to die for the people.)

Peter denies Jesus

[15] Simon Peter and another disciple followed Jesus. Because this other disciple was known to the high priest, he went with Jesus into the high priest's courtyard. [16] However, Peter stood outside near the gate. Then the other disciple (the one known to the high priest) came out and spoke to the woman stationed at the gate, and she brought Peter in. [17] The servant woman stationed at the gate asked Peter, "Aren't you one of this man's disciples?"

"I'm not," he replied. [18] The servants and the guards had made a fire because it was cold. They were standing around it, warming themselves. Peter joined them there, standing by the fire and warming himself.

Jesus testifies

[19] Meanwhile, the chief priest questioned Jesus about his disciples and his teaching. [20] Jesus answered, "I've spoken openly to the world. I've always taught in synagogues and in the temple, where all the Jews gather. I've said nothing in private. [21] Why ask me? Ask those who heard what I told them. They know what I said."

[22] After Jesus spoke, one of the guards standing there slapped Jesus in the face. "Is that how you would answer the high priest?" he asked.

[23] Jesus replied, "If I speak wrongly, testify about what was wrong. But if I speak correctly, why do you strike me?" [24] Then Annas sent him, bound, to Caiaphas the high priest.

Peter denies Jesus again

[25] Meanwhile, Simon Peter was still standing with the guards, warming himself. They asked, "Aren't you one of his disciples?"

Peter denied it, saying, "I'm not."

[26] A servant of the high priest, a relative of the one whose ear Peter had cut off, said to him, "Didn't I see you in the garden with him?" [27] Peter denied it again, and immediately a rooster crowed.

Trial before Pilate

[28] The Jewish leaders led Jesus from Caiaphas to the Roman governor's palace.[d] It was early in the morning. So that they could eat the Passover, the Jewish leaders wouldn't enter the palace; entering the palace would have made them ritually impure.

[29] So Pilate went out to them and asked, "What charge do you bring against this man?"

[30] They answered, "If he had done nothing wrong, we wouldn't have handed him over to you."

[31] Pilate responded, "Take him yourselves and judge him according to your Law."

The Jewish leaders replied, "The Law doesn't allow us to kill anyone." ([32] This was so that Jesus' word might be fulfilled when he indicated how he was going to die.)

Pilate questions Jesus

[33] Pilate went back into the palace. He summoned Jesus and asked, "Are you the king of the Jews?"

[34] Jesus answered, "Do you say this on your own or have others spoken to you about me?"

[d] Or praetorium

³⁵Pilate responded, "I'm not a Jew, am I? Your nation and its chief priests handed you over to me. What have you done?"

³⁶Jesus replied, "My kingdom doesn't originate from this world. If it did, my guards would fight so that I wouldn't have been arrested by the Jewish leaders. My kingdom isn't from here."

³⁷"So you are a king?" Pilate said.

Jesus answered, "You say that I am a king. I was born and came into the world for this reason: to testify to the truth. Whoever accepts the truth listens to my voice."

³⁸"What is truth?" Pilate asked.

Release of Barabbas

After Pilate said this, he returned to the Jewish leaders and said, "I find no grounds for any charge against him. ³⁹You have a custom that I release one prisoner for you at Passover. Do you want me to release for you the king of the Jews?"

⁴⁰They shouted, "Not this man! Give us Barabbas!" (Barabbas was an outlaw.)

Jesus is whipped and mocked as king

19 Then Pilate had Jesus taken and whipped. ²The soldiers twisted together a crown of thorns and put it on his head, and dressed him in a purple robe. ³Over and over they went up to him and said, "Greetings, king of the Jews!" And they slapped him in the face.

⁴Pilate came out of the palace again and said to the Jewish leaders, "Look! I'm bringing him out to you to let you know that I find no grounds for a charge against him." ⁵When Jesus came out, wearing the crown of thorns and the purple robe, Pilate said to them, "Here's the man."

⁶When the chief priests and their deputies saw him, they shouted out, "Crucify, crucify!"

Pilate told them, "You take him and crucify him. I don't find any grounds for a charge against him."

⁷The Jewish leaders replied, "We have a Law, and according to this Law we ought to die because he made himself out to be God's Son."

Pilate questions Jesus again

⁸When Pilate heard this word, he was even more afraid. ⁹He went back into the residence and spoke to Jesus, "Where are you from?" Jesus didn't answer. ¹⁰So Pilate said, "You won't speak to me? Don't you know that I have authority to release you and also to crucify you?"

¹¹Jesus replied, "You would have no authority over me if it had not been given to you from above. That's why the one who handed me over to you has the greater sin." ¹²From that moment on, Pilate wanted to release Jesus.

However, the Jewish leaders cried out, saying, "If you release this man, you aren't a friend of the emperor! Anyone who makes himself out to be a king opposes the emperor!"

¹³When Pilate heard these words, he led Jesus out and seated him on the judge's bench at the place called Stone Pavement (in Aramaic, *Gabbatha*). ¹⁴It was about noon on the Preparation Day for the Passover. Pilate said to the Jewish leaders, "Here's your king."

¹⁵The Jewish leaders cried out, "Take him away! Take him away! Crucify him!"

Pilate responded, "What? Do you want me to crucify your king?"

"We have no king except the emperor," the chief priests answered. [16] Then Pilate handed Jesus over to be crucified.

Crucifixion

The soldiers took Jesus prisoner. [17] Carrying his cross by himself, he went out to a place called Skull Place (in Aramaic, *Golgotha*). [18] That's where they crucified him—and two others with him, one on each side and Jesus in the middle. [19] Pilate had a public notice written and posted on the cross. It read "Jesus the Nazarene, the king of the Jews." [20] Many of the Jews read this sign, for the place where Jesus was crucified was near the city and it was written in Aramaic, Latin, and Greek. [21] Therefore, the Jewish chief priests complained to Pilate, "Don't write, 'The king of the Jews' but 'This man said, "I am the king of the Jews."'"

[22] Pilate answered, "What I've written, I've written."

[23] When the soldiers crucified Jesus, they took his clothes and his sandals, and divided them into four shares, one for each soldier. His shirt was seamless, woven as one piece from the top to the bottom. [24] They said to each other, "Let's not tear it. Let's cast lots to see who will get it." This was to fulfill the scripture,

> They divided my clothes
> among themselves,
> and they cast lots for my clothing.[e]

That's what the soldiers did.

[25] Jesus' mother and his mother's sister, Mary the wife of Clopas, and Mary Magdalene stood near the cross. [26] When Jesus saw his mother and the disciple whom he loved standing nearby, he said to his mother, "Woman, here is your son." [27] Then he said to the disciple, "Here is your mother." And from that time on, this disciple took her into his home.

[28] After this, knowing that everything was already completed, in order to fulfill the scripture, Jesus said, "I am thirsty." [29] A jar full of sour wine was nearby, so the soldiers soaked a sponge in it, placed it on a hyssop branch, and held it up to his lips. [30] When he had received the sour wine, Jesus said, "It is completed." Bowing his head, he gave up his life.

Witness at the cross

[31] It was the Preparation Day and the Jewish leaders didn't want the bodies to remain on the cross on the Sabbath, especially since that Sabbath was an important day. So they asked Pilate to have the legs of those crucified broken and the bodies taken down. [32] Therefore, the soldiers came and broke the legs of the two men who were crucified with Jesus. [33] When they came to Jesus, they saw that he was already dead so they didn't break his legs. [34] However, one of the soldiers pierced his side with a spear, and immediately blood and water came out. [35] The one who saw this has testified, and his testimony is true. He knows that he speaks the truth, and he has testified so that you also can believe. [36] These things happened to fulfill the scripture, *They won't break any of his bones.*[f] [37] And another scripture says, *They will look at him whom they have pierced.*[g]

Jesus' body is buried

[38] After this Joseph of Arimathea asked Pilate if he could take away the

[e] Ps 22:18 [f] Exod 12:46 [g] Zech 12:10

body of Jesus. Joseph was a disciple of Jesus, but a secret one because he feared the Jewish authorities. Pilate gave him permission, so he came and took the body away. ³⁹Nicodemus, the one who at first had come to Jesus at night, was there too. He brought a mixture of myrrh and aloe, nearly seventy-five pounds in all.ʰ ⁴⁰Following Jewish burial customs, they took Jesus' body and wrapped it, with the spices, in linen cloths. ⁴¹There was a garden in the place where Jesus was crucified, and in the garden was a new tomb in which no one had ever been laid. ⁴²Because it was the Jewish Preparation Day and the tomb was nearby, they laid Jesus in it.

Empty tomb

20 Early in the morning of the first day of the week, while it was still dark, Mary Magdalene came to the tomb and saw that the stone had been taken away from the tomb. ²She ran to Simon Peter and the other disciple, the one whom Jesus loved, and said, "They have taken the Lord from the tomb, and we don't know where they've put him." ³Peter and the other disciple left to go to the tomb. ⁴They were running together, but the other disciple ran faster than Peter and was the first to arrive at the tomb. ⁵Bending down to take a look, he saw the linen cloths lying there, but he didn't go in. ⁶Following him, Simon Peter entered the tomb and saw the linen cloths lying there. ⁷He also saw the face cloth that had been on Jesus' head. It wasn't with the other clothes but was folded up in its own place. ⁸Then the other disciple, the one who arrived at the tomb first,

also went inside. He saw and believed. ⁹They didn't yet understand the scripture that Jesus must rise from the dead. ¹⁰Then the disciples returned to the place where they were staying.

Jesus appears to Mary

¹¹Mary stood outside near the tomb, crying. As she cried, she bent down to look into the tomb. ¹²She saw two angels dressed in white, seated where the body of Jesus had been, one at the head and one at the foot. ¹³The angels asked her, "Woman, why are you crying?"

She replied, "They have taken away my Lord, and I don't know where they've put him." ¹⁴As soon as she had said this, she turned around and saw Jesus standing there, but she didn't know it was Jesus.

¹⁵Jesus said to her, "Woman, why are you crying? Who are you looking for?"

Thinking he was the gardener, she replied, "Sir, if you have carried him away, tell me where you have put him and I will get him."

¹⁶Jesus said to her, "Mary."

She turned and said to him in Aramaic, "Rabbouni" (which means *Teacher*).

¹⁷Jesus said to her, "Don't hold on to me, for I haven't yet gone up to my Father. Go to my brothers and sisters and tell them, 'I'm going up to my Father and your Father, to my God and your God.'"

¹⁸Mary Magdalene left and announced to the disciples, "I've seen the Lord." Then she told them what he said to her.

Jesus appears to the disciples

¹⁹It was still the first day of the week. That evening, while the disciples were

---

ʰOr *one hundred litra*; that is, one hundred Roman pounds

behind closed doors because they were afraid of the Jewish authorities, Jesus came and stood among them. He said, "Peace be with you." ²⁰After he said this, he showed them his hands and his side. When the disciples saw the Lord, they were filled with joy. ²¹Jesus said to them again, "Peace be with you. As the Father sent me, so I am sending you." ²²Then he breathed on them and said, "Receive the Holy Spirit. ²³If you forgive anyone's sins, they are forgiven; if you don't forgive them, they are forgiven."

Jesus appears to Thomas and the disciples

²⁴Thomas, the one called Didymus,[i] one of the Twelve, wasn't with the disciples when Jesus came. ²⁵The other disciples told him, "We've seen the Lord!"

But he replied, "Unless I see the nail marks in his hands, put my finger in the wounds left by the nails, and put my hand into his side, I won't believe."

²⁶After eight days his disciples were again in a house and Thomas was with them. Even though the doors were locked, Jesus entered and stood among them. He said, "Peace be with you." ²⁷Then he said to Thomas, "Put your finger here. Look at my hands. Put your hand into my side. No more disbelief. Believe!"

²⁸Thomas responded to Jesus, "My Lord and my God!"

²⁹Jesus replied, "Do you believe because you see me? Happy are those who don't see and yet believe."

³⁰Then Jesus did many other miraculous signs in his disciples' presence, signs that aren't recorded in this scroll.

³¹But these things are written so that you will believe that Jesus is the Christ, God's Son, and that believing, you will have life in his name.

Jesus appears again to the disciples

21 Later, Jesus himself appeared again to his disciples at the Sea of Tiberias. This is how it happened: ²Simon Peter, Thomas (called Didymus[j]), Nathanael from Cana in Galilee, Zebedee's sons, and two other disciples were together. ³Simon Peter told them, "I'm going fishing."

They said, "We'll go with you." They set out in a boat, but throughout the night they caught nothing. ⁴Early in the morning, Jesus stood on the shore, but the disciples didn't realize it was Jesus.

⁵Jesus called to them, "Children, have you caught anything to eat?"

They answered him, "No."

⁶He said, "Cast your net on the right side of the boat and you will find some."

So they did, and there were so many fish that they couldn't haul in the net. ⁷Then the disciple whom Jesus loved said to Peter, "It's the Lord!" When Simon Peter heard it was the Lord, he wrapped his coat around himself (for he was naked) and jumped into the water. ⁸The other disciples followed in the boat, dragging the net full of fish, for they weren't far from shore, only about one hundred yards.

⁹When they landed, they saw a fire there, with fish on it, and some bread. ¹⁰Jesus said to them, "Bring some of the fish that you've just caught." ¹¹Simon Peter got up and pulled the net to shore. It was full of large fish,

[i] Or the twin [j] Or the twin

one hundred fifty-three of them. Yet the net hadn't torn, even with so many fish. [12]Jesus said to them, "Come and have breakfast." None of the disciples could bring themselves to ask him, "Who are you?" They knew it was the Lord. [13]Jesus came, took the bread, and gave it to them. He did the same with the fish. [14]This was now the third time Jesus appeared to his disciples after he was raised from the dead.

Jesus and Peter

[15]When they finished eating, Jesus asked Simon Peter, "Simon son of John, do you love me more than these?"

Simon replied, "Yes, Lord, you know I love you."

Jesus said to him, "Feed my lambs." [16]Jesus asked a second time, "Simon son of John, do you love me?"

Simon replied, "Yes, Lord, you know I love you."

Jesus said to him, "Take care of my sheep." [17]He asked a third time, "Simon son of John, do you love me?"

Peter was sad that Jesus asked him a third time, "Do you love me?" He replied, "Lord, you know everything; you know I love you."

Jesus said to him, "Feed my sheep. [18]I assure you that when you were younger you tied your own belt and walked around wherever you wanted.

When you grow old, you will stretch out your hands and another will tie your belt and lead you where you don't want to go." [19]He said this to show the kind of death by which Peter would glorify God. After saying this, Jesus said to Peter, "Follow me."

Jesus and the disciple whom he loved

[20]Peter turned around and saw the disciple whom Jesus loved following them. This was the one who had leaned against Jesus at the meal and asked him, "Lord, who is going to betray you?" [21]When Peter saw this disciple, he said to Jesus, "Lord, what about him?"

[22]Jesus replied, "If I want him to remain until I come, what difference does that make to you? You must follow me." [23]Therefore, the word spread among the brothers and sisters that this disciple wouldn't die. However, Jesus didn't say he wouldn't die, but only, "If I want him to remain until I come, what difference does that make to you?" [24]This is the disciple who testifies concerning these things and who wrote them down. We know that his testimony is true. [25]Jesus did many other things as well. If all of them were recorded, I imagine the world itself wouldn't have enough room for the scrolls that would be written.

ACTS OF THE APOSTLES

The risen Jesus with his disciples

1 Theophilus, the first scroll I wrote concerned everything Jesus did and taught from the beginning, [2]right up to the day when he was taken up into heaven. Before he was taken up,

working in the power of the Holy Spirit, Jesus instructed the apostles he had chosen. [3]After his suffering, he showed them that he was alive with many convincing proofs. He appeared to them over a period of forty days, speaking to them about God's kingdom. [4]While they were eating together, he ordered them not to leave Jerusalem but to wait for what the Father had promised. He said, "This is what you heard from me: [5]John baptized with water, but in only a few days you will be baptized with the Holy Spirit."

[6]As a result, those who had gathered together asked Jesus, "Lord, are you going to restore the kingdom to Israel now?"

[7]Jesus replied, "It isn't for you to know the times or seasons that the Father has set by his own authority. [8]Rather, you will receive power when the Holy Spirit has come upon you, and you will be my witnesses in Jerusalem, in all Judea and Samaria, and to the end of the earth."

[9]After Jesus said these things, as they were watching, he was lifted up and a cloud took him out of their sight. [10]While he was going away and as they were staring toward heaven, suddenly two men in white robes stood next to them. [11]They said, "Galileans, why are you standing here, looking toward heaven? This Jesus, who was taken up from you into heaven, will come in the same way that you saw him go into heaven."

Jesus' followers in Jerusalem

[12]Then they returned to Jerusalem from the Mount of Olives, which is near Jerusalem—a sabbath day's journey away. [13]When they entered the city, they went to the upstairs room where they were staying. Peter, John, James, and Andrew; Philip and Thomas; Bartholomew and Matthew; James,

Alphaeus' son; Simon the zealot; and Judas, James' son— [14]all were united in their devotion to prayer, along with some women, including Mary the mother of Jesus, and his brothers.

A replacement for Judas

[15]During this time, the family of believers was a company of about one hundred twenty persons. Peter stood among them and said, [16]"Brothers and sisters, the scripture that the Holy Spirit announced beforehand through David had to be fulfilled. This was the scripture concerning Judas, who became a guide for those who arrested Jesus. [17]This happened even though he was one of us and received a share of this ministry. ([18]In fact, he bought a field with the payment he received for his injustice. Falling headfirst, he burst open in the middle and all his intestines spilled out. [19]This became known to everyone living in Jerusalem, so they called that field in their own language Hakeldama, or "Field of Blood.") [20]"It is written in the Psalms scroll,

Let his home become deserted
*   and let there be no one living in it;*[a]
and
Give his position of leadership
*   to another.*[b]

[21]"Therefore, we must select one of those who have accompanied us during the whole time the Lord Jesus lived among us, [22]beginning from the baptism of John until the day when Jesus was taken from us. This person must become along with us a witness to his resurrection." [23]So they nominated two: Joseph called Barsabbas, who was also known as Justus, and Matthias.

---

[a]Ps 69:25 [b]Ps 109:8

²⁴They prayed, "Lord, you know everyone's deepest thoughts and desires. Show us clearly which one you have chosen from among these two ²⁵to take the place of this ministry and apostleship, from which Judas turned away to go to his own place." ²⁶When they cast lots, the lot fell on Matthias. He was added to the eleven apostles.

Pentecost

2 When Pentecost Day arrived, they were all together in one place. ²Suddenly a sound from heaven like the howling of a fierce wind filled the entire house where they were sitting. ³They saw what seemed to be individual flames of fire alighting on each one of them. ⁴They were all filled with the Holy Spirit and began to speak in other languages as the Spirit enabled them to speak.

⁵There were pious Jews from every nation under heaven living in Jerusalem. ⁶When they heard this sound, a crowd gathered. They were mystified because everyone heard them speaking in their native languages. ⁷They were surprised and amazed, saying, "Look, aren't all the people who are speaking Galileans, every one of them? ⁸How then can each of us hear them speaking in our native language? ⁹Parthians, Medes, and Elamites; as well as residents of Mesopotamia, Judea, and Cappadocia, Pontus and Asia, ¹⁰Phrygia and Pamphylia, Egypt and the regions of Libya bordering Cyrene; and visitors from Rome (both Jews and converts to Judaism), ¹¹Cretans and Arabs—we hear them declaring the mighty works of God in our own languages!" ¹²They

were all surprised and bewildered. Some asked each other, "What does this mean?" ¹³Others jeered at them, saying, "They're full of new wine!"

¹⁴Peter stood with the other eleven apostles. He raised his voice and declared, "Judeans and everyone living in Jerusalem! Know this! Listen carefully to my words! ¹⁵These people aren't drunk, as you suspect; after all, it's only nine o'clock in the morning! ¹⁶Rather, this is what was spoken through the prophet Joel:

¹⁷ *In the last days, God says,*
   I will pour out my Spirit on all people.
   Your sons and daughters
      will prophesy.
   Your young will see visions.
   Your elders will dream dreams.
¹⁸ *Even upon my servants,*
      men and women,
   I will pour out my Spirit
      in those days,
      and they will prophesy.
¹⁹ *I will cause wonders to occur*
      in the heavens above
      and signs on the earth below,
      blood and fire and a cloud of smoke.
²⁰ *The sun will be changed into darkness,*
      and the moon will be changed
      into blood,
      before the great and spectacular day
      of the Lord comes.
²¹ *And everyone who calls on the name*
      *of the Lord will be saved.*ᶜ

²²"Fellow Israelites, listen to these words! Jesus the Nazarene was a man whose credentials God proved to you through miracles, wonders, and signs, which God performed through him among you. You yourselves know this. ²³In accordance with God's established

ᶜJoel 2:28-32

plan and foreknowledge, he was betrayed. You, with the help of wicked men, had Jesus killed by nailing him to a cross. ²⁴God raised him up! God freed him from death's dreadful grip, since it was impossible for death to hang on to him. ²⁵David says about him,

I foresaw that the Lord
    was always with me;
    because he is at my right hand
    I won't be shaken.
²⁶ Therefore, my heart was glad
    and my tongue rejoiced.
Moreover, my body will live in hope,
    ²⁷ because you won't abandon me
      to the grave,
    nor permit your holy one
      to experience decay.
²⁸ You have shown me the paths of life;
    your presence will fill me
      with happiness.ᵈ

²⁹"Brothers and sisters, I can speak confidently about the patriarch David. He died and was buried, and his tomb is with us to this very day. ³⁰Because he was a prophet, he knew that God promised him with a solemn pledge to seat one of his descendants on his throne. ³¹Having seen this beforehand, David spoke about the resurrection of Christ, that he wasn't abandoned to the grave, nor did his body experience decay.ᵉ ³²This Jesus God raised up. We are all witnesses to that fact. ³³He was exalted to God's right side and received from the Father the promised Holy Spirit. He poured out this Spirit, and you are seeing and hearing the results of his having done so. ³⁴David didn't ascend into heaven. Yet he says,

The Lord said to my Lord,
    'Sit at my right side,

³⁵ until I make your enemies
    a footstool for your feet.'ᶠ

³⁶"Therefore, let all Israel know beyond question that God has made this Jesus, whom you crucified, both Lord and Christ."

³⁷When the crowd heard this, they were deeply troubled. They said to Peter and the other apostles, "Brothers, what should we do?"

³⁸Peter replied, "Change your hearts and lives. Each of you must be baptized in the name of Jesus Christ for the forgiveness of your sins. Then you will receive the gift of the Holy Spirit. ³⁹This promise is for you, your children, and for all who are far away—as many as the Lord our God invites." ⁴⁰With many other words he testified to them and encouraged them, saying, "Be saved from this perverse generation." ⁴¹Those who accepted Peter's message were baptized. God brought about three thousand people into the community on that day.

Community of believers

⁴²The believers devoted themselves to the apostles' teaching, to the community, to their shared meals, and to their prayers. ⁴³A sense of awe came over everyone. God performed many wonders and signs through the apostles. ⁴⁴All the believers were united and shared everything. ⁴⁵They would sell pieces of property and possessions and distribute the proceeds to everyone who needed them. ⁴⁶Every day, they met together in the temple and ate in their homes. They shared food with gladness and simplicity. ⁴⁷They praised God and demonstrated God's goodness

ᵈPs 16:8-11 ᵉPs 16:10 ᶠPs 110:1

to everyone. The Lord added daily to the community those who were being saved.

Healing of a crippled man

3 Peter and John were going up to the temple at three o'clock in the afternoon, the established prayer time. [2] Meanwhile, a man crippled since birth was being carried in. Every day, people would place him at the temple gate known as the Beautiful Gate so he could ask for money from those entering the temple. [3] When he saw Peter and John about to enter, he began to ask them for a gift. [4] Peter and John stared at him. Peter said, "Look at us!" [5] So the man gazed at them, expecting to receive something from them. [6] Peter said, "I don't have any money, but I will give you what I do have. In the name of Jesus Christ the Nazarene, rise up and walk!" [7] Then he grasped the man's right hand and raised him up. At once his feet and ankles became strong. [8] Jumping up, he began to walk around. He entered the temple with them, walking, leaping, and praising God. [9] All the people saw him walking and praising God. [10] They recognized him as the same one who used to sit at the temple's Beautiful Gate asking for money. They were filled with amazement and surprise at what had happened to him.

[11] While the healed man clung to Peter and John, all the people rushed toward them at Solomon's Porch, completely amazed. [12] Seeing this, Peter addressed the people: "You Israelites, why are you amazed at this? Why are you staring at us as if we made him walk by our own power or piety? [13] The God of Abraham, Isaac, and Jacob—the God of our ancestors—has glorified his servant Jesus. This is the one you handed over and denied in Pilate's presence, even though he had already decided to release him. [14] You rejected the holy and righteous one, and asked that a murderer be released to you instead. [15] You killed the author of life, the very one whom God raised from the dead. We are witnesses of this. [16] His name itself has made this man strong. That is, because of faith in Jesus' name, God has strengthened this man whom you see and know. The faith that comes through Jesus gave him complete health right before your eyes.

[17] "Brothers and sisters, I know you acted in ignorance. So did your rulers. [18] But this is how God fulfilled what he foretold through all the prophets: that his Christ would suffer. [19] Change your hearts and lives! Turn back to God so that your sins may be wiped away. [20] Then the Lord will provide a season of relief from the distress of this age and he will send Jesus, whom he handpicked to be your Christ. [21] Jesus must remain in heaven until the restoration of all things, about which God spoke long ago through his holy prophets. [22] Moses said, *The Lord your God will raise up from your own people a prophet like me. Listen to whatever he tells you.* [23] *Whoever doesn't listen to that prophet will be totally cut off from the people.*[g] [24] All the prophets who spoke—from Samuel forward—announced these days. [25] You are the heirs of the prophets and the covenant that God made with your ancestors when he told Abraham, *Through your descendants, all the*

[g] Deut 18:15, 19

families on earth will be blessed.[h] [26]After God raised his servant, he sent him to you first—to bless you by enabling each of you to turn from your evil ways."

Peter and John questioned

4 While Peter and John were speaking to the people, the priests, the captain of the temple guard, and the Sadducees confronted them. [2]They were incensed that the apostles were teaching the people and announcing that the resurrection of the dead was happening because of Jesus. [3]They seized Peter and John and put them in prison until the next day. (It was already evening.) [4]Many who heard the word became believers, and their number grew to about five thousand.

[5]The next day the leaders, elders, and legal experts gathered in Jerusalem, [6]along with Annas the high priest, Caiaphas, John, Alexander, and others from the high priest's family. [7]They had Peter and John brought before them and asked, "By what power or in what name did you do this?"

[8]Then Peter, inspired by the Holy Spirit, answered, "Leaders of the people and elders, [9]are we being examined today because something good was done for a sick person, a good deed that healed him? [10]If so, then you and all the people of Israel need to know that this man stands healthy before you because of the name of Jesus Christ the Nazarene—whom you crucified but whom God raised from the dead. [11]This Jesus is the stone you builders rejected; he has become the cornerstone! [12]Salvation can be found in no one else. Throughout the whole world, no other name has been given among humans through which we must be saved."

[13]The council was caught by surprise by the confidence with which Peter and John spoke. After all, they understood that these apostles were uneducated and inexperienced. They also recognized that they had been followers of Jesus. [14]However, since the healed man was standing with Peter and John before their own eyes, they had no rebuttal. [15]After ordering them to wait outside, the council members began to confer with each other. [16]"What should we do with these men? Everyone living in Jerusalem is aware of the sign performed through them. It's obvious to everyone and we can't deny it. [17]To keep it from spreading further among the people, we need to warn them not to speak to anyone in this name." [18]When they called Peter and John back, they demanded that they stop all speaking and teaching in the name of Jesus.

[19]Peter and John responded, "It's up to you to determine whether it's right before God to obey you rather than God. [20]As for us, we can't stop speaking about what we have seen and heard." [21]They threatened them further, then released them. Because of public support for Peter and John, they couldn't find a way to punish them. Everyone was praising God for what had happened, [22]because the man who had experienced this sign of healing was over 40 years old.

The believers pray

[23]After their release, Peter and John returned to the brothers and sisters and reported everything the chief priests

[h]Gen 22:18; 26:4

and elders had said. [24]They listened, then lifted their voices in unison to God, "Master, you are the one who created the heaven, the earth, the sea, and everything in them. [25]You are the one who spoke by the Holy Spirit through our ancestor David, your servant:

> Why did the Gentiles rage,
>   and the peoples plot in vain?
> [26] The kings of the earth took their stand
>   and the rulers gathered together
>   as one
>   against the Lord
>   and against his Christ.[1]

[27]Indeed, both Herod and Pontius Pilate, with Gentiles and Israelites, did gather in this city against your holy servant Jesus, whom you anointed. [28]They did what your power and plan had already determined would happen. [29]Now, Lord, take note of their threats and enable your servants to speak your word with complete confidence. [30]Stretch out your hand to bring healing and enable signs and wonders to be performed through the name of Jesus, your holy servant." [31]After they prayed, the place where they were gathered was shaken. They were all filled with the Holy Spirit and began speaking God's word with confidence.

Sharing among the believers

[32]The community of believers was one in heart and mind. None of them would say, "This is mine!" about any of their possessions, but held everything in common. [33]The apostles continued to bear powerful witness to the resurrection of the Lord Jesus, and an abundance of grace was at work among them all. [34]There were no needy persons among them. Those who owned properties or houses would sell them, bring the proceeds from the sales, [35]and place them in the care and under the authority of the apostles. Then it was distributed to anyone who was in need.

[36]Joseph, whom the apostles nicknamed Barnabas (that is, "one who encourages"), was a Levite from Cyprus. [37]He owned a field, sold it, brought the money, and placed it in the care and under the authority of the apostles.

Pretenders of sharing

However, a man named Ananias, along with his wife Sapphira, sold a piece of property. [2]With his wife's knowledge, he withheld some of the proceeds from the sale. He brought the rest and placed it in the care and under the authority of the apostles. [3]Peter asked, "Ananias, how is it that Satan has influenced you to lie to the Holy Spirit by withholding some of the proceeds from the sale of your land? [4]Wasn't that property yours to keep? After you sold it, wasn't the money yours to do with whatever you wanted? What made you think of such a thing? You haven't lied to other people but to God!" [5]When Ananias heard these words, he dropped dead. Everyone who heard this conversation was terrified. [6]Some young men stood up, wrapped up his body, carried him out, and buried him.

[7]About three hours later, his wife entered, but she didn't know what had happened to her husband. [8]Peter asked her, "Tell me, did you and your husband receive this price for the field?"

She responded, "Yes, that's the amount."

---

[1]Or anointed one; Ps 2:1-2

⁹He replied, "How could you scheme with each other to challenge the Lord's Spirit? Look! The feet of those who buried your husband are at the door. They will carry you out too." ¹⁰At that very moment, she dropped dead at his feet. When the young men entered and found her dead, they carried her out and buried her with her husband. ¹¹Trepidation and dread seized the whole church and all who heard what had happened.

Responses to the church

¹²The apostles performed many signs and wonders among the people. They would come together regularly at Solomon's Porch. ¹³No one from outside the church dared to join them, even though the people spoke highly of them. ¹⁴Indeed, more and more believers in the Lord, large numbers of both men and women, were added to the church. ¹⁵As a result, they would even bring the sick out into the main streets and lay them on cots and mats so that at least Peter's shadow could fall on some of them as he passed by. ¹⁶Even large numbers of persons from towns around Jerusalem would gather, bringing the sick and those harassed by unclean spirits. Everyone was healed.

The Jerusalem Council harasses the apostles

¹⁷The high priest, together with his allies, the Sadducees, was overcome with jealousy. ¹⁸They seized the apostles and made a public show of putting them in prison. ¹⁹An angel from the Lord opened the prison doors during the night and led them out. The angel told them, ²⁰"Go, take your place in the temple, and tell the people everything about this new life." ²¹Early in the morning, they went into the temple as they had been told and began to teach.

When the high priest and his colleagues gathered, they convened the Jerusalem Council, that is, the full assembly of Israel's elders. They sent word to the prison to have the apostles brought before them. ²²However, the guards didn't find them in the prison. They returned and reported, ²³"We found the prison locked and well-secured, with guards standing at the doors, but when we opened the doors we found no one inside!" ²⁴When they received this news, the captain of the temple guard and the chief priests were baffled and wondered what might be happening. ²⁵Just then, someone arrived and announced, "Look! The people you put in prison are standing in the temple and teaching the people!" ²⁶Then the captain left with his guards and brought the apostles back. They didn't use force because they were afraid the people would stone them.

²⁷The apostles were brought before the council where the high priest confronted them: ²⁸"In no uncertain terms, we demanded that you not teach in this name. And look at you! You have filled Jerusalem with your teaching. And you are determined to hold us responsible for this man's death."

²⁹Peter and the apostles replied, "We must obey God rather than humans! ³⁰The God of our ancestors raised Jesus from the dead—whom you killed by hanging him on a tree. ³¹God has exalted Jesus to his right side as leader and savior so that he could enable Israel to change its heart and life and to find forgiveness for sins. ³²We are witnesses of such things, as is the Holy Spirit,

whom God has given to those who obey him."

33When the council members heard this, they became furious and wanted to kill the apostles. 34One council member, a Pharisee and teacher of the Law named Gamaliel, well-respected by all the people, stood up and ordered that the men be taken outside for a few moments. 35He said, "Fellow Israelites, consider carefully what you intend to do to these people. 36Some time ago, Theudas appeared, claiming to be somebody, and some four hundred men joined him. After he was killed, all of his followers scattered, and nothing came of that. 37Afterward, at the time of the census, Judas the Galilean appeared and got some people to follow him in a revolt. He was killed too, and all his followers scattered far and wide. 38Here's my recommendation in this case: Distance yourselves from these men. Let them go! If their plan or activity is of human origin, it will end in ruin. 39If it originates with God, you won't be able to stop them. Instead, you would actually find yourselves fighting God!" The council was convinced by his reasoning. 40After calling the apostles back, they had them beaten. They ordered them not to speak in the name of Jesus, then let them go. 41The apostles left the council rejoicing because they had been regarded as worthy to suffer disgrace for the sake of the name. 42Every day they continued to teach and proclaim the good news that Jesus is the Christ, both in the temple and in houses.

Selection of seven to serve

6 About that time, while the number of disciples continued to increase, a complaint arose. Greek-speaking disciples accused the Aramaic-speaking disciples because their widows were being overlooked in the daily food service. 2The Twelve called a meeting of all the disciples and said, "It isn't right for us to set aside proclamation of God's word in order to serve tables. 3Brothers and sisters, carefully choose seven well-respected men from among you. They must be well-respected and endowed by the Spirit with exceptional wisdom. We will put them in charge of this concern. 4As for us, we will devote ourselves to prayer and the service of proclaiming the word." 5This proposal pleased the entire community. They selected Stephen, a man endowed by the Holy Spirit with exceptional faith, Philip, Prochorus, Nicanor, Timon, Parmenas, and Nicolaus from Antioch, a convert to Judaism. 6The community presented these seven to the apostles, who prayed and laid their hands on them. 7God's word continued to grow. The number of disciples in Jerusalem increased significantly. Even a large group of priests embraced the faith.

Arrest and murder of Stephen

8Stephen, who stood out among the believers for the way God's grace was at work in his life and for his exceptional endowment with divine power, was doing great wonders and signs among the people. 9Opposition arose from some who belonged to the so-called Synagogue of Former Slaves. Members from Cyrene, Alexandria, Cilicia, and Asia entered into debate with Stephen. 10However, they couldn't resist the wisdom the Spirit gave him as he spoke. 11Then they secretly enticed some people to claim, "We heard him insult Moses and God." 12They stirred up the people, the elders, and the legal experts. They caught Stephen, dragged him away, and brought him before the Jerusalem Council. ¹³Before the council, they presented false witnesses who testified, "This man never stops speaking against this holy place and the Law. ¹⁴In fact, we heard him say that this man Jesus of Nazareth will destroy this place and alter the customary practices Moses gave us." ¹⁵Everyone seated in the council stared at Stephen, and they saw that his face was radiant, just like an angel's.

7 The high priest asked, "Are these accusations true?"

²Stephen responded, "Brothers and fathers, listen to me. Our glorious God appeared to our ancestor Abraham while he was still in Mesopotamia, before he settled in Haran. ³God told him, 'Leave your homeland and kin, and go to the land that I will show you.'ʲ ⁴So Abraham left the land of the Chaldeans and settled in Haran. After Abraham's father died, God had him resettle in this land where you now live. ⁵God didn't give him an inheritance here, not even a square foot of land. However, God did promise to give the land as his possession to him and to his descendants, even though Abraham had no child. ⁶God put it this way: *His descendants will be strangers in a land that belongs to others, who will enslave them and abuse them for four hundred years.*ᵏ ⁷*And I will condemn the nation they serve as slaves,* God said, *and afterward they will leave*ˡ that land and serve me in this place. ⁸God gave him the covenant confirmed through circumcision. Accordingly, eight days after Isaac's birth, Abraham

circumcised him. Isaac did the same with Jacob, and Jacob with the twelve patriarchs.

⁹"Because the patriarchs were jealous of Joseph, they sold him into slavery in Egypt. God was with him, however, ¹⁰and rescued him from all his troubles. The grace and wisdom he gave Joseph were recognized by Pharaoh, king of Egypt, who appointed him ruler over Egypt and over his whole palace. ¹¹A famine came upon all Egypt and Canaan, and great hardship came with it. Our ancestors had nothing to eat. ¹²When Jacob heard there was grain in Egypt, he sent our ancestors there for the first time. ¹³During their second visit, Joseph told his brothers who he was, and Pharaoh learned about Joseph's family. ¹⁴Joseph sent for his father Jacob and all his relatives—seventy-five in all—and invited them to live with him. ¹⁵So Jacob went down to Egypt, where he and our ancestors died. ¹⁶Their bodies were brought back to Shechem and placed in the tomb that Abraham had purchased for a certain sum of money from Hamor's children, who lived in Shechem.

¹⁷"When it was time for God to keep the promise he made to Abraham, the number of our people in Egypt had greatly expanded. ¹⁸But then *another king rose to power over Egypt who didn't know anything about Joseph.*ᵐ ¹⁹He exploited our people and abused our ancestors. He even forced them to abandon their newly born babies so they would die. ²⁰That's when Moses was born. He was highly favored by God, and for three months his parents cared for him in their home. ²¹After he

ʲGen 12:1 ᵏGen 15:13 ˡGen 15:14 ᵐExod 1:8

was abandoned, Pharaoh's daughter adopted and cared for him as though he were her own son. [22]Moses learned everything Egyptian wisdom had to offer, and he was a man of powerful words and deeds.

[23]"When Moses was 40 years old, he decided to visit his family, the Israelites. [24]He saw one of them being wronged so he came to his rescue and evened the score by killing the Egyptian. [25]He expected his own kin to understand that God was using him to rescue them, but they didn't. [26]The next day he came upon some Israelites who were caught up in an argument. He tried to make peace between them by saying, 'You are brothers! Why are you harming each other?' [27]The one who started the fight against his neighbor pushed Moses aside and said, *'Who appointed you as our leader and judge?* [28]*Are you planning to kill me like you killed that Egyptian yesterday?'*[n] [29]When Moses heard this, he fled to Midian, where he lived as an immigrant and had two sons.

[30]"Forty years later, an angel appeared to Moses in the flame of a burning bush in the wilderness near Mount Sinai. [31]Enthralled by the sight, Moses approached to get a closer look and he heard the Lord's voice: [32]*I am the God of your ancestors, the God of Abraham, Isaac, and Jacob.*[o] Trembling with fear, Moses didn't dare to investigate any further. [33]The Lord continued, *'Remove the sandals from your feet, for the place where you are standing is holy ground.* [34]*I have clearly seen the oppression my people have experienced in Egypt, and I have heard their groaning. I have come*

down to rescue them. Come! I am sending you to Egypt.'[p]

[35]"This is the same Moses whom they rejected when they asked, 'Who appointed you as our leader and judge?' This is the Moses whom God sent as leader and deliverer. God did this with the help of the angel who appeared before him in the bush. [36]This man led them out after he performed wonders and signs in Egypt at the Red Sea and for forty years in the wilderness. [37]This is the Moses who told the Israelites, *'God will raise up for you a prophet like me from your own people.*[q] [38]This is the one who was in the assembly in the wilderness with our ancestors and with the angel who spoke to him on Mount Sinai. He is the one who received life-giving words to give to us. [39]He's also the one whom our ancestors refused to obey. Instead, they pushed him aside and, in their thoughts and desires, returned to Egypt. [40]They told Aaron, *'Make us gods that will lead us. As for this Moses who led us out of Egypt, we don't know what's happened to him!'*[r] [41]That's when they made an idol in the shape of a calf, offered a sacrifice to it, and began to celebrate what they had made with their own hands. [42]So God turned away from them and handed them over to worship the stars in the sky, just as it is written in the scroll of the Prophets:

> Did you bring sacrifices
>   and offerings to me
>   for forty years in the wilderness,
>   house of Israel?
>
> [43] No! Instead, you took the tent
>   of Moloch with you,
>   and the star of your god Rephan,

---

[n]Exod 2:14   [o]Exod 3:6   [p]Exod 3:5, 7   [q]Deut 18:15   [r]Exod 32:1

*the images that you made in order
to worship them.
Therefore, I will send you far away,
farther than Babylon.*[s]

[44]"The tent of testimony was with our ancestors in the wilderness. Moses built it just as he had been instructed by the one who spoke to him and according to the pattern he had seen. [45]In time, when they had received the tent, our ancestors carried it with them when, under Joshua's leadership, they took possession of the land from the nations whom God expelled. This tent remained in the land until the time of David. [46]God approved of David, who asked that he might provide a dwelling place for the God of Jacob.[t] [47]But it was Solomon who actually built a house for God. [48]However, the Most High doesn't live in houses built by human hands. As the prophet says,

[49] *Heaven is my throne,
    and the earth is my footstool.
'What kind of house will you build
    for me,' says the Lord,
    'or where is my resting place?
[50] Didn't I make all these things
    with my own hand?'*[u]

[51]"You stubborn people! In your thoughts and hearing, you are like those who have had no part in God's covenant! You continuously set yourself against the Holy Spirit, just like your ancestors did. [52]Was there a single prophet your ancestors didn't harass? They even killed those who predicted the coming of the righteous one, and you've betrayed and murdered him! [53]You received the Law given by angels, but you haven't kept it."

[54]Once the council members heard these words, they were enraged and began to grind their teeth at Stephen. [55]But Stephen, enabled by the Holy Spirit, stared into heaven and saw God's majesty and Jesus standing at God's right side. [56]He exclaimed, "Look! I can see heaven on display and the Human One[v] standing at God's right side!" [57]At this, they shrieked and covered their ears. Together, they charged at him, [58]threw him out of the city, and began to stone him. The witnesses placed their coats in the care of a young man named Saul. [59]As they battered him with stones, Stephen prayed, "Lord Jesus, accept my life!" [60]Falling to his knees, he shouted, "Lord, don't hold this sin against them!" Then he died.

8 Saul was in full agreement with Stephen's murder.

The church scatters

At that time, the church in Jerusalem began to be subjected to vicious harassment. Everyone except the apostles was scattered throughout the regions of Judea and Samaria. [2]Some pious men buried Stephen and deeply grieved over him. [3]Saul began to wreak havoc against the church. Entering one house after another, he would drag off both men and women and throw them into prison.

Philip in Samaria

[4]Those who had been scattered moved on, preaching the good news along the way. [5]Philip went down to a city in Samaria[w] and began to preach Christ to them. [6]The crowds were

---

[s]Amos 5:25-27   [t]Critical editions of the Gk New Testament read *house of Jacob*.   [u]Isa 66:1-2
[v]Or *Son of Man*   [w]Or *the city of Samaria*

united by what they heard Philip say and the signs they saw him perform, and they gave him their undivided attention. [7] With loud shrieks, unclean spirits came out of many people, and many who were paralyzed or crippled were healed. [8] There was great rejoicing in that city.

[9] Before Philip's arrival, a certain man named Simon had practiced sorcery in that city and baffled the people of Samaria. He claimed to be a great person. [10] Everyone, from the least to the greatest, gave him their undivided attention and referred to him as "the power of God called Great." [11] He had their attention because he had baffled them with sorcery for a long time. [12] After they came to believe Philip, who preached the good news about God's kingdom and the name of Jesus Christ, both men and women were baptized. [13] Even Simon himself came to believe and was baptized. Afterward, he became one of Philip's supporters. As he saw firsthand the signs and great miracles that were happening, he was astonished.

[14] When word reached the apostles in Jerusalem that Samaria had accepted God's word, they commissioned Peter and John to go to Samaria. [15] Peter and John went down to Samaria where they prayed that the new believers would receive the Holy Spirit. ([16] This was because the Holy Spirit had not yet fallen on any of them; they had only been baptized in the name of the Lord Jesus.) [17] So Peter and John laid their hands on them, and they received the Holy Spirit.

[18] When Simon perceived that the Spirit was given through the laying on of the apostles' hands, he offered them money. [19] He said, "Give me this authority too so that anyone on whom I lay my hands will receive the Holy Spirit."

[20] Peter responded, "May your money be condemned to hell along with you because you believed you could buy God's gift with money! [21] You can have no part or share in God's word because your heart isn't right with God. [22] Therefore, change your heart and life! Turn from your wickedness! Plead with the Lord in the hope that your wicked intent can be forgiven, [23] for I see that your bitterness has poisoned you and evil has you in chains."

[24] Simon replied, "All of you, please, plead to the Lord for me so that nothing of what you have said will happen to me!" [25] After the apostles had testified and proclaimed the Lord's word, they returned to Jerusalem, preaching the good news to many Samaritan villages along the way.

Philip and the Ethiopian eunuch

[26] An angel from the Lord spoke to Philip, "At noon, take[x] the road that leads from Jerusalem to Gaza." (This is a desert road.) [27] So he did. Meanwhile, an Ethiopian man was on his way home from Jerusalem, where he had come to worship. He was a eunuch and an official responsible for the entire treasury of Candace. (Candace is the title given to the Ethiopian queen.) [28] He was reading the prophet Isaiah while sitting in his carriage. [29] The Spirit told Philip, "Approach this carriage and stay with it."

[30] Running up to the carriage, Philip heard the man reading the prophet Isaiah. He asked, "Do you really understand what you are reading?"

x Or travel south along

³¹The man replied, "Without someone to guide me, how could I?" Then he invited Philip to climb up and sit with him. ³²This was the passage of scripture he was reading:

> Like a sheep he was led
>   to the slaughter
> and like a lamb before its shearer
>   is silent
> so he didn't open his mouth.
>
> ³³ In his humiliation
>   justice was taken away from him.
> Who can tell the story
>   of his descendants
>   because his life was taken
>   from the earth?ʸ

³⁴The eunuch asked Philip, "Tell me, about whom does the prophet say this? Is he talking about himself or someone else?" ³⁵Starting with that passage, Philip proclaimed the good news about Jesus to him. ³⁶As they went down the road, they came to some water.

The eunuch said, "Look! Water! What would keep me from being baptized?"ᶻ ³⁸He ordered that the carriage halt. Both Philip and the eunuch went down to the water, where Philip baptized him. ³⁹When they came up out of the water, the Lord's Spirit suddenly took Philip away. The eunuch never saw him again but went on his way rejoicing. ⁴⁰Philip found himself in Azotus. He traveled through that area, preaching the good news in all the cities until he reached Caesarea.

Saul encounters the risen Jesus

9 Meanwhile, Saul was still spewing out murderous threats against the Lord's disciples. He went to the high priest, ²seeking letters to the synagogues in Damascus. If he found persons who belonged to the Way, whether men or women, these letters would authorize him to take them as prisoners to Jerusalem. ³During the journey, as he approached Damascus, suddenly a light from heaven encircled him. ⁴He fell to the ground and heard a voice asking him, "Saul, Saul, why are you harassing me?"

⁵Saul asked, "Who are you, Lord?"

"I am Jesus, whom you are harassing," came the reply. ⁶"Now get up and enter the city. You will be told what you must do."

⁷Those traveling with him stood there speechless; they heard the voice but saw no one. ⁸After they picked Saul up from the ground, he opened his eyes but he couldn't see. So they led him by the hand into Damascus. ⁹For three days he was blind and neither ate nor drank anything.

¹⁰In Damascus there was a certain disciple named Ananias. The Lord spoke to him in a vision, "Ananias!"

He answered, "Yes, Lord."

¹¹The Lord instructed him, "Go to Judas' house on Straight Street and ask for a man from Tarsus named Saul. He is praying. ¹²In a vision he has seen a man named Ananias enter and put his hands on him to restore his sight."

¹³Ananias countered, "Lord, I have heard many reports about this man. People say he has done horrible things to your holy people in Jerusalem. ¹⁴He's here with authority from the chief

---

ʸIsa 53:7-8 ᶻCritical editions of the Gk New Testament do not include 8:37 *Philip said to him, "If you believe with all your heart, you can be." The eunuch answered, "I believe that Jesus Christ is God's Son."*

priests to arrest everyone who calls on your name."

¹⁵The Lord replied, "Go! This man is the agent I have chosen to carry my name before Gentiles, kings, and Israelites. ¹⁶I will show him how much he must suffer for the sake of my name."

¹⁷Ananias went to the house. He placed his hands on Saul and said, "Brother Saul, the Lord sent me—Jesus, who appeared to you on the way as you were coming here. He sent me so that you could see again and be filled with the Holy Spirit." ¹⁸Instantly, flakes fell from Saul's eyes and he could see again. He got up and was baptized. ¹⁹After eating, he regained his strength.

He stayed with the disciples in Damascus for several days. ²⁰Right away, he began to preach about Jesus in the synagogues. "He is God's Son," he declared.

²¹Everyone who heard him was baffled. They questioned each other, "Isn't he the one who was wreaking havoc among those in Jerusalem who called on this name? Hadn't he come here to take those same people as prisoners to the chief priests?"

²²But Saul grew stronger and stronger. He confused the Jews who lived in Damascus by proving that Jesus is the Christ.

²³After this had gone on for some time, the Jews hatched a plot to kill Saul. ²⁴However, he found out about their scheme. They were keeping watch at the city gates around the clock so they could assassinate him. ²⁵But his disciples took him by night and lowered him in a basket through an opening in the city wall.

²⁶When Saul arrived in Jerusalem, he tried to join the disciples, but they were all afraid of him. They didn't believe he was really a disciple. ²⁷Then Barnabas brought Saul to the apostles and told them the story about how Saul saw the Lord on the way and that the Lord had spoken to Saul. He also told them about the confidence with which Saul had preached in the name of Jesus in Damascus. ²⁸After this, Saul moved freely among the disciples in Jerusalem and was speaking with confidence in the name of the Lord. ²⁹He got into debates with the Greek-speaking Jews as well, but they tried to kill him. ³⁰When the family of believers learned about this, they escorted him down to Caesarea and sent him off to Tarsus.

³¹Then the church throughout Judea, Galilee, and Samaria enjoyed a time of peace. God strengthened the church, and its life was marked by reverence for the Lord. Encouraged by the Holy Spirit, the church continued to grow in numbers.

Peter heals and raises the dead

³²As Peter toured the whole region, he went to visit God's holy people in Lydda. ³³There he found a man named Aeneas who had been paralyzed and had been confined to his bed for eight years. ³⁴Peter said to him, "Aeneas, Jesus Christ heals you! Get up and make your bed." At once he got up. ³⁵Everyone who lived in Lydda and Sharon saw him and turned to the Lord.

³⁶In Joppa there was a disciple named Tabitha (in Greek her name is Dorcas). Her life overflowed with good works and compassionate acts on behalf of those in need. ³⁷About that time, though, she became so ill that she died. After they washed her body, they laid her in an upstairs room. ³⁸Since

Lydda was near Joppa, when the disciples heard that Peter was there, they sent two people to Peter. They urged, "Please come right away!" ³⁹Peter went with them. Upon his arrival, he was taken to the upstairs room. All the widows stood beside him, crying as they showed the tunics and other clothing Dorcas made when she was alive.

⁴⁰Peter sent everyone out of the room, then knelt and prayed. He turned to the body and said, "Tabitha, get up!" She opened her eyes, saw Peter, and sat up. ⁴¹He gave her his hand and raised her up. Then he called God's holy people, including the widows, and presented her alive to them. ⁴²The news spread throughout Joppa, and many put their faith in the Lord. ⁴³Peter stayed for some time in Joppa with a certain tanner named Simon.

Peter, Cornelius, and the Gentiles

10 There was a man in Caesarea named Cornelius, a centurion in the Italian Company.ᵃ ²He and his whole household were pious, Gentile God-worshippers. He gave generously to those in need among the Jewish people and prayed to God constantly. ³One day at nearly three o'clock in the afternoon, he clearly saw an angel from God in a vision. The angel came to him and said, "Cornelius!"

⁴Startled, he stared at the angel and replied, "What is it, Lord?"

The angel said, "Your prayers and your compassionate acts are like a memorial offering to God. ⁵Send messengers to Joppa at once and summon a certain Simon, the one known as Peter. ⁶He is a guest of Simon the tanner, whose house is near the seacoast." ⁷When the angel who was speaking to him had gone, Cornelius summoned two of his household servants along with a pious soldier from his personal staff. ⁸He explained everything to them, then sent them to Joppa.

⁹At noon on the following day, as their journey brought them close to the city, Peter went up on the roof to pray. ¹⁰He became hungry and wanted to eat. While others were preparing the meal, he had a visionary experience. ¹¹He saw heaven opened up and something like a large linen sheet being lowered to the earth by its four corners. ¹²Inside the sheet were all kinds of four-legged animals, reptiles, and wild birds.ᵇ ¹³A voice told him, "Get up, Peter! Kill and eat!"

¹⁴Peter exclaimed, "Absolutely not, Lord! I have never eaten anything impure or unclean."

¹⁵The voice spoke a second time, "Never consider unclean what God has made pure." ¹⁶This happened three times, then the object was suddenly pulled back into heaven.

¹⁷Peter was bewildered about the meaning of the vision. Just then, the messengers sent by Cornelius discovered the whereabouts of Simon's house and arrived at the gate. ¹⁸Calling out, they inquired whether the Simon known as Peter was a guest there.

¹⁹While Peter was brooding over the vision, the Spirit interrupted him, "Look! Three people are looking for you. ²⁰Go downstairs. Don't ask questions; just go with them because I have sent them."

²¹So Peter went downstairs and told them, "I'm the one you are looking for. Why have you come?"

ᵃOr *cohort* (approximately six hundred soldiers) ᵇOr *birds in the sky*

²²They replied, "We've come on behalf of Cornelius, a centurion and righteous man, a God-worshipper who is well-respected by all Jewish people. A holy angel directed him to summon you to his house and to hear what you have to say." ²³Peter invited them into the house as his guests.

The next day he got up and went with them, together with some of the believers from Joppa. ²⁴They arrived in Caesarea the following day. Anticipating their arrival, Cornelius had gathered his relatives and close friends. ²⁵As Peter entered the house, Cornelius met him and fell at his feet in order to honor him. ²⁶But Peter lifted him up, saying, "Get up! Like you, I'm just a human." ²⁷As they continued to talk, Peter went inside and found a large gathering of people. ²⁸He said to them, "You all realize that it is forbidden for a Jew to associate or visit with outsiders. However, God has shown me that I should never call a person impure or unclean. ²⁹For this reason, when you sent for me, I came without objection. I want to know, then, why you sent for me."

³⁰Cornelius answered, "Four days ago at this same time, three o'clock in the afternoon, I was praying at home. Suddenly a man in radiant clothing stood before me. ³¹He said, 'Cornelius, God has heard your prayers, and your compassionate acts are like a memorial offering to him. ³²Therefore, send someone to Joppa and summon Simon, who is known as Peter. He is a guest in the home of Simon the tanner, located near the seacoast.' ³³I sent for you right away, and you were kind enough to come. Now, here we are, gathered in the presence of God to listen to everything the Lord has directed you to say."

³⁴Peter said, "I really am learning that God doesn't show partiality to one group of people over another. ³⁵Rather, in every nation, whoever worships him and does what is right is acceptable to him. ³⁶This is the message of peace he sent to the Israelites by proclaiming the good news through Jesus Christ: He is Lord of all! ³⁷You know what happened throughout Judea, beginning in Galilee after the baptism John preached. ³⁸You know about Jesus of Nazareth, whom God anointed with the Holy Spirit and endowed with power. Jesus traveled around doing good and healing everyone oppressed by the devil because God was with him. ³⁹We are witnesses of everything he did, both in Judea and in Jerusalem. They killed him by hanging him on a tree, ⁴⁰but God raised him up on the third day and allowed him to be seen, ⁴¹not by everyone but by us. We are witnesses whom God chose beforehand, who ate and drank with him after God raised him from the dead. ⁴²He commanded us to preach to the people and to testify that he is the one whom God appointed as judge of the living and the dead. ⁴³All the prophets testify about him that everyone who believes in him receives forgiveness of sins through his name."

⁴⁴While Peter was still speaking, the Holy Spirit fell on everyone who heard the word. ⁴⁵The circumcised believers who had come with Peter were astonished that the gift of the Holy Spirit had been poured out even on the Gentiles. ⁴⁶They heard them speaking in other languages and praising God. Peter asked, ⁴⁷"These people have received the Holy Spirit just as we have. Surely no one can stop them from being baptized with water, can they?" ⁴⁸He

directed that they be baptized in the name of Jesus Christ. Then they invited Peter to stay for several days.

Jerusalem church questions Peter

11 The apostles and the brothers and sisters throughout Judea heard that even the Gentiles had welcomed God's word. ²When Peter went up to Jerusalem, the circumcised believers criticized him. ³They accused him, "You went into the home of the uncircumcised and ate with them!"

⁴Step-by-step, Peter explained what had happened. ⁵"I was in the city of Joppa praying when I had a visionary experience. In my vision, I saw something like a large linen sheet being lowered from heaven by its four corners. It came all the way down to me. ⁶As I stared at it, wondering what it was, I saw four-legged animals—including wild beasts—as well as reptiles and wild birds.ᶜ ⁷I heard a voice say, 'Get up, Peter! Kill and eat!' ⁸I responded, 'Absolutely not, Lord! Nothing impure or unclean has ever entered my mouth.' ⁹The voice from heaven spoke a second time, 'Never consider unclean what God has made pure.' ¹⁰This happened three times, then everything was pulled back into heaven. ¹¹At that moment three men who had been sent to me from Caesarea arrived at the house where we were staying. ¹²The Spirit told me to go with them even though they were Gentiles. These six brothers also went with me, and we entered that man's house. ¹³He reported to us how he had seen an angel standing in his house and saying, 'Send to Joppa and summon Simon, who is known as Peter. ¹⁴He will tell

you how you and your entire household can be saved.' ¹⁵When I began to speak, the Holy Spirit fell on them, just as the Spirit fell on us in the beginning. ¹⁶I remembered the Lord's words: 'John will baptize with water, but you will be baptized with the Holy Spirit.' ¹⁷If God gave them the same gift he gave us who believed in the Lord Jesus Christ, then who am I? Could I stand in God's way?"

¹⁸Once the apostles and other believers heard this, they calmed down. They praised God and concluded, "So then God has enabled Gentiles to change their hearts and lives so that they might have new life."

The Antioch church

¹⁹Now those who were scattered as a result of the trouble that occurred because of Stephen traveled as far as Phoenicia, Cyprus, and Antioch. They proclaimed the word only to Jews. ²⁰Among them were some people from Cyprus and Cyrene. They entered Antioch and began to proclaim the good news about the Lord Jesus also to Gentiles. ²¹The Lord's power was with them, and a large number came to believe and turned to the Lord.

²²When the church in Jerusalem heard about this, they sent Barnabas to Antioch. ²³When he arrived and saw evidence of God's grace, he was overjoyed and encouraged everyone to remain fully committed to the Lord. ²⁴Barnabas responded in this way because he was a good man, whom the Holy Spirit had endowed with exceptional faith. A considerable number of people were added to the Lord. ²⁵Barnabas went to Tarsus in search of Saul. ²⁶When he

---

ᶜOr birds in the sky

found him, he brought him to Antioch. They were there for a whole year, meeting with the church and teaching large numbers of people. It was in Antioch where the disciples were first labeled "Christians."

²⁷About that time, some prophets came down from Jerusalem to Antioch. ²⁸One of them, Agabus, stood up and, inspired by the Spirit, predicted that a severe famine would overtake the entire Roman world. (This occurred during Claudius' rule.) ²⁹The disciples decided they would send support to the brothers and sisters in Judea, with everyone contributing to this ministry according to each person's abundance. ³⁰They sent Barnabas and Saul to take this gift to the elders.

Herod imprisons Peter

12 About that time King Herod began to harass some who belonged to the church. ²He had James, John's brother, killed with a sword. ³When he saw that this pleased the Jews, he arrested Peter as well. This happened during the Festival of Unleavened Bread. ⁴He put Peter in prison, handing him over to four squads of soldiers, sixteen in all, who guarded him. He planned to charge him publicly after the Passover. ⁵While Peter was held in prison, the church offered earnest prayer to God for him.

⁶The night before Herod was going to bring Peter's case forward, Peter was asleep between two soldiers and bound with two chains, with soldiers guarding the prison entrance. ⁷Suddenly an angel from the Lord appeared and a light shone in the prison cell. After nudging Peter on his side to awaken him, the angel raised him up and said,

"Quick! Get up!" The chains fell from his wrists. ⁸The angel continued, "Get dressed. Put on your sandals." Peter did as he was told. The angel said, "Put on your coat and follow me." ⁹Following the angel, Peter left the prison. However, he didn't realize the angel had actually done all this. He thought he was seeing a vision. ¹⁰They passed the first and second guards and came to the iron gate leading to the city. It opened for them by itself. After leaving the prison, they proceeded the length of one street, when abruptly the angel was gone.

¹¹At that, Peter came to his senses and remarked, "Now I'm certain that the Lord sent his angel and rescued me from Herod and from everything the Jewish people expected." ¹²Realizing this, he made his way to Mary's house. (Mary was John's mother; he was also known as Mark.) Many believers had gathered there and were praying. ¹³When Peter knocked at the outer gate, a female servant named Rhoda went to answer. ¹⁴She was so overcome with joy when she recognized Peter's voice that she didn't open the gate. Instead, she ran back in and announced that Peter was standing at the gate.

¹⁵"You've lost your mind!" they responded. She stuck by her story with such determination that they began to say, "It must be his guardian angel." ¹⁶Meanwhile, Peter remained outside, knocking at the gate. They finally opened the gate and saw him there, and they were astounded.

¹⁷He gestured with his hand to quiet them down, then recounted how the Lord led him out of prison. He said, "Tell this to James and the brothers and sisters." Then he left for another place.

¹⁸The next morning the soldiers were flustered about what had happened to Peter. ¹⁹Herod called for a thorough search. When Peter didn't turn up, Herod interrogated the guards and had them executed. Afterward, Herod left Judea in order to spend some time in Caesarea.

²⁰Herod had been furious with the people of Tyre and Sidon for some time. They made a pact to approach him together, since their region depended on the king's realm for its food supply. They persuaded Blastus, the king's personal attendant, to join their cause, then appealed for an end to hostilities. ²¹On the scheduled day Herod dressed himself in royal attire, seated himself on the throne, and gave a speech to the people. ²²Those assembled kept shouting, over and over, "This is a god's voice, not the voice of a mere human!" ²³Immediately an angel from the Lord struck Herod down, because he didn't give the honor to God. He was eaten by worms and died.

²⁴God's word continued to grow and increase. ²⁵Barnabas and Saul returned to Antioch from Jerusalem[d] after completing their mission, bringing with them John, who was also known as Mark.

Barnabas and Saul sent to minister

13 The church at Antioch included prophets and teachers: Barnabas, Simeon (nicknamed Niger), Lucius from Cyrene, Manaen (a childhood friend of Herod the ruler), and Saul. ²As they were worshipping the Lord and fasting, the Holy Spirit said, "Appoint Barnabas and Saul to the work I have called them to undertake." ³After they fasted and prayed, they laid their hands on these two and sent them off.

Serving in Cyprus

⁴After the Holy Spirit sent them on their way, they went down to Seleucia. From there they sailed to Cyprus. ⁵In Salamis they proclaimed God's word in the Jewish synagogues. John was with them as their assistant. ⁶They traveled throughout the island until they arrived at Paphos. There they found a certain man named Bar-Jesus, a Jew who was a false prophet and practiced sorcery. ⁷He kept company with the governor of that province, an intelligent man named Sergius Paulus. The governor sent for Barnabas and Saul since he wanted to hear God's word. ⁸But Elymas the sorcerer[e] (for that's what people understood his name meant) opposed them, trying to steer the governor away from the faith. ⁹Empowered by the Holy Spirit, Saul, also known as Paul, glared at Bar-Jesus and ¹⁰said, "You are a deceiver and trickster! You devil! You attack anything that is right! Will you never stop twisting the straight ways of the Lord into crooked paths? ¹¹Listen! The Lord's power is set against you. You will be blind for a while, unable even to see the daylight." At once, Bar-Jesus' eyes were darkened, and he began to grope about for someone to lead him around by the hand. ¹²When the governor saw what had taken place, he came to believe, for he was astonished by the teaching about the Lord.

[d]Critical editions of the Gk New Testament read *returned to Jerusalem*. [e]Or *magician* (Gk *magos*)

Paul and Barnabas in Pisidian Antioch

¹³Paul and his companions sailed from Paphos to Perga in Pamphylia. John deserted them there and returned to Jerusalem. ¹⁴They went on from Perga and arrived at Antioch in Pisidia. On the Sabbath, they entered and found seats in the synagogue there. ¹⁵After the reading of the Law and the Prophets, the synagogue leaders invited them, "Brothers, if one of you has a sermon for the people, please speak."

¹⁶Standing up, Paul gestured with his hand and said, "Fellow Israelites and Gentile God-worshippers, please listen to me. ¹⁷The God of this people Israel chose our ancestors. God made them a great people while they lived as strangers in the land of Egypt. With his great power, he led them out of that country. ¹⁸For about forty years, God put up with them in the wilderness. ¹⁹God conquered seven nations in the land of Canaan and gave the Israelites their land as an inheritance. ²⁰This happened over a period of about four hundred fifty years.

"After this, he gave them judges until the time of the prophet Samuel. ²¹The Israelites requested a king, so God gave them Saul, Kish's son, from the tribe of Benjamin, and he served as their king for forty years. ²²After God removed him, he raised up David to be their king. God testified concerning him, 'I have found David, Jesse's son, *a man who shares my desires.*[f] Whatever my will is, he will do.' ²³From this man's descendants, God brought to Israel a savior, Jesus, just as he promised. ²⁴Before Jesus' appearance, John proclaimed to all the Israelites a baptism to show they

were changing their hearts and lives. ²⁵As John was completing his mission, he said, 'Who do you think I am? I'm not the one you think I am, but he is coming after me. I'm not worthy to loosen his sandals.'

²⁶"Brothers, children of Abraham's family, and you Gentile God-worshippers, the message about this salvation has been sent to us. ²⁷The people in Jerusalem and their leaders didn't recognize Jesus. By condemning him they fulfilled the words of the prophets that are read every Sabbath. ²⁸Even though they didn't find a single legal basis for the death penalty, they asked Pilate to have him executed. ²⁹When they finished doing everything that had been written about him, they took him down from the cross[g] and laid him in a tomb. ³⁰But God raised him from the dead! ³¹He appeared over many days to those who had traveled with him from Galilee to Jerusalem. They are now his witnesses to the people.

³²"We proclaim to you the good news. What God promised to our ancestors, ³³he has fulfilled for us, their children, by raising up Jesus. As it was written in the second psalm, *You are my son; today I have become your father.*[h] ³⁴"God raised Jesus from the dead, never again to be subjected to death's decay. Therefore, God said, *I will give to you the holy and firm promises I made to David.*[i] ³⁵In another place it is said, *You will not let your holy one experience death's decay.*[j] ³⁶David served God's purpose in his own generation, then he died and was buried with his ancestors. He experienced death's decay, ³⁷but the one whom God has raised up didn't experience death's decay.

[f]Tg 1 Sam 13:14   [g]Or *tree*   [h]Ps 2:7   [i]Isa 55:3   [j]Ps 16:10

[38]"Therefore, brothers and sisters, know this: Through Jesus we proclaim forgiveness of sins to you. From all those sins from which you couldn't be put in right relationship with God through Moses' Law, [39]through Jesus everyone who believes is put in right relationship with God. [40]Take care that the prophets' words don't apply to you:

[41]   Look, you scoffers,
    marvel and die.
    I'm going to do work in your day —
    a work you won't believe
    even if someone told you."[k]

[42]As Paul and Barnabas were leaving the synagogue, the people urged them to speak about these things again on the next Sabbath. [43]When the people in the synagogue were dismissed, many Jews and devout converts to Judaism accompanied Paul and Barnabas, who urged them to remain faithful to the message of God's grace.

[44]On the next Sabbath, almost everyone in the city gathered to hear the Lord's word. [45]When the Jews saw the crowds, they were overcome with jealousy. They argued against what Paul was saying by slandering him. [46]Speaking courageously, Paul and Barnabas said, "We had to speak God's word to you first. Since you reject it and show that you are unworthy to receive eternal life, we will turn to the Gentiles. [47]This is what the Lord commanded us:

    I have made you a light for the Gentiles,
    so that you could bring salvation to the
    end of the earth."[l]

[48]When the Gentiles heard this, they rejoiced and honored the Lord's word. Everyone who was appointed for eternal life believed, [49]and the Lord's word

was broadcast throughout the entire region. [50]However, the Jews provoked the prominent women among the Gentile God-worshippers, as well as the city's leaders. They instigated others to harass Paul and Barnabas, and threw them out of their district. [51]Paul and Barnabas shook the dust from their feet and went to Iconium. [52]Because of the abundant presence of the Holy Spirit in their lives, the disciples were overflowing with happiness.

Paul and Barnabas in Iconium

14 The same thing happened in Iconium. Paul and Barnabas entered the Jewish synagogue and spoke as they had before. As a result, a huge number of Jews and Greeks believed. [2]However, the Jews who rejected the faith stirred up the Gentiles, poisoning their minds against the brothers. [3]Nevertheless, Paul and Barnabas stayed there for quite some time, confidently speaking about the Lord. And the Lord confirmed the word about his grace by the signs and wonders he enabled them to perform. [4]The people of the city were divided—some siding with the Jews, others with the Lord's messengers. [5]Then some Gentiles and Jews, including their leaders, hatched a plot to mistreat and stone Paul and Barnabas. [6]When they learned of it, these two messengers fled to the Lycaonian cities of Lystra and Derbe and the surrounding area, [7]where they continued to proclaim the good news.

Healing a crippled man in Lystra

[8]In Lystra there was a certain man who lacked strength in his legs. He had

[k]Hab 1:5   [l]Isa 49:6

been crippled since birth and had never walked. Sitting there, he [9]heard Paul speaking. Paul stared at him and saw that he believed he could be healed.

[10]Raising his voice, Paul said, "Stand up straight on your feet!" He jumped up and began to walk.

[11]Seeing what Paul had done, the crowd shouted in the Lycaonian language, "The gods have taken human form and come down to visit us!" [12]They referred to Barnabas as Zeus and to Paul as Hermes, since Paul was the main speaker. [13]The priest of Zeus, whose temple was located just outside the city, brought bulls and wreaths to the city gates. Along with the crowds, he wanted to offer sacrifices to them.

[14]When the Lord's messengers Barnabas and Paul found out about this, they tore their clothes in protest and rushed out into the crowd. They shouted, [15]"People, what are you doing? We are humans too, just like you! We are proclaiming the good news to you: turn to the living God and away from such worthless things. He *made the heaven, the earth, the sea, and everything in them.*[m] [16]In the past, he permitted every nation to go its own way. [17]Nevertheless, he hasn't left himself without a witness. He has blessed you by giving you rain from above as well as seasonal harvests, and satisfying you with food and happiness." [18]Even with these words, they barely kept the crowds from sacrificing to them.

[19]Jews from Antioch and Iconium arrived and won the crowds over. They stoned Paul and dragged him out of the city, supposing he was dead. [20]When the disciples surrounded him, he got up

and entered the city again. The following day he left with Barnabas for Derbe.

Returning to Antioch

[21]Paul and Barnabas proclaimed the good news to the people in Derbe and made many disciples. Then they returned to Lystra, Iconium, and Antioch, where [22]they strengthened the disciples and urged them to remain firm in the faith. They told them, "If we are to enter God's kingdom, we must pass through many troubles." [23]They appointed elders for each church. With prayer and fasting, they committed these elders to the Lord, in whom they had placed their trust.

[24]After Paul and Barnabas traveled through Pisidia, they came to Pamphylia. [25]They proclaimed the word in Perga, then went down to Attalia. [26]From there they sailed to Antioch, where they had been entrusted to God's grace to the work they had now completed. [27]On their arrival, they gathered the church together and reported everything that God had accomplished through their activity, and how God had opened a door of faith for the Gentiles. [28]They stayed with the disciples a long time.

The Jerusalem Council

15 Some people came down from Judea teaching the family of believers, "Unless you are circumcised according to the custom we've received from Moses, you can't be saved." [2]Paul and Barnabas took sides against these Judeans and argued strongly against their position.

The church at Antioch appointed

[m]Ps 146:6

Paul, Barnabas, and several others from Antioch to go up to Jerusalem to set this question before the apostles and the elders. [3] The church sent this delegation on their way. They traveled through Phoenicia and Samaria, telling stories about the conversion of the Gentiles to everyone. Their reports thrilled the brothers and sisters. [4] When they arrived in Jerusalem, the church, the apostles, and the elders all welcomed them. They gave a full report of what God had accomplished through their activity. [5] Some believers from among the Pharisees stood up and claimed, "The Gentiles must be circumcised. They must be required to keep the Law from Moses."

[6] The apostles and the elders gathered to consider this matter. [7] After much debate, Peter stood and addressed them, "Fellow believers, you know that, early on, God chose me from among you as the one through whom the Gentiles would hear the word of the gospel and come to believe. [8] God, who knows people's deepest thoughts and desires, confirmed this by giving them the Holy Spirit, just as he did to us. [9] He made no distinction between us and them, but purified their deepest thoughts and desires through faith. [10] Why then are you now challenging God by placing a burden on the shoulders of these disciples that neither we nor our ancestors could bear? [11] On the contrary, we believe that we and they are saved in the same way, by the grace of the Lord Jesus."

[12] The entire assembly fell quiet as they listened to Barnabas and Paul describe all the signs and wonders God did among the Gentiles through their activity. [13] When Barnabas and Paul also fell silent, James responded, "Fellow believers, listen to me. [14] Simon reported how, in his kindness, God came to the Gentiles in the first place, to raise up from them a people of God. [15] The prophets' words agree with this; as it is written,

[16] After this I will return,
     and I will rebuild David's fallen tent;
     I will rebuild what has been
        torn down.
     I will restore it
  [17] so that the rest of humanity
     will seek the Lord,
     even all the Gentiles who belong
        to me.
  The Lord says this,
     the one who does these things[n]
[18] known from earliest times.

[19] "Therefore, I conclude that we shouldn't create problems for Gentiles who turn to God. [20] Instead, we should write a letter, telling them to avoid the pollution associated with idols, sexual immorality, eating meat from strangled animals, and consuming blood. [21] After all, Moses has been proclaimed in every city for a long time, and is read aloud every Sabbath in every synagogue."

Letter to the Gentile believers

[22] The apostles and the elders, along with the entire church, agreed to send some delegates chosen from among themselves to Antioch, together with Paul and Barnabas. They selected Judas Barsabbas and Silas, who were leaders among the brothers and sisters. [23] They were to carry this letter:

The apostles and the elders, to the Gentile brothers and sisters in

---

[n] Amos 9:11-12

Antioch, Syria, and Cilicia. Greetings! [24]"We've heard that some of our number have disturbed you with unsettling words we didn't authorize. [25]We reached a unified decision to select some delegates and send them to you along with our dear friends Barnabas and Paul. [26]These people have devoted their lives to the name of our Lord Jesus Christ. [27]Therefore, we are sending Judas and Silas. They will confirm what we have written. [28]The Holy Spirit has led us to the decision that no burden should be placed on you other than these essentials: [29]refuse food offered to idols, blood, the meat from strangled animals, and sexual immorality. You will do well to avoid such things. Farewell."

[30]When Barnabas, Paul, and the delegates were sent on their way, they went down to Antioch. They gathered the believers and delivered the letter. [31]The people read it, delighted with its encouraging message. [32]Judas and Silas were prophets, and they said many things that encouraged and strengthened the brothers and sisters. [33]Judas and Silas stayed there awhile, then were sent back with a blessing of peace from the brothers and sisters to those who first sent them.[o] [35]Paul and Barnabas stayed in Antioch, where, together with many others, they taught and proclaimed the good news of the Lord's word.

Paul and Barnabas part company

[36]Some time later, Paul said to Barnabas, "Let's go back and visit all the brothers and sisters in every city where we preached the Lord's word. Let's see how they are doing." [37]Barnabas wanted to take John Mark with them. [38]Paul insisted that they shouldn't take him along, since he had deserted them in Pamphylia and hadn't continued with them in their work. [39]Their argument became so intense that they went their separate ways. Barnabas took Mark and sailed to Cyprus. [40]Paul chose Silas and left, entrusted by the brothers and sisters to the Lord's grace. [41]He traveled through Syria and Cilicia, strengthening the churches.

Paul adds Timothy

16 Paul reached Derbe, and then Lystra, where there was a disciple named Timothy. He was the son of a believing Jewish woman and a Greek father. [2]The brothers and sisters in Lystra and Iconium spoke well of him. [3]Paul wanted to take Timothy with him, so he circumcised him. This was because of the Jews who lived in those areas, for they all knew Timothy's father was Greek. [4]As Paul and his companions traveled through the cities, they instructed Gentile believers to keep the regulations put in place by the apostles and elders in Jerusalem. [5]So the churches were strengthened in the faith and every day their numbers flourished.

Vision of the Macedonian

[6]Paul and his companions traveled throughout the regions of Phrygia and Galatia because the Holy Spirit kept them from speaking the word in the province of Asia. [7]When they

---

[o]Critical editions of the Gk New Testament do not include 15:34 *Silas decided to remain there.*

approached the province of Mysia, they tried to enter the province of Bithynia, but the Spirit of Jesus wouldn't let them. [8] Passing by Mysia, they went down to Troas instead. [9] A vision of a man from Macedonia came to Paul during the night. He stood urging Paul, "Come over to Macedonia and help us!" [10] Immediately after he saw the vision, we prepared to leave for the province of Macedonia, concluding that God had called us to proclaim the good news to them.

Lydia's conversion

[11] We sailed from Troas straight for Samothrace and came to Neapolis the following day. [12] From there we went to Philippi, a city of Macedonia's first district and a Roman colony. We stayed in that city several days. [13] On the Sabbath we went outside the city gate to the riverbank, where we thought there might be a place for prayer. We sat down and began to talk with the women who had gathered. [14] One of those women was Lydia, a Gentile God-worshipper from the city of Thyatira, a dealer in purple cloth. As she listened, the Lord enabled her to embrace Paul's message. [15] Once she and her household were baptized, she urged, "Now that you have decided that I am a believer in the Lord, come and stay in my house." And she persuaded us.

Paul and Silas in prison

[16] One day, when we were on the way to the place for prayer, we met a slave woman. She had a spirit that enabled her to predict the future. She made a lot of money for her owners through fortune-telling. [17] She began following Paul and us, shouting, "These people

are servants of the Most High God! They are proclaiming a way of salvation to you!" [18] She did this for many days.

This annoyed Paul so much that he finally turned and said to the spirit, "In the name of Jesus Christ, I command you to leave her!" It left her at that very moment.

[19] Her owners realized that their hope for making money was gone. They grabbed Paul and Silas and dragged them before the officials in the city center. [20] When her owners approached the legal authorities, they said, "These people are causing an uproar in our city. They are Jews [21] who promote customs that we Romans can't accept or practice." [22] The crowd joined in the attacks against Paul and Silas, so the authorities ordered that they be stripped of their clothes and beaten with a rod. [23] When Paul and Silas had been severely beaten, the authorities threw them into prison and ordered the jailer to secure them with great care. [24] When he received these instructions, he threw them into the innermost cell and secured their feet in stocks.

[25] Around midnight Paul and Silas were praying and singing hymns to God, and the other prisoners were listening to them. [26] All at once there was such a violent earthquake that it shook the prison's foundations. The doors flew open and everyone's chains came loose. [27] When the jailer awoke and saw the open doors of the prison, he thought the prisoners had escaped, so he drew his sword and was about to kill himself. [28] But Paul shouted loudly, "Don't harm yourself! We're all here!"

[29] The jailer called for some lights, rushed in, and fell trembling before

Paul and Silas. [30]He led them outside and asked, "Honorable masters, what must I do to be rescued?"

[31]They replied, "Believe in the Lord Jesus, and you will be saved—you and your entire household. [32]They spoke the Lord's word to him and everyone else in his house. [33]Right then, in the middle of the night, the jailer welcomed them and washed their wounds. He and everyone in his household were immediately baptized. [34]He brought them into his home and gave them a meal. He was overjoyed because he and everyone in his household had come to believe in God.

[35]The next morning the legal authorities sent the police to the jailer with the order "Release those people."

[36]So the jailer reported this to Paul, informing him, "The authorities sent word that you both are to be released. You can leave now. Go in peace."

[37]Paul told the police, "Even though we are Roman citizens, they beat us publicly without first finding us guilty of a crime, and they threw us into prison. And now they want to send us away secretly? No way! They themselves will have to come and escort us out." [38]The police reported this to the legal authorities, who were alarmed to learn that Paul and Silas were Roman citizens. [39]They came and consoled Paul and Silas, escorting them out of prison and begging them to leave the city.

[40]Paul and Silas left the prison and made their way to Lydia's house where they encouraged the brothers and sisters. Then they left Philippi.

More troubles for Paul

17 Paul and Silas journeyed through Amphipolis and Apollonia, then came to Thessalonica, where there was a Jewish synagogue. [2]As was Paul's custom, he entered the synagogue and for three Sabbaths interacted with them on the basis of the scriptures. [3]Through his interpretation of the scriptures, he demonstrated that the Christ had to suffer and rise from the dead. He declared, "This Jesus whom I proclaim to you is the Christ." [4]Some were convinced and joined Paul and Silas, including a larger number of Greek God-worshippers and quite a few prominent women.

[5]But the Jews became jealous and brought along some thugs who were hanging out in the marketplace. They formed a mob and started a riot in the city. They attacked Jason's house, intending to bring Paul and Silas before the people. [6]When they didn't find them, they dragged Jason and some believers before the city officials. They were shouting, "These people who have been disturbing the peace throughout the empire have also come here. [7]What is more, Jason has welcomed them into his home. Every one of them does what is contrary to Caesar's decrees by naming someone else as king: Jesus." [8]This provoked the crowd and the city officials even more. [9]After Jason and the others posted bail, they released them.

[10]As soon as it was dark, the brothers and sisters sent Paul and Silas on to Beroea. When they arrived, they went to the Jewish synagogue. [11]The Beroean Jews were more honorable than those in Thessalonica. This was evident in the great eagerness with which they accepted the word and examined the scriptures each day to see whether Paul and Silas' teaching was true. [12]Many came to believe, including a number

of reputable Greek women and many Greek men.

[13]The Jews from Thessalonica learned that Paul also proclaimed God's word in Beroea, so they went there too and were upsetting and disturbing the crowds. [14]The brothers and sisters sent Paul away to the seacoast at once, but Silas and Timothy remained at Beroea. [15]Those who escorted Paul led him as far as Athens, then returned with instructions for Silas and Timothy to come to him as quickly as possible.

[16]While Paul waited for them in Athens, he was deeply distressed to find that the city was flooded with idols. [17]He began to interact with the Jews and Gentile God-worshippers in the synagogue. He also addressed whoever happened to be in the marketplace each day. [18]Certain Epicurean and Stoic philosophers engaged him in discussion too. Some said, "What an amateur! What's he trying to say?" Others remarked, "He seems to be a proclaimer of foreign gods." (They said this because he was preaching the good news about Jesus and the resurrection.) [19]They took him into custody and brought him to the council on Mars Hill. "What is this new teaching? Can we learn what you are talking about? [20]You've told us some strange things and we want to know what they mean." ([21]They said this because all Athenians as well as the foreigners who live in Athens used to spend their time doing nothing but talking about or listening to the newest thing.)

[22]Paul stood up in the middle of the council on Mars Hill and said, "People of Athens, I see that you are very religious in every way. [23]As I was walking through town and carefully observing your objects of worship, I even found an altar with this inscription: 'To an unknown God.' What you worship as unknown, I now proclaim to you. [24]God, who made the world and everything in it, is Lord of heaven and earth. He doesn't live in temples made with human hands. [25]Nor is God served by human hands, as though he needed something, since he is the one who gives life, breath, and everything else. [26]From one person God created every human nation to live on the whole earth, having determined their appointed times and the boundaries of their lands. [27]God made the nations so they would seek him, perhaps even reach out to him and find him. In fact, God isn't far away from any of us. [28]In God we live, move, and exist. As some of your own poets said, 'We are his offspring.'

[29]"Therefore, as God's offspring, we have no need to imagine that the divine being is like a gold, silver, or stone image made by human skill and thought. [30]God overlooks ignorance of these things in times past, but now directs everyone everywhere to change their hearts and lives. [31]This is because God has set a day when he intends to judge the world justly by a man he has appointed. God has given proof of this to everyone by raising him from the dead."

[32]When they heard about the resurrection from the dead, some began to ridicule Paul. However, others said, "We'll hear from you about this again." [33]At that, Paul left the council. [34]Some people joined him and came to believe, including Dionysius, a member of the council on Mars Hill, a woman named Damaris, and several others.

Paul in Corinth

18 After this, Paul left Athens and went to Corinth. [2] There he found a Jew named Aquila, a native of Pontus. He had recently come from Italy with his wife Priscilla because Claudius had ordered all Jews to leave Rome. Paul visited with them. [3] Because they practiced the same trade, he stayed and worked with them. They all worked with leather. [4] Every Sabbath he interacted with people in the synagogue, trying to convince both Jews and Greeks. [5] Once Silas and Timothy arrived from Macedonia, Paul devoted himself fully to the word, testifying to the Jews that Jesus was the Christ. [6] When they opposed and slandered him, he shook the dust from his clothes in protest and said to them, "You are responsible for your own fates! I'm innocent! From now on I'll go to the Gentiles!" [7] He left the synagogue and went next door to the home of Titius Justus, a Gentile God-worshipper. [8] Crispus, the synagogue leader, and his entire household came to believe in the Lord. Many Corinthians believed and were baptized after listening to Paul.

[9] One night the Lord said to Paul in a vision, "Don't be afraid. Continue speaking. Don't be silent. [10] I'm with you and no one who attacks you will harm you, for I have many people in this city." [11] So he stayed there for eighteen months, teaching God's word among them.

[12] Now when Gallio was the governor of the province of Achaia, the Jews united in their opposition against Paul and brought him before the court. [13] "This man is persuading others to worship God unlawfully," they declared. [14] Just as Paul was about to speak, Gallio said to the Jews, "If there had been some sort of injury or criminal behavior, I would have reason to accept your complaint. [15] However, since these are squabbles about a message, names, and your own Law, deal with them yourselves. I have no desire to sit in judgment over such things." [16] He expelled them from the court, [17] but everyone seized Sosthenes, the synagogue leader, and gave him a beating in the presence of the governor. None of this mattered to Gallio.

[18] After Paul stayed in Corinth for some time, he said good-bye to the brothers and sisters. At the Corinthian seaport of Cenchreae he had his head shaved, since he had made a solemn promise. Then, accompanied by Priscilla and Aquila, he sailed away to Syria. [19] After they arrived in Ephesus, he left Priscilla and Aquila and entered the synagogue and interacted with the Jews. [20] They asked him to stay longer, but he declined. [21] As he said farewell to them, though, he added, "God willing, I will return." Then he sailed off from Ephesus. [22] He arrived in Caesarea, went up to Jerusalem and greeted the church, and then went down to Antioch.

[23] After some time there he left and traveled from place to place in the region of Galatia and the district of Phrygia, strengthening all the disciples.

Apollos and his ministry

[24] Meanwhile, a certain Jew named Apollos arrived in Ephesus. He was a native of Alexandria and was well-educated and effective in his use of the scriptures. [25] He had been instructed in the way of the Lord and spoke as one stirred up by the Spirit. He taught accurately the things about Jesus, even

though he was aware only of the baptism John proclaimed and practiced. 26 He began speaking with confidence in the synagogue. When Priscilla and Aquila heard him, they received him into their circle of friends and explained to him God's way more accurately. 27 When he wanted to travel to Achaia, the brothers and sisters encouraged him and wrote to the disciples so they would open their homes to him. Once he arrived, he was of great help to those who had come to believe through grace. 28 He would vigorously defeat Jewish arguments in public debate, using the scriptures to prove that Jesus was the Christ.

Paul in Ephesus

19 While Apollos was in Corinth, Paul took a route through the interior and came to Ephesus, where he found some disciples. 2 He asked them, "Did you receive the Holy Spirit when you came to believe?"

They replied, "We've not even heard that there is a Holy Spirit."

3 Then he said, "What baptism did you receive, then?"

They answered, "John's baptism."

4 Paul explained, "John baptized with a baptism by which people showed they were changing their hearts and lives. It was a baptism that told people about the one who was coming after him. This is the one in whom they were to believe. This one is Jesus." 5 After they listened to Paul, they were baptized in the name of the Lord Jesus. 6 When Paul placed his hands on them, the Holy Spirit came on them, and they began speaking in other languages and prophesying. 7 Altogether, there were about twelve people.

8 Paul went to the synagogue and spoke confidently for the next three months. He interacted with those present and offered convincing arguments concerning the nature of God's kingdom. 9 Some people had closed their minds, though. They refused to believe and publicly slandered the Way. As a result, Paul left them, took the disciples with him, and continued his daily interactions in Tyrannus' lecture hall. 10 This went on for two years, so that everyone living in the province of Asia—both Jews and Greeks—heard the Lord's word.

11 God was doing unusual miracles through Paul. 12 Even the small towels and aprons that had touched his skin were taken to the sick, and their diseases were cured and the evil spirits left them.

13 There were some Jews who traveled around throwing out evil spirits. They tried to use the power of the name of the Lord Jesus against some people with evil spirits. They said, "In the name of the Jesus whom Paul preaches, I command you!" 14 The seven sons of Sceva, a Jewish chief priest, were doing this.

15 The evil spirit replied, "I know Jesus and I'm familiar with Paul, but who are you?" 16 The person who had an evil spirit jumped on them and overpowered them all with such force that they ran out of that house naked and wounded. 17 This became known to the Jews and Greeks living in Ephesus. Everyone was seized with fear and they held the name of the Lord Jesus in the highest regard.

18 Many of those who had come to believe came, confessing their past practices. 19 This included a number of people who practiced sorcery. They

collected their sorcery texts and burned them publicly. The value of those materials was calculated at more than someone might make if they worked for one hundred sixty-five years.P [20] In this way the Lord's word grew abundantly and strengthened powerfully.

[21] Once these things had come to an end, Paul, guided by the Spirit, decided to return to Jerusalem, taking a route that would carry him through the provinces of Macedonia and Achaia. He said, "After I have been there, I must visit Rome as well." [22] He sent two of his assistants, Timothy and Erastus, to Macedonia, while he remained awhile in the province of Asia.

[23] At that time a great disturbance erupted about the Way. [24] There was a silversmith named Demetrius. He made silver models of Artemis' temple, and his business generated a lot of profit for the craftspeople. [25] He called a meeting with these craftspeople and others working in related trades and said, "Friends, you know that we make an easy living from this business. [26] And you can see and hear that this Paul has convinced and misled a lot of people, not only in Ephesus but also throughout most of the province of Asia. He says that gods made by human hands aren't really gods. [27] This poses a danger not only by discrediting our trade but also by completely dishonoring the great goddess Artemis. The whole province of Asia—indeed, the entire civilized world—worships her, but her splendor will soon be extinguished."

[28] Once they heard this, they were beside themselves with anger and be-

gan to shout, "Great is Artemis of the Ephesians!"

[29] The city was thrown into turmoil. They rushed as one into the theater. They seized Gaius and Aristarchus, Paul's traveling companions from the province of Macedonia. [30] Paul wanted to appear before the assembly, but the disciples wouldn't allow him. [31] Even some officials of the province of Asia, who were Paul's friends, sent word to him, urging him not to risk going into the theater. [32] Meanwhile, the assembly was in a state of confusion. Some shouted one thing, others shouted something else, and most of the crowd didn't know why they had gathered. [33] The Jews sent Alexander to the front, and some of the crowd directed their words toward him. He gestured that he wanted to offer a defense before the assembly, [34] but when they realized he was a Jew, they all shouted in unison, "Great is Artemis of the Ephesians!" This continued for about two hours.

[35] The city manager brought order to the crowd and said, "People of Ephesus, doesn't everyone know that the city of Ephesus is guardian of the temple of the great Artemis and of her image, which fell from heaven? [36] Therefore, since these facts are undeniable, you must calm down. Don't be reckless. [37] The men you brought here have neither robbed the temple nor slandered our goddess. [38] Therefore, if Demetrius and the craftspeople with him have a charge against anyone, the courts are in session and governors are available. They can press charges against each other there. [39] Additional disputes can

---

P Or *fifty thousand silver drachmen* (a drachme is equivalent in value to a denarion, a typical day's wage).

be resolved in a legal assembly. [40]As for us, we are in danger of being charged with rioting today, since we can't justify this unruly gathering." [41]After he said this, he dismissed the assembly.

Paul visits Macedonia and Greece

20 When the riot was over, Paul sent for the disciples, encouraged them, said good-bye, and left for the province of Macedonia. [2]He traveled through that region with a message of encouragement. When he came to Greece, [3]he stayed for three months. Because the Jews hatched a plot against Paul as he was about to sail for Syria, he decided instead to return through Macedonia. [4]He was accompanied by Sopater, Pyrrhus' son from Beroea, Aristarchus and Secundus from Thessalonica, Gaius from Derbe, Timothy, and Tychicus and Trophimus from the province of Asia. [5]They went on ahead and waited for us in Troas. [6]We sailed from Philippi after the Festival of Unleavened Bread and met them five days later in Troas, where we stayed for a week.

Meeting with believers in Troas

[7]On the first day of the week, as we gathered together for a meal, Paul was holding a discussion with them. Since he was leaving the next day, he continued talking until midnight. [8]There were many lamps in the upstairs room where we had gathered. [9]A young man named Eutychus was sitting in the window. He was sinking into a deep sleep as Paul talked on and on. When he was sound asleep, he fell from the third floor and died. [10]Paul went down, fell on him and embraced him, then said, "Don't be alarmed. He's alive!" [11]Then Paul went

back upstairs and ate. He talked for a long time—right up until daybreak—then he left. [12]They took the young man away alive, and they were greatly comforted.

Farewell to the Ephesian leaders

[13]We went on to the ship and sailed for Assos, where we intended to take Paul on board. Paul had arranged this, since he intended to make his way there by land. [14]When he met us at Assos, we took him aboard and went on to Mitylene. [15]The next day we sailed from there and arrived opposite Chios. On the day after, we sailed to Samos, and on the following day we came to Miletus. [16]Paul had decided to sail past Ephesus so that he wouldn't need to spend too much time in the province of Asia. He was hurrying to reach Jerusalem, if possible, by Pentecost Day.

[17]From Miletus he sent a message to Ephesus calling for the church's elders to meet him. [18]When they arrived, he said to them, "You know how I lived among you the whole time I was with you, beginning with the first day I arrived in the province of Asia. [19]I served the Lord with great humility and with tears in the midst of trials that came upon me because of the Jews' schemes. [20]You know I held back nothing that would be helpful so that I could proclaim to you and teach you both publicly and privately in your homes. [21]You know I have testified to both Jews and Greeks that they must change their hearts and lives as they turn to God and have faith in our Lord Jesus. [22]Now, compelled by the Spirit, I'm going to Jerusalem. I don't know what will happen to me there. [23]What I do know is that the Holy Spirit testifies to me from city

to city that prisons and troubles await me. ²⁴But nothing, not even my life, is more important than my completing my mission. This is nothing other than the ministry I received from the Lord Jesus: to testify about the good news of God's grace.

²⁵"I know that none of you will see me again—you among whom I traveled and proclaimed the kingdom. ²⁶Therefore, today I testify to you that I'm not responsible for anyone's fate. ²⁷I haven't avoided proclaiming the entire plan of God to you. ²⁸Watch yourselves and the whole flock, in which the Holy Spirit has placed you as supervisors, to shepherd God's church, which he obtained with the death of his own Son.�q ²⁹I know that, after my departure, savage wolves will come in among you and won't spare the flock. ³⁰Some of your own people will distort the word in order to lure followers after them. ³¹Stay alert! Remember that for three years I constantly and tearfully warned each one of you. I never stopped warning you! ³²Now I entrust you to God and the message of his grace, which is able to build you up and give you an inheritance among all whom God has made holy. ³³I haven't craved anyone's silver, gold, or clothing. ³⁴You yourselves know that I have provided for my own needs and for those of my companions with my own hands. ³⁵In everything I have shown you that, by working hard, we must help the weak. In this way we remember the Lord Jesus' words: 'It is more blessed to give than to receive.'"

³⁶After he said these things, he knelt down with all of them to pray. ³⁷They cried uncontrollably as everyone embraced and kissed Paul. ³⁸They were especially grieved by his statement that they would never see him again. Then they accompanied him to the ship.

Paul travels to Jerusalem

21 After we tore ourselves away from them, we set sail on a straight course to Cos, reaching Rhodes the next day, and then Patara. ²We found a ship crossing over to Phoenicia, boarded, and put out to sea. ³We spotted Cyprus, but passed by it on our left. We sailed on to the province of Syria and landed in Tyre, where the ship was to unload its cargo. ⁴We found the disciples there and stayed with them for a week. Compelled by the Spirit, they kept telling Paul not to go to Jerusalem. ⁵When our time had come to an end, we departed. All of them, including women and children, accompanied us out of town where we knelt on the beach and prayed. ⁶We said good-bye to each other, then we boarded the ship and they returned to their homes.

⁷Continuing our voyage, we sailed from Tyre and arrived in Ptolemais. We greeted the brothers and sisters there and spent a day with them. ⁸The next day we left and came to Caesarea. We went to the house of Philip the evangelist, one of the Seven, and stayed with him. ⁹He had four unmarried daughters who were involved in the work of prophecy. ¹⁰After staying there for several days, a prophet named Agabus came down from Judea. ¹¹He came to us, took Paul's belt, tied his own feet and hands, and said, "This is what the Holy Spirit says: 'In Jerusalem the Jews will bind the man who owns this belt,

---

�q Or with the death of his own, or with his own death

and they will hand him over to the Gentiles.'" [12]When we heard this, we and the local believers urged Paul not to go up to Jerusalem.

[13]Paul replied, "Why are you doing this? Why are you weeping and breaking my heart? I'm ready not only to be arrested but even to die in Jerusalem for the sake of the name of the Lord Jesus."

[14]Since we couldn't talk him out of it, the only thing we could say was, "The Lord's will be done."

[15]After this, we got ready and made our way up to Jerusalem. [16]Some of the disciples from Caesarea accompanied us and led us to Mnason's home, where we were guests. He was from Cyprus and had been a disciple a long time. [17]When we arrived in Jerusalem, the brothers and sisters welcomed us warmly.

Meeting the Jerusalem church leaders

[18]On the next day Paul and the rest of us went to see James. All of the elders were present. [19]After greeting them, he gave them a detailed report of what God had done among the Gentiles through his ministry. [20]Those who heard this praised God. Then they said to him, "Brother, you see how many thousands of Jews have become believers, and all of them keep the Law passionately. [21]They have been informed that you teach all the Jews who live among the Gentiles to reject Moses, telling them not to circumcise their children nor to live according to our customs. [22]What about this? Without a doubt, they will hear that you have arrived. [23]You must therefore do what we tell you. Four men among us have made a solemn promise. [24]Take them with

you, go through the purification ritual with them, and pay the cost of having their heads shaved. Everyone will know there is nothing to those reports about you but that you too live a life in keeping with the Law. [25]As for the Gentile believers, we wrote a letter about what we decided, that they avoid food offered to idols, blood, the meat from strangled animals, and sexual immorality." [26]The following day Paul took the men with him and went through the purification ritual with them. He entered the temple and publicly announced the completion of the days of purification, when the offering would be presented for each one of them.

Paul seized by the people

[27]When the seven days of purification were almost over, the Jews from the province of Asia saw Paul in the temple. Grabbing him, they threw the whole crowd into confusion by shouting, [28]"Fellow Israelites! Help! This is the man who teaches everyone everywhere against our people, the Law, and this place. Not only that, he has even brought Greeks into the temple and defiled this holy place." ([29]They said this because they had seen Trophimus the Ephesian in the city with him earlier, and they assumed Paul had brought him into the temple.) [30]The entire city was stirred up. The people came rushing, seized Paul, and dragged him out of the temple. Immediately the gates were closed. [31]While they were trying to kill him, a report reached the commander of a company of soldiers that all Jerusalem was in a state of confusion. [32]Without a moment's hesitation, he took some soldiers and officers and ran down to the mob. When the mob

saw the commander and his soldiers, they stopped beating Paul. 33When the commander arrived, he arrested Paul and ordered him to be bound with two chains. Only then did he begin to ask who Paul was and what he had done.

34Some in the crowd shouted one thing, others shouted something else. Because of the commotion, he couldn't learn the truth, so he ordered that Paul be taken to the military headquarters. 35When Paul reached the steps, he had to be carried by the soldiers in order to protect him from the violence of the crowd. 36The mob that followed kept screaming, "Away with him!"

37As Paul was about to be taken into the military headquarters, he asked the commander, "May I speak with you?"

He answered, "Do you know Greek? 38Aren't you the Egyptian who started a revolt and led four thousand terrorists into the desert some time ago?"

39Paul replied, "I'm a Jew from Tarsus in Cilicia, a citizen of an important city. Please, let me speak to the people." 40With the commander's permission, Paul stood on the steps and gestured to the people. When they were quiet, he addressed them in Aramaic.

Paul's defense before his accusers

22 "Brothers and fathers, listen now to my defense." 2When they heard him address them in Aramaic, they became even more quiet. 3Paul continued, "I'm a Jew, born in Tarsus in Cilicia but raised in this city. Under Gamaliel's instruction, I was trained in the strict interpretation of our ancestral Law. I am passionately loyal to God, just like you who are gathered here today. 4I harassed those who followed this Way to their death, arresting and delivering both men and women into prison. 5The high priest and the whole Jerusalem Council can testify about me. I received letters from them, addressed to our associates in Damascus, then went there to bring those who were arrested to Jerusalem so they could be punished.

6"During that journey, about noon, as I approached Damascus, suddenly a bright light from heaven encircled me. 7I fell to the ground and heard a voice asking me, 'Saul, Saul, why are you harassing me?' 8I answered, 'Who are you, Lord?' 'I am Jesus the Nazarene, whom you are harassing,' he replied. 9My traveling companions saw the light, but they didn't hear the voice of the one who spoke to me. 10I asked, 'What should I do, Lord?' 'Get up,' the Lord replied, 'and go into Damascus. There you will be told everything you have been appointed to do.' 11I couldn't see because of the brightness of that light, so my companions led me by the hand into Damascus.

12"There was a certain man named Ananias. According to the standards of the Law, he was a pious man who enjoyed the respect of all the Jews living there. 13He came and stood beside me. 'Brother Saul, receive your sight!' he said. Instantly, I regained my sight and I could see him. 14He said, 'The God of our ancestors has selected you to know his will, to see the righteous one, and to hear his voice. 15You will be his witness to everyone concerning what you have seen and heard. 16What are you waiting for? Get up, be baptized, and wash away your sins as you call on his name.'

17"When I returned to Jerusalem and was praying in the temple, I had a visionary experience. 18I saw the Lord speaking to me. 'Hurry!' he said. 'Leave

Jerusalem at once because they won't accept your testimony about me.' ¹⁹I responded, 'Lord, these people know I used to go from one synagogue to the next, beating those who believe in you and throwing them into prison. ²⁰When Stephen your witness was being killed, I stood there giving my approval, even watching the clothes that belonged to those who were killing him.' ²¹Then the Lord said to me, 'Go! I will send you far away to the Gentiles.'"

²²The crowd listened to Paul until he said this. Then they shouted, "Away with this man! He's not fit to live!" ²³As they were screaming, throwing off their garments, and flinging dust into the air, ²⁴the commander directed that Paul be taken into the military headquarters. He ordered that Paul be questioned under the whip so that he could find out why they were shouting at him like this.

²⁵As they were stretching him out and tying him down with straps, Paul said to the centurion standing there, "Can you legally whip a Roman citizen who hasn't been found guilty in court?"

²⁶When the centurion heard this, he went to the commander and reported it. He asked, "What are you about to do? This man is a Roman citizen!"

²⁷The commander went to Paul and demanded, "Tell me! Are you a Roman citizen?"

He said, "Yes."

²⁸The commander replied, "It cost me a lot of money to buy my citizenship."

Paul said, "I'm a citizen by birth." ²⁹At once those who were about to examine him stepped away. The commander was alarmed when he realized he had bound a Roman citizen.

Paul appears before the Jewish council

³⁰The commander still wanted to know the truth about why Paul was being accused by the Jews. Therefore, the next day he ordered the chief priests and the entire Jerusalem Council to assemble. Then he took Paul out of prison and had him stand before them.

23 Paul stared at the council and said, "Brothers, I have lived my life with an altogether clear conscience right up to this very day." ²The high priest Ananias ordered those standing beside Paul to strike him in the mouth. ³Then Paul said to him, "God is about to strike you, you whitewashed wall! You sit and judge according to the Law, yet disobey the Law by ordering that I be struck."

⁴Those standing near him asked, "You dare to insult God's high priest?"

⁵Paul replied, "Brothers, I wasn't aware that he was the high priest. It is written, *You will not speak evil about a ruler of your people.*"[r]

⁶Knowing that some of them were Sadducees and the others Pharisees, Paul exclaimed in the council, "Brothers, I'm a Pharisee and a descendant of Pharisees. I am on trial because of my hope in the resurrection of the dead!"

⁷These words aroused a dispute between the Pharisees and Sadducees, and the assembly was divided. ⁸This is because Sadducees say that there's no resurrection, angel, or spirit, but Pharisees affirm them all. ⁹Council members were shouting loudly. Some Pharisees who were legal experts stood up and insisted forcefully, "We find nothing wrong with this man! What if a spirit or

[r]Exod 22:28

angel has spoken to him?" ¹⁰ The dispute became so heated that the commander feared they might tear Paul to pieces. He ordered soldiers to go down and remove him by force from their midst. Then they took him back to the military headquarters.

¹¹ The following night the Lord stood near Paul and said, "Be encouraged! Just as you have testified about me in Jerusalem, so too you must testify in Rome."

A murder plot discovered

¹² The next morning some Jewish leaders formulated a plot and solemnly promised that they wouldn't eat or drink until they had killed Paul. ¹³ More than forty people were involved in the conspiracy. ¹⁴ They went to the chief priests and elders and said, "We have solemnly promised to eat nothing until we have killed Paul. ¹⁵ You and the council must explain to the commander that you need Paul brought down to you. Pretend that you want to examine his case more closely. We're prepared to kill him before he arrives."

¹⁶ Paul's sister had a son who heard about the ambush and he came to the military headquarters and reported it to Paul. ¹⁷ Paul called for one of the centurions and said, "Take this young man to the commander because he has something to report to him."

¹⁸ He took him to the commander and said, "The prisoner Paul asked me to bring this young man to you. He has something to tell you."

¹⁹ The commander took him by the hand and withdrew to a place where they could speak privately. He asked, "What do you have to report to me?"

²⁰ He replied, "The Jewish leaders have conspired to ask that you bring Paul down to the council tomorrow. They will pretend that they want to investigate his case more closely. ²¹ Don't fall for it! More than forty of them are waiting to ambush him. They have solemnly promised not to eat or drink until they have killed him. They are ready now, awaiting your consent."

²² The commander dismissed the young man, ordering him, "Don't tell anyone that you brought this to my attention."

²³ The commander called two centurions and said, "Prepare two hundred soldiers, seventy horsemen, and two hundred spearmen to leave for Caesarea at nine o'clock tonight. ²⁴ Have horses ready for Paul to ride, so they may take him safely to Governor Felix." ²⁵ He wrote the following letter:

²⁶ Claudius Lysias, to the most honorable Governor Felix: Greetings. ²⁷ This man was seized by the Jews and was almost killed by them. I was nearby with a unit of soldiers, and I rescued him when I discovered that he was a Roman citizen. ²⁸ I wanted to find out why they were accusing him, so I brought him to their council. ²⁹ I discovered that they were accusing him about questions related to their Law. I found no charge deserving of death or imprisonment. ³⁰ When I was informed of a conspiracy against his life, I sent him to you at once and ordered his accusers to bring their case against him before you.

³¹ Following their orders, the soldiers took Paul during the night and brought him to Antipatris. ³² The following day they let the horsemen continue on with

Paul while they returned to the military headquarters in Jerusalem. ³³The horsemen entered Caesarea, delivered the letter to the governor, and brought Paul before him. ³⁴After he read the letter, he asked Paul about his home province. When he learned that he was from Cilicia, ³⁵the governor said, "I will hear your case when your accusers arrive." Then he ordered that Paul be kept in custody in Herod's palace.

Paul's trial before Felix

24 Five days later the high priest Ananias came down with some elders and a lawyer named Tertullus. They pressed charges against Paul before the governor. ²After the governor summoned Paul, Tertullus began to make his case against him. He declared, "Under your leadership, we have experienced substantial peace, and your administration has brought reforms to our nation. ³Always and everywhere, most honorable Felix, we acknowledge this with deep gratitude. ⁴I don't want to take too much of your time, so I ask that you listen with your usual courtesy to our brief statement of the facts. ⁵We have found this man to be a troublemaker who stirs up riots among all the Jews throughout the empire. He's a ringleader of the Nazarene faction ⁶and even tried to defile the temple. That's when we arrested him.ˢ ⁸By examining him yourself, you will be able to verify the allegations we are bringing against him." ⁹The Jews reinforced the action against Paul, affirming the truth of these accusations.

¹⁰The governor nodded at Paul, giving him permission to speak.

He responded, "I know that you have been judge over this nation for many years, so I gladly offer my own defense. ¹¹You can verify that I went up to worship in Jerusalem no more than twelve days ago. ¹²They didn't find me arguing with anyone in the temple or stirring up a crowd, whether in the synagogue or anywhere else in the city. ¹³Nor can they prove to you the allegations they are now bringing against me. ¹⁴I do admit this to you, that I am a follower of the Way, which they call a faction. Accordingly, I worship the God of our ancestors and believe everything set out in the Law and written in the Prophets. ¹⁵The hope I have in God I also share with my accusers, that there will be a resurrection of both the righteous and the unrighteous. ¹⁶On account of this, I have committed myself to maintaining a clear conscience before God and with all people. ¹⁷After an absence of several years, I came to Jerusalem to bring gifts for the poor of my nation and to offer sacrifices. ¹⁸When they found me in the temple, I was ritually pure. There was no crowd and no disturbance. ¹⁹But there were some Jews from the province of Asia. They should be here making their accusations, if indeed they have something against me. ²⁰In their absence, have these people who are here declare what crime they found when I stood before the Jerusalem Council. ²¹Perhaps it concerns this one statement that I blurted out when I was with them: 'I am on trial before

---

ˢCritical editions of the Gk New Testament do not include *We wanted to put him on trial according to our Law, ⁷ but Lysias the commander arrived and took him from our hands with great force. ⁸ Then he ordered his accusers to appear before you.*

you today because of the resurrection of the dead.'"

²²Felix, who had an accurate understanding of the Way, adjourned the meeting. He said, "When Lysias the commander arrives from Jerusalem, I will decide this case." ²³He arranged for a centurion to guard Paul. He was to give Paul some freedom, and his friends were not to be hindered in their efforts to provide for him.

Paul in custody

²⁴After several days, Felix came with his wife Drusilla, who was Jewish, and summoned Paul. He listened to him talk about faith in Christ Jesus. ²⁵When he spoke about upright behavior, self-control, and the coming judgment, Felix became fearful and said, "Go away for now! When I have time, I'll send for you." ²⁶At the same time, he was hoping that Paul would offer him some money, so he often sent for him and talked with him.

²⁷When two years had passed, Felix was succeeded by Porcius Festus. Since Felix wanted to grant a favor to the Jews, he left Paul in prison.

Paul appeals to Caesar

25 Three days after arriving in the province, Festus went up to Jerusalem from Caesarea. ²The chief priests and Jewish leaders presented their case against Paul. Appealing to him, ³they asked as a favor from Festus that he summon Paul to Jerusalem. They were planning to ambush and kill him along the way. ⁴But Festus responded by keeping Paul in Caesarea, since he was to return there very soon himself. ⁵"Some of your leaders can come down with me," he said. "If he's done

anything wrong, they can bring charges against him."

⁶He stayed with them for no more than eight or ten days, then went down to Caesarea. The following day he took his seat in the court and ordered that Paul be brought in. ⁷When he arrived, many Jews who had come down from Jerusalem surrounded him. They brought serious charges against him, but they couldn't prove them. ⁸In his own defense, Paul said, "I've done nothing wrong against the Jewish Law, against the temple, or against Caesar."

⁹Festus, wanting to put the Jews in his debt, asked Paul, "Are you willing to go up to Jerusalem to stand trial before me concerning these things?"

¹⁰Paul replied, "I'm standing before Caesar's court. I ought to be tried here. I have done nothing wrong to the Jews, as you well know. ¹¹If I'm guilty and have done something that deserves death, then I won't try to avoid death. But if there is nothing to their accusations against me, no one has the authority to hand me over to them. I appeal to Caesar!"

¹²After Festus conferred with his advisors, he responded, "You have appealed to Caesar. To Caesar you will go."

King Agrippa informed about Paul

¹³After several days had passed, King Agrippa and Bernice arrived in Caesarea to welcome Festus. ¹⁴Since they were staying there for many days, Festus discussed the case against Paul with the king. He said, "There is a man whom Felix left in prison. ¹⁵When I was in Jerusalem, the Jewish chief priests and elders brought charges against him and requested a guilty verdict in his case. ¹⁶I told them it is contrary to Roman

practice to hand someone over before they have faced their accusers and had opportunity to offer a defense against the charges. [17]When they came here, I didn't put them off. The very next day I took my seat in the court and ordered that the man be brought before me. [18]When the accusers took the floor, they didn't charge him with any of the crimes I had expected. [19]Instead, they quibbled with him about their own religion and about some dead man named Jesus, who Paul claimed was alive. [20]Since I had no idea how to investigate these matters, I asked if he would be willing to go to Jerusalem to stand trial there on these issues. [21]However, Paul appealed that he be held in custody pending a decision from His Majesty the emperor, so I ordered that he be held until I could send him to Caesar."

[22]Agrippa said to Festus, "I want to hear the man myself."

"Tomorrow," Festus replied, "you will hear him."

[23]The next day Agrippa and Bernice came with great fanfare. They entered the auditorium with the military commanders and the city's most prominent men. Festus then ordered that Paul be brought in. [24]Festus said, "King Agrippa and everyone present with us: You see this man! The entire Jewish community, both here and in Jerusalem, has appealed to me concerning him. They've been calling for his immediate death. [25]I've found that he has done nothing deserving death. When he appealed to His Majesty, I decided to send him to Rome. [26]I have nothing definite to write to our lord emperor. Therefore, I've brought him before all of you, and especially before you, King Agrippa, so that after this

investigation, I might have something to write. [27]After all, it would be foolish to send a prisoner without specifying the charges against him."

Paul's defense before Agrippa

26 Agrippa said to Paul, "You may speak for yourself."

So Paul gestured with his hand and began his defense. [2]"King Agrippa, I consider myself especially fortunate that I stand before you today as I offer my defense concerning all the accusations the Jews have brought against me. [3]This is because you understand well all the Jewish customs and controversies. Therefore, I ask you to listen to me patiently. [4]Every Jew knows the way of life I have followed since my youth because, from the beginning, I was among my people and in Jerusalem. [5]They have known me for a long time. If they wanted to, they could testify that I followed the way of life set out by the most exacting group of our religion. I am a Pharisee. [6]Today I am standing trial because of the hope in the promise God gave our ancestors. [7]This is the promise our twelve tribes hope to receive as they earnestly worship night and day. The Jews are accusing me, King Agrippa, because of this hope! [8]Why is it inconceivable to you that God raises the dead?

[9]"I really thought that I ought to oppose the name of Jesus the Nazarene in every way possible. [10]And that's exactly what I did in Jerusalem. I locked up many of God's holy people in prison under the authority of the chief priests. When they were condemned to death, I voted against them. [11]In one synagogue after another—indeed, in all the synagogues—I would often torture

them, compelling them to slander God. My rage bordered on the hysterical as I pursued them, even to foreign cities.

[12]"On one such journey, I was going to Damascus with the full authority of the chief priests. [13]While on the road at midday, King Agrippa, I saw a light from heaven shining around me and my traveling companions. That light was brighter than the sun. [14]We all fell to the ground, and I heard a voice that said to me in Aramaic, 'Saul, Saul, why are you harassing me? It's hard for you to kick against a spear.'[t] [15]Then I said, 'Who are you, Lord?' The Lord replied, 'I am Jesus, whom you are harassing. [16]Get up! Stand on your feet! I have appeared to you for this purpose: to appoint you as my servant and witness of what you have seen and what I will show you. [17]I will rescue you from your own people and from the Gentiles. I am sending you [18]to open their eyes. Then they can turn from darkness to light and from the power of Satan to God, and receive forgiveness of sins and a place among those who are made holy by faith in me.'

[19]"So, King Agrippa, I wasn't disobedient to that heavenly vision. [20]Instead, I proclaimed first to those in Damascus and Jerusalem, then to the whole region of Judea and to the Gentiles. My message was that they should change their hearts and lives and turn to God, and that they should demonstrate this change in their behavior. [21]Because of this, some Jews seized me in the temple and tried to murder me. [22]God has helped me up to this very day. Therefore, I stand here and bear witness to the lowly and the great. I'm saying

nothing more than what the Prophets and Moses declared would happen: [23]that the Christ would suffer and that, as the first to rise from the dead, he would proclaim light both to my people and to the Gentiles."

[24]At this point in Paul's defense, Festus declared with a loud voice, "You've lost your mind, Paul! Too much learning is driving you mad!"

[25]But Paul replied, "I'm not mad, most honorable Festus! I'm speaking what is sound and true. [26]King Agrippa knows about these things, and I have been speaking openly to him. I'm certain that none of these things have escaped his attention. This didn't happen secretly or in some out-of-the-way place. [27]King Agrippa, do you believe the prophets? I know you do."

[28]Agrippa said to Paul, "Are you trying to convince me that, in such a short time, you've made me a Christian?"

[29]Paul responded, "Whether it is a short or a long time, I pray to God that not only you but also all who are listening to me today will become like me, except for these chains."

[30]The king stood up, as did the governor, Bernice, and those sitting with them. [31]As they left, they were saying to each other, "This man is doing nothing that deserves death or imprisonment."

[32]Agrippa said to Festus, "This man could have been released if he hadn't appealed to Caesar."

Paul's voyage to Rome

27 When it was determined that we were to sail to Italy, Paul and some other prisoners were placed in the custody of a centurion named Julius of

[t]Or goads

the Imperial Company.[u] [2]We boarded a ship from Adramyttium that was about to sail for ports along the coast of the province of Asia. So we put out to sea. Aristarchus, a Macedonian from Thessalonica, came with us. [3]The next day we landed in Sidon. Julius treated Paul kindly and permitted him to go to some friends so they could take care of him. [4]From there we sailed off. We passed Cyprus, using the island to shelter us from the headwinds. [5]We sailed across the open sea off the coast of Cilicia and Pamphylia, and landed in Myra in Lycia. [6]There the centurion found an Alexandrian ship headed for Italy and put us on board. [7]After many days of slow and difficult sailing, we arrived off the coast of Cnidus. The wind wouldn't allow us to go farther, so we sailed under the shelter of Crete off Salmone. [8]We sailed along the coast only with difficulty until we came to a place called Good Harbors,[v] near the city of Lasea.

[9]Much time had been lost, and the voyage was now dangerous since the Day of Reconciliation had already passed. Paul warned them, [10]"Men, I see that our voyage will suffer damage and great loss, not only for the cargo and ship but also for our lives." [11]But the centurion was persuaded more by the ship's pilot and captain than by Paul's advice. [12]Since the harbor was unsuitable for spending the winter, the majority supported a plan to put out to sea from there. They thought they might reach Phoenix in Crete and spend the winter in its harbor, which faced southwest and northwest.

[13]When a gentle south wind began to blow, they thought they could carry out their plan. They pulled up anchor and sailed closely along the coast of Crete. [14]Before long, a hurricane-strength wind known as a northeaster swept down from Crete. [15]The ship was caught in the storm and couldn't be turned into the wind. So we gave in to it, and it carried us along. [16]After sailing under the shelter of an island called Cauda, we were able to control the lifeboat only with difficulty. [17]They brought the lifeboat aboard, then began to wrap the ship with cables to hold it together. Fearing they might run aground on the sandbars of the Gulf of Syrtis, they lowered the anchor and let the ship be carried along. [18]We were so battered by the violent storm that the next day the men began throwing cargo overboard. [19]On the third day, they picked up the ship's gear and hurled it into the sea. [20]When neither the sun nor the moon appeared for many days and the raging storm continued to pound us, all hope of our being saved from this peril faded.

[21]For a long time no one had eaten. Paul stood up among them and said, "Men, you should have complied with my instructions not to sail from Crete. Then we would have avoided this damage and loss. [22]Now I urge you to be encouraged. Not one of your lives will be lost, though we will lose the ship. [23]Last night an angel from the God to whom I belong and whom I worship stood beside me. [24]The angel said, 'Don't be afraid, Paul! You must stand before Caesar! Indeed, God has also graciously given you everyone sailing with you.' [25]Be encouraged, men! I have faith in God that it will be exactly as he told me. [26]However, we must run aground on some island."

[u]Or cohort (approximately six hundred soldiers)   [v]Or Fair Havens

²⁷On the fourteenth night, we were being carried across the Adriatic Sea. Around midnight the sailors began to suspect that land was near. ²⁸They dropped a weighted line to take soundings and found the water to be about one hundred twenty feet deep. After proceeding a little farther, we took soundings again and found the water to be about ninety feet deep. ²⁹Afraid that we might run aground somewhere on the rocks, they hurled out four anchors from the stern and began to pray for daylight. ³⁰The sailors tried to abandon the ship by lowering the lifeboat into the sea, pretending they were going to lower anchors from the bow. ³¹Paul said to the centurion and his soldiers, "Unless they stay in the ship, you can't be saved from peril." ³²The soldiers then cut the ropes to the lifeboat and let it drift away.

³³Just before daybreak, Paul urged everyone to eat. He said, "This is the fourteenth day you've lived in suspense, and you've not had even a bite to eat. ³⁴I urge you to take some food. Your health depends on it. None of you will lose a single hair from his head." ³⁵After he said these things, he took bread, gave thanks to God in front of them all, then broke it and began to eat. ³⁶Everyone was encouraged and took some food. (³⁷In all, there were two hundred seventy-six of us on the ship.) ³⁸When they had eaten as much as they wanted, they lightened the ship by throwing the grain into the sea.

³⁹In the morning light they saw a bay with a sandy beach. They didn't know what land it was, but they thought they might possibly be able to run the ship aground. ⁴⁰They cut the anchors loose and left them in the sea. At the same time, they untied the ropes that ran back to the rudders. They raised the foresail to catch the wind and made for the beach. ⁴¹But they struck a sandbar and the ship ran aground. The bow was stuck and wouldn't move, and the stern was broken into pieces by the force of the waves. ⁴²The soldiers decided to kill the prisoners to keep them from swimming to shore and escaping. ⁴³However, the centurion wanted to save Paul, so he stopped them from carrying out their plan. He ordered those who could swim to jump overboard first and head for land. ⁴⁴He ordered the rest to grab hold of planks or debris from the ship. In this way, everyone reached land safely.

On the Island of Malta

28 After reaching land safely, we learned that the island was called Malta. ²The islanders showed us extraordinary kindness. Because it was rainy and cold, they built a fire and welcomed all of us. ³Paul gathered a bunch of dry sticks and put them on the fire. As he did, a poisonous snake, driven out by the heat, latched on to his hand. ⁴When the islanders saw the snake hanging from his hand, they said to each other, "This man must be a murderer! He was rescued from the sea, but the goddess Justice hasn't let him live!" ⁵Paul shook the snake into the fire and suffered no harm. ⁶They expected him to swell up with fever or suddenly drop dead. After waiting a long time and seeing nothing unusual happen to him, they changed their minds and began to claim that he was a god.

⁷Publius, the island's most prominent person, owned a large estate in that area. He welcomed us warmly into

his home as his guests for three days. [8]Publius' father was bedridden, sick with a fever and dysentery. Paul went to see him and prayed. He placed his hand on him and healed him. [9]Once this happened, the rest of the sick on the island came to him and were healed. [10]They honored us in many ways. When we were getting ready to sail again, they supplied us with what we needed.

Paul makes it to Rome

[11]After three months we put out to sea in a ship that had spent the winter at the island. It was an Alexandrian ship with carvings of the twin gods Castor and Pollux as its figurehead. [12]We landed in Syracuse where we stayed three days. [13]From there we sailed to Rhegium. After one day a south wind came up, and we arrived on the second day in Puteoli. [14]There we found brothers and sisters who urged us to stay with them for a week. In this way we came to Rome. [15]When the brothers and sisters there heard about us, they came as far as the Forum of Appius and the Three Taverns to meet us. When Paul saw them, he gave thanks to God and was encouraged. [16]When we entered Rome, Paul was permitted to live by himself, with a soldier guarding him.

Paul meets Jewish leaders in Rome

[17]Three days later, Paul called the Jewish leaders together. When they gathered, he said, "Brothers, although I have done nothing against our people or the customs of our ancestors, I'm a prisoner from Jerusalem. They handed me over to the Romans, [18]who intended to release me after they examined me, because they couldn't find any reason

for putting me to death. [19]When the Jews objected, I was forced to appeal to Caesar. Don't think I appealed to Caesar because I had any reason to bring charges against my nation. [20]This is why I asked to see you and speak with you: it's because of the hope of Israel that I am bound with this chain."

[21]They responded, "We haven't received any letters about you from Judea, nor have any of our brothers come and reported or said anything bad about you. [22]But we think it's important to hear what you think, for we know that people everywhere are speaking against this faction."

[23]On the day scheduled for this purpose, many people came to the place where he was staying. From morning until evening, he explained and testified concerning God's kingdom and tried to convince them about Jesus through appealing to the Law from Moses and the Prophets. [24]Some were persuaded by what he said, but others refused to believe. [25]They disagreed with each other and were starting to leave when Paul made one more statement: "The Holy Spirit spoke correctly when he said to your ancestors through Isaiah the prophet,

[26] *Go to this people and say:*
   You will hear, to be sure,
      but never understand;
   and you will certainly see
      but never recognize
      what you are seeing.
[27] *This people's senses*
      have become calloused,
   and they've become
      hard of hearing,
   and they've shut their eyes
      so that they won't see
      with their eyes

or hear with their ears
    or understand with their minds,
        and change their hearts
            and lives that I may heal them.[W]
28"Therefore, be certain of this: God's salvation has been sent to the Gentiles. They will listen!"[X]

Paul's ministry in Rome

30 Paul lived in his own rented quarters for two full years and welcomed everyone who came to see him. 31 Unhindered and with complete confidence, he continued to preach God's kingdom and to teach about the Lord Jesus Christ.

ROMANS

Greeting

1 From Paul, a slave of Christ Jesus, called to be an apostle and set apart for God's good news. 2-3 God promised this good news about his Son ahead of time through his prophets in the holy scriptures. His Son was descended from David. 4 He was publicly identified as God's Son with power through his resurrection from the dead, which was based on the Spirit of holiness. This Son is Jesus Christ our Lord. 5 Through him we have received God's grace and our appointment to be apostles. This was to bring all Gentiles to faithful obedience for his name's sake. 6 You who are called by Jesus Christ are also included among these Gentiles.

7 To those in Rome who are dearly loved by God and called to be God's people.

Grace to you and peace from God our Father and the Lord Jesus Christ.

Thanksgiving and Paul's plans to visit

8 First of all, I thank my God through Jesus Christ for all of you, because the news about your faithfulness is being spread throughout the whole world. 9 I serve God in my spirit by preaching the good news about God's Son, and God is my witness that I continually mention you 10 in all my prayers. I'm always asking that somehow, by God's will, I might succeed in visiting you at last. 11 I really want to see you to pass along some spiritual gift to you so that you can be strengthened. 12 What I mean is that we can mutually encourage each other while I am with you. We can be encouraged by the faithfulness we find in each other, both your faithfulness and mine.

13 I want you to know, brothers and sisters, that I planned to visit you many times, although I have been prevented from coming until now. I want to harvest some fruit among you, just as I have done among the other Gentiles. 14 I have a responsibility both to Greeks and to those who don't speak Greek, both to the wise and to the foolish.

[W]Isa 6:9-10 [X]Critical editions of the Gk New Testament do not include 28:29 After he said this, the Jews left, debating among themselves.

God's righteousness is revealed

15That's why I'm ready to preach the gospel also to you who are in Rome. 16I'm not ashamed of the gospel: it is God's own power for salvation to all who have faith in God, to the Jew first and also to the Greek. 17God's righteousness is being revealed in the gospel, from faithfulness[a] for faith,[b] as it is written, *The righteous person will live by faith.*[c]

Gentiles are without excuse

18God's wrath is being revealed from heaven against all the ungodly behavior and the injustice of human beings who silence the truth with injustice. 19This is because what is known about God should be plain to them because God made it plain to them. 20Ever since the creation of the world, God's invisible qualities—God's eternal power and divine nature—have been clearly seen, because they are understood through the things God has made. So humans are without excuse. 21Although they knew God, they didn't honor God as God or thank him. Instead, their reasoning became pointless, and their foolish hearts were darkened. 22While they were claiming to be wise, they made fools of themselves. 23They exchanged the glory of the immortal God for images that look like mortal humans: birds, animals, and reptiles. 24So God abandoned them to their hearts' desires, which led to the moral corruption of degrading their own bodies with each other. 25They traded God's truth for a lie, and they worshipped and served the creation instead of the creator, who is blessed forever. Amen.

26That's why God abandoned them to degrading lust. Their females traded natural sexual relations for unnatural sexual relations. 27Also, in the same way, the males traded natural sexual relations with females, and burned with lust for each other. Males performed shameful actions with males, and they were paid back with the penalty they deserved for their mistake in their own bodies. 28Since they didn't think it was worthwhile to acknowledge God, God abandoned them to a defective mind to do inappropriate things. 29So they were filled with all injustice, wicked behavior, greed, and evil behavior. They are full of jealousy, murder, fighting, deception, and malice. They are gossips, 30they slander people, and they hate God. They are rude and proud, and they brag. They invent ways to be evil, and they are disobedient to their parents. 31They are without understanding, disloyal, without affection, and without mercy. 32Though they know God's decision that those who persist in such practices deserve death, they not only keep doing these things but also approve others who practice them.

Jews are without excuse

2 So every single one of you who judge others is without any excuse. You condemn yourself when you judge another person because the one who is judging is doing the same things. 2We know that God's judgment agrees with the truth, and his judgment is against those who do these kinds of things. 3If you judge those who do these kinds of things while you do the same things yourself, think about this: Do

[a]Or faith [b]Or faithfulness [c]Hab 2:4

you believe that you will escape God's judgment? [4]Or do you have contempt for the riches of God's generosity, tolerance, and patience? Don't you realize that God's kindness is supposed to lead you to change your heart and life? [5]You are storing up wrath for yourself because of your stubbornness and your heart that refuses to change. God's just judgment will be revealed on the day of wrath. [6]*God will repay everyone based on their works.*[d] [7]On the one hand, he will give eternal life to those who look for glory, honor, and immortality based on their patient good work. [8]But on the other hand, there will be wrath and anger for those who obey wickedness instead of the truth because they are acting out of selfishness and disobedience. [9]There will be trouble and distress for every human being who does evil, for the Jew first and also for the Greek. [10]But there will be glory, honor, and peace for everyone who does what is good, for the Jew first and also for the Greek. [11]God does not have favorites.

[12]Those who have sinned outside the Law will also die outside the Law, and those who have sinned under the Law will be judged by the Law. [13]It isn't the ones who hear the Law who are righteous in God's eyes. It is the ones who do what the Law says who will be treated as righteous. [14]Gentiles don't have the Law. But when they instinctively do what the Law requires they are a Law in themselves, though they don't have the Law. [15]They show the proof of the Law written on their hearts, and their consciences affirm it. Their conflicting thoughts will accuse them, or even make a defense for them, [16]on

the day when, according to my gospel, God will judge the hidden truth about human beings through Christ Jesus.

Jews will be judged as well

[17]But,

if you call yourself a Jew;
if you rely on the Law;
if you brag about your relationship
to God;
[18]if you know the will of God;
if you are taught by the Law
so that you can figure out
the things that really matter;
[19]if you have persuaded yourself
that you are:
a guide for the blind;
a light to those
who are in darkness;
[20]an educator of the foolish;
a teacher of infants
(since you have
the full content of knowledge
and truth in the Law);
[21]then why don't you
who are teaching others
teach yourself?
If you preach, "No stealing,"
do you steal?
[22]If you say, "No adultery,"
do you commit adultery?
If you hate idols,
do you rob temples?
[23]If you brag about the Law, do you
shame God by breaking the Law? [24]As it
is written: *The name of God is discredited
by the Gentiles because of you.*[e]

[25]Circumcision is an advantage
if you do what the Law says. But if
you are a person who breaks the Law,
your status of being circumcised has
changed into not being circumcised.

[d]Ps 62:12; Prov 24:12   [e]Isa 52:5 LXX

²⁶So if the person who isn't circumcised keeps the Law, won't his status of not being circumcised be counted as if he were circumcised? ²⁷The one who isn't physically circumcised but keeps the Law will judge you. You became a law-breaker after you had the written Law and circumcision. ²⁸It isn't the Jew who maintains outward appearances who will receive praise from God, and it isn't people who are outwardly circumcised on their bodies. ²⁹Instead, it is the person who is a Jew inside, who is circumcised in spirit, not literally. That person's praise doesn't come from people but from God.

God's faithfulness and justice

3 So what's the advantage of being a Jew? Or what's the benefit of circumcision? ²Plenty in every way. First of all, the Jews were trusted with God's revelations. ³What does it matter, then, if some weren't faithful? Their lack of faith won't cancel God's faithfulness, will it? ⁴Absolutely not! God must be true, even if every human being is a liar, as it is written,

So that it can show that you are right
   in your words;
and you will triumph
   when you are judged.ᶠ

⁵But if our lack of righteousness confirms God's justice, what will we say? That God, who brings wrath upon us, isn't just (I'm speaking rhetorically)? ⁶Absolutely not! If God weren't just, how could he judge the world? ⁷But if God's truth is demonstrated by my lie and it increases his glory, why am I still judged as a sinner? ⁸Why not say, "Let's do evil things so that good things

will come out of it"? (Some people who slander us accuse us of saying that, but these people deserve criticism.)

All are under the power of sin

⁹So what are we saying? Are we better off? Not at all. We have already stated the charge: both Jews and Greeks are all under the power of sin. ¹⁰As it is written,

There is no righteous person,
   not even one.
¹¹ There is no one who understands.
   There is no one who looks for God.
¹² They all turned away.
   They have become
      worthless together.
   There is no one who shows kindness.
   There is not even one.ᵍ
¹³ Their throat is a grave
      that has been opened.
   They are deceitful with their tongues,
      and the poison of vipers
      is under their lips.ʰ
¹⁴ Their mouths are full of cursing
      and bitterness.ⁱ
¹⁵ Their feet are quick to shed blood;
¹⁶   destruction and misery
      are in their ways;
¹⁷   and they don't know
      the way of peace.ʲ
¹⁸ There is no fear of God in their view
      of the world.ᵏ

¹⁹Now, we know that whatever the Law says, it speaks to those who are under the Law, in order to shut every mouth and make it so the whole world has to answer to God. ²⁰It follows that no human being will be treated as righteous in his presence by doing what the Law says, because the knowledge of sin comes through the Law.

ᶠPs 51:4 ᵍPs 14:1-3 ʰPs 5:9 ⁱPs 10:7 ʲIsa 59:7-8 ᵏPs 36:1

God's righteousness through faithfulness of Christ

²¹ But now God's righteousness has been revealed apart from the Law, which is confirmed by the Law and the Prophets. ²² God's righteousness comes through the faithfulness of Jesus Christ for all who have faith in him. There's no distinction. ²³ All have sinned and fall short of God's glory, ²⁴ but all are treated as righteous freely by his grace because of a ransom that was paid by Christ Jesus. ²⁵ Through his faithfulness, God displayed Jesus as the place of sacrifice where mercy is found by means of his blood. He did this to demonstrate his righteousness in passing over sins that happened before, ²⁶ during the time of God's patient tolerance. He also did this to demonstrate that he is righteous in the present time, and to treat the one who has faith in Jesus as righteous.

²⁷ What happens to our bragging? It's thrown out. With which law? With what we have accomplished under the Law? ²⁸ No, not at all, but through the law of faith. We consider that a person is treated as righteous by faith, apart from what is accomplished under the Law. ²⁹ Or is God the God of Jews only? Isn't God the God of Gentiles also? Yes, God is also the God of Gentiles. ³⁰ Since God is one, then the one who makes the circumcised righteous by faith will also make the one who isn't circumcised righteous through faith. ³¹ Do we then cancel the Law through this faith? Absolutely not! Instead, we confirm the Law.

Abraham's faith was credited as righteousness

4 So what are we going to say? Are we going to find that Abraham is our ancestor on the basis of genealogy? ² Because if Abraham was made righteous because of his actions, he would have had a reason to brag, but not in front of God. ³ What does the scripture say? *Abraham had faith in God, and it was credited to him as righteousness.*¹ ⁴ Workers' salaries aren't credited to them on the basis of an employer's grace but rather on the basis of what they deserve. ⁵ But faith is credited as righteousness to those who don't work, because they have faith in God who makes the ungodly righteous. ⁶ In the same way, David also pronounces a blessing on the person to whom God credits righteousness apart from actions:

⁷ *Happy are those whose actions outside*
    the Law are forgiven,
    and whose sins are covered.

⁸ *Happy are those whose sin*
    isn't counted against them
    *by the Lord.*ᵐ

⁹ Is this state of happiness only for the circumcised or is it also for those who aren't circumcised? We say, "Faith was credited to Abraham as righteousness." ¹⁰ So how was it credited? When he was circumcised, or when he wasn't circumcised? In fact, it was credited while he still wasn't circumcised, not after he was circumcised. ¹¹ He received the sign of circumcision as a seal of the righteousness that comes from the faith he had while he still wasn't circumcised. It happened this way so that Abraham could be the ancestor of all those people who aren't circumcised, who have faith in God, and so are counted as righteous. ¹² He could also be the ancestor of those circumcised

¹Gen 15:6 ᵐPs 32:1-2

people, who aren't only circumcised but who also walk in the path of faith, like our ancestor Abraham did while he wasn't circumcised.

Abraham's promise is received through faith

[13] The promise to Abraham and to his descendants, that he would inherit the world, didn't come through the Law but through the righteousness that comes from faith. [14] If they inherit because of the Law, then faith has no effect and the promise has been canceled. [15] The Law brings about wrath. But when there isn't any law, there isn't any violation of the law. [16] That's why the inheritance comes through faith, so that it will be on the basis of God's grace. In that way, the promise is secure for all of Abraham's descendants, not just for those who are related by Law but also for those who are related by the faith of Abraham, who is the father of all of us. [17] As it is written: *I have appointed you to be the father of many nations.*[n] So Abraham is our father in the eyes of God in whom he had faith, the God who gives life to the dead and calls things that don't exist into existence. [18] When it was beyond hope, he had faith in the hope that he would become the father of many nations, in keeping with the promise God spoke to him: *That's how many descendants you will have.*[o] [19] Without losing faith, Abraham, who was nearly 100 years old, took into account his own body, which was as good as dead, and Sarah's womb, which was dead. [20] He didn't hesitate with a lack of faith in God's promise, but he grew strong in faith and gave glory

to God. [21] He was fully convinced that God was able to do what he promised. [22] Therefore, it was credited to him as righteousness.

[23] But the scripture that says *it was credited to him*[p] wasn't written only for Abraham's sake. [24] It was written also for our sake, because it is going to be credited to us too. It will be credited to those of us who have faith in the one who raised Jesus our Lord from the dead. [25] He was handed over because of our mistakes, and he was raised to meet the requirements of righteousness for us.

Therefore, we have peace with God

5 Therefore, since we have been made righteous through his faithfulness,[q] we have peace with God through our Lord Jesus Christ. [2] We have access by faith into this grace in which we stand through him, and we boast in the hope of God's glory. [3] But not only that! We even take pride in our problems, because we know that trouble produces endurance, [4] endurance produces character, and character produces hope. [5] This hope doesn't put us to shame, because the love of God has been poured out in our hearts through the Holy Spirit, who has been given to us.

[6] While we were still weak, at the right moment, Christ died for ungodly people. [7] It isn't often that someone will die for a righteous person, though maybe someone might dare to die for a good person. [8] But God shows his love for us, because while we were still sinners Christ died for us. [9] So, now that we have been made righteous by his blood, we can be even more certain

[n] Gen 17:5 [o] Gen 15:5 [p] Gen 15:6 [q] Or *faith*

that we will be saved from God's wrath through him. [10]If we were reconciled to God through the death of his Son while we were still enemies, now that we have been reconciled, how much more certain is it that we will be saved by his life? [11]And not only that: we even take pride in God through our Lord Jesus Christ, the one through whom we now have a restored relationship with God.

Grace now rules

[12]Just as through one human being sin came into the world, and death came through sin, so death has come to everyone, since everyone has sinned. [13]Although sin was in the world, since there was no Law, it wasn't taken into account until the Law came. [14]But death ruled from Adam until Moses, even over those who didn't sin in the same way Adam did—Adam was a type of the one who was coming.

[15]But the free gift of Christ isn't like Adam's failure. If many people died through what one person did wrong, God's grace is multiplied even more for many people with the gift—of comes the one person Jesus Christ—that comes through grace. [16]The gift isn't like the consequences of one person's sin. The judgment that came from one person's sin led to punishment, but the free gift that came out of many failures led to the verdict of acquittal. [17]If death ruled because of one person's failure, those who receive the multiplied grace and the gift of righteousness will even more certainly rule in life through the one person Jesus Christ.

[18]So now the righteous requirements necessary for life are met for everyone through the righteous act of one person, just as judgment fell on everyone through the failure of one person. [19]Many people were made righteous through the obedience of one person, just as many people were made sinners through the disobedience of one person. [20]The Law stepped in to amplify the failure, but where sin increased, grace multiplied even more. [21]The result is that grace will rule through God's righteousness, leading to eternal life through Jesus Christ our Lord, just as sin ruled in death.

Our new life in Christ

6 So what are we going to say? Should we continue sinning so grace will multiply? [2]Absolutely not! All of us died to sin. How can we still live in it? [3]Or don't you know that all who were baptized into Christ Jesus were baptized into his death? [4]Therefore, we were buried together with him through baptism into his death, so that just as Christ was raised from the dead through the glory of the Father, we too can walk in newness of life. [5]If we were united together in a death like his, we will also be united together in a resurrection like his. [6]This is what we know: the person that we used to be was crucified with him in order to get rid of the corpse that had been controlled by sin. That way we wouldn't be slaves to sin anymore, [7]because a person who has died has been freed from sin's power. [8]But if we died with Christ, we have faith that we will also live with him. [9]We know that Christ has been raised from the dead and he will never die again. Death no longer has power over him. [10]He died to sin once and for all with his death, but he lives for God with his life. [11]In the same way, you also should consider yourselves dead to sin but alive for God in Christ Jesus.

^{12}So then, don't let sin rule your body, so that you do what it wants. ^{13}Don't offer parts of your body to sin, to be used as weapons to do wrong. Instead, present yourselves to God as people who have been brought back to life from the dead, and offer all the parts of your body to God to be used as weapons to do right. ^{14}Sin will have no power over you, because you aren't under Law but under grace.

Freedom from sin

^{15}So what? Should we sin because we aren't under Law but under grace? Absolutely not! ^{16}Don't you know that if you offer yourselves to someone as obedient slaves, that you are slaves of the one whom you obey? That's true whether you serve as slaves of sin, which leads to death, or as slaves of the kind of obedience that leads to righteousness. ^{17}But thank God that although you used to be slaves of sin, you gave wholehearted obedience to the teaching that was handed down to you, which provides a pattern. ^{18}Now that you have been set free from sin, you have become slaves of righteousness. ^{19}(I'm speaking with ordinary metaphors because of your limitations.) Once, you offered the parts of your body to be used as slaves to impurity and to lawless behavior that leads to still more lawless behavior. Now, you should present the parts of your body as slaves to righteousness, which makes your lives holy. ^{20}When you were slaves of sin, you were free from the control of righteousness. ^{21}What consequences did you get from doing things that you are now ashamed of? The outcome of

those things is death. ^{22}But now that you have been set free from sin and become slaves to God, you have the consequence of a holy life, and the outcome is eternal life. ^{23}The wages that sin pays are death, but God's gift is eternal life in Christ Jesus our Lord.

Freedom from the Law

7Brothers and sisters, I'm talking to you as people who know the Law. Don't you know that the Law has power over someone only as long as he or she lives? ^{2}A married woman is united with her husband under the Law while he is alive. But if her husband dies, she is released from the Law concerning her husband. ^{3}So then, if she lives with another man while her husband is alive, she's committing adultery. But if her husband dies, she's free from the Law, so she won't be committing adultery if she marries someone else. ^{4}Therefore, my brothers and sisters, you also died with respect to the Law through the body of Christ, so that you could be united with someone else. You are united with the one who was raised from the dead so that we can bear fruit for God. ^{5}When we were self-centered, the sinful passions aroused through the Law were at work in all the parts of our body, so that we bore fruit for death. ^{6}But now we have been released from the Law. We have died with respect to the thing that controlled us, so that we can be slaves in the new life under the Spirit, not in the old life under the written Law.

The function of the Law

^{7}So what are we going to say? That the Law is sin? Absolutely not! But I wouldn't have known sin except through the Law. I wouldn't have known the desire for what others have if the Law had not said, *Don't desire to take what others have.*[r] ⁸But sin seized the opportunity and used this commandment to produce all kinds of desires in me. Sin is dead without the Law. ⁹I used to be alive without the Law, but when the commandment came, sin sprang to life, ¹⁰and I died. So the commandment that was intended to give life brought death. ¹¹Sin seized the opportunity through the commandment, deceived me, and killed me. ¹²So the Law itself is holy, and the commandment is holy, righteous, and good.

Living under the Law

¹³So did something good bring death to me? Absolutely not! But sin caused my death through something good so that sin would be exposed as sin. That way sin would become even more thoroughly sinful through the commandment. ¹⁴We know that the Law is spiritual, but I'm made of flesh and blood, and I'm sold as a slave to sin. ¹⁵I don't know what I'm doing, because I don't do what I want to do. Instead, I do the thing that I hate. ¹⁶But if I'm doing the thing that I don't want to do, I'm agreeing that the Law is right. ¹⁷But now I'm not the one doing it anymore. Instead, it's sin that lives in me. I know that good doesn't live in me—that is, in my body. The desire to do good is inside of me, but I can't do it. ¹⁹I don't do the good that I want to do, but I do the evil that I don't want to do. ²⁰But if I do the very thing that I don't want to do, then I'm not the one doing it anymore. Instead, it is sin that lives in me that is doing it.

²¹So I find that, as a rule, when I want to do what is good, evil is right there with me. ²²I gladly agree with the Law on the inside, ²³but I see a different law at work in my body. It wages a war against the law of my mind and takes me prisoner with the law of sin that is in my body. ²⁴I'm a miserable human being. Who will deliver me from this dead corpse? ²⁵Thank God through Jesus Christ our Lord! So then I'm a slave to God's Law in my mind, but I'm a slave to sin's law in my body.

Set free by the Spirit

8 So now there isn't any condemnation for those who are in Christ Jesus. ²The law of the Spirit of life in Christ Jesus has set you free from the law of sin and death. ³God has done what was impossible for the Law, since it was weak because of selfishness. God condemned sin in the body by sending his own Son to deal with sin in the same body as humans, who are controlled by sin. ⁴He did this so that the righteous requirement of the Law might be fulfilled in us. Now the way we live is based on the Spirit, not based on selfishness. ⁵People whose lives are based on selfishness think about selfish things, but people whose lives are based on the Spirit think about things that are related to the Spirit. ⁶The attitude that comes from selfishness leads to death, but the attitude that comes from the Spirit leads to life and peace. ⁷So the attitude that comes from selfishness is hostile to God. It doesn't submit to God's Law, because it can't. ⁸People who are self-centered aren't able to please God.

[r] Exod 20:17; Deut 5:21

9 But you aren't self-centered. Instead you are in the Spirit, if in fact God's Spirit lives in you. If anyone doesn't have the Spirit of Christ, they don't belong to him. 10 If Christ is in you, the Spirit is your life because of God's righteousness, but the body is dead because of sin. 11 If the Spirit of the one who raised Jesus from the dead lives in you, the one who raised Christ from the dead will give life to your human bodies also, through his Spirit that lives in you.

12 So then, brothers and sisters, we have an obligation, but it isn't an obligation to ourselves to live our lives on the basis of selfishness. 13 If you live on the basis of selfishness, you are going to die. But if by the Spirit you put to death the actions of the body, you will live. 14 All who are led by God's Spirit are God's sons and daughters. 15 You didn't receive a spirit of slavery to lead you back again into fear, but you received a Spirit that shows you are adopted as his children. With this Spirit, we cry, "Abba, Father." 16 The same Spirit agrees with our spirit, that we are God's children. 17 But if we are children, we are also heirs. We are God's heirs and fellow heirs with Christ, if we really suffer with him so that we can also be glorified with him.

Our suffering and our hope

18 I believe that the present suffering is nothing compared to the coming glory that is going to be revealed to us. 19 The whole creation waits breathless with anticipation for the revelation of God's sons and daughters. 20 Creation was subjected to frustration, not by its own choice—it was the choice of the one who subjected it—but in the hope 21 that the creation itself will be set free from slavery to decay and brought into the glorious freedom of God's children. 22 We know that the whole creation is groaning together and suffering labor pains up until now. 23 And it's not only the creation. We ourselves who have the Spirit as the first crop of the harvest also groan inside as we wait to be adopted and for our bodies to be set free. 24 We were saved in hope. If we see what we hope for, that isn't hope. Who hopes for what they already see? 25 But if we hope for what we don't see, we wait for it with patience.

26 In the same way, the Spirit comes to help our weakness. We don't know what we should pray, but the Spirit himself pleads our case with unexpressed groans. 27 The one who searches hearts knows how the Spirit thinks, because he pleads for the saints, consistent with God's will. 28 We know that God works all things together for good for the ones who love God, for those who are called according to his purpose. 29 We know this because God knew them in advance, and he decided in advance that they would be conformed to the image of his Son. That way his Son would be the first of many brothers and sisters. 30 Those who God decided in advance would be conformed to his Son, he also called. Those whom he called, he also made righteous. Those whom he made righteous, he also glorified.

31 So what are we going to say about these things? If God is for us, who is against us? 32 He didn't spare his own Son but gave him up for us all. Won't he also freely give us all things with him? 33 Who will bring a charge against God's elect people? It is God who acquits them. 34 Who is going to convict them? It is Christ Jesus who died, even

more, who was raised, and who also is at God's right side. It is Christ Jesus who also pleads our case for us.

³⁵Who will separate us from Christ's love? Will we be separated by trouble, or distress, or harassment, or famine, or nakedness, or danger, or sword? ³⁶As it is written,

> We are being put to death all day long
> for your sake.
> We are treated like sheep for slaughter.ˢ

³⁷But in all these things we win a sweeping victory through the one who loved us. ³⁸I'm convinced that nothing can separate us from God's love in Christ Jesus our Lord: not death or life, not angels or rulers, not present things or future things, not powers ³⁹or height or depth, or any other thing that is created.

The tragedy of Israel's unbelief

9 I'm speaking the truth in Christ—I'm not lying, as my conscience assures me with the Holy Spirit: ²I have great sadness and constant pain in my heart. ³I wish I could be cursed, cut off from Christ if it helped my brothers and sisters, who are my flesh-and-blood relatives. ⁴They are Israelites. The adoption as God's children, the glory, the covenants, the giving of the Law, the worship, and the promises belong to them. ⁵The Jewish ancestors are theirs, and the Christ descended from those ancestors. He is the one who rules over all things, who is God, and who is blessed forever. Amen.

Israel and God's choice

⁶But it's not as though God's word has failed. Not all who are descended from Israel are part of Israel. ⁷Not all

of Abraham's children are called Abraham's descendants, but instead *your descendants will be named through Isaac.*ᵗ ⁸That means it isn't the natural children who are God's children, but it is the children from the promise who are counted as descendants. ⁹The words in the promise were: *A year from now I will return, and Sarah will have a son.*ᵘ

¹⁰Not only that, but also Rebecca conceived children with one man, our ancestor Isaac. ¹¹When they hadn't been born yet and when they hadn't yet done anything good or bad, it was shown that God's purpose would continue because it was based on his choice. ¹²It wasn't because of what was done but because of God's call. This was said to her: *The older child will be a slave to the younger one.*ᵛ ¹³As it is written, *I loved Jacob, but I hated Esau.*ʷ

¹⁴So what are we going to say? Isn't this unfair on God's part? Absolutely not! ¹⁵He says to Moses, *I'll have mercy on whomever I choose to have mercy, and I'll show compassion to whomever I choose to show compassion.*ˣ ¹⁶So then, it doesn't depend on a person's desire or effort. It depends entirely on God, who shows mercy. ¹⁷Scripture says to Pharaoh, *I have put you in this position for this very thing: so I can show my power in you and so that my name can be spread through the entire earth.*ʸ ¹⁸So then, God has mercy on whomever he wants to, but he makes resistant whomever he wants to.

¹⁹So you are going to say to me, "Then why does he still blame people? Who has ever resisted his will?" ²⁰You are only a human being. Who do you think you are to talk back to God? *Does the clay*

ˢPs 44:22 ᵗGen 21:12 ᵘGen 18:10, 14 ᵛGen 25:23 ʷMal 1:2-3 ˣExod 33:19 ʸExod 9:16

say to the potter, "Why did you make me like this?"[z] 21Doesn't the potter have the power over the clay to make one pot for special purposes and another for garbage from the same lump of clay? 22What if God very patiently puts up with pots made for wrath that were designed for destruction, because he wanted to show his wrath and to make his power known? 23What if he did this to make the wealth of his glory known toward pots made for mercy, which he prepared in advance for glory? 24We are the ones God has called. We don't come only from the Jews but we also come from the Gentiles. 25As it says also in Hosea,

I will call "my people"
        those who aren't my people,
    and the one who isn't well loved,
        I will call "loved one."[a]

26And in the place where it was said to them,

"You aren't my people,"
    there they will be called
        "the living God's children."[b]

27But Isaiah cries out for Israel,
Though the number of Israel's children
        will be like the sand of the sea,
    only a remaining part will be saved,
28 because the Lord does what he says
        completely and quickly.[c]

29As Isaiah prophesied,
If the Lord of the heavenly forces
        had not left descendants for us,
    we would have been like Sodom,
    and we would have become
        like Gomorrah.[d]

Israel and God's righteousness

30So what are we going to say? Gentiles who weren't striving for righ-

teousness achieved righteousness, the righteousness that comes from faith. 31But though Israel was striving for a Law of righteousness, they didn't arrive. 32Why? It's because they didn't go for it by faith but they went for it as if it could be reached by doing something. They have tripped over a stumbling block. 33As it is written:

Look! I'm putting a stumbling block
        in Zion,
    which is a rock that offends people.
    And the one who has faith in him will
        not be put to shame.[e]

10 Brothers and sisters, my heart's desire is for Israel's salvation. That's my prayer to God for them. 2I can vouch for them: they are enthusiastic about God. However, it isn't informed by knowledge. 3They don't submit to God's righteousness because they don't understand his righteousness, and they try to establish their own righteousness. 4Christ is the goal of the Law, which leads to righteousness for all who have faith in God.

5Moses writes about the righteousness that comes from the Law: *The person who does these things will live by them.*[f] 6But the righteousness that comes from faith talks like this: *Don't say in your heart, "Who will go up into heaven?"*[g] (that is, to bring Christ down) 7or *"Who will go down into the region below?"*[h] (that is, to bring Christ up from the dead). 8But what does it say? *The word is near you, in your mouth and in your heart*[i] (that is, the message of faith that we preach). 9Because if you confess with your mouth "Jesus is Lord" and in your heart you have faith

[z]Isa 29:16; 45:9 [a]Hos 2:23 [b]Hos 1:10 [c]Isa 10:22-23 LXX [d]Isa 1:9 [e]Isa 28:16; 8:14
[f]Lev 18:5 [g]Deut 9:4; 30:12 [h]Deut 30:13 [i]Deut 30:14

that God raised him from the dead, you will be saved. ¹⁰ Trusting with the heart leads to righteousness, and confessing with the mouth leads to salvation. ¹¹ The scripture says, *All who have faith in him won't be put to shame.*ʲ ¹² There is no distinction between Jew and Greek, because the same Lord is Lord of all, who gives richly to all who call on him. ¹³ *All who call on the Lord's name will be saved.*ᵏ

¹⁴ So how can they call on someone they don't have faith in? And how can they have faith in someone they haven't heard of? And how can they hear without a preacher? ¹⁵ And how can they preach unless they are sent? As it is written, *How beautiful are the feet of those who announce the good news.*ˡ

¹⁶ But everyone hasn't obeyed the good news. As Isaiah says, *Lord, who has had faith in our message?*ᵐ ¹⁷ So, faith comes from listening, but it's listening by means of Christ's message. ¹⁸ But I ask you, didn't they hear it? Definitely! *Their voice has gone out into the entire earth, and their message has gone out to the corners of the inhabited world.*ⁿ ¹⁹ But I ask you again, didn't Israel understand? First, Moses says, *I will make you jealous of those who aren't a people, of a people without understanding.*ᵒ ²⁰ And Isaiah even dares to say, *I was found by those who didn't look for me; I revealed myself to those who didn't ask for me.*ᵖ ²¹ But he says about Israel, *All day long I stretched out my hands to a disobedient and contrary people.*�q

Israel and God's faithfulness

11 So I ask you, has God rejected his people? Absolutely not! I'm an Israelite, a descendant of Abraham, from the tribe of Benjamin. ² God hasn't rejected his people, whom he knew in advance. Or don't you know what the scripture says in the case of Elijah, when he pleads with God against Israel? ³ *Lord, they have killed your prophets, and they have torn down your altars. I'm the only one left, and they are trying to take my life.*ʳ ⁴ But what is God's reply to him? *I have kept for myself seven thousand people who haven't bowed their knees to Baal.*ˢ ⁵ So also in the present time there is a remaining group by the choice of God's grace. ⁶ But if it is by grace, it isn't by what's done anymore. If it were, God's grace wouldn't be grace.

⁷ So what? Israel didn't find what it was looking for. Those who were chosen found it, but the others were resistant. ⁸ As it is written, *God gave them a dull spirit, so that their eyes would not see and their ears not hear, right up until the present day.*ᵗ ⁹ And David says,

> *Their table should become a pitfall and a trap,*
> *a stumbling block and payback to them for what they have done.*
> ¹⁰ *Their eyes should be darkened so they can't see,*
> *and their backs always bent.*ᵘ

¹¹ So I'm asking you: They haven't stumbled so that they've fallen permanently, have they? Absolutely not! But salvation has come to the Gentiles by their failure, in order to make Israel jealous. ¹² But if their failure brings riches to the world, and their defeat brings riches to the Gentiles, how much more will come from the completion of their number! ¹³ I'm speaking to you

ʲIsa 28:16 ᵏJoel 2:32 ˡIsa 52:7; Nah 1:15 ᵐIsa 53:1 ⁿPs 19:4 ᵒDeut 32:21 ᵖIsa 65:1
qIsa 65:2 ʳ1 Kgs 19:10, 14 ˢ1 Kgs 18:18 ᵗDeut 29:4; Isa 29:10 ᵘPs 69:22-23

Gentiles. Considering that I'm an apostle to the Gentiles, I publicize my own ministry [14]in the hope that somehow I might make my own people jealous and save some of them. [15]If their rejection has brought about a close relationship between God and the world, how can their acceptance mean anything less than life from the dead?

[16]But if part of a batch of dough is offered to God as holy, the whole batch of dough is holy too. If a root is holy, the branches will be holy too. [17]If some of the branches were broken off, and you were a wild olive branch, and you were grafted in among the other branches and shared the root that produces the rich oil of the olive tree, [18]then don't brag like you're better than the other branches. If you do brag, be careful: it's not you that sustains the root, but it's the root that sustains you. [19]You will say then, "Branches were broken off so that I could be grafted in." [20]Fine. They were broken off because they weren't faithful, but you stand only by your faithfulness.[v] So don't think in a proud way; instead be afraid. [21]If God didn't spare the natural branches, he won't spare you either. [22]So look at God's kindness and harshness. It's harshness toward those who fell, but it's God's kindness to you, provided you continue in his kindness; otherwise, you could be cut off too. [23]And even those who were cut off will be grafted back in if they don't continue to be unfaithful, because God is able to graft them in again. [24]If you were naturally part of a wild olive tree and you were cut off from it, and then, contrary to nature, you were grafted into the cultivated olive tree, won't these natural branches stand an even better chance of being grafted back onto their own olive tree?

All Israel will be saved

[25]I don't want you to be unaware of this secret,[w] brothers and sisters. That way you won't think too highly of yourselves. A part of Israel has become resistant until the full number of the Gentiles comes in. [26]In this way, all Israel will be saved, as it is written:

The deliverer will come from Zion.
  He will remove ungodly behavior
    from Jacob.
[27] This is my covenant with them,
  when I take away their sins.[x]

[28]According to the gospel, they are enemies for your sake, but according to God's choice, they are loved for the sake of their ancestors. [29]God's gifts and calling can't be taken back. [30]Once you were disobedient to God, but now you have mercy because they were disobedient. [31]In the same way, they have also been disobedient because of the mercy that you received, so now they can receive mercy too. [32]God has locked up all people in disobedience, in order to have mercy on all of them.

[33]God's riches, wisdom, and knowledge are so deep! They are as mysterious as his judgments, and they are as hard to track as his paths!
[34] Who has known the Lord's mind?
  Or who has been his mentor?[y]
[35] Or who has given him a gift
    and has been paid back by him?[z]
[36] All things are from him
  and through him and for him.
  May the glory be to him forever.
    Amen.

---

[v]Or faith [w]Or mystery [x]Isa 59:20-21; 27:9; Jer 31:33-34 [y]Isa 40:13 [z]Job 41:11

Living sacrifice and transformed lives

12 So, brothers and sisters, because of God's mercies, I encourage you to present your bodies as a living sacrifice that is holy and pleasing to God. This is your appropriate priestly service. ²Don't be conformed to the patterns of this world, but be transformed by the renewing of your minds so that you can figure out what God's will is—what is good and pleasing and mature.

Transformed relationships

³Because of the grace that God gave me, I can say to each one of you: don't think of yourself more highly than you ought to think. Instead, be reasonable since God has measured out a portion of faith to each one of you. ⁴We have many parts in one body, but the parts don't all have the same function. ⁵In the same way, though there are many of us, we are one body in Christ, and individually we belong to each other. ⁶We have different gifts that are consistent with God's grace that has been given to us. If your gift is prophecy, you should prophesy in proportion to your faith. ⁷If your gift is service, devote yourself to serving. If your gift is teaching, devote yourself to teaching. ⁸If your gift is encouragement, devote yourself to encouraging. The one giving should do it with no strings attached. The leader should lead with passion. The one showing mercy should be cheerful.

⁹Love should be shown without pretending. Hate evil, and hold on to what is good. ¹⁰Love each other like the members of your family. Be the best at showing honor to each other. ¹¹Don't hesitate to be enthusiastic—be on fire in the Spirit as you serve the Lord! ¹²Be happy in your hope, stand your ground when you're in trouble, and devote yourselves to prayer. ¹³Contribute to the needs of God's people, and welcome strangers into your home. ¹⁴Bless people who harass you—bless and don't curse them. ¹⁵Be happy with those who are happy, and cry with those who are crying. ¹⁶Consider everyone as equal, and don't think that you're better than anyone else. Instead, associate with people who have no status. Don't think that you're so smart. ¹⁷Don't pay back anyone for their evil actions with evil actions, but show respect for what everyone else believes is good.

¹⁸If possible, to the best of your ability, live at peace with all people. ¹⁹Don't try to get revenge for yourselves, my dear friends, but leave room for God's wrath. It is written, *Revenge belongs to me; I will pay it back, says the Lord.*[a] ²⁰Instead, *If your enemy is hungry, feed him; if he is thirsty, give him a drink. By doing this, you will pile burning coals of fire upon his head.*[b] ²¹Don't be defeated by evil, but defeat evil with good.

13 Every person should place themselves under the authority of the government. There isn't any authority unless it comes from God, and the authorities that are there have been put in place by God. ²So anyone who opposes the authority is standing against what God has established. People who take this kind of stand will get punished. ³The authorities don't frighten people who are doing the right thing. Rather, they frighten people who are doing

[a]Deut 32:35 [b]Prov 25:21-22

wrong. Would you rather not be afraid of authority? Do what's right, and you will receive its approval. ⁴It is God's servant given for your benefit. But if you do what's wrong, be afraid because it doesn't have weapons to enforce the law for nothing. It is God's servant put in place to carry out his punishment on those who do what is wrong. ⁵That is why it is necessary to place yourself under the government's authority, not only to avoid God's punishment but also for the sake of your conscience. ⁶You should also pay taxes for the same reason, because the authorities are God's assistants, concerned with this very thing. ⁷So pay everyone what you owe them. Pay the taxes you owe, pay the duties you are charged, give respect to those you should respect, and honor those you should honor.

⁸Don't be in debt to anyone, except for the obligation to love each other. Whoever loves another person has fulfilled the Law. ⁹The commandments, *Don't commit adultery, don't murder, don't steal, don't desire what others have,*ᶜ and any other commandments, are all summed up in one word: *You must love your neighbor as yourself.*ᵈ ¹⁰Love doesn't do anything wrong to a neighbor; therefore, love is what fulfills the Law.

The day is near

¹¹As you do all this, you know what time it is. The hour has already come for you to wake up from your sleep. Now our salvation is nearer than when we first had faith. ¹²The night is almost over, and the day is near. So let's get rid of the actions that belong to the darkness and put on the weapons of light.

¹³Let's behave appropriately as people who live in the day, not in partying and getting drunk, not in sleeping around and obscene behavior, not in fighting and obsession. ¹⁴Instead, dress yourself with the Lord Jesus Christ, and don't plan to indulge your selfish desires.

Welcoming each other like Christ

14 Welcome the person who is weak in faith—but not in order to argue about differences of opinion. ²One person believes in eating everything, while the weak person eats only vegetables. ³Those who eat must not look down on the ones who don't, and the ones who don't eat must not judge the ones who do, because God has accepted them. ⁴Who are you to judge someone else's servants? They stand or fall before their own Lord (and they will stand, because the Lord has the power to make them stand). ⁵One person considers some days to be more sacred than others, while another person considers all days to be the same. Each person must have their own convictions. ⁶Someone who thinks that a day is sacred, thinks that way for the Lord. Those who eat, eat for the Lord, because they thank God. And those who don't eat, don't eat for the Lord, and they thank the Lord too. ⁷We don't live for ourselves and we don't die for ourselves. ⁸If we live, we live for the Lord, and if we die, we die for the Lord. Therefore, whether we live or die, we belong to God. ⁹This is why Christ died and lived: so that he might be Lord of both the dead and the living. ¹⁰But why do you judge your brother or sister? Or why do you look down on your brother or sister? We all will stand in front of

ᶜExod 20:13-15, 17; Deut 5:17-19, 21   ᵈLev 19:18

the judgment seat of God. [11]Because it is written,

As I live, says the Lord,
every knee will bow to me,
and every tongue will give praise
to God.[e]

[12]So then, each of us will give an account of ourselves to God.

[13]So stop judging each other. Instead, this is what you should decide: never put a stumbling block or obstacle in the way of your brother or sister. [14]I know and I'm convinced in the Lord Jesus that nothing is wrong to eat in itself. But if someone thinks something is wrong to eat, it becomes wrong for that person. [15]If your brother or sister is upset by your food, you are no longer walking in love. Don't let your food destroy someone for whom Christ died. [16]And don't let something you consider to be good be criticized as wrong. [17]God's kingdom isn't about eating food and drinking but about righteousness, peace, and joy in the Holy Spirit. [18]Whoever serves Christ this way pleases God and gets human approval.

[19]So let's strive for the things that bring peace and the things that build each other up. [20]Don't destroy what God has done because of food. All food is acceptable, but it's a bad thing if it trips someone else. [21]It's a good thing not to eat meat or drink wine or to do anything that trips your brother or sister. [22]Keep the belief that you have to yourself—it's between you and God. People are blessed who don't convict themselves by the things they approve. [23]But those who have doubts are convicted if they go ahead and eat, because

they aren't acting on the basis of faith. Everything that isn't based on faith is sin.

15 We who are powerful need to be patient with the weakness of those who don't have power, and not please ourselves. [2]Each of us should please our neighbors for their good in order to build them up. [3]Christ didn't please himself, but, as it is written, *The insults of those who insulted you fell on me.*[f] [4]Whatever was written in the past was written for our instruction so that we could have hope through endurance and through the encouragement of the scriptures. [5]May the God of endurance and encouragement give you the same attitude toward each other, similar to Christ Jesus' attitude. [6]That way you can glorify the God and Father of our Lord Jesus Christ together with one voice.

[7]So welcome each other, in the same way that Christ also welcomed you, for God's glory. [8]I'm saying that Christ became a servant of those who are circumcised for the sake of God's truth, in order to confirm the promises given to the ancestors, [9]and so that the Gentiles could glorify God for his mercy. As it is written,

Because of this I will confess you
among the Gentiles,
and I will sing praises
to your name.[g]

[10]And again, it says,

Rejoice, Gentiles, with his people.[h]

[11]And again,

Praise the Lord, all you Gentiles,
and all the people should
sing his praises.[i]

[12]And again, Isaiah says,

[e]Isa 45:23 [f]Ps 69:9 [g]Ps 18:49 [h]Deut 32:43 [i]Ps 117:1

There will be a root of Jesse,
    who will also rise
        to rule the Gentiles.
    The Gentiles will place their hope
        in him.[j]

¹³May the God of hope fill you with all joy and peace in faith so that you overflow with hope by the power of the Holy Spirit.

Paul's ministry to the Gentiles

¹⁴My brothers and sisters, I myself am convinced that you yourselves are full of goodness, filled with all knowledge, and are able to teach each other. ¹⁵But I've written to you in a sort of daring way, partly to remind you of what you already know. I'm writing to you in this way because of the grace that was given to me by God. ¹⁶It helps me to be a minister of Christ Jesus to the Gentiles. I'm working as a priest of God's gospel so that the offering of the Gentiles can be acceptable and made holy by the Holy Spirit. ¹⁷So in Christ Jesus I brag about things that have to do with God. ¹⁸I don't dare speak about anything except what Christ has done through me to bring about the obedience of the Gentiles. He did it by what I've said and what I've done, ¹⁹by the power of signs and wonders, and by the power of God's Spirit. So I've completed the circuit of preaching Christ's gospel from Jerusalem all the way around to Illyricum. ²⁰In this way, I have a goal to preach the gospel where they haven't heard of Christ yet, so that I won't be building on someone else's foundation. ²¹Instead, as it's written, *Those who hadn't been told about him will see, and those who hadn't heard will understand.*[k]

Travel plans to visit Rome

²²That's why I've been stopped so many times from coming to see you. ²³But now, since I don't have any place to work in these regions anymore, and since I've wanted to come to see you for many years, ²⁴I'll visit you when I go to Spain. I hope to see you while I'm passing through. And I hope you will send me on my way there, after I have first been reenergized by some time in your company.

²⁵But now I'm going to Jerusalem, to serve God's people. ²⁶Macedonia and Achaia have been happy to make a contribution for the poor among God's people in Jerusalem. ²⁷They were happy to do this, and they are actually in debt to God's people in Jerusalem. If the Gentiles got a share of the Jewish people's spiritual resources, they ought to minister to them with material resources. ²⁸So then after I have finished this job and have safely delivered the final amount of Gentiles' offering to them, I will leave for Spain, visiting you on the way. ²⁹And I know that when I come to you I will come with the fullest blessing of Christ.

³⁰Brothers and sisters, I urge you, through our Lord Jesus Christ and through the love of the Spirit, to join me in my struggles in your prayers to God for me. ³¹Pray that I will be rescued from the people in Judea who don't believe. Also, pray that my service for Jerusalem will be acceptable to God's people there ³²so that I can come to you with joy by God's will and be reenergized with your company. ³³May the God of peace be with you all. Amen.

[j]Isa 11:10 [k]Isa 52:15

Introduction to Phoebe

16 I'm introducing our sister Phoebe to you, who is a servant[1] of the church in Cenchreae. [2]Welcome her in the Lord in a way that is worthy of God's people, and give her whatever she needs from you, because she herself has been a sponsor of many people, myself included.

Greetings to Roman Christians

[3]Say hello to Prisca and Aquila, my coworkers in Christ Jesus, [4]who risked their own necks for my life. I'm not the only one who thanks God for them, but all the churches of the Gentiles do the same. [5]Also say hello to the church that meets in their house. Say hello to Epaenetus, my dear friend, who was the first convert[m] in Asia for Christ. [6]Say hello to Mary, who has worked very hard for you. [7]Say hello to Andronicus and Junia, my relatives and my fellow prisoners. They are prominent among the apostles, and they were in Christ before me. [8]Say hello to Ampliatus, my dear friend in the Lord. [9]Say hello to Urbanus, our coworker in Christ, and my dear friend Stachys. [10]Say hello to Apelles, who is tried and true in Christ. Say hello to the members of the household of Aristobulus. [11]Say hello to my relative Herodion. Say hello to the members of the household of Narcissus who are in the Lord. [12]Say hello to Tryphaena and Tryphosa, who are workers for the Lord. Say hello to my dear friend Persis, who has worked hard in the Lord. [13]Say hello to Rufus, who is an outstanding believer, along with his mother and mine. [14]Say hello

to Asyncritus, Phlegon, Hermes, Patrobas, Hermas, and the brothers and sisters who are with them. [15]Say hello to Philologus and Julia, Nereus and his sister, and Olympas, and all the saints who are with them. [16]Say hello to each other with a holy kiss. All the churches of Christ say hello to you.

Warning against divisions

[17]Brothers and sisters, I urge you to watch out for people who create divisions and problems against the teaching that you learned. Keep away from them. [18]People like that aren't serving the Lord. They are serving their own feelings. They deceive the hearts of innocent people with smooth talk and flattery. [19]The news of your obedience has reached everybody, so I'm happy for you. But I want you to be wise about what's good, and innocent about what's evil. [20]The God of peace will soon crush Satan[n] under your feet. The grace of our Lord Jesus Christ be with you.

Greetings from Paul's coworkers

[21]Timothy my coworker says hello to you, and Lucius, Jason, and Sosipater, my relatives. [22]I'm Tertius, and I'm writing this letter to you in the Lord—hello! [23]Gaius, who is host to me and to the whole church, says hello to you. Erastus the city treasurer says hello to you, along with our brother Quartus.[o]

Final prayer

[25]May the glory be to God who can strengthen you with my good news and the message that I preach about Jesus Christ. He can strengthen you with the

[1]Or *deacon* [m]Or *is the firstfruits* [n]Or *the Adversary* [o]Critical editions of the Gk New Testament do not include 16:24 *The grace of our Lord Jesus Christ be with you.*

announcement of the secret[p] that was kept quiet for a long time. [26]Now that secret is revealed through what the prophets wrote. It is made known to the Gentiles[q] in order to lead to their faithful obedience based on the command of the eternal God. [27]May the glory be to God, who alone is wise! May the glory be to him through Jesus Christ forever! Amen.

1 CORINTHIANS

Greeting

[1]From Paul, called by God's will to be an apostle of Jesus Christ, and from Sosthenes our brother.

[2]To God's church that is in Corinth:

To those who have been made holy to God in Christ Jesus, who are called to be God's people.

Together with all those who call upon the name of our Lord Jesus Christ in every place—he's their Lord and ours!

[3]Grace to you and peace from God our Father and the Lord Jesus Christ.

Thanksgiving for the Corinthians

[4]I thank my God always for you, because of God's grace that was given to you in Christ Jesus. [5]That is, you were made rich through him in everything: in all your communication and every kind of knowledge, [6]in the same way that the testimony about Christ was confirmed with you. [7]The result is that you aren't missing any spiritual gift while you wait for our Lord Jesus Christ to be revealed. [8]He will also confirm your testimony about Christ until the end so that you will be blameless on the day of our Lord Jesus Christ. [9]God is faithful, and you were called by him to partnership with his Son, Jesus Christ our Lord.

Rival groups in Corinth

[10]Now I encourage you, brothers and sisters, in the name of our Lord Jesus Christ: Agree with each other and don't be divided into rival groups. Instead, be restored with the same mind and the same purpose. [11]My brothers and sisters, Chloe's people gave me some information about you, that you're fighting with each other. [12]What I mean is this: that each one of you says, "I belong to Paul," "I belong to Apollos," "I belong to Cephas," "I belong to Christ." [13]Has Christ been divided? Was Paul crucified for you, or were you baptized in Paul's name? [14]Thank God that I didn't baptize any of you, except Crispus and Gaius, [15]so that nobody can say that you were baptized in my name! [16]Oh, I baptized the house of Stephanas too. Otherwise, I don't know if I baptized anyone else. [17]Christ didn't send me to baptize but to preach the good news. And Christ didn't send me to preach the good news with clever words so that Christ's cross won't be emptied of its meaning.

[p]Or *mystery*   [q]Or *all the Gentiles*

Human wisdom versus the cross

[18]The message of the cross is foolishness to those who are being destroyed. But it is the power of God for those of us who are being saved. [19]It is written in scripture: *I will destroy the wisdom of the wise, and I will reject the intelligence of the intelligent.*[a] [20]Where are the wise? Where are the legal experts? Where are today's debaters? Hasn't God made the wisdom of the world foolish? [21]In God's wisdom, he determined that the world wouldn't come to know him through its wisdom. Instead, God was pleased to save those who believe through the foolishness of preaching. [22]Jews ask for signs, and Greeks look for wisdom, [23]but we preach Christ crucified, which is a scandal to Jews and foolishness to Gentiles. [24]But to those who are called—both Jews and Greeks—Christ is God's power and God's wisdom. [25]This is because the foolishness of God is wiser than human wisdom, and the weakness of God is stronger than human strength.

[26]Look at your situation when you were called, brothers and sisters! By ordinary human standards not many were wise, not many were powerful, not many were from the upper class. [27]But God chose what the world considers foolish to shame the wise. God chose what the world considers weak to shame the strong. [28]And God chose what the world considers low-class and low-life—what is considered to be nothing—to reduce what is considered to be something to nothing. [29]So no human being can brag in God's presence. [30]It is because of God that you are in Christ Jesus. He became wisdom from God for us. This means that he made us righteous and holy, and delivered us. [31]This is consistent with what was written: *The one who brags should brag in the Lord!*[b]

2 When I came to you, brothers and sisters, I didn't come preaching God's secrets to you like I was an expert in speech or wisdom. [2]I had made up my mind not to think about anything while I was with you except Jesus Christ, and to preach him as crucified. [3]I stood in front of you with weakness, fear, and a lot of shaking. [4]My message and my preaching weren't presented with convincing wise words but with a demonstration of the Spirit and of power. [5]I did this so that your faith might not depend on the wisdom of people but on the power of God.

Definition of wisdom

[6]What we say is wisdom to people who are mature. It isn't a wisdom that comes from the present day or from today's leaders who are being reduced to nothing. [7]We talk about God's wisdom, which has been hidden as a secret. God determined this wisdom in advance, before time began, for our glory. [8]It is a wisdom that none of the present-day rulers have understood, because if they did understand it, they would never have crucified the Lord of glory! [9]But this is precisely what is written: *God has prepared things for those who love him that no eye has seen, or ear has heard, or that haven't crossed the mind of any human being.*[c] [10]God has revealed these things to us through the Spirit. The Spirit searches everything, including the depths of God. [11]Who knows a

[a]Isa 29:14 [b]Jer 9:24 [c]Isa 64:4

person's depths except their own spirit that lives in them? In the same way, no one has known the depths of God except God's Spirit. [12]We haven't received the world's spirit but God's Spirit so that we can know the things given to us by God. [13]These are the things we are talking about—not with words taught by human wisdom but with words taught by the Spirit—we are interpreting spiritual things to spiritual people. [14]But people who are unspiritual don't accept the things from God's Spirit. They are foolishness to them and can't be understood, because they can only be comprehended in a spiritual way. [15]Spiritual people comprehend everything, but they themselves aren't understood by anyone. [16]*Who has known the mind of the Lord, who will advise him?*[d] But we have the mind of Christ.

Wisdom applied to divisions in the church

3 Brothers and sisters, I couldn't talk to you like spiritual people but like unspiritual people, like babies in Christ. [2]I gave you milk to drink instead of solid food, because you weren't up to it yet. [3]Now you are still not up to it because you are still unspiritual. When jealousy and fighting exist between you, aren't you unspiritual and living by human standards? [4]When someone says, "I belong to Paul," and someone else says, "I belong to Apollos," aren't you acting like people without the Spirit? [5]After all, what is Apollos? What is Paul? They are servants who helped you to believe. Each one had a role given to them by the Lord: [6]I planted, Apollos watered, but God made it grow. [7]Because of this,

neither the one who plants nor the one who waters is anything, but the only one who is anything is God who makes it grow. [8]The one who plants and the one who waters work together, but each one will receive their own reward for their own labor. [9]We are God's co-workers, and you are God's field, God's building.

[10]I laid a foundation like a wise master builder according to God's grace that was given to me, but someone else is building on top of it. Each person needs to pay attention to the way they build on it. [11]No one can lay any other foundation besides the one that is already laid, which is Jesus Christ. [12]So, whether someone builds on top of the foundation with gold, silver, precious stones, wood, grass, or hay, [13]each one's work will be clearly shown. The day will make it clear, because it will be revealed with fire—the fire will test the quality of each one's work. [14]If anyone's work survives, they'll get a reward. [15]But if anyone's work goes up in flames, they'll lose it. However, they themselves will be saved as if they had gone through a fire. [16]Don't you know that you are God's temple and God's Spirit lives in you? [17]If someone destroys God's temple, God will destroy that person, because God's temple is holy, which is what you are.

[18]Don't fool yourself. If some of you think they are worldly-wise, then they should become foolish so that they can become wise. [19]This world's wisdom is foolishness to God. As it's written, *He catches the wise in their cleverness.*[e] [20]And also, *The Lord knows that the thoughts of the wise are silly.*[f] [21]So then,

[d]Isa 40:13　[e]Job 5:13　[f]Ps 94:11

no one should brag about human beings. Everything belongs to you— [22] Paul, Apollos, Cephas, the world, life, death, things in the present, things in the future—everything belongs to you, [23] but you belong to Christ, and Christ belongs to God.

Paul's role as an apostle

4 So a person should think about us this way—as servants of Christ and managers of God's secrets. [2] In this kind of situation, what is expected of a manager is that they prove to be faithful. [3] I couldn't care less if I'm judged by you or by any human court; I don't even judge myself. [4] I'm not aware of anything against me, but that doesn't make me innocent, because the Lord is the one who judges me. [5] So don't judge anything before the right time—wait until the Lord comes. He will bring things that are hidden in the dark to light, and he will make people's motivations public. Then there will be recognition for each person from God.

[6] Brothers and sisters, I have applied these things to myself and Apollos for your benefit. I've done this so that you can learn what it means not to go beyond what has been written and so none of you will become arrogant by supporting one of us against the other. [7] Who says that you are better than anyone else? What do you have that you didn't receive? And if you received it, then why are you bragging as if you didn't receive it? [8] You've been filled already! You've become rich already! You rule like kings without us! I wish you did rule so that we could be kings with you! [9] I suppose that God has shown that we apostles are at the end of the line. We are like prisoners sentenced to death, because we have become a spectacle in the world, both to angels and to humans. [10] We are fools for Christ, but you are wise through Christ! We are weak, but you are strong! You are honored, but we are dishonored! [11] Up to this very moment we are hungry, thirsty, wearing rags, abused, and homeless. [12] We work hard with our own hands. When we are insulted, we respond with a blessing; when we are harassed, we put up with it; [13] when our reputation is attacked, we are encouraging. We have become the scum of the earth, the waste that runs off everything, up to the present time.

[14] I'm not writing these things to make you ashamed but to warn you, since you are my loved children. [15] You may have ten thousand mentors in Christ, but you don't have many fathers. I gave birth to you in Christ Jesus through the gospel, [16] so I encourage you to follow my example. [17] This is why I've sent Timothy to you; he's my loved and trusted child in the Lord; he'll remind you about my way of life in Christ Jesus. He'll teach the same way as I teach everywhere in every church. [18] Some have become arrogant as if I'm not coming to see you. [19] But, if the Lord is willing, I'll come to you soon. Then I won't focus on what these arrogant people say, but I'll find out what power they possess. [20] God's kingdom isn't about words but about power. [21] Which do you want? Should I come to you with a big stick to punish you, or with love and a gentle spirit?

Confronting sexual immorality in the church

5 Everyone has heard that there is sexual immorality among you. This

is a type of immorality that isn't even heard of among the Gentiles—a man is having sex with his father's wife! [2]And you're proud of yourselves instead of being so upset that the one who did this thing is expelled from your community. [3]Though I'm absent physically, I'm present in the spirit and I've already judged the man who did this as if I were present. [4]When you meet together in the name of our Lord Jesus, I'll be present in spirit with the power of our Lord Jesus. [5]At that time we need to hand this man over to Satan to destroy his human weakness so that a spirit might be saved on the day of the Lord.

[6]Your bragging isn't good! Don't you know that a tiny grain of yeast makes a whole batch of dough rise? [7]Clean out the old yeast so you can be a new batch of dough, given that you're supposed to be unleavened bread. Christ our Passover lamb has been sacrificed, [8]so let's celebrate the feast with the unleavened bread of honesty and truth, not with old yeast or with the yeast of evil and wickedness.

[9]I wrote to you in my earlier letter not to associate with sexually immoral people. [10]But I wasn't talking about the sexually immoral people in the outside world by any means—or the greedy, or the swindlers, or people who worship false gods—otherwise, you would have to leave the world entirely! [11]But now I'm writing to you not to associate with anyone who calls themselves "brother" or "sister" who is sexually immoral, greedy, someone who worships false gods, an abusive person, a drunk, or a swindler. Don't even eat with anyone like this. [12]What do I care about judging

outsiders? Isn't it your job to judge insiders? [13]God will judge outsiders. *Expel the evil one from among you!*[g]

Confronting lawsuits in the church

6 When someone in your assembly has a legal case against another member, do they dare to take it to court to be judged by people who aren't just, instead of by God's people? [2]Or don't you know that God's people will judge the world? If the world is to be judged by you, are you incompetent to judge trivial cases? [3]Don't you know that we will judge angels? Why not ordinary things? [4]So then if you have ordinary lawsuits, do you appoint people as judges who aren't respected by the church? [5]I'm saying this because you should be ashamed of yourselves! Isn't there one person among you who is wise enough to pass judgment between believers? [6]But instead, does a brother or sister have a lawsuit against another brother or sister, and do they do this in front of unbelievers? [7]The fact that you have lawsuits against each other means that you've already lost your case. Why not be wronged instead? Why not be cheated? [8]But instead you are doing wrong and cheating—and you're doing it to your own brothers and sisters.

[9]Don't you know that people who are unjust won't inherit God's kingdom? Don't be deceived. Those who are sexually immoral, those who worship false gods, adulterers, both participants in same-sex intercourse,[h] [10]thieves, the greedy, drunks, abusive people, and swindlers won't inherit God's kingdom. [11]That is what some of you used to be! But you were washed clean, you

---

[g]Deut 17:7; 19:19; 22:21, 24; 24:7   [h]*Or submissive and dominant male sexual partners*

were made holy to God, and you were made right with God in the name of the Lord Jesus Christ and in the Spirit of our God.

Avoid sexual immorality

[12] I have the freedom to do anything, but not everything is helpful. I have the freedom to do anything, but I won't be controlled by anything. [13] Food is for the stomach and the stomach is for food, and yet God will do away with both. The body isn't for sexual immorality but for the Lord, and the Lord is for the body. [14] God has raised the Lord and will raise us through his power. [15] Don't you know that your bodies are parts of Christ? So then, should I take parts of Christ and make them a part of someone who is sleeping around?[i] No way! [16] Don't you know that anyone who is joined to someone who is sleeping around is one body with that person? The scripture says, *The two will become one flesh.*[j] [17] The one who is joined to the Lord is one spirit with him. [18] Avoid sexual immorality! Every sin that a person can do is committed outside the body, except those who engage in sexual immorality commit sin against their own bodies. [19] Or don't you know that your body is a temple of the Holy Spirit who is in you? Don't you know that you have the Holy Spirit from God, and you don't belong to yourselves? [20] You have been bought and paid for, so honor God with your body.

Marriage and celibacy

7 Now, about what you wrote: "It's good for a man not to have sex with a woman." [2] Each man should have his own wife, and each woman should have her own husband because of sexual immorality. [3] The husband should meet his wife's sexual needs, and the wife should do the same for her husband. [4] The wife doesn't have authority over her own body, but the husband does. Likewise, the husband doesn't have authority over his own body, but the wife does. [5] Don't refuse to meet each other's needs unless you both agree for a short period of time to devote yourselves to prayer. Then come back together again so that Satan might not tempt you because of your lack of self-control. [6] I'm saying this to give you permission; it's not a command. [7] I wish all people were like me, but each has a particular gift from God: one has this gift, and another has that one.

[8] I'm telling those who are single and widows that it's good for them to stay single like me. [9] But if they can't control themselves, they should get married, because it's better to marry than to burn with passion. [10] I'm passing on the Lord's command to those who are married: A wife shouldn't leave her husband, [11] but if she does leave him, then she should stay single or be reconciled to her husband. And a man shouldn't divorce his wife.

[12] I'm telling everyone else (the Lord didn't say this specifically): If a believer has a wife who doesn't believe, and she agrees to live with him, then he shouldn't divorce her. [13] If a woman has a husband who doesn't believe and he agrees to live with him, then she shouldn't divorce him. [14] The husband

---

[i] Or *a prostitute*; commonly, women who sell their bodies to multiple sex partners but includes those who are sexually immoral   [j] Gen 2:24

who doesn't believe belongs to God because of his wife, and the wife who doesn't believe belongs to God because of her husband. Otherwise, your children would be contaminated by the world, but now they are spiritually set apart. ¹⁵But if a spouse who doesn't believe chooses to leave, then let them leave. The brother or sister isn't tied down in these circumstances. God has called you to peace. ¹⁶How do you know as a wife if you will save your husband? Or how do you know as a husband if you will save your wife?

¹⁷Nevertheless, each person should live the kind of life that the Lord assigned when he called each one. This is what I teach in all the churches. ¹⁸If someone was circumcised when called, he shouldn't try to reverse it. If someone wasn't circumcised when he was called, he shouldn't be circumcised. ¹⁹Circumcision is nothing; not being circumcised is nothing. What matters is keeping God's commandments. ²⁰Each person should stay in the situation they were in when they were called. ²¹If you were a slave when you were called, don't let it bother you. But if you are actually able to be free, take advantage of the opportunity. ²²Anyone who was a slave when they were called by the Lord has the status of being the Lord's free person. In the same way, anyone who was a free person when they were called is Christ's slave. ²³You were bought and paid for. Don't become slaves of people. ²⁴So then, brothers and sisters, each of you should stay with God in the situation you were in when you were called.

²⁵I don't have a command from the Lord about people who have never been married,ᵏ but I'll give you my opinion as someone you can trust because of the Lord's mercy. ²⁶So I think this advice is good because of the present crisis: Stay as you are. ²⁷If you are married, don't get a divorce. If you are divorced, don't try to find a spouse. ²⁸But if you do marry, you haven't sinned; and if someone who hasn't been married gets married, they haven't sinned. But married people will have a hard time, and I'm trying to spare you that. ²⁹This is what I'm saying, brothers and sisters: The time has drawn short. From now on, those who have wives should be like people who don't have them. ³⁰Those who are sad should be like people who aren't crying. Those who are happy should be like people who aren't happy. Those who buy something should be like people who don't have possessions. ³¹Those who use the world should be like people who aren't preoccupied with it, because this world in its present form is passing away.

³²I want you to be free from concerns. A man who isn't married is concerned about the Lord's concerns—how he can please the Lord. ³³But a married man is concerned about the world's concerns—how he can please his wife. ³⁴His attention is divided. A woman who isn't married or who is a virgin is concerned about the Lord's concerns so that she can be dedicated to God in both body and spirit. But a married woman is concerned about the world's concerns—how she can please her husband. ³⁵I'm saying this for your own advantage. It's not to restrict you but rather to promote effective and consistent service to the Lord without distraction.

ᵏOr *virgins*

36If someone thinks he is acting inappropriately toward an unmarried woman whom he knows, and if he has strong feelings and it seems like the right thing to do, he should do what he wants—he's not sinning—they should get married. 37But if a man stands firm in his decision, and doesn't feel the pressure, but has his own will under control, he does right if he decides in his own heart not to marry the woman. 38Therefore, the one who marries the unmarried woman does right, and the one who doesn't get married will do even better. 39A woman is obligated to stay in her marriage as long as her husband is alive. But if her husband dies, she is free to marry whomever she wants, only it should be a believer in the Lord. 40But in my opinion, she will be happier if she stays the way she is. And I think that I have God's Spirit too.

Meat sacrificed to false gods

8 Now concerning meat that has been sacrificed to a false god: We know that we all have knowledge. Knowledge makes people arrogant, but love builds people up. 2If anyone thinks they know something, they don't yet know as much as they should know. 3But if someone loves God, then they are known by God.

4So concerning the actual food involved in these sacrifices to false gods, we know that a false god isn't anything in this world, and that there is no God except for the one God. 5Granted, there are so-called "gods," in heaven and on the earth, as there are many gods and many lords. 6However, for us believers,

There is one God the Father.
    All things come from him,
    and we belong to him.

And there is one Lord Jesus Christ.
    All things exist through him,
    and we live through him.

7But not everybody knows this. Some are eating this food as though it really is food sacrificed to a real idol, because they were used to idol worship until now. Their conscience is weak because it has been damaged. 8Food won't bring us close to God. We're not missing out if we don't eat, and we don't have any advantage if we do eat. 9But watch out or else this freedom of yours might be a problem for those who are weak. 10Suppose someone sees you (the person who has knowledge) eating in an idol's temple. Won't the person with a weak conscience be encouraged to eat the meat sacrificed to false gods? 11The weak brother or sister for whom Christ died is destroyed by your knowledge. 12You sin against Christ if you sin against your brothers and sisters and hurt their weak consciences this way. 13This is why, if food causes the downfall of my brother or sister, I won't eat meat ever again, or else I may cause my brother or sister to fall.

Waiving rights for the gospel

9 Am I not free? Am I not an apostle? Haven't I seen Jesus our Lord? Aren't you my work in the Lord? 2If I'm not an apostle to others, at least I am to you! You are the seal that shows I'm an apostle. 3This is my defense against those who criticize me. 4Don't we have the right to eat and drink? 5Don't we have the right to travel with a wife who believes like the rest of the apostles, the Lord's brothers, and Cephas? 6Or is it only I and Barnabas who don't have the right to not work for our living? 7Who joins the army and pays their own way?

Who plants a vineyard and doesn't eat its fruit? Who shepherds a flock and doesn't drink its milk? [8]I'm not saying these things just based on common sense, am I? Doesn't the Law itself say these things? [9]In Moses' Law it's written: *You will not muzzle the ox when it is threshing.*[l] Is God worried about oxen, [10]or did he say this entirely for our sake? It was written for our sake because the one who plows and the one who threshes should each do so with the hope of sharing the produce. [11]If we sowed spiritual things in you, is it so much to ask to harvest some material things from you?

[12]If others have these rights over you, don't we deserve them all the more? However, we haven't made use of this right, but we put up with everything so we don't put any obstacle in the way of the gospel of Christ. [13]Don't you know that those who serve in the temple have to eat food from the temple, and those who serve at the altar share part of what is sacrificed on the altar? [14]In the same way, the Lord commanded that those who preach the gospel should get their living from the gospel. [15]But I haven't taken advantage of this. And I'm not writing this so that it will be done for me. It's better for me to die than to lose my right to brag about this! [16]If I preach the gospel, I have no reason to brag, since I'm obligated to do it. I'm in trouble if I don't preach the gospel. [17]If I do this voluntarily, I get rewarded for it. But if I'm forced to do it, then I've been charged with a responsibility. [18]What reward do I get? That when I preach, I offer the good news free of charge. That's why I don't use

the rights to which I'm entitled through the gospel.

[19]Although I'm free from all people, I make myself a slave to all people, to recruit more of them. [20]I act like a Jew to the Jews, so I can recruit Jews. I act like I'm under the Law to those under the Law, so I can recruit those who are under the Law (though I myself am not under the Law). [21]I act like I'm outside the Law to those who are outside the Law, so I can recruit those outside the Law (though I'm not outside the law of God but rather under the law of Christ). [22]I act weak to the weak, so I can recruit the weak. I have become all things to all people, so I could save some by all possible means. [23]All the things I do are for the sake of the gospel, so I can be a partner with it.

[24]Don't you know that all the runners in the stadium run, but only one gets the prize? So run to win. [25]Everyone who competes practices self-discipline in everything. The runners do this to get a crown of leaves that shrivel up and die, but we do it to receive a crown that never dies. [26]So now this is how I run—not without a clear goal in sight. I fight like a boxer in the ring, not like someone who is shadowboxing. [27]Rather, I'm landing punches on my own body and subduing it like a slave. I do this to be sure that I myself won't be disqualified after preaching to others.

Warning from the wilderness generation

10Brothers and sisters, I want you to be sure of the fact that our ancestors were all under the cloud and they all went through the sea. [2]All were

[l]Deut 25:4

baptized into Moses in the cloud and in the sea. [3] All ate the same spiritual food, [4] and all drank the same spiritual drink. They drank from a spiritual rock that followed them, and the rock was Christ. [5] However, God was unhappy with most of them, and they were struck down in the wilderness. [6] These things were examples for us, so we won't crave evil things like they did. [7] Don't worship false gods like some of them did, as it is written, *The people sat down to eat and drink and they got up to play.*[m] [8] Let's not practice sexual immorality, like some of them did, and twenty-three thousand died in one day. [9] Let's not test Christ, like some of them did, and were killed by the snakes. [10] Let's not grumble, like some of them did, and were killed by the destroyer. [11] These things happened to them as an example and were written as a warning for us to whom the end of time has come. [12] So those who think they are standing need to watch out or else they may fall. [13] No temptation has seized you that isn't common for people. But God is faithful. He won't allow you to be tempted beyond your abilities. Instead, with the temptation, God will also supply a way out so that you will be able to endure it.

Avoid false gods to glorify God

[14] So then, my dear friends, run away from the worship of false gods! [15] I'm talking to you like you are sensible people. Think about what I'm saying. [16] Isn't the cup of blessing that we bless a sharing in the blood of Christ? Isn't the loaf of bread that we break a sharing in the body of Christ? [17] Since there is one loaf of bread, we who are many

are one body, because we all share the one loaf of bread. [18] Look at the people of Israel. Don't those who eat the sacrifices share from the altar? [19] What am I saying then? That food sacrificed to a false god is anything, or that a false god is anything? [20] No, but this kind of sacrifice is sacrificed to demons and not to God. I don't want you to be sharing in demons. [21] You can't drink the cup of the Lord and the cup of demons; you can't participate in the table of the Lord and the table of demons. [22] Or should we make the Lord jealous? We aren't stronger than he is, are we?

[23] Everything is permitted, but everything isn't beneficial. Everything is permitted, but everything doesn't build others up. [24] No one should look out for their own advantage, but they should look out for each other. [25] Eat everything that is sold in the marketplace, without asking questions about it because of your conscience. [26] *The earth and all that is in it belong to the Lord.*[n] [27] If an unbeliever invites you to eat with them and you want to go, eat whatever is served, without asking questions because of your conscience. [28] But if someone says to you, "This meat was sacrificed in a temple," then don't eat it for the sake of the one who told you and for the sake of conscience. [29] Now when I say "conscience" I don't mean yours but the other person's. Why should my freedom be judged by someone else's conscience? [30] If I participate with gratitude, why should I be blamed for food I thank God for? [31] So, whether you eat or drink or whatever you do, you should do it all for God's glory. [32] Don't offend either Jews or

[m]Exod 32:6 [n]Ps 24:1

Greeks, or God's church. ³³This is the same thing that I do. I please everyone in everything I do. I don't look out for my own advantage, but I look out for many people so that they can be saved. **11** Follow my example, just like I follow Christ's.

Appropriate dress in worship

²I praise you because you remember all my instructions, and you hold on to the traditions exactly as I handed them on to you. ³Now I want you to know that the head of every man is Christ, and the head of the woman is the man, and the head of Christ is God. ⁴Every man who prays or prophesies with his head covered shames his head. ⁵Every woman who prays or prophesies with her head uncovered disgraces her head. It is the same thing as having her head shaved. ⁶If a woman doesn't cover her head, then she should have her hair cut off. If it is disgraceful for a woman to have short hair or to be shaved, then she should keep her head covered. ⁷A man shouldn't have his head covered, because he is the image and glory of God; but the woman is man's glory. ⁸Man didn't have his origin from woman, but woman from man; ⁹and man wasn't created for the sake of the woman, but the woman for the sake of the man. ¹⁰Because of this a woman should have authority over her head, because of the angels. ¹¹However, woman isn't independent from man, and man isn't independent from woman in the Lord. ¹²As woman came from man so also man comes from woman. But everything comes from God. ¹³Judge for yourselves: Is it appropriate for a woman to pray to God with her head uncovered? ¹⁴Doesn't nature itself teach you that if a man has long hair, it is a disgrace to him; ¹⁵but if a woman has long hair, it is her glory? This is because her long hair is given to her for a covering. ¹⁶But if someone wants to argue about this, we don't have such a custom, nor do God's churches.

The community meal

¹⁷Now I don't praise you as I give the following instruction because when you meet together, it does more harm than good. ¹⁸First of all, when you meet together as a church, I hear that there are divisions among you, and I partly believe it. ¹⁹It's necessary that there are groups among you, to make it clear who is genuine. ²⁰So when you get together in one place, it isn't to eat the Lord's meal. ²¹Each of you goes ahead and eats a private meal. One person goes hungry while another is drunk. ²²Don't you have houses to eat and drink in? Or do you look down on God's churches and humiliate those who have nothing? What can I say to you? Will I praise you? No, I don't praise you in this.

²³I received a tradition from the Lord, which I also handed on to you: on the night on which he was betrayed, the Lord Jesus took bread. ²⁴After giving thanks, he broke it and said, "This is my body, which is for you; do this to remember me." ²⁵He did the same thing with the cup, after they had eaten, saying, "This cup is the new covenant in my blood. Every time you drink it, do this to remember me." ²⁶Every time you eat this bread and drink this cup, you broadcast the death of the Lord until he comes.

²⁷This is why those who eat the bread or drink the cup of the Lord inappropriately will be guilty of the Lord's body

and blood. [28] Each individual should test himself or herself, and eat from the bread and drink from the cup in that way. [29] Those who eat and drink without correctly understanding the body are eating and drinking their own judgment. [30] Because of this, many of you are weak and sick, and quite a few have died. [31] But if we had judged ourselves, we wouldn't be judged. [32] However, we are disciplined by the Lord when we are judged so that we won't be judged and condemned along with the whole world. [33] For these reasons, my brothers and sisters, when you get together to eat, wait for each other. [34] If some of you are hungry, they should eat at home so that getting together doesn't lead to judgment. I will give directions about the other things when I come.

Spiritual gifts

12 Brothers and sisters, I don't want you to be ignorant about spiritual gifts. [2] You know that when you were Gentiles you were often misled by false gods that can't even speak. [3] So I want to make it clear to you that no one says, "Jesus is cursed!" when speaking by God's Spirit, and no one can say, "Jesus is Lord," except by the Holy Spirit. [4] There are different spiritual gifts but the same Spirit; [5] and there are different ministries and the same Lord; [6] and there are different activities but the same God who produces all of them in everyone. [7] A demonstration of the Spirit is given to each person for the common good. [8] A word of wisdom is given by the Spirit to one person, a word of knowledge to another according to the same Spirit, [9] faith to still

another by the same Spirit, gifts of healing to another in the one Spirit, [10] performance of miracles to another, prophecy to another, the ability to tell spirits apart to another, different kinds of tongues° to another, and the interpretation of the tongues to another. [11] All these things are produced by the one and same Spirit who gives what he wants to each person.

[12] Christ is just like the human body—a body is a unit and has many parts; and all the parts of the body are one body, even though there are many. [13] We were all baptized by one Spirit into one body, whether Jew or Greek, or slave or free, and we all were given one Spirit to drink. [14] Certainly the body isn't one part but many. [15] If the foot says, "I'm not part of the body because I'm not a hand," does that mean it's not part of the body? [16] If the ear says, "I'm not part of the body because I'm not an eye," does that mean it's not part of the body? [17] If the whole body were an eye, what would happen to the hearing? And if the whole body were an ear, what would happen to the sense of smell? [18] But as it is, God has placed each one of the parts in the body just like he wanted. [19] If all were one and the same body part, what would happen to the body? [20] But as it is, there are many parts but one body. [21] So the eye can't say to the hand, "I don't need you," or in turn, the head can't say to the feet, "I don't need you." [22] Instead, the parts of the body that people think are the weakest are the most necessary. [23] The parts of the body that we think are less honorable are the ones we honor the most. The private parts of our body

°Or *ecstatic speech* or *languages* could be used for *tongues* or *tongue* throughout chaps 12–14.

that aren't presentable are the ones that are given the most dignity. ²⁴The parts of our body that are presentable don't need this. But God has put the body together, giving greater honor to the part with less honor ²⁵so that there won't be division in the body and so the parts might have mutual concern for each other. ²⁶If one part suffers, all the parts suffer with it; if one part gets the glory, all the parts celebrate with it. ²⁷You are the body of Christ and parts of each other. ²⁸In the church, God has appointed first apostles, second prophets, third teachers, then miracles, then gifts of healing, the ability to help others, leadership skills, different kinds of tongues. ²⁹All aren't apostles, are they? All aren't prophets, are they? All aren't teachers, are they? All don't perform miracles, do they? ³⁰All don't have gifts of healing, do they? All don't speak in different tongues, do they? All don't interpret, do they? ³¹Use your ambition to try to get the greater gifts. And I'm going to show you an even better way.

Love: the universal spiritual gift

13 If I speak in tongues of human beings and of angels but I don't have love, I'm a clanging gong or a clashing cymbal. ²If I have the gift of prophecy and I know all the mysteries and everything else, and if I have such complete faith that I can move mountains but I don't have love, I'm nothing. ³If I give away everything that I have and hand over my own body to feel good about what I've done but I don't have love, I receive no benefit whatsoever.

⁴Love is patient, love is kind, it isn't jealous, it doesn't brag, it isn't arrogant, ⁵it isn't rude, it doesn't seek its own advantage, it isn't irritable, it doesn't keep a record of complaints, ⁶it isn't happy with injustice, but it is happy with the truth. ⁷Love puts up with all things, trusts in all things, hopes for all things, endures all things.

⁸Love never fails. As for prophecies, they will be brought to an end. As for tongues, they will stop. As for knowledge, it will be brought to an end. ⁹We know in part and we prophesy in part; ¹⁰but when the perfect comes, what is partial will be brought to an end. ¹¹When I was a child, I used to speak like a child, reason like a child, think like a child. But now that I have become a man, I've put an end to childish things. ¹²Now we see a reflection in a mirror; then we will see face-to-face. Now I know partially, but then I will know completely in the same way that I have been completely known. ¹³Now faith, hope, and love remain—these three things—and the greatest of these is love.

Spiritual gifts and church order

14 Pursue love, and use your ambition to try to get spiritual gifts but especially so that you might prophesy. ²This is because those who speak in a tongue don't speak to people but to God; no one understands it—they speak mysteries by the Spirit. ³Those who prophesy speak to people, building them up, and giving them encouragement and comfort. ⁴People who speak in a tongue build up themselves; those who prophesy build up the church. ⁵I wish that all of you spoke in tongues, but I'd rather you could prophesy. Those who prophesy are more important than those who speak in tongues, unless they are able to interpret them so that the church might be built up. ⁶After all, brothers and sisters, if I come to you speaking in tongues, how will I help you unless I speak to you with a revelation, some knowledge, a prophecy, or a teaching? [7]Likewise, things that aren't alive like a harp or a lyre can make a sound, but if there aren't different notes in the sounds they make, how will the tune from the harp or the lyre be recognized? [8]And if a trumpet call is unrecognizable, then who will prepare for battle? [9]It's the same way with you: If you don't use language that is easy to understand when you speak in a tongue, then how will anyone understand what is said? [10]It will be as if you are speaking into the air! There are probably many language families in the world, and none of them are without meaning. [11]So if I don't know the meaning of the language, then I will be like a foreigner to those who speak it, and they will be like foreigners to me. [12]The same holds true for you: since you are ambitious for spiritual gifts, use your ambition to try to work toward being the best at building up the church.

[13]Therefore, those who speak in a tongue should pray to be able to interpret. [14]If I pray in a tongue, my spirit prays but my mind isn't productive. [15]What should I do? I'll pray in the Spirit, but I'll pray with my mind too; I'll sing a psalm in the Spirit, but I'll sing the psalm with my mind too. [16]After all, if you praise God in the Spirit, how will the people who aren't trained in that language say "Amen!" to your thanksgiving, when they don't know what you are saying? [17]You may offer a beautiful prayer of thanksgiving, but the other

person is not being built up. [18]I thank God that I speak in tongues more than all of you. [19]But in the church I'd rather speak five words in my right mind than speak thousands of words in a tongue so that I can teach others.

[20]Brothers and sisters, don't be like children in the way you think. Well, be babies when it comes to evil, but be adults in your thinking. [21]In the Law it is written: *I will speak to this people with foreign languages and foreigners' lips, but they will not even listen to me this way,*[p] says the Lord. [22]So then, tongues are a sign for those who don't believe, not for those who believe. But prophecy is a sign for believers, not for those who don't believe. [23]So suppose that the whole church is meeting and everyone is speaking in tongues. If people come in who are outsiders or unbelievers, won't they say that you are out of your minds? [24]But if everyone is prophesying when an unbeliever or outsider comes in, they are tested by all and called to account by all. [25]The secrets of their hearts are brought to light. When that happens, they will fall on their faces and worship God, proclaiming out loud that truly God is among you!

[26]What is the outcome of this, brothers and sisters? When you meet together, each one has a psalm, a teaching, a revelation, a tongue, or an interpretation. All these things must be done to build up the church. [27]If some speak in a tongue, then let two or at most three speak, one at a time, and someone must interpret. [28]However, if there is no interpreter, then they should keep quiet in the meeting. They should speak privately to themselves

[p]Isa 28:11-12

and to God. [29]In the case of prophets, let two or three speak and have the rest evaluate what is said. [30]And if some revelation comes to someone else who is sitting down, the first one should be quiet. [31]You can all prophesy one at a time so that everyone can learn and be encouraged. [32]The spirits of prophets are under the control of the prophets. [33]God isn't a God of disorder but of peace. Like in all the churches of God's people, [34]the women should be quiet during the meeting. They are not allowed to talk. Instead, they need to get under control, just as the Law says. [35]If they want to learn something, they should ask their husbands at home. It is disgraceful for a woman to talk during the meeting.

[36]Did the word of God originate with you? Has it come only to you? [37]If anyone thinks that they are prophets or "spiritual people," then let them recognize that what I'm writing to you is the Lord's command. [38]If someone doesn't recognize this, they aren't recognized. [39]So then, brothers and sisters, use your ambition to try to get the gift of prophecy, but don't prevent speaking in tongues. [40]Everything should be done with dignity and in proper order.

The resurrection

15 Brothers and sisters, I want to call your attention to the good news that I preached to you, which you also received and in which you stand. [2]You are being saved through it if you hold on to the message I preached to you, unless somehow you believed it for nothing. [3]I passed on to you as most important what I also received: Christ died for our sins in line with the scriptures, [4]he was buried, and he rose on the third day in line with the scriptures. [5]He appeared to Cephas, then to the Twelve, [6]and then he appeared to more than five hundred brothers and sisters at once—most of them are still alive to this day, though some have died. [7]Then he appeared to James, then to all the apostles, [8]and last of all he appeared to me, as if I were born at the wrong time. [9]I'm the least important of the apostles. I don't deserve to be called an apostle, because I harassed God's church. [10]I am what I am by God's grace, and God's grace hasn't been for nothing. In fact, I have worked harder than all the others—that is, it wasn't me but the grace of God that is with me. [11]So then, whether you heard the message from me or them, this is what we preach and this is what you have believed.

[12]So if the message that is preached says that Christ has been raised from the dead, then how can some of you say, "There's no resurrection of the dead"? [13]If there's no resurrection of the dead, then Christ hasn't been raised either. [14]If Christ hasn't been raised, then our preaching is useless and your faith is useless. [15]We are found to be false witnesses about God, because we testified against God that he raised Christ, when he didn't raise him if it's the case that the dead aren't raised. [16]If the dead aren't raised, then Christ hasn't been raised either. [17]If Christ hasn't been raised, then your faith is worthless; you are still in your sins, [18]and what's more, those who have died in Christ are gone forever. [19]If we have a hope in Christ only in this life, then we deserve to be pitied more than anyone else.

²⁰But in fact Christ has been raised from the dead. He's the first crop of the harvest⁹ of those who have died. ²¹Since death came through a human being, the resurrection of the dead came through one too. ²²In the same way that everyone dies in Adam, so also everyone will be given life in Christ. ²³Each event will happen in the right order: Christ, the first crop of the harvest,ʳ then those who belong to Christ at his coming, ²⁴and then the end, when Christ hands over the kingdom to God the Father, when he brings every form of rule, every authority and power to an end. ²⁵It is necessary for him to rule until *he puts all enemies under his feet.*ˢ ²⁶Death is the last enemy to be brought to an end, ²⁷since he has brought everything under control under his feet. When it says that everything has been brought under his control, this clearly means everything except for the one who placed everything under his control. ²⁸But when all things have been brought under his control, then the Son himself will also be under the control of the one who gave him control over everything so that God may be all in all.

²⁹Otherwise, what are those who are getting baptized for the dead doing? If the dead aren't raised, then why are they being baptized for them? ³⁰And what about us? Why are we in danger all day every day? ³¹Brothers and sisters, I swear by the pride I have in you in Christ Jesus our Lord, I'm facing death every day. ³²From a human point of view, what good does it do me if I fought wild animals in Ephesus? If the dead aren't raised, *let's eat and drink because tomorrow we'll die.*ᵗ ³³Don't be

deceived, bad company corrupts good character. ³⁴Sober up by acting like you should and don't sin. Some of you are ignorant about God—I say this because you should be ashamed of yourselves!

³⁵But someone will say, "How are the dead raised? What kind of body will they have when they come back?" ³⁶Look, fool! When you put a seed into the ground, it doesn't come back to life unless it dies. ³⁷What you put in the ground doesn't have the shape that it will have, but it's a bare grain of wheat or some other seed. ³⁸God gives it the sort of shape that he chooses, and he gives each of the seeds its own shape. ³⁹All flesh isn't alike. Humans have one kind of flesh, animals have another kind of flesh, birds have another kind of flesh, and fish have another kind. ⁴⁰There are heavenly bodies and earthly bodies. The heavenly bodies have one kind of glory, and the earthly bodies have another kind of glory. ⁴¹The sun has one kind of glory, the moon has another kind of glory, and the stars have another kind of glory (but one star is different from another star in its glory). ⁴²It's the same with the resurrection of the dead: a rotting body is put into the ground, but what is raised won't ever decay. ⁴³It's degraded when it's put into the ground, but it's raised in glory. It's weak when it's put into the ground, but it's raised in power. ⁴⁴It's a physical body when it's put into the ground, but it's raised as a spiritual body.

If there's a physical body, there's also a spiritual body. ⁴⁵So it is also written, *The first human, Adam, became a living person,*ᵘ and the last Adam became a spirit that gives life. ⁴⁶But

---

⁹*Or firstfruits*   ʳ*Or firstfruits*   ˢPs 110:1   ᵗIsa 22:13   ᵘGen 2:7

the physical body comes first, not the spiritual one—the spiritual body comes afterward. [47] The first human was from the earth made from dust; the second human is from heaven. [48] The nature of the person made of dust is shared by people who are made of dust, and the nature of the heavenly person is shared by heavenly people. [49] We will look like[v] the heavenly person in the same way as we have looked like the person made from dust.

[50] This is what I'm saying, brothers and sisters: Flesh and blood can't inherit God's kingdom. Something that rots can't inherit something that doesn't decay. [51] Listen, I'm telling you a secret: All of us won't die, but we will all be changed— [52] in an instant, in the blink of an eye, at the final trumpet. The trumpet will blast, and the dead will be raised with bodies that won't decay, and we will be changed. [53] It's necessary for this rotting body to be clothed with what can't decay, and for the body that is dying to be clothed in what can't die. [54] And when the rotting body has been clothed in what can't decay, and the dying body has been clothed in what can't die, then this statement in scripture will happen:

> Death has been swallowed up
>   by a victory.[w]
> [55] Where is your victory, Death?
>   Where is your sting, Death?[x]

([56] Death's sting is sin, and the power of sin is the Law.) [57] Thanks be to God, who gives us this victory through our Lord Jesus Christ! [58] As a result of all this, my loved brothers and sisters, you must stand firm, unshakable, excelling in the work of the Lord as always, because you know that your labor isn't going to be for nothing in the Lord.

Collection for Jerusalem

16 Concerning the collection of money for God's people: You should do what I have directed the churches in Galatia to do. [2] On the first day of the week, each of you should set aside whatever you can afford from what you earn so that the collection won't be delayed until I come. [3] Then when I get there, I'll send whomever you approve to Jerusalem with letters of recommendation to bring your gift. [4] If it seems right for me to go too, they'll travel with me.

Plans to visit

[5] I'll come to you after I go through Macedonia, and because I'm going through Macedonia, [6] I may stay with you or even spend the winter there in Corinth so that you can send me on my way to wherever I'm off to next. [7] I don't want to make a quick visit to you, since I hope to spend some time with you if the Lord lets it happen. [8] I'll stay here in Ephesus until the Festival of Pentecost. [9] In spite of the fact that there are many opponents, a big and productive opportunity has opened up for my mission here.

[10] If Timothy comes to you, be sure that he has no reason to be afraid while he's with you, because he does the work of the Lord just like I do. [11] So don't let anyone disrespect him, but send him on in peace so he can join me. I'm waiting for him along with the brothers and sisters. [12] Concerning Apollos our brother: I strongly encouraged him to visit you with the brothers and sisters, but he

[v]Or bear the image of   [w]Isa 25:8   [x]Hos 13:14

didn't want to go now. He'll come when he has an opportunity.

Final greeting

[13]Stay awake, stand firm in your faith, be brave, be strong. [14]Everything should be done in love.

[15]Brothers and sisters, I encourage you to do something else. You know that the people in Stephanas' household were the first crop of the harvest to come from the mission to Achaia. They have dedicated themselves to the service of God's people. [16]So accept the authority of people like them and of anyone who cooperates and works hard. [17]I'm so happy that Stephanas, Fortunatus, and Achaicus have arrived; they've made up for my missing you. [18]Indeed they've provided my spirit and yours with a much-needed rest. Therefore, give them proper recognition.

[19]The churches in the province of Asia greet you. Aquila and Prisca greet you warmly in the Lord, together with the church that meets in their house. [20]All the brothers and sisters greet you. You in turn should greet each other with a holy kiss. [21]Here is my greeting in my own handwriting—Paul.

[22]A curse on anyone who doesn't love the Lord. Come, Lord! [23]The grace of the Lord Jesus be with you. [24]My love is with all of you in Christ Jesus.

2 CORINTHIANS

Greeting

1 From Paul, an apostle of Christ Jesus by God's will, and Timothy our brother.

To God's church that is in Corinth, along with all of God's people throughout Achaia.

[2]Grace to you and peace from God our Father and from our Lord Jesus Christ.

God's comfort in trouble

[3]May the God and Father of our Lord Jesus Christ be blessed! He is the compassionate Father and God of all comfort. [4]He's the one who comforts us in all our trouble so that we can comfort other people who are in every kind of trouble. We offer the same comfort that we ourselves received from God. [5]That is because we receive so much comfort through Christ in the same way that we share so many of Christ's sufferings. [6]So if we have trouble, it is to bring you comfort and salvation. If we are comforted, it is to bring you comfort from the experience of endurance while you go through the same sufferings that we also suffer. [7]Our hope for you is certain, because we know that as you are partners in suffering, so also you are partners in comfort.

[8]Brothers and sisters, we don't want you to be unaware of the troubles that we went through in Asia. We were weighed down with a load of suffering that was so far beyond our strength that we were afraid we might not survive. [9]It certainly seemed to us as if we had gotten the death penalty. This was so that we would have confidence in God, who raises the dead, instead of ourselves. [10]God rescued us from a terrible death, and he will rescue us. We have set our hope on him that he will rescue us again, [11]since you are helping

with your prayer for us. Then many people can thank God on our behalf for the gift that was given to us through the prayers of many people.

Paul explains his change of plans

[12]We have conducted ourselves with godly sincerity and pure motives in the world, and especially toward you. This is why we are confident, and our conscience confirms this. We didn't act with human wisdom but we relied on the grace of God. [13]We don't write anything to you except what you can read and also understand. I hope that you will understand totally [14]since you have already understood us partly. Understand that in the day of our Lord Jesus, we will make you proud as you will also make us proud.

[15]Because I was sure of this, I wanted to visit you first so that you could have a second opportunity to see me. [16]I wanted to visit you on my way to Macedonia, and then come to you again on my way back from Macedonia, at which point I was hoping you would help me on my way to Judea.

[17]So I wasn't unreliable when I planned to do this, was I? Or do I make decisions with a substandard human process so that I say "Yes, yes" and "No, no" at the same time? [18]But as God is faithful, our message to you isn't both yes and no. [19]God's Son, Jesus Christ, is the one who was preached among you by us—through me, Silvanus, and Timothy—he wasn't yes and no. In him it is always yes. [20]All of God's promises have their yes in him. That is why we say Amen through him to the glory of God. [21]God is the one who establishes us with you in Christ and who anointed us. [22]God also sealed us and gave the Spirit as a down payment in our hearts. [23]I call on God as my witness—I didn't come again to Corinth because I wanted to spare you. [24]It isn't that we are trying to control your faith, but we are working with you for your happiness, because you stand firm in your faith.

2 So I decided that, for my own sake, I wouldn't visit you again while I was upset. [2]If I make you sad, who will be there to make me glad when you are sad because of me?

Paul's former letter

[3]That's why I wrote this very thing to you, so that when I came I wouldn't be made sad by the ones who ought to make me happy. I have confidence in you, that my happiness means your happiness. [4]I wrote to you in tears, with a very troubled and anxious heart. I didn't write to make you sad but so you would know the overwhelming love that I have for you.

[5]But if someone has made anyone sad, that person hasn't hurt me but all of you to some degree (not to exaggerate). [6]The punishment handed out by the majority is enough for this person. [7]This is why you should try your best to forgive and to comfort this person now instead, so that this person isn't overwhelmed by too much sorrow. [8]So I encourage you to show your love for this person.

[9]This is another reason why I wrote you. I wanted to test you and see if you are obedient in everything. [10]If you forgive anyone for anything, I do too. And whatever I've forgiven (if I've forgiven anything), I did it for you in the presence of Christ. [11]This is so that we won't be taken advantage of by Satan, because we are well aware of his schemes.

Paul's ministry

[12]When I came to Troas to preach Christ's gospel, the Lord gave me an opportunity to preach. [13]But I was worried because I couldn't find my brother Titus there. So I said good-bye to them and went on to Macedonia.

[14]But thank God, who is always leading us around through Christ as if we were in a parade. He releases the fragrance of the knowledge of him everywhere through us. [15]We smell like the aroma of Christ's offering to God, both to those who are being saved and to those who are on the road to destruction. [16]We smell like a contagious dead person to those who are dying, but we smell like the fountain of life to those who are being saved.

Who is qualified for this kind of ministry? [17]We aren't like so many people who hustle the word of God to make a profit. We are speaking through Christ in the presence of God, as those who are sincere and as those who are sent from God.

3 Are we starting to commend ourselves again? We don't need letters of introduction to you or from you like other people, do we? [2]You are our letter, written on our hearts, known and read by everyone. [3]You show that you are Christ's letter, delivered by us. You weren't written with ink but with the Spirit of the living God. You weren't written on tablets of stone but on tablets of human hearts.

[4]This is the confidence that we have through Christ in the presence of God. [5]It isn't that we ourselves are qualified to claim that anything came from us. No, our qualification is from God. [6]He has qualified us as ministers of a new covenant, not based on what is written but on the Spirit, because what is written kills, but the Spirit gives life.

Ministers of the new covenant

[7]The ministry that brought death was carved in letters on stone tablets. It came with such glory that the Israelites couldn't look for long at Moses' face because his face was shining with glory, even though it was a fading glory. [8]Won't the ministry of the Spirit be much more glorious? [9]If the ministry that brought condemnation has glory, how much more glorious is the ministry that brings righteousness? [10]In fact, what was glorious isn't glorious now, because of the glory that is brighter. [11]If the glory that fades away was glorious, how much more glorious is the one that lasts!

[12]So, since we have such a hope, we act with great confidence. [13]We aren't like Moses, who used to put a veil over his face so that the Israelites couldn't watch the end of what was fading away. [14]But their minds were closed. Right up to the present day the same veil remains when the old covenant is read. The veil is not removed because it is taken away by Christ. [15]Even today, whenever Moses is read, a veil lies over their hearts. [16]But whenever someone turns back to the Lord, the veil is removed. [17]The Lord is the Spirit, and where the Lord's Spirit is, there is freedom. [18]All of us are looking with unveiled faces at the glory of the Lord as if we were looking in a mirror. We are being transformed into that same image from one degree of glory to the next degree of glory. This comes from the Lord, who is the Spirit.

4 This is why we don't get discouraged, given that we received this ministry

in the same way that we received God's mercy. [2]Instead, we reject secrecy and shameful actions. We don't use deception, and we don't tamper with God's word. Instead, we commend ourselves to everyone's conscience in the sight of God by the public announcement of the truth. [3]And even if our gospel is veiled, it is veiled to those who are on the road to destruction. [4]The god of this age has blinded the minds of those who don't have faith so they couldn't see the light of the gospel that reveals Christ's glory. Christ is the image of God.

[5]We don't preach about ourselves. Instead, we preach about Jesus Christ as Lord, and we describe ourselves as your slaves for Jesus' sake. [6]God said that light should shine out of the darkness. He is the same one who shine in our hearts to give us the light of the knowledge of God's glory in the face of Jesus Christ.

Physical bodies and eternal glory

[7]But we have this treasure in clay pots so that the awesome power belongs to God and doesn't come from us. [8]We are experiencing all kinds of trouble, but we aren't crushed. We are confused, but we aren't depressed. [9]We are harassed, but we aren't abandoned. We are knocked down, but we aren't knocked out.

[10]We always carry Jesus' death around in our bodies so that Jesus' life can also be seen in our bodies. [11]We who are alive are always being handed over to death for Jesus' sake so that Jesus' life can also be seen in our bodies that are dying. [12]So death is at work in us, but life is at work in you.

[13]We have the same faithful spirit as what is written in scripture: *I had faith, and so I spoke.*[a] We also have faith, and so we also speak. [14]We do this because we know that the one who raised the Lord Jesus will also raise us with Jesus, and he will bring us into his presence along with you. [15]All these things are for your benefit. As grace increases to benefit more and more people, it will cause gratitude to increase, which results in God's glory.

[16]So we aren't depressed. But even if our bodies are breaking down on the outside, the person that we are on the inside is being renewed every day. [17]Our temporary minor problems are producing an eternal stockpile of glory for us that is beyond all comparison. [18]We don't focus on the things that can be seen but on the things that can't be seen. The things that can be seen don't last, but the things that can't be seen are eternal.

5 We know that if the tent that we live in on earth is torn down, we have a building from God. It's a house that isn't handmade, which is eternal and located in heaven. [2]We groan while we live in this residence. We really want to dress ourselves with our building from heaven— [3]since we assume that when we take off this tent, we won't find out that we are naked. [4]Yes, while we are in this tent we groan, because we are weighed down. We want to be dressed not undressed, so that what is dying can be swallowed up by life. [5]Now the one who prepared us for this very thing is God, and God gave us the Spirit as a down payment for our home.

[6]So we are always confident, because

---

[a]Ps 116:10 (115:1 LXX)

we know that while we are living in the body, we are away from our home with the Lord. [7]We live by faith and not by sight. [8]We are confident, and we would prefer to leave the body and to be at home with the Lord. [9]So our goal is to be acceptable to him, whether we are at home or away from home. [10]We all must appear before Christ in court so that each person can be paid back for the things that were done while in the body, whether they were good or bad.

Ministry of reconciliation

[11]So we try to persuade people, since we know what it means to fear the Lord. We are well known by God, and I hope that in your heart we are well known by you as well. [12]We aren't trying to commend ourselves to you again. Instead, we are giving you an opportunity to be proud of us so that you could answer those who take pride in superficial appearance, and not in what is in the heart.

[13]If we are crazy, it's for God's sake. If we are rational, it's for your sake. [14]The love of Christ controls us, because we have concluded this: one died for the sake of all; therefore, all died. [15]He died for the sake of all so that those who are alive should live not for themselves but for the one who died for them and was raised.

[16]So then, from this point on we won't recognize people by human standards. Even though we used to know Christ by human standards, that isn't how we know him now. [17]So then, if anyone is in Christ, that person is part of the new creation. The old things have gone away, and look, new things have arrived!

[18]All of these new things are from God, who reconciled us to himself through Christ and who gave us the ministry of reconciliation. [19]In other words, God was reconciling the world to himself through Christ, by not counting people's sins against them. He has trusted us with this message of reconciliation.

[20]So we are ambassadors who represent Christ. God is negotiating with you through us. We beg you as Christ's representatives, "Be reconciled to God!" [21]God caused the one who didn't know sin to be sin for our sake so that through him we could become the righteousness of God.

6 Since we work together with him, we are also begging you not to receive the grace of God in vain. [2]He says, *I listened to you at the right time, and I helped you on the day of salvation.*[b] Look, now is the right time! Look, now is the day of salvation!

[3]We don't give anyone any reason to be offended about anything so that our ministry won't be criticized. [4]Instead, we commend ourselves as ministers of God in every way. We did this with our great endurance through problems, disasters, and stressful situations. [5]We went through beatings, imprisonments, and riots. We experienced hard work, sleepless nights, and hunger. [6]We displayed purity, knowledge, patience, and generosity. We served with the Holy Spirit, genuine love, [7]telling the truth, and God's power. We carried the weapons of righteousness in our right hand and our left hand. [8]We were treated with honor and dishonor and with verbal abuse and good evaluation. We were

[b]Isa 49:8

seen as both fake and real, [9] as unknown and well known, as dying—and look, we are alive! We were seen as punished but not killed, [10] as going through pain but always happy, as poor but making many rich, and as having nothing but owning everything.

Call to relationship and holiness

[11] Corinthians, we have spoken openly to you, and our hearts are wide open. [12] There are no limits to the affection that we feel for you. You are the ones who placed boundaries on your affection for us. [13] But as a fair trade—I'm talking to you like you are children—open your hearts wide too.

[14] Don't be tied up as equal partners with people who don't believe. What does righteousness share with that which is outside the Law? What relationship does light have with darkness? [15] What harmony does Christ have with Satan?[c] What does a believer have in common with someone who doesn't believe? [16] What agreement can there be between God's temple and idols? Because we are the temple of the living God. Just as God said, *I live with them, and I will move among them. I will be their God, and they will be my people.*[d] [17] Therefore, *come out from among them and be separated, says the Lord. Don't touch what is unclean. Then I will welcome you.*[e] [18] *I will be a father to you, and you will be my sons and daughters, says the Lord Almighty.*[f]

7 My dear friends, since we have these promises, let's cleanse ourselves from anything that contaminates our body or spirit so that we make our holiness complete in the fear of God.

[2] Make room in your hearts for us. We didn't do anything wrong to anyone. We didn't ruin anyone. We didn't take advantage of anyone. [3] I'm not saying this to make you feel guilty. I've already said that you are in our hearts so that we die and live together with you. [4] I have every confidence in you. I'm terribly proud of you. I'm filled with encouragement. I'm overwhelmed with happiness while in the middle of our problems.

Titus' good report

[5] Even after we arrived in Macedonia, we couldn't rest physically. We were surrounded by problems. There was external conflict, and there were internal fears. [6] However, God comforts people who are discouraged, and he comforted us by Titus' arrival. [7] We weren't comforted only by his arrival but also by the comfort he had received from you. He told us about your desire to see me, how you were sorry, and about your concern for me, so that I was even happier.

[8] Even though my letter hurt you, I don't regret it. Well—I did regret it just a bit because I see that that letter made you sad, though only for a short time. [9] Now I'm glad—not because you were sad but because you were made sad enough to change your hearts and lives. You felt godly sadness so that no one was harmed by us in any way. [10] Godly sadness produces a changed heart and life that leads to salvation and leaves no regrets, but sorrow under the influence of the world produces death. [11] Look at what this very experience of godly sadness has produced in you: such enthusiasm, what a desire to clear yourselves

---

[c] Or *Beliah*   [d] Lev 26:11-12   [e] Isa 52:11; Ezek 20:34, 41   [f] 2 Sam 7:14

of blame, such indignation, what fear, what purpose, such concern, what justice! In everything you have shown yourselves to be innocent in the matter. [12]So although I wrote to us, it wasn't for the sake of the one who did wrong, or for the sake of the one who was wronged, but to show you your own enthusiasm for us in the sight of God. [13]Because of this we have been encouraged. And in addition to our own encouragement, we were even more pleased at how happy Titus was. His mind has been put at rest by all of you. [14]If I've bragged about you to him in any way, I haven't been embarrassed. Instead, our bragging to Titus has also been proven to be true, just like everything we said to you was true. [15]His devotion to you is growing even more as he remembers how all of you were obedient when you welcomed him with fear and trembling. [16]I'm happy, because I can completely depend on you.

Encouragement to give generously

8 Brothers and sisters, we want to let you know about the grace of God that was given to the churches of Macedonia. [2]While they were being tested by many problems, their extra amount of happiness and their extreme poverty resulted in a surplus of rich generosity. [3]I assure you that they gave what they could afford and even more than they could afford, and they did it voluntarily. [4]They urgently begged us for the privilege[g] of sharing in this service for the saints. [5]They even exceeded our expectations, because they gave themselves to the Lord first and to us, consistent with God's will. [6]As a result, we

challenged Titus to finish this work of grace with you the way he had started it. [7]Be the best in this work of grace in the same way that you are the best in everything, such as faith, speech, knowledge, total commitment, and the love we inspired in you. [8]I'm not giving an order, but by mentioning the commitment of others, I'm trying to prove the authenticity of your love also. [9]You know the grace of our Lord Jesus Christ. Although he was rich, he became poor for our sakes, so that you could become rich through his poverty.

[10]I'm giving you my opinion about this. It's to your advantage to do this, since you not only started to do it last year but you wanted to do it too. [11]Now finish the job as well so that you finish it with as much enthusiasm as you started, given what you can afford. [12]A gift is appreciated because of what a person can afford, not because of what that person can't afford, if it's apparent that it's done willingly. [13]It isn't that we want others to have financial ease and you financial difficulties, but it's a matter of equality. [14]At the present moment, your surplus can fill their deficit so that in the future their surplus can fill your deficit. In this way there is equality. [15]As it is written, *The one who gathered more didn't have too much, and the one who gathered less didn't have too little.*[h]

Plans for the Collection

[16]But thank God, who put the same commitment that I have for you in Titus' heart. [17]Not only has he accepted our challenge but he's on his way to see you voluntarily, and he's excited. [18]We

[g]Or *grace*   [h]Exod 16:18

are sending the brother who is famous in all the churches because of his work for the gospel along with him.

¹⁹In addition to this, he is chosen by the churches to be our traveling companion in this work of grace, which we are taking care of for the sake of the glory of the Lord himself, and to show our desire to help. ²⁰We are trying to avoid being blamed by anyone for the way we take care of this large amount of money. ²¹We care about doing the right thing, not only in the Lord's eyes but also in the eyes of other people.

²²We are sending our brother with them. We have tested his commitment in many ways and many times. Now he's even more committed, because he has so much confidence in you. ²³If there is any question about Titus, he is my partner and coworker among you. If there is any question about our brothers, they are the churches' apostles and an honor to Christ. ²⁴So show them the proof of your love and the reason we are so proud of you, in such a way that the churches can see it.

9It's unnecessary for me to write to you about this service for God's people. ²I know about your willingness to help. I brag about you to the Macedonians, saying, "Greece has been ready since last year," and your enthusiasm has motivated most of them.

³But I'm sending the brothers so that our bragging about you in this case won't be empty words, and so that you can be prepared, just as I keep telling them you will be. ⁴If some Macedonians should come with me and find out that you aren't ready, we (not to mention you) would be embarrassed as far as this project goes.

⁵This is why I thought it was necessary to encourage the brothers to go to you ahead of time and arrange in advance the generous gift you have already promised. I want it to be a real gift from you. I don't want you to feel like you are being forced to give anything. ⁶What I mean is this: the one who sows a small number of seeds will also reap a small crop, and the one who sows a generous amount of seeds will also reap a generous crop.

⁷Everyone should give whatever they have decided in their heart. They shouldn't give with hesitation or because of pressure. God loves a cheerful giver. ⁸God has the power to provide you with more than enough of every kind of grace. That way, you will all have everything you need always and in everything to provide more than enough for every kind of good work. ⁹As it is written, *He scattered everywhere; he gave to the needy; his righteousness remains forever.*[i]

¹⁰The one who supplies seed for planting and bread for eating will supply and multiply your seed and will increase your crop, which is righteousness. ¹¹You will be made rich in every way so that you can be generous in every way. Such generosity produces thanksgiving to God through us. ¹²Your ministry of this service to God's people isn't only fully meeting their needs but it is also multiplying in many expressions of thanksgiving to God. ¹³They will give honor to God for your obedience to your confession of Christ's gospel. They will do this because this service provides evidence of your obedience, and because of your generosity in

[i]Ps 112:9

sharing with them and with everyone. [14]They will also pray for you, and they will care deeply for you because of the outstanding grace that God has given to you. [15]Thank God for his gift that words can't describe!

Paul's personal request for obedience

10[1]I, Paul, make a personal request to you with the gentleness and kindness of Christ. I'm shy when I'm with you, but I'm bossy when I'm away from you! [2]I beg you that when I'm with you in person, I won't have to boss you around. I'm afraid that I may have to use that kind of behavior with those people who think we live by human standards. [3]Although we live in the world, we don't fight our battles with human methods. [4]Our weapons that we fight with aren't human, but instead they are powered by God for the destruction of fortresses. They destroy arguments, [5]and every defense that is raised up to oppose the knowledge of God. They capture every thought to make it obedient to Christ. [6]Once your obedience is complete, we are ready to punish any disobedience.

[7]Look at what is right in front of you! If anyone is sure about belonging to Christ, that person should think again. We belong to Christ just like that person. [8]Even if I went on to brag about our authority, I wouldn't be ashamed of it. The Lord gave us that authority to build you up and not to destroy you.

[9]I don't want it to seem like I'm trying to intimidate you with my letters. [10]I know what some people are saying: "His letters are severe and powerful,

but in person he is weak and his speech is worth nothing." [11]These people need to think about this—that when we are with you, our actions will show that we are the same as the words we wrote when we were away from you. [12]We won't dare to place ourselves in the same league or to compare ourselves with some of those who are promoting themselves. When they measure themselves by themselves, and compare themselves with themselves, they have no understanding.

[13]We won't take pride in anything more than what is appropriate. Let's look at the boundaries of our work area that God has assigned to us. It's an area that includes you. [14]We aren't going out of bounds, as if our work area doesn't extend as far as you. We were the first ones to travel as far as Corinth with the gospel of Christ. [15]We don't take pride in what other people do outside of our boundaries. We hope that our work will be extended even more by you as your faith grows, until it expands fully (within the boundaries, of course). [16]We hope that our work grows even to the point of the gospel being preached in places beyond Corinth, without bragging about what has already been done in another person's work area. [17]But, *the one who brags should brag in the Lord.*[j] [18]It isn't the person who promotes himself or herself who is approved but the person whom the Lord commends.

Confrontation of the super-apostles

11I hope that you will put up with me while I act like a fool. Well, in fact,

[j]Jer 9:24

you are putting up with me! [2] I'm deeply concerned about you with the same concern that God has. As your father, I promised you in marriage to one husband. I promised to present you as an innocent virgin to Christ himself. [3] But I'm afraid that your minds might be seduced in the same way as the snake deceived Eve with his devious tricks. You might be unable to focus completely on a genuine and innocent commitment to Christ.

[4] If a person comes and preaches some other Jesus than the one we preached, or if you receive a different Spirit than the one you had received, or a different gospel than the one you embraced, you put up with it so easily! [5] I don't consider myself as second-rate in any way compared to the "super-apostles." [6] But even if I'm uneducated in public speaking, I'm not uneducated in knowledge. We have shown this to you in every way and in everything we have done. [7] Did I commit a sin by humbling myself to give you an advantage because I preached the gospel of God to you free of charge? [8] I robbed other churches by taking a salary from them in order to serve you! [9] While I was with you, I didn't burden any of you even though I needed things. The believers who came from Macedonia gave me everything I needed. I kept myself from being a financial drain on you in any way, and I will continue to keep myself from being a burden.

[10] Since Christ's truth is in me, I won't stop telling the entire area of Greece that I'm proud of what I did. [11] Why? Is it because I don't love you? God knows that I do! [12] But I'm going to continue to do what I'm doing. I want to contradict the claims of the people who want to be treated like they are the same as us because of what they brag about. [13] Such people are false apostles and dishonest workers who disguise themselves as apostles of Christ. [14] And no wonder! Even Satan disguises himself as an angel of light. [15] It is no great surprise then that his servants also disguise themselves as servants of righteousness. Their end will be what their actions deserve.

Paul defends himself

[16] I repeat, no one should take me for a fool. But if you do, then allow me to be a fool so that I can brag like a fool for a bit. [17] I'm not saying what I'm saying because the Lord tells me to. I'm saying it like I'm a fool. I'm putting my confidence in this business of bragging. [18] Since so many people are bragging based on human standards, that is how I'm going to brag too. [19] Because you, who are so wise, are happy to put up with fools. [20] You put up with it if someone enslaves you, if someone exploits you, if someone takes advantage of you, if someone places themselves over you, or if someone hits you in the face. [21] I'm ashamed to say that we have been weak in comparison! But in whatever they challenge me, I challenge them (I'm speaking foolishly).

[22] Are they Hebrews? So am I. Are they Israelites? So am I. Are they descendants of Abraham? So am I. [23] Are they ministers of Christ? I'm speaking like a crazy person. What I've done goes well beyond what they've done. I've worked much harder. I've been imprisoned much more often. I've been beaten more times than I can count. I've faced death many times. [24] I received the "forty lashes minus

one" from the Jews five times. [25]I was beaten with rods three times. I was stoned once. I was shipwrecked three times. I spent a day and a night on the open sea. [26]I've been on many journeys. I faced dangers from rivers, robbers, my people, and Gentiles. I faced dangers in the city, in the desert, on the sea, and from false brothers and sisters. [27]I faced these dangers with hard work and heavy labor, many sleepless nights, hunger and thirst, often without food, and in the cold without enough clothes.

[28]Besides all the other things I could mention, there's my daily stress because I'm concerned about all the churches. [29]Who is weak without me being weak? Who is led astray without me being furious about it? [30]If it's necessary to brag, I'll brag about my weaknesses. [31]The God and Father of the Lord Jesus, the one who is blessed forever, knows that I'm not lying. [32]At Damascus the governor under King Aretas was guarding the city of Damascus in order to capture me, [33]but I got away from him by being lowered in a basket through a window in the city wall.

Paul's visions and revelations from the Lord

12 It is necessary to brag, not that it does any good. I'll move on to visions and revelations from the Lord. [2]I know a man in Christ who was caught up into the third heaven fourteen years ago. I don't know whether it was in the body or out of the body. God knows. [3, 4]I know that this man was caught up into paradise and that he heard unspeakable words that were things no one is allowed to repeat. I don't know whether it was in the body or apart from the body. God knows. [5]I'll brag about this man,

but I won't brag about myself, except to brag about my weaknesses.

[6]If I did want to brag, I wouldn't make a fool of myself because I'd tell the truth. I'm holding back from bragging so that no one will give me any more credit than what anyone sees or hears about me. [7]I was given a thorn in my body because of the outstanding revelations I've received so that I wouldn't be conceited. It's a messenger from Satan sent to torment me so that I wouldn't be conceited.

[8]I pleaded with the Lord three times for it to leave me alone. [9]He said to me, "My grace is enough for you, because power is made perfect in weakness." So I'll gladly spend my time bragging about my weaknesses so that Christ's power can rest on me. [10]Therefore, I'm all right with weaknesses, insults, disasters, harassments, and stressful situations for the sake of Christ, because when I'm weak, then I'm strong.

[11]I've become a fool! You made me do it. Actually, I should have been commended by you. I'm not inferior to the super-apostles in any way, even though I'm a nonentity. [12]The signs of an apostle were performed among you with continuous endurance through signs, wonders, and miracles. [13]How were you treated worse than the other churches, except that I myself wasn't a financial burden on you? Forgive me for this wrong!

Paul's plans to visit and a warning

[14]Look, I'm ready to visit you a third time, and I won't be a burden on you. I don't want your things; I want you. It isn't the children's responsibility to save up for their parents but parents for children. [15]I will very gladly spend and be spent for your sake. If I love you more, will you love me less?

[16] We all know that I didn't place a burden on you, but in spite of that you think I'm a con artist who fooled you with a trick. [17] I haven't taken advantage of you through any of the people I sent to you, have I? [18] I strongly encouraged Titus to go to you and sent the brother with him. Titus didn't take advantage of you, did he? Didn't we live by the same Spirit? Didn't we walk in the same footsteps?

[19] Have you been thinking up to now that we are defending ourselves to you? Actually, we are speaking in the sight of God and in Christ. Dear friends, everything is meant to build you up. [20] I'm afraid that maybe when I come you will be different from the way I want you to be, and that I'll be different from the way you want me to be. I'm afraid that there might be fighting, obsession, losing your temper, competitive opposition, backstabbing, gossip, conceit, and disorderly conduct. [21] I'm afraid that when I come again, my God may embarrass me in front of you. I might have to go into mourning over all the people who have sinned before and haven't changed their hearts and lives from what they used to practice: moral corruption, sexual immorality, and doing whatever feels good.

13 This is the third time that I'm coming to visit you. Every matter is settled on the evidence of two or three witnesses. [2] When I was with you on my second visit, I already warned those who continued to sin. Now I'm repeating that warning to all the rest of you while I'm at a safe distance: if I come again, I won't spare anyone. [3] Since you are demanding proof that Christ

speaks through me, Christ isn't weak in dealing with you but shows his power among you. [4] Certainly he was crucified because of weakness, but he lives by the power of God. Certainly we also are weak in him, but we will live together with him, because of God's power that is directed toward you.

[5] Examine yourselves to see if you are in the faith. Test yourselves. Don't you understand that Jesus Christ is in you? Unless, of course, you fail the test. [6] But I hope that you will realize that we don't fail the test. [7] We pray to God that you don't do anything wrong, not because we want to appear to pass the test but so that you might do the right thing, even if we appear to fail.

[8] We can't do anything against the truth but only to help the truth. [9] We are happy when we are weak but you are strong. We pray for this: that you will be made complete. [10] This is why I'm writing these things while I'm away. I'm writing so that I won't need to act harshly when I'm with you by using the authority that the Lord gave me. He gave it to me so that I could build you up, not tear you down.

Final greeting

[11] Finally, brothers and sisters, goodbye. Put things in order, respond to my encouragement, be in harmony with each other, and live in peace—and the God of love and peace will be with you.

[12] Say hello to each other with a holy kiss.[k] All of God's people say hello to you.

[13] The grace of the Lord Jesus Christ, the love of God, and the fellowship of the Holy Spirit be with you all.

[k] 2 Cor 13:12-13 is in some versions equivalent to 13:12-14.

GALATIANS

Greeting

1 From Paul, an apostle who is not sent from human authority or commissioned through human agency, but sent through Jesus Christ and God the Father who raised him from the dead; ² and from all the brothers and sisters with me.

To the churches in Galatia.

³ Grace and peace to you from God the Father and the Lord Jesus Christ. ⁴ He gave himself for our sins, so he could deliver us from this present evil age, according to the will of our God and Father. ⁵ To God be the glory forever and always! Amen.

The gospel challenged in Galatia

⁶ I'm amazed that you are so quickly deserting the one who called you by the grace of Christ to follow another gospel. ⁷ It's not really another gospel, but certain people are confusing you and they want to change the gospel of Christ. ⁸ However, even if we ourselves or a heavenly angel should ever preach anything different from what we preached to you, they should be under a curse. ⁹ I'm repeating what we've said before: if anyone preaches something different from what you received, they should be under a curse!

Paul's leadership

¹⁰ Am I trying to win over human beings or God? Or am I trying to please people? If I were still trying to please people, I wouldn't be Christ's slave.

¹¹ Brothers and sisters, I want you to know that the gospel I preached isn't human in origin. ¹² I didn't receive it or learn it from a human. It came through a revelation from Jesus Christ.

¹³ You heard about my previous life in Judaism, how severely I harassed God's church and tried to destroy it. ¹⁴ I advanced in Judaism beyond many of my peers, because I was much more militant about the traditions of my ancestors. ¹⁵ But God had set me apart from birth and called me through his grace. He was pleased ¹⁶ to reveal his Son to me, so that I might preach about him to the Gentiles. I didn't immediately consult with any human being. ¹⁷ I didn't go up to Jerusalem to see the men who were apostles before me either, but I went away into Arabia and I returned again to Damascus. ¹⁸ Then after three years I went up to Jerusalem to visit Cephas and stayed with him fifteen days. ¹⁹ But I didn't see any other of the apostles except James the brother of the Lord. ²⁰ Before God, I'm not lying about the things that I'm writing to you! ²¹ Then I went into the regions of Syria and Cilicia, ²² but I wasn't known personally by the Christian churches in Judea. ²³ They only heard a report about me: "The man who used to harass us now preaches the faith that he once tried to destroy." ²⁴ So they were glorifying God because of me.

Confirmation of Paul's leadership

2 Then after fourteen years I went up to Jerusalem again with Barnabas, and I took Titus along also. ² I went there because of a revelation, and I laid out the gospel that I preach to the Gentiles for them. But I did it privately with the influential leaders to make sure that I wouldn't be working or that I hadn't worked for nothing. ³However, not even Titus, who was with me and who was a Greek, was required to be circumcised. ⁴But false brothers and sisters, who were brought in secretly, slipped in to spy on our freedom, which we have in Christ Jesus, and to make us slaves. ⁵We didn't give in and submit to them for a single moment, so that the truth of the gospel would continue to be with you.

⁶The influential leaders didn't add anything to what I was preaching—and whatever they were makes no difference to me, because God doesn't show favoritism. ⁷But on the contrary, they saw that I had been given the responsibility to preach the gospel to the people who aren't circumcised, just as Peter had been to the circumcised. ⁸The one who empowered Peter to become an apostle to the circumcised empowered me also to be one to the Gentiles. ⁹James, Cephas, and John, who are considered to be key leaders, shook hands with me and Barnabas as equals when they recognized the grace that was given to me. So it was agreed that we would go to the Gentiles, while they continue to go to the people who were circumcised. ¹⁰They asked only that we would remember the poor, which was certainly something I was willing to do.

The Jewish-Gentile controversy

¹¹But when Cephas came to Antioch, I opposed him to his face, because he was wrong. ¹²He had been eating with the Gentiles before certain people came from James. But when they came, he began to back out and separate himself, because he was afraid of the people who promoted circumcision. ¹³And the rest of the Jews also joined him in this hypocrisy so that even Barnabas got carried away with them in their hypocrisy. ¹⁴But when I saw that they weren't acting consistently with the truth of the gospel, I said to Cephas in front of everyone, "If you, though you're a Jew, live like a Gentile and not like a Jew, how can you require the Gentiles to live like Jews?"

¹⁵We are born Jews—we're not Gentile sinners. ¹⁶However, we know that a person isn't made righteous by the works of the Law but rather through the faithfulness of Jesus Christ. We ourselves believed in Christ Jesus so that we could be made righteous by the faithfulness of Christ and not by the works of the Law—because no one will be made righteous by the works of the Law. ¹⁷But if it is discovered that we ourselves are sinners while we are trying to be made righteous in Christ, then is Christ a servant of sin? Absolutely not! ¹⁸If I rebuild the very things that I tore down, I show that I myself am breaking the Law. ¹⁹I died to the Law through the Law, so that I could live for God. ²⁰I have been crucified with Christ and I no longer live, but Christ lives in me. And the life that I now live in my body, I live by faith, indeed, by the faithfulness of God's Son, who loved me and gave himself for me. ²¹I don't ignore the grace of God, because if we become righteous through the Law, then Christ died for no purpose.

Works versus the Spirit

3 You irrational Galatians! Who put a spell on you? Jesus Christ was put

on display as crucified before your eyes! [2]I just want to know this from you: Did you receive the Spirit by doing the works of the Law or by believing what you heard? [3]Are you so irrational? After you started with the Spirit, are you now finishing up with your own human effort? [4]Did you experience so much for nothing? I wonder if it really was for nothing. [5]So does the one providing you with the Spirit and working miracles among you do this by you doing the works of the Law or by you believing what you heard?

Abraham: an example of righteousness

[6]Understand that in the same way that Abraham *believed God and it was credited to him as righteousness,*[a] [7]those who believe are the children of Abraham. [8]But when it saw ahead of time that God would make the Gentiles righteous on the basis of faith, scripture preached the gospel in advance to Abraham: *All the Gentiles will be blessed in you.*[b] [9]Therefore, those who believe are blessed together with Abraham who believed.

[10]All those who rely on the works of the Law are under a curse, because it is written, *Everyone is cursed who does not keep on doing all the things that have been written in the Law scroll.*[c] [11]But since no one is made righteous by the Law as far as God is concerned, it is clear that *the righteous one will live on the basis of faith.*[d] [12]The Law isn't based on faith; rather, *the one doing these things will live by them.*[e] [13]Christ redeemed us from the curse of the Law by becoming a curse for us—because it is

written, *Everyone who is hung on a tree is cursed.*[f] [14]He redeemed us so that the blessing of Abraham would come to the Gentiles through Christ Jesus, and that we would receive the promise of the Spirit through faith.

[15]Brothers and sisters, I'll use an example from human experience. No one ignores or makes additions to a validated will. [16]The promises were made to Abraham and to his descendant. It doesn't say, "and to the descendants," as if referring to many rather than just one. It says, "and to your descendant," who is Christ. [17]I'm saying this: the Law, which came four hundred thirty years later, doesn't invalidate the agreement that was previously validated by God so that it cancels the promise. [18]If the inheritance were based upon the Law, it would no longer be from the promise. But God has given it graciously to Abraham through a promise.

The Law's origin and purpose

[19]So why was the Law given? It was added because of offenses, until the descendant would come to whom the promise had been made. It was put in place through angels by the hand of a mediator. [20]Now the mediator does not take one side; but God is one. [21]So, is the Law against the promises of God? Absolutely not! If a Law had been given that was able to give life, then righteousness would in fact have come from the Law. [22]But scripture locked up all things under sin, so that the promise based on the faithfulness of Jesus Christ might be given to those who have faith. [23]Before faith came, we were guarded under the Law, locked up

[a]Gen 15:6 [b]Gen 12:3 [c]Deut 27:26 [d]Hab 2:4 [e]Lev 18:5 [f]Deut 21:23

until faith that was coming would be revealed, [24]so that the Law became our custodian until Christ so that we might be made righteous by faith.

God's children are heirs in Christ

[25]But now that faith has come, we are no longer under a custodian.

[26]You are all God's children through faith in Christ Jesus. [27]All of you who were baptized into Christ have clothed yourselves with Christ. [28]There is neither Jew nor Greek; there is neither slave nor free; nor is there male and female, for you are all one in Christ Jesus. [29]Now if you belong to Christ, then indeed you are Abraham's descendants, heirs according to the promise.

4 I'm saying that as long as the heirs are minors, they are no different from slaves, though they really are the owners of everything. [2]However, they are placed under trustees and guardians until the date set by the parents. [3]In the same way, when we were minors, we were also enslaved by this world's system. [4]But when the fulfillment of the time came, God sent his Son, born through a woman, and born under the Law. [5]This was so he could redeem those under the Law so that we could be adopted. [6]Because you are sons and daughters, God sent the Spirit of his Son into our hearts, crying, "Abba, Father!" [7]Therefore, you are no longer a slave but a son or daughter, and if you are his child, then you are also an heir through God.

Paul's concern for the Galatians

[8]At the time, when you didn't know God, we were enslaved by things that aren't gods by nature. [9]But now, after knowing God (or rather, being known by God), how can you turn back again to the weak and worthless world system? Do you want to be slaves to it again? [10]You observe religious days and months and seasons and years. [11]I'm afraid for you! Perhaps my hard work for you has been for nothing.

[12]I beg you to be like me, brothers and sisters, because I have become like you! You haven't wronged me. [13]You know that I first preached the gospel to you because of an illness. [14]Though my poor health burdened you, you didn't look down on me or reject me, but you welcomed me as if I were an angel from God, or as if I were Christ Jesus! [15]Where then is the great attitude that you had? I swear that, if possible, you would have dug out your eyes and given them to me. [16]So then, have I become your enemy by telling you the truth? [17]They are so concerned about you, though not with good intentions. Rather, they want to shut you out so that you would run after them. [18]However, it's always good to have people concerned about you with good intentions, and not just when I'm there with you. [19]My little children, I'm going through labor pains again until Christ is formed in you. [20]But I wish I could be with you now and change how I sound, because I'm at a loss about you.

Slave versus free

[21]Tell me—those of you who want to be under the Law—don't you listen to the Law? [22]It's written that Abraham had two sons, one by the slave woman and one by the free woman. [23]The son by the slave woman was conceived the normal way, but the son by the free woman was conceived through a promise. [24]These things are an allegory:

the women are two covenants. One is from Mount Sinai, which gives birth to slave children; this is Hagar. [25]Hagar is Mount Sinai in Arabia, and she corresponds to the present-day Jerusalem, because the city is in slavery with her children. [26]But the Jerusalem that is above is free, and she is our mother. [27]It's written,

Rejoice, barren woman,
  you who have not given birth.
  Break out with a shout,
    you who have not suffered
    labor pains;
  because the woman
    who has been deserted
    will have many more children
    than the woman
    who has a husband.[g]

[28]Brothers and sisters, you are children of the promise like Isaac. [29]But just as it was then, so it is now also: the one who was conceived the normal way harassed the one who was conceived by the Spirit. [30]But what does the scripture say? *Throw out the slave woman and her son, because the slave woman's son won't share the inheritance with the free woman's son.*[h] [31]Therefore, brothers and sisters, we aren't the slave woman's children, but we are the free woman's children.

5 Christ has set us free for freedom. Therefore, stand firm and don't submit to the bondage of slavery again.

Arguments against being circumcised

[2]Look, I, Paul, am telling you that if you have yourselves circumcised, having Christ won't help you. [3]Again I swear to every man who has himself circumcised that he is required to do the whole Law. [4]You people who are trying to be made righteous by the Law have been estranged from Christ. You have fallen away from grace! [5]We eagerly wait for the hope of righteousness through the Spirit by faith. [6]Being circumcised or not being circumcised doesn't matter in Christ Jesus, but faith working through love does matter.

[7]You were running well—who stopped you from obeying the truth? [8]This line of reasoning doesn't come from the one who calls you. [9]A little yeast works through the whole lump of dough. [10]I'm convinced about you in the Lord that you won't think any other way. But the one who is confusing you will pay the penalty, whoever that may be. [11]Brothers and sisters, if I'm still preaching circumcision, why am I still being harassed? In that case, the offense of the cross would be canceled. [12]I wish that the ones who are upsetting you would castrate themselves!

[13]You were called to freedom, brothers and sisters; only don't let this freedom be an opportunity to indulge your selfish impulses, but serve each other through love. [14]All the Law has been fulfilled in a single statement: *Love your neighbor as yourself.*[i] [15]But if you bite and devour each other, be careful that you don't get eaten up by each other!

Two different ways of living

[16]I say be guided by the Spirit and you won't carry out your selfish desires. [17]A person's selfish desires are set against the Spirit, and the Spirit is set against one's selfish desires. They are opposed to each other, so you

[g]Isa 54:1 [h]Gen 21:10 [i]Lev 19:18

shouldn't do whatever you want to do. ¹⁸But if you are being led by the Spirit, you aren't under the Law. ¹⁹The actions that are produced by selfish motives are obvious, since they include sexual immorality, moral corruption, doing whatever feels good, ²⁰idolatry, drug use and casting spells, hate, fighting, obsession, losing your temper, competitive opposition, conflict, selfishness, group rivalry, ²¹jealousy, drunkenness, partying, and other things like that. I warn you as I have already warned you, that those who do these kinds of things won't inherit God's kingdom.

²²But the fruit of the Spirit is love, joy, peace, patience, kindness, goodness, faithfulness, ²³gentleness, and self-control. There is no law against things like this. ²⁴Those who belong to Christ Jesus have crucified the self with its passions and its desires.

²⁵If we live by the Spirit, let's follow the Spirit. ²⁶Let's not become arrogant, make each other angry, or be jealous of each other.

Caring and sharing

6 Brothers and sisters, if a person is caught doing something wrong, you who are spiritual should restore someone like this with a spirit of gentleness. Watch out for yourselves so you won't be tempted too. ²Carry each other's burdens and so you will fulfill the law of Christ. ³If anyone thinks they are important when they aren't, they're fooling themselves. ⁴Each person should test their own work and be happy with

doing a good job and not compare themselves with others. ⁵Each person will have to carry their own load.

⁶Those who are taught the word should share all good things with their teacher. ⁷Make no mistake, God is not mocked. A person will harvest what they plant. ⁸Those who plant only for their own benefit will harvest devastation from their selfishness, but those who plant for the benefit of the Spirit will harvest eternal life from the Spirit. ⁹Let's not get tired of doing good, because in time we'll have a harvest if we don't give up. ¹⁰So then, let's work for the good of all whenever we have an opportunity, and especially for those in the household of faith.

Final greeting

¹¹Look at the large letters I'm making with my own handwriting! ¹²Whoever wants to look good by human standards will try to get you to be circumcised, but only so they won't be harassed for the cross of Christ. ¹³Those who are circumcised don't observe the Law themselves, but they want you to be circumcised, so they can boast about your physical body.ʲ ¹⁴But as for me, God forbid that I should boast about anything except for the cross of our Lord Jesus Christ. The world has been crucified to me through him, and I have been crucified to the world. ¹⁵Being circumcised or not being circumcised doesn't mean anything. What matters is a new creation. ¹⁶May peace and mercy be on whoever follows this rule and on God's Israel.

ʲIn Gk the word traditionally rendered as *flesh* is rendered here as *physical body*, but it has a wide range of meaning. Gal 5:13-25; 6:8, 12 contain nine close occurrences of the same word in Gk, but it is rendered as *selfish* in regard to impulses, desires, motives, or benefit, and *human standards* in 6:12.

¹⁷From now on, no one should bother me because I bear the marks of Jesus on my body.

¹⁸Brothers and sisters, may the grace of our Lord Jesus Christ be with your spirit. Amen.

EPHESIANS

Greeting

1 From Paul, an apostle of Christ Jesus by God's will.

To the holy and faithful people in Christ Jesus in Ephesus.ᵃ ²Grace and peace to you from God our Father and our Lord Jesus Christ.

The believers' blessings

³Bless the God and Father of our Lord Jesus Christ! He has blessed us in Christ with every spiritual blessing that comes from heaven. ⁴God chose us in Christ to be holy and blameless in God's presence before the creation of the world. ⁵God destined us to be his adopted children through Jesus Christ because of his love. This was according to his goodwill and plan ⁶and to honor his glorious grace that he has given to us freely through the Son whom he loves. ⁷We have been ransomed through his Son's blood, and we have forgiveness for our failures based on his overflowing grace, ⁸which he poured over us with wisdom and understanding. ⁹God revealed his hidden designᵇ to us, which is according to his goodwill and the plan that he intended to accomplish through his Son. ¹⁰This is what God planned for the climax of all times:ᶜ to bring all things together in Christ, the

things in heaven along with the things on earth. ¹¹We have also received an inheritance in Christ. We were destined by the plan of God, who accomplishes everything according to his design. ¹²We are called to be an honor to God's glory because we were the first to hope in Christ. ¹³You too heard the word of truth in Christ, which is the good news of your salvation. You were sealed with the promised Holy Spirit because you believed in Christ. ¹⁴The Holy Spirit is the down payment on our inheritance, which is applied toward our redemption as God's own people, resulting in the honor of God's glory.

Paul's prayer for the Ephesians

¹⁵Since I heard about your faith in the Lord Jesus and your love for all God's people, this is the reason that ¹⁶I don't stop giving thanks to God for you when I remember you in my prayers. ¹⁷I pray that the God of our Lord Jesus Christ, the Father of glory, will give you a spirit of wisdom and revelation that makes God known to you. ¹⁸I pray that the eyes of your heart will have enough light to see what is the hope of God's call, what is the richness of God's glorious inheritance among believers, ¹⁹and what is the overwhelming greatness of God's power that is working

---

ᵃThe location of Ephesus was added in some later manuscripts, probably to make the opening of this letter similar to the others in the collection of Paul's letters. ᵇOr *mystery* ᶜOr *the fullness of times* among us believers. This power is conferred by the energy of God's powerful strength. [20]God's power was at work in Christ when God raised him from the dead and sat him at God's right side in the heavens, [21]far above every ruler and authority and power and angelic power, any power that might be named not only now but in the future. [22]God put everything under Christ's feet and made him head of everything in the church, [23]which is his body. His body, the church, is the fullness of Christ, who fills everything in every way.

Saved from sin to life

2At one time you were like a dead person because of the things you did wrong and your offenses against God. [2]You used to live like people of this world. You followed the rule of a destructive spiritual power. This is the spirit of disobedience to God's will that is now at work in persons whose lives are characterized by disobedience. [3]At one time you were like those persons. All of you used to do whatever felt good and whatever you thought you wanted so that you were children headed for punishment just like everyone else.

[4-5]However, God is rich in mercy. He brought us to life with Christ while we were dead as a result of those things that we did wrong. He did this because of the great love that he has for us. You are saved by God's grace! [6]And God raised us up and seated us in the heavens with Christ Jesus. [7]God did this to show future generations the greatness of his grace by the goodness that God has shown us in Christ Jesus.

[8]You are saved by God's grace because of your faith.[d] This salvation is God's gift. It's not something you possessed. [9]It's not something you did that you can be proud of. [10]Instead, we are God's accomplishment, created in Christ Jesus to do good things. God planned for these good things to be the way that we live our lives.

The reconciliation of God's people

[11]So remember that once you were Gentiles by physical descent, who were called "uncircumcised" by Jews who are physically circumcised. [12]At that time you were without Christ. You were aliens rather than citizens of Israel, and strangers to the covenants of God's promise. In this world you had no hope and no God. [13]But now, thanks to Christ Jesus, you who once were so far away have been brought near by the blood of Christ.

[14]Christ is our peace. He made both Jews and Gentiles into one group. With his body, he broke down the barrier of hatred that divided us. [15]He canceled the detailed rules of the Law so that he could create one new person out of the two groups, making peace. [16]He reconciled them both as one body to God by the cross, which ended the hostility to God.

[17]When he came, he announced the good news of peace to you who were far away from God and to those who were near. [18]We both have access to the Father through Christ by the one Spirit. [19]So now you are no longer strangers and aliens. Rather, you are fellow citizens with God's people, and you belong to God's household. [20]As God's household, you are built on the foundation of

[d]Or through his faithfulness

the apostles and prophets with Christ Jesus himself as the cornerstone. [21]The whole building is joined together in him, and it grows up into a temple that is dedicated to the Lord. [22]Christ is building you into a place where God lives through the Spirit.

Paul, apostle to the Gentiles

3 This is why I, Paul, am a prisoner of Christ for you Gentiles.

[2]You've heard, of course, about the responsibility to distribute God's grace, which God gave to me for you, right? [3]God showed me his secret plane[e] in a revelation, as I mentioned briefly before ([4]when you read this, you'll understand my insight into the secret plan[f] about Christ). [5]Earlier generations didn't know this hidden plan that God has now revealed to his holy apostles and prophets through the Spirit. [6]This plan is that the Gentiles would be co-heirs and parts of the same body, and that they would share with the Jews in the promises of God in Christ Jesus through the gospel. [7]I became a servant of the gospel because of the grace that God showed me through the exercise of his power.

[8]God gave his grace to me, the least of all God's people, to preach the good news about the immeasurable riches of Christ to the Gentiles. [9]God sent me to reveal the secret plan[g] that had been hidden since the beginning of time by God, who created everything. [10]God's purpose is now to show the rulers and powers in the heavens the many different varieties of his wisdom through the church. [11]This was consistent with the plan he had from the beginning of time

that he accomplished through Christ Jesus our Lord. [12]In Christ we have bold and confident access to God through faith in him.[h] [13]So then, I ask you not to become discouraged by what I'm suffering for you, which is your glory.

Paul's prayer for the Ephesians

[14]This is why I kneel before the Father. [15]Every ethnic group in heaven or on earth is recognized by him. [16]I ask that he will strengthen you in your inner selves from the riches of his glory through the Spirit. [17]I ask that Christ will live in your hearts through faith. As a result of having strong roots in love, [18]I ask that you'll have the power to grasp love's width and length, height and depth, together with all believers. [19]I ask that you'll know the love of Christ that is beyond knowledge so that you will be filled entirely with the fullness of God.

[20]Glory to God, who is able to do far beyond all that we could ask or imagine by his power at work within us; [21]glory to him in the church and in Christ Jesus for all generations, forever and always. Amen.

Unity of the body of Christ

4 Therefore, as a prisoner for the Lord, I encourage you to live as people worthy of the call you received from God. [2]Conduct yourselves with all humility, gentleness, and patience. Accept each other with love, [3]and make an effort to preserve the unity of the Spirit with the peace that ties you together. [4]You are one body and one spirit, just as God also called you in one hope. [5]There is one Lord, one faith, one baptism,

---

[e]Or *mystery*   [f]Or *mystery*   [g]Or *mystery*   [h]Or *through his faithfulness*

⁶and one God and Father of all, who is over all, through all, and in all.

⁷God has given his grace to each one of us measured out by the gift that is given by Christ. ⁸That's why scripture says, *When he climbed up to the heights, he captured prisoners, and he gave gifts to people.*[i]

⁹What does the phrase "he climbed up" mean if it doesn't mean that he had first gone down into the lower regions, the earth? ¹⁰The one who went down is the same one who climbed up above all the heavens so that he might fill everything.

¹¹He gave some apostles, some prophets, some evangelists, and some pastors and teachers. ¹²His purpose was to equip God's people for the work of serving and building up the body of Christ ¹³until we all reach the unity of faith and knowledge of God's Son. God's goal is for us to become mature adults—to be fully grown, measured by the standard of the fullness of Christ. ¹⁴As a result, we aren't supposed to be infants any longer who can be tossed and blown around by every wind that comes from teaching with deceitful scheming and the tricks people play to deliberately mislead others. ¹⁵Instead, by speaking the truth with love, let's grow in every way into Christ, ¹⁶who is the head. The whole body grows from him, as it is joined and held together by all the supporting ligaments. The body makes itself grow in that it builds itself up with love as each one does its part.

The old and new life

¹⁷So I'm telling you this, and I insist on it in the Lord: you shouldn't live your life like the Gentiles anymore. They base their lives on pointless thinking, ¹⁸and they are in the dark in their reasoning. They are disconnected from God's life because of their ignorance and their closed hearts. ¹⁹They are people who lack all sense of right and wrong, and who have turned themselves over to doing whatever feels good and to practicing every sort of corruption along with greed.

²⁰But you didn't learn that sort of thing from Christ. ²¹Since you really listened to him and you were taught how the truth is in Jesus, ²²change the former way of life that was part of the person you once were, corrupted by deceitful desires. ²³Instead, renew the thinking in your mind by the Spirit ²⁴and clothe yourself with the new person created according to God's image in justice and true holiness.

²⁵Therefore, after you have gotten rid of lying, *Each of you must tell the truth to your neighbor*[j] because we are parts of each other in the same body. ²⁶*Be angry without sinning.*[k] Don't let the sun set on your anger. ²⁷Don't provide an opportunity for the devil. ²⁸Thieves should no longer steal. Instead, they should go to work, using their hands to do good so that they will have something to share with whoever is in need.

²⁹Don't let any foul words come out of your mouth. Only say what is helpful when it is needed for building up the community so that it benefits those who hear what you say. ³⁰Don't make the Holy Spirit of God unhappy—you were sealed by him for the day of redemption. ³¹Put aside all bitterness, losing your temper, anger, shouting,

[i]Ps 68:18 [j]Zech 8:16 [k]Ps 4:4

and slander, along with every other evil. [32]Be kind, compassionate, and forgiving to each other, in the same way God forgave you in Christ.

5 Therefore, imitate God like dearly loved children. [2]Live your life with love, following the example of Christ, who loved us and gave himself for us. He was a sacrificial offering that smelled sweet to God.

[3]Sexual immorality, and any kind of impurity or greed, shouldn't even be mentioned among you, which is right for holy persons. [4]Obscene language, silly talk, or vulgar jokes aren't acceptable for believers. Instead, there should be thanksgiving. [5]Because you know for sure that persons who are sexually immoral, impure, or greedy—which happens when things become gods—those persons won't inherit the kingdom of Christ and God.

Be children of light

[6]Nobody should deceive you with stupid ideas. God's anger comes down on those who are disobedient because of this kind of thing. [7]So you shouldn't have anything to do with them. [8]You were once darkness, but now you are light in the Lord, so live your life as children of light. [9]Light produces fruit that consists of every sort of goodness, justice, and truth. [10]Therefore, test everything to see what's pleasing to the Lord, [11]and don't participate in the unfruitful actions of darkness. Instead, you should reveal the truth about them. [12]It's embarrassing to even talk about what certain persons do in secret. [13]But everything exposed to the light is revealed by the light. [14]Everything that is

revealed by the light is light. Therefore, it says, *Wake up, sleeper!*[l] *Get up from the dead,*[m] *and Christ will shine on you.*[n]

Be filled with the Spirit

[15]So be careful to live your life wisely, not foolishly. [16]Take advantage of every opportunity because these are evil times. [17]Because of this, don't be ignorant, but understand the Lord's will. [18]Don't get drunk on wine, which produces depravity. Instead, be filled with the Spirit in the following ways: [19]speak to each other with psalms, hymns, and spiritual songs; sing and make music to the Lord in your hearts; [20]always give thanks to God the Father for everything in the name of our Lord Jesus Christ; [21]and submit to each other out of respect for Christ. [22]For example, wives should submit to their husbands as if to the Lord. [23]A husband is the head of his wife like Christ is head of the church, that is, the savior of the body. [24]So wives submit to their husbands in everything like the church submits to Christ. [25]As for husbands, love your wives just like Christ loved the church and gave himself for her. [26]He did this to make her holy by washing her in a bath of water with the word. [27]He did this to present himself with a splendid church, one without any sort of stain or wrinkle on her clothes, but rather one that is holy and blameless. [28]That's how husbands ought to love their wives—in the same way as they do their own bodies. Anyone who loves his wife loves himself. [29]No one ever hates his own body, but feeds it and takes care of it just like Christ does for the church [30]because we are parts of

---

[l]Isa 26:19; 51:17; 52:1; 60:1   [m]Isa 26:19   [n]Isa 60:1

his body. [31]*This is why a man will leave his father and mother and be united with his wife, and the two of them will be one body.*[o] [32]Marriage is a significant allegory,[p] and I'm applying it to Christ and the church. [33]In any case, as for you individually, each one of you should love his wife as himself, and wives should respect[q] their husbands.

6 As for children, obey your parents in the Lord, because it is right. [2]The commandment *Honor your father and mother* is the first one with a promise attached: [3]*so that things will go well for you, and you will live for a long time in the land.*[r] [4]As for parents, don't provoke your children to anger, but raise them with discipline and instruction about the Lord.

[5]As for slaves, obey your human masters with fear and trembling and with sincere devotion to Christ. [6]Don't work to make yourself look good and try to flatter people, but act like slaves of Christ carrying out God's will from the heart. [7]Serve your owners enthusiastically, as though you were serving the Lord and not human beings. [8]You know that the Lord will reward every person who does what is right, whether that person is a slave or a free person. [9]As for masters, treat your slaves in the same way. Stop threatening them, because you know that both you and your slaves have a master in heaven. He doesn't distinguish between people on the basis of status.

Put on the armor of God

[10]Finally, be strengthened by the Lord and his powerful strength. [11]Put on God's armor so that you can make a stand against the tricks of the devil. [12]We aren't fighting against human enemies but against rulers, authorities, forces of cosmic darkness, and spiritual powers of evil in the heavens. [13]Therefore, pick up the full armor of God so that you can stand your ground on the evil day and after you have done everything possible to still stand. [14]So stand with the belt of truth around your waist, justice as your breastplate, [15]and put shoes on your feet so that you are ready to spread the good news of peace. [16]Above all, carry the shield of faith so that you can extinguish the flaming arrows of the evil one. [17]Take the helmet of salvation and the sword of the Spirit, which is God's word.

[18]Offer prayers and petitions in the Spirit all the time. Stay alert by hanging in there and praying for all believers. [19]As for me, pray that when I open my mouth, I'll get a message that confidently makes this secret plan[s] of the gospel known. [20]I'm an ambassador in chains for the sake of the gospel. Pray so that the Lord will give me the confidence to say what I have to say.

Final greeting

[21]Tychicus, my loved brother and faithful servant of the Lord, can inform you about my situation and what I'm doing. [22]I've sent him for this reason—so that you will know about us. He can reassure you.

[23]May there be peace with the brothers and sisters as well as love with the faith that comes from God the Father and the Lord Jesus Christ. [24]May grace be with all those who love our Lord Jesus Christ forever.

[o]Gen 2:24 [p]Or *mystery* [q]Or *fear* [r]Exod 20:12; Deut 5:16 [s]Or *mystery*

PHILIPPIANS

Greeting

1 From Paul and Timothy, slaves of Christ Jesus.

To all those in Philippi who are God's people in Christ Jesus, along with your supervisors[a] and servants.[b]

[2] May the grace and peace from God our Father and the Lord Jesus Christ be with you.

Thanksgiving and prayer

[3] I thank my God every time I mention you in my prayers. [4] I'm thankful for all of you every time I pray, and it's always a prayer full of joy. [5] I'm glad because of the way you have been my partners in the ministry of the gospel from the time you first believed it until now. [6] I'm sure about this: the one who started a good work in you will stay with you to complete the job by the day of Christ Jesus. [7] I have good reason to think this way about all of you because I keep you in my heart. You are all my partners in God's grace, both during my time in prison and in the defense and support of the gospel. [8] God is my witness that I feel affection for all of you with the compassion of Christ Jesus.

[9] This is my prayer: that your love might become even more and more rich with knowledge and all kinds of insight. [10] I pray this so that you will be able to decide what really matters and so you will be sincere and blameless on the day of Christ. [11] I pray that you will then be filled with the fruit of righteousness, which comes from Jesus Christ, in order to give glory and praise to God.

Priority of the gospel

[12] Brothers and sisters, I want you to know that the things that have happened to me have actually advanced the gospel. [13] The whole Praetorian Guard and everyone else knows that I'm in prison for Christ. [14] Most of the brothers and sisters have had more confidence through the Lord to speak the word boldly and bravely because of my jail time. [15] Some certainly preach Christ with jealous and competitive motives, but others preach with good motives. [16] They are motivated by love, because they know that I'm put here to give a defense of the gospel; [17] the others preach Christ because of their selfish ambition. They are insincere, hoping to cause me more pain while I'm in prison.

[18] What do I think about this? Just this: since Christ is proclaimed in every possible way, whether from dishonest or true motives, I'm glad and I'll continue to be glad. [19] I'm glad because I know that this will result in my release through your prayers and the help of the Spirit of Jesus Christ. [20] It is my expectation and hope that I won't be put to shame in anything. Rather, I hope with daring courage that Christ's greatness will be seen in my body, now as always, whether I live or die. [21] Because for me, living serves Christ and dying is even better. [22] If I continue to live in this world, I get results from my work.

---

[a] Or overseers, bishops [b] Or deacons

23But I don't know what I prefer. I'm torn between the two because I want to leave this life and be with Christ, which is far better. 24However, it's more important for me to stay in this world for your sake. 25I'm sure of this: I will stay alive and remain with all of you to help your progress and the joy of your faith, 26and to increase your pride in Christ Jesus through my presence when I visit you again.

Live worthy of the gospel

27Most important, live together in a manner worthy of Christ's gospel. Do this, whether I come and see you or I'm absent and hear about you. Do this so that you stand firm, united in one spirit and mind as you struggle together to remain faithful to the gospel. 28That way, you won't be afraid of anything your enemies do. Your faithfulness and courage are a sign of their coming destruction and your salvation, which is from God. 29God has generously granted you the privilege, not only of believing in Christ but also of suffering for Christ's sake. 30You are having the same struggle that you saw me face and now hear that I'm still facing.

Imitate Christ

2Therefore, if there is any encouragement in Christ, any comfort in love, any sharing in the Spirit, any sympathy, 2complete my joy by thinking the same way, having the same love, being united, and agreeing with each other. 3Don't do anything for selfish purposes, but with humility think of others as better than yourselves. 4Instead of each person watching out for their own good, watch out for what is better for others. 5Adopt the attitude that was in Christ Jesus:

6 Though he was in the form of God,
　he did not consider
　　being equal with God
　　something to exploit.
7 But he emptied himself
　by taking the form of a slave
　and by becoming
　　like human beings.
When he found himself
　in the form of a human,
8 he humbled himself
　by becoming obedient
　to the point of death,
　even death on a cross.
9 Therefore, God highly honored him
　and gave him a name
　above all names,
10 so that at the name of Jesus everyone
　in heaven, on earth,
　　and under the earth might bow
11 and every tongue confess
　that Jesus Christ is Lord,
　to the glory of God the Father.

Carry out your salvation

12Therefore, my loved ones, just as you always obey me, not just when I am present but now even more while I am away, carry out your own salvation with fear and trembling. 13God is the one who enables you both to want and to actually live out his good purposes. 14Do everything without grumbling and arguing 15so that you may be blameless and pure, innocent children of God surrounded by people who are crooked and corrupt. Among these people you shine like stars in the world 16because you hold on to the word of life. This will allow me to say on the day of Christ that I haven't run for nothing or worked for nothing. 17But even if I am poured out like a drink offering upon the altar of service for your faith,

I am glad. I'm glad with all of you. [18]You should be glad about this in the same way. Be glad with me!

Sending Timothy and Epaphroditus

[19]I hope in the Lord Jesus to send Timothy to see you soon so that I may be encouraged by hearing about you. [20]I have no one like him. He is a person who genuinely cares about your wellbeing. [21]All the others put their own business ahead of Jesus Christ's business. [22]You know his character, how he labors with me for the gospel like a son works with his father. [23]So he is the one that I hope to send as soon as I find out how things turn out here for me. [24]I trust in the Lord that I also will visit you soon.

[25]I think it is also necessary to send Epaphroditus to you. He is my brother, coworker, and fellow soldier; and he is your representative who serves my needs. [26]He misses you all, and he was upset because you heard he was sick. [27]In fact, he was so sick that he nearly died. But God had mercy on him—and not just on him but also on me, because his death would have caused me great sorrow. [28]Therefore, I am sending him immediately so that when you see him again you can be glad and I won't worry. [29]So welcome him in the Lord with great joy and show great respect for people like him. [30]He risked his life and almost died for the work of Christ, and he did this to make up for the help you couldn't give me.

Values and priorities

3 So then, my brothers and sisters, be glad in the Lord. It's no trouble for me to repeat the same things to you because they will help keep you on track.

[2]Watch out for the "dogs." Watch out for people who do evil things. Watch out for those who insist on circumcision, which is really mutilation. [3]We are the circumcision. We are the ones who serve by God's Spirit and who boast in Christ Jesus. We don't put our confidence in rituals performed on the body, [4]though I have good reason to have this kind of confidence. If anyone else has reason to put their confidence in physical advantages, I have even more:

[5]I was circumcised on the eighth day.

I am from the people of Israel and the tribe of Benjamin.

I am a Hebrew of the Hebrews.

With respect to observing the Law, I'm a Pharisee.

[6]With respect to devotion to the faith, I harassed the church.

With respect to righteousness under the Law, I'm blameless.

[7]These things were my assets, but I wrote them off as a loss for the sake of Christ. [8]But even beyond that, I consider everything a loss in comparison with the superior value of knowing Christ Jesus my Lord. I have lost everything for him, but what I lost I think of as sewer trash, so that I might gain Christ [9]and be found in him. In Christ I have a righteousness that is not my own and that does not come from the Law but rather from the faithfulness of Christ. It is the righteousness of God that is based on faith. [10]The righteousness that I have comes from knowing Christ, the power of his resurrection, and the participation in his sufferings. It includes being conformed to his death [11]so that I may perhaps reach the goal of the resurrection of the dead.

[12]It's not that I have already reached this goal or have already been perfected,

but I pursue it, so that I may grab hold of it because Christ grabbed hold of me for just this purpose. [13]Brothers and sisters, I myself don't think I've reached it, but I do this one thing: I forget about the things behind me and reach out for the things ahead of me. [14]The goal I pursue is the prize of God's upward call in Christ Jesus. [15]So all of us who are spiritually mature should think this way, and if anyone thinks differently, God will reveal it to him or her. [16]Only let's live in a way that is consistent with whatever level we have reached.

Imitate Paul

[17]Brothers and sisters, become imitators of me and watch those who live this way—you can use us as models. [18]As I have told you many times and now say with deep sadness, many people live as enemies of the cross. [19]Their lives end with destruction. Their god is their stomach, and they take pride in their disgrace because their thoughts focus on earthly things. [20]Our citizenship is in heaven. We look forward to a savior that comes from there—the Lord Jesus Christ. [21]He will transform our humble bodies so that they are like his glorious body, by the power that also makes him able to subject all things to himself.

Stand firm in the Lord

4 Therefore, my brothers and sisters whom I love and miss, who are my joy and crown, stand firm in the Lord.

Loved ones, [2]I urge Euodia and I urge Syntyche to come to an agreement in the Lord. [3]Yes, and I'm also asking you, loyal friend, to help these women who have struggled together with me in the ministry of the gospel, along with Clement and the rest of my coworkers whose names are in the scroll of life.

[4]Be glad in the Lord always! Again I say, be glad! [5]Let your gentleness show in your treatment of all people. The Lord is near. [6]Don't be anxious about anything; rather, bring up all of your requests to God in your prayers and petitions, along with giving thanks. [7]Then the peace of God that exceeds all understanding will keep your hearts and minds safe in Christ Jesus.

[8]From now on, brothers and sisters, if anything is excellent and if anything is admirable, focus your thoughts on these things: all that is true, all that is holy, all that is just, all that is pure, all that is lovely, and all that is worthy of praise. [9]Practice these things: whatever you learned, received, heard, or saw in us. The God of peace will be with you.

Paul's thanks for gifts

[10]I was very glad in the Lord because now at last you have shown concern for me again. (Of course you were always concerned but had no way to show it.) [11]I'm not saying this because I need anything, for I have learned how to be content in any circumstance. [12]I know the experience of being in need and of having more than enough; I have learned the secret to being content in any and every circumstance, whether full or hungry or whether having plenty or being poor. [13]I can endure all these things through the power of the one who gives me strength. [14]Still, you have done well to share my distress.

[15]You Philippians know from the time of my first mission work in Macedonia how no church shared in supporting my ministry except you. [16]You sent contributions repeatedly to take care of my needs even while I was in

Thessalonica. [17]I'm not hoping for a gift, but I am hoping for a profit that accumulates in your account. [18]I now have plenty and it is more than enough. I am full to overflowing because I received the gifts that you sent from Epaphroditus. Those gifts give off a fragrant aroma, an acceptable sacrifice that pleases God. [19]My God will meet your every need out of his riches in the glory that is found in Christ Jesus. [20]Let glory

be given to God our Father forever and always. Amen.

Final greeting

[21]Greet all God's people in Christ Jesus. The brothers and sisters with me send you their greeting. [22]All God's people here, especially those in Caesar's household, send you their greeting. [23]The grace of the Lord Jesus Christ be with your spirits.

COLOSSIANS

Greeting

1 From Paul, an apostle of Christ Jesus by God's will, and Timothy our brother.
[2]To the holy and faithful brothers and sisters in Christ in Colossae. Grace and peace to you from God our Father.

Thanksgiving and prayer for the Colossians

[3]We always give thanks to God, the Father of our Lord Jesus Christ, when we pray for you. [4]We've done this since we heard of your faith in Christ Jesus and your love for all God's people. [5]You have this faith and love because of the hope reserved for you in heaven. You previously heard about this hope through the true message, the good news, [6]which has come to you. This message has been bearing fruit and growing among you since the day you heard and truly understood God's grace, in the same way that it is bearing fruit and growing in the whole world. [7]You learned it from Epaphras, who is

the fellow slave we love and Christ's faithful minister for your sake. [8]He informed us of your love in the Spirit.

[9]Because of this, since the day we heard about you, we haven't stopped praying for you and asking for you to be filled with the knowledge of God's will, with all wisdom and spiritual understanding. [10]We're praying this so that you can live lives that are worthy of the Lord and pleasing to him in every way: by producing fruit in every good work and growing in the knowledge of God; [11]by being strengthened through his glorious might so that you endure everything and have patience; [12]and by giving thanks with joy to the Father. He made it so you could take part in the inheritance, in light granted to God's holy people. [13]He rescued us from the control of darkness and transferred us into the kingdom of the Son he loves. [14]He set us free through the Son and forgave our sins.

Hymn about Christ's work

[15]The Son is the image
    of the invisible God,

the one who is first
over all creation,[a]

[16] Because all things were created
by him:
    both in the heavens
    and on the earth,
    the things that are visible
    and the things that are invisible.
    Whether they are thrones
        or powers,
    or rulers or authorities,
    all things were created
        through him and for him.

[17] He existed before all things,
    and all things are held together
    in him.

[18] He is the head of the body,
    the church,
who is the beginning,
    the one who is firstborn
    from among the dead[b]
    so that he might occupy
        the first place in everything.

[19] Because all the fullness of God
    was pleased to live in him,
    [20] and he reconciled all things
    to himself through him—
        whether things on earth
        or in the heavens.
    He brought peace
        through the blood of his cross.

[21] Once you were alienated from God
and you were enemies with him in your
minds, which was shown by your evil
actions. [22] But now he has reconciled
you by his physical body through death,
to present you before God as a people

who are holy, faultless, and without
blame. [23] But you need to remain well
established and rooted in faith and not
shift away from the hope given in the
good news that you heard. This message has been preached throughout all
creation under heaven. And I, Paul, became a servant of this good news.

Paul's service for the church

[24] Now I'm happy to be suffering for
you. I'm completing what is missing
from Christ's sufferings with my own
body. I'm doing this for the sake of his
body, which is the church. [25] I became
a servant of the church by God's commission, which was given to me for you,
in order to complete God's word. [26] I'm
completing it with a secret plan[c] that
has been hidden for ages and generations but which has now been revealed
to his holy people. [27] God wanted to
make the glorious riches of this secret
plan[d] known among the Gentiles, which
is Christ living in you, the hope of glory.
[28] This is what we preach as we warn and
teach every person with all wisdom so
that we might present each one mature
in Christ. [29] I work hard and struggle for
this goal with his energy, which works
in me powerfully.

2 I want you to know how much I
struggle for you, for those in Laodicea, and for all who haven't known me
personally. [2] My goal is that their hearts
would be encouraged and united together in love so that they might have
all the riches of assurance that come
with understanding, so that they might
have the knowledge of the secret plan[e]
of God, namely Christ. [3] All the treasures of wisdom and knowledge are

---

[a] Or firstborn of all creation   [b] Or first over the dead   [c] Or mystery   [d] Or mystery   [e] Or mystery

hidden in him. [4]I'm telling you this so that no one deceives you with convincing arguments, [5]because even though I am absent physically, I'm with you in spirit. I'm happy to see the discipline and stability of your faith in Christ.

Error threatening the church

[6]So live in Christ Jesus the Lord in the same way as you received him. [7]Be rooted and built up in him, be established in faith, and overflow with thanksgiving just as you were taught. [8]See to it that nobody enslaves you with philosophy and foolish deception, which conform to human traditions and the way the world thinks and acts rather than Christ. [9]All the fullness of deity lives in Christ's body. [10]And you have been filled by him, who is the head of every ruler and authority. [11]You were also circumcised by him. This wasn't performed by human hands—the whole body was removed through this circumcision by Christ. [12]You were buried with him through baptism and raised with him through faith in the power of God, who raised him from the dead. [13]When you were dead because of the things you had done wrong and because your body wasn't circumcised, God made you alive with Christ and forgave all the things you had done wrong. [14]He destroyed the record of the debt we owed, with its requirements that worked against us. He canceled it by nailing it to the cross. [15]When he disarmed the rulers and authorities, he exposed them to public disgrace by leading them in a triumphal parade.

[16]So don't let anyone judge you about eating or drinking or about a festival, a new moon observance, or sabbaths. [17]These religious practices are only a shadow of what was coming—the body that cast the shadow is Christ. [18]Don't let anyone who wants to practice harsh self-denial and worship angels rob you of the prize. They go into detail about what they have seen in visions and have become unjustifiably arrogant by their selfish way of thinking. [19]They don't stay connected to the head. The head nourishes and supports the whole body through the joints and ligaments, so the body grows with a growth that is from God.

[20]If you died with Christ to the way the world thinks and acts, why do you submit to rules and regulations as though you were living in the world? [21]"Don't handle!" "Don't taste!" "Don't touch!" [22]All these things cease to exist when they are used. Such rules are human commandments and teachings. [23]They look like they are wise with this self-made religion and their self-denial by the harsh treatment of the body, but they are no help against indulging in selfish immoral behavior.

Your life hidden in Christ

3 Therefore, if you were raised with Christ, look for the things that are above, where Christ is sitting at God's right side. [2]Think about the things above and not things on earth. [3]You died, and your life is hidden with Christ in God. [4]When Christ, who is your life, is revealed, then you also will be revealed with him in glory.

[5]So put to death the parts of your life that belong to the earth, such as sexual immorality, moral corruption, lust, evil desire, and greed (which is idolatry). [6]The wrath of God is coming upon disobedient people because of these things. [7]You used to live this way,

when you were alive to these things. ⁸But now set aside these things, such as anger, rage, malice, slander, and obscene language. ⁹Don't lie to each other. Take off the old human nature with its practices ¹⁰and put on the new nature, which is renewed in knowledge by conforming to the image of the one who created it. ¹¹In this image there is neither Greek nor Jew, circumcised nor uncircumcised, barbarian, Scythian, slave nor free, but Christ is all things and in all people.

¹²Therefore, as God's choice, holy and loved, put on compassion, kindness, humility, gentleness, and patience. ¹³Be tolerant with each other and, if someone has a complaint against anyone, forgive each other. As the Lord forgave you, so also forgive each other. ¹⁴And over all these things put on love, which is the perfect bond of unity. ¹⁵The peace of Christ must control your hearts—a peace into which you were called in one body. And be thankful people. ¹⁶The word of Christ must live in you richly. Teach and warn each other with all wisdom by singing psalms, hymns, and spiritual songs. Sing to God with gratitude in your hearts. ¹⁷Whatever you do, whether in speech or action, do it all in the name of the Lord Jesus and give thanks to God the Father through him.

¹⁸Wives, submit to your husbands in a way that is appropriate in the Lord. ¹⁹Husbands, love your wives and don't be harsh with them. ²⁰Children, obey your parents in everything, because this pleases the Lord. ²¹Parents, don't provoke your children in a way that ends up discouraging them.

²²Slaves, obey your masters on earth in everything. Don't just obey like people pleasers when they are watching. Instead, obey with the single motivation of fearing the Lord. ²³Whatever you do, do it from the heart for the Lord and not for people. ²⁴You know that you will receive an inheritance as a reward. You serve the Lord Christ. ²⁵But evildoers will receive their reward for their evil actions. There is no discrimination.

4 Masters, be just and fair to your slaves, knowing that you yourselves have a master in heaven.

²Keep on praying and guard your prayers with thanksgiving. ³At the same time, pray for us also. Pray that God would open a door for the word so we can preach the secret plan[f] of Christ—which is why I'm in chains. ⁴Pray that I might be able to make it as clear as I ought to when I preach. ⁵Act wisely toward outsiders, making the most of the opportunity. ⁶Your speech should always be gracious and sprinkled with insight so that you may know how to respond to every person.

Final greeting

⁷Tychicus, our dearly loved brother, faithful minister, and fellow slave in the Lord, will inform you about everything that has happened to me. ⁸This is why I sent him to you, so that you'll know all about us and so he can encourage your hearts. ⁹I sent him with Onesimus, our faithful and dearly loved brother, who is one of you. They will let you know about everything here.

¹⁰Aristarchus, my fellow prisoner, says hello to you. So does Mark,

[f]Or *mystery*

Barnabas' cousin (you received instructions about him; if he comes to you, welcome him). ¹¹Jesus, called Justus, also says hello. These are my only fellow workers for God's kingdom who are Jewish converts. They have been an encouragement to me. ¹²Epaphras, who is one of you, says hello. He's a slave of Christ Jesus who always wrestles for you in prayers so that you will stand firm and be fully mature and complete in the entire will of God. ¹³I can vouch for him that he has worked hard for you and for those in Laodicea

and Hierapolis. ¹⁴Luke, the dearly loved physician, and Demas say hello.

¹⁵Say hello to the brothers and sisters in Laodicea, along with Nympha and the church that meets in her house. ¹⁶After this letter has been read to you publicly, make sure that the church in Laodicea reads it and that you read the one from Laodicea. ¹⁷And tell Archippus, "See to it that you complete the ministry that you received in the Lord."

¹⁸I, Paul, am writing this greeting personally. Remember that I'm in prison. Grace be with you.

1 THESSALONIANS

Greeting

1 From Paul, Silvanus, and Timothy.

To the Thessalonians' church that is in God the Father and the Lord Jesus Christ.

Grace and peace to all of you.

Thanksgiving to God

²We always thank God for all of you when we mention you constantly in our prayers. ³This is because we remember your work that comes from faith,ᵃ your effort that comes from love, and your perseverance that comes from hope in our Lord Jesus Christ in the presence of our God and Father. ⁴Brothers and sisters, you are loved by God, and we know that he has chosen you. ⁵We know this because our good news didn't come to you just in speech but also with power and the Holy Spirit and with deep conviction. You know as well as we do what kind of people we were when we were

with you, which was for your sake. ⁶You became imitators of us and of the Lord when you accepted the message that came from the Holy Spirit with joy in spite of great suffering. ⁷As a result you became an example to all the believers in Macedonia and Achaia. ⁸The message about the Lord rang out from you, not only in Macedonia and Achaia but in every place. The news about your faithfulness to God has spread so that we don't even need to mention it. ⁹People tell us about what sort of welcome we had from you and how you turned to God from idols. As a result, you are servingᵇ the living and true God, ¹⁰and you are waiting for his Son from heaven. His Son is Jesus, who is the one he raised from the dead and who is the one who will rescue us from the coming wrath.

Paul's ministry in Thessalonica

2 As you yourselves know, brothers and sisters, our visit with you wasn't

ᵃOr faithfulness ᵇOr to become slaves of

a waste of time. ²On the contrary, we had the courage through God to speak God's good news in spite of a lot of opposition, although we had already suffered and were publicly insulted in Philippi, as you know. ³Our appeal isn't based on false information, the wrong motives, or deception. ⁴Rather, we have been examined and approved by God to be trusted with the good news, and that's exactly how we speak. We aren't trying to please people, but we are trying to please God, who continues to examine our hearts. ⁵As you know, we never used flattery, and God is our witness that we didn't have greedy motives. ⁶We didn't ask for special treatment from people—not from you or from others— ⁷although we could have thrown our weight around as Christ's apostles. Instead, we were gentle with you like a nursing mother caring for her own children. ⁸We were glad to share not only God's good news with you but also our very lives because we cared for you so much. ⁹You remember, brothers and sisters, our efforts and hard work. We preached God's good news to you, while we worked night and day so we wouldn't be a burden on any of you. ¹⁰You and God are witnesses of how holy, just, and blameless we were toward you believers. ¹¹Likewise, you know how we treated each of you like a father treats his own children. ¹²We appealed to you, encouraged you, and pleaded with you to live lives worthy of the God who is calling you into his own kingdom and glory.

How the Thessalonians received God's message

¹³We also thank God constantly for this: when you accepted God's word that you heard from us, you welcomed it for what it truly is. Instead of accepting it as a human message, you accepted it as God's message, and it continues to work in you who are believers. ¹⁴Brothers and sisters, you became imitators of the churches of God in Judea, which are in Christ Jesus. This was because you also suffered the same things from your own people as they did from the Jews. ¹⁵They killed both the Lord Jesus and the prophets and drove us out. They don't please God, and they are hostile to the entire human race ¹⁶when they try to stop us from speaking to the Gentiles so they can be saved. Their sins are constantly pushing the limit.ᶜ God's wrath has caught up with them in the end.

Paul's desire to visit

¹⁷Brothers and sisters, we were separated from you for a while physically but not in our hearts. We made every effort in our desire to see you again face-to-face. ¹⁸We wanted to come to you—I, Paul, tried over and over again—and Satan stopped us. ¹⁹What is our hope, joy, or crown that we can brag about in front of our Lord Jesus when he comes? Isn't it all of you? ²⁰You are our glory and joy!

3 So when we couldn't stand it any longer, we thought it was a good idea to stay on in Athens by ourselves, ²and we sent you Timothy, who is our brother and God's coworker in the good news about Christ. We sent him to strengthen and encourage you in your faithfulness. ³We didn't want any of you to be shaken by these problems. You know very well that we were meant

ᶜOr They constantly fill up the measure of their sin.

to go through this. [4]In fact, when we were with you, we kept on predicting that we were going to face problems exactly like what happened, as you know. [5]That's why I sent Timothy to find out about your faithfulness when I couldn't stand it anymore. I was worried that the tempter might have tempted you so that our work would have been a waste of time.

Paul's prayer for the Thessalonians

[6]Now Timothy has returned to us from you and has given us good news about your faithfulness and love! He says that you always have good memories about us and that you want to see us as much as we want to see you. [7]Because of this, brothers and sisters, we were encouraged in all our distress and trouble through your faithfulness. [8]For now we are alive if you are standing your ground in the Lord. [9]How can we thank God enough for you, given all the joy we have because of you before our God? [10]Night and day, we pray more than ever to see all of you in person and to complete whatever you still need for your faith. [11]Now may our God and Father himself and our Lord Jesus guide us on our way back to you. [12]May the Lord cause you to increase and enrich your love for each other and for everyone in the same way as we also love you. [13]May the love cause your hearts to be strengthened, to be blameless in holiness before our God and Father when our Lord Jesus comes with all his people. Amen.

Living that pleases God

4 So then, brothers and sisters, we ask and encourage you in the Lord Jesus to keep living the way you already are and even do better in how you live and please God—just as you learned from us. [2]You know the instructions we gave you through the Lord Jesus. [3]God's will is that your lives are dedicated to him.[d] This means that you stay away from sexual immorality [4]and learn how to control your own body in a pure[e] and respectable way. [5]Don't be controlled by your sexual urges like the Gentiles who don't know God. [6]No one should mistreat or take advantage of their brother or sister in this issue. The Lord punishes people for all these things, as we told you before and sternly warned you. [7]God didn't call us to be immoral but to be dedicated to him.[f] [8]Therefore, whoever rejects these instructions isn't rejecting a human authority. They are rejecting God, who gives his Holy Spirit to you.

[9]You don't need us to write about loving your brothers and sisters because God has already taught you to love each other. [10]In fact, you are doing loving deeds for all the brothers and sisters throughout Macedonia. Now we encourage you, brothers and sisters, to do so even more. [11]Aim to live quietly, mind your own business, and earn your own living, just as I told you. [12]That way you'll behave appropriately toward outsiders, and you won't be in need.

Believers who have died

[13]Brothers and sisters, we want you to know about people who have died[g] so that you won't mourn like others who don't have any hope. [14]Since we believe that Jesus died and rose, so we also believe that God will bring with him

---

[d]Or holy, sanctified [e]Or holy, sanctified [f]Or holy, sanctified [g]Or fallen asleep

those who have died in Jesus. ¹⁵What we are saying is a message from the Lord: we who are alive and still around at the Lord's coming definitely won't go ahead of those who have died. ¹⁶This is because the Lord himself will come down from heaven with the signal of a shout by the head angel and a blast on God's trumpet. First, those who are dead in Christ will rise. ¹⁷Then, we who are living and still around will be taken up together with them in the clouds to meet the Lord in the air. That way we will always be with the Lord. ¹⁸So encourage each other with these words.

The Lord's coming

5 We don't need to write to you about the timing and dates, brothers and sisters. ²You know very well that the day of the Lord is going to come like a thief in the night. ³When they are saying, "There is peace and security," at that time sudden destruction will attack them, like labor pains start with a pregnant woman, and they definitely won't escape. ⁴But you aren't in darkness, brothers and sisters, so the day won't catch you by surprise like a thief. ⁵All of you are children of light and children of the day. We don't belong to night or darkness. ⁶So then, let's not sleep like the others, but let's stay awake and stay sober. ⁷People who sleep sleep at night, and people who get drunk get drunk at night. ⁸Since we belong to the day, let's stay sober, wearing faithfulness and love as a piece of armor that protects our body[h] and the hope of salvation as a helmet. ⁹God didn't intend for us to suffer his wrath but rather to possess salvation through

our Lord Jesus Christ. ¹⁰Jesus died for us so that, whether we are awake or asleep, we will live together with him. ¹¹So continue encouraging each other and building each other up, just like you are doing already.

Final instructions and blessing

¹²Brothers and sisters, we ask you to respect those who are working with you, leading you, and instructing you. ¹³Think of them highly with love because of their work. Live in peace with each other. ¹⁴Brothers and sisters, we urge you to warn those who are disorderly. Comfort the discouraged. Help the weak. Be patient with everyone. ¹⁵Make sure no one repays a wrong with a wrong, but always pursue the good for each other and everyone else. ¹⁶Rejoice always. ¹⁷Pray continually. ¹⁸Give thanks in every situation because this is God's will for you in Christ Jesus. ¹⁹Don't suppress the Spirit. ²⁰Don't brush off Spirit-inspired messages, ²¹but examine everything carefully and hang on to what is good. ²²Avoid every kind of evil. ²³Now, may the God of peace himself cause you to be completely dedicated to him; and may your spirit, soul, and body be kept intact and blameless at our Lord Jesus Christ's coming. ²⁴The one who is calling you is faithful and will do this.

Final greeting

²⁵Brothers and sisters, pray for us. ²⁶Greet all the brothers and sisters with a holy kiss. ²⁷By the Lord's authority, I order all of you to have this letter read aloud to all the brothers and sisters. ²⁸The grace of our Lord Jesus Christ be with all of you.

[h]Or breastplate

2 THESSALONIANS

Greeting

1 From Paul, Silvanus, and Timothy:

To the church of the Thessalonians, which is in God our Father, and in the Lord Jesus Christ.

² Grace and peace to all of you from God our Father and the Lord Jesus Christ.

Thanksgiving and encouragement

³ Brothers and sisters, we must always thank God for you. This is only right because your faithfulness is growing by leaps and bounds, and the love that all of you have for each other is increasing. ⁴ That's why we ourselves are bragging about you in God's churches. We tell about your endurance and faithfulness in all the harassments and trouble that you have put up with. ⁵ This shows that God's judgment is right, and that you will be considered worthy of God's kingdom for which you are suffering. ⁶ After all, it's right for God to pay back the ones making trouble for you with trouble ⁷ and to pay back you who are having trouble with relief along with us. This payback will come when the Lord Jesus is revealed from heaven with his powerful angels. ⁸ He will give justice with blazing fire to those who don't recognize God and don't obey the good news of our Lord Jesus. ⁹ They will pay the penalty of eternal destruction away from the Lord's presence and away from his mighty glory. ¹⁰ This will happen when he comes on that day to receive honor from his holy people and to be admired by everyone who has believed—and our testimony to you was believed.

¹¹ We are constantly praying for you for this: that our God will make you worthy of his calling and accomplish every good desire and faithful work by his power. ¹² Then the name of our Lord Jesus will be honored by you, and you will be honored by him, consistent with the grace of our God and the Lord Jesus Christ.

Day of the Lord

2 Brothers and sisters, we have a request for you concerning our Lord Jesus Christ's coming and when we are gathered together to be with him. ² We don't want you to be easily confused in your mind or upset if you hear that the day of the Lord is already here, whether you hear it through some spirit, a message, or a letter supposedly from us. ³ Don't let anyone deceive you in any way. That day won't come unless the rebellion comes first and the person who is lawless is revealed, who is headed for destruction. ⁴ He is the opponent of every so-called god or object of worship and promotes himself over them. So he sits in God's temple, displaying himself to show that he is God. ⁵ You remember that I used to tell you these things while I was with you, don't you? ⁶ Now you know what holds him back so that he can be revealed when his time comes. ⁷ The hidden plan to live without any law is at work now, but it will be secret only until the one who is holding it back is out of the way. ⁸ Then the person who is lawless will be revealed. The Lord Jesus will destroy him with the breath

from his mouth. When the Lord comes, his appearance will put an end to him. [9]When the person who is lawless comes, it will happen through Satan's effort, with all kinds of fake power, signs, and wonders. [10]It will happen with every sort of wicked deception of those who are heading toward destruction because they have refused to love the truth that would allow them to be saved. [11]This is why God will send them an influence that will mislead them so that they will believe the lie. [12]The result will be that everyone will be judged who is not convinced by the truth but is happy with injustice.

Prayer of thanks and encouragement

[13]But we always must thank God for you, brothers and sisters who are loved by God. This is because he chose you from the beginning to be the first crop of the harvest. This brought salvation, through your dedication to God by the Spirit and through your belief in the truth. [14]God called all of you through our good news so you could possess the honor of our Lord Jesus Christ. [15]So then, brothers and sisters, stand firm and hold on to the traditions we taught you, whether we taught you in person or through our letter. [16]Our Lord Jesus Christ himself and God our Father loved us and through grace gave us eternal comfort and a good hope. [17]May he encourage your hearts and give you strength in every good thing you do or say.

Prayer request

3 Finally, brothers and sisters, pray for us so that the Lord's message will spread quickly and be honored, just like

it happened with you. [2]Pray too that we will be rescued from inappropriate and evil people since everyone that we meet won't respond with faith. [3]But the Lord is faithful and will give you strength and protect you from the evil one. [4]We are confident about you in the Lord— that you are doing and will keep doing what we tell you to do. [5]May the Lord lead your hearts to express God's love and Christ's endurance.

Discipline for the undisciplined

[6]Brothers and sisters, we command you in the name of our Lord Jesus Christ to stay away from every brother or sister who lives an undisciplined life that is not in line with the traditions that you received from us. [7]You yourselves know how you need to imitate us because we were not undisciplined when we were with you. [8]We didn't eat anyone's food without paying for it. Instead, we worked night and day with effort and hard work so that we would not impose on you. [9]We did this to give you an example to imitate, not because we didn't have a right to insist on financial support. [10]Even when we were with you we were giving you this command: "If anyone doesn't want to work, they shouldn't eat." [11]We hear that some of you are living an undisciplined life. They aren't working, but they are meddling in other people's business. [12]By the Lord Jesus Christ, we command and encourage such people to work quietly and put their own food on the table. [13]Brothers and sisters, don't get discouraged in doing what is right. [14]Take note of anyone who doesn't obey what we have said in this letter. Don't associate with them so they will be ashamed of themselves. [15]Don't treat

them like enemies, but warn them like you would do for a brother or sister.

Final greeting

[16] May the Lord of peace himself give you peace always in every way. The Lord be with all of you. [17] I, Paul, am writing this greeting with my own hand. This verifies that the letter is from me, as in every letter of mine. This is how I write. [18] The grace of our Lord Jesus Christ be with all of you.

1 TIMOTHY

Greeting

1 From Paul, who is an apostle of Jesus Christ by the command of God our savior and of Christ Jesus our hope. [2] To Timothy, my true child in the faith.

Grace, mercy, and peace from God the Father and from Christ Jesus our Lord.

Timothy's purpose in Ephesus

[3] When I left for Macedonia, I asked you to stay behind in Ephesus so that you could instruct certain individuals not to spread wrong teaching. [4] They shouldn't pay attention to myths and endless genealogies. Their teaching only causes useless guessing games instead of faithfulness to God's way of doing things. [5] The goal of instruction is love from a pure heart, a good conscience, and a sincere faith. [6] Because they missed this goal, some people have been distracted by talk that doesn't mean anything. [7] They want to be teachers of Law without understanding either what they are saying or what they are talking about with such confidence. [8] Now we know that the Law is good if used appropriately. [9] We understand this: the Law isn't established for a righteous person but for people who live without laws and without obeying any authority. They are the ungodly and the sinners. They are people who are not spiritual, and nothing is sacred to them. They kill their fathers and mothers, and murder others. [10] They are people who are sexually unfaithful, and people who have intercourse with the same sex. They are kidnappers,[a] liars, individuals who give false testimonies in court, and those who do anything else that is opposed to sound teaching. [11] Sound teaching agrees with the glorious gospel of the blessed God that has been trusted to me.

Thanksgiving

[12] I thank Christ Jesus our Lord, who has given me strength because he considered me faithful. So he appointed me to ministry [13] even though I used to speak against him, attack his people, and I was proud. But I was shown mercy because I acted in ignorance and without faith. [14] Our Lord's favor poured all over me along with the faithfulness and love that are in Christ Jesus. [15] This saying is reliable and deserves full acceptance: "Christ Jesus came into the world to save sinners"—and I'm the biggest sinner of all. [16] But this is why I

[a] Or *slave dealers*

was shown mercy, so that Christ Jesus could show his endless patience to me first of all. So I'm an example for those who are going to believe in him for eternal life. [17] Now to the king of the ages, to the immortal, invisible, and only God, may honor and glory be given to him forever and always! Amen.

Importance of faith and a good conscience

[18] Timothy, my child, I'm giving you these instructions based on the prophecies that were once made about you. So if you follow them, you can wage a good war [19] because you have faith and a good conscience. Some people have ruined their faith because they refused to listen to their conscience, [20] such as Hymenaeus and Alexander. I've handed them over to Satan so that they can be taught not to speak against God.

Prayer for everyone

2 First of all, then, I ask that requests, prayers, petitions, and thanksgiving be made for all people. [2] Pray for kings and everyone who is in authority so that we can live a quiet and peaceful life in complete godliness and dignity. [3] This is right and it pleases God our savior, [4] who wants all people to be saved and to come to a knowledge of the truth. [5] There is one God and one mediator between God and humanity, the human Christ Jesus, [6] who gave himself as a payment to set all people free. This was a testimony that was given at the right time. [7] I was appointed to be a preacher and apostle of this testimony—I'm telling the truth and I'm not lying!

I'm a teacher of the Gentiles in faith and truth.

Instructions for men and women

[8] Therefore, I want men to pray everywhere by lifting up hands that are holy, without anger or argument. [9] In the same way, I want women to enhance their appearance with clothing that is modest and sensible, not with elaborate hairstyles, gold, pearls, or expensive clothes. [10] They should make themselves attractive by doing good, which is appropriate for women who claim to honor God.

[11] A wife[b] should learn quietly with complete submission. [12] I don't allow a wife[c] to teach or to control her husband.[d] Instead, she should be a quiet listener. [13] Adam was formed first, and then Eve. [14] Adam wasn't deceived, but rather his wife[e] became the one who stepped over the line because she was completely deceived. [15] But a wife[f] will be brought safely through childbirth,[g] if they both continue in faith, love, and holiness, together with self-control.

Supervisors in God's household

3 This saying is reliable: if anyone has a goal to be a supervisor[h] in the church, they want a good thing. [2] So the church's supervisor must be without fault. They should be faithful to their spouse, sober, modest, and honest. They should show hospitality and be skilled at teaching. [3] They shouldn't be addicted to alcohol or be a bully. Instead, they should be gentle, peaceable, and not greedy. [4] They should manage

[b] Or a woman [c] Or a woman [d] Or a man [e] Or the woman [f] Or a woman [g] Or saved through childbearing [h] Or bishop, overseer

their own household well—they should see that their children are obedient with complete respect, [5]because if they don't know how to manage their own household, how can they take care of God's church? [6]They shouldn't be new believers so that they won't become proud and fall under the devil's spell. [7]They should also have a good reputation with those outside the church so that they won't be embarrassed and fall into the devil's trap.

Servants in God's household

[8]In the same way, servants[i] in the church should be dignified, not two-faced, heavy drinkers, or greedy for money. [9]They should hold on to the faith that has been revealed with a clear conscience. [10]They should also be tested and then serve if they are without fault. [11]In the same way, women who are servants[j] in the church should be dignified and not gossip. They should be sober and faithful in everything they do. [12]Servants[k] must be faithful to their spouse and manage their children and their own households well. [13]Those who have served well gain a good standing and considerable confidence in the faith that is in Christ Jesus.

Leading God's household

[14]I hope to come to you quickly. But I'm writing these things to you so that [15]if I'm delayed, you'll know how you should behave in God's household. It is the church of the living God and the backbone and support of the truth. [16]Without question, the mystery of godliness is great: he was revealed as a human, declared righteous by

the Spirit, seen by angels, preached throughout the nations, believed in around the world, and taken up in glory.

4 The Spirit clearly says that in latter times some people will turn away from the faith. They will pay attention to spirits that deceive and to the teaching of demons. [2]They will be controlled by the pretense of lying, and their own consciences will be seared. [3]They will prohibit marriage and eating foods that God created—and he intended them to be accepted with thanksgiving by those who are faithful and have come to know the truth. [4]Everything that has been created by God is good, and nothing that is received with thanksgiving should be rejected. [5]These things are made holy by God's word and prayer. [6]If you point these things out to the believers, you will be a good servant of Christ Jesus who has been trained by the words of faith and the good teaching that you've carefully followed. [7]But stay away from the godless myths that are passed down from the older women.

Practices of spiritual leadership

Train yourself for a holy life! [8]While physical training has some value, training in holy living is useful for everything. It has promise for this life now and the life to come. [9]This saying is reliable and deserves complete acceptance. [10]We work and struggle for this: "Our hope is set on the living God, who is the savior of all people, especially those who believe." [11]Command these things. Teach them. [12]Don't let anyone look down on you because you are young. Instead, set an example for the believers through your speech, behavior,

[i]Or deacons   [j]Or wives, omit who are servants   [k]Or deacons

love, faith, and by being sexually pure. [13]Until I arrive, pay attention to public reading, preaching, and teaching. [14]Don't neglect the spiritual gift in you that was given through prophecy when the elders laid hands on you. [15]Practice these things, and live by them so that your progress will be visible to all. [16]Focus on working on your own development and on what you teach. If you do this, you will save yourself and those who hear you.

Caring for God's family

5 Don't correct an older man, but encourage him like he's your father; treat younger men like your brothers, [2]treat older women like your mother, and treat younger women like your sisters with appropriate respect.

[3]Take care of widows who are truly needy. [4]But if a particular widow has children or grandchildren, they should first learn to respect their own family and repay their parents, because this pleases God. [5]A widow who is truly needy and all alone puts her hope in God and keeps on going with requests and prayers, night and day. [6]But a widow who tries to live a life of luxury is dead even while she is alive. [7]Teach these things so that the families[l] will be without fault. [8]But if someone doesn't provide for their own family, and especially for a member of their household, they have denied the faith. They are worse than those who have no faith.

[9]Put a widow on the list who is older than 60 years old and who was faithful to her husband. [10]She should have a reputation for doing good: raising children, providing hospitality to strangers,

washing the feet of the saints, helping those in distress, and dedicating herself to every kind of good thing. [11]But don't accept younger widows for the list. When their physical desires distract them from Christ, they will want to get married. [12]Then they will be judged for setting aside their earlier commitment. [13]Also, they learn to be lazy by going from house to house. They are not only lazy, but they also become gossips and busybodies, talking about things they shouldn't. [14]So I want younger widows to marry, have children, and manage their homes so that they won't give the enemy any reason to slander us. ([15]Some have already turned away to follow Satan.) [16]If any woman who is a believer has widows in her family, she should take care of them and not burden the church, so that it can help other widows who are truly needy.

Instructions for elders

[17]Elders who lead well should be paid double, especially those who work with public speaking and teaching. [18]The scripture says, *Don't put a muzzle on an ox while it treads grain,*[m] and *Workers deserve their pay.*[n] [19]Don't accept an accusation made against an elder unless it is confirmed by two or three witnesses. [20]Discipline those who are sinning in front of everyone so that all the others will be afraid. [21]I charge you before God and Christ Jesus and the elect angels to follow these practices without bias, and without playing favorites. [22]Don't rush to commission anyone to leadership, and don't participate in the sins of others. Keep yourself morally pure.

[23]Don't drink water anymore, but use

[l]Or *they* [m]Deut 25:4 [n]Luke 10:7

a little wine because of your stomach problems and your frequent illnesses. [24]The sins of some people are obvious, and the sins are judged before the people must face judgment, but the sins of other people show up later. [25]In the same way, the good that people do is also obvious and can't be hidden.

Conduct of Christian slaves

6 Those who are under the bondage of slavery should consider their own masters as worthy of full respect so that God's name and our teaching won't get a bad reputation. [2]And those who have masters who are believers shouldn't look down on them because they are brothers. Instead, they should serve them more faithfully, because the people who benefit from your good service are believers who are loved. Teach and encourage these things.

Warning about false teachers

[3]If anyone teaches anything different and doesn't agree with sound teaching about our Lord Jesus Christ and teaching that is consistent with godliness, [4]that person is conceited. They don't understand anything but have a sick obsession with debates and arguments. This creates jealousy, conflict, verbal abuse, and evil suspicions. [5]There is constant bickering between people whose minds are ruined and who have been robbed of the truth. They think that godliness is a way to make money! [6]Actually, godliness is a great source of profit when it is combined with being happy with what you already have. [7]We didn't bring anything into the world and so we can't take anything out of it: [8]we'll be happy with food and clothing. [9]But people who are trying to get rich

fall into temptation. They are trapped by many stupid and harmful passions that plunge people into ruin and destruction. [10]The love of money is the root of all kinds of evil. Some have wandered away from the faith and have impaled themselves with a lot of pain because they made money their goal.

[11]But as for you, man of God, run away from all these things. Instead, pursue righteousness, holy living, faithfulness, love, endurance, and gentleness. [12]Compete in the good fight of faith. Grab hold of eternal life—you were called to it, and you made a good confession of it in the presence of many witnesses. [13]I command you in the presence of God, who gives life to all things, and Christ Jesus, who made the good confession when testifying before Pontius Pilate. [14]Obey this order without fault or failure until the appearance of our Lord Jesus Christ. [15]The timing of this appearance is revealed by God alone, who is the blessed and only master, the King of kings and Lord of lords. [16]He alone has immortality and lives in light that no one can come near. No human being has ever seen or is able to see him. Honor and eternal power belong to him. Amen.

Wealth of good works

[17]Tell people who are rich at this time not to become egotistical and not to place their hope on their finances, which are uncertain. Instead, they need to hope in God, who richly provides everything for our enjoyment. [18]Tell them to do good, to be rich in the good things they do, to be generous, and to share with others. [19]When they do these things, they will save a treasure for themselves that is a good foundation

for the future. That way they can take hold of what is truly life.

Protect the tradition

²⁰Timothy, protect what has been given to you in trust. Avoid godless and pointless discussions and the contradictory claims of so-called "knowledge." ²¹When some people adopted this false knowledge, they missed the goal of faith.

May grace be with you all.

2 TIMOTHY

Greeting

¹From Paul, an apostle of Christ Jesus by God's will, to promote the promise of life that is in Christ Jesus.

²To Timothy, my dear child.

Grace, mercy, and peace from God the Father and Christ Jesus our Lord.

Thanksgiving and prayer

³I'm grateful to God, whom I serve with a good conscience as my ancestors did. I constantly remember you in my prayers day and night. ⁴When I remember your tears, I long to see you so that I can be filled with happiness. ⁵I'm reminded of your authentic faith, which first lived in your grandmother Lois and your mother Eunice. I'm sure that this faith is also inside you. ⁶Because of this, I'm reminding you to revive God's gift that is in you through the laying on of my hands. ⁷God didn't give us a spirit that is timid but one that is powerful, loving, and self-controlled.

Don't be ashamed of the testimony

⁸So don't be ashamed of the testimony about the Lord or of me, his prisoner. Instead, share the suffering for the good news, depending on God's power. ⁹God is the one who saved and called us with a holy calling. This wasn't based on what we have done, but it was based on his own purpose and grace that he gave us in Christ Jesus before time began. ¹⁰Now his grace is revealed through the appearance of our savior, Christ Jesus. He destroyed death and brought life and immortality into clear focus through the good news. ¹¹I was appointed a messenger, apostle, and teacher of this good news. ¹²This is also why I'm suffering the way I do, but I'm not ashamed. I know the one in whom I've placed my trust. I'm convinced that God is powerful enough to protect what he has placed in my trust until that day. ¹³Hold on to the pattern of sound teaching that you heard from me with the faith and love that are in Christ Jesus. ¹⁴Protect this good thing that has been placed in your trust through the Holy Spirit who lives in us.

¹⁵You know that everyone in Asia has turned away from me, including Phygelus and Hermogenes. ¹⁶May the Lord show mercy to Onesiphorus' household, because he supported me many times and he wasn't ashamed of my imprisonment. ¹⁷After I arrived in Rome, he quickly looked for me and found me. ¹⁸May the Lord allow him to find his mercy on that day (and you know very well how much he served me in Ephesus).

Pass on the message and share suffering

2 So, my child, draw your strength from the grace that is in Christ Jesus. [2] Take the things you heard me say in front of many other witnesses and pass them on to faithful people who are also capable of teaching others.

[3] Accept your share of suffering like a good soldier of Christ Jesus. [4] Nobody who serves in the military gets tied up with civilian matters, so that they can please the one who recruited them. [5] Also in the same way, athletes don't win unless they follow the rules. [6] A hardworking farmer should get the first share of the crop. [7] Think about what I'm saying; the Lord will give you understanding about everything.

[8] Remember Jesus Christ, who was raised from the dead and descended from David. This is my good news. [9] This is the reason I'm suffering to the point that I'm in prison like a common criminal. But God's word cannot be imprisoned. [10] This is why I endure everything for the sake of those who are chosen by God so that they too may experience salvation in Christ Jesus with eternal glory. [11] This saying is reliable:

"If we have died together,
   we will also live together.
[12] If we endure,
   we will also rule together.
If we deny him, he will also deny us.
[13] If we are disloyal, he stays faithful"
   because he can't be anything else
   than what he is.

Speak, instruct, and act correctly

[14] Remind them of these things and warn them in the sight of God not to engage in battles over words that aren't helpful and only destroy those who hear them. [15] Make an effort to present yourself to God as a tried-and-true worker, who doesn't need to be ashamed but is one who interprets the message of truth correctly. [16] Avoid their godless discussions, because they will lead many people into ungodly behavior, [17] and their ideas will spread like an infection. This includes Hymenaeus and Philetus, [18] who have deviated from the truth by claiming that the resurrection has already happened. This has undermined some people's faith.

[19] God's solid foundation is still standing with this sign: *The Lord knows the people who belong to him,*[a] and *Everyone who confesses the Lord's name must avoid wickedness.*[b] [20] In a mansion, there aren't just gold and silver bowls but also some bowls that are made of wood and clay. Some are meant for special uses, some garbage.[c] [21] So if anyone washes filth off themselves, they will be set apart as a "special bowl." They will be useful to the owner of the mansion for every sort of good work.

Avoid conflict with opponents

[22] Run away from adolescent cravings. Instead, pursue righteousness, faith, love, and peace together with those who confess the Lord with a clean heart. [23] Avoid foolish and thoughtless discussions, since you know that they produce conflicts. [24] God's slave shouldn't be argumentative but should be kind toward all people, able to teach, patient, [25] and should correct opponents with gentleness. Perhaps God will change their mind and give them

[a]Num 16:5 LXX   [b]Possibly modeled on Isa 26:13   [c]Or *dishonorable purposes*

a knowledge of the truth. ²⁶They may come to their senses and escape from the devil's trap that holds them captive to do his will.

Avoid people like this

3 Understand that the last days will be dangerous times. ²People will be selfish and love money. They will be the kind of people who brag and who are proud. They will slander others, and they will be disobedient to their parents. They will be ungrateful, unholy, ³unloving, contrary, and critical. They will be without self-control and brutal, and they won't love what is good. ⁴They will be people who are disloyal, reckless, and conceited. They will love pleasure instead of loving God. ⁵They will look like they are religious but deny God's power. Avoid people like this. ⁶Some will slither into households and control immature women who are burdened with sins and driven by all kinds of desires. ⁷These women are always learning, but they can never arrive at an understanding of the truth. ⁸These people oppose the truth in the same way that Jannes and Jambres opposed Moses. Their minds are corrupt and their faith is counterfeit. ⁹But they won't get very far. Their foolishness will become obvious to everyone like those others.

Take Paul as your model

¹⁰But you have paid attention to my teaching, conduct, purpose, faithfulness, patience, love, and endurance. ¹¹You have seen me experience physical abuse and ordeals in places such as Antioch, Iconium, and Lystra. I put up with all sorts of abuse, and the Lord rescued me from it all! ¹²In fact, anyone who wants to live a holy life in Christ Jesus will be harassed. ¹³But evil people and swindlers will grow even worse, as they deceive others while being deceived themselves.

¹⁴But you must continue with the things you have learned and found convincing. You know who taught you. ¹⁵Since childhood you have known the holy scriptures that help you to be wise in a way that leads to salvation through faith that is in Christ Jesus. ¹⁶Every scripture is inspired by God and is useful for teaching, for showing mistakes, for correcting, and for training character, ¹⁷so that the person who belongs to God can be equipped to do everything that is good.

Timothy's commission and Paul's departure

4 I'm giving you this commission in the presence of God and of Christ Jesus, who is coming to judge the living and the dead, and by his appearance and his kingdom. ²Preach the word. Be ready to do it whether it is convenient or inconvenient. Correct, confront, and encourage with patience and instruction. ³There will come a time when people will not tolerate sound teaching. They will collect teachers who say what they want to hear because they are self-centered. ⁴They will turn their back on the truth and turn to myths. ⁵But you must keep control of yourself in all circumstances. Endure suffering, do the work of a preacher of the good news, and carry out your service fully.

⁶I'm already being poured out like a sacrifice to God, and the time of my death is near. ⁷I have fought the good fight, finished the race, and kept the faith. ⁸At last the champion's wreath

that is awarded for righteousness[d] is waiting for me. The Lord, who is the righteous[e] judge, is going to give it to me on that day. He's giving it not only to me but also to all those who have set their heart on waiting for his appearance.

Final instructions

[9] Do your best to come to me quickly. [10] Demas has fallen in love with the present world and has deserted me and has gone to Thessalonica. Crescens has gone to Galatia, and Titus has gone to Dalmatia. [11] Only Luke is with me. Get Mark, and bring him with you. He has been a big help to me in the ministry. [12] I sent Tychicus to Ephesus. [13] When you come, bring along the coat I left with Carpus in Troas. Also bring the scrolls and especially the parchments. [14] Alexander, the craftsman who works with metal, has really hurt me. The Lord will pay him back for what he has done. [15] But watch out for him, because he opposes your teaching.

[16] No one took my side at my first court hearing. Everyone deserted me. I hope that God doesn't hold it against them! [17] But the Lord stood by me and gave me strength, so that the entire message would be preached through me and so all the nations could hear it. I was also rescued from the lion's mouth! [18] The Lord will rescue me from every evil action and will save me for his heavenly kingdom. To him be the glory forever and always. Amen.

Final greetings

[19] Say hello to Prisca and Aquila and the household of Onesiphorus. [20] Erastus stayed in Corinth, and I left Trophimus in Miletus because of his illness. [21] Try hard to come to me before winter. Eubulus, Pudens, Linus, Claudia, and all the brothers and sisters say hello.

[22] The Lord be with your spirit. Grace be with you all.

TITUS

Greeting

1 From Paul, a slave of God and an apostle of Jesus Christ. I'm sent to bring about the faith of God's chosen people and a knowledge of the truth that agrees with godliness. [2] Their faith and this knowledge are based on the hope of eternal life that God, who doesn't lie, promised before time began. [3] God revealed his message at the appropriate time through

preaching, and I was trusted with preaching this message by the command of God our savior. [4] To Titus, my true child in a common faith.

Grace and peace from God the Father and Christ Jesus our savior.

Appointing elders

[5] The reason I left you behind in Crete was to organize whatever needs to be done and to appoint elders in each city, as I told you. [6] Elders should

---

[d] Or justice   [e] Or just

be without fault. They should be faithful to their spouse,[a] and have faithful children who can't be accused of self-indulgence or rebelliousness. [7]This is because supervisors[b] should be without fault as God's managers: they shouldn't be stubborn, irritable, addicted to alcohol, a bully, or greedy. [8]Instead, they should show hospitality, love what is good, and be reasonable, ethical, godly, and self-controlled. [9]They must pay attention to the reliable message as it has been taught to them so that they can encourage people with healthy instruction and refute those who speak against it.

Correcting rebellious people

[10]In fact, there are many who are rebellious people, loudmouths, and deceivers, especially some of those who are Jewish believers.[c] [11]They must be silenced because they upset entire households. They teach what they shouldn't to make money dishonestly. [12]Someone who is one of their own prophets said, "People from Crete are always liars, wild animals, and lazy gluttons." [13]This statement is true. Because of this, correct them firmly, so that they can be healthy in their faith. [14]They shouldn't pay attention to Jewish myths and commands from people who reject the truth. [15]Everything is clean to those who are clean, but nothing is clean to those who are corrupt and without faith. Instead, their mind and conscience are corrupted. [16]They claim to know God, but they deny God by the things that they do. They are detestable, disobedient, and disqualified to do anything good.

Teaching all people how to be godly

2 But you should talk in a way that is consistent with sound teaching. [2]Tell the older men to be sober, dignified, sensible, and healthy in respect to their faith, love, and patience.

[3]Likewise, tell the older women to be reverent in their behavior, teaching what is good, rather than being gossips or addicted to heavy drinking. [4]That way they can mentor young women to love their husbands and children, [5]and to be sensible, morally pure, working at home, kind and submissive to their own husbands, so that God's word won't be ridiculed. [6]Likewise, encourage the younger men to be sensible [7]in every way. Offer yourself as a role model of good actions. Show integrity, seriousness, [8]and a sound message that is above criticism when you teach, so that any opponent will be ashamed because they won't find anything bad to say about us.

[9]Tell slaves to submit to their own masters and please them in everything they do. They shouldn't talk back [10]or steal. Instead, they should show that they are completely reliable in everything so that they might make the teaching about God our savior attractive in every way.

[11]The grace of God has appeared, bringing salvation to all people. [12]It educates us so that we can live sensible, ethical, and godly lives right now by rejecting ungodly lives and the desires of this world. [13]At the same time we wait for the blessed hope and the glorious appearance of our great God and savior Jesus Christ. [14]He gave himself for us in order to rescue us from every kind of

---

[a]Or they should be a one-woman man. [b]Or overseers, bishops [c]Or from the circumcision

lawless behavior, and cleanse a special people for himself who are eager to do good actions.

¹⁵Talk about these things. Encourage and correct with complete authority. Don't let anyone disrespect you.

3 Remind them to submit to rulers and authorities. They should be obedient and ready to do every good thing. ²They shouldn't speak disrespectfully about anyone, but they should be peaceful, kind, and show complete courtesy toward everyone. ³We were once foolish, disobedient, deceived, and slaves to our desires and various pleasures too. We were spending our lives in evil behavior and jealousy. We were disgusting, and we hated other people. ⁴But "when God our savior's kindness and love appeared, ⁵he saved us because of his mercy, not because of righteous things we had done. He did it through the washing of new birth and the renewing by the Holy Spirit, ⁶which God poured out upon us generously through Jesus Christ our savior. ⁷So, since we have been made righteous by his grace, we can inherit the hope for eternal life."

⁸This saying is reliable. And I want you to insist on these things, so that those who have come to believe in God might give careful attention to doing good. These things are good and useful for everyone.

Final instructions and greetings

⁹Avoid stupid controversies, genealogies, and fights about the Law, because they are useless and worthless. ¹⁰After a first and second warning, have nothing more to do with a person who causes conflict, ¹¹because you know that someone like this is twisted and sinful—so they condemn themselves.

¹²When I send Artemas or Tychicus to you, try to come to me in Nicopolis, because I've decided to spend the winter there. ¹³Help Zenas the lawyer and Apollos on their journey with enthusiasm so that they won't need anything. ¹⁴But our people should also learn to devote themselves to doing good in order to meet pressing needs so they aren't unproductive.

¹⁵Everyone with me greets you; greet those who love us faithfully.

Grace be with all of you.

PHILEMON

Greeting

¹From Paul, who is a prisoner for the cause of Christ Jesus, and our brother Timothy.

To Philemon our dearly loved co-worker, ²Apphia our sister, Archippus our fellow soldier, and the church that meets in your house.

³May the grace and peace from God our Father and the Lord Jesus Christ be with you.

Paul's prayer for Philemon

⁴Philemon, I thank my God every time I mention you in my prayers ⁵because I've heard of your love and faithfulness, which you have both for the Lord Jesus and for all God's people. ⁶I pray that your partnership in the faith might become effective by an understanding of all that is good among us in Christ. ⁷I have great joy and encouragement because of your love, since the

hearts of God's people are refreshed by your actions, my brother.

Paul's appeal for Onesimus

[8]Therefore, though I have enough confidence in Christ to command you to do the right thing, [9]I would rather appeal to you through love. I, Paul—an old man, and now also a prisoner for Christ Jesus—[10]appeal to you for my child Onesimus. I became his father in the faith during my time in prison. [11]He was useless to you before, but now he is useful to both of us. [12]I'm sending him back to you, which is like sending you my own heart. [13]I considered keeping him with me so that he might serve me in your place during my time in prison because of the gospel. [14]However, I didn't want to do anything without your consent so that your act of kindness would occur willingly and not under pressure. [15]Maybe this is the reason that Onesimus was separated from you for a while so that you might have him back forever—[16]no longer as a slave but more than a slave—that is, as a dearly loved brother. He is especially a dearly loved brother to me. How much more can he become a brother to you, personally and spiritually in the Lord!

[17]So, if you really consider me a partner, welcome Onesimus as if you were welcoming me. [18]If he has harmed you in any way or owes you money, charge it to my account. [19]I, Paul, will pay it back to you (I'm writing this with my own hand). Of course, I won't mention that you owe me your life.

[20]Yes, brother, I want this favor from you in the Lord! Refresh my heart in Christ. [21]I'm writing to you, confident of your obedience and knowing that you will do more than what I ask. [22]Also, one more thing—prepare a guest room for me. I hope that I will be released from prison to be with you because of your prayers.

Final greeting

[23]Epaphras, who is in prison with me for the cause of Christ Jesus, greets you, [24]as well as my coworkers Mark, Aristarchus, Demas, and Luke. [25]May the grace of the Lord Jesus Christ be with your spirit.

HEBREWS

The Son is God's ultimate messenger

[1]In the past, God spoke through the prophets to our ancestors in many times and many ways. [2]In these final days, though, he spoke to us through a Son. God made his Son the heir of everything and created the world through him. [3]The Son is the light of God's glory and the imprint of God's being. He maintains everything with his powerful message. After he carried out the cleansing of people from their sins, he sat down at the right side of the highest majesty. [4]And the Son became so much greater than the other messengers, such as angels, that he received a more important title than theirs.

Speaking to the Son and angels

[5]After all, when did God ever say to any of the angels:

You are my Son.
  Today I have become your Father?[a]
Or, even,
I will be his Father,
  and he will be my Son?[b]
[6] But then, when he brought his first-born into the world, he said,

All of God's angels must worship him.[c]

[7] He talks about the angels:
He's the one who uses the spirits
  for his messengers
  and who uses flames of fire
  as ministers.[d]

[8] But he says to his Son,
God, your throne is forever
  and your kingdom's scepter
  is a rod of justice.

[9] *You loved righteousness*
  and hated lawless behavior.
  That is why God, your God,
  has anointed you with oil
    instead of your companions.[e]

[10] And he says,
You, Lord, laid the earth's foundations
  in the beginning,
  and the heavens are made
  by your hands.

[11] *They will pass away,*
  but you remain.
They will all wear out like old clothes.
[12] *You will fold them up like a coat.*
They will be changed
  like a person changes clothes,
  but you stay the same,
  and the years of your life
    won't come to an end.[f]

[13] When has he ever said to any of the angels,

Sit at my right side
  until I put your enemies
    under your feet like a footstool?[g]

[14] Aren't all the angels ministering spirits who are sent to serve those who are going to inherit salvation?

Listen to the Son's message

2 This is why it's necessary for us to pay more attention to what we have heard, or else we may drift away from it. [2] If the message that was spoken by angels was reliable, and every offense and act of disobedience received an appropriate consequence, [3] how will we escape if we ignore such a great salvation? It was first announced through the Lord, and then it was confirmed by those who heard him. [4] God also vouched for their message with signs, amazing things, various miracles, and gifts from the Holy Spirit, which were handed out the way he wanted.

Jesus is the enthroned human being

[5] God didn't put the world that is coming (the world we are talking about) under the angels' control. [6] Instead, someone declared somewhere,

What is humanity
  that you think about them?
  Or what are human beings
    that you care about them?
[7] *For a while you made them*
  lower than angels.
  You crowned the human beings
    with glory and honor.
[8] *You put everything*
  under their control.[h]

When he puts everything under their control, he doesn't leave anything out of control. But right now, we don't see everything under their control yet.

[a] Ps 2:7 [b] 2 Sam 7:14; 1 Chron 17:13 [c] Deut 32:43 and Ps 97:7 LXX [d] Ps 104:4 [e] Ps 45:6-7
[f] Ps 102:25-27 [g] Ps 110:1 [h] Ps 8:4-6

⁹However, we do see the one who was made lower in order than the angels for a little while—it's Jesus! He's the one who is now crowned with glory and honor because of the suffering of his death. He suffered death so that he could taste death for everyone through God's grace.

Qualified to be a high priest

¹⁰It was appropriate for God, for whom and through whom everything exists, to use experiences of suffering to make perfect the pioneer of salvation. This salvation belongs to many sons and daughters whom he's leading to glory. ¹¹This is because the one who makes people holy and the people who are being made holy all come from one source. That is why Jesus isn't ashamed to call them brothers and sisters when he says,

¹² *I will publicly announce your name*
    to my brothers and sisters.
  I will praise you in the middle
    of the assembly.[i]
¹³He also says,
  I will rely on him.[j]
And also,
  Here I am with the children whom God
    has given to me.[k]

¹⁴Therefore, since the children share in flesh and blood, he also shared the same things in the same way. He did this to destroy the one who holds the power over death—the devil—by dying. ¹⁵He set free those who were held in slavery their entire lives by their fear of death. ¹⁶Of course, he isn't trying to help angels, but rather he's helping Abraham's descendants. ¹⁷Therefore, he had to be made like his brothers and sisters in every way. This was so that he could become a merciful and faithful high priest in things relating to God, in order to wipe away the sins of the people. ¹⁸He's able to help those who are being tempted, since he himself experienced suffering when he was tempted.

We are Jesus' house

3 Therefore, brothers and sisters who are partners in the heavenly calling, think about Jesus, the apostle and high priest of our confession. ²Jesus was faithful to the one who appointed him just like Moses was faithful in God's house. ³But he deserves greater glory than Moses in the same way that the builder of the house deserves more honor than the house itself. ⁴Every house is built by someone, and God is the builder of everything. ⁵Moses was faithful in all God's house as a servant in order to affirm the things that would be spoken later. ⁶But Jesus was faithful over God's house as a Son. We are his house if we hold on to the confidence and the pride that our hope gives us.

Respond to Jesus' voice now

⁷So, as the Holy Spirit says,
  Today, if you hear his voice,
⁸ *don't have stubborn hearts*
    as they did in the rebellion,
  on the day when they tested me
    in the desert.
⁹ *That is where your ancestors challenged*
    and tested me,
  though they had seen my work
    for forty years.
¹⁰ *So I was angry with them.*
  I said, "Their hearts always go off course,
    and they don't know my ways."

[i]Ps 22:22 [j]Isa 8:17 LXX [k]Isa 8:18

[11] *Because of my anger I swore:*
    "They will never enter my rest!"[l]
[12] Watch out, brothers and sisters, so that none of you have an evil, unfaithful heart that abandons the living God. [13] Instead, encourage each other every day, as long as it's called "today," so that none of you become insensitive to God because of sin's deception. [14] We are partners with Christ, but only if we hold on to the confidence we had in the beginning until the end.

[15] When it says,

Today, if you hear his voice,
    don't have stubborn hearts
        as they did in the rebellion.[m]

[16] Who was it who rebelled when they heard his voice? Wasn't it all of those who were brought out of Egypt by Moses? [17] And with whom was God angry for forty years? Wasn't it with the ones who sinned, whose bodies fell in the desert? [18] And against whom did he swear that they would never enter his rest, if not against the ones who were disobedient? [19] We see that they couldn't enter because of their lack of faith.

Enter the rest

4 Therefore, since the promise that we can enter into rest is still open, let's be careful so that none of you will appear to miss it. [2] We also had the good news preached to us, just as the Israelites did. However, the message they heard didn't help them, because they weren't united in faith with the ones who listened to it. [3] We who have faith are entering the rest. As God said,

And because of my anger I swore:
    "They will never enter into my rest!"[n]

And yet God's works were completed at the foundation of the world. [4] Then somewhere he said this about the seventh day of creation: *God rested on the seventh day from all his works.*[o] [5] But again, in the passage above, God said, *They will never enter my rest!*[p] [6] Therefore, it's left open for some to enter it, and the ones who had the good news preached to them before didn't enter because of disobedience. [7] Just as it says in the passage above, God designates a certain day as "today," when he says through David much later,

Today, if you hear his voice,
    don't have stubborn hearts.[q]

[8] If Joshua gave the Israelites rest, God wouldn't have spoken about another day later on. [9] So you see that a sabbath rest is left open for God's people. [10] The one who entered God's rest also rested from his works, just as God rested from his own.

First summary of the message

[11] Therefore, let's make every effort to enter that rest so that no one will fall by following the same example of disobedience, [12] because God's word is living, active, and sharper than any two-edged sword. It penetrates to the point that it separates the soul from the spirit and the joints from the marrow. It's able to judge the heart's thoughts and intentions. [13] No creature is hidden from it, but rather everything is naked and exposed to the eyes of the one to whom we have to give an answer.

[14] Also, let's hold on to the confession since we have a great high priest who passed through the heavens, who is Jesus, God's Son; [15] because we don't

[l]Ps 95:7-11 [m]Ps 95:7-8 [n]Ps 95:11 [o]Gen 2:2 [p]Ps 95:11 [q]Ps 95:7-8

have a high priest who can't sympathize with our weaknesses but instead one who was tempted in every way that we are, except without sin.

[16] Finally, let's draw near to the throne of favor with confidence so that we can receive mercy and find grace when we need help.

Introduction to a deeper teaching

5 Every high priest is taken from the people and put in charge of things that relate to God for their sake, in order to offer gifts and sacrifices for sins. [2] The high priest is able to deal gently with the ignorant and those who are misled since he himself is prone to weakness. [3] Because of his weakness, he must offer sacrifices for his own sins as well as for the people. [4] No one takes this honor for themselves but takes it only when they are called by God, just like Aaron.

[5] In the same way Christ also didn't promote himself to become high priest. Instead, it was the one who said to him,

You are my Son.
Today I have become your Father,
[6] as he also says in another place,
You are a priest forever,
according to the order
of Melchizedek.[ᵀ]

[7] During his days on earth, Christ offered prayers and requests with loud cries and tears as his sacrifices to the one who was able to save him from death. He was heard because of his godly devotion. [8] Although he was a Son, he learned obedience from what he suffered. [9] After he had been made perfect, he became the source of eternal salvation for everyone who obeys

him. [10] He was appointed by God to be a high priest according to the order of Melchizedek.

[11] We have a lot to say about this topic, and it's difficult to explain, because you have been lazy and you haven't been listening. [12] Although you should have been teachers by now, you need someone to teach you an introduction to the basics about God's message. You have come to the place where you need milk instead of solid food. [13] Everyone who lives on milk is not used to the word of righteousness, because they are babies. [14] But solid food is for the mature, whose senses are trained by practice to distinguish between good and evil.

Let's press on to maturity

6 So let's press on to maturity, by moving on from the basics about Christ's word. Let's not lay a foundation of turning away from dead works, of faith in God, [2] of teaching about ritual ways to wash with water, laying on of hands, the resurrection from the dead, and eternal judgment—all over again. [3] We're going to press on, if God allows it.

[4] Because it's impossible to restore people to changed hearts and lives who turn away once they have seen the light, tasted the heavenly gift, become partners with the Holy Spirit, [5] and tasted God's good word and the powers of the coming age. [6] They are crucifying God's Son all over again and exposing him to public shame. [7] The ground receives a blessing from God when it drinks up the rain that regularly comes and falls on it and yields a useful crop for those people for whom it is being farmed. [8] But if it produces thorns and thistles, it's useless and close to being cursed. It ends up being burned.

ᵀPs 110:4

Make your hope sure

⁹But we are convinced of better things in your case, brothers and sisters, even though we are talking this way—things that go together with salvation. ¹⁰God isn't unjust so that he forgets your efforts and the love you have shown for his name's sake when you served and continue to serve God's holy people. ¹¹But we desperately want each of you to show the same effort to make your hope sure until the end. ¹²This is so you won't be lazy but follow the example of the ones who inherit the promises through faith and patience.

Our hope in Jesus' priesthood

¹³When God gave Abraham his promise, he swore by himself since he couldn't swear by anyone greater. ¹⁴He said, *I will certainly bless you and multiply your descendants.*ˢ ¹⁵So Abraham obtained the promise by showing patience. ¹⁶People pledge by something greater than themselves. A solemn pledge guarantees what they say and shuts down any argument. ¹⁷When God wanted to further demonstrate to the heirs of the promise that his purpose doesn't change, he guaranteed it with a solemn pledge. ¹⁸So these are two things that don't change, because it's impossible for God to lie. He did this so that we, who have taken refuge in him, can be encouraged to grasp the hope that is lying in front of us. ¹⁹This hope, which is a safe and secure anchor for our whole being, enters the sanctuary behind the curtain. ²⁰That's where Jesus went in advance and entered for us, since he became a high priest according to the order of Melchizedek.

7This Melchizedek, who was king of Salem and priest of the Most High God, met Abraham as he returned from the defeat of the kings, and Melchizedek blessed him. ²Abraham gave a tenth of everything to him. His name means first "king of righteousness," and then "king of Salem," that is, "king of peace." ³He is without father or mother or any family. He has no beginning or end of life, but he's like God's Son and remains a priest for all time.

A priest like Melchizedek

⁴See how great Melchizedek was! Abraham, the father of the people, gave him a tenth of everything he captured. ⁵The descendants of Levi who receive the office of priest have a commandment under the Law to collect a tenth of everything from the people who are their brothers and sisters, though they also are descended from Abraham. ⁶But Melchizedek, who isn't related to them, received a tenth of everything from Abraham and blessed the one who had received the promises. ⁷Without question, the less important person is blessed by the more important person. ⁸In addition, in one case a tenth is received by people who die, and in the other case, the tenth is received by someone who continues to live, according to the record. ⁹It could be said that Levi, who received a tenth, paid a tenth through Abraham ¹⁰because he was still in his ancestor's body when Abraham paid the tenth to Melchizedek.

¹¹So if perfection came through the levitical office of priest (for the people received the Law under the priests), why was there still a need to speak about

ˢGen 22:17

raising up another priest according to the order of Melchizedek rather than one according to the order of Aaron? [12]When the order of the priest changes, there has to be a change in the Law as well. [13]The person we are talking about belongs to another tribe, and no one ever served at the altar from that tribe. [14]It's clear that our Lord came from the tribe of Judah, but Moses never said anything about priests from that tribe. [15]And it's even clearer if another priest appears who is like Melchizedek. [16]He has become a priest by the power of a life that can't be destroyed, rather than a legal requirement about physical descent. [17]This is confirmed:

> You are a priest forever,
>   according to the order
>   of Melchizedek.[t]

Able to save completely

[18]On the one hand, an earlier command is set aside because it was weak and useless [19](because the Law made nothing perfect). On the other hand, a better hope is introduced, through which we draw near to God. [20]And this was not done without a solemn pledge! The others have become priests without a solemn pledge, [21]but this priest was affirmed with a solemn pledge by the one who said,

> The Lord has made a solemn pledge
>   and will not change his mind:
> You are a priest forever.[u]

[22]As a result, Jesus has become the guarantee of a better covenant. [23]The others who became priests are numerous because death prevented them from continuing to serve. [24]In contrast, he holds the office of priest permanently because he continues to serve forever. [25]This is why he can completely save those who are approaching God through him, because he always lives to speak with God for them.

[26]It's appropriate for us to have this kind of high priest: holy, innocent, incorrupt, separate from sinners, and raised high above the heavens. [27]He doesn't need to offer sacrifices every day like the other high priests, first for their own sins and then for the sins of the people. He did this once for all when he offered himself. [28]The Law appoints people who are prone to weakness as high priests, but the content of the solemn pledge, which came after the Law, appointed a Son who has been made perfect forever.

Meeting tents, sacrifices, and covenants

8 Now the main point of what we are saying is this: We have this kind of high priest. He sat down at the right side of the throne of the majesty in the heavens. [2]He's serving as a priest in the holy place, which is the true meeting tent that God, not any human being, set up. [3]Every high priest is appointed to offer gifts and sacrifices. So it's necessary for this high priest also to have something to offer. [4]If he was located on earth, he wouldn't be a priest because there are already others who offer gifts based on the Law. [5]They serve in a place that is a copy and shadow of the heavenly meeting tent. This is indicated when Moses was warned by God when he was about to set up the meeting tent: See that you follow the pattern that I showed you on the mountain in every

---

detail.ᵛ ⁶But now, Jesus has received a superior priestly service just as he arranged a better covenant that is enacted with better promises.

⁷If the first covenant had been without fault, it wouldn't have made sense to expect a second. ⁸But God did find fault with them, since he says,

Look, the days are coming,
    says the Lord,
    when I will make a covenant
        with the house of Israel,
    and I will make a new covenant
        with the house of Judah.
⁹ It will not be like the covenant
    that I made with their ancestors
    on the day I took them by the hand
        to lead them out of the land
        of Egypt,
    because they did not continue
        to keep my covenant,
    and I lost interest in them,
        says the Lord.
¹⁰ This is the covenant that I will make
    with the house of Israel
        after those days, says the Lord.
    I will place my laws in their minds,
        and write them on their hearts.
    I will be their God,
        and they will be my people.
¹¹ And each person won't ever teach
        a neighbor
    or their brother or sister, saying,
        "Know the Lord,"
    because they will all know me,
        from the least important of them
            to the most important;
¹² because I will be lenient
        toward their unjust actions,
    and I won't remember
        their sins anymore.ʷ
¹³When it says new, it makes the first

obsolete. And if something is old and outdated, it's close to disappearing.

Christ's service in the heavenly meeting tent

9 So then the first covenant had regulations for the priests' service and the holy place on earth. ²They pitched the first tent called the holy place. It contained the lampstand, the table, and the loaves of bread presented to God. ³There was a tent behind the second curtain called the holy of holies. ⁴It had the gold altar for incense and the chest containing the covenant, which was covered with gold on all sides. In the chest there was a gold jar containing manna, Aaron's rod that budded, and the stone tablets of the covenant. ⁵Above the chest there were magnificent winged creaturesˣ casting their shadow over the seat of the chest, where sin is taken care of. Right now we can't talk about these things in detail. ⁶When these things have been prepared in this way, priests enter the first tent all the time as they perform their service. ⁷But only the high priest enters the second tent once a year. He never does this without blood, which he offers for himself and for the sins the people committed in ignorance. ⁸With this, the Holy Spirit is showing that the way into the holy place hadn't been revealed yet while the first tent was standing. ⁹This is a symbol for the present time. It shows that the gifts and sacrifices that are being offered can't perfect the conscience of the one who is serving. ¹⁰These are superficial regulations that are only about food, drink, and various ritual ways to wash with water. They

are regulations that have been imposed until the time of the new order.

[11] But Christ has appeared as the high priest of the good things that have happened. He passed through the greater and more perfect meeting tent, which isn't made by human hands (that is, it's not a part of this world). [12] He entered the holy of holies once for all by his own blood, not by the blood of goats or calves, securing our deliverance for all time. [13] If the blood of goats and bulls and the sprinkled ashes of cows made spiritually contaminated people holy and clean, [14] how much more will the blood of Jesus wash our consciences clean from dead works in order to serve the living God? He offered himself to God through the eternal Spirit as a sacrifice without any flaw.

Christ's death and the new covenant

[15] This is why he's the mediator of a new covenant (which is a will): so that those who are called might receive the promise of the eternal inheritance on the basis of his death. His death occurred to set them free from the offenses committed under the first covenant. [16] When there is a will, you need to confirm the death of the one who made the will. [17] This is because a will takes effect only after a death, since it's not in force while the one who made the will is alive. [18] So not even the first covenant was put into effect without blood. [19] Moses took the blood of calves and goats, along with water, scarlet wool, and hyssop, and sprinkled both the Law scroll itself and all the people after he had proclaimed every command of the

Law to all the people. [20] While he did it, he said, *This is the blood of the covenant that God established for you.*[y] [21] And in the same way he sprinkled the meeting tent and also all the equipment that would be used in the priests' service with blood. [22] Almost everything is cleansed by blood, according to the Law's regulations, and there is no forgiveness without blood being shed.

[23] So it was necessary for the copies of the heavenly things to be cleansed with these sacrifices, but the heavenly things had to be cleansed with better sacrifices than these. [24] Christ didn't enter the holy place (which is a copy of the true holy place) made by human hands, but into heaven itself, so that he now appears in God's presence for us. [25] He didn't enter to offer himself over and over again, like the high priest enters the earthly holy place every year with blood that isn't his. [26] If that were so, then Jesus would have to suffer many times since the foundation of the world. Instead, he has now appeared once at the end of the ages to get rid of sin by sacrificing himself. [27] People are destined to die once and then face judgment. [28] In the same way, Christ was also offered once to take on himself the sins of many people. He will appear a second time, not to take away sin but to save those who are eagerly waiting for him.

Christ's once-for-all sacrifice

10 The Law is a shadow of the good things that are coming, not the real things themselves. It never can perfect the ones who are trying to draw near to God through the same sacrifices that are offered continually every

[y] Exod 24:8

year. [2]Otherwise, wouldn't they have stopped being offered? If the people carrying out their religious duties had been completely cleansed once, no one would have been aware of sin anymore. [3]Instead, these sacrifices are a reminder of sin every year, [4]because it's impossible for the blood of bulls and goats to take away sins.

[5]Therefore, when he comes into the world he says,

You didn't want a sacrifice
or an offering,
  but you prepared a body for me;
[6]*you weren't pleased*
  with entirely burned offerings
  or a sin offering.
[7]*So then I said,*
  "Look, I've come to do your will, God.
  This has been written about me
    in the scroll."[a]

[8]He says above, *You didn't want* and *you weren't pleased with a sacrifice or an offering or with entirely burned offerings or a purification offering,*[a] which are offered because the Law requires them. [9]Then he said, *Look, I've come to do your will.*[b] He puts an end to the first to establish the second. [10]We have been made holy by God's will through the offering of Jesus Christ's body once for all.

[11]Every priest stands every day serving and offering the same sacrifices over and over, sacrifices that can never take away sins. [12]But when this priest offered one sacrifice for sins for all time, he sat down at the right side of God. [13]Since then, he's waiting until his enemies are made into a footstool for his feet, [14]because he perfected the people who are being made holy with one offering for all time.

[15]The Holy Spirit affirms this when saying,

[16]*This is the covenant that I will make*
  with them.
After these days, says the Lord,
I will place my laws in their hearts
  and write them on their minds.
[17]*And I won't remember their sins*
  and their lawless behavior anymore.[c]

[18]When there is forgiveness for these things, there is no longer an offering for sin.

Second summary of the message

[19]Brothers and sisters, we have confidence that we can enter the holy of holies by means of Jesus' blood, [20]through a new and living way that he opened up for us through the curtain, which is his body, [21]and we have a great high priest over God's house.

[22]Therefore, let's draw near with a genuine heart with the certainty that our faith gives us, since our hearts are sprinkled clean from an evil conscience and our bodies are washed with pure water.

[23]Let's hold on to the confession of our hope without wavering, because the one who made the promises is reliable.

[24]And let us consider each other carefully for the purpose of sparking love and good deeds. [25]Don't stop meeting together with other believers, which some people have gotten into the habit of doing. Instead, encourage each other, especially as you see the day drawing near.

Judgment for intentional sin

[26]If we make the decision to sin after we receive the knowledge of the truth, there isn't a sacrifice for sins left any

---

[z]Ps 40:6-8   [a]Ps 40:6   [b]Ps 40:7-8   [c]Jer 31:33-34

longer. [27]There's only a scary expectation of judgment and of a burning fire that's going to devour God's opponents. [28]When someone rejected the Law from Moses, they were put to death without mercy on the basis of the testimony of two or three witnesses. [29]How much worse punishment do you think is deserved by the person who walks all over God's Son, who acts as if the blood of the covenant that made us holy is just ordinary blood, and who insults the Spirit of grace? [30]We know the one who said,

Judgment is mine;

I will pay people back.[d]

And he also said,

The Lord will judge his people.[e]

[31]It's scary to fall into the hands of the living God!

Confidence and faith to endure

[32]But remember the earlier days, after you saw the light. You stood your ground while you were suffering from an enormous amount of pressure. [33]Sometimes you were exposed to insults and abuse in public. Other times you became partners with those who were treated that way. [34]You even showed sympathy toward people in prison and accepted the confiscation of your possessions with joy, since you knew that you had better and lasting possessions. [35]So don't throw away your confidence—it brings a great reward. [36]You need to endure so that you can receive the promises after you do God's will.

[37]In a little while longer,

the one who is coming will come
and won't delay;

[38]but my righteous one will live by faith,
and my whole being won't be pleased
with anyone who shrinks back.[f]

[39]But we aren't the sort of people who timidly draw back and end up being destroyed. We're the sort of people who have faith so that our whole beings are preserved.

Description of faith

11 Faith is the reality of what we hope for, the proof of what we don't see. [2]The elders in the past were approved because they showed faith.

Acts of faith by God's people

[3]By faith we understand that the universe has been created by a word from God so that the visible came into existence from the invisible.

[4]By faith Abel offered a better sacrifice to God than Cain, which showed that he was righteous, since God gave approval to him for his gift. Though he died, he's still speaking through faith.

[5]By faith Enoch was taken up so that he didn't see death, and he wasn't found because God took him up.[g] He was given approval for having pleased God before he was taken up. [6]It's impossible to please God without faith because the one who draws near to God must believe that he exists and that he rewards people who try to find him.

[7]By faith Noah responded with godly fear when he was warned about events he hadn't seen yet. He built an ark to deliver his household. With his faith, he criticized the world and became an heir of the righteousness that comes from faith.

[8]By faith Abraham obeyed when he

---

[d]Deut 32:35 [e]Deut 32:36; Ps 135:14 [f]Hab 2:3-4 [g]Gen 5:24

was called to go out to a place that he was going to receive as an inheritance. He went out without knowing where he was going.

⁹By faith he lived in the land he had been promised as a stranger. He lived in tents along with Isaac and Jacob, who were coheirs of the same promise. ¹⁰He was looking forward to a city that has foundations, whose architect and builder is God.

¹¹By faith even Sarah received the ability to have a child, though she herself was barren and past the age for having children, because she believed that the one who promised was faithful. ¹²So descendants were born from one man (and he was as good as dead). They were as many as the number of the stars in the sky and as countless as the grains of sand on the seashore. ¹³All these people died in faith without receiving the promises, but they saw the promises from a distance and welcomed them. They confessed that they were strangers and immigrants on earth. ¹⁴People who say this kind of thing make it clear that they are looking for a homeland. ¹⁵If they had been thinking about the country that they had left, they would have had the opportunity to return to it. ¹⁶But at this point in time, they are longing for a better country, that is, a heavenly one. Therefore, God isn't ashamed to be called their God—he has prepared a city for them.

¹⁷By faith Abraham offered Isaac when he was tested. The one who received the promises was offering his only son. ¹⁸He had been told concerning him, *Your legitimate descendants will*

*come from Isaac.*ʰ ¹⁹He figured that God could even raise him from the dead. So in a way he did receive him back from the dead.

²⁰By faith Isaac also blessed Jacob and Esau concerning their future.

²¹By faith Jacob blessed each of Joseph's sons as he was dying and *bowed in worship over the head of his staff.*ⁱ

²²By faith Joseph recalled the exodus of the Israelites at the end of his life, and gave instructions about burying his bones.

²³By faith Moses was hidden by his parents for three months when he was born, because they saw that the child was beautiful and they weren't afraid of the king's orders.

²⁴By faith Moses refused to be called the son of Pharaoh's daughter when he was grown up. ²⁵He chose to be mistreated with God's people instead of having the temporary pleasures of sin. ²⁶He thought that the abuses he suffered for Christ were more valuable than the treasures of Egypt, since he was looking forward to the reward.

²⁷By faith he left Egypt without being afraid of the king's anger. He kept on going as if he could see what is invisible.

²⁸By faith he kept the Passover and the sprinkling of blood, in order that the destroyer could not touch their firstborn children.

²⁹By faith they crossed the Red Sea as if they were on dry land, but when the Egyptians tried it, they were drowned.

³⁰By faith Jericho's walls fell after the people marched around them for seven days.

³¹By faith Rahab the prostitute wasn't

ʰGen 21:12 ⁱGen 47:31 LXX

killed with the disobedient because she welcomed the spies in peace.

³²What more can I say? I would run out of time if I told you about Gideon, Barak, Samson, Jephthah, David, Samuel, and the prophets. ³³Through faith they conquered kingdoms, brought about justice, realized promises, shut the mouths of lions, ³⁴put out raging fires, escaped from the edge of the sword, found strength in weakness, were mighty in war, and routed foreign armies. ³⁵Women received back their dead by resurrection. Others were tortured and refused to be released so they could gain a better resurrection.

³⁶But others experienced public shame by being taunted and whipped; they were even put in chains and in prison. ³⁷They were stoned to death, they were cut in two, and they died by being murdered with swords. They went around wearing the skins of sheep and goats, needy, oppressed, and mistreated. ³⁸The world didn't deserve them. They wandered around in deserts, mountains, caves, and holes in the ground.

³⁹All these people didn't receive what was promised, though they were given approval for their faith. ⁴⁰God provided something better for us so they wouldn't be made perfect without us.

Let's also run the race

12 So then, with endurance, let's also run the race that is laid out in front of us, since we have such a great cloud of witnesses surrounding us. Let's throw off any extra baggage, get rid of the sin that trips us up, ²and fix our eyes on Jesus, faith's pioneer and perfecter. He endured the cross, ignoring the shame, for the sake of the joy that was laid out in front of him, and sat down at the right side of God's throne.

Run the race with discipline

³Think about the one who endured such opposition from sinners so that you won't be discouraged and you won't give up. ⁴In your struggle against sin, you haven't resisted yet to the point of shedding blood, ⁵and you have forgotten the encouragement that addresses you as sons and daughters:

My child, don't make light
 of the Lord's discipline
 or give up when you are corrected
 by him,
⁶ because the Lord disciplines
 whomever he loves,
 and he punishes every son
 or daughter whom he accepts.ʲ

⁷Bear hardship for the sake of discipline. God is treating you like sons and daughters! What child isn't disciplined by his or her father? ⁸But if you don't experience discipline, which happens to all children, then you are illegitimate and not real sons and daughters. ⁹What's more, we had human parents who disciplined us, and we respected them for it. How much more should we submit to the Father of spirits and live? ¹⁰Our human parents disciplined us for a little while, as it seemed best to them, but God does it for our benefit so that we can share his holiness. ¹¹No discipline is fun while it lasts, but it seems painful at the time. Later, however, it yields the peaceful fruit of righteousness for those who have been trained by it.

ʲProv 3:11-12

¹²So strengthen your drooping hands and weak knees! ¹³Make straight paths for your feet so that if any part is lame, it will be healed rather than injured more seriously. ¹⁴Pursue the goal of peace along with everyone—and holiness as well, because no one will see the Lord without it. ¹⁵Make sure that no one misses out on God's grace. Make sure that no root of bitterness grows up that might cause trouble and pollute many people. ¹⁶Make sure that no one becomes sexually immoral or ungodly like Esau. He sold his inheritance as the oldest son for one meal. ¹⁷You know that afterward, when he wanted to inherit the blessing, he was rejected because he couldn't find a way to change his heart and life, though he looked for it with tears.

Priestly service in heavenly Jerusalem

¹⁸You haven't drawn near to something that can be touched: a burning fire, darkness, shadow, a whirlwind, ¹⁹a blast of a trumpet, and a sound of words that made the ones who heard it beg that there wouldn't be one more word. ²⁰They couldn't stand the command, *If even a wild animal touches the mountain, it must be stoned.*ᵏ ²¹The sight was so frightening that Moses said, "I'm terrified and shaking!"

²²But you have drawn near to Mount Zion, the city of the living God, heavenly Jerusalem, to countless angels in a festival gathering, ²³to the assembly of God's firstborn children who are registered in heaven, to God the judge of all, to the spirits of the righteous who have been made perfect, ²⁴to Jesus the

mediator of the new covenant, and to the sprinkled blood that speaks better than Abel's blood.

²⁵See to it that you don't resist the one who is speaking. If the people didn't escape when they refused to listen to the one who warned them on earth, how will we escape if we reject the one who is warning from heaven? ²⁶His voice shook the earth then, but now he has made a promise: *Still once more I will shake not only the earth but heaven also.*ˡ ²⁷The words "still once more" reveal the removal of what is shaken—the things that are part of this creation—so that what isn't shaken will remain. ²⁸Therefore, since we are receiving a kingdom that can't be shaken, let's continue to express our gratitude.ᵐ With this gratitude, let's serveⁿ in a way that is pleasing to God with respect and awe, ²⁹because our God really is a consuming fire.

Our acts of service and sacrifice

13Keep loving each other like family. ²Don't neglect to open up your homes to guests, because by doing this some have been hosts to angels without knowing it. ³Remember prisoners as if you were in prison with them, and people who are mistreated as if you were in their place. ⁴Marriage must be honored in every respect, with no cheating on the relationship, because God will judge the sexually immoral person and the person who commits adultery. ⁵Your way of life should be free from the love of money, and you should be content with what you have. After all, he has said, *I will never leave*

ᵏExod 19:12-13 ˡExod 19:18 ᵐOr *hold on to grace* ⁿOr *offer priestly service* you or abandon you.° ⁶ This is why we can confidently say,

> The Lord is my helper,
>> and I won't be afraid.
> What can people do to me?ᵖ

⁷ Remember your leaders who spoke God's word to you. Imitate their faith as you consider the way their lives turned out. ⁸ Jesus Christ is the same yesterday, today, and forever!

⁹ Don't be misled by the many strange teachings out there. It's a good thing for the heart to be strengthened by grace rather than by food. Food doesn't help those who live in this context. ¹⁰ We have an altar, and those who serve as priests in the meeting tent don't have the right to eat from it. ¹¹ The blood of the animals is carried into the holy of holies by the high priest as an offering for sin, and their bodies are burned outside the camp. ¹² And so Jesus also suffered outside the city gate to make the people holy with his own blood.

¹³ So now, let's go to him outside the camp, bearing his shame. ¹⁴ We don't have a permanent city here, but rather we are looking for the city that is still to come.

¹⁵ So let's continually offer up a sacrifice of praise through him, which is the fruit from our lips that confess his name. ¹⁶ Don't forget to do good and to share what you have because God is pleased with these kinds of sacrifices.

Closing greeting and blessing

¹⁷ Rely on your leaders and defer to them, because they watch over your whole being as people who are going to be held responsible for you. They need to be able to do this with pleasure and not with complaints about you, because that wouldn't help you. ¹⁸ Pray for us. We're sure that we have a good conscience, and we want to do the right thing in every way. ¹⁹ I'm particularly asking you to do this so that I can be returned to you quickly.

²⁰ May the God of peace,
>> who brought back
>>> the great shepherd of the sheep,
>> our Lord Jesus,
>>> from the dead by the blood
>>> of the eternal covenant,
²¹ equip you with every good thing
>> to do his will,
>>> by developing in us what pleases
>>> him through Jesus Christ.
> To him be the glory
>> forever and always. Amen.

²² I urge you, brothers and sisters, to put up with this message of encouragement, since I've only written a short letter to you! ²³ You should know that our brother Timothy has been set free. If he comes soon, we will travel together to see you.

²⁴ Greet your leaders and all of God's holy people. The group from Italy greets you.

²⁵ May grace be with all of you.

°Deut 31:6; Gen 28:15   ᵖPs 118:6

JAMES

Greeting

1 From James, a slave of God and of the Lord Jesus Christ.

To the twelve tribes who are scattered outside the land of Israel. Greetings!

Stand firm

2 My brothers and sisters, think of the various tests you encounter as occasions for joy. 3 After all, you know that the testing of your faith produces endurance. 4 Let this endurance complete its work so that you may be fully mature, complete, and lacking in nothing. 5 But anyone who needs wisdom should ask God, whose very nature is to give to everyone without a second thought, without keeping score. Wisdom will certainly be given to those who ask. 6 Whoever asks shouldn't hesitate. They should ask in faith, without doubting. Whoever doubts is like the surf of the sea, tossed and turned by the wind. 7 People like that should never imagine that they will receive anything from the Lord. 8 They are double-minded, unstable in all their ways.

9 Brothers and sisters who are poor should find satisfaction in their high status. 10 Those who are wealthy should find satisfaction in their low status, because they will die off like wildflowers. 11 The sun rises with its scorching heat and dries up the grass so that its flowers fall and its beauty is lost. Just like that, in the midst of their daily lives, the wealthy will waste away. 12 Those who stand firm during testing are blessed. They are tried and true. They will receive the life God has promised to those who love him as their reward.

Our cravings versus God's gifts

13 No one who is tested should say, "God is tempting me!" This is because God is not tempted by any form of evil, nor does he tempt anyone. 14 Everyone is tempted by their own cravings; they are lured away and enticed by them. 15 Once those cravings conceive, they give birth to sin; and when sin grows up, it gives birth to death.

16 Don't be misled, my dear brothers and sisters. 17 Every good gift, every perfect gift, comes from above. These gifts come down from the Father, the creator of the heavenly lights, in whose character there is no change at all. 18 He chose to give us birth by his true word, and here is the result: we are like the first crop from the harvest of everything he created.

Welcoming and doing the word

19 Know this, my dear brothers and sisters: everyone should be quick to listen, slow to speak, and slow to grow angry. 20 This is because an angry person doesn't produce God's righteousness. 21 Therefore, with humility, set aside all moral filth and the growth of wickedness, and welcome the word planted deep inside you—the very word that is able to save you.

22 You must be doers of the word and not only hearers who mislead themselves. 23 Those who hear but don't do the word are like those who look at their faces in a mirror. 24 They look at themselves, walk away, and immediately forget what they were like. 25 But there are those who study the perfect law, the law of freedom, and continue

to do it. They don't listen and then forget, but they put it into practice in their lives. They will be blessed in whatever they do.

²⁶If those who claim devotion to God don't control what they say, they mislead themselves. Their devotion is worthless. ²⁷True devotion, the kind that is pure and faultless before God the Father, is this: to care for orphans and widows in their difficulties and to keep the world from contaminating us.

Don't show favoritism

2 My brothers and sisters, when you show favoritism you deny the faithfulness of our Lord Jesus Christ, who has been resurrected in glory. ²Imagine two people coming into your meeting. One has a gold ring and fine clothes, while the other is poor, dressed in filthy rags. ³Then suppose that you were to take special notice of the one wearing fine clothes, saying, "Here's an excellent place. Sit here." But to the poor person you say, "Stand over there"; or, "Here, sit at my feet." ⁴Wouldn't you have shown favoritism among yourselves and become evil-minded judges?

⁵My dear brothers and sisters, listen! Hasn't God chosen those who are poor by worldly standards to be rich in terms of faith? Hasn't God chosen the poor as heirs of the kingdom he has promised to those who love him? ⁶But you have dishonored the poor. Don't the wealthy make life difficult for you? Aren't they the ones who drag you into court? ⁷Aren't they the ones who insult the good name spoken over you at your baptism?

⁸You do well when you really fulfill the royal law found in scripture, *Love your neighbor as yourself.*ᵃ ⁹But when you show favoritism, you are committing a sin, and by that same law you are exposed as a lawbreaker. ¹⁰Anyone who tries to keep all of the Law but fails at one point is guilty of failing to keep all of it. ¹¹The one who said, *Don't commit adultery,* also said, *Don't commit murder.*ᵇ So if you don't commit adultery but do commit murder, you are a lawbreaker. ¹²In every way, then, speak and act as people who will be judged by the law of freedom. ¹³There will be no mercy in judgment for anyone who hasn't shown mercy. Mercy overrules judgment.

Showing faith

¹⁴My brothers and sisters, what good is it if people say they have faith but do nothing to show it? Claiming to have faith can't save anyone, can it? ¹⁵Imagine a brother or sister who is naked and never has enough food to eat. ¹⁶What if one of you said, "Go in peace! Stay warm! Have a nice meal!"? What good is it if you don't actually give them what their bodies need? ¹⁷In the same way, faith is dead when it doesn't result in faithful activity.

¹⁸Someone might claim, "You have faith and I have action." But how can I see your faith apart from your actions? Instead, I'll show you my faith by putting it into practice in faithful action. ¹⁹It's good that you believe that God is one. Ha! Even the demons believe this, and they tremble with fear. ²⁰Are you so slow? Do you need to be shown that faith without actions has no value at all? ²¹What about Abraham, our father?

ᵃLev 19:18 ᵇExod 20:13, 15 LXX (English: 20:13-14); Deut 5:17-18

Wasn't he shown to be righteous through his actions when he offered his son Isaac on the altar? [22]See, his faith was at work along with his actions. In fact, his faith was made complete by his faithful actions. [23]So the scripture was fulfilled that says, *Abraham believed God, and God regarded him as righteous.*[c] What is more, Abraham was called God's friend. [24]So you see that a person is shown to be righteous through faithful actions and not through faith alone. [25]In the same way, wasn't Rahab the prostitute shown to be righteous when she received the messengers as her guests and then sent them on by another road? [26]As the lifeless body is dead, so faith without actions is dead.

Taming the tongue

3 My brothers and sisters, not many of you should become teachers, because we know that we teachers will be judged more strictly. [2]We all make mistakes often, but those who don't make mistakes with their words have reached full maturity. Like a bridled horse, they can control themselves entirely. [3]When we bridle horses and put bits in their mouths to lead them wherever we want, we can control their whole bodies.

[4]Consider ships: They are so large that strong winds are needed to drive them. But pilots direct their ships wherever they want with a little rudder. [5]In the same way, even though the tongue is a small part of the body, it boasts wildly.

Think about this: A small flame can set a whole forest on fire. [6]The tongue is a small flame of fire, a world of evil at work in us. It contaminates our entire lives. Because of it, the circle of life is set on fire. The tongue itself is set on fire by the flames of hell.

[7]People can tame and already have tamed every kind of animal, bird, reptile, and fish. [8]No one can tame the tongue, though. It is a restless evil, full of deadly poison. [9]With it we both bless the Lord and Father and curse human beings made in God's likeness. [10]Blessing and cursing come from the same mouth. My brothers and sisters, it just shouldn't be this way!

[11]Both fresh water and salt water don't come from the same spring, do they? [12]My brothers and sisters, can a fig tree produce olives? Can a grapevine produce figs? Of course not, and fresh water doesn't flow from a saltwater spring either.

Wisdom from above

[13]Are any of you wise and understanding? Show that your actions are good with a humble lifestyle that comes from wisdom. [14]However, if you have bitter jealousy and selfish ambition in your heart, then stop bragging and living in ways that deny the truth. [15]This is not the wisdom that comes down from above. Instead, it is from the earth, natural and demonic. [16]Wherever there is jealousy and selfish ambition, there is disorder and everything that is evil. [17]What of the wisdom from above? First, it is pure, and then peaceful, gentle, obedient, filled with mercy and good actions, fair, and genuine. [18]Those who make peace sow the seeds of justice by their peaceful acts.

Conflict with people and God

4 What is the source of conflict among you? What is the source of your

disputes? Don't they come from your cravings that are at war in your own lives? ²You long for something you don't have, so you commit murder. You are jealous for something you can't get, so you struggle and fight. You don't have because you don't ask. ³You ask and don't have because you ask with evil intentions, to waste it on your own cravings.

⁴You unfaithful people! Don't you know that friendship with the world means hostility toward God? So whoever wants to be the world's friend becomes God's enemy. ⁵Or do you suppose that scripture is meaningless? Doesn't God long for our faithfulness in[d] the life he has given us to us? ⁶But he gives us more grace. This is why it says, *God stands against the proud, but favors the humble.*[f] ⁷Therefore, submit to God. Resist the devil, and he will run away from you. ⁸Come near to God, and he will come near to you. Wash your hands, you sinners. Purify your hearts, you double-minded. ⁹Cry out in sorrow, mourn, and weep! Let your laughter become mourning and your joy become sadness. ¹⁰Humble yourselves before the Lord, and he will lift you up.

¹¹Brothers and sisters, don't say evil things about each other. Whoever insults or criticizes a brother or sister insults and criticizes the Law. If you find fault with the Law, you are not a doer of the Law but a judge over it. ¹²There is only one lawgiver and judge, and he is able to save and to destroy. But you who judge your neighbor, who are you?

Warning the proud and wealthy

¹³Pay attention, you who say, "Today or tomorrow we will go to such-and-such a town. We will stay there a year, buying and selling, and making a profit." ¹⁴You don't really know about tomorrow. What is your life? You are a mist that appears for only a short while before it vanishes. ¹⁵Here's what you ought to say: "If the Lord wills, we will live and do this or that." ¹⁶But now you boast and brag, and all such boasting is evil. ¹⁷It is a sin when someone knows the right thing to do and doesn't do it.

5 Pay attention, you wealthy people! Weep and moan over the miseries coming upon you. ²Your riches have rotted. Moths have destroyed your clothes. ³Your gold and silver have rusted, and their rust will be evidence against you. It will eat your flesh like fire. Consider the treasure you have hoarded in the last days. ⁴Listen! Hear the cries of the wages of your field hands. These are the wages you stole from those who harvested your fields. The cries of the harvesters have reached the ears of the Lord of heavenly forces. ⁵You have lived a self-satisfying life on this earth, a life of luxury. You have stuffed your hearts in preparation for the day of slaughter. ⁶You have condemned and murdered the righteous one, who doesn't oppose you.

Courageous patience

⁷Therefore, brothers and sisters, you must be patient as you wait for the coming of the Lord. Consider the farmer who waits patiently for the coming of rain in the fall and spring, looking forward to the precious fruit of the earth. ⁸You also must wait patiently, strengthening your resolve, because

---

[d]Or *jealously longs for* [e]Or *Doesn't the spirit that God placed in us have jealous desires?*
[f]Prov 3:34

the coming of the Lord is near. [9]Don't complain about each other, brothers and sisters, so that you won't be judged. Look! The judge is standing at the door!

[10]Brothers and sisters, take the prophets who spoke in the name of the Lord as an example of patient resolve and steadfastness. [11]Look at how we honor those who have practiced endurance. You have heard of the endurance of Job. And you have seen what the Lord has accomplished, for the Lord is full of compassion and mercy.

Final instructions

[12]Most important, my brothers and sisters, never make a solemn pledge—neither by heaven nor earth, nor by anything else. Instead, speak with a simple "Yes" or "No," or else you may fall under judgment.

[13]If any of you are suffering, they should pray. If any of you are happy, they should sing. [14]If any of you are sick, they should call for the elders of the church, and the elders should pray over them, anointing them with oil in the name of the Lord. [15]Prayer that comes from faith will heal the sick, for the Lord will restore them to health. And if they have sinned, they will be forgiven. [16]For this reason, confess your sins to each other and pray for each other so that you may be healed. The prayer of the righteous person is powerful in what it can achieve. [17]Elijah was a person just like us. When he earnestly prayed that it wouldn't rain, no rain fell for three and a half years. [18]He prayed again, God sent rain, and the earth produced its fruit.

[19]My brothers and sisters, if any of you wander from the truth and someone turns back the wanderer, [20]recognize that whoever brings a sinner back from the wrong path will save them from death and will bring about the forgiveness of many sins.

1 PETER

Greeting

1 Peter, an apostle of Jesus Christ,
To God's chosen strangers who live in the world of the diaspora, who live in Pontus, Galatia, Cappadocia, Asia, and Bithynia. [2]God the Father chose you because of what he knew beforehand. He chose you through the Holy Spirit's work of making you holy and because of the faithful obedience and sacrifice of Jesus Christ.

May God's grace and peace be multiplied to you.

Thanksgiving

[3]May the God and Father of our Lord Jesus Christ be blessed! On account of his vast mercy, he has given us new birth. You have been born anew into a living hope through the resurrection of Jesus Christ from the dead. [4]You have a pure and enduring inheritance that cannot perish—an inheritance that is presently kept safe in heaven for you. [5]Through his faithfulness, you are guarded by God's power so that you can receive the salvation he is ready to reveal in the last time.

[6]You now rejoice in this hope, even

if it's necessary for you to be distressed for a short time by various trials. [7]This is necessary so that your faith may be found genuine. (Your faith is more valuable than gold, which will be destroyed even though it is itself tested by fire.) Your genuine faith will result in praise, glory, and honor for you when Jesus Christ is revealed. [8]Although you've never seen him, you love him. Even though you don't see him now, you trust him and so rejoice with a glorious joy that is too much for words. [9]You are receiving the goal of your faith: your salvation.

[10]The prophets, who long ago foretold the grace that you've received, searched and explored, inquiring carefully about this salvation. [11]They wondered what the Spirit of Christ within them was saying when he bore witness beforehand about the suffering that would happen to Christ and the glory that would follow. They wondered what sort of person or what sort of time they were speaking about. [12]It was revealed to them that in their search they were not serving themselves but you. These things, which even angels long to examine, have now been proclaimed to you by those who brought you the good news. They did this in the power of the Holy Spirit, who was sent from heaven.

Response of obedience

[13]Therefore, once you have your minds ready for action and you are thinking clearly, place your hope completely on the grace that will be brought to you when Jesus Christ is revealed. [14]Don't be conformed to your former desires, those that shaped you when you were ignorant. But, as obedient children, [15]you must be holy in every aspect of your lives, just as the one who called you is holy. [16]It is written, *You will be holy, because I am holy.*[a] [17]Since you call upon a Father who judges all people according to their actions without favoritism, you should conduct yourselves with reverence during the time of your dwelling in a strange land. [18]Live in this way, knowing that you were not liberated by perishable things like silver or gold from the empty lifestyle you inherited from your ancestors. [19]Instead, you were liberated by the precious blood of Christ, like that of a flawless, spotless lamb. [20]Christ was chosen before the creation of the world, but was only revealed at the end of time. This was done for you, [21]who through Christ are faithful to the God who raised him from the dead and gave him glory. So now, your faith and hope should rest in God.

[22]As you set yourselves apart by your obedience to the truth so that you might have genuine affection for your fellow believers, love each other deeply and earnestly. [23]Do this because you have been given new birth—not from the type of seed that decays but from seed that doesn't. This seed is God's lifegiving and enduring word. [24]Thus,

*All human life on the earth
    is like grass,
    and all human glory
      is like a flower in a field.
The grass dries up
    and its flower falls off,*
[25] *but the Lord's word endures forever.*[b]
This is the word that was proclaimed to you as good news.

[a]Lev 19:2 [b]Isa 40:6-8

Your identity as believers

2 Therefore, get rid of all ill will and all deceit, pretense, envy, and slander. ²Instead, like a newborn baby, desire the pure milk of the word. Nourished by it, you will grow into salvation, ³since you have tasted that the Lord is good.

⁴Now you are coming to him as to a living stone. Even though this stone was rejected by humans, from God's perspective it is chosen, valuable. ⁵You yourselves are being built like living stones into a spiritual temple. You are being made into a holy priesthood to offer up spiritual sacrifices that are acceptable to God through Jesus Christ. ⁶Thus it is written in scripture, *Look! I am laying a cornerstone in Zion, chosen, valuable. The person who believes in him will never be shamed.*ᶜ ⁷So God honors you who believe. For those who refuse to believe, though, the stone the builders tossed aside has become the capstone. ⁸This is a stone that makes people stumble and a rock that makes them fall. Because they refuse to believe in the word, they stumble. Indeed, this is the end to which they were appointed. ⁹But you are a chosen race, a royal priesthood, a holy nation, a people who are God's own possession. You have become this people so that you may speak of the wonderful acts of the one who called you out of darkness into his amazing light. ¹⁰Once you weren't a people, but now you are God's people. Once you hadn't received mercy, but now you have received mercy.

Life as strangers in the world

¹¹Dear friends, since you are immigrants and strangers in the world, I urge that you avoid worldly desires that wage war against your lives. ¹²Live honorably among the unbelievers. Today, they defame you, as if you were doing evil. But in the day when God visits to judge they will glorify him, because they have observed your honorable deeds.

¹³For the sake of the Lord submit to every human institution. Do this whether it means submitting to the emperor as supreme ruler, ¹⁴or to governors as those sent by the emperor. They are sent to punish those doing evil and to praise those doing good. ¹⁵Submit to them because it's God's will that by doing good you will silence the ignorant talk of foolish people. ¹⁶Do this as God's slaves, and yet also as free people, not using your freedom as a cover-up for evil. ¹⁷Honor everyone. Love the family of believers. Have respectful fear of God. Honor the emperor.

¹⁸Household slaves, submit by accepting the authority of your masters with all respect. Do this not only to good and kind masters but also to those who are harsh. ¹⁹Now, it is commendable if, because of one's understanding of God, someone should endure pain through suffering unjustly. ²⁰But what praise comes from enduring patiently when you have sinned and are beaten for it? But if you endure steadfastly when you've done good and suffer for it, this is commendable before God.

²¹You were called to this kind of endurance, because Christ suffered on your behalf. He left you an example so that you might follow in his footsteps. ²²He committed no sin, nor did he ever speak in ways meant to deceive. ²³When he was insulted, he did not

ᶜIsa 28:16

reply with insults. When he suffered, he did not threaten revenge. Instead, he entrusted himself to the one who judges justly. [24] He carried in his own body on the cross the sins we committed. He did this so that we might live in righteousness, having nothing to do with sin. By his wounds you were healed. [25] Though you were like straying sheep, you have now returned to the shepherd and guardian of your lives.

3 Wives, likewise, submit to your husbands. Do this so that even if some of them refuse to believe the word, they may be won without a word by their wives' way of life. [2] After all, they will have observed the reverent and holy manner of your lives. [3] Don't try to make yourselves beautiful on the outside, with stylish hair or by wearing gold jewelry or fine clothes. [4] Instead, make yourselves beautiful on the inside, in your hearts, with the enduring quality of a gentle, peaceful spirit. This type of beauty is very precious in God's eyes. [5] For it was in this way that holy women who trusted in God used to make themselves beautiful, accepting the authority of their own husbands. [6] For example, Sarah accepted Abraham's authority when she called him *master*. You have become her children when you do good and don't respond to threats with fear.

[7] Husbands, likewise, submit by living with your wife in ways that honor her, knowing that she is the weaker partner. Honor her all the more, as she is also a coheir of the gracious care of life. Do this so that your prayers won't be hindered.

[8] Finally, all of you be of one mind, sympathetic, lovers of your fellow believers, compassionate, and modest in your opinion of yourselves. [9] Don't pay back evil for evil or insult for insult. Instead, give blessing in return. You were called to do this so that you might inherit a blessing. [10] For

> those who want to love life
> and see good days
> should keep their tongue
> from evil speaking
> and their lips from speaking lies.
> [11] They should shun evil and do good;
> seek peace and chase after it.
> [12] The Lord's eyes are on the righteous
> and his ears are open to their prayers.
> But the Lord cannot tolerate those
> who do evil.[d]

[13] Who will harm you if you are zealous for good? [14] But happy are you, even if you suffer because of righteousness! Don't be terrified or upset by them. [15] Instead, regard Christ as holy in your hearts. Whenever anyone asks you to speak of your hope, be ready to defend it. [16] Yet do this with respectful humility, maintaining a good conscience. Act in this way so that those who malign your good lifestyle in Christ may be ashamed when they slander you. [17] It is better to suffer for doing good (if this could possibly be God's will) than for doing evil.

[18] Christ himself suffered on account of sins, once for all, the righteous one on behalf of the unrighteous. He did this in order to bring you into the presence of God. Christ was put to death as a human, but made alive by the Spirit. [19] And it was by the Spirit that he went to preach to the spirits in prison. [20] In the past, these spirits

[d] Ps 34:12-16

were disobedient—when God patiently waited during the time of Noah. Noah built an ark in which a few (that is, eight) lives were rescued through water. [21]Baptism is like that. It saves you now—not because it removes dirt from your body but because it is the mark of a good conscience toward God. Your salvation comes through the resurrection of Jesus Christ, [22]who is at God's right side. Now that he has gone into heaven, he rules over all angels, authorities, and powers.

4 Therefore, since Christ suffered as a human, you should also arm yourselves with his way of thinking. This is because whoever suffers is finished with sin. [2]As a result, they don't live the rest of their human lives in ways determined by human desires but in ways determined by God's will. [3]You have wasted enough time doing what unbelievers desire—living in their unrestrained immorality and lust, their drunkenness and excessive feasting and wild parties, and their forbidden worship of idols. [4]They think it's strange that you don't join in these activities with the same flood of unrestrained wickedness. So they slander you. [5]They will have to reckon with the one who is ready to judge the living and the dead. [6]Indeed, this is the reason the good news was also preached to the dead. This happened so that, although they were judged as humans according to human standards, they could live by the Spirit according to divine standards.

[7]The end of everything has come. Therefore, be self-controlled and clearheaded so you can pray. [8]Above all, show sincere love to each other, because love brings about the forgiveness of many

sins. [9]Open your homes to each other without complaining. [10]And serve each other according to the gift each person has received, as good managers of God's diverse gifts. [11]Whoever speaks should do so as those who speak God's word. Whoever serves should do so from the strength that God furnishes. Do this so that in everything God may be honored through Jesus Christ. To him be honor and power forever and always. Amen.

Stand firm in the last times

[12]Dear friends, don't be surprised about the fiery trials that have come among you to test you. These are not strange happenings. [13]Instead, rejoice as you share Christ's suffering. You share his suffering now so that you may also have overwhelming joy when his glory is revealed. [14]If you are mocked because of Christ's name, you are blessed, for the Spirit of glory—indeed, the Spirit of God—rests on you.

[15]Now none of you should suffer as a murderer or thief or evildoer or rebel. [16]But don't be ashamed if you suffer as one who belongs to Christ. Rather, honor God as you bear Christ's name. Give honor to God, [17]because it's time for judgment to begin with God's own household. But if judgment starts with us, what will happen to those who refuse to believe God's good news? [18]If the righteous are barely rescued, what will happen to the godless and sinful? [19]So then, those who suffer because they follow God's will should commit their lives to a trustworthy creator by doing what is right.

5 Therefore, I have a request for the elders among you. (I ask this as a fellow elder and a witness of Christ's sufferings, and as one who shares in the glory that is about to be revealed.) I urge the elders: [2] Like shepherds, tend the flock of God among you. Watch over it. Don't shepherd because you must, but do it voluntarily for God. Don't shepherd greedily, but do it eagerly. [3] Don't shepherd by ruling over those entrusted to your care, but become examples to the flock. [4] And when the chief shepherd appears, you will receive an unfading crown of glory.

[5] In the same way, I urge you who are younger: accept the authority of the elders. And everyone, clothe yourselves with humility toward each other. God stands against the proud, but he gives favor to the humble.

[6] Therefore, humble yourselves under God's power so that he may raise you up in the last day. [7] Throw all your anxiety onto him, because he cares about you. [8] Be clearheaded. Keep alert. Your accuser, the devil, is on the prowl like a roaring lion, seeking someone to devour. [9] Resist him, standing firm in the faith. Do so in the knowledge that your fellow believers are enduring the same suffering throughout the world. [10] After you have suffered for a little while, the God of all grace, the one who called you into his eternal glory in Christ Jesus, will himself restore, empower, strengthen, and establish you. [11] To him be power forever and always. Amen.

Final greeting

[12] I have written and sent these few lines to you by Silvanus. I consider him to be a faithful brother. In these lines I have urged and affirmed that this is the genuine grace of God. Stand firm in it. [13] The fellow-elect church in Babylon greets you, and so does my son Mark. [14] Greet each other with the kiss of love. Peace to you all who are in Christ.

2 PETER

Greeting

1 From Simon Peter, a slave and apostle of Jesus Christ.
To those who received a faith equal to ours through the justice of our God and savior Jesus Christ.
[2] May you have more and more grace and peace through the knowledge of God and Jesus our Lord.

Christian life in outline

[3] By his divine power the Lord has given us everything we need for life and godliness through the knowledge of the one who called us by his own honor and glory. [4] Through his honor and glory he has given us his precious and wonderful promises, that you may share the divine nature and escape from the world's immorality that sinful craving produces.

[5] This is why you must make every effort to add moral excellence to your faith; and to moral excellence, knowledge; [6] and to knowledge, self-control; and to self-control, endurance; and to endurance, godliness; [7] and to godliness, affection for others; and to affection for others, love. [8] If all these are yours and they are growing in you, they'll keep you from becoming inactive and unfruitful in the knowledge of our Lord Jesus Christ. [9] Whoever lacks

these things is shortsighted and blind, forgetting that they were cleansed from their past sins.

[10]Therefore, brothers and sisters, be eager to confirm your call and election. Do this and you will never ever be lost. [11]In this way you will receive a rich welcome into the everlasting kingdom of our Lord and savior Jesus Christ.

Reminder of the Christian life

[12]So I'll keep reminding you about these things, although you already know them and stand secure in the truth you have. [13]I think it's right that I keep stirring up your memory, as long as I'm alive. [14]After all, our Lord Jesus Christ has shown me that I am about to depart from this life. [15]I'm eager for you always to remember these things after my death.

Christ's return is true

[16]We didn't repeat crafty myths when we told you about the powerful coming of our Lord Jesus Christ. Quite the contrary, we witnessed his majesty with our own eyes. [17]He received honor and glory from God the Father when a voice came to him from the magnificent glory, saying, "This is my dearly loved Son, with whom I am well-pleased." [18]We ourselves heard this voice from heaven while we were with him on the holy mountain. [19]In addition, we have a most reliable prophetic word, and you would do well to pay attention to it, just as you would to a lamp shining in a dark place, until the day dawns and the morning star rises in your hearts. [20]Most important, you must know that no prophecy of scripture represents the prophet's own understanding of things, [21]because no prophecy ever came by

human will. Instead, men and women led by the Holy Spirit spoke from God.

Appearance of false teachers

2But false prophets also arose among the people. In the same way, false teachers will come among you. They will introduce destructive opinions and deny the master who bought them, bringing quick destruction on themselves. [2]Many will follow them in their unrestrained immorality, and because of these false teachers the way of truth will be slandered. [3]In their greed they will take advantage of you with lies. The judgment pronounced against them long ago hasn't fallen idle, nor is their destruction sleeping.

Active judgment of God

[4]God didn't spare the angels when they sinned but cast them into the lowest level of the underworld and committed them to chains of darkness, keeping them there until the judgment. [5]And he didn't spare the ancient world when he brought a flood on the world of ungodly people, even though he protected Noah, a preacher of righteousness, along with seven others. [6]God condemned the cities of Sodom and Gomorrah to total destruction, reducing them to ashes as a warning to ungodly people. [7]And he rescued righteous Lot, who was made miserable by the unrestrained immorality of unruly people. ([8]While that righteous man lived among them he felt deep distress every day on account of the immoral actions he saw and heard.) [9]These things show that the Lord knows how to rescue the godly from their trials, and how to keep the unrighteous for punishment on the Judgment Day. [10]This is especially true

for those who follow after the corrupt cravings of the sinful nature and defy the Lord's authority.

Evil character of the false teachers

These reckless, brash people aren't afraid to insult the glorious ones, [11]yet angels, who are stronger and more powerful, don't use insults when pronouncing the Lord's judgment on them. [12]These false teachers are like irrational animals, mere creatures of instinct, born to be captured and destroyed. They slander what they don't understand and, like animals, they will be destroyed. [13]In this way, they will receive payment for their wrongdoing.

They even enjoy unruly parties in broad daylight. They are blots and blemishes, taking delight in their seductive pleasures while feasting with you. [14]They are always looking for someone with whom to commit adultery. They are always on the lookout for opportunities to sin. They ensnare people whose faith is weak. They have hearts trained in greed. They are under God's curse. [15]Leaving the straight path, they have gone off course, following the way of Balaam son of Bosor, who loved the payment of doing wrong. [16]But Balaam was rebuked for his wrongdoing. A donkey, which has no voice, spoke with a human voice and put a stop to the prophet's madness.

[17]These false teachers are springs without water, mists driven by the wind. The underworld has been reserved for them. [18]With empty, self-important speech, they use sinful cravings and unrestrained immorality to ensnare people who have only just escaped life with those who have wandered from the truth. [19]These false

teachers promise freedom, but they themselves are slaves of immorality; whatever overpowers you, enslaves you. [20]If people escape the moral filth of this world through the knowledge of our Lord and savior Jesus Christ, then get tangled up in it again and are overcome by it, they are worse off than they were before. [21]It would be better for them never to have known the way of righteousness than, having come to know it, to turn back from the holy commandment entrusted to them. [22]They demonstrate the truth of the proverb: "A dog returns to its own vomit, and a washed sow wallows in the mud."

Delay of Christ's coming in judgment

3 My dear friends, this is now my second letter to you. I have written both letters to stir up your sincere understanding with a reminder. [2]I want you to recall what the holy prophets foretold as well as what the Lord and savior commanded through your apostles. [3]Most important, know this: in the last days scoffers will come, jeering, living by their own cravings, [4]and saying, "Where is the promise of his coming? After all, nothing has changed—not since the beginning of creation, nor even since the ancestors died."

[5]But they fail to notice that, by God's word, heaven and earth were formed long ago out of water and by means of water. [6]And it was through these that the world of that time was flooded and destroyed. [7]But by the same word, heaven and earth are now held in reserve for fire, kept for the Judgment Day and destruction of ungodly people.

⁸Don't let it escape your notice, dear friends, that with the Lord a single day is like a thousand years and a thousand years are like a single day. ⁹The Lord isn't slow to keep his promise, as some think of slowness, but he is patient toward you, not wanting anyone to perish but all to change their hearts and lives. ¹⁰But the Day of the Lord will come like a thief. On that day the heavens will pass away with a dreadful noise, the elements will be consumed by fire, and the earth and all the works done on it will be exposed.

¹¹Since everything will be destroyed in this way, what sort of people ought you to be? You must live holy and godly lives, ¹²waiting for and hastening the coming day of God. Because of that day, the heavens will be destroyed by fire and the elements will melt away in the flames. ¹³But according to his promise we are waiting for a new heaven and a new earth, where righteousness is at home.

Preparing for Christ's coming in judgment

¹⁴Therefore, dear friends, while you are waiting for these things to happen, make every effort to be found by him in peace—pure and faultless. ¹⁵Consider the patience of our Lord to be salvation, just as our dear friend and brother Paul wrote to you according to the wisdom given to him, ¹⁶speaking of these things in all his letters. Some of his remarks are hard to understand, and people who are ignorant and whose faith is weak twist them to their own destruction, just as they do the other scriptures.

Final instruction

¹⁷Therefore, dear friends, since you have been warned in advance, be on guard so that you aren't led off course into the error of sinful people, and lose your own safe position. ¹⁸Instead, grow in the grace and knowledge of our Lord and savior Jesus Christ. To him belongs glory now and forever. Amen.

1 JOHN

Announcement about the word of life

1 We announce to you what existed from the beginning, what we have heard, what we have seen with our eyes, what we have seen and our hands handled, about the word of life. ²The life was revealed, and we have seen, and we testify and announce to you the eternal life that was with the Father and was revealed to us. ³What we have seen and heard, we also announce it to you so that you can have fellowship with us. Our fellowship is with the Father and with his Son, Jesus Christ. ⁴We are

writing these things so that our joy can be complete.

The message: God is light

⁵This is the message that we have heard from him and announce to you: "God is light and there is no darkness in him at all." ⁶If we claim, "We have fellowship with him," and live in darkness, we are lying and do not act truthfully. ⁷But if we live in the light in the same way as he is in the light, we have fellowship with each other, and the blood of Jesus, his Son, cleanses us from every sin. ⁸If we claim, "We

don't have any sin," we deceive ourselves and the truth is not in us. ⁹But if we confess our sins, he is faithful and just to forgive us our sins and cleanse us from everything we've done wrong. ¹⁰If we claim, "We have never sinned," we make him a liar and his word is not in us.

Living in the light

2 My little children, I'm writing these things to you so that you don't sin. But if you do sin, we have an advocate with the Father, Jesus Christ the righteous one. ²He is God's way of dealing with our sins, not only ours but the sins of the whole world. ³This is how we know that we know him: if we keep his commandments. ⁴The one who claims, "I know him," while not keeping his commandments, is a liar, and the truth is not in this person. ⁵But the love of God is truly perfected in whoever keeps his word. This is how we know we are in him. ⁶The one who claims to remain in him ought to live in the same way as he lived.

⁷Dear friends, I'm not writing a new commandment to you, but an old commandment that you had from the beginning. The old commandment is the message you heard. ⁸On the other hand, I am writing a new commandment to you, which is true in him and in you, because the darkness is passing away and the true light already shines. ⁹The one who claims to be in the light while hating a brother or sister is in the darkness even now. ¹⁰The person loving a brother and sister stays in the light, and there is nothing in the light that causes a person to stumble. ¹¹But the person who hates a brother or sister is in the darkness and lives in the darkness, and doesn't know where to go because the darkness blinds the eyes.

Motivations for writing

¹²Little children, I'm writing to you because your sins have been forgiven through Jesus' name. ¹³Parents, I'm writing to you because you have known the one who has existed from the beginning. Young people, I'm writing to you because you have conquered the evil one. ¹⁴Little children, I write to you because you know the Father. Parents, I write to you because you have known the one who has existed from the beginning. Young people, I write to you because you are strong, the word of God remains in you, and you have conquered the evil one.

Warning about the world

¹⁵Don't love the world or the things in the world. If anyone loves the world, the love of the Father is not in them. ¹⁶Everything that is in the world—the craving for whatever the body feels, the craving for whatever the eyes see and the arrogant pride in one's possessions—is not of the Father but is of the world. ¹⁷And the world and its cravings are passing away, but the person who does the will of God remains forever.

Remaining in the truth

¹⁸Little children, it is the last hour. Just as you have heard that the antichrist is coming, so now many antichrists have appeared. This is how we know it is the last hour. ¹⁹They went out from us, but they were not really part of us. If they had been part of us, they would have stayed with us. But by going out from us, they showed they all

are not part of us. [20] But you have an anointing from the holy one, and all of you know the truth. [21] I don't write to you because you don't know the truth but because you know it. You know that no lie comes from the truth. [22] Who is the liar? Isn't it the person who denies that Jesus is the Christ? This person is the antichrist: the one who denies the Father and the Son. [23] Everyone who denies the Son does not have the Father, but the one who confesses the Son has the Father also.

[24] As for you, what you heard from the beginning must remain in you. If what you heard from the beginning remains in you, you will also remain in relationship to the Son and in the Father. [25] This is the promise that he himself gave us: eternal life. [26] I write these things to you about those who are attempting to deceive you. [27] As for you, the anointing that you received from him remains on you, and you don't need anyone to teach you the truth. But since his anointing teaches you about all things (it's true and not a lie), remain in relationship to him just as he taught you.

Remaining until Jesus appears

[28] And now, little children, remain in relationship to Jesus, so that when he appears we can have confidence and not be ashamed in front of him when he comes. [29] If you know that he is righteous, you also know that every person who practices righteousness is born from him.

3 See what kind of love the Father has given to us in that we should be called God's children, and that is what

we are! Because the world didn't recognize him, it doesn't recognize us.

[2] Dear friends, now we are God's children, and it hasn't yet appeared what we will be. We know that when he appears we will be like him because we'll see him as he is. [3] And all who have this hope in him purify themselves even as he is pure. [4] Every person who practices sin commits an act of rebellion, and sin is rebellion. [5] You know that he appeared to take away sins, and there is no sin in him. [6] Every person who remains in relationship to him does not sin. Any person who sins has not seen him or known him.

Practicing sin or righteousness

[7] Little children, make sure no one deceives you. The person who practices righteousness is righteous, in the same way that Jesus is righteous. [8] The person who practices sin belongs to the devil, because the devil has been sinning since the beginning. God's Son appeared for this purpose: to destroy the works of the devil. [9] Those born from God don't practice sin because God's DNA[a] remains in them. They can't sin because they are born from God. [10] This is how God's children and the devil's children are apparent: everyone who doesn't practice righteousness is not from God, including the person who doesn't love a brother or sister. [11] This is the message that you heard from the beginning: love each other. [12] Don't behave like Cain, who belonged to the evil one and murdered his brother. And why did he kill him? He killed him because his own works were evil, but the works of his brother were righteous.

---

[a] Or genetic character

Loving each other

¹³Don't be surprised, brothers and sisters, if the world hates you. ¹⁴We know that we have transferred from death to life, because we love the brothers and sisters. The person who does not love remains in death. ¹⁵Everyone who hates a brother or sister is a murderer, and you know that murderers don't have eternal life residing in them. ¹⁶This is how we know love: Jesus laid down his life for us, and we ought to lay down our lives for our brothers and sisters. ¹⁷But if someone has material possessions and sees a brother or sister in need but refuses to help—how can the love of God dwell in a person like that?

¹⁸Little children, let's not love with words or speech but with action and truth. ¹⁹This is how we will know that we belong to the truth and reassure our hearts in God's presence. ²⁰Even if our hearts condemn us, God is greater than our hearts and knows all things. ²¹Dear friends, if our hearts don't condemn us, we have confidence in relationship to God. ²²We receive whatever we ask from him because we keep his commandments and do what pleases him. ²³This is his commandment, that we believe in the name of his Son, Jesus Christ, and love each other as he commanded us. ²⁴Those who keep his commandments dwell in God and God dwells in them. This is how we know that he dwells in us, because of the Spirit he has given us.

Testing the spirits

4 Dear friends, don't believe every spirit. Test the spirits to see if they are from God because many false prophets have gone into the world. ²This is how you know if a spirit comes from God: every spirit that confesses that Jesus Christ has come as a human[b] is from God, ³and every spirit that doesn't confess Jesus is not from God. This is the spirit of the antichrist, which you have heard is coming and is now already in the world. ⁴You are from God, little children, and you have defeated these people because the one who is in you is greater than the one who is in the world. ⁵They are from the world. So they speak from the world's point of view and the world listens to them. ⁶We are from God. The person who knows God listens to us. Whoever is not from God doesn't listen to us. This is how we recognize the Spirit of truth and the spirit of error.

Love and God

⁷Dear friends, let's love each other, because love is from God, and everyone who loves is born from God and knows God. ⁸The person who doesn't love does not know God, because God is love. ⁹This is how the love of God is revealed to us: God has sent his only Son into the world so that we can live through him. ¹⁰This is love: it is not that we loved God but that he loved us and sent his Son as the sacrifice that deals with our sins. ¹¹Dear friends, if God loved us this way, we also ought to love each other. ¹²No one has ever seen God. If we love each other, God remains in us and his love is made perfect in us. ¹³This is how we know we remain in him and he remains in us, because he has given us a measure of his Spirit. ¹⁴We have seen and testify that the Father has sent

b Or come in the flesh

the Son to be the savior of the world. ¹⁵If any of us confess that Jesus is God's Son, God remains in us and we remain in God. ¹⁶We have known and have believed the love that God has for us.

God is love, and those who remain in love remain in God and God remains in them. ¹⁷This is how love has been perfected in us, so that we can have confidence on the Judgment Day, because we are exactly the same as God is in this world. ¹⁸There is no fear in love, but perfect love drives out fear, because fear expects punishment. The person who is afraid has not been made perfect in love. ¹⁹We love because God first loved us. ²⁰Those who say, "I love God" and hate their brothers or sisters are liars. After all, those who don't love their brothers or sisters whom they have seen can hardly love God whom they have not seen! ²¹This commandment we have from him: Those who claim to love God ought to love their brother and sister also.

5 Everyone who believes that Jesus is the Christ has been born from God. Whoever loves someone who is a parent loves the child born to the parent. ²This is how we know that we love the children of God: when we love God and keep God's commandments. ³This is the love of God: we keep God's commandments. God's commandments are not difficult, ⁴because everyone who is born from God defeats the world. And this is the victory that has defeated the world: our faith. ⁵Who defeats the world? Isn't it the one who believes that Jesus is God's Son?

Testimony about Jesus

⁶This is the one who came by water and blood: Jesus Christ. Not by water only but by water and blood. And the Spirit is the one who testifies, because the Spirit is the truth. ⁷The three are testifying—⁸the Spirit, the water, and the blood—and the three are united in agreement. ⁹If we receive human testimony, God's testimony is greater, because this is what God testified: he has testified about his Son. ¹⁰The one who believes in God's Son has the testimony within; the one who doesn't believe God has made God a liar, because that one has not believed the testimony that God gave about his Son. ¹¹And this is the testimony: God gave eternal life to us, and this life is in his Son. ¹²The one who has the Son has life. The one who doesn't have God's Son does not have life.

Confidence in prayer

¹³I write these things to you who believe in the name of God's Son so that you can know that you have eternal life. ¹⁴This is the confidence that we have in our relationship with God: If we ask for anything in agreement with his will, he listens to us. ¹⁵If we know that he listens to whatever we ask, we know that we have received what we asked from him. ¹⁶If anyone sees a brother or sister committing a sin that does not result in death, they should pray, and God will give life to them—that is, to those who commit sins that don't result in death. There is a sin that results in death—I'm not saying that you should pray about that. ¹⁷Every unrighteous action is sin, but there is a sin that does not result in death.

Be on guard

¹⁸We know that everyone born from God does not sin, but the ones born from

God guard themselves,[c] and the evil one cannot touch them. [19]We know we are from God, and the whole world lies in the power of the evil one. [20]We know that God's Son has come and has given us understanding to know the one who is true. We are in the one who is true by being in his Son, Jesus Christ. This is the true God and eternal life. [21]Little children, guard yourselves from idols!

2 JOHN

Greeting

[1]From the elder.

To the chosen gentlewoman and her children, whom I truly love (and I am not the only one, but also all who know the truth), [2]because of the truth that remains with us and will be with us forever.

[3]Grace, mercy, and peace from God the Father and from Jesus Christ, the Son of the Father, will be ours who live in truth and love.

Love each other

[4]I was overjoyed to find some of your children living in the truth, just as we had been commanded by the Father. [5]Now, dear friends, I am requesting that we love each other. It's not as though I'm writing a new command to you, but it's one we have had from the beginning. [6]This is love: that we live according to his commands. This is the command that you heard from the beginning: live in love.

Reject false teachers

[7]Many deceivers have gone into the world who do not confess that Jesus Christ came as a human being. This kind of person is the deceiver and the antichrist. [8]Watch yourselves so that you don't lose what we've worked for but instead receive a full reward. [9]Anyone who goes too far and does not continue in the teaching about Christ does not have God. Whoever continues in this teaching has both the Father and the Son. [10]Whoever comes to you who does not affirm this teaching should neither be received nor welcomed into your home, [11]because welcoming people like that is the same thing as sharing in their evil actions.

Plans to visit

[12]I have a lot to tell you. I don't want to use paper and ink, but I hope to visit you and talk with you face-to-face, so that our joy can be complete.

Final greeting

[13]Your chosen sister's children greet you.

[c]Or but the one who is born from God guards him from sin

3 JOHN

Greeting

¹From the elder.

To my dear friend Gaius, whom I truly love.

²Dear friend, I'm praying that all is well with you and that you enjoy good health in the same way that you prosper spiritually.

Encouragement for Gaius

³I was overjoyed when the brothers and sisters arrived and spoke highly of your faithfulness to the truth, shown by how you live according to the truth. ⁴I have no greater joy than this: to hear that my children are living according to the truth. ⁵Dear friend, you act faithfully in whatever you do for our brothers and sisters, even though they are strangers. ⁶They spoke highly of your love in front of the church. You all would do well to provide for their journey in a way that honors God, ⁷because they left on their journey for the sake of Jesus Christ without accepting any support from the Gentiles. ⁸Therefore, we ought to help people like this so that we can be coworkers with the truth.

Criticism of Diotrephes

⁹I wrote something to the church, but Diotrephes, who likes to put himself first, doesn't welcome us. ¹⁰Because of this, if I come, I will bring up what he has done—making unjustified and wicked accusations against us. And as if that were not enough, he not only refuses to welcome the brothers and sisters but stops those who want to do so and even throws them out of the church! ¹¹Dear friend, don't imitate what is bad but what is good. Whoever practices what is good belongs to God. Whoever practices what is bad has not seen God.

Approval of Demetrius

¹²Everyone speaks highly of Demetrius, even the truth itself. We also speak highly of him, and you know that what we say is true.

Final greeting

¹³I have a lot to say to you, but I don't want to use pen and ink. ¹⁴I hope to see you soon, and we will speak face-to-face. ¹⁵Peace be with you. Your friends here greet you. Greet our friends there by name.

JUDE

Greeting

¹Jude, a slave of Jesus Christ and brother of James.

To those who are called, loved by God the Father and kept safe by Jesus Christ.

²May you have more and more mercy, peace, and love.

Certain judgment of the false teachers

³Dear friends, I wanted very much to write to you concerning the salvation we share. Instead, I must write to urge you to fight for the faith delivered once and for all to God's holy people. ⁴Godless people have slipped in among you. They turn the

grace of our God into unrestrained immorality and deny our only master and Lord, Jesus Christ. Judgment was passed against them a long time ago.

[5] I want to remind you of something you already know very well. The Lord, who once saved a people out of Egypt, later destroyed those who didn't maintain their faith. [6] I remind you too of the angels who didn't keep their position of authority but deserted their own home. The Lord has kept them in eternal chains in the underworld until the judgment of the great day. [7] In the same way, Sodom and Gomorrah and neighboring towns practiced immoral sexual relations and pursued other sexual urges. By undergoing the punishment of eternal fire, they serve as a warning.

[8] Yet, even knowing this, these dreamers in the same way pollute themselves, reject authority, and slander the angels. [9] The archangel Michael, when he argued with the devil about Moses' body, did not dare charge him with slander. Instead, he said, "The Lord rebuke you!" [10] But these people slander whatever they don't understand. They are destroyed by what they know instinctively, as though they were irrational animals.

Prophecies about the false teachers

[11] They are damned, for they follow in the footsteps of Cain. For profit they give themselves over to Balaam's error. They are destroyed in the uprising of Korah. [12] These people are like jagged rocks just below the surface of the water waiting to snag you when they join your love feasts. They feast with you without reverence. They care only for themselves. They are waterless clouds carried along by the winds; fruitless autumn trees,

twice dead, uprooted; [13] wild waves of the sea foaming up their own shame; wandering stars for whom the darkness of the underworld is reserved forever.

[14] Enoch, who lived seven generations after Adam, prophesied about these people when he said, "See, the Lord comes with his countless holy ones, [15] to execute judgment on everyone and to convict everyone about every ungodly deed they have committed in their ungodliness as well as all the harsh things that sinful ungodly people have said against him." [16] These are faultfinding grumblers, living according to their own desires. They speak arrogant words and they show partiality to people when they want a favor in return.

[17] But you, dear friends, remember the words spoken beforehand by the apostles of our Lord Jesus Christ. [18] They said to you, "In the end time scoffers will come living according to their own ungodly desires." [19] These people create divisions. Since they don't have the Spirit, they are worldly.

A strategy for the faithful

[20] But you, dear friends: build each other up on the foundation of your most holy faith, pray in the Holy Spirit, [21] keep each other in the love of God, wait for the mercy of our Lord Jesus Christ, who will give you eternal life. [22] Have mercy on those who doubt. [23] Save some by snatching them from the fire. Fearing God, have mercy on some, hating even the clothing contaminated by their sinful urges.

Blessing

[24] To the one who is able
    to protect you from falling,
    and to present you blameless

and rejoicing before
his glorious presence,
²⁵ to the only God our savior,
through Jesus Christ our Lord,

belong glory, majesty, power,
and authority,
before all time, now and forever.
Amen.

REVELATION

Greetings

1 A revelation of Jesus Christ, which God gave him to show his servants what must soon take place. Christ made it known by sending it through his angel to his servant John, ²who bore witness to the word of God and to the witness of Jesus Christ, including all that John saw. ³Favored is the one who reads the words of this prophecy out loud, and favored are those who listen to it being read, and keep what is written in it, for the time is near.

⁴John, to the seven churches that are in Asia:

Grace and peace to you from the one who is and was and is coming, and from the seven spirits that are before God's throne, ⁵and from Jesus Christ—the faithful witness, the firstborn from among the dead, and the ruler of the kings of the earth.

To the one who loves us and freed us from our sins by his blood, ⁶who made us a kingdom, priests to his God and Father—to him be glory and power forever and always. Amen.

⁷ Look, he is coming with the clouds! Every eye will see him, including those who pierced him, and all the tribes of the earth will mourn because of him. This is so. Amen. ⁸"I am the Alpha and the Omega," says the Lord God, "the one who is and was and is coming, the Almighty."

Christ appears to John

⁹I, John, your brother who shares with you in the hardship, kingdom, and endurance that we have in Jesus, was on the island called Patmos because of the word of God and my witness about Jesus. ¹⁰I was in a Spirit-inspired trance on the Lord's day, and I heard behind me a loud voice that sounded like a trumpet. ¹¹It said, "Write down on a scroll whatever you see, and send it to the seven churches: to Ephesus, Smyrna, Pergamum, Thyatira, Sardis, Philadelphia, and Laodicea."

¹²I turned to see who was speaking to me, and when I turned, I saw seven oil lamps burning on top of seven gold stands. ¹³In the middle of the lampstands I saw someone who looked like the Human One.ᵃ He wore a robe that stretched down to his feet, and he had a gold sash around his chest. ¹⁴His head and hair were white as white wool—like snow—and his eyes were like a fiery flame. ¹⁵His feet were like fine brass that has been purified in a furnace, and his voice sounded like rushing water. ¹⁶He held seven stars in his right hand, and from his mouth came a sharp, two-edged sword. His appearance was like the sun shining with all its power.

ᵃOr Son of Man

¹⁷When I saw him, I fell at his feet like a dead man. But he put his right hand on me and said, "Don't be afraid. I'm the first and the last, ¹⁸and the living one. I was dead, but look! Now I'm alive forever and always. I have the keys of Death and the Grave. ¹⁹So write down what you have seen, both the scene now before you and the things that are about to unfold after this. ²⁰As for the mystery of the seven stars that you saw in my right hand and the seven gold lampstands, here is what they mean: the seven stars are the angels of the seven churches, and the seven lampstands are the seven churches.

Message to Ephesus

2 "Write this to the angel of the church in Ephesus:
These are the words of the one who holds the seven stars in his right hand and walks among the seven gold lampstands: ²I know your works, your labor, and your endurance. I also know that you don't put up with those who are evil. You have tested those who say they are apostles but are not, and you have found them to be liars. ³You have shown endurance and put up with a lot for my name's sake, and you haven't gotten tired. ⁴But I have this against you: you have let go of the love you had at first. ⁵So remember the high point from which you have fallen. Change your hearts and lives and do the things you did at first. If you don't, I'm coming to you. I will move your lampstand from its place if you don't change your hearts and lives. ⁶But you have this in your favor: you hate what the Nicolaitans are doing, which I also hate. ⁷If you can hear, listen to what the Spirit is saying to the churches. I will allow those who

emerge victorious to eat from the tree of life, which is in God's paradise.

Message to Smyrna

⁸"Write this to the angel of the church in Smyrna:
These are the words of the one who is the first and the last, who died and came back to life: ⁹I know your hardship and poverty (though you are actually rich). I also know the hurtful things that have been spoken about you by those who say they are Jews (though they are not, but are really Satan's synagogue). ¹⁰Don't be afraid of what you are going to suffer. Look! The devil is going to throw some of you into prison in order to test you. You will suffer hardship for ten days. Be faithful even to the point of death, and I will give you the crown of life. ¹¹If you can hear, listen to what the Spirit is saying to the churches. Those who emerge victorious won't be hurt by the second death.

Message to Pergamum

¹²"Write this to the angel of the church in Pergamum:
These are the words of the one who has the sharp, two-edged sword: ¹³I know that you are living right where Satan's throne is. You are holding on to my name, and you didn't break faith with me even at the time that Antipas, my faithful witness, was killed among you, where Satan lives. ¹⁴But I have a few things against you, because you have some there who follow Balaam's teaching. Balaam had taught Balak to trip up the Israelites so that they would eat food sacrificed to idols and commit sexual immorality. ¹⁵In the same way, you have some who follow the Nicolaitans' teaching. ¹⁶So change your hearts

and lives. If you don't, I am coming to you soon, and I will make war on them with the sword that comes from my mouth. [17] If you can hear, listen to what the Spirit is saying to the churches. I will give those who emerge victorious some of the hidden manna to eat. I will also give to each of them a white stone with a new name written on it, which no one knows except the one who receives it.

Message to Thyatira

[18] "Write this to the angel of the church in Thyatira:

These are the words of God's Son, whose eyes are like a fiery flame, and whose feet are like fine brass. [19] I know your works, your love and faithfulness, your service and endurance. I also know that the works you have done most recently are even greater than those you did at first. [20] But I have this against you: you put up with that woman, Jezebel, who calls herself a prophet. You allow her to teach and to mislead my servants into committing sexual immorality and eating food sacrificed to idols. [21] I gave her time to change her heart and life, but she refuses to change her life of prostitution. [22] Look! I'm throwing her onto a sickbed. I am casting those who have committed adultery with her into terrible hardship—if they don't change their hearts from following her practices—[23] and I will even put her children to death with disease. Then all the churches will know that I'm the one who examines minds and hearts, and that I will give to each of you what your actions deserve. [24] As for the rest of you in Thyatira—those of you who don't follow this teaching and haven't learned the so-called "deep secrets" of Satan—I won't burden you with anything else.

[25] Just hold on to what you have until I come. [26] To those who emerge victorious, keeping my practices until the end, I will give authority over the nations—[27] to rule the nations with an iron rod and smash them like pottery—[28] just as I received authority from my Father. I will also give them the morning star. [29] If you can hear, listen to what the Spirit is saying to the churches.

Message to Sardis

3 "Write this to the angel of the church in Sardis:

These are the words of the one who holds God's seven spirits and the seven stars: I know your works. You have the reputation of being alive, and you are in fact dead. [2] Wake up and strengthen whatever you have left, teetering on the brink of death, for I've found that your works are far from complete in the eyes of my God. [3] So remember what you received and heard. Hold on to it and change your hearts and lives. If you don't wake up, I will come like a thief, and you won't know what time I will come upon you. [4] But you do have a few people in Sardis who haven't stained their clothing. They will walk with me clothed in white because they are worthy. [5] Those who emerge victorious will wear white clothing like this. I won't scratch out their names from the scroll of life, but will declare their names in the presence of my Father and his angels. [6] If you can hear, listen to what the Spirit is saying to the churches.

Message to Philadelphia

[7] "Write this to the angel of the church in Philadelphia:

These are the words of the one who is holy and true, who has the key of David. Whatever he opens, no one will shut;

and whatever he shuts, no one opens. [8] I know your works. Look! I have set in front of you an open door that no one can shut. You have so little power, and yet you have kept my word and haven't denied my name. [9] Because of this I will make the people from Satan's synagogue (who say they are Jews and really aren't, but are lying)—I will make them come and bow down at your feet and realize that I have loved you. [10] Because you kept my command to endure, I will keep you safe through the time of testing that is about to come over the whole world, to test those who live on earth. [11] I'm coming soon. Hold on to what you have so that no one takes your crown. [12] As for those who emerge victorious, I will make them pillars in the temple of my God, and they will never leave it. I will write on them the name of my God and the name of the city of my God, the New Jerusalem that comes down out of heaven from my God. I will also write on them my own new name. [13] If you can hear, listen to what the Spirit is saying to the churches.

Message to Laodicea

[14] "Write this to the angel of the church in Laodicea:

These are the words of the Amen, the faithful and true witness, the ruler[b] of God's creation. [15] I know your works. You are neither cold nor hot. I wish that you were either cold or hot. [16] So because you are lukewarm, and neither hot nor cold, I'm about to spit you out of my mouth. [17] After all, you say, 'I'm rich, and I've grown wealthy, and I don't need a thing.' You don't realize that you are miserable, pathetic, poor, blind, and naked. [18] My advice is that you buy

gold from me that has been purified by fire so that you may be rich, and white clothing to wear so that your nakedness won't be shamefully exposed, and ointment to put on your eyes so that you may see. [19] I correct and discipline those whom I love. So be earnest and change your hearts and lives. [20] Look! I'm standing at the door and knocking. If any hear my voice and open the door, I will come in to be with them, and will have dinner with them, and they will have dinner with me. [21] As for those who emerge victorious, I will allow them to sit with me on my throne, just as I emerged victorious and sat down with my Father on his throne. [22] If you can hear, listen to what the Spirit is saying to the churches."

John sees God's heavenly throne

4 After this I looked and there was a door that had been opened in heaven. The first voice that I had heard, which sounded like a trumpet, said to me, "Come up here, and I will show you what must take place after this." [2] At once I was in a Spirit-inspired trance and I saw a throne in heaven, and someone was seated on the throne. [3] The one seated there looked like jasper and carnelian, and surrounding the throne was a rainbow that looked like an emerald. [4] Twenty-four thrones, with twenty-four elders seated upon them, surrounded the throne. The elders were dressed in white clothing and had gold crowns on their heads. [5] From the throne came lightning, voices, and thunder. In front of the throne were seven flaming torches, which are the seven spirits of God. [6] Something like

[b] Or beginning

a glass sea, like crystal, was in front of the throne.

In the center, by the throne, were four living creatures encircling the throne. These creatures were covered with eyes on the front and on the back. [7]The first living creature was like a lion. The second living creature was like an ox. The third living creature had a face like a human being. And the fourth living creature was like an eagle in flight. [8]Each of the four living creatures had six wings, and each was covered all around and on the inside with eyes. They never rest day or night, but keep on saying,

"Holy, holy, holy is the Lord
God Almighty,
who was and is and is coming."

[9]Whenever the living creatures give glory, honor, and thanks to the one seated on the throne, who lives forever and always, [10]the twenty-four elders fall before the one seated on the throne. They worship the one who lives forever and always. They throw down their crowns before the throne and say,

[11]"You are worthy, our Lord and God,
to receive glory and honor
and power,
because you created all things.
It is by your will
that they existed
and were created."

The Lamb takes the scroll

5Then I saw a scroll in the right hand of the one seated on the throne. It had writing on the front and the back, and it was sealed with seven seals. [2]I saw a powerful angel, who proclaimed in a loud voice, "Who is worthy to open the scroll and break its seals?" [3]But no one in heaven or on earth or under the earth could open the scroll

or look inside it. [4]So I began to weep and weep, because no one was found worthy to open the scroll or to look inside it. [5]Then one of the elders said to me, "Don't weep. Look! The Lion of the tribe of Judah, the Root of David, has emerged victorious so that he can open the scroll and its seven seals."

[6]Then, in between the throne and the four living creatures and among the elders, I saw a Lamb, standing as if it had been slain. It had seven horns and seven eyes, which are God's seven spirits, sent out into the whole earth. [7]He came forward and took the scroll from the right hand of the one seated on the throne. [8]When he took the scroll, the four living creatures and the twenty-four elders fell down before the Lamb. Each held a harp and gold bowls full of incense, which are the prayers of the saints. [9]They took up a new song, saying,

"You are worthy to take the scroll
and open its seals,
because you were slain,
and by your blood you purchased
for God
persons from every tribe,
language, people, and nation.
[10]You made them a kingdom and
priests to our God,
and they will rule on earth."

[11]Then I looked, and I heard the sound of many angels surrounding the throne, the living creatures, and the elders. They numbered in the millions—thousands upon thousands. [12]They said in a loud voice,

"Worthy is the slaughtered Lamb
to receive power, wealth, wisdom,
and might,
and honor, glory, and blessing."

[13]And I heard every creature in heaven and on earth and under the

earth and in the sea—I heard everything everywhere say,

"Blessing, honor, glory,
and power belong
to the one seated on the throne
and to the Lamb
forever and always."

[14] Then the four living creatures said, "Amen," and the elders fell down and worshipped.

Opening the first six seals

6 Then I looked on as the Lamb opened one of the seven seals. I heard one of the four living creatures say in a voice like thunder, "Come!" [2] So I looked, and there was a white horse. Its rider held a bow and was given a crown. And he went forth from victory to victory.

[3] When the Lamb opened the second seal, I heard the second living creature say, "Come!" [4] Out came another horse, fiery red. Its rider was allowed to take peace from the earth so that people would kill each other. He was given a large sword.

[5] When he opened the third seal, I heard the third living creature say, "Come!" So I looked, and there was a black horse. Its rider held a balance for weighing in his hand. [6] I heard what sounded like a voice from among the four living creatures. It said, "A quart of wheat for a denarion,[c] and three quarts of barley for a denarion, but don't damage the olive oil and the wine."

[7] When he opened the fourth seal, I heard the voice of the fourth living creature say, "Come!" [8] So I looked, and there was a pale green horse. Its rider's name was Death, and the Grave was following right behind. They were given authority over a fourth of the earth, to kill by sword, famine, disease, and the wild animals of the earth.

[9] When he opened the fifth seal, I saw under the altar those who had been slaughtered on account of the word of God and the witness they had given. [10] They cried out with a loud voice, "Holy and true Master, how long will you wait before you pass judgment? How long before you require justice for our blood, which was shed by those who live on earth?" [11] Each of them was given a white robe, and they were told to rest a little longer, until their fellow servants and brothers and sisters—who were about to be killed as they were—were finished.

[12] I looked on as he opened the sixth seal, and there was a great earthquake. The sun became black as funeral clothing, and the entire moon turned red as blood. [13] The stars of the sky fell to the earth as a fig tree drops its fruit when shaken by a strong wind. [14] The sky disappeared like a scroll being rolled up, and every mountain and island was moved from its place. [15] Then the kings of the earth, the officials and the generals, the rich and the powerful, and everyone, slave and free, hid themselves in caves and in the rocks of the mountains. [16] They called to the mountains and the rocks, "Fall on us and hide us from the face of the one seated on the throne and from the Lamb's wrath! [17] The great day of their wrath has come, and who is able to stand?"

One hundred forty-four thousand sealed

7 After this I saw four angels standing at the four corners of the earth. They

---

[c] A denarion was a day's pay for a laborer.

held back the earth's four winds so that no wind would blow against the earth, the sea, or any tree. [2] I saw another angel coming up from the east, holding the seal of the living God. He cried out with a loud voice to the four angels who had been given the power to damage the earth and sea. [3] He said, "Don't damage the earth, the sea, or the trees until we have put a seal on the foreheads of those who serve our God."

[4] Then I heard the number of those who were sealed: one hundred forty-four thousand, sealed from every tribe of the Israelites:

[5] From the tribe of Judah,
twelve thousand were sealed;
    from the tribe of Reuben,
twelve thousand;
    from the tribe of Gad,
twelve thousand;
[6] from the tribe of Asher,
twelve thousand;
    from the tribe of Naphtali,
twelve thousand;
    from the tribe of Manasseh,
twelve thousand;
[7] from the tribe of Simeon,
twelve thousand;
    from the tribe of Levi,
twelve thousand;
    from the tribe of Issachar,
twelve thousand;
[8] from the tribe of Zebulun,
twelve thousand;
    from the tribe of Joseph,
twelve thousand;
    from the tribe of Benjamin,
twelve thousand were sealed.

The great crowd and seventh seal

[9] After this I looked, and there was a great crowd that no one could number. They were from every nation, tribe, people, and language. They were standing before the throne and before the Lamb. They wore white robes and held palm branches in their hands. [10] They cried out with a loud voice:

"Victory belongs to our God
    who sits on the throne,
        and to the Lamb."

[11] All the angels stood in a circle around the throne, and around the elders and the four living creatures. They fell facedown before the throne and worshipped God, [12] saying,

"Amen! Blessing and glory
    and wisdom and thanksgiving
    and honor and power and might
        be to our God forever
        and always. Amen."

[13] Then one of the elders said to me, "Who are these people wearing white robes, and where did they come from?"

[14] I said to him, "Sir, you know."

Then he said to me, "These people have come out of great hardship. They have washed their robes and made them white in the Lamb's blood. [15] This is the reason they are before God's throne. They worship him day and night in his temple, and the one seated on the throne will shelter them. [16] They won't hunger or thirst anymore. No sun or scorching heat will beat down on them, [17] because the Lamb who is in the midst of the throne will shepherd them. He will lead them to the springs of life-giving water,[d] and God will wipe away every tear from their eyes."

8 Then, when the Lamb opened the seventh seal, there was silence in heaven for about half an hour.

[d] Or the water of life

The first four trumpet plagues

[2]Then I saw the seven angels who stand before God, and seven trumpets were given to them. [3]Another angel came and stood at the altar, and he held a gold bowl for burning incense. He was given a large amount of incense, in order to offer it on behalf of the prayers of all the saints on the gold altar in front of the throne. [4]The smoke of the incense offered for the prayers of the saints rose up before God from the angel's hand. [5]Then the angel took the incense container and filled it with fire from the altar. He threw it down to the earth, and there were thunder, voices, lightning, and an earthquake.

[6]Then the seven angels who held the seven trumpets got ready to blow them. [7]The first angel blew his trumpet, and hail and fire mixed with blood appeared, and was thrown down to the earth. A third of the earth was burned up. A third of the trees were burned up. All the green grass was burned up. [8]Then the second angel blew his trumpet, and something like a huge mountain burning with fire was thrown down into the sea. A third of the sea became blood, [9]a third of the creatures living in the sea died, and a third of the ships were destroyed. [10]Then the third angel blew his trumpet, and a great star, burning like a torch, fell from heaven. It fell on a third of the rivers and springs of water. [11]The star's name is Wormwood, and a third of the waters became wormwood, and many people died from the water, because it became so bitter. [12]Then the fourth angel blew his trumpet, and a third of the sun was struck, and a third of the moon, and a third of the stars so that a third of them became dark. The day lost a third of its light, and the night lost a third of its light too.

[13]Then I looked and I heard an eagle flying high overhead. It said with a loud voice, "Horror, horror, oh! The horror for those who live on earth because of the blasts of the remaining trumpets that the three angels are about to blow!"

The fifth and sixth trumpet plagues

9 Then the fifth angel blew his trumpet, and I saw a star that had fallen from heaven to earth, and he was given the key to the shaft of the abyss. [2]He opened the shaft of the abyss; and smoke rose up from the shaft, like smoke from a huge furnace. The sun and air were darkened by the smoke from the shaft. [3]Then locusts came forth from the smoke and onto the earth. They were given power like the power that scorpions have on the earth. [4]They were told not to hurt the grass of the earth or any green plant or any tree. They could only hurt the people who didn't have the seal of God on their foreheads. [5]The locusts weren't allowed to kill them, but only to make them suffer for five months—and the suffering they inflict is like that of a scorpion when it strikes a person. [6]In those days people will seek death, but they won't find it. They will want to die, but death will run away from them.

[7]The locusts looked like horses ready for battle. On their heads were what seemed to be gold crowns. Their faces were like human faces, [8]their hair was like women's hair, and their teeth were like lions' teeth. [9]In front they had what seemed to be iron armor upon their chests, and the sound of their wings was like the sound of many chariots and horses racing into battle.

[10]They also have tails with stingers, just like scorpions; and in their tails is their power to hurt people for five months. [11]Their king is an angel from the abyss, whose Hebrew name is Abaddon,[e] and whose Greek name is Apollyon.[f]

[12]The first horror has passed. Look! Two horrors are still coming after this.

[13]Then the sixth angel blew his trumpet, and I heard a voice from the four horns of the gold altar that is before God. [14]It said to the sixth angel, who had the trumpet, "Release the four angels who are bound at the great river Euphrates." [15]Then the four angels who had been made ready for that hour, day, month, and year were released to kill a third of humankind. [16]The number of cavalry troops was two hundred million. I heard their number. [17]And this is the way I saw the horses and their riders in the vision: they had breastplates that were fiery red, dark blue, and yellow as sulfur. The horses' heads were like lions' heads, and out of their mouths came fire, smoke, and sulfur. [18]By these three plagues a third of humankind was killed: by the fire, smoke, and sulfur coming out of their mouths. [19]The horses' power is in their mouths and their tails, for their tails are like snakes with heads that inflict injuries.

[20]The rest of humankind, who weren't killed by these plagues, didn't change their hearts and lives and turn from their handiwork. They didn't stop worshipping demons and idols made of gold, silver, bronze, stone, and wood—idols that can't see or hear or walk. [21]They didn't turn away from their murders, their spells and drugs, their sexual immorality, or their stealing.

John receives the open scroll

10 Then I saw another powerful angel coming down from heaven. He was robed with a cloud, with a rainbow over his head. His face was like the sun, and his feet were like fiery pillars. [2]He held an open scroll in his hand. He put his right foot on the sea and his left foot on the land. [3]He called out with a loud voice like a lion roaring, and when he called out, the seven thunders raised their voices. [4]When the seven thunders spoke, I was about to write, but I heard a voice from heaven say, "Seal up what the seven thunders have said, and don't write it down."

[5]Then the angel I saw standing on the sea and on the land raised his right hand to heaven. [6]He swore by the one who lives forever and always, who created heaven and what is in it, the earth and what is in it, and the sea and what is in it, and said, "The time is up. [7]In the days when the seventh angel blows his trumpet, God's mysterious purpose will be accomplished, fulfilling the good news he gave to his servants the prophets."

[8]Then the voice I heard from heaven spoke to me again and said, "Go, take the opened scroll from the hand of the angel who stands on the sea and on the land." [9]So I went to the angel and told him to give me the scroll. He said to me, "Take it and eat it. It will make you sick to your stomach, but sweet as honey in your mouth." [10]So I took the scroll from the angel's hand and ate it. And it was sweet as honey in my mouth, but when I swallowed it, it made my stomach churn. [11]I was told, "You must prophesy again about many peoples, nations, languages, and kings."

[e]Destruction　[f]Destroyer

Two witnesses

11 Then I was given a measuring rod, which was like a pole. And I was told, "Get up and measure God's temple, the altar, and those who worship there. ²But don't measure the court outside the temple. Leave that out, because it has been given to the nations, and they will trample the holy city underfoot for forty-two months.

³"And I will allow my two witnesses to prophesy for one thousand two hundred sixty days, wearing mourning clothes. ⁴These are the two olive trees and the two lampstands that stand before the Lord of the earth. ⁵If anyone wants to hurt them, fire comes out of their mouth and burns up their enemies. So if anyone wants to hurt them, they have to be killed in this way. ⁶They have the power to close up the sky so that no rain will fall for as long as they prophesy. They also have power over the waters, to turn them into blood, and to strike the earth with any plague, as often as they wish.

⁷"When they have finished their witnessing, the beast that comes up from the abyss will make war on them, gain victory over them, and kill them. ⁸Their dead bodies will lie on the street of the great city that is spiritually called Sodom and Egypt, where also their Lord was crucified. ⁹And for three and a half days, members of the peoples, tribes, languages, and nations will look at their dead bodies, but they won't let their dead bodies be put in a tomb. ¹⁰Those who live on earth will rejoice over them. They will celebrate and give each other gifts, because these two prophets had brought such pain to those who live on earth.

¹¹"But after three and a half days, the breath of life from God entered them, and they stood on their feet. Great fear came over those who saw them. ¹²Then they heard a loud voice from heaven say to them, 'Come up here.' And they went up to heaven in a cloud, while their enemies watched them. ¹³At that hour there was a great earthquake, and a tenth of the city fell. Seven thousand people were killed by the earthquake, and the rest were afraid and gave glory to the God of heaven."

¹⁴The second horror is over. The third horror is coming soon.

Seventh trumpet

¹⁵Then the seventh angel blew his trumpet, and there were loud voices in heaven saying,

"The kingdom of the world
    has become
    the kingdom of our Lord
    and his Christ,
    and he will rule
    forever and always."

¹⁶Then the twenty-four elders, who were seated on their thrones before God, fell on their faces and worshipped God. ¹⁷They said,

"We give thanks to you,
    Lord God Almighty,
    who is and was,
    for you have taken
    your great power
    and enforced your rule.
¹⁸The nations were enraged,
    but your wrath came.
The time came for the dead
    to be judged.
The time came to reward
    your servants, the prophets
    and saints,
    and those who fear your name,
    both small and great,

and to destroy those who
destroy the earth."

19 Then God's temple in heaven was opened, and the chest containing his covenant appeared in his temple. There were lightning, voices, thunder, an earthquake, and large hail.

A woman, her child, and the dragon

12 Then a great sign appeared in heaven: a woman clothed with the sun, with the moon under her feet and a crown of twelve stars on her head. 2 She was pregnant, and she cried out because she was in labor, in pain from giving birth. 3 Then another sign appeared in heaven: it was a great fiery red dragon, with seven heads and ten horns, and seven royal crowns on his heads. 4 His tail swept down a third of heaven's stars and threw them to the earth. The dragon stood in front of the woman who was about to give birth so that when she gave birth, he might devour her child. 5 She gave birth to a son, a male child who is to rule all the nations with an iron rod. Her child was snatched up to God and his throne. 6 Then the woman fled into the desert, where God has prepared a place for her. There she will be taken care of for one thousand two hundred sixty days.

Michael and the dragon

7 Then there was war in heaven: Michael and his angels fought the dragon. The dragon and his angels fought back, 8 but they did not prevail, and there was no longer any place for them in heaven. 9 So the great dragon was thrown down. The old snake, who is called the devil and Satan, the deceiver of the whole world, was thrown down to the earth;

and his angels were thrown down with him. 10 Then I heard a loud voice in heaven say,

"Now the salvation and power
　and kingdom of our God,
　　and the authority of his Christ
　　have come.
The accuser of our brothers
　and sisters,
　　who accuses them day and night
　　before our God,
　　has been thrown down.
11 They gained the victory over him
　on account of the blood of the Lamb
　and the word of their witness.
Love for their own lives
　didn't make them afraid to die.
12 Therefore, rejoice, you heavens and
　you who dwell in them.
But oh! The horror for the earth
　and sea!
　　The devil has come down to you
　　with great rage,
　　for he knows that he only
　　has a short time."

The dragon pursues the woman

13 When the dragon saw that he had been thrown down to the earth, he chased the woman who had given birth to the male child. 14 But the woman was given the two wings of the great eagle so that she could fly to her place in the desert. There she would be taken care of—out of the snake's reach—for a time and times and half a time. 15 Then from his mouth the snake poured a river of water after the woman so that the river would sweep her away. 16 But the earth helped the woman. The earth opened its mouth and swallowed the river that the dragon poured out of his mouth. 17 So the dragon was furious with the woman, and he went off to

make war on the rest of her children, on those who keep God's commandments and hold firmly to the witness of Jesus.

The beast from the sea

¹⁸Then the dragon stood on the seashore, **13** ¹and I saw a beast coming up out of the sea. It had ten horns and seven heads. Each of its horns was decorated with a royal crown, and on its heads were blasphemous names. ²The beast I saw was like a leopard. Its feet were like a bear's, and its mouth was like a lion's mouth. The dragon gave it his power, throne, and great authority. ³One of its heads appeared to have been slain and killed, but its deadly wound was healed. So the whole earth was amazed and followed the beast. ⁴They worshipped the dragon because it had given the beast its authority. They worshipped the beast and said, "Who is like the beast, and who can fight against it?"

⁵The beast was given a mouth that spoke boastful and blasphemous things, and it was given authority to act for forty-two months. ⁶It opened its mouth to speak blasphemies against God. It blasphemed God's name and his dwelling place (that is, those who dwell in heaven).

⁷It was also allowed to make war on the saints and to gain victory over them. It was given authority over every tribe, people, language, and nation. ⁸All who live on earth worshipped it, all whose names hadn't been written—from the time the earth was made—in the scroll of life of the Lamb who was slain. ⁹Whoever has ears must listen: ¹⁰If any are to be taken captive, then into captivity they will go. If any are to be killed by the sword, then by the sword they will be killed. This calls for endurance and faithfulness on the part of the saints.

The beast from the land

¹¹Then I saw another beast coming up from the earth. It had two horns like a lamb, but it was speaking like a dragon. ¹²It exercises all the authority of the first beast in its presence. It also makes the earth and those who live in it worship the first beast, whose fatal wound was healed. ¹³It does great signs so that it even makes fire come down from heaven to earth in the presence of the people. ¹⁴It deceives those who live on earth by the signs that it was allowed to do in the presence of the beast. It told those who live on earth to make an image for the beast who had been wounded by the sword and yet came to life again. ¹⁵It was allowed to give breath to the beast's image so that the beast's image would even speak and cause anyone who didn't worship the beast's image to be put to death. ¹⁶It forces everyone—the small and great, the rich and poor, the free and slaves—to have a mark put on their right hand or on their forehead. ¹⁷It will not allow anyone to make a purchase or sell anything unless the person has the mark with the beast's name or the number of its name. ¹⁸This calls for wisdom. Let the one who understands calculate the beast's number, for it's a human being's number. Its number is six hundred sixty-six.

The Lamb and the one hundred forty-four thousand

14 Then I looked, and there was the Lamb, standing on Mount Zion. With him were one hundred forty-four thousand who had his name and his Father's name written on their foreheads. [2]I heard a sound from heaven that was like the sound of rushing water and loud thunder. The sound I heard was like that of harpists playing their harps. [3]They sing a new song in front of the throne, the four living creatures, and the elders. And no one could learn the song except the one hundred forty-four thousand who had been purchased from the earth. [4]They weren't defiled with women, for these people who follow the Lamb wherever he goes are virgins. They were purchased from among humankind as early produce for God and the Lamb. [5]No lie came from their mouths; they are blameless.

Messages of three angels

[6]Then I saw another angel flying high overhead with eternal good news to proclaim to those who live on earth, and to every nation, tribe, language, and people. [7]He said in a loud voice, "Fear God and give him glory, for the hour of his judgment has come. Worship the one who made heaven and earth, the sea and springs of water."

[8]Another angel, a second one, followed and said, "Fallen, fallen is Babylon the great! She made all the nations drink the wine of her lustful passion."

[9]Then another angel, a third one, followed them and said in a loud voice, "If any worship the beast and its image, and receive a mark on their foreheads or their hands, [10]they themselves will also drink the wine of God's passionate anger, poured full strength into the cup of his wrath. They will suffer the pain of fire and sulfur in the presence of the holy angels and the Lamb. [11]The smoke of their painful suffering goes up forever and always. There is no rest day or night for those who worship the beast and its image, and those who receive the mark of its name."

[12]This calls for the endurance of the saints, who keep God's commandments and keep faith with Jesus.

[13]And I heard a voice from heaven say, "Write this: Favored are the dead who die in the Lord from now on."

"Yes," says the Spirit, "so they can rest from their labors, because their deeds follow them."

Two harvests of the earth

[14]Then I looked, and there was a white cloud. On the cloud was seated someone who looked like the Human One.[g] He had a gold crown on his head and a sharp sickle in his hand. [15]Another angel came out of the temple, calling in a loud voice to the one seated on the cloud: "Use your sickle to reap the harvest, for the time to harvest has come, and the harvest of the earth is ripe." [16]So the one seated on the cloud swung his sickle over the earth, and the earth was harvested.

[17]Then another angel came out of the temple in heaven, and he also had a sharp sickle. [18]Still another angel, who has power over fire, came out from the altar. He said in a loud voice to the one who had the sharp sickle, "Use your sharp sickle to cut the clusters in the vineyard of the earth, because its grapes are ripe." [19]So the angel swung his sickle into the earth, and cut the vineyard of the earth, and he put what

[g]Or Son of Man

he reaped into the great winepress of God's passionate anger. [20] Then the winepress was trampled outside the city, and the blood came out of the winepress as high as the horses' bridles for almost two hundred miles.[h]

Song of Moses and the Lamb

15 Then I saw another great and awe-inspiring sign in heaven. There were seven angels with seven plagues—and these are the last, for with them God's anger is brought to an end. [2] Then I saw what appeared to be a sea of glass mixed with fire. Those who gained victory over the beast, its image, and the number of its name were standing by the glass sea, holding harps from God. [3] They sing the song of Moses, God's servant, and the song of the Lamb, saying,

> "Great and awe-inspiring
>   are your works,
>   Lord God Almighty.
> Just and true are your ways,
>   king of the nations.
> [4] Who won't fear you, Lord,
>   and glorify your name?
>   You alone are holy.
> All nations will come and fall down
>   in worship before you,
>   for your acts of justice
>   have been revealed."

Seven bowl plagues

[5] After this I looked, and the temple in heaven—that is, the tent of witness—was opened. [6] The seven angels, who have the seven plagues, came out of the temple. They were clothed in pure bright linen and had gold sashes around their waists. [7] Then one of the four living creatures gave the seven angels seven gold bowls full of the anger of the God who lives forever and always. [8] The temple was filled with smoke from God's glory and power, and no one could go into the temple until the seven plagues of the seven last angels were brought to an end.

16 Then I heard a loud voice from the temple say to the seven angels, "Go and pour out the seven bowls of God's anger on the earth." [2] So the first angel poured his bowl on the earth, and a nasty and terrible sore appeared on the people who had the beast's mark and worshipped its image. [3] The second angel poured his bowl into the sea, and the sea turned into blood, like the blood of a corpse, and every living thing in the sea died. [4] The third angel poured his bowl into the rivers and springs of water, and they turned into blood. [5] Then I heard the angel of the waters say,

> "You are just, holy one,
>   who is and was,
> because you have given
>   these judgments.
> [6] They poured out the blood of saints
>   and prophets,
> and you have given them blood
>   to drink. They deserve it!"

[7] And I heard the altar say,

> "Yes, Lord God Almighty,
>   your judgments are true
>   and just."

[8] The fourth angel poured his bowl on the sun, and it was allowed to burn people with fire. [9] The people were burned by intense heat, and they cursed the name of the God who had power over these plagues. But they

---

[h]Or one thousand six hundred stades

didn't change their hearts and lives and give him glory. ¹⁰The fifth angel poured his bowl over the beast's throne, and darkness covered its kingdom. People bit their tongues because of their pain, ¹¹and they cursed the God of heaven because of their pains and sores; but they didn't turn away from what they had done.

¹²Then the sixth angel poured his bowl on the great river Euphrates. Its water was dried up so that the way was ready for the kings from the east. ¹³Then I saw three unclean spirits, like frogs, come from the dragon's mouth, the beast's mouth, and the mouth of the false prophet. ¹⁴These are demonic spirits that do signs. They go out to the kings of the whole world, to gather them for battle on the great day of God the Almighty. (¹⁵Look! I'm coming like a thief! Favored are those who stay awake and clothed so that they don't go around naked and exposed to shame.) ¹⁶The spirits gathered them at the place that is called in Hebrew, Harmagedon.¹

¹⁷Then the seventh angel poured his bowl into the air, and a loud voice came out from the temple, from the throne, saying, "It is done!" ¹⁸There were lightning strikes, voices, and thunder, and a great earthquake occurred. The earthquake was greater than any that have occurred since there have been people on earth. ¹⁹The great city split into three parts, and the cities of the nations fell. God remembered Babylon the great so that he gave her the wine cup of his furious anger. ²⁰Every island fled, and the mountains disappeared. ²¹Huge hailstones weighing about one hundred pounds came down from heaven on the people. They cursed God for the plague of hail, because the plague was so terrible.

Babylon and the beast

17Then one of the seven angels who had the seven bowls spoke with me. "Come," he said, "I will show you the judgment upon the great prostitute, who is seated on deep waters. ²The kings of the earth have committed sexual immorality with her, and those who live on earth have become drunk with the wine of her whoring."

³Then he brought me in a Spirit-inspired trance to a desert. There I saw a woman seated on a scarlet beast that was covered with blasphemous names. It had seven heads and ten horns. ⁴The woman wore purple and scarlet clothing, and she glittered with gold and jewels and pearls. In her hand she held a gold cup full of the vile and impure things that came from her activity as a prostitute. ⁵A name—a mystery—was written on her forehead: "Babylon the great, the mother of prostitutes and the vile things of the earth." ⁶I saw that the woman was drunk on the blood of the saints and the blood of Jesus' witnesses. I was completely stunned when I saw her.

⁷Then the angel said to me, "Why are you amazed? I will tell you the mystery of the woman and the seven-headed, ten-horned beast that carries her. ⁸The beast that you saw was and is not, and is about to come up out of the abyss and go to destruction. Those who live on earth, whose names haven't been written in the scroll of life from the time the earth was made, will be amazed when

---

¹Or *Armageddon*

they see the beast, because it was and is not and will again be present. ⁹This calls for an understanding mind. The seven heads are seven mountains on which the woman is seated. They are also seven kings. ¹⁰Five kings have fallen, the one is, and the other hasn't yet come. When that king comes, he must remain for only a short time. ¹¹As for the beast that was and is not, it is itself an eighth king that belongs to the seven, and it is going to destruction. ¹²The ten horns that you saw are ten kings, who haven't yet received royal power. But they will receive royal authority for an hour, along with the beast. ¹³These kings will be of one mind, and they will give their power and authority to the beast. ¹⁴They will make war on the Lamb, but the Lamb will emerge victorious, for he is Lord of lords and King of kings. Those with him are called, chosen, and faithful."

¹⁵Then he said to me, "The waters that you saw, where the prostitute is seated, are peoples, crowds, nations, and languages. ¹⁶As for the ten horns that you saw, they and the beast will hate the prostitute. They will destroy her and strip her bare. They will devour her flesh and burn her with fire ¹⁷because God moved them to carry out his purposes. That is why they will be of one mind and give their royal power to the beast, until God's words have been accomplished. ¹⁸The woman whom you saw is the great city that rules over the kings of the earth."

Babylon's fall

18 After this I saw another angel coming down from heaven. He had great authority, and the earth was filled with light because of his glory. ²He called out with a loud voice, saying, "Fallen, fallen is Babylon the great! She has become a home for demons and a lair for every unclean spirit. She is a lair for every unclean bird, and a lair for every unclean and disgusting beast ³because all the nations have fallen[j] due to the wine of her lustful passion. The kings of the earth committed sexual immorality with her, and the merchants of the earth became rich from the power of her loose and extravagant ways."

⁴Then I heard another voice from heaven say, "Come out of her, my people, so that you don't take part in her sins and don't receive any of her plagues. ⁵Her sins have piled up as high as heaven, and God remembered her unjust acts. ⁶Give her what she has given to others. Give her back twice as much for what she has done. In the cup that she has poured, pour her twice as much. ⁷To the extent that she glorified herself and indulged her loose and extravagant ways, give her pain and grief. In her heart she says, 'I sit like a queen! I'm not a widow. I'll never see grief.' ⁸This is why her plagues will come in a single day—deadly disease, grief, and hunger. She will be consumed by fire because the Lord God who judges her is powerful.

⁹"The kings of the earth, who committed sexual immorality with her and shared her loose and extravagant ways, will weep and mourn over her when they see the smoke from her burning. ¹⁰They will stand a long way off because they are afraid of the pain she suffers, and they will say, 'Oh, the horror!

---

[j]Critical editions of the Gk New Testament read *have drunk.*

Babylon, you great city, you powerful city! In a single hour your judgment has come.'

[11]"The merchants of the earth will weep and mourn over her, for no one buys their cargoes anymore—[12]cargoes of gold, silver, jewels, and pearls; fine linen, purple, silk, and scarlet; all those things made of scented wood, ivory, fine wood, bronze, iron, and marble; [13]cinnamon, incense, fragrant ointment, and frankincense; wine, oil, fine flour, and wheat; cattle, sheep, horses, and carriages; and slaves, even human lives. [14]The fruit your whole being craved has gone from you. All your glitter and glamour are lost to you, never ever to be found again.'

[15]"The merchants who sold these things, and got so rich by her, will stand a long way off because they fear the pain she suffers. They will weep and mourn, and say, [16]'Oh, the horror! The great city that wore fine linen, purple, and scarlet, who glittered with gold, jewels, and pearls—[17]in just one hour such great wealth was destroyed.'

"Every sea captain, every seafarer, sailors, and all who make their living on the sea stood a long way off. [18]They cried out as they saw the smoke from her burning and said, 'What city was ever like the great city?' [19]They threw dust on their heads, and they cried out, weeping and mourning. They said, 'Oh, the horror! The great city, where all who have ships at sea became so rich by her prosperity—in just one hour she was destroyed. [20]Rejoice over her, heaven—you saints, apostles, and prophets—because God has condemned her as she condemned you.'"

[21]Then a powerful angel picked up a stone that was like a huge millstone and threw it into the sea, saying, "With such violent force the great city of Babylon will be thrown down, and it won't be found anymore. [22]The sound of harpists and musicians, of pipers and trumpeters, will never be heard among you again. No craftsman of any kind will ever be found among you again. The sound of the hand mill will never be heard among you again. [23]The light of a lamp will never shine among you again. The sound of a bridegroom and bride will never be heard among you again because your merchants ran the world, because all the nations were deceived by the spell you cast, and because [24]the blood of prophets, of saints, and of all who have been slaughtered on the earth was found among you."[k]

Celebration in heaven

19 After this I heard what sounded like a huge crowd in heaven. They said,

"Hallelujah! The salvation and glory
    and power of our God!
[2] His judgments are true and just,
    because he judged
        the great prostitute,
        who ruined the earth
            by her whoring,
    and he exacted the penalty
        for the blood of his servants
        from her hand."

[3]Then they said a second time,

"Hallelujah! Smoke goes up
    from her forever and always."

[4]The twenty-four elders and the four living creatures fell down and worshipped God, who is seated on the throne, and they said, "Amen. Hallelujah!"

[k]Or her

[5]Then a voice went out from the throne and said,

"Praise our God, all you his servants,
    and you who fear him, both small
    and great."

[6]And I heard something that sounded like a huge crowd, like rushing water and powerful thunder. They said,

"Hallelujah! The Lord our God,
    the Almighty,
    exercised his royal power!

[7] Let us rejoice and celebrate,
    and give him the glory,
    for the wedding day of the Lamb
        has come,
    and his bride has made
        herself ready.

[8] She was given fine,
    pure white linen to wear,
    for the fine linen is the saints' acts
        of justice."

[9]Then the angel said to me, "Write this: Favored are those who have been invited to the wedding banquet of the Lamb." He said to me, "These are the true words of God." [10]Then I fell at his feet to worship him. But he said, "Don't do that! I'm a servant just like you and your brothers and sisters who hold firmly to the witness of Jesus. Worship God! The witness of Jesus is the spirit of prophecy!"

Christ defeats the beast

[11]Then I saw heaven opened, and there was a white horse. Its rider was called Faithful and True, and he judges and makes war justly. [12]His eyes were like a fiery flame, and on his head were many royal crowns. He has a name written on him that no one knows but he himself. [13]He wore a robe dyed[1] with blood, and his name was called the Word of God. [14]Heaven's armies, wearing fine linen that was white and pure, were following him on white horses. [15]From his mouth comes a sharp sword that he will use to strike down the nations. He is the one who will rule them with an iron rod. And he is the one who will trample the winepress of the Almighty God's passionate anger. [16]He has a name written on his robe and on his thigh: King of kings and Lord of lords.

[17]Then I saw an angel standing in the sun, and he called out with a loud voice and said to all the birds flying high overhead, "Come and gather for God's great supper. [18]Come and eat the flesh of kings, the flesh of generals, the flesh of the powerful, and the flesh of horses and their riders. Come and eat the flesh of all, both free and slave, both small and great." [19]Then I saw that the beast and the kings of the earth and their armies had gathered to make war against the rider on the horse and his army. [20]But the beast was seized, along with the false prophet who had done signs in the beast's presence. (He had used the signs to deceive people into receiving the beast's mark and into worshipping the beast's image.) The two of them were thrown alive into the fiery lake that burns with sulfur. [21]The rest were killed by the sword that comes from the mouth of the rider on the horse, and all the birds ate their fill of their flesh.

Satan confined

20 Then I saw an angel coming down from heaven, holding in his hand

---

[1]Critical editions of the Gk New Testament read *dipped* or *covered with*.

the key to the abyss and a huge chain. [2]He seized the dragon, the old snake, who is the devil and Satan, and bound him for a thousand years. [3]He threw him into the abyss, then locked and sealed it over him. This was to keep him from continuing to deceive the nations until the thousand years were over. After this he must be released for a little while.

The saints rule with Christ

[4]Then I saw thrones, and people took their seats on them, and judgment was given in their favor.[m] They were the ones who had been beheaded for their witness to Jesus and God's word, and those who hadn't worshipped the beast or its image, who hadn't received the mark on their forehead or hand. They came to life and ruled with Christ for one thousand years. [5]The rest of the dead didn't come to life until the thousand years were over. This is the first resurrection. [6]Favored and holy are those who have a share in the first resurrection. The second death has no power over them, but they will be priests of God and of Christ, and will rule with him for one thousand years.

Satan's defeat

[7]When the thousand years are over, Satan will be released from his prison. [8]He will go out to deceive the nations that are at the four corners of the earth—Gog and Magog. He will gather them for battle. Their number is like the sand of the sea. [9]They came up across the whole earth and surrounded the saints' camp, the city that God loves. But fire came down from heaven and consumed them. [10]Then the devil, who had deceived them, was thrown into the lake of fire and sulfur, where the beast and the false prophet also were. There painful suffering will be inflicted upon them day and night, forever and always.

Final judgment

[11]Then I saw a great white throne and the one who is seated on it. Before his face both earth and heaven fled away, and no place was found for them. [12]I saw the dead, the great and the small, standing before the throne, and scrolls were opened. Another scroll was opened too; this is the scroll of life. And the dead were judged on the basis of what was written in the scrolls about what they had done. [13]The sea gave up the dead that were in it, and Death and the Grave gave up the dead that were in them, and people were judged by what they had done. [14]Then Death and the Grave were thrown into the fiery lake. This, the fiery lake, is the second death. [15]Then anyone whose name wasn't found written in the scroll of life was thrown into the fiery lake.

New heaven and new earth

21 Then I saw a new heaven and a new earth, for the former heaven and the former earth had passed away, and the sea was no more. [2]I saw the holy city, New Jerusalem, coming down out of heaven from God, made ready as a bride beautifully dressed for her husband. [3]I heard a loud voice from the throne say, "Look! God's dwelling is here with humankind. He will dwell with them, and they will be his peoples. God himself will be with them as their

[m]Or to them

God. [4] He will wipe away every tear from their eyes. Death will be no more. There will be no mourning, crying, or pain anymore, for the former things have passed away." [5] Then the one seated on the throne said, "Look! I'm making all things new." He also said, "Write this down, for these words are trustworthy and true." [6] Then he said to me, "All is done. I am the Alpha and the Omega, the beginning and the end. To the thirsty I will freely give water from the life-giving spring. [7] Those who emerge victorious will inherit these things. I will be their God, and they will be my sons and daughters. [8] But for the cowardly, the faithless, the vile, the murderers, those who commit sexual immorality, those who use drugs and cast spells, the idolaters and all liars—their share will be in the lake that burns with fire and sulfur. This is the second death."

New Jerusalem

[9] Then one of the seven angels who had the seven bowls full of the seven last plagues spoke with me. "Come," he said, "I will show you the bride, the Lamb's wife." [10] He took me in a Spirit-inspired trance to a great, high mountain, and he showed me the holy city, Jerusalem, coming down out of heaven from God. [11] The city had God's glory. Its brilliance was like a priceless jewel, like jasper that was as clear as crystal. [12] It had a great high wall with twelve gates. By the gates were twelve angels, and on the gates were written the names of the twelve tribes of Israel's sons. [13] There were three gates on the east, three gates on the north, three gates on the south, and three gates on the west.

[14] The city wall had twelve foundations, and on them were the twelve names of the Lamb's twelve apostles.

[15] The angel who spoke to me had a gold measuring rod with which to measure the city, its gates, and its wall. [16] Now the city was laid out as a square. Its length was the same as its width. He measured the city with the rod, and it was fifteen hundred miles.[n] Its length and width and height were equal. [17] He also measured the thickness of its wall. It was two hundred sixteen feet[o] thick, as a person—or rather, an angel—measures things. [18] The wall was built of jasper, and the city was pure gold, like pure glass. [19] The city wall's foundations were decorated with every kind of jewel. The first foundation was jasper, the second was sapphire, the third was chalcedony, and the fourth was emerald. [20] The fifth was sardonyx, the sixth was carnelian, the seventh was chrysolite, and the eighth was beryl. The ninth was topaz, the tenth was chrysoprase, the eleventh was jacinth, and the twelfth was amethyst. [21] The twelve gates were twelve pearls; each one of the gates was made from a single pearl. And the city's main street was pure gold, as transparent as glass.

[22] I didn't see a temple in the city, because its temple is the Lord God Almighty and the Lamb. [23] The city doesn't need the sun or the moon to shine on it, because God's glory is its light, and its lamp is the Lamb. [24] The nations will walk by its light, and the kings of the earth will bring their glory into it. [25] Its gates will never be shut by day, and there will be no night there. [26] They will bring the glory and honor of the nations into

---

[n]Or twelve thousand stades   [o]Or one hundred forty-four pechon (cubits)

it. ²⁷Nothing unclean will ever enter it, nor anyone who does what is vile and deceitful, but only those who are registered in the Lamb's scroll of life.

22 Then the angel showed me the river of life-giving water,ᵖ shining like crystal, flowing from the throne of God and the Lamb ²through the middle of the city's main street. On each side of the river is the tree of life, which produces twelve crops of fruit, bearing its fruit each month. The tree's leaves are for the healing of the nations. ³There will no longer be any curse. The throne of God and the Lamb will be in it, and his servants will worship him. ⁴They will see his face, and his name will be on their foreheads. ⁵Night will be no more. They won't need the light of a lamp or the light of the sun, for the Lord God will shine on them, and they will rule forever and always.

Jesus is coming soon

⁶Then he said to me, "These words are trustworthy and true. The Lord, the God of the spirits of the prophets, sent his angel to show his servants what must soon take place.

⁷"Look! I'm coming soon. Favored is the one who keeps the words of the prophecy contained in this scroll."

⁸I, John, am the one who heard and saw these things. When I heard and saw them, I fell down to worship at the feet of the angel who had shown them to me. ⁹But he said to me, "Don't do that! I'm a servant just like you and your brothers and sisters, the prophets, and those who keep the words of this scroll. Worship God!" ¹⁰Then he said to me, "Don't seal up the words of the prophecy contained in this scroll, because the time is near. ¹¹Let those who do wrong keep doing what is wrong. Let the filthy still be filthy. Let those who are righteous keep doing what is right. Let those who are holy still be holy.

¹²"Look! I'm coming soon. My reward is with me, to repay all people as their actions deserve. ¹³I am the alpha and the omega, the first and the last, the beginning and the end. ¹⁴Favored are those who wash their robes so that they may have the right of access to the tree of life and may enter the city by the gates. ¹⁵Outside are the dogs, the drug users and spell-casters, those who commit sexual immorality, the murderers, the idolaters, and all who love and practice deception.

¹⁶"I, Jesus, have sent my angel to bear witness to all of you about these things for the churches. I'm the root and descendant of David, the bright morning star. ¹⁷The Spirit and the bride say, 'Come!' Let the one who hears say, 'Come!' And let the one who is thirsty come! Let the one who wishes receive life-giving water�q as a gift."

¹⁸Now I bear witness to everyone who hears the words of the prophecy contained in this scroll: If anyone adds to them, God will add to that person the plagues that are written in this scroll. ¹⁹If anyone takes away from the words of this scroll of prophecy, God will take away that person's share in the tree of life and the holy city, which are described in this scroll.

²⁰The one who bears witness to these things says, "Yes, I'm coming soon." Amen. Come, Lord Jesus!

²¹The grace of the Lord Jesus be with all.

ᵖOr *the water of life*   qOr *the water of life*

Psalms and Proverbs

PSALMS

BOOK I
(Psalms 1–41)

Psalm 1

[1] The truly happy person
    doesn't follow wicked advice,
    doesn't stand on the road
      of sinners,
    and doesn't sit
      with the disrespectful.
[2] Instead of doing those things,
    these persons
    love the LORD's Instruction,
    and they recite God's Instruction
      day and night!
[3] They are like a tree
    replanted by streams of water,
    which bears fruit
      at just the right time
    and whose leaves don't fade.
      Whatever they do succeeds.

[4] That's not true for the wicked!
    They are like dust
      that the wind blows away.
[5] And that's why the wicked
    will have no standing
      in the court of justice—
    neither will sinners
      in the assembly of the righteous.
[6] The LORD is intimately acquainted
    with the way of the righteous,
    but the way of the wicked
      is destroyed.

Psalm 2

[1] Why do the nations rant?
    Why do the peoples rave uselessly?

[2] The earth's rulers take their stand;
    the leaders scheme together
      against the LORD and
    against his anointed one.
[3] "Come!" they say.
    "We will tear off their ropes
      and throw off their chains!"
[4] The one who rules in heaven laughs;
    my Lord makes fun of them.
[5] But then God speaks to them angrily;
    then he terrifies them with his fury:
[6] "I hereby appoint my king on Zion,
    my holy mountain!"

[7] I will announce the LORD's decision:
    He said to me, "You are my son,
      today I have become your father.
[8] Just ask me,
    and I will make the nations
      your possession;
    the far corners of the earth
      will be your property.
[9] You will smash them
    with an iron rod;
    you will shatter them
      like a pottery jar."

[10] So kings, wise up!
    Be warned, you rulers of the earth!
[11] Serve the LORD reverently—
    trembling, [12] kiss his feet[a]
    or else he will become angry,
      and your way will be destroyed
    because his anger ignites
      in an instant.

But all who take refuge in the LORD
    are truly happy!

---

[a] Correction; Heb uncertain; MT *rejoice with trembling, kiss the son* (but with *son* in Aram, not Heb)

Psalm 3

*A psalm of David, when he fled
from his son Absalom.*

¹ LORD, I have so many enemies!
So many are standing against me.
² So many are talking about me:
"Even God won't help him." *Selah*[b]
³ But you, LORD, are my shield!
You are my glory!
You are the one who restores me.
⁴ I cry out loud to the LORD,
and he answers me
from his holy mountain. *Selah*
⁵ I lie down, sleep, and wake up
because the LORD helps me.
⁶ I won't be afraid of thousands
of people
surrounding me on all sides.

⁷ Stand up, LORD!
Save me, my God!
In fact, hit all my enemies on the jaw;
shatter the teeth of the wicked!
⁸ Rescue comes from the LORD!
May your blessing
be on your people! *Selah*

Psalm 4

*For the music leader.
With stringed instruments.
A psalm of David.*

¹ Answer me when I cry out,
my righteous God!
Set me free from my troubles!
Have mercy on me!
Listen to my prayer!

² How long, you people,
will my reputation be insulted?
How long will you continue
to love what is worthless
and go after lies? *Selah*

³ Know this: the LORD takes
personal care of the faithful.
The LORD will hear me
when I cry out to him.
⁴ So be afraid, and don't sin!
Think hard about it in your bed
and weep over it! *Selah*
⁵ Bring righteous offerings,
and trust the LORD!

⁶ Many people say,
"We can't find goodness anywhere.
The light of your face has left us,
LORD!"[c]
⁷ But you have filled my heart
with more joy
than when their wheat and wine
are everywhere!
⁸ I will lie down and fall asleep in peace
because you alone, LORD,
let me live in safety.

Psalm 5

*For the music leader. For the
flutes. A psalm of David.*

¹ Hear my words, LORD!
Consider my groans!
² Pay attention to the sound
of my cries, my king and my God,
because I am praying to you!
³ LORD, in the morning
you hear my voice.
In the morning I lay it all out
before you.
Then I wait expectantly.
⁴ Because you aren't a God
who enjoys wickedness;
evil doesn't live with you.
⁵ Arrogant people won't last long
in your sight;
you hate all evildoers;
⁶ you destroy liars.

---

[b] Heb uncertain; probably a musical term [c] Correction; MT *Shine the light of your face on us,
LORD!*

The LORD despises people
  who are violent and dishonest.

⁷ But me? I will enter your house
    because of your abundant,
      faithful love;
  I will bow down at your holy temple,
    honoring you.
⁸ LORD, because of many enemies,
    please lead me in your righteousness.
  Make your way clear,
    right in front of me.
⁹ Because there's no truth
    in my enemies' mouths,
  all they have inside them
    is destruction.
  Their throats are open graves;
    their tongues slick with talk.
¹⁰ Condemn them, God!
    Let them fail by their own plans.
  Throw them out for their many sins
    because they've rebelled against you.
¹¹ But let all who take refuge
    in you celebrate.
  Let them sing out loud forever!
  Protect them
    so that all who love your name
      can rejoice in you.
¹² Because you, LORD,
    bless the righteous.
  You cover them with favor
    like a shield.

Psalm 6
*For the music leader.
On stringed instruments.
According to the eighth.*ᵈ
A psalm of David.

¹ Please, LORD,
    don't punish me when you are angry;
    don't discipline me
      when you are furious.

² Have mercy on me, LORD,
    because I'm frail.
  Heal me, LORD,
    because my bones
      are shaking in terror!
³ My whole bodyᵉ is completely terrified!
  But you, LORD!
    How long will this last?
⁴ Come back to me, LORD! Deliver me!
  Save me for the sake
    of your faithful love!
⁵ No one is going to praise you
    when they are dead.
  Who gives you thanks
    from the grave?ᶠ

⁶ I'm worn out from groaning.
  Every night, I drench my bed
    with tears;
  I soak my couch all the way through.
⁷ My vision fails because of my grief;
    it's weak because of all my distress.
⁸ Get away from me, all you evildoers,
    because the LORD
      has heard me crying!
⁹ The LORD has listened to my request.
  The LORD accepts my prayer.
¹⁰ All my enemies will be ashamed
    and completely terrified;
  they will be defeated
    and ashamed instantly.

Psalm 7
*A shiggayonᵍ of David,
which he sang to the LORD
about Cush, a Benjaminite.*
¹ I take refuge in you, LORD, my God.
  Save me from all who chase me!
    Rescue me!
² Otherwise, they will rip me apart,
    dragging me off
      with no chance of rescue.

ᵈPerhaps a reference to an eight-string instrument; also in Ps 12 ᵉOr *soul*; also in 6:4
ᶠHeb *Sheol* ᵍPerhaps *lament*

³ LORD, my God, if I have done this—
  if my hands have done
    anything wrong,
⁴ if I have repaid a friend with evil
  or oppressed a foe for no reason—
⁵ then let my enemy
  not only chase but catch me,
    trampling my life into the ground,
  laying my reputation
    in the dirt.   *Selah*

⁶ Get up, LORD; get angry!
  Stand up against the fury of my foes!
  Wake up, my God;ʰ
    you command that justice be done!
⁷ Let the assembled peoples
    surround you.
  Rule them from on high!ⁱ
⁸ The LORD will judge the peoples.
  Establish justice for me, LORD,
    according to my righteousness
    and according to my integrity.
⁹ Please let the evil of the wicked
    be over,
  but set the righteous firmly in place
    because you, the righteous God,
  are the one who examines
    hearts and minds.

¹⁰ God is my shield;
  he saves those whose heart is right.
¹¹ God is a righteous judge,
  a God who is angry at evilʲ
    every single day.
¹² If someone doesn't change their ways,
  God will sharpen his sword,
    will bend his bow,
    will string an arrow.
¹³ God has deadly weapons in store
    for those who won't change;
  he gets his flaming arrows ready!

¹⁴ But look how the wicked hatch evil,
  conceive trouble, give birth to lies!
¹⁵ They make a pit, dig it all out,
  and then fall right into the hole
    that they've made!
¹⁶ The trouble they cause
    will come back on their own heads;
  the violence they commit
    will come down
      on their own skulls.
¹⁷ But I will thank the LORD
    for his righteousness;
  I will sing praises
    to the name of the LORD
      Most High.

Psalm 8

For the music leader.
*According to the Gittith.*ᵏ
A psalm of David.

¹ LORD, our Lord, how majestic
  is your name throughout the earth!
  You made your glory
    higher than heaven!ˡ
² From the mouths of nursing babies
  you have laid a strong foundation
    because of your foes,
  in order to stop vengeful enemies.
³ When I look up at your skies,
  at what your fingers made—
    the moon and the stars
    that you set firmly in place—
⁴ what are human beings
  that you think about them;
  what are human beings
    that you pay attention to them?
⁵ You've made them only slightly
    less than divine,
  crowning them with
    glory and grandeur.

ʰOr *for my sake* ⁱCorrection; MT *Come back to be exalted over them.* ʲHeb lacks *at evil.*
ᵏPerhaps the name of an instrument (Tg) or melody. LXX *About the winepresses;* or *About the Gittite;* also in Pss 81 and 84 ˡCorrection; Heb uncertain

⁶ You've let them rule over
    your handiwork,
    putting everything
    under their feet—
⁷ all sheep and all cattle,
    the wild animals too,
⁸ the birds in the sky,
    the fish of the ocean,
    everything that travels
    the pathways of the sea.
⁹ LORD, our Lord, how majestic
    is your name throughout the earth!

Psalm 9ᵐ

For the music leader.
According to Muth-labben.ⁿ
A psalm of David.

א ¹ I will thank you, LORD,
    with all my heart;
    I will talk about
    all your wonderful acts.
² I will celebrate and rejoice in you;
    I will sing praises to your name,
    Most High.

ב ³ When my enemies turn and retreat,
    they fall down and die
    right in front of you
⁴ because you have established justice
    for me and my claim,
    because you rule from the throne,
    establishing justice rightly.

ג ⁵ You've denounced the nations,
    destroyed the wicked.
    You've erased their names
    for all time.
⁶ Every enemy is wiped out,
    like something ruined forever.

You've torn down their cities—
    even the memory of them is dead.

ה ⁷ But the LORD rules forever!
    He assumes his throne
    for the sake of justice.
⁸ He will establish justice
    in the world rightly;
    he will judge all people fairly.

ו ⁹ The LORD is a safe place
    for the oppressed—
    a safe place in difficult times.
¹⁰ Those who know your name
    trust you
    because you have not abandoned
    any who seek you, LORD.

ז ¹¹ Sing praises to the LORD,
    who lives in Zion!
    Proclaim his mighty acts
    among all people!
¹² Because the one who
    avenges bloodshed
    remembers those who suffer;
    the LORD hasn't forgotten
    their cries for help.

ח ¹³ Have mercy on me, LORD!
    Just look how I suffer
    because of those who hate me.
    But you are the one
    who brings me back
    from the very gates of death
¹⁴ so I can declare all your praises,
    so I can rejoice in your salvation
    in the gates of Daughter Zion.

ט ¹⁵ The nations have fallen
    into the hole
    they themselves made!

ᵐPs 9 is an alphabetic acrostic poem (cf Ps 119) in Heb, with successive letters of the alphabet
beginning every few lines, with only a few exceptions. Only ten letters are found in Ps 9;
the sequence may be continued in Ps 10, suggesting that Pss 9–10 are a single poem.
ⁿOr *Almuth labben*; Heb uncertain, perhaps a reference to the melody; cf Pss 46:1; 48:14

Their feet are caught
        in the very net
            they themselves hid!
¹⁶ The LORD is famous for the justice
        he has done;
    it's his own doing
        that the wicked are trapped.
                            Higgayon.° *Selah*

ˀ ¹⁷ Let the wicked
        go straight to the grave,ᴾ
    the same for every nation
        that forgets God.

 כ ¹⁸ Because the poor
        won't be forgotten forever,
    the hope of those who suffer
        won't be lost for all time.

¹⁹ Get up, LORD!
    Don't let people prevail!
    Let the nations be judged
        before you.
²⁰ Strike them with fear, LORD.
    Let the nations know
        they are only human.   *Selah*

Psalm 10�q

ל ¹ Why do you stand so far away, LORD,
        hiding yourself in troubling times?
² Meanwhile, the wicked are proudly
        in hot pursuit of those who suffer.
    Let them get caught
        in the very same schemes
            they've thought up!

³ The wicked brag
        about their body'sʳ cravings;
    the greedy reject the LORD,
        cursing.

⁴ At the peak of their wrath,
        the wicked don't seek God:
    There's no God—
        that's what they
            are always thinking.
⁵ Their ways are always twisted.
        Your rules are too lofty for them.
    They snort at all their foes.
⁶ They think to themselves,
        We'll never stumble.
    We'll never encounter
        any resistance.

פ ⁷ Their mouths are filled
        with curses, dishonesty, violence.
    Under their tongues lie
        troublemaking and wrongdoing.
⁸ They wait in a place
        perfect for ambush;ˢ
    from their hiding places
        they kill innocent people;
ע   their eyes spot those
        who are helpless.
⁹ They lie in ambush
        in secret places,
    like a lion in its lair.
    They lie in ambush
        so they can seize those who suffer!
    They seize the poor, all right,
        dragging them off in their nets.
¹⁰ Their helpless victims are crushed;
        they collapse, falling prey
            to the strength of the wicked.
¹¹ The wicked think to themselves:
        God has forgotten.
    God has hidden his face.
    God never sees anything!

ק ¹² Get up, LORD!
    Get your fist ready, God!

°Heb uncertain; or *recitation* (see Pss 1:2; 19:14) or *melody* (see Ps 92:3). ᴾHeb *Sheol* qPss 9
and 10 contain part of an acrostic poem and might originally be one poem in Heb. ʳOr *soul's*
ˢHeb uncertain

Don't forget the ones who suffer!
¹³Why do the wicked reject God?
    Why do they think to themselves
    that you won't find out?
ר ¹⁴But you do see!
    You do see troublemaking
        and grief,
    and you do something about it!
    The helpless leave it all to you.
    You are the orphan's helper.

ש ¹⁵Break the arms of those
    who are wicked and evil.
    Seek out their wickedness
    until there's no more to find.
¹⁶The LORD rules forever and always!
    The nations will vanish
    from his land.

ת ¹⁷LORD, you listen to the desires
    of those who suffer.
    You steady their hearts;
    you listen closely to them,
¹⁸to establish justice
    for the orphan and the oppressed,
    so that people of the land
    will never again be terrified.

Psalm 11

For the music leader. Of David.
¹I have taken refuge in the LORD.
    So how can you say to me,ᵗ
    "Flee to the hills like a bird
    ²because the wicked
    have already bent their bows;
    they've already strung
        their arrows;
    they are ready to secretly shoot
    those whose heart is right"?
³When the very bottom of things
    falls out,

what can a righteous person
    possibly accomplish?

⁴But the LORD is in his holy temple.
    The LORD! His throne is in heaven.
    His eyes see—
    his vision examines all of humanity.
⁵The LORD examines
    both the righteous and the wicked;
    his very beingᵘ hates
    anyone who loves violence.
⁶God will rain fiery coals and sulfur
    on the wicked;
    their cups will be filled
        with nothing
    but a scorching hot wind
⁷because the LORD is righteous!
    He loves righteous deeds.
    Those whose heart is right
    will see God's face.ᵛ

Psalm 12

For the music leader.
According to the Sheminith.ʷ
A psalm of David.
¹Help, LORD,
    because the godly are all gone;
    the faithful have
        completely disappeared
    from the human race!
²Everyone tells lies to everyone else;
    they talk with slick speech
    and divided hearts.
³Let the LORD cut off all
    slick-talking lips
    and every tongue that brags
        and brags,
⁴that says, "We're unbeatable
    with our tongues!
    Who could get the best of us
    with lips like ours?"

ᵗOr *my soul* ᵘOr *soul* ᵛHeb lacks *heart*, but see 11:2 and Pss 7:10; 32:11; 36:10. ʷPerhaps a reference to an eight-string instrument; also in Ps 6

⁵ But the LORD says,
   "Because the poor are oppressed,
   because of the groans of the needy,
   I'm now standing up.
   I will provide the help
      they are gasping for."ˣ

⁶ The LORD's promises are pure,
   like silver that's been refined
      in an oven,
   purified seven times over!

⁷ You, LORD, will keep us,ʸ
   protecting us
      from this generation forever.

⁸ The wicked roam all over the place,
   while depravity is praised
      by human beings.

Psalm 13
*For the music leader.
A song of David.*

¹ How long will you forget me, LORD?
   Forever?
   How long will you hide your face
      from me?

² How long will I be left
   to my own wits,
   agony filling my heart? Daily?
   How long will my enemy keep
      defeating me?

³ Look at me!
   Answer me, LORD my God!
   Restore sight to my eyes!
   Otherwise, I'll sleep the sleep
      of death,

⁴ and my enemy will say, "I won!"
   My foes will rejoice
      over my downfall.

⁵ But I have trusted
   in your faithful love.
   My heart will rejoice
      in your salvation.

⁶ Yes, I will sing to the LORD
   because he has been good to me.

Psalm 14
For the music leader. Of David.

¹ Fools say in their hearts,
   There is no God.
   They are corrupt and do evil things;
   not one of them
      does anything good.

² The LORD looks down
   from heaven on humans
   to see if anyone is wise,
   to see if anyone seeks God,
      ³ but all of them have turned bad.
   Everyone is corrupt.
   No one does good—
      not even one person!

⁴ Are they dumb, all these evildoers,
   devouring my people
   like they are eating bread
      but never calling on the LORD?

⁵ Count on it:ᶻ
   they will be in utter panic
   because God is with
      the righteous generation.

⁶ You evildoers may humiliate
   the plans of those who suffer,
      but the LORD is their refuge.

⁷ Let Israel's salvation come out
      of Zion!
   When the LORD changes
      his people's circumstances
      for the better,
   Jacob will rejoice;
   Israel will celebrate!

ˣHeb uncertain ʸLXX; MT *keep them* ᶻOr *There they will be; cf 53:5*

Psalm 15
A psalm of David.

[1] Who can live in your tent, LORD?
Who can dwell
on your holy mountain?

[2] The person who
lives free of blame,
does what is right,
and speaks the truth sincerely;

[3] who does no damage
with their talk,
does no harm to a friend,
doesn't insult a neighbor;

[4] someone who despises
those who act wickedly,
but who honors those
who honor the LORD;
someone who keeps their promise
even when it hurts;

[5] someone who doesn't lend money
with interest,
who won't accept a bribe
against any innocent person.
Whoever does these things
will never stumble.

Psalm 16
A miktam[a] of David.

[1] Protect me, God,
because I take refuge in you.

[2] I say to the LORD, "You are my Lord.
Apart from you,
I have nothing good."

[3] Now as for the "holy ones"
in the land,
the "magnificent ones"
that I was so happy about;

[4] let their suffering increase because
they hurried after a different god.[b]
I won't participate
in their blood offerings;

[5] You, LORD, are my portion, my cup;
you control my destiny.

[6] The property lines have fallen
beautifully for me;
yes, I have a lovely home.

[7] I will bless the LORD who advises me;
even at night I am instructed
in the depths of my mind.

[8] I always put the LORD in front of me;
I will not stumble
because he is on my right side.

[9] That's why my heart celebrates
and my mood is joyous;
yes, my whole body will rest
in safety

[10] because you won't abandon
my life[c] to the grave;[d]
you won't let your faithful follower
see the pit.

[11] You teach me the way of life.
In your presence
is total celebration.
Beautiful things are always
in your right hand.

Psalm 17
A prayer of David.

[1] Listen to what's right, LORD;
pay attention to my cry!
Listen closely to my prayer;
it's spoken by lips that don't lie!

[2] My justice comes from you;
let your eyes see what is right!

[3] You have examined my heart,
testing me at night.
You've looked me over closely,
but haven't found anything wrong.
My mouth doesn't sin.

[a]Perhaps *inscription* [b]Heb uncertain in 16:3-4; Heb lacks *because* and *god* in 16:4. [c]Or *my soul* [d]Heb *Sheol*

⁴ But these other people's deeds?
    I have avoided such violent ways
    by the command from your lips.
⁵ My steps are set firmly on your paths;
    my feet haven't slipped.

⁶ I cry out to you
    because you answer me.
    So tilt your ears toward me now—
    listen to what I'm saying!
⁷ Manifest your faithful love
    in amazing ways
    because you are the one
    who saves those
        who take refuge in you,
    saving them from their attackers
    by your strong hand.
⁸ Watch me with the very pupil
        of your eye!
    Hide me in the protection
        of your wings,
⁹   away from the wicked
        who are out to get me,
    away from my deadly enemies
        who are all around me!
¹⁰ They have no pity;ᵉ
    their mouths speak arrogantly.
¹¹ They track me down—
    suddenly, they surround me!
    They make their plans
        to put me in the dirt.
¹² They are like a lion
    eager to rip its prey;
    they are like a strong young lion
        lying in wait.

¹³ Get up, LORD!
    Confront them!
    Bring them down!
    Rescue my life from the wicked—
        use your sword!

¹⁴ Rescue me from these people—
    use your own hands, LORD!
    Rescue me from these people
    whose only possession
        is their fleeting life.ᶠ
    But fill the stomachs
        of your cherished ones;
    let their children be filled full
    so that they have leftovers
        enough for their babies.

¹⁵ But me? I will see your face
        in righteousness;
    when I awake, I will be filled full
        by seeing your image.

Psalm 18ᵍ

For the music leader.
Of David the LORD's servant,
who spoke the words of this song
to the LORD after the LORD
delivered him from the power
of all his enemies and from Saul.
¹ He said: I love you, LORD,
    my strength.

² The LORD is my solid rock,
    my fortress, my rescuer.
    My God is my rock—
    I take refuge in him!—
        he's my shield,
        my salvation's strength,
        my place of safety.
³ Because he is praiseworthy,ʰ
    I cried out to the LORD,
    and I was saved from my enemies.
⁴ Death's cords were wrapped
        around me;
    rivers of wickedness terrified me.
⁵ The cords of the graveⁱ
        surrounded me;
    death's traps held me tight.

ᵉHeb uncertain ᶠHeb uncertain ᵍThis poem also occurs in 2 Sam 22 with some variations.
ʰHeb uncertain ⁱHeb *Sheol*

⁶ In my distress I cried out
  to the LORD;
  I called to my God for help.
 God heard my voice from his temple;
  I called to him for help,
  and my call reached his ears.

⁷ The earth rocked and shook;
  the bases of the mountains
   trembled and reeled
  because of God's anger.

⁸ Smoke went up from God's nostrils;
  out of his mouth
   came a devouring fire;
  flaming coals blazed out
   in front of him!

⁹ God parted the skies and came down;
  thick darkness was beneath
   his feet.

¹⁰ God mounted the heavenly
   creatures and flew;
  he soared on the wings of the wind.

¹¹ God made darkness cloak him;
  his covering was dark water
   and dense cloud.

¹² God's clouds went ahead
  of the brightness before him;
  hail and coals of fire went too.

¹³ The LORD thundered in heaven;
  the Most High made
   his voice heard
  with hail and coals of fire.

¹⁴ God shot his arrows,
  scattering the enemy;
  he sent the lightning and
   threw them into confusion.

¹⁵ The seabeds were exposed;
  the earth's foundations
   were laid bare
  at your rebuke, LORD,
  at the angry blast of air coming
   from your nostrils.

¹⁶ From on high God reached down
  and grabbed me;

he took me out of all that water.

¹⁷ God saved me
  from my powerful enemy,
  saved me from my foes,
  who were too much for me.

¹⁸ They came at me on the very day
  of my distress,
  but the LORD was my support.

¹⁹ He brought me out
  to wide-open spaces;
  he pulled me out safe
  because he is pleased with me.

²⁰ The LORD rewarded me
  for my righteousness;
  he restored me
  because my hands are clean,

²¹ because I have kept
  the LORD's ways.
 I haven't acted wickedly
  against my God.

²² All his rules are right in front of me;
 I haven't turned away from
   any of his laws.

²³ I have lived with integrity
  before him;
 I've kept myself from wrongdoing.

²⁴ And so the LORD restored me
  for my righteousness
  because my hands are clean
   in his eyes.

²⁵ You deal faithfully with the faithful;
  you show integrity
   toward the one
    who has integrity.

²⁶ You are pure toward the pure,
  but toward the crooked,
   you are tricky.

²⁷ You are the one who saves
  people who suffer
  and brings down those
   with proud eyes.

²⁸ You are the one
  who lights my lamp—

the LORD my God
illumines my darkness.

²⁹ With you I can charge into battle;
with my God I can leap over a wall.

³⁰ God! His way is perfect;
the LORD's word is tried and true.
He is a shield
for all who take refuge in him.

³¹ Now really, who is divine
except the LORD?
And who is a rock but our God?

³² Only God! The God
who equips me with strength
and makes my way perfect,

³³ who makes my step
as sure as the deer's,
who lets me stand securely
on the heights,

³⁴ who trains my hands for war
so my arms can bend
a bronze bow.

³⁵ You've given me the shield
of your salvation;
your strong hand has supported me;
your help has made me great.

³⁶ You've let me walk fast and safe,
without even twisting an ankle.

³⁷ I chased my enemies
and caught them!
I didn't come home
until I finished them off.

³⁸ I struck them down;
they couldn't get up again;
they fell under my feet.

³⁹ You equipped me with strength
for war;
you brought my adversaries
down underneath me.

⁴⁰ You made my enemies turn tail
from me;
I destroyed my foes.

⁴¹ They cried for help,
but there was no one
to save them.
They cried for help to the LORD,
but he wouldn't answer them.

⁴² I crushed them
like dust blown away by the wind;
I threw them out
like mud dumped in the streets.

⁴³ You delivered me from struggles
with many people;
you appointed me the leader
of many nations.
Strangers come to serve me.

⁴⁴ After hearing about me,
they obey me;
foreigners grovel before me.

⁴⁵ Foreigners lose their nerve;
they come trembling
out of their fortresses.ʲ

⁴⁶ The LORD lives! Bless God, my rock!
Let the God of my salvation
be lifted high!

⁴⁷ This is the God who avenges
on my behalf,
who subdues people before me,

⁴⁸ who delivers me from my enemies.
Yes, you lifted me high
above my adversaries;
you delivered me
from violent people.

⁴⁹ That's why I thank you, LORD,
in the presence of the nations.
That's why I sing praises
to your name.

⁵⁰ You are the one who gives
great victories to your king,
who shows faithful love
to your anointed one—
to David and to his
descendants forever.

ʲ Or prisons

Psalm 19

For the music leader.
A psalm of David.

¹Heaven is declaring God's glory;
   the sky is proclaiming
   his handiwork.
² One day gushes the news to the next,
   and one night informs another
   what needs to be known.
³ Of course, there's no speech,
   no words—
   their voices can't be heard—
⁴ but their sound^k extends
   throughout the world;
   their words reach the ends
   of the earth.

God has made a tent in heaven
   for the sun.
⁵ The sun is like a groom
   coming out of
   his honeymoon suite;
   like a warrior,
   it thrills at running its course.
⁶ It rises in one end of the sky;
   its circuit is complete at the other.
   Nothing escapes its heat.

⁷ The LORD's Instruction is perfect,
   reviving one's very being.^l
   The LORD's laws are faithful,
   making naive people wise.
⁸ The LORD's regulations are right,
   gladdening the heart.
   The LORD's commands are pure,
   giving light to the eyes.
⁹ Honoring the LORD is correct,
   lasting forever.
   The LORD's judgments are true.
   All of these are righteous!
¹⁰ They are more desirable than gold—
   than tons of pure gold!

They are sweeter than honey—
   even dripping off the honeycomb!
¹¹ No doubt about it:
   your servant is enlightened
   by them;
   there is great reward
   in keeping them.
¹² But can anyone know
   what they've accidentally
   done wrong?
   Clear me of any unknown sin
¹³ and save your servant
   from willful sins.
   Don't let them rule me.
   Then I'll be completely blameless;
   I'll be innocent of great wrongdoing.

¹⁴ Let the words of my mouth
   and the meditations of my heart
   be pleasing to you,
   LORD, my rock and my redeemer.

Psalm 20

For the music leader.
A psalm of David.

¹ I pray that the LORD answers you
   whenever you are in trouble.
   Let the name of Jacob's God
   protect you.
² Let God send help to you
   from the sanctuary
   and support you from Zion.
³ Let God recall your many
   grain offerings;
   let him savor your
   entirely burned offerings.   *Selah*
⁴ Let God grant what is in your heart
   and fulfill all your plans.
⁵ Then we will rejoice
   that you've been helped.
   We will fly our flags
   in the name of our God.
   Let the LORD fulfill all your requests!

^k LXX, Vulg, Sym; MT *line or string*   ^l Or *soul*

⁶ Now I know that the LORD saves
    his anointed one;
  God answers his anointed one
    from his heavenly sanctuary,
    answering with mighty acts
    of salvation
    achieved by his strong hand.
⁷ Some people trust in chariots,
    others in horses;
  but we praise the LORD's name.
⁸ They will collapse and fall,
    but we will stand up straight
    and strong.

⁹ LORD, save the king!
  Let him answer us when we cry out!

Psalm 21

For the music leader.
A psalm of David.

¹ The king celebrates your strength,
    LORD;
  look how happy he is
    about your saving help!
² You've given him
    what his heart desires;
  you haven't denied
    what his lips requested.   *Selah*
³ You bring rich blessings right to him;
    you put a crown of pure gold
    on his head.
⁴ He asked you for life,
    and you gave it to him, all right—
    long days, forever and always!
⁵ The king's reputation is great
    because of your saving help;
  you've conferred on him
    glory and grandeur.
⁶ You grant him blessings forever;
    you make him happy
    with the joy of your presence.
⁷ Because the king trusts the LORD,
    and because of the Most High's
    faithful love,
    he will not stumble.

⁸ Your hand will catch
    all your enemies;
  your strong hand will catch
    all who hate you.
⁹ When you appear, LORD,
    you will light them up
    like an oven on fire.
  God will eat them whole
    in his anger;
  fire will devour them.
¹⁰ You will destroy their offspring
    from the land;
  destroy their descendants
    from the human race.
¹¹ Because they sought to do you harm,
    they devised a wicked plan—
    but they will fail!
¹² Because you will make them
    turn and run
  when you aim your bow
    straight at their faces!

¹³ Be exalted, LORD, in your strength!
  We will sing and praise your power!

Psalm 22

For the music leader.
According to the "Doe of Dawn."
A psalm of David.

¹ My God! My God,
    why have you left me all alone?
  Why are you so far
    from saving me—
    so far from my anguished groans?
² My God, I cry out during the day,
    but you don't answer;
  even at nighttime I don't stop.
³ You are the holy one, enthroned.
  You are Israel's praise.
⁴ Our ancestors trusted you—
    they trusted
    and you rescued them;
⁵ they cried out to you
    and they were saved;

they trusted you
and they weren't ashamed.

⁶ But I'm just a worm, less than human;
insulted by one person,
despised by another.
⁷ All who see me make fun of me—
they gape, shaking their heads:
⁸ "He committed himself to the LORD,
so let God rescue him;
let God deliver him
because God likes him so much."
⁹ But you are the one who pulled me
from the womb,
placing me safely
at my mother's breasts.
¹⁰ I was thrown on you from birth;
you've been my God
since I was in my mother's womb.
¹¹ Please don't be far from me,
because trouble is near
and there's no one to help.

¹² Many bulls surround me;
mighty bulls from Bashan
encircle me.
¹³ They open their mouths at me
like a lion ripping and roaring!
¹⁴ I'm poured out like water.
All my bones have fallen apart.
My heart is like wax;
it melts inside me.
¹⁵ My strength is dried up
like a piece of broken pottery.
My tongue sticks
to the roof of my mouth;
you've set me down
in the dirt of death.
¹⁶ Dogs surround me;
a pack of evil people circle me
like a lion—
oh, my poor hands and feet!

¹⁷ I can count all my bones!
Meanwhile, they just stare at me,
watching me.
¹⁸ They divvy up my garments
among themselves;
they cast lots for my clothes.

¹⁹ But you, LORD! Don't be far away!
You are my strength!
Come quick and help me!
²⁰ Deliver me^m from the sword.
Deliver my life from the power
of the dog.
²¹ Save me from the mouth
of the lion.
From the horns of the wild oxen
you have answered me!

²² I will declare your name
to my brothers and sisters;
I will praise you in the very center
of the congregation.
²³ All of you who revere the LORD—
praise him!
All of you who are Jacob's
descendants—honor him!
All of you who are all Israel's
offspring—
stand in awe of him!
²⁴ Because he didn't despise or detest
the suffering of the one
who suffered—
he didn't hide his face from me.
No, he listened when I cried out to
him for help.

²⁵ I offer praise
in the great congregation
because of you;
I will fulfill my promises
in the presence of those
who honor God.

^m Or *my soul*; also in 22:29

²⁶ Let all those who are suffering
      eat and be full!
   Let all who seek the LORD
      praise him!
   I pray your hearts live forever!
²⁷ Every part of the earth
      will remember and come back
      to the LORD;
   every family among all the nations
      will worship you.
²⁸ Because the right to rule
      belongs to the LORD,
   he rules all nations.
²⁹ Indeed, all the earth's powerful
      will worship him;ⁿ
   all who are descending
      to the dust
      will kneel before him;
   my being also lives for him.ᵒ
³⁰ Future descendants will serve him;
   generations to come will be told
      about my Lord.
³¹ They will proclaim
      God's righteousness
   to those not yet born,
      telling them what God has done.

Psalm 23
A psalm of David.

¹ The LORD is my shepherd.
   I lack nothing.
² He lets me rest in grassy meadows;
   he leads me to restful waters;
³ he keeps meᵖ alive.
   He guides me in proper paths
      for the sake of his good name.

⁴ Even when I walk
      through the darkest valley,
   I fear no danger
      because you are with me.

Your rod and your staff—
      they protect me.

⁵ You set a table for me
      right in front of my enemies.
   You bathe my head in oil;
      my cup is so full it spills over!
⁶ Yes, goodness and faithful love
      will pursue me all the days
      of my life,
   and I will live�q in the LORD's house
      as long as I live.

Psalm 24
A psalm of David.

¹ The earth is the LORD's
      and everything in it,
   the world and its inhabitants too.
² Because God is the one
      who established it on the seas;
   God set it firmly on the waters.

³ Who can ascend
      the LORD's mountain?
   Who can stand
      in his holy sanctuary?
⁴ Only the one with clean hands
      and a pure heart;
   the one who hasn't made
      false promises,
   the one who hasn't
      sworn dishonestly.
⁵ That kind of person receives
      blessings from the LORD
   and righteousness
      from the God who saves.
⁶ And that's how things are
      with the generation
      that seeks him—
   that seeks the face
      of Jacob's God.ʳ   *Selah*

ⁿCorrection; MT *All the earth's powerful have eaten and will worship.* ᵒCorrection with LXX;
Heb uncertain ᵖOr *my soul* qLXX; MT *I will return* ʳLXX, Syr; MT *seek your face, Jacob*

⁷ Mighty gates: lift up your heads!
  Ancient doors: rise up high!
   So the glorious king can enter!
⁸ Who is this glorious king?
  The LORD—strong and powerful!
  The LORD—powerful in battle!
⁹ Mighty gates: lift up your heads!
  Ancient doors: rise up high!
   So the glorious king can enter!
¹⁰ Who is this glorious king?
  The LORD of heavenly forces—
   he is the glorious king!   *Selah*

Psalm 25ᵃ
Of David.

א ¹ I offer my lifeᵇ to you, LORD.
ב ² My God, I trust you.
   Please don't let me be put to shame!
   Don't let my enemies rejoice
    over me!
ג ³ For that matter,
    don't let anyone who hopes in you
    be put to shame;
   instead, let those who are
    treacherous without excuse
    be put to shame.

ד ⁴ Make your ways known to me,
    LORD;
   teach me your paths.
ה ⁵ Lead me in your truth—
   teach it to me—
   because you are the God
    who saves me.
ו   I put my hope in you all day long.
ז ⁶ LORD, remember your compassion
    and faithful love—
   they are forever!
ח ⁷ But don't remember the sins
    of my youth or my wrongdoing.
   Remember me only
    according to your faithful love

for the sake of your goodness,
    LORD.

ט ⁸ The LORD is good
    and does the right thing;
   he teaches sinners which way
    they should go.
י ⁹ God guides the weak to justice,
    teaching them his way.
כ ¹⁰ All the LORD's paths
    are loving and faithful
   for those who keep his covenant
    and laws.

ל ¹¹ Please, for the sake
    of your good name,
   LORD, forgive my sins,
    which are many!

מ ¹² Where are the ones
    who honor the LORD?
   God will teach them which path
    to take.
נ ¹³ They will live a good life,
    and their descendants
    will possess the land.
ס ¹⁴ The LORD counsels those
    who honor him;
   he makes his covenant known
    to them.
ע ¹⁵ My eyes are always looking
    to the LORD
   because he will free my feet
    from the net.

פ ¹⁶ Turn to me, God,
    and have mercy on me
   because I'm alone and suffering.
צ ¹⁷ My heart's troubles
    keep getting bigger—
   set me free from my distress!
¹⁸ Look at my suffering and trouble—
    forgive all my sins!

ᵃPs 25 is an alphabetic acrostic poem; see the note at Pss 9–10. ᵇOr *soul*; also in 25:13, 20

^ר¹⁹ Look at how many enemies I have
and how violently they hate me!
^ש²⁰ Please protect my life! Deliver me!
Don't let me be put to shame
because I take refuge in you.
^ת²¹ Let integrity and virtue guard me
because I hope in you.

²² Please, God, save Israel
from all its troubles!

Psalm 26
Of David.

¹ Establish justice for me, LORD,
because I have walked with integrity.
I've trusted the LORD
without wavering.
² Examine me, LORD;
put me to the test!
Purify[u] my mind[v] and my heart.
³ Because your faithful love
is right in front of me—
I walk in your truth!
⁴ I don't spend time with people
up to no good;
I don't keep company with liars.
⁵ I detest the company of evildoers,
and I don't sit with wicked people.
⁶ I wash my hands—they are innocent!
I walk all around your altar, LORD,
⁷ proclaiming out loud my thanks,
declaring all your wonderful deeds!
⁸ I love the beauty[w] of your house, LORD;
I love the place
where your glory resides.

⁹ Don't gather me[x] up with the sinners,
taking my life along with
violent people
¹⁰ in whose hands are evil schemes,
whose strong hands
are full of bribes.

¹¹ But me? I walk with integrity.
Save me! Have mercy on me!

¹² My feet now stand on level ground.
I will bless the LORD
in the great congregation.

Psalm 27
Of David.

¹ The LORD is my light
and my salvation.
Should I fear anyone?
The LORD is a fortress
protecting my life.
Should I be frightened
of anything?
² When evildoers come at me
trying to eat me up—
it's they, my foes and my enemies,
who stumble and fall!
³ If an army camps against me,
my heart won't be afraid.
If war comes up against me,
I will continue to trust in this:
⁴ I have asked one thing
from the LORD—
it's all I seek:
to live in the LORD's house
all the days of my life,
seeing the LORD's beauty
and constantly adoring
his temple.
⁵ Because he will shelter me
in his own dwelling
during troubling times;
he will hide me in a secret place
in his own tent;
he will set me up high,
safe on a rock.

⁶ Now my head is higher
than the enemies surrounding me,

^uLXX or *investigate* ^vOr *kidneys* ^wLXX; MT *the dwelling of your house* ^xOr *my soul*

and I will offer sacrifices
  in God's tent—
    sacrifices with shouts of joy!
  I will sing and praise the LORD.

[7] LORD, listen to my voice
  when I cry out—
  have mercy on me and answer me!
[8] Come, my heart says, seek God's face.[y]
  LORD, I do seek your face!
[9] Please don't hide it from me!
  Don't push your servant
    aside angrily—
    you have been my help!
  God who saves me,
    don't neglect me!
    Don't leave me all alone!
[10] Even if my father and mother
    left me all alone,
  the LORD would take me in.
[11] LORD, teach me your way;
  because of my opponents,
    lead me on a good path.
[12] Don't give me over
  to the desires of my enemies,
  because false witnesses
    and violent accusers
  have taken their stand against me.
[13] But I have sure faith
  that I will experience
    the LORD's goodness
  in the land of the living!

[14] Hope in the LORD!
  Be strong!
  Let your heart take courage!
  Hope in the LORD!

Psalm 28
Of David.

[1] I cry out to you, LORD.
  You are my rock;
    don't refuse to hear me.

If you won't talk to me,
    I'll be just like those
      going down to the pit.
[2] Listen to my request for mercy
  when I cry out to you,
    when I lift up my hands
      to your holy inner sanctuary.
[3] Don't drag me off with the wicked
    and those who do evil;
  the type who talk nice
    to their friends
  while evil thoughts
    are in their hearts!
[4] Pay them back
    for what they've done!
  Pay them back
    for their evil deeds!
  Pay them back
    for their handiwork!
  Give back to them exactly
    what they deserve!
[5] Because they have no regard
    for what the LORD has done,
  no regard for his handiwork,
  God will tear them down
    and never rebuild!

[6] Bless the LORD
  because he has listened
    to my request for mercy!
[7] The LORD is my strength
    and my shield.
  My heart trusts him.
    I was helped, my heart rejoiced,
    and I thank him with my song.
[8] The LORD is his people's strength;
  he is a fortress of protection
    for his anointed one.
[9] Save your people, God!
  Bless your possession!
  Shepherd them
    and carry them for all time!

[y] Correction; MT *My heart says to/of you . . . see my face!*

Psalm 29

A psalm of David.

[1] You, divine beings!
  Give to the LORD—
  give to the LORD glory and power!
[2] Give to the LORD
  the glory due his name!
  Bow down to the LORD
  in holy splendor!

[3] The LORD's voice is over the waters;
  the glorious God thunders;
  the LORD is over
  the mighty waters.
[4] The LORD's voice is strong;
  the LORD's voice is majestic.
[5] The LORD's voice breaks cedar trees—
  yes, the LORD shatters
  the cedars of Lebanon.
[6] He makes Lebanon jump around
  like a young bull,
  makes Sirion jump around
  like a young wild ox.
[7] The LORD's voice unleashes
  fiery flames;
  [8] the LORD's voice
  shakes the wilderness—
  yes, the LORD shakes
  the wilderness of Kadesh.
[9] The LORD's voice convulses the oaks,
  strips the forests bare,
  but in his temple
  everyone shouts, "Glory!"

[10] The LORD sits enthroned
  over the floodwaters;
  the LORD sits enthroned—
  king forever!

[11] Let the LORD give strength
  to his people!
  Let the LORD bless his people
  with peace!

Psalm 30

*A psalm. A song for the
temple dedication. Of David.*

[1] I exalt you, LORD,
  because you pulled me up;
  you didn't let my enemies
  celebrate over me.
[2] LORD, my God,
  I cried out to you for help,
  and you healed me.
[3] LORD, you brought me[z] up
  from the grave,[a]
  brought me back to life
  from among those
  going down to the pit.

[4] You who are faithful to the LORD,
  sing praises to him;
  give thanks to his holy name!
[5] His anger lasts for only a second,
  but his favor lasts a lifetime.
  Weeping may stay all night,
  but by morning, joy!

[6] When I was comfortable, I said,
  "I will never stumble."
[7] Because it pleased you, LORD,
  you made me a strong mountain.
  But then you hid your presence.
  I was terrified.
[8] I cried out to you, LORD.
  I begged my Lord for mercy:
[9] "What is to be gained
  by my spilled blood,
  by my going down into the pit?
  Does dust thank you?
  Does it proclaim your faithfulness?
[10] LORD, listen and have mercy on me!
  LORD, be my helper!"

[11] You changed my mourning
  into dancing.

---

[z]Or *my soul* [a]Heb *Sheol*

You took off my funeral clothes
and dressed me up in joy
¹² so that my whole being
might sing praises to you
and never stop.
LORD, my God,
I will give thanks to you forever.

Psalm 31
For the music leader.
A psalm of David.

¹ I take refuge in you, LORD.
Please never let me be put to shame.
Rescue me by your righteousness!
² Listen closely to me!
Deliver me quickly;
be a rock that protects me;
be a strong fortress that saves me!
³ You are definitely my rock
and my fortress.
Guide me and lead me
for the sake of your good name!
⁴ Get me out of this net
that's been set for me
because you are my
protective fortress.
⁵ I entrust my spirit into your hands;
you, LORD, God of faithfulness—
you have saved me.
⁶ I hate those who embrace
what is completely worthless.
I myself trust the LORD.
⁷ I rejoice and celebrate
in your faithful love
because you saw my suffering—
you were intimately acquainted
with my deep distress.
⁸ You didn't hand me over to the enemy,
but set my feet in wide-open spaces.

⁹ Have mercy on me, LORD,
because I'm depressed.

My vision fails because of my grief,
as do my spirit and my body.
¹⁰ My life is consumed with sadness;
my years are consumed
with groaning.
Strength fails me
because of my suffering;ᵇ
my bones dry up.
¹¹ I'm a joke to all my enemies,
still worse to my neighbors.
I scare my friends,
and whoever sees me in the street
runs away!
¹² I am forgotten, like I'm dead,
completely out of mind;
I am like a piece of pottery,
destroyed.
¹³ Yes, I've heard all the gossiping,
terror all around;
so many gang up together
against me,
they plan to take my life!

¹⁴ But me? I trust you, LORD!
I affirm, "You are my God."
¹⁵ My future is in your hands.
Don't hand me over to my enemies,
to all who are out to get me!
¹⁶ Shine your face on your servant;
save me by your faithful love!
¹⁷ LORD, don't let me be put to shame
because I have cried out to you.
Let the wicked be put to shame;
let them be silenced
in death's domain!ᶜ
¹⁸ Let their lying lips be shut up
whenever they speak arrogantly
against the righteous
with pride and contempt!
¹⁹ How great is the goodness
that you've reserved
for those who honor you,

ᵇLXX, Syr; MT *my sin* ᶜHeb *Sheol*

that you commit to those
who take refuge in you—
in the sight of everyone!
²⁰ You hide them
in the shelter of your wings,ᵈ
safe from human scheming.
You conceal them in a shelter,
safe from accusing tongues.

²¹ Bless the LORD,
because he has wondrously revealed
his faithful love to me
when I was like a city under siege!
²² When I was panicked, I said,
"I'm cut off from your eyes!"
But you heard my request
for mercy
when I cried out to you for help.

²³ All you who are faithful,
love the LORD!
The LORD protects
those who are loyal,
but he pays the proud back
to the fullest degree.
²⁴ All you who wait for the LORD,
be strong and let your heart
take courage.

Psalm 32

A maskilᵉ of David.

¹ The one whose wrongdoing
is forgiven,
whose sin is covered over,
is truly happy!
² The one the LORD
doesn't consider guilty—
in whose spirit
there is no dishonesty—
that one is truly happy!

³ When I kept quiet,
my bones wore out;
I was groaning all day long—
every day, every night!—
⁴ because your hand
was heavy upon me.
My energy was sapped as if in
a summer drought.   *Selah*

⁵ So I admitted my sin to you;
I didn't conceal my guilt.
"I'll confess my sins to the LORD,"
is what I said.
Then you removed the guilt
of my sin.   *Selah*

⁶ That's why all the faithful
should pray to you
during troubled times,ᶠ
so that a great flood of water
won't reach them.
⁷ You are my secret hideout!
You protect me from trouble.
You surround me
with songs of rescue!   *Selah*

⁸ I will instruct you and teach you
about the direction you should go.
I'll advise you
and keep my eye on you.
⁹ Don't be like some senseless
horse or mule,
whose movement
must be controlled
with a bit and a bridle,ᵍ
Don't be anything like that!ʰ
¹⁰ The pain of the wicked is severe,
but faithful love surrounds
the one who trusts the LORD.
¹¹ You who are righteous,
rejoice in the LORD and be glad!

ᵈCorrection; see Ps 61:5; MT *in the hiding place of your face.* ᵉPerhaps *instruction* ᶠCorrection; MT *at a time of finding only* ᵍHeb uncertain ʰHeb uncertain

All you whose hearts are right,
  sing out in joy!

Psalm 33

[1] All you who are righteous,
  shout joyfully to the LORD!
It's right for those who do right
  to praise God.
[2] Give thanks to the LORD
  with the lyre!
Sing praises to him
  with the ten-stringed harp!
[3] Sing to him a new song!
  Play your best with joyful shouts!
[4] Because the LORD's word is right,
  his every act is done in good faith.
[5] He loves righteousness and justice;
  the LORD's faithful love
  fills the whole earth.
[6] The skies were made
  by the LORD's word,
all their starry multitude
  by the breath of his mouth.
[7] He gathered the ocean waters
  into a heap;
he put the deep seas
  into storerooms.
[8] All the earth honors the LORD;
  all the earth's inhabitants
  stand in awe of him.
[9] Because when he spoke,
  it happened!
When he commanded, there it was!
[10] The LORD overrules
  what the nations plan;
he frustrates what the peoples
  intend to do.
[11] But the LORD's plan stands forever;
  what he intends to do lasts
  from one generation to the next.
[12] The nation whose God is the LORD,

the people whom God has chosen
  as his possession,
is truly happy!
[13] The LORD looks down from heaven;
  he sees every human being.
[14] From his dwelling place
  God observes
all who live on earth.
[15] God is the one who made
  all their hearts,
the one who knows
  everything they do.

[16] Kings aren't saved by the strength
  of their armies;
warriors aren't rescued
  by how much power they have.
[17] A warhorse is a bad bet for victory;
  it can't save despite
  its great strength.
[18] But look here: the LORD's eyes watch
  all who honor him,
all who wait for his faithful love,
[19] to deliver their lives[j] from death
  and keep them alive
  during a famine.

[20] We put our hope in the LORD.
  He is our help and our shield.
[21] Our heart rejoices in God
  because we trust his holy name.
[22] LORD, let your faithful love
  surround us
because we wait for you.

Psalm 34[j]

*Of David, when he pretended
to be crazy before Abimelech,
who banished him so that he left.*

א [1] I will bless the LORD at all times;
  his praise will always be
  in my mouth.

---

[i] Or *souls*; also in 33:20   [j] Ps 34 is an alphabetic acrostic poem; see the note at Pss 9–10.

ב ²I[k] praise the LORD—
    let the suffering listen and rejoice.
ג ³ Magnify the LORD with me!
    Together let us lift
        his name up high!

ד ⁴ I sought the LORD
    and he answered me.
    He delivered me
        from all my fears.
ה ⁵ Those who look to God will shine;
    their faces are never ashamed.
ז ⁶ This suffering person cried out:
    the LORD listened and saved him
        from every trouble.
ח ⁷ On every side, the LORD's
    messenger protects those who
        honor God;
    and he delivers them.
ט ⁸ Taste and see how good
    the LORD is!
    The one who takes refuge in him
        is truly happy!
י ⁹ You who are the LORD's holy ones,
    honor him,
    because those who honor him
        don't lack a thing.
כ ¹⁰ Even strong young lions
    go without and get hungry,
    but those who seek the LORD
        lack no good thing.

ל ¹¹ Come, children, listen to me.
    Let me teach you
        how to honor the LORD:
מ ¹² Do you love life;
    do you relish the chance
        to enjoy good things?
נ ¹³ Then you must keep your tongue
    from evil
    and keep your lips
        from speaking lies!

ס ¹⁴ Turn away from evil! Do good!
    Seek peace and go after it!

ע ¹⁵ The LORD's eyes
    watch the righteous,
    his ears listen
        to their cries for help.
פ ¹⁶ But the LORD's face is set against
    those who do evil,
    to eliminate even the memory
        of them from the earth.
צ ¹⁷ When the righteous cry out,
    the LORD listens;
    he delivers them
        from all their troubles.
ק ¹⁸ The LORD is close
    to the brokenhearted;
    he saves those whose spirits
        are crushed.

ר ¹⁹ The righteous have many problems,
    but the LORD delivers them
        from every one.
ש ²⁰ He protects all their bones;
    not even one will be broken.
ת ²¹ But just one problem
    will kill the wicked,
    and those who hate the righteous
        will be held responsible.
²² The LORD saves his servants' lives;
    all those who take refuge in him
    won't be held responsible
        for anything.

Psalm 35
Of David.

¹ LORD, argue with those
    who argue with me;
    fight with those
        who fight against me!
² Grab a shield and armor;
    stand up and help me!

---

[k]Or *my soul*; also in 34:22

3 Use your spear and ax[l]
   against those who are out
      to get me!
   Say to me:[m] "I'm your salvation!"
4 Let those who want me dead
   be humiliated and put to shame.
   Let those who intend to hurt me
   be thoroughly frustrated
      and disgraced.
5 Let them be like dust on the wind—
   and let the LORD's messenger
      be the one who does the blowing!
6 Let their path be
   dark and slippery—
   and let the LORD's messenger
      be the one who does the chasing!
7 Because they hid their net for me
   for no reason,
   they dug a pit for me for no reason.
8 Let disaster come to them
   when they don't suspect it.
   Let the net they hid
      catch them instead!
   Let them fall into it—
      to their disaster!

9 But I will rejoice in the LORD;
   I will celebrate his salvation.
10 All my bones will say,
   "LORD, who could compare to you?
   You rescue the weak
      from those who overpower them;
   you rescue the weak and the needy
      from those who plunder them."

11 Violent witnesses stand up.
   They question me about things
      I know nothing about.
12 They pay me back evil for good,
   leaving me stricken with grief.
13 But when they were sick,
   I wore clothes for grieving,

and I kept a strict fast.
   When my prayer
   came back unanswered,[n]
14 I would wander around like
   I was grieving a friend or a brother.
   I was weighed down, sad,
      like I was a mother in mourning.
15 But when I stumbled,
   they celebrated and
   gathered together—
   they gathered together against me!
   Strangers[o] I didn't know tore me
      to pieces and wouldn't quit.
16 They ridiculed me
   over and over again,
   like godless people would do,
   grinding their teeth at me.

17 How long, my Lord,
   will you watch this happen?
   Rescue me from their attacks;
   rescue my precious life
      from these predatory lions!
18 Then I will thank you
   in the great assembly;
   I will praise you
      in a huge crowd of people.
19 Don't let those who are my enemies
   without cause celebrate over me;
   don't let those who hate me
   for no reason
      wink at my demise.
20 They don't speak the truth;
   instead, they plot false accusations
   against innocent people
      in the land.
21 They speak out against me;
   saying, "Yes! Oh, yes! We've seen it
   with our own eyes!"

22 But you've seen it too, LORD.
   Don't keep quiet about it.

[l]Correction   [m]Or *my soul*; also in 35:4, 7, 9, 12, 13, 17, 24   [n]Heb uncertain   [o]Correction

Please don't be far from me,
my Lord.
²³ Wake up! Get up and do justice
for me;
argue my case,
my Lord and my God!
²⁴ Establish justice for me
according to your righteousness,
LORD, my God.
Don't let them celebrate over me.
²⁵ Don't let them say to themselves,
Yes! Exactly what we wanted!
Don't let them say,
"We ate him up!"
²⁶ Let all those who celebrate
my misfortune be disgraced
and put to shame!
Let those who exalt themselves
over me
be dressed up in shame
and dishonor!
²⁷ But let those who want things
to be set right for me
shout for joy and celebrate!
Let them constantly say,
"The LORD is great—
God wants his servant
to be at peace."
²⁸ Then my tongue will talk
all about your righteousness;
it will talk
about your praise all day long.

Psalm 36

For the music leader.
Of the LORD's servant David.
¹ I know the sinful utterance
of the wicked;^p
No fear of God
confronts their own eyes,
² because in their own eyes
they are slick with talk

about their guilt ever being
found out and despised.^q
³ The words of their mouths
are evil and dishonest.
They have stopped being wise
and stopped doing good.
⁴ They plot evil even while
resting in bed!
They commit themselves
to a path that is no good.
They don't reject what is evil.

⁵ But your loyal love, LORD,
extends to the skies;
your faithfulness
reaches the clouds.
⁶ Your righteousness is
like the strongest mountains;
your justice is like the deepest sea.
LORD, you save both humans
and animals.
⁷ Your faithful love is priceless, God!
Humanity finds refuge
in the shadow of your wings.
⁸ They feast on the bounty
of your house;
you let them drink
from your river of pure joy.
⁹ Within you is the spring of life.
In your light, we see light.

¹⁰ Extend your faithful love
to those who know you;
extend your righteousness
to those whose heart is right.
¹¹ Don't let the feet of arrogant people
walk all over me;
don't let the hands of the wicked
drive me off.
¹² Look—right there is where
the evildoers have fallen,
pushed down, unable to get up!

---

^pHeb uncertain   ^qHeb uncertain

Psalm 37ʳ

Of David.

א ¹ Don't get upset over evildoers;
don't be jealous of those
who do wrong,
² because they will fade fast,
like grass;
they will wither
like green vegetables.

ב ³ Trust the LORD and do good;
live in the land,
and farm faithfully.
⁴ Enjoy the LORD,
and he will give
what your heart asks.

ג ⁵ Commit your way to the LORD!
Trust him! He will act
⁶ and will make your righteousness
shine like the dawn,
your justice like high noon.

ד ⁷ Be still before the LORD,
and waitˢ for him.
Don't get upset when
someone gets ahead—
someone who invents
evil schemes.

ה ⁸ Let go of anger
and leave rage behind!
Don't get upset—
it will only lead to evil.
⁹ Because evildoers
will be eliminated,
but those who hope in the LORD—
they will possess the land.

ו ¹⁰ In just a little while
the wicked won't exist!
If you go looking around
their place,
they won't be there.
¹¹ But the weak will inherit the land;

they will enjoy a surplus of peace.

ז ¹² The wicked plot
against the righteous,
grinding their teeth at them.
¹³ But my Lord just laughs at them
because he knows
that their day is coming.

ח ¹⁴ The wicked draw their swords
and bend their bows
to bring down the weak
and the needy,
to slaughter those
whose way is right.
¹⁵ But the sword of the wicked
will enter their own hearts!
Their bows will be broken!

ט ¹⁶ Better is the little
that the righteous have
than the overabundant wealth
of the wicked.ᵗ
¹⁷ The arms of the wicked
will be broken,
but the LORD supports
the righteous.

י ¹⁸ The LORD is intimately acquainted
with the lives of the blameless;
their heritage will last forever.
¹⁹ They won't be ashamed
in troubling times,
and in a period of famine
they will eat their fill.

כ ²⁰ But the wicked will die,
the LORD's enemies
will disappear—
disappear like the beauty
of a meadow—in smoke.

ל ²¹ The wicked borrow
and don't pay it back,
but the righteous are generous
and giving.

ʳPs 37 is an alphabetic acrostic poem; see the note at Pss 9–10.   ˢCorrection with LXX, Vulg
ᵗLXX, Vulg, Syr; MT *abundant wealth of many wicked*

²² Those blessed by God
    will possess the land,
    but those cursed by God
      will be cut off.

ם²³ A person's steps are made secure
      by the LORD
    when they delight in his way.
²⁴ Though they trip up,
    they won't be thrown down,
    because the LORD
      holds their hand.

נ²⁵ I was young and now I'm old,
    but I have never seen
      the righteous left all alone,
    have never seen their children
      begging for bread.
²⁶ They are always gracious
      and generous.
    Their children are a blessing.

ס²⁷ Turn away from evil! Do good!
    Then you will live
    in the land forever.
²⁸ The LORD loves justice.
    He will never leave his faithful
      all alone.
ע   They are guarded forever,
      but the children of the wicked
      are eliminated.
²⁹ The righteous will possess the land;
    they will live on it forever.

פ³⁰ The mouths of the righteous
      recite wisdom;
    their tongues discuss justice.
³¹ The Instruction of their God
      is in their hearts;
    they don't miss a step.
צ³² The wicked, on the other hand,
      target the righteous,
    seeking to kill them.

³³ But the LORD won't leave
      the righteous
    to the power of the wicked,
    and won't let the righteous
      be found guilty
    when they are judged.

ק³⁴ Hope in the LORD
    and keep his way!
    He will lift you up
      so you can possess the land.
    When the wicked
      are eliminated,
    you will see it for yourself!

ר³⁵ I myself have seen
      wicked powerful people,
    exalting themselves
      like a stately cedar.ᵘ
³⁶ But when Iᵛ came back,
      they were gone!
    I looked all over for them,
    but they couldn't be found!

ש³⁷ Observe those who have integrity
    and watch those whose heart
      is right
    because the future belongs
      to persons of peace.
³⁸ But wrongdoers will be destroyed
      all together;
    the future of the wicked
      will be cut short.

ת³⁹ The salvation of the righteous
      comes from the LORD;
    he is their refuge
      in times of trouble.
⁴⁰ The LORD will help them
    and rescue them—
    rescue them from the wicked—
    and he will save them
    because they have taken refuge
      in him.

ᵘLXX   ᵛLXX, Syr, Vulg

Psalm 38

A psalm of David.
For the memorial offering.

¹ Please, LORD, don't punish me
    when you are mad;
    don't discipline me
      when you are furious.
² Your arrows have pierced me;
    your fist has come down hard on me.
³ There's nothing in my body
    that isn't broken
      because of your rage;
    there's no health in my bones
      because of my sin.
⁴ My wrongdoings are
    stacked higher than my head;
    they are a weight
      that's way too heavy for me.
⁵ My wounds reek; they are all infected
    because of my stupidity.
⁶ I am hunched over, completely down;
    I wander around all day long, sad.
⁷ My insides are burning up;
    there's nothing in my body
      that isn't broken.
⁸ I'm worn out, completely crushed;
    I groan because of
      my miserable heart.

⁹ Everything I long for
    is laid out before you, my Lord;
    my sighs aren't hidden from you.
¹⁰ My heart pounds;
    my strength abandons me.
    Even the light of my eyes is gone.
¹¹ My loved ones and friends
    keep their distance
      from me in my sickness;
    those who were near me
      now stay far away.
¹² Those who want me dead lay traps;
    those who want me harmed
      utter threats,
      muttering lies all day long.

¹³ But I'm like someone who is deaf,
    who can't hear;
    like someone who can't speak,
      whose mouth won't open.
¹⁴ I've become like a person
    who doesn't hear what is being said,
    whose mouth has
      no good comeback.
¹⁵ But I wait for you, LORD!
    You will answer, my Lord, my God!
¹⁶ Because I prayed:
    "Don't let them celebrate over me
    or exalt themselves over me
      when my foot slips,"
¹⁷ because I'm very close to falling,
    and my pain is always with me.
¹⁸ Yes, I confess my wrongdoing;
    I'm worried about my sin.
¹⁹ But my mortal enemies
    are so strong;
    those who hate me for no reason
      seem countless.
²⁰ Those who give,
    repay good with evil;
    they oppose me for pursuing good.

²¹ Don't leave me all alone, LORD!
    Please, my God,
      don't be far from me!
²² Come quickly and help me,
    my Lord, my salvation!

Psalm 39

For the music leader. To Jeduthun.
A psalm of David.

¹ I promised I would watch my steps
    so as not to sin with my tongue;
    promised to keep my mouth shut
    as long as the wicked were
      in my presence.
² So I was completely quiet, silent.
    I kept my peace, but it did no good.
    My pain got worse.
³ My heart got hot inside me;

while stewing over it,
the fire burned.
Then I spoke out with my tongue:
⁴ "Let me know my end, LORD.
How many days do I have left?
I want to know how brief
my time is."

⁵ You've made my days so short;
my lifetime is like nothing
in your eyes.
Yes, a human life is nothing
but a puff of air! *Selah*

⁶ Yes, people wander around
like shadows;
yes, they hustle and bustle,
but pointlessly;
they don't even know who will get
the wealth they've amassed.

⁷ So now, Lord,
what should I be waiting for?
My hope is set on you.
⁸ Deliver me from all my sins;
don't make me
some foolish person's joke.
⁹ I am completely silent;
I won't open my mouth
because you have acted.
¹⁰ Get this plague of yours off me!
I'm being destroyed by the blows
from your fist.
¹¹ You discipline people for their sin,
punishing them;
like a moth, you ruin
what they treasure.
Yes, a human life is just
a puff of air! *Selah*

¹² Hear my prayer, LORD!
Listen closely to my cry for help!
Please don't ignore my tears!
I'm just a foreigner—
an immigrant staying with you,
just like all my ancestors were.

¹³ Look away from me
so I can be happy again
before I pass away and am gone.

Psalm 40
*For the music leader. Of David.
A psalm.*

¹ I put all my hope in the LORD.
He leaned down to me;
he listened to my cry for help.
² He lifted me out of the pit of death,
out of the mud and filth,
and set my feet on solid rock.
He steadied my legs.
³ He put a new song in my mouth,
a song of praise for our God.
Many people will learn of this
and be amazed;
they will trust the LORD.
⁴ Those who put their trust in the LORD,
who pay no attention to the proud
or to those who follow lies,
are truly happy!

⁵ You, LORD my God!
You've done so many things—
your wonderful deeds
and your plans for us—
no one can compare with you!
If I were to proclaim
and talk about all of them,
they would be too numerous
to count!
⁶ You don't relish sacrifices
or offerings;
you don't require
entirely burned offerings
or compensation offerings—
but you have given me ears!
⁷ So I said, "Here I come!
I'm inscribed in the written scroll.
⁸ I want to do your will, my God.
Your Instruction is deep
within me."

⁹ I've told the good news
of your righteousness
in the great assembly.
I didn't hold anything back—
as you well know, LORD!
¹⁰ I didn't keep your righteousness
only to myself.
I declared your faithfulness
and your salvation.
I didn't hide your loyal love
and trustworthiness
from the great assembly.

¹¹ So now you, LORD—
don't hold back
any of your compassion from me.
Let your loyal love and faithfulness
always protect me,
¹² because countless evils surround me.
My wrongdoings have caught up
with me—
I can't see a thing!
There's more of them
than hairs on my head—
my courage leaves me.
¹³ Favor me, LORD, and deliver me!
LORD, come quickly and help me!
¹⁴ Let those who seek my life,
who want me dead,
be disgraced and put to shame.
Let those who want to do me harm
be thoroughly frustrated
and humiliated.
¹⁵ Let those who say to me,
"Yes! Oh, yes!"ʷ
be destroyed by their shame.
¹⁶ But let all who seek you
celebrate and rejoice in you.
Let those who love your salvation
always say,
"The LORD is great!"
¹⁷ But me? I'm weak and needy.

Let my Lord think of me.
You are my help and my rescuer.
My God, don't wait any longer!

Psalm 41
*For the music leader.
A psalm of David.*

¹ Those who pay close attention
to the poor are truly happy!
The LORD rescues them
during troubling times.
² The LORD protects them
and keeps them alive;
they are widely regarded
throughout the land
as happy people.
Youˣ won't hand them over
to the will of their enemies.
³ The LORD will strengthen them
when they are lying in bed, sick.
You will completely transform
the place where they lie ill.

⁴ But me? I said,
"LORD, have mercy on me!
Heal me because I have sinned
against you."
⁵ My enemies speak maliciously
about me:
"When will he die
and his name disappear?"
⁶ Whenever they come to visit,
they say nothing of value.
Their hearts collect evil gossip;
once they leave,
they tell it to everybody.
⁷ All of those who hate me
talk about me,
whispering to each other,
plotting evil against me:
⁸ "Some horrible thing
has been poured into him;

ʷSee Ps 35:21, 25. ˣLXX, Syr; Vulg *God won't*

the next time he lies down,
  he won't get up."
⁹ Even my good friend,
  the one I trusted,
  who shared my food,
  has kicked me with his heel—
  a betrayer!
¹⁰ But you, LORD, please have mercy
  on me and lift me up
  so I can pay them back!
¹¹ Then I'll know you are pleased
  with me
  because my enemy won't be
  shouting in triumph over me.
¹² You support me in my integrity;
  you put me in
  your presence forever.
¹³ Bless the LORD, the God of Israel,
  from forever to forever!
  Amen and Amen!

BOOK II
(Psalms 42–72)

Psalm 42 ʸ
*For the music leader.
A maskil*ᶻ *of the Korahites.*
¹ Just like a deer that craves
  streams of water,
  my whole being ᵃ craves you, God.
² My whole being thirsts for God,
  for the living God.
  When will I come
  and see God's face?ᵇ
³ My tears have been my food
  both day and night,
  as people constantly questioned me,
  "Where's your God now?"

⁴ But I remember these things
  as I bare my soul:

how I made my way
  to the mighty one's abode,ᶜ
to God's own house,
  with joyous shouts
  and thanksgiving songs—
  a huge crowd celebrating
  the festival!
⁵ Why, I ask myself,
  are you so depressed?
  Why are you so upset inside?
Hope in God!
  Because I will again give him thanks,
  my saving presence and ⁶my God.

My whole being is depressed.
  That's why I remember you
  from the land of Jordan
  and Hermon,
  from Mount Mizar.
⁷ Deep called to deep
  at the noise of your waterfalls;
  all your massive waves surged
  over me.
⁸ By day the LORD commands
  his faithful love;
  by night his song is with me—
  a prayer to the God of my life.

⁹ I will say to God, my solid rock,
  "Why have you forgotten me?
  Why do I have to walk around,
  sad, oppressed by enemies?"
¹⁰ With my bones crushed,
  my foes make fun of me,
  constantly questioning me:
  "Where's your God now?"

¹¹ Why, I ask myself,
  are you so depressed?
  Why are you so upset inside?
Hope in God!

ʸPss 42–43 form one single poem; cf the note at Pss 9–10. ᶻPerhaps *instruction* ᵃOr *soul*; also in 42:2, 4, 5, 6, 11; 43:5 ᵇSyr, Tg; MT *and appear before God?* ᶜHeb uncertain

Because I will again
     give him thanks,
my saving presence and my God.

Psalm 43

[1] Establish justice for me, God!
     Argue my case
          against ungodly people!
     Rescue me from the dishonest
          and unjust!
[2] Because you are my God,
     my protective fortress!
     Why have you rejected me?
     Why do I have to walk around,
          sad, oppressed by enemies?
[3] Send your light and truth—
     those will guide me!
     Let them bring me
          to your holy mountain,
          to your dwelling place.
[4] Let me come to God's altar—
     let me come to God, my joy,
          my delight—
     then I will give you thanks
          with the lyre,
     God, my God!

[5] Why, I ask myself,
     are you so depressed?
     Why are you so upset inside?
     Hope in God!
          Because I will again
          give him thanks,
     my saving presence and my God.

Psalm 44

*For the music leader.
A maskil[d] of the Korahites.*

[1] We have heard it, God,
     with our own ears;
     our ancestors told us about it:
     about the deeds you did
          in their days,

in days long past.
[2] You, by your own hand,
     removed all the nations,
          but you planted our ancestors.
     You crushed all the peoples,
          but you set our ancestors free.
[3] No, not by their own swords
     did they take possession
          of the land—
          their own arms didn't save them.
     No, it was your strong hand,
          your arm,
     and the light of your face
          because you were pleased
               with them.
[4] It's you, God! You who are my king,
     the one who orders salvation
          for Jacob.
[5] We've pushed our foes away
     by your help;
     we've trampled our enemies
          by your name.
[6] No, I won't trust in my bow;
     my sword won't save me
[7] because it's you who saved us
     from our foes,
     you who put those who hate us
          to shame.
[8] So we glory in God at all times
     and give thanks
          to your name forever.   *Selah*

[9] But now you've rejected
     and humiliated us.
     You no longer accompany
          our armies.
[10] You make us retreat
     from the enemy;
     our adversaries plunder us.
[11] You've handed us over
     like sheep for butchering;
     you've scattered us
          among the nations.

---

[d] Perhaps *instruction*

¹² You've sold your people for nothing,
        not even bothering
            to set a decent price.
¹³ You've made us a joke to all our
        neighbors;
    we're mocked and ridiculed
        by everyone around us.
¹⁴ You've made us a bad joke
        to the nations,
    something to be laughed at
        by all peoples.
¹⁵ All day long my disgrace confronts me,
    and shame covers my face
¹⁶ because of the voices of those
        who make fun of me
    and bad-mouth me,
        because of the enemy who is out
            for revenge.

¹⁷ All this has come upon us,
    but we haven't forgotten you
        or broken your covenant.
¹⁸ Our hearts haven't turned away,
    neither have our steps
        strayed from your way.
¹⁹ But you've crushed us in the place
        where jackals^e live,
    covering us with deepest darkness.
²⁰ If we had forgotten
        the name of our God
    or spread out our hands
        to some strange deity,
²¹ wouldn't God have discovered it?
    After all, God knows every secret
        of the heart.
²² No, God, it's because of you
    that we are getting killed every day—
        it's because of you
    that we are considered sheep
        ready for slaughter.

²³ Wake up! Why are you sleeping, Lord?
    Get up! Don't reject us forever!

²⁴ Why are you hiding your face,
        forgetting our suffering
            and oppression?
²⁵ Look: we're going down to the dust;
    our stomachs are flat
        on the ground!
²⁶ Stand up! Help us!
    Save us for the sake
        of your faithful love.

Psalm 45

For the music leader. According to
"The Lilies." Of the Korahites.
A maskil.^f A love song.

¹ A marvelous word
        has stirred my heart
    as I mention my works
        to the king.
    My tongue is the pen
        of a skillful scribe.

² You are the most handsome of men;
    grace has been poured out
        on your lips.
    No wonder God has blessed
        you forever!
³ Strap on your sword, great warrior,
    with your glory and grandeur.
⁴ Go and succeed in your grandeur!
    Ride out on behalf of truth,
        humility, and righteousness!
    Let your strong hand perform
        awesome deeds.^g
⁵ Let the peoples fall beneath you.
    May your sharp arrows pierce
        the hearts of the king's enemies.
⁶ Your divine throne
        is eternal and everlasting.
    Your royal scepter
        is a scepter of justice.
⁷ You love righteousness
    and hate wickedness.

---

^e Or *the sea monster(s)*   ^f Perhaps *instruction*   ^g Heb uncertain

No wonder God, your God,
   has anointed you
with the oil of joy
   more than all your companions!
8 All your clothes have
   the pleasing scent of myrrh, aloes,
   and cinnamon.
   The music of stringed instruments
      coming from ivory palaces
   entertains you.
9 The royal princess is standing
   in your precious jewels;[h]
   the queen stands at your right,
      dressed in the gold of Ophir.

10 Listen, daughter; pay attention,
   and listen closely!
   Forget your people
   and your father's house.
11 Let the king desire your beauty.
   Because he is your master,
   bow down to him now.
12 The city of Tyre, the wealthiest of all,
   will seek your favor with gifts,
13 with riches of every sort
   for the royal princess,
      dressed in pearls,[i]
   her robe embroidered with gold.
14 In robes of many colors,
   she is led to the king.
   Her attendants,
      the young women servants
      following her,
   are presented to you as well.
15 As they enter the king's palace,
   they are led in with celebration
      and joy.

16 Your sons, great king,
   will succeed your fathers;[j]
   you will appoint them as princes
      throughout the land.

17 I will perpetuate your name
   from one generation to the next
so the peoples will praise you
   forever and always.

Psalm 46
*For the music leader.
Of the Korahites.
According to Alamoth.[k] A song.*
1 God is our refuge and strength,
   a help always near
   in times of great trouble.
2 That's why we won't be afraid
   when the world falls apart,
   when the mountains crumble
      into the center of the sea,
3 when its waters roar and rage,
   when the mountains shake
      because of its surging waves.   *Selah*

4 There is a river whose streams
   gladden God's city,
   the holiest dwelling
      of the Most High.
5 God is in that city.
   It will never crumble.
   God will help it
      when morning dawns.
6 Nations roar; kingdoms crumble.
   God utters his voice;
      the earth melts.
7 The LORD of heavenly forces
   is with us!
   The God of Jacob is our place
      of safety.   *Selah*

8 Come, see the LORD's deeds,
   what devastation he has imposed
      on the earth—
9 bringing wars to an end
   in every corner of the world,

[h]Syr; MT *royal princess is among your precious ones.* [i]Correction; Heb lacks *for*; Heb uncertain in 45:12–13. [j]Heb lacks *great king.* [k]Heb uncertain; see note at Pss 9–10.

breaking the bow
   and shattering the spear,
   burning chariots with fire.

10 "That's enough!
   Now know that I am God!
   I am exalted among all nations;
    I am exalted throughout
     the world!"

11 The LORD of heavenly forces
   is with us!
   The God of Jacob is our place
   of safety.   *Selah*

Psalm 47
For the music leader.
A psalm of the Korahites.

1 Clap your hands, all you people!
   Shout joyfully to God
   with a joyous shout!
2 Because the LORD Most High
   is awesome,
   he is the great king
   of the whole world.
3 He subdues the nations under us,
   subdues all people beneath our feet.
4 He chooses our inheritance for us:
   the heights of Jacob,
    which he loves.   *Selah*

5 God has gone up
   with a joyous shout—
   the LORD with the blast
   of the ram's horn.
6 Sing praises to God! Sing praises!
   Sing praises to our king!
    Sing praises
   7 because God is king
   of the whole world!
   Sing praises with a song
   of instruction![1]

8 God is king over the nations.
   God sits on his holy throne.
9 The leaders of all people are gathered
   with the people of Abraham's God
   because the earth's guardians
    belong to God;
   God is exalted beyond all.

Psalm 48
A song. A psalm of the Korahites.

1 In the city belonging to our God,
   the LORD is great
   and so worthy of praise!
His holy mountain
   2 is a beautiful summit,
   the joy of the whole world.
Mount Zion, in the far north,
   is the city of the great king.
3 God is in its fortifications,
   revealing himself as a place
   of safety.

4 Look: the kings
   assembled themselves,
   advancing all together—
   5 when they saw it,
   they were stunned;
   they panicked and
   ran away frightened.
6 Trembling took hold of them
   right there—
   like a woman giving birth,
   7 or like the east wind
   when it smashes
   the ships of Tarshish.
8 Just like we had heard,
   now we've seen it for ourselves
   in the city of the LORD
   of heavenly forces,
   in the city of our God.
   May God make it secure forever!
         Selah

---

[1] Or *Sing praises with understanding* or *wisely* (cf LXX, Vulg); Heb *maskil*; see the note at Ps 32.

in their hearts will rule
over them come morning!—
their forms wasting away
in the grave
rather than having
some dignified residence.P

¹⁵ But God will save my life
from the power of the grave,
because he will take me.   *Selah*

¹⁶ Don't be overly impressed
when someone becomes rich,
their house swelling
to fantastic proportions,
¹⁷ because when they die,
they won't take any of it
with them.
Their fantastic things won't
accompany them down under.
¹⁸ Though they consider themselves
blessed during their lives,
and even thank you
when you deal well with them,q
¹⁹ they too will join the ancestors
who've gone ahead;
they too will never
see the light again.
²⁰ Wealthy people?
They just don't understand;
they're just like the animals
that pass away.

Psalm 50

A psalm of Asaph.

¹ From the rising of the sun
to where it sets,
God, the LORD God, speaks,
calling out to the earth.
² From Zion, perfect in beauty,
God shines brightly.
³ Our God is coming;
he won't keep quiet.

A devouring fire is before him;
a storm rages all around him.
⁴ God calls out to the skies above
and to the earth
in order to judge his people:
⁵ "Bring my faithful to me,
those who made a covenant
with me by sacrifice."
⁶ The skies proclaim his righteousness
because God himself is the judge.
Selah

⁷ "Listen, my people, I will now speak;
Israel, I will now testify against you.
I am God—your God!
⁸ I'm not punishing you
for your sacrifices
or for your entirely
burned offerings,
which are always before me.
⁹ I won't accept bulls from your house
or goats from your corrals
¹⁰ because every forest animal
already belongs to me,
as do the cattle on a thousand hills.
¹¹ I know every mountain bird;
even the insects in the fields
are mine.
¹² Even if I were hungry,
I wouldn't tell you
because the whole world
and everything in it
already belong to me.
¹³ Do I eat bulls' meat?
Do I drink goats' blood?
¹⁴ Offer God a sacrifice of thanksgiving!
Fulfill the promises
you made to the Most High!
¹⁵ Cry out to me
whenever you are in trouble;
I will deliver you,
then you will honor me."

PHeb uncertain in 49:13-14   qLXX, Syr

9 We dwell on your faithful love, God,
    in your temple.
10 Your praise, God,
    just like your reputation,
    extends to the far corners
        of the earth.
    Your strong hand is filled
        with righteousness.
11 Let Mount Zion be glad;
    let the towns of Judah rejoice
    because of your acts of justice!

12 Walk around Zion;
    go all the way around it;
    count its towers.
13 Examine its defenses closely;
    tour its fortifications
    so that you may tell
        future generations:
14 "This is God,
    our God, forever and always!
    He is the one who will lead us
    even to the very end."m

Psalm 49

For the music leader.
A psalm of the Korahites.

1 Listen to this, all you people!
    Listen closely,
    all you citizens of the world—
2 people of every kind,
    rich and poor alike!
3 My mouth speaks wisdom;
    my heart's meditation
    is full of insight.
4 I will pay close attention
    to a proverb;
    I will explain my riddle on the lyre.

5 Why should I be afraid
    in times of trouble,

when the wrongdoing
    of my bullies engulfs me—
6 those people who trust
    in their fortunes
    and boast of their fantastic wealth?
7 Wealth? It can't save a single person!
    It can't pay a life's ransom-price
    to God.
8 The price to save someone's life
    is too high—
    wealth will never be enough—
9 no one can live forever
    without experiencing the pit.

10 Everyone knows
    that the wise die too,
    just like foolish
    and stupid people do,
    all of them leaving their fortunes
        to others.
11 Their gravesn are
    their eternal homes,
    the place they live
    for all generations,
    even if they had counties
        named after them!
12 People won't live any longer
    because of wealth;
    they're just like the animals
        that pass away.

13 That's how it goes
    for those who are foolish,
    as well as for those
    who follow their lead,
    pleased with their talk.   *Selah*
14 Like sheep, they're headed
    straight for the grave.o
    Death will be their shepherd—
    but those who do right

---

mLXX; Heb uncertain; Heb *al muth* (*unto death* or *against death*), but see the notes at Pss 9–10, 46—the words might belong in the heading of Ps 49. nCorrection with LXX oHeb *Sheol*; also again in 49:7, 15

16 But to the wicked God says,
  "Why do you talk about my laws?
    Why do you even mention
      my covenant?
17 You hate discipline, and
    you toss my words
      behind your back.
18 You make friends with thieves
    whenever you see one;
    you spend your time
      with adulterers.
19 You set your mouth free to do evil,
    then harness your tongue
      to tell lies.
20 You sit around,
    talking about your own siblings;
    you find fault with the children
      of your very own mother.
21 You've done these things
    and I've kept quiet.
  You thought I was just like you!
    But now I'm punishing you;
    I'm laying it all out,
      right in front of your face.
22 So consider this carefully,
  all you who forget God,
    or I'll rip you to pieces
      with no one to deliver you:
23 The one who offers
    a sacrifice of thanksgiving
    is the one who honors me.
  And it is to the one who charts
      the correct path that
    I will show divine salvation."

Psalm 51

*For the music leader.
A psalm of David, when the prophet
Nathan came to him just after
he had been with Bathsheba.*
1 Have mercy on me, God,
    according to your faithful love!

Wipe away my wrongdoings
    according to your
      great compassion!
2 Wash me completely clean
    of my guilt;
    purify me from my sin!
3 Because I know my wrongdoings,
    my sin is always
      right in front of me.
4 I've sinned against you—you alone.
  I've committed evil in your sight.
    That's why you are justified
      when you render your verdict,
    completely correct
      when you issue your judgment.
5 Yes, I was born in guilt, in sin,
    from the moment my mother
      conceived me.
6 And yes, you want truth
    in the most hidden places;
    you teach me wisdom
      in the most secret space.ʳ
7 Purify me with hyssop
    and I will be clean;
    wash me and I will be
      whiter than snow.
8 Let me hear joy
    and celebration again;
    let the bones you crushed
      rejoice once more.
9 Hide your face from my sins;
    wipe away all my guilty deeds!
10 Create a clean heart for me, God;
    put a new, faithful spirit
      deep inside me!
11 Please don't throw me
    out of your presence;
    please don't take your holy spirit
      away from me.
12 Return the joy
    of your salvation to me
    and sustain me
      with a willing spirit.

ʳHeb uncertain

¹³ Then I will teach wrongdoers
   your ways,
   and sinners will come back to you.

¹⁴ Deliver me from violence, God,
   God of my salvation,
   so that my tongue can sing
   of your righteousness.

¹⁵ Lord, open my lips,
   and my mouth
   will proclaim your praise.

¹⁶ You don't want sacrifices.
   If I gave an entirely burned offering,
   you wouldn't be pleased.

¹⁷ A broken spirit is my sacrifice, God.ˢ
   You won't despise a heart, God,
   that is broken and crushed.

¹⁸ Do good things for Zion
   by your favor.
   Rebuild Jerusalem's walls.

¹⁹ Then you will again want
   sacrifices of righteousness—
   entirely burned offerings
   and complete offerings.
   Then bulls will again be sacrificed
   on your altar.

Psalm 52

For the music leader.
A maskilᵗ of David,
when Doeg the Edomite came
and told Saul, "David has gone
to Ahimelech's house."

¹ Hey, powerful person!
   Why do you brag about evil?
   God's faithful love
   lasts all day long.

² Your tongue devises destruction:
   it's like a sharpened razor,
   causing deception.

³ You love evil more than good;
   you love lying more than
   speaking what is right.   *Selah*

⁴ You love all destructive words;
   you love the deceiving tongue.

⁵ But God will
   take you down permanently;
   he will snatch you up,
   tear you out of your tent,
   and uproot you from the land
   of the living!   *Selah*

⁶ The righteous will see and be in awe;
   they will laugh at those people:

⁷ "Look at them!
   They didn't make God their refuge.
   Instead, they trusted in
   their own great wealth.
   They sought refuge in it—
   to their own destruction!"

⁸ But I am like a green olive tree
   in God's house;
   I trust in God's faithful love
   forever and always.

⁹ I will give thanks to you,
   God, forever,
   because you have acted.
   In the presence
   of your faithful people,
   I will hope in your name
   because it's so good.

Psalm 53

For the music leader,
according to the mahalath.
A maskilᵘ of David.

¹ Fools say in their hearts,
   There's no God.
   They are corrupt
   and do horrible deeds;

ˢCorrection   ᵗPerhaps *instruction*   ᵘPerhaps *instruction*

not one of them
   does anything good.

² God looks down from heaven
      on humans
   to see if anyone is wise,
   to see if anyone seeks God.
³ But all have turned away.
   Everyone is corrupt.
   No one does good—
      not even one person!

⁴ Are they dumb—these evildoers—
      devouring my people
      like they are eating bread
   but never calling on God?

⁵ There, where there was nothing
      to fear,
   they will be in utter panic
   because God will scatter the bones
      of those who attacked you.
   You will put them to shame
   because God has rejected them.

⁶ Let Israel's salvation
      come out of Zion!
   When God changes
      his people's circumstances
      for the better,
   Jacob will rejoice;
   Israel will celebrate!

Psalm 54

*For the music leader.
With stringed instruments.
A maskil[v] of David, when the
Ziphites came and said to Saul,
"Isn't David hiding among us?"*
¹ God! Save me by your name;
   defend me by your might!

² God! Hear my prayer;
   listen to the words of my mouth!

³ The proud have come up
      against me;
   violent people want me dead.
   They pay no attention to God.

Selah

⁴ But look here: God is my helper;
   my Lord sustains my life.
⁵ He will bring disaster
      on my opponents.
   By your faithfulness, God,
      destroy them!

⁶ I will sacrifice to you freely;
   I will give thanks
      to your name, LORD,
   because it's so good,
      ⁷ and because God has delivered me
      from every distress.
   My eyes have seen
      my enemies' defeat.[w]

Psalm 55

*For the music leader.
With stringed instruments.
A maskil[x] of David.*
¹ God, listen to my prayer;
   don't avoid my request!
² Pay attention! Answer me!
   I can't sit still while complaining.
   I'm beside myself
      ³ over the enemy's noise,
   at the wicked person's racket,
   because they bring disaster on me
   and harass me furiously.

⁴ My heart pounds in my chest
   because death's terrors
   have reached me.

ᵛPerhaps *instruction* ʷHeb lacks *defeat.* ˣPerhaps *instruction*

⁵ Fear and trembling
   have come upon me;
   I'm shaking all over.
⁶ I say to myself,
   I wish I had wings like a dove!
   I'd fly away and rest.
⁷ I'd run so far away!
   I'd live in the desert.   *Selah*
⁸ I'd hurry to my hideout,
   far from the rushing wind
   and storm.

⁹ Baffle them, my Lord!
   Confuse their language
   because I see violence and conflict
      in the city.
¹⁰ Day and night they make
   their rounds on its walls,
   and evil and misery live inside it.
¹¹ Disaster lives inside it;
   oppression and fraud
      never leave the town square.

¹² It's not an enemy
   that is insulting me—
   I could handle that.
   It's not someone who hates me
      who is exalted over me—
   I could hide from them.
¹³ No. It's you, my equal,
   my close companion,
      my good friend!
¹⁴ It was so pleasant when
   together we entered God's house
      with the crowd.

¹⁵ Let death devastate my enemies;
   let them go to the grave^y alive
   because evil lives with them—
      even inside them!
¹⁶ But I call out to God,
   and the LORD will rescue me.

¹⁷ At evening, morning, and midday
   I complain and moan
   so that God will hear my voice.
¹⁸ He saves me,^z unharmed,
   from my struggle,
   though there are many
      who are out to get me.
¹⁹ God, who is enthroned
   from ancient days,
   will hear and humble them   *Selah*
   because they don't change
   and they don't worship God.

²⁰ My friend attacked his allies,
   breaking his covenant.
²¹ Though his talk is smoother
      than butter,
   war is in his heart;
   though his words are more
      silky than oil,
   they are really drawn swords:
²² "Cast your burden on the LORD—
   he will support you!
   God will never let the righteous
      be shaken!"

²³ But you, God, bring the wicked
   down to the deepest pit.
   Let bloodthirsty
   and treacherous people
   not live out even half their days.
   But me? I trust in you!

Psalm 56

*For the music leader. According to
"The Silent Dove of Distant Places."
A miktam^a of David, when the
Philistines seized him in Gath.*
¹ God, have mercy on me
   because I'm being trampled.
   All day long the enemy
      oppresses me.

^yHeb *Sheol*   ^zOr *my life or soul*   ^aPerhaps *inscription*

² My attackers trample me
    all day long
    because I have so many enemies.
Exalted one, ³ whenever I'm afraid,
    I put my trust in you—
    ⁴ in God, whose word I praise.
    I trust in God; I won't be afraid.
    What can mere flesh do to me?

⁵ All day long they frustrate
    my pursuits;
    all their thoughts
    are evil against me.
⁶ They get together
    and set an ambush—
    they are watching my steps,
    hoping for my death.
⁷ Don't rescue them for any reason!
    In wrath bring down
    the people, God!

⁸ You yourself have kept track
    of my misery.
    Put my tears into your bottle—
    aren't they on your scroll already?
⁹ Then my enemies will retreat
    when I cry out.
    I know this because God is mine.
¹⁰ God: whose word I praise.
    The LORD: whose word I praise.
¹¹ I trust in God; I won't be afraid.
    What can anyone do to me?

¹² I will fulfill my promises
    to you, God.
    I will present
    thanksgiving offerings to you
¹³ because you have saved my life
    from death,
    saved my feet from stumbling
    so that I can walk before God
    in the light of life.

Psalm 57

*For the music leader.
Do not destroy.
A miktam[b] of David, when he fled
from Saul into the cave.*

¹ Have mercy on me, God;
    have mercy on me
    because I[c] have taken refuge in you.
I take refuge
    in the shadow of your wings
    until destruction passes by.
² I call out to God Most High—
    to God, who comes through for me.
³ He sends orders from heaven
    and saves me,
    rebukes the one who tramples me.
            Selah

    God sends his loyal love
    and faithfulness.

⁴ My life is in the middle
    of a pack of lions.
    I lie down among those
    who devour humans.
    Their teeth are spears and arrows;
    their tongues
    are sharpened swords.
⁵ Exalt yourself, God,
    higher than heaven!
    Let your glory be over all the earth!
⁶ They laid a net for my feet
    to bring me down;
    they dug a pit for me,
    but they fell into it instead!   *Selah*

⁷ My heart is unwavering, God—
    my heart is unwavering.
    I will sing and make music.
    ⁸ Wake up, my glory!
    Wake up, harp and lyre!
    I will wake the dawn itself!
⁹ I will give thanks to you, my Lord,

---

[b]Perhaps *inscription*   [c]Or *my soul*

among all the peoples;
  I will make music to you
  among the nations
¹⁰because your faithful love
  is as high as heaven;
  your faithfulness reaches the clouds.
¹¹Exalt yourself, God,
  higher than heaven!
  Let your glory be over all the earth!

Psalm 58

For the music leader.
Do not destroy.
A psalm of David, a miktam.^d
¹Do you really speak what is right,
  you gods?
  Do you really judge humans fairly?
²No: in your hearts you plan injustice;
  your hands do violence on the earth.

³The wicked backslide from the womb;
  liars go astray from birth.
⁴Their venom is like
  a snake's venom—
  like a deaf cobra's—
  one that shuts its ears
⁵so it can't hear
  the snake charmer's voice
  or the spells of a skillful enchanter.

⁶God, break their teeth
  out of their mouths!
  Tear out the lions' jawbones, LORD!
⁷Let them dissolve
  like water flowing away.
  When they bend the bow,
  let their arrows
  be like headless shafts.^e
⁸Like the snail that dissolves
  into slime,
  like a woman's stillborn child,
  let them never see the sun.

⁹Before your pots feel the thorns,
  whether green or burned up,
  God will sweep them away!^f

¹⁰But the righteous will rejoice
  when they see vengeance done,
  when they wash their feet
  in the blood of the wicked.
¹¹Then it will be said:
  "Yes, there is a reward
  for the righteous!
  Yes, there is a God
  who judges people on the earth."

Psalm 59

For the music leader.
Do not destroy.
A miktam^g *of David, when Saul*
sent men to watch the house
in order to kill him.
¹Oh, my God, deliver me
  from my enemies;
  put me out of reach from those
  who rise up against me.
²Deliver me from evildoers;
  save me from the bloodthirsty.
³Look at how they lie in ambush
  for my life!
  Powerful people are attacking me,
  LORD—
  but not because of any error
  or sin of mine.
⁴They run and take their stand—
  but not because of any fault
  of mine.

Get up when I cry out to you!
  Look at what's happening!
⁵You are the LORD God
  of heavenly forces,
  the God of Israel!
  Wake up and punish all the nations!

^dPerhaps *inscription* ^eHeb uncertain ^fHeb uncertain ^gPerhaps *inscription*

Grant no mercy
to any wicked traitor!   *Selah*

⁶ They come back every evening,
growling like dogs,
prowling around the city.

⁷ See what they belch out
with their mouths:
swords are between their lips!
Who can listen to them?ʰ

⁸ But you, LORD, laugh at them.
You mock all the nations.

⁹ I keep looking for you, my strength,
because God is my stronghold.

¹⁰ My loving God will come to meet me.
God will allow me to look down
on my enemies.

¹¹ Don't kill them,
or my people might forget;
instead, by your power
shake them up
and bring them down,
you who are our shield
and my Lord.

¹² For the sin of their mouths,
the words that they speak,
let them be captured in their pride.
For the curses and lies they repeat,
¹³ finish them off in anger;
finish them off until they are gone!
Then let it be known
to the ends of the earth
that God rules over Jacob.   *Selah*

¹⁴ They come back every evening,
growling like dogs,
prowling around the city.

¹⁵ They roam about for food,
and if they don't get their fill,
they stay all night.

¹⁶ But me? I will sing of your strength!

In the morning I will shout out loud
about your faithful love
because you have been
my stronghold,
my shelter when I was distraught.

¹⁷ I will sing praises to you, my strength,
because God is my stronghold,
my loving God.

Psalm 60

*For the music leader.
According to "Lily."
A testimony. A miktamⁱ of David.
For instruction, when he went
to war with Aram-naharaim
and Aram-sobah, and when Joab
returned and defeated Edom,
killing twelve thousand
in the Salt Valley.*

¹ God, you have rejected us—
shattered us.
You've been so angry.
Now restore us!

² You've made the ground quake,
splitting it open.
Now repair its cracks
because it's shaking apart!

³ You've made your people
suffer hardship;
you've given us wine
and we stagger.

⁴ Give a flag to those who honor you,
so they can rally around it,
safe from attack.ʲ   *Selah*

⁵ Save us by your power and answer us
so that the people you love
might be rescued.

⁶ God has spoken in his sanctuary:
"I will celebrate
as I divide up Shechem
and portion out the Succoth Valley.

ʰHeb uncertain   ⁱPerhaps *inscription*   ʲOr *the bow*; Heb uncertain

⁷ Gilead is mine;
  Manasseh is mine;
  Ephraim is my helmet;
  Judah is my scepter.
⁸ But Moab is my washbowl;
  I'll throw my shoe at Edom.
  I shout in triumph over Philistia!ᵏ
⁹ I wish someone would bring me
    to a fortified city!
  I wish someone would lead me
    to Edom!"

¹⁰ But you have rejected us, God,
    haven't you?
  God, you no longer accompany
    our armies.
¹¹ Give us help against the enemy;
    human help is worthless.
¹² With God we will triumph;
    he's the one who will trample
    our adversaries.

Psalm 61
For the music leader,
with stringed instruments.
Of David.

¹ God, listen to my cry;
    pay attention to my prayer!
² When my heart is weak,
  I cry out to you
    from the very ends of the earth.
  Lead me to the rock
    that is higher than I am
³ because you have been my refuge,
  a tower of strength
    in the face of the enemy.
⁴ Please let me live in your tent forever!
  Please let me take refuge
    in the shelter of your wings! *Selah*
⁵ Because you, God,
    have heard my promises;

you've given meˡ
  the same possession
  as those who honor your name.

⁶ Add days to the king's life!
  Let his years extend
    for many generations!
⁷ Let him be enthroned forever
    before God!
  Make it so love and faithfulness
    watch over him!
⁸ Then I will sing praises
    to your name forever,
  and I will do what I promised
    every single day.

Psalm 62
For the music leader.
According to Jeduthun.
A psalm of David.

¹ Only in God do Iᵐ find rest;
    my salvation comes from him.
² Only God is my rock
    and my salvation—
    my stronghold!—
  I won't be shaken anymore.

³ How long will all of you attack others;
  how long will you tear them downⁿ
    as if they were leaning walls
    or broken-down fences?
⁴ The only desire of this people
    is to bring others down low;
  they delight in deception.
  With their mouths they bless,
    but inside they are cursing. *Selah*

⁵ Oh, Iᵒ must find rest in God only,
    because my hope comes from him!
⁶ Only God is my rock
    and my salvation—

ᵏSyr, Ps 108:9; MT *Celebrate over me, Philistia!* ˡHeb lacks *me.* ᵐOr *my soul* ⁿCorrection; MT *kill them* ᵒOr *my soul*

my stronghold!—
  I will not be shaken.
⁷ My deliverance and glory
    depend on God.
  God is my strong rock.
  My refuge is in God.
⁸ All you people:
    Trust in him at all times!
  Pour out your hearts before him!
  God is our refuge!   *Selah*

⁹ Human beings are nothing
    but a breath.
  Human beings are nothing but lies.
  They don't even register on a scale;
    taken all together
    they are lighter than a breath!
¹⁰ Don't trust in violence;
    don't set false hopes in robbery.
  When wealth bears fruit,
    don't set your heart on it.
¹¹ God has spoken one thing—
    make it two things—
    that I myself have heard:
    that strength belongs to God,
¹² and faithful love comes from you,
    my Lord—
  and that you will repay
    everyone according to their deeds.

Psalm 63
A psalm of David,
when he was in the Judean desert.
¹ God! My God! It's you—
    I search for you!
  My whole being[p] thirsts for you!
  My body desires you
    in a dry and tired land,
    no water anywhere.
² Yes, I've seen you in the sanctuary;
    I've seen your power and glory.
³ My lips praise you

because your faithful love
    is better than life itself!
⁴ So I will bless you as long as I'm alive;
    I will lift up my hands in your name.

⁵ I'm fully satisfied—
    as with a rich dinner.
  My mouth speaks praise
    with joy on my lips—
⁶ whenever I ponder you on my bed,
    whenever I meditate on you
    in the middle of the night—
⁷ because you've been a help to me
    and I shout for joy in the protection
    of your wings.
⁸ My whole being clings to you;
    your strong hand upholds me.

⁹ But what about those people
    who want to destroy me?
  Let them go into the bowels
    of the earth!
¹⁰ Let their blood flow by the sword!
    Let them be food for wild jackals!
¹¹ But the king should rejoice in God;
    everyone who swears by God
    should give praise
  when the mouths of liars
    are shut for good.

Psalm 64
For the music leader.
A psalm of David.
¹ Listen to me when I complain, God!
    Protect my life
    from the enemy's terror!
² Hide me from the secret plots
    of wicked people;
  hide me from the schemes
    of evildoers
³ who sharpen their tongues
    like swords.

[p] Or *my soul;* also in 63:5, 8

Psalm 64:4

They aim their arrow—
   a cruel word—
⁴ from their hiding places
   so as to shoot an innocent person.
   They shoot without warning
   and without fear.
⁵ They encourage themselves
   with evil words.
   They plan on laying traps in secret.
   "Who will be able to see them?"
     they ask.
⁶ "Let someone try
   to expose our crimes!
   We've devised a perfect plot!
   It's deep within
     the human mind and heart."�q

⁷ But God will shoot them
   with an arrow!
   Without warning,
   they will be wounded.
⁸ The LORD will make them trip
   over their own tongues;
   everyone who sees them
   will just shake their heads.
⁹ Then all people will honor God,
   will announce the act of God,
   will understand it was God's work.
¹⁰ Let the righteous rejoice in the LORD;
   let them take refuge in him;
   let everyone whose heart is
   in the right place give praise!

Psalm 65
*For the music leader.
A psalm of David. A song.*
¹ God of Zion,
   to you even silence is praise.
   Promises made to you are kept—
² you listen to prayer—
   and all living things come to you.
³ When wrongdoings become
   too much for me,

you forgive our sins.
⁴ How happy is the one you choose
   to bring close,
   the one who lives
   in your courtyards!
We are filled full
   by the goodness of your house,
   by the holiness of your temple.

⁵ In righteousness you answer us,
   by your awesome deeds,
   God of our salvation—
   you, who are the security
   of all the far edges of the earth,
   even the distant seas.
⁶ You establish the mountains
   by your strength;
   you are dressed in raw power.
⁷ You calm the roaring seas;
   calm the roaring waves,
   calm the noise of the nations.
⁸ Those who dwell on the far edges
   stand in awe of your acts.
You make the gateways
   of morning and evening
   sing for joy.
⁹ You visit the earth
   and make it abundant,
   enriching it greatly
   by God's stream, full of water.
You provide people with grain
   because that is what you've decided.
¹⁰ Drenching the earth's furrows,
   leveling its ridges,
   you soften it with rain showers;
   you bless its growth.
¹¹ You crown the year
   with your goodness;
   your paths overflow with rich food.
¹² Even the desert pastures drip with it,
   and the hills are dressed
   in pure joy.

qHeb uncertain

13 The meadowlands are covered
   with flocks,
   the valleys decked out in grain—
      they shout for joy;
      they break out in song!

Psalm 66
For the music leader.
A song. A psalm.

1 Shout joyfully to God,
   all the earth!
2 Sing praises to the glory
   of God's name!
   Make glorious his praise!
3 Say to God:
   "How awesome are your works!
   Because of your great strength,
      your enemies cringe before you.
4 All the earth worships you,
   sings praises to you,
      sings praises to your name!" *Selah*

5 Come and see God's deeds;
   his works for human beings
      are awesome:
6 He turned the sea into dry land
   so they could cross the river
      on foot.
   Right there we rejoiced in him!
7 God rules with power forever;
   keeps a good eye on the nations.
      So don't let the rebellious
      exalt themselves.   *Selah*

8 All you nations, bless our God!
   Let the sound of his praise
      be heard!
9 God preserved us among the living;
   he didn't let our feet slip a bit.

10 But you, God, have tested us—
   you've refined us like silver,
11 trapped us in a net,
   laid burdens on our backs,

12 let other people run
   right over our heads—
      we've been through fire and water.

But you brought us out to freedom!
13 So I'll enter your house
   with entirely burned offerings.
   I'll keep the promises I made to you,
14 the ones my lips uttered,
   the ones my mouth spoke
      when I was in deep trouble.
15 I will offer the best burned offerings
   to you
   along with the smoke
      of sacrificed rams.
   I will offer both bulls and goats,
                              Selah

16 Come close and listen,
   all you who honor God;
   I will tell you
      what God has done for me:
17 My mouth cried out to him
   with praise on my tongue.
18 If I had cherished evil in my heart,
   my Lord would not have listened.
19 But God definitely listened.
   He heard the sound of my prayer.
20 Bless God!
   He didn't reject my prayer;
   he didn't withhold
      his faithful love from me.

Psalm 67
For the music leader,
with stringed instruments.
A psalm. A song.

1 Let God grant us grace and bless us;
   let God make his face shine on us,
                              Selah
2 so that your way becomes known
   on earth,
   so that your salvation becomes
      known among all the nations.

³ Let the people thank you, God!
  Let all the people thank you!
⁴ Let the people celebrate
  and shout with joy
  because you judge
    the nations fairly
  and guide all nations
    on the earth.   Selah
⁵ Let the people thank you, God!
  Let all the people thank you!

⁶ The earth has yielded its harvest.
  God blesses us—
    our God blesses us!
⁷ Let God continue to bless us;
  let the far ends of the earth
    honor him.

Psalm 68

For the music leader. Of David.
A psalm. A song.

¹ Let God rise up;
  let his enemies scatter;
  let those who hate him
    run scared before him!
² Like smoke is driven away,
    drive them away!
  Like wax melting before fire,
    let the wicked perish before God!
³ But let the righteous be glad
  and celebrate before God.
  Let them rejoice with gladness!
⁴ Sing to God! Sing praises to his name!
  Exalt the one
    who rides the clouds!
  The LORD is his name.
    Celebrate before him!

⁵ Father of orphans
  and defender of widows
  is God in his holy habitation!
⁶ God settles the lonely in their homes;

he sets prisoners free
  with happiness,ʳ
  but the rebellious dwell
    in a parched land.

⁷ When you went forth
  before your people, God,
  when you marched
    through the wasteland,   Selah
⁸ the earth shook!
  Yes, heaven poured down
  before God, the one from Sinai—
  before God, the God of Israel!
⁹ You showered down
    abundant rain, God;
  when your inheritance grew weary,
    you restored it yourself,
¹⁰ and your creatures settled in it.
  In your goodness, God,
    you provided for the poor.

¹¹ My Lord gives the command—
  many messengers are
    bringing good news:
¹² "The kings of armies are on the run!
  The women back home
    divide the spoil.
¹³ Even if you lie down
    among the sheepfolds,
  there are wings of a dove
    covered with silver;
  its pinions covered
    in precious gold."ˢ
¹⁴ When the Almightyᵗ
  scattered the kings there,
  snow fell on Mount Zalmon.

¹⁵ Mighty mountain, Mount Bashan;
  many-peaked mountain,
    Mount Bashan!
¹⁶ You many-peaked mountain:
  Why do you look with envy

ʳOr *skillfully*; LXX, Vulg *with strength*; Heb uncertain   ˢHeb uncertain   ᵗHeb *Shaddai*

at the mountain
  God desired for his dwelling,
  the mountain
    where the LORD dwells forever?

¹⁷ God's chariots are
  twice ten thousand—
  countless thousands!
  My Lord came from Sinai^u
  into the sanctuary.
¹⁸ You ascended the heights,
  leading away your captives,
  receiving tribute from people,
  even from those who rebel
    against the LORD God's
    dwelling there.
¹⁹ Bless the Lord!
  The God of our salvation
  supports us day after day!   *Selah*
²⁰ Our God is the God of salvation,
  and escape from certain death
  comes through God my LORD.

²¹ Yes, God will shatter
  the heads of his enemies—
  the very skulls of those
  who walk in guilt.
²² My Lord has spoken:
  "From Bashan I will bring
    those people back.
  I will bring them back
    from the ocean's depths
²³ so that you can wash your feet
    in their blood,
  so that your dogs' tongues
    can lap up their share
    of your enemies."

²⁴ They saw your procession, God—
  the procession of my God,
  my king, into the sanctuary.
²⁵ First came the singers,

then the musicians;
  between them the young women
    were playing hand drums:
²⁶ "Bless God in the great congregation;
  bless the LORD
    from Israel's fountain!"
²⁷ There's Benjamin leading them,
  though he's little;
  then the princes of Judah,
    their speaker;
  then the princes of Zebulun
  and the princes of Naphtali.

²⁸ Summon your strength, God!
  Show how strong you are, God,
    just as you've done for us before,
  ²⁹ from your temple above Jerusalem,
    where kings bring you gifts.
³⁰ Rebuke the wild animals
    of the marshland,
  the herd of bulls
    among the calves of the peoples.
  Trample those who delight in money;
  scatter the peoples
    who take pleasure in battles.
³¹ Let ambassadors come from Egypt;
  let Cush stretch out its hands
    to God.

³² Sing to God,
  all kingdoms of the earth!
  Sing praises to my Lord.   *Selah*
³³ Sing to the one
  who rides through heaven,
    the most ancient heaven.
  Look! God sends forth his voice,
    his mighty voice.
³⁴ Recognize how strong God is!
  His majesty extends over Israel;
  his strength is in the clouds.
³⁵ You are awesome, God,
  in your sanctuaries—

---

^uCorrection; MT *My Lord was among them, the one from Sinai, in holiness.*

the God of Israel who gives
  strength and power to his people!

Bless God!

Psalm 69

*For the music leader. According to
"The Lilies." Of David.*

¹ Save me, God,
  because the waters
    have reached my neck!
² I have sunk into deep mud.
  My feet can't touch the bottom!
  I have entered deep water;
    the flood has swept me up.
³ I am tired of crying.
  My throat is hoarse.
  My eyes are exhausted
    with waiting for my God.

⁴ More numerous than the hairs
    on my head
  are those who hate me
    for no reason.
  My treacherous enemies,
    those who would destroy me,
    are countless.
  Must I now give back
    what I didn't steal
    in the first place?
⁵ God, you know my foolishness;
  my wrongdoings aren't hidden
    from you.

⁶ LORD God of heavenly forces!—
  don't let those who hope in you
    be put to shame because of me.
  God of Israel!—
  don't let those who seek you
    be disgraced because of me.
⁷ I am insulted because of you.
  Shame covers my face.
⁸ I have become a stranger
  to my own brothers,

an immigrant
  to my mother's children.
⁹ Because passion for your house
    has consumed me,
  the insults of those who insult you
    have fallen on me!
¹⁰ I wept while I fasted—
  even for that I was insulted.
¹¹ When I wore funeral clothes,
  people made fun of me.
¹² Those who sit at the city gate
    muttered things about me;
  drunkards made up rude songs.

¹³ But me?
  My prayer reaches you, LORD,
    at just the right time.
  God, in your great and faithful love,
    answer me with your
    certain salvation!
¹⁴ Save me from the mud!
  Don't let me drown!
  Let me be saved from those
    who hate me
  and from these watery depths!
¹⁵ Don't let me be swept away
    by the floodwaters!
  Don't let the abyss swallow me up!
  Don't let the pit close its mouth
    over me!
¹⁶ Answer me, LORD,
  for your faithful love is good!
  Turn to me
    in your great compassion!
¹⁷ Don't hide your face from me,
    your servant,
  because I'm in deep trouble.
  Answer me quickly!
¹⁸ Come close to me!
  Redeem me!
  Save me because of my enemies!

¹⁹ You know full well the insults
  I've received;

you know my shame
and my disgrace.
All my adversaries are right there
in front of you.
²⁰ Insults have broken my heart.
I'm sick about it.
I hoped for sympathy,
but there wasn't any;
I hoped for comforters,
but couldn't find any.
²¹ They gave me poison for food.
To quench my thirst
they gave me vinegar to drink.

²² Let the table before them
become a trap,
their offerings a snare.
²³ Let their eyes grow too dim to see;
make their insides
tremble constantly.
²⁴ Pour out your anger on them—
let your burning fury catch them.
²⁵ Let their camp be devastated;
let no one dwell in their tents.
²⁶ Because they go after those
you've already struck;
they talk about the pain
of those you've already pierced.
²⁷ Pile guilt on top of their guilt!
Don't let them come
into your righteousness!
²⁸ Let them be wiped out
of the scroll of life!
Let them not be recorded
along with the righteous!
²⁹ And me? I'm afflicted.
I'm full of pain.
Let your salvation
keep me safe, God!

³⁰ I will praise God's name with song;
I will magnify him with thanks
³¹ because that is more pleasing
to the LORD than an ox,
more pleasing than a young bull
with full horns and hooves.
³² Let the afflicted see it and be glad!
You who seek God—
let your hearts beat strong again
³³ because the LORD listens
to the needy
and doesn't despise his captives.

³⁴ Let heaven and earth praise God,
the oceans too,
and all that moves within them!
³⁵ God will most certainly save Zion
and will rebuild Judah's cities
so that God's servants
can live there and possess it.
³⁶ The offspring of God's servants
will inherit Zion,
and those who love God's name
will dwell there.

Psalm 70

For the music leader. Of David.
For the memorial offering.

¹ Hurry, God, to deliver me;
hurry, LORD, to help me!
² Let those who seek my life
be ashamed and humiliated!
Let them fall back
and be disgraced—
those people who delight
in my downfall!
³ Let those who say, "Aha! Aha!"
stop because of their
shameful behavior.
⁴ But let all who seek you
rejoice and be glad in you,
and let those who love your saving
help say again and again:
"God is great!"
⁵ But me? I'm poor and needy.
Hurry to me, God!
You are my helper and my deliverer.
Oh, LORD, don't delay!

Psalm 71

¹ I've taken refuge in you, LORD.
    Don't let me ever be put to shame!
² Deliver me and rescue me
    by your righteousness!
    Bend your ear toward me
        and save me!
³ Be my rock of refuge
    where I can always escape.
You commanded that my life
    be saved
    because you are my rock
    and my fortress.

⁴ My God, rescue me
    from the power of the wicked;
    rescue me from the grip
        of the wrongdoer and
        the oppressor
   ⁵ because you are my hope, Lord.
You, LORD, are the one I've trusted
    since childhood.
⁶ I've depended on you from birth—
    you cut the cord when I came
        from my mother's womb.
    My praise is always about you.
⁷ I've become an example
    to many people
    because you are my strong refuge.
⁸ My mouth is filled with your praise,
    glorifying you all day long.
⁹ Don't cast me off in old age.
    Don't abandon me when
    my strength is used up!

¹⁰ Yes, my enemies have been
    talking about me;
    those who stalk me plot together:
¹¹ "God has abandoned him!
    Pursue him!
    Grab him
        because no one will deliver him!"

¹² Don't be far from me, God!
    My God, hurry to help me!
¹³ Let my accusers be put to shame,
    completely finished off!
    Let those who seek my downfall
    be dressed in insults and disgrace!

¹⁴ But me? I will hope. Always.
    I will add to all your praise.
¹⁵ My mouth will repeat
    your righteous acts
    and your saving deeds all day long.
    I don't even know
    how many of those there are!
¹⁶ I will dwell on your mighty acts,
    my Lord.
    LORD, I will help others remember
    nothing but your righteous deeds.
¹⁷ You've taught me since my youth, God,
    and I'm still proclaiming
    your wondrous deeds!
¹⁸ So, even in my old age
    with gray hair,
    don't abandon me, God!
    Not until I tell generations
    about your mighty arm,
    tell all who are yet to come
        about your strength,
   ¹⁹ and about your
    ultimate righteousness, God,
    because you've done
    awesome things!
Who can compare to you, God?
²⁰ You, who have shown me
    many troubles and calamities,
    will revive me once more.^v
    From the depths of the earth,
    you will raise me up one more time.
²¹ Please increase my honor
    and comfort me all around.
²² Then I'll give you thanks
    with a harp—

^vQere; Kethib *who have shown us . . . will revive us*

I will thank you
  for your faithfulness, my God.
I will make music for you
  with the lyre, holy one of Israel.
²³ My lips will rejoice aloud
  when I make music for you;
  my whole being,ʷ which you saved,
  will do the same.
²⁴ My tongue, also, will tell
  of your righteousness all day long,
  because those who seek
  my downfall
  have been put to shame
  and disgraced.

Psalm 72
Of Solomon.

¹ God, give your judgments
  to the king.
  Give your righteousness
  to the king's son.
² Let him judge your people
  with righteousness
  and your poor ones with justice.
³ Let the mountains bring peace
  to the people;
  let the hills bring righteousness.
⁴ Let the king bring justice
  to people who are poor;
  let him save the children
  of those who are needy,
  but let him crush oppressors!
⁵ Let the king liveˣ as long as the sun,
  as long as the moon,
  generation to generation.
⁶ Let him fall like rain
  upon fresh-cut grass,
  like showers that water the earth.
⁷ Let the righteous flourish
  throughout their lives,
  and let peace prosper
  until the moon is no more.

⁸ Let the king rule from sea to sea,
  from the river to the ends
  of the earth.
⁹ Let the desert dwellers
  bow low before him;
  let his enemies lick the dust.
¹⁰ Let the kings of Tarshish
  and the islands bring tribute;
  let the kings of Sheba and Seba
  present gifts.
¹¹ Let all the kings bow down
  before him;
  let all the nations serve him.

¹² Let it be so, because he delivers
  the needy who cry out,
  the poor, and those who
  have no helper.
¹³ He has compassion on the weak
  and the needy;
  he saves the lives of those
  who are in need.
¹⁴ He redeems their lives
  from oppression and violence;
  their blood is precious in his eyes.

¹⁵ Let the king live long!
  Let Sheba's gold be given to him!
  Let him be prayed for always!
  Let him be blessed all day long!
¹⁶ Let there be abundant grain
  in the land.
  Let it wave on the mountaintops.
  Let its fruit flourish like Lebanon.
  Let it thrive like grass on the land.
¹⁷ Let the king's name last forever.
  Let his name endure
  as long as the sun.
  Let all the nations be blessed
  through him and call him happy.

¹⁸ Bless the LORD God,
  the God of Israel—

ʷ Or soul ˣ LXX; MT *May they fear you.*

the only one
who does wondrous things!

[19] Bless God's glorious name forever;
let his glory fill all the earth!
Amen and Amen!

[20] The prayers of David, Jesse's son,
are ended.

BOOK III
(Psalms 73–89)

Psalm 73
A psalm of Asaph.

[1] Truly God is good to Israel,
to those who have a pure heart.
[2] But me? My feet had almost stumbled;
my steps had nearly slipped
[3] because I envied the arrogant;
I observed how the wicked
are well off:
[4] They suffer no pain;
their bodies are fit and strong.
[5] They are never in trouble;
they aren't weighed down
like other people.
[6] That's why they wear arrogance
like a necklace,
why violence covers them
like clothes.
[7] Their eyes bulge out
from eating so well;
their hearts overflow
with delusions.
[8] They scoff and talk so cruel;
from their privileged positions
they plan oppression.
[9] Their mouths dare to speak
against heaven!
Their tongues roam the earth!
[10] That's why people keep going back
to them,
keep approving what they say.[y]

[11] And what they say is this:
"How could God possibly know!
Does the Most High
know anything at all!"
[12] Look at these wicked ones,
always relaxed,
piling up the wealth!

[13] Meanwhile, I've kept my heart pure
for no good reason;
I've washed my hands
to stay innocent for nothing.
[14] I'm weighed down all day long.
I'm punished every morning.
[15] If I said, "I will talk about all this,"
I would have been unfaithful
to your children.
[16] But when I tried to understand
these things,
it just seemed like hard work
[17] until I entered God's sanctuary
and understood what would
happen to the wicked.
[18] You will definitely put them
on a slippery path;
you will make them fall
into ruin!
[19] How quickly they are devastated,
utterly destroyed by terrors!
[20] As quickly as a dream departs
from someone waking up,
my Lord,
when you are stirred up,
you make them disappear.[z]

[21] When my heart was bitter,
when I was all cut up inside,
[22] I was stupid and ignorant.
I acted like nothing
but an animal toward you.
[23] But I was still always with you!
You held my strong hand!

---

[y]Heb uncertain   [z]Heb uncertain

²⁴You have guided me
  with your advice;
  later you will receive me
    with glory.
²⁵Do I have anyone else in heaven?
  There's nothing on earth I desire
    except you.
²⁶My body and my heart fail,
  but God is my heart's rock
    and my share forever.
²⁷Look! Those far from you die;
  you annihilate all those
    who are unfaithful to you.
²⁸But me? It's good for me
  to be near God.
  I have taken my refuge in you,
    my Lᴏʀᴅ God,
  so I can talk all about your works!

Psalm 74
A maskil[a] *of Asaph.*

¹God, why have you
  abandoned us forever?
  Why does your anger smolder
    at the sheep of your own pasture?
²Remember your congregation
  that you took as your own
    long ago,
  that you redeemed to be the tribe
    of your own possession—
  remember Mount Zion,
    where you dwell.
³March to the unending ruins,
  to all that the enemy destroyed
    in the sanctuary.

⁴Your enemies roared
  in your own meeting place;
  they set up their own signs there!
⁵It looked like axes raised
  against a thicket of trees.[b]
⁶And then all its carvings

they hacked down with hatchet
  and pick.
⁷They set fire to your sanctuary,
  burned it to the ground;
  they defiled the dwelling place
    of your name.
⁸They said in their hearts,
  We'll kill all of them together!
  They burned all of God's
    meeting places in the land.
⁹We don't see our own signs anymore.
  No prophet is left.
  And none of us know
    how long it will last.

¹⁰How long, God, will foes insult you?
  Are enemies going to abuse
    your name forever?
¹¹Why do you pull your hand back?
  Why do you hold your strong hand
    close to your chest?

¹²Yet God has been my king
  from ancient days—
  God, who makes salvation happen
    in the heart of the earth!
¹³You split the sea with your power.
  You shattered the heads
    of the sea monsters on the water.
¹⁴You crushed Leviathan's heads.
  You gave it to the desert dwellers
    for food!
¹⁵You split open springs and streams;
  you made strong-flowing rivers
    dry right up.
¹⁶The day belongs to you!
  The night too!
  You established both the moon
    and the sun.
¹⁷You set all the boundaries
  of the earth in place.
  Summer and winter?
    You made them!

---

[a]Perhaps *instruction*   [b]Heb uncertain

¹⁸ So remember this, LORD:
  how enemies have insulted you,
  how unbelieving fools
    have abused your name.
¹⁹ Don't deliver the life of your dove
    to wild animals!
  Don't forget the lives
    of your afflicted people forever!
²⁰ Consider the covenant!
  Because the land's dark places
    are full of violence.
²¹ Don't let the oppressed
    live in shame.
  No, let the poor and needy
    praise your name!

²² God, rise up! Make your case!
  Remember how unbelieving fools
    insult you all day long.
²³ Don't forget the voices
    of your enemies,
  the racket of your adversaries
    that never quits.

Psalm 75
*For the music leader.
Do not destroy.
A psalm of Asaph. A song.*
¹ We give thanks to you, God.
  Yes, we give thanks!
  Your name is near.
  Your marvelous deeds
    are declared.

² God says,ᶜ
  "When I decide the time is right,
    I will establish justice just so.
³ The earth and all its inhabitants
    will melt,
  but I will keep its pillars steady."
                              Selah

⁴ I said to the arrogant,
    "Don't be arrogant!"
  To the wicked I said,
    "Don't exalt your strength!
⁵ Don't exalt your strength
    so highly.
  Don't speak so arrogantly
    against the rock."ᵈ
⁶ Because what exalts someone
    doesn't come from the east or west;
  it's not from the south either.
⁷ Rather it is God who is the judge.
  He brings this person down,
    but that person he lifts up.
⁸ Indeed, there's a cup
    in the LORD's hand
  full of foaming wine,
    mixed with spice.
  He will pour it out,
  and all of the earth's wicked people
    must drink it;
  they must drink every last drop!

⁹ But I will rejoiceᵉ always;
  I will sing praises to Jacob's God!
¹⁰ God says:ᶠ
  "I will demolish every bit
    of the wicked's power,
  but the strength of the righteous
    will be lifted up."

Psalm 76
*For the music leader.
With stringed instruments.
A psalm of Asaph. A song.*
¹ God is known in Judah;
  his name is great in Israel.
² His dwelling place became Salem;
  his habitation was Zion.
³ It was there that he broke
  the fiery shafts of the bow,

ᶜHeb lacks *God says.*   ᵈLXX *against God;* MT *speak with an arrogant neck*   ᵉLXX; MT *I will declare*
ᶠHeb lacks *God says.*

you have demonstrated
your strength among all peoples.
[15] With your mighty arm
you redeemed your people;
redeemed the children of
Jacob and Joseph.   *Selah*

[16] The waters saw you, God—
the waters saw you and reeled!
Even the deep depths shook!
[17] The clouds poured water,
the skies cracked thunder;
your arrows were flying
all around!
[18] The crash of your thunder
was in the swirling storm;
lightning lit up the whole world;
the earth shook and quaked.
[19] Your way went straight through
the sea;
your pathways went right through
the mighty waters.
But your footprints left no trace!
[20] You led your people like sheep
under the care of Moses and Aaron.

Psalm 78

A maskil[j] of Asaph.

[1] Listen, my people, to my teaching;
tilt your ears toward
the words of my mouth.
[2] I will open my mouth with a proverb.
I'll declare riddles
from days long gone—
[3] ones that we've heard
and learned about,
ones that our ancestors told us.
[4] We won't hide them
from their descendants;
we'll tell the next generation
all about the praise due the LORD
and his strength—
the wondrous works God has done.

[5] He established a law for Jacob
and set up Instruction for Israel,
ordering our ancestors
to teach them to their children.
[6] This is so that the next generation
and children not yet born
will know these things,
and so they can rise up
and tell their children
[7] to put their hope in God—
never forgetting God's deeds,
but keeping
God's commandments—
[8] and so that they won't become
like their ancestors:
a rebellious, stubborn generation,
a generation whose heart
wasn't set firm
and whose spirit
wasn't faithful to God.

[9] The children of Ephraim,
armed with bows,
retreated on the day of battle.
[10] They didn't keep God's covenant;
they refused to walk
in his Instruction.
[11] They forgot God's deeds
as well as the wondrous works
he showed them.
[12] But God performed wonders
in their ancestors' presence—
in the land of Egypt,
in the field of Zoan.
[13] God split the sea
and led them through,
making the waters
stand up like a wall.
[14] God led them with the cloud by day;
by the lightning all through
the night.
[15] God split rocks open
in the wilderness,

---

[j] Perhaps *instruction*

the shield, the sword—
even the battle itself!   *Selah*

⁴ You are ablaze with light,
mightier than the mountains
that give food.
⁵ The bravehearted lie plundered.
They sank into deep lethargy.
All the strong troops
couldn't even lift their hands!
⁶ At your rebuke, Jacob's God,
both chariot and horse
were stopped dead-still.

⁷ You! You are awesome!
Who can stand before you
when you are angry?
⁸ You have announced judgment
from heaven.
The earth grew afraid and fell silent
⁹ when God rose up to establish justice,
when God rose up to save
all of the earth's poor.   *Selah*

¹⁰ Even human rage will turn
to your praise
when you dress yourself
with whatever remains
of your wrath.ᵍ
¹¹ Make promises to the LORD
your God and keep them!
Let all around him bring gifts
to the awesome one.
¹² He breaks the spirit of princes.
He is terrifying to all the kings
of the earth.

Psalm 77
*For the music leader.
According to Jeduthun.
Of Asaph. A psalm.*
¹ I cry out loud to God—
out loud to God
so that he can hear me!

² During the day when I'm in trouble
I look for my Lord.
At night my hands
are still outstretched
and don't grow numb;
my whole beingʰ refuses
to be comforted.
³ I remember God and I moan.
I complain,
and my spirit grows tired.   *Selah*

⁴ You've kept my eyelids from closing.
I'm so upset I can't even speak.
⁵ I think about days long past;
I remember years that seem
an eternity in the past.
⁶ I meditate with my heart at night;ⁱ
I complain, and my spirit
keeps searching:

⁷ "Will my Lord reject me forever?
Will he never be pleased again?
⁸ Has his faithful love
come to a complete end?
Is his promise over
for future generations?
⁹ Has God forgotten
how to be gracious?
Has he angrily stopped up
his compassion?"   *Selah*

¹⁰ It's my misfortune, I thought,
that the strong hand
of the Most High is different now.

¹¹ But I will remember the LORD's deeds;
yes, I will remember
your wondrous acts
from times long past.
¹² I will meditate on all your works;
I will ponder your deeds.
¹³ God, your way is holiness!
Who is as great a god as you, God?
¹⁴ You are the God who works wonders;

ᵍHeb uncertain   ʰOr soul   ⁱLXX; MT *I remember my song in the night.*

gave them plenty to drink—
as if from the deep itself!
¹⁶ God made streams flow
from the rock,
made water run like rivers.

¹⁷ But they continued to sin
against God,
rebelling against the Most High
in the desert.
¹⁸ They tested God in their hearts,
demanded food for their stomachs.
¹⁹ They spoke against God!
"Can God set a dinner table
in the wilderness?" they asked.
²⁰ "True, God struck the rock
and water gushed
and streams flowed,
but can he give bread too?
Can he provide meat
for his people?"
²¹ When the LORD heard this,
he became furious.
A fire was ignited against Jacob;
wrath also burned against Israel
²² because they had no faith in God,
because they didn't trust
his saving power.
²³ God gave orders to the skies above,
opened heaven's doors,
²⁴ and rained manna on them
so they could eat.
He gave them
the very grain of heaven!
²⁵ Each person ate the bread
of the powerful ones;^k
God sent provisions
to satisfy them.
²⁶ God set the east wind moving
across the skies
and drove the south wind
by his strength.

²⁷ He rained meat on them
as if it were dust in the air;
he rained as many birds
as the sand on the seashore!
²⁸ God brought the birds down
in the center of their camp,
all around their dwellings.
²⁹ So they ate
and were completely satisfied;
God gave them exactly
what they had craved.
³⁰ But they didn't stop craving—
even with the food
still in their mouths!
³¹ So God's anger came up against them:
he killed the most hearty of them;
he cut down Israel's youth
in their prime.
³² But in spite of all that,
they kept sinning
and had no faith
in God's wondrous works.
³³ So God brought their days to an end,
like a puff of air,
and their years in total ruin.
³⁴ But whenever God killed them,
they went after him!
They would turn
and earnestly search for God.
³⁵ They would remember that God
was their rock,
that the Most High
was their redeemer.
³⁶ But they were just flattering him
with lip service.
They were lying to him
with their tongues.
³⁷ Their hearts weren't firmly set
on him;
they weren't faithful
to his covenant.
³⁸ But God, being compassionate,

^kOr *everyone ate the bread from heaven*; Heb uncertain

kept forgiving their sins,
kept avoiding destruction;
he took back his anger
　　so many times,
wouldn't stir up all his wrath!
[39] God kept remembering
that they were just flesh,
just breath that passes
　　and doesn't come back.

[40] How often they rebelled
against God in the wilderness
and distressed him in the desert!
[41] Time and time again
they tested God,
provoking the holy one of Israel.
[42] They didn't remember
God's power—
the day when he saved them
　　from the enemy;
　[43] how God performed
his signs in Egypt,
his marvelous works
　　in the field of Zoan.
[44] God turned their rivers into blood;
they couldn't drink
from their own streams.
[45] God sent swarms against them
to eat them up,
frogs to destroy them.
[46] God handed over their crops
to caterpillars,
their land's produce to locusts.
[47] God killed their vines with hail,
their sycamore trees with frost.
[48] God delivered their cattle
over to disease,[1]
their herds to plagues.
[49] God unleashed his burning anger
against them—
fury, indignation, distress,
a troop of evil messengers.

[50] God blazed a path for his wrath.
He didn't save them from death,
but delivered their lives
　　over to disease.
[51] God struck down
all of Egypt's oldest males;
in Ham's tents,
he struck their pride and joy.
[52] God led his own people
out like sheep,
guiding them like a flock
　　in the wilderness.
[53] God led them in safety—
they were not afraid!
But the sea engulfed their enemies!
[54] God brought them
to his holy territory,
to the mountain that his own
　　strong hand had acquired.
[55] God drove out the nations
before them
and apportioned property
　　for them;
he settled Israel's tribes
　　in their tents.

[56] But they tested and defied
the Most High God;
they didn't pay attention
to his warnings.
[57] They turned away, became faithless
just like their ancestors;
they twisted away
like a defective bow.
[58] They angered God
with their many shrines;
they angered him with their idols.
[59] God heard and became enraged;
he rejected Israel utterly.
[60] God abandoned the sanctuary
at Shiloh,
the tent where he had lived
with humans.

---

[1] Correction; MT *to hailstones*

⁶¹ God let his power be held captive,
    let his glory go
        to the enemy's hand.
⁶² God delivered his people
        up to the sword;
    he was enraged
        at his own possession.
⁶³ Fire devoured his young men,
    and his young women
        had no wedding songs.
⁶⁴ God's priests were killed by the sword,
    and his widows couldn't even cry.
⁶⁵ But then my Lord woke up—
    as if he'd been sleeping!
    Like a warrior shaking off wine,
⁶⁶ God beat back his foes;
    he made them
        an everlasting disgrace.

⁶⁷ God rejected the tent of Joseph
    and didn't choose
        the tribe of Ephraim.
⁶⁸ Instead, he chose the tribe of Judah,
    the mountain of Zion,
        which he loves.
⁶⁹ God built his sanctuary
    like the highest heaven
    and like the earth,
        which he established forever.
⁷⁰ And God chose David, his servant,
    taking him from the sheepfolds.
⁷¹ God brought him
    from shepherding nursing ewes
    to shepherd his people Jacob,
    to shepherd his inheritance, Israel.
⁷² David shepherded them
    with a heart of integrity;
    he led them with the skill
        of his hands.

Psalm 79
A psalm of Asaph.

¹ The nations have come
    into your inheritance, God!
    They've defiled your holy temple.
They've made Jerusalem
    a bunch of ruins.
² They've left your servants' bodies
    as food for the birds;
    they've left the flesh
        of your faithful
    to the wild animals of the earth.
³ They've poured out the blood
        of the faithful
    like water all around Jerusalem,
    and there's no one left to bury them.
⁴ We've become a joke to our neighbors,
    nothing but objects of ridicule
    and disapproval to those around us.

⁵ How long will you rage, LORD?
        Forever?
    How long will your anger
        burn like fire?
⁶ Pour out your wrath on the nations
    who don't know you,
    on the kingdoms
        that haven't called on your name.
⁷ They've devoured Jacob
    and demolished his pasture.
⁸ Don't remember the iniquities
    of past generations;
    let your compassion hurry
        to meet us
    because we've been brought so low.
⁹ God of our salvation, help us
    for the glory of your name!
    Deliver us and cover our sins
    for the sake of your name!
¹⁰ Why should the nations say,
    "Where's their God now?"
    Let vengeance for the spilled blood
        of your servants
    be known among the nations
    before our very eyes!
¹¹ Let the prisoners' groaning
        reach you.
    With your powerful arm
        spare those who are destined to die.

¹² Pay back our neighbors
  seven times over,
  right where it hurts,
  for the insults
    they used on you, Lord.
¹³ We are, after all, your people
  and the sheep
    of your very own pasture.
We will give you thanks forever;
  we will proclaim your praises
  from one generation to the next.

Psalm 80

*For the music leader.
According to "Lotus Blossoms."
A testimony of Asaph. A psalm.*

¹ Shepherd of Israel, listen!
  You, the one who leads Joseph
    as if he were a sheep.
  You, who are enthroned upon
    the winged heavenly creatures.
  Show yourself ² before Ephraim,
    Benjamin, and Manasseh!
  Wake up your power!
  Come to save us!
³ Restore us, God!
  Make your face shine
    so that we can be saved!

⁴ LORD God of heavenly forces,
  how long will you fume
    against your people's prayer?
⁵ You've fed them bread
    made of tears;
  you've given them tears
    to drink three times over!
⁶ You've put us at odds
    with our neighbors;
  our enemies make fun of us.
⁷ Restore us, God of heavenly forces!
  Make your face shine
    so that we can be saved!

⁸ You brought a vine out of Egypt.
  You drove out the nations
    and planted it.
⁹ You cleared the ground for it;
  then it planted its roots deep,
    filling the land.
¹⁰ The mountains were covered
    by its shade;
  the mighty cedars were covered
    by its branches.
¹¹ It sent its branches
    all the way to the sea;
  its shoots went all the way
    to the Euphrates River.^m
¹² So why have you now torn down
    its walls
  so that all who come along
    can pluck its fruit,
¹³ so that any boar from the forest
    can tear it up,
  so that the bugs can feed on it?

¹⁴ Please come back,
    God of heavenly forces!
  Look down from heaven
    and perceive it!
  Attend to this vine,
¹⁵ this root that you planted
    with your strong hand,
  this son whom you secured
    as your very own.
¹⁶ It is burned with fire.
  It is chopped down.
  They die at the rebuke
    coming from you.
¹⁷ Let your hand be
  with the one on your right side—
  with the one whom you secured
    as your own—
¹⁸ then we will not turn away
    from you!
  Revive us
  so that we can call on your name.

^m Or *the Great River*

¹⁹ Restore us,
    LORD God of heavenly forces!
    Make your face shine
        so that we can be saved!

Psalm 81

For the music leader.
According to the Gittith. Of Asaph.

¹ Rejoice out loud to God,
    our strength!
    Shout for joy to Jacob's God!
² Take up a song and strike the drum!
    Sweet lyre along with harp!
³ Blow the horn on the new moon,
        at the full moon,
    for our day of celebration!
⁴ Because this is the law for Israel;
    this is a rule of Jacob's God.
⁵ He made it a decree for Joseph
    when he went out
        against the land of Egypt,
    when I heard a language
        I did not yet know:

⁶ "I lifted the burden off your shoulders;
    your hands are free
        of the brick basket!
⁷ In distress you cried out,
        so I rescued you.
    I answered you
        in the secret of thunder.
    I tested you at the waters
        of Meribah.   *Selah*
⁸ Listen, my people, I'm warning you!
    If only you would listen to me, Israel.
⁹ There must be no foreign god
        among you.
    You must not bow down
        to any strange deity.
¹⁰ I am the LORD your God,
    who brought you up
        from Egypt's land.
    Open your mouth wide—
        I will fill it up!

¹¹ "But my people wouldn't listen
        to my voice.
    Israel simply wasn't agreeable
        toward me.
¹² So I sent them off
        to follow their willful hearts;
    they followed their own advice.
¹³ How I wish my people
        would listen to me!
    How I wish Israel would walk
        in my ways!
¹⁴ Then I would subdue their enemies
        in a second;
    I would turn my hand
        against their foes.
¹⁵ Those who hate the LORD
        would grovel before me,
    and their doom would last forever!
¹⁶ But I would feed you
        with the finest wheat.
    I would satisfy you with honey
        from the rock."

Psalm 82

A psalm of Asaph.

¹ God takes his stand
        in the divine council;
    he gives judgment
        among the gods:
² "How long will you judge unjustly
    by granting favor to the wicked?
                                Selah
³ Give justice to the lowly
        and the orphan;
    maintain the right of the poor
        and the destitute!
⁴ Rescue the lowly and the needy.
    Deliver them
        from the power of the wicked!"

⁵ They don't know;
    they don't understand;
    they wander around in the dark.
    All the earth's foundations shake.

⁶ I hereby declare, "You are gods,
children of the Most High—
all of you!
⁷ But you will die like mortals;
you will fall down like any prince."

⁸ Rise up, God! Judge the earth
because you hold all nations
in your possession!

Psalm 83

A song. A psalm of Asaph.

¹ God, don't be silent!
Don't be quiet or sit still, God,
² because—look!—
your enemies are growling;
those who hate you
are acting arrogantly.
³ They concoct crafty plans
against your own people;
they plot against
the people you favor.
⁴ "Come on," they say,
"let's wipe them out as a nation!
Let the name Israel
be remembered no more!"
⁵ They plot with a single-minded heart;
they make a covenant against you.
⁶ They are the clans
of Edom and the Ishmaelites,
Moab and the Hagrites,
⁷ Gebal, Ammon, Amalek,
Philistia along with the citizens
of Tyre.
⁸ Assyria too has joined them—
they are the strong arm
for Lot's children.   *Selah*

⁹ Do to them what you did to Midian,
to Sisera, and to Jabin
at the Kishon River.
¹⁰ They were destroyed at Endor;

they became fertilizer
for the ground.
¹¹ Make their officials
like Oreb and Zeeb,
all their princes
like Zebah and Zalmunna—
¹² those who said, "Let's take
God's pastures for ourselves."
¹³ My God, make them
like tumbleweeds,
like chaff blown by wind.
¹⁴ Just like a fire consumes a forest,
just like flames set
mountains ablaze,
¹⁵ pursue them with your storm,
terrify them with your hurricane.
¹⁶ Cover their faces with shame,
LORD, so that they might
seek your name.
¹⁷ Let them be shamed
and terrified forever.
Let them die in disgrace.
¹⁸ Let them know that you—
your name is the LORD!—
you alone are Most High
over all the earth.

Psalm 84

For the music leader.
According to the Gittith.
Of the Korahites. A psalm.

¹ How lovely is your dwelling place,
LORD of heavenly forces!
² My very being[n] longs, even yearns,
for the LORD's courtyards.
My heart and my body
will rejoice out loud
to the living God!

³ Yes, the sparrow too
has found a home there;
the swallow has found herself a nest

[n] Or *soul*

where she can lay her young
  beside your altars,
  Lord of heavenly forces,
  my king, my God!
⁴Those who live in your house
  are truly happy;
  they praise you constantly.   *Selah*

⁵Those who put their strength in you
  are truly happy;
  pilgrimage is in their hearts.
⁶As they pass through the
  Baca Valley,°
  they make it a spring of water.
  Yes, the early rain covers it
  with blessings.
⁷They go from strength to strength,
  until they see the supreme God
  in Zion.ᴾ
⁸Lord God of heavenly forces,
  hear my prayer;
  listen closely, Jacob's God!   *Selah*
⁹Look at our shield, God;
  pay close attention
  to the face of your anointed one!

¹⁰Better is a single day
  in your courtyards
  than a thousand days
  anywhere else!
  I would prefer to stand outside
  the entrance of my God's house
  than live comfortably
  in the tents of the wicked!
¹¹The Lord is a sun and shield;
  God is favor and glory.
  The Lord gives—
  doesn't withhold!—good things
  to those who walk with integrity.
¹²Lord of heavenly forces,
  those who trust in you
  are truly happy!

Psalm 85

For the music leader.
Of the Korahites. A psalm.

¹Lord, you've been kind to your land;
  you've changed Jacob's circumstances
  for the better.
²You've forgiven
  your people's wrongdoing;
  you've covered all their sins.   *Selah*
³You've stopped being furious;
  you've turned away
  from your burning anger.
⁴You, the God who can save us,
  restore us!
  Stop being angry with us!
⁵Will you be mad at us forever?
  Will you prolong your anger
  from one generation to the next?
⁶Won't you bring us
  back to life again
  so that your people
  can rejoice in you?
⁷Show us your faithful love, Lord!
  Give us your salvation!

⁸Let me hear what the Lord God says,
  because he speaks peace
  to his people and
  to his faithful ones.
  Don't let them return
  to foolish ways.
⁹God's salvation is very close
  to those who honor him
  so that his glory can live
  in our land.
¹⁰Faithful love and truth have met;
  righteousness and peace
  have kissed.
¹¹Truth springs up from the ground;
  righteousness gazes
  down from heaven.
¹²Yes, the Lord gives what is good,
  and our land yields its produce.

°LXX; Vulg *Valley of Tears*   ᴾCorrection; MT *the God of gods will be seen in Zion*

¹³ Righteousness walks before God,
   making a road for his steps.

Psalm 86

A prayer of David.

¹ LORD, listen closely to me
   and answer me,
   because I am poor and in need.
² Guard my life because I am faithful.
   Save your servant
   who trusts in you—you! My God!
³ Have mercy on me, Lord,
   because I cry out to you all day long.
⁴ Make your servant's life�q
   happy again
   because, my Lord,
   I offer my life to you,
⁵ because, my Lord,
   you are good and forgiving,
   full of faithful love
   for all those who cry out to you.
⁶ Listen closely to my prayer, LORD;
   pay close attention to the sound
   of my requests for mercy.
⁷ Whenever I am in trouble,
   I cry out to you,
   because you will answer me.

⁸ My Lord! There is no one like you
   among the gods!
   There is nothing that can compare
   to your works!
⁹ All the nations that you've made
   will come
   and bow down before you, Lord;
   they will glorify your name,
¹⁰ because you are awesome
   and a wonder-worker.
   You are God. Just you.

¹¹ Teach me your way, LORD,
   so that I can walk in your truth.
   Make my heart focused
   only on honoring your name.
¹² I give thanks to you,
   my Lord, my God,
   with all my heart,
   and I will glorify your name forever,
¹³ because your faithful love
   toward me is awesome
   and because you've rescued my life
   from the lowest part of hell.ʳ

¹⁴ The arrogant rise up against me, God.
   A gang of violent people
   want me dead.
   They don't give a thought for you.
¹⁵ But you, my Lord,
   are a God of compassion and mercy;
   you are very patient
   and full of faithful love.
¹⁶ Come back to me!
   Have mercy on me!
   Give your servant your strength;
   save this child of your servant!
¹⁷ Show me a sign of your goodness
   so that those who hate me
   will see it and be put to shame—
   show a sign that you, LORD,
   have helped me and comforted me.

Psalm 87

A psalm of the Korahites. A song.

¹ God's foundation is set
   on the holy mountains.
² The LORD loves Zion's gates
   more than all of Jacob's
   houses combined.
³ Glorious things are said about you,
   the city of God!   *Selah*
⁴ I count Rahab and Babel
   among those who know me;
   also Philistia and Tyre,
   along with Cush—
   each of these was born there.

�q Or *soul*; also in 86:4*b*, 13   ʳ Heb *Sheol*

5 And of Zion it is said:
"Each person was born in it,
but the one who will establish it
is the Most High."
6 The LORD makes a record
as he registers the peoples:
"Each one was born there."   *Selah*
7 And while they dance, people sing:
"The source of my life
comes from you."

Psalm 88

A song. A psalm of the Korahites.
For the music leader.
According to "Mahalath Leannoth."[s]
A maskil[t] *of Heman the Ezrahite.*
1 LORD, God of my salvation,
by day I cry out,
even at night, before you—
2 let my prayer reach you!
Turn your ear to my outcry
3 because my whole being[u]
is filled with distress;
my life is at the very brink of hell.[v]

4 I am considered as one
of those plummeting into the pit.
I am like those who are beyond help,
5 drifting among the dead,
lying in the grave,
like dead bodies—
those you don't remember anymore,
those who are cut off
from your power.
6 You placed me down
in the deepest pit,
in places dark and deep.
7 Your anger smothers me;
you subdue me with it,
wave after wave.   *Selah*
8 You've made my friends distant.

You've made me disgusting to them.
I can't escape. I'm trapped!
9 My eyes are tired of looking
at my suffering.
I've been calling out
to you every day, LORD—
I've had my hands outstretched
to you!

10 Do you work wonders for the dead?
Do ghosts rise up
and give you thanks?   *Selah*
11 Is your faithful love
proclaimed in the grave,
your faithfulness
in the underworld?[w]
12 Are your wonders known
in the land of darkness,
your righteousness
in the land of oblivion?

13 But I cry out to you, LORD!
My prayer meets you
first thing in the morning!
14 Why do you reject my very being,
LORD?
Why do you hide your face
from me?
15 Since I was young I've been afflicted,
I've been dying.
I've endured your terrors.
I'm lifeless.
16 Your fiery anger
has overwhelmed me;
your terrors have destroyed me.
17 They surround me all day long
like water;
they engulf me completely.
18 You've made my loved ones
and companions distant.
My only friend is darkness.

---

[s] Heb uncertain   [t] Perhaps *instruction*   [u] Or *soul*, also in 88:14   [v] Heb *Sheol*   [w] Heb *Abaddon*

Psalm 89

A maskil[x] of Ethan the Ezrahite.

¹ I will sing of the LORD's
loyal love forever.
I will proclaim your faithfulness
with my own mouth
from one generation to the next.

² That's why I say,
"Your[y] loyal love is rightly built—
forever!
You establish your faithfulness
in heaven."

³ You said,[z] "I made a covenant
with my chosen one;
I promised my servant David:

⁴ 'I will establish
your offspring forever;
I will build up your throne from
one generation to the next.'"

Selah

⁵ Heaven thanks you
for your wondrous acts, LORD—
for your faithfulness too—
in the assembly of the holy ones.

⁶ Is there any in the sky
who could compare to the LORD?
Who among the gods
is equal to the LORD?

⁷ God is respected
in the council of the holy ones;
God is awesome and revered
more than all those around him.

⁸ Who is like you,
LORD God of heavenly forces?
Mighty LORD, your faithfulness
surrounds you!

⁹ You rule over the surging sea:
When its waves rise up,
it's you who makes them still.

¹⁰ It's you who crushed Rahab
like a dead body;

you scattered your enemies
with your strong arm.

¹¹ Heaven is yours! The earth too!
The world and all that fills it—
you made all of it!

¹² North and south—you created them!
The mountains Tabor and Hermon
shout praises to your name.

¹³ You have a powerful arm;
your hand is strong;
your strong hand is raised high!

¹⁴ Your throne is built
on righteousness and justice;
loyal love and faithfulness
stand in front of you.

¹⁵ The people who know the celebratory
shout are truly happy!
They walk in the light of your
presence, LORD!

¹⁶ They rejoice in your name
all day long
and are uplifted
by your righteousness

¹⁷ because you are the splendor
of their strength.
By your favor you make us strong

¹⁸ because our shield
is the LORD's own;
our king belongs
to the holy one of Israel!

¹⁹ Once you spoke in a vision
to your faithful servants:
I placed a crown on a strong man.
I raised up someone
specially chosen from the people.

²⁰ I discovered my servant David.
I anointed him with my holy oil.

²¹ My hand will sustain him—
yes, my arm will strengthen him!

²² No enemy will oppress him;

no wicked person
  will make him suffer.
²³ I will crush all his foes
  in front of him.
  I will strike down
    all those who hate him.
²⁴ My faithfulness and my loyal love
  will be with him.
  He will be strengthened
    by my name.
²⁵ I will set his hand on the sea.
  I will set his strong hand
    on the rivers.
²⁶ He will cry out to me:
  "You are my father,
    my God, the rock of my salvation."
²⁷ Yes, I'll make him
    the one born first—
  I'll make him the high king
    of all earth's kings.
²⁸ I will always guard my loyal love
  toward him.
  My covenant with him
    will last forever.
²⁹ I will establish his dynasty
    for all time.
  His throne will last
    as long as heaven does.
³⁰ But if his children ever
    abandon my Instruction,
  stop following my rules—
³¹ if they treat my statutes like dirt,
  stop keeping
    my commandments—
³² then I will punish their sin
    with a stick,
  and I will punish their wrongdoing
    with a severe beating.
³³ But even then I won't withdraw
  my loyal love from him.
  I won't betray my faithfulness.
³⁴ I won't break my covenant.
  I won't renege on what
    crossed my lips.

³⁵ By my own holiness
    I've sworn one thing:
  I will not lie to David.
³⁶ His dynasty will last forever.
  His throne will be like the sun,
    always before me.
³⁷ It will be securely
    established forever;
  like the moon, a faithful witness
    in the sky.   *Selah*

³⁸ But you, God, have rejected
    and despised him.
  You've become infuriated
    with your anointed one.
³⁹ You've canceled the covenant
    with your servant.
  You've thrown his crown
    in the dirt.
⁴⁰ You've broken through all his walls.
  You've made his strongholds
    a pile of ruins.
⁴¹ All those who pass by plunder him.
  He's nothing but a joke
    to his neighbors.
⁴² You lifted high his foes' strong hand.
  You gave all his enemies
    reason to celebrate.
⁴³ Yes, you dulled the edge of his sword
  and didn't support him in battle.
⁴⁴ You've put an end to his splendor.
  You've thrown his throne
    to the ground.
⁴⁵ You've shortened the prime
    of his life.
  You've wrapped him up in shame.
                        Selah

⁴⁶ How long will it last, LORD?
  Will you hide yourself forever?
  How long will your wrath
    burn like fire?
⁴⁷ Remember how short my life is!
  Have you created humans
    for no good reason?

⁴⁸Who lives their life
    without seeing death?
  Who is ever rescued
    from the grip of the grave?ᵃ *Selah*

⁴⁹Where now are your loving acts
    from long ago, my Lord—
  the same ones you promised
    to David
  by your own faithfulness?

⁵⁰Remember your servant's abuse,
    my Lord!
  Remember how I bear in my heart
    all the insults of the nations,ᵇ
⁵¹the ones your enemies,
    LORD, use—
  the ones they use to abuse
    every step your anointed one takes.

⁵²Bless the LORD forever!
    Amen and Amen!

BOOK IV
(Psalms 90–106)

Psalm 90

A prayer of Moses, the man of God.

¹Lord, you have been our help,
    generation after generation.
²Before the mountains were born,
    before you birthed the earth
    and the inhabited world—
  from forever in the past
    to forever in the future, you are God.

³You return people to dust,
    saying, "Go back, humans,"
⁴because in your perspective
    a thousand years
    are like yesterday past,
  like a short period
    during the night watch.
⁵You sweep humans away
    like a dream,

like grass that is renewed
    in the morning.
⁶True, in the morning it thrives,
    renewed,
  but come evening it withers,
    all dried up.

⁷Yes, we are wasting away
    because of your wrath;
  we are paralyzed with fear
    on account of your rage.
⁸You put our sins
    right in front of you,
  set our hidden faults
    in the light from your face.
⁹Yes, all our days slip away
    because of your fury;
  we finish up our years
    with a whimper.
¹⁰We live at best
    to be seventy years old,
  maybe eighty, if we're strong.
  But their duration brings
    hard work and trouble
  because they go by so quickly.
    And then we fly off.
¹¹Who can comprehend
    the power of your anger?
  The honor that is due you
    corresponds to your wrath.
¹²Teach us to number our days
    so we can have a wise heart.

¹³Come back to us, LORD!
    Please, quick!
  Have some compassion
    for your servants!
¹⁴Fill us full every morning
    with your faithful love
  so we can rejoice and celebrate
    our whole life long.
¹⁵Make us happy
    for the same amount of time
    that you afflicted us—

ᵃHeb *Sheol* ᵇCorrection; MT *all of many peoples*

for the same number of years
  that we saw only trouble.
[16] Let your acts be seen by your servants;
    let your glory be seen
    by their children.
[17] Let the kindness of the Lord our God
    be over us.
  Make the work of our hands last.
  Make the work of our hands last!

Psalm 91

[1] Living in the Most High's shelter,
    camping in the Almighty's[c] shade,
[2] I say to the LORD, "You are my refuge,
    my stronghold!
  You are my God—the one I trust!"

[3] God will save you
    from the hunter's trap
    and from deadly sickness.
[4] God will protect you with his pinions;
    you'll find refuge under his wings.
  His faithfulness is
    a protective shield.
[5] Don't be afraid of terrors at night,
    arrows that fly in daylight,
[6] or sickness that prowls in the dark,
    destruction that ravages
    at noontime.
[7] Even if one thousand people
    fall dead next to you,
    ten thousand right beside you—
    it won't happen to you.
[8] Just look with your eyes,
    and you will see
    the wicked punished.
[9] Because you've made the LORD
    my refuge,
    the Most High,
    your place of residence—
[10] no evil will happen to you;
    no disease will come close
    to your tent.

[11] Because he will order his messengers
    to help you,
    to protect you wherever you go.
[12] They will carry you
    with their own hands
    so you don't bruise your foot
    on a stone.
[13] You'll march on top of lions
    and vipers;
    you'll trample young lions
    and serpents underfoot.

[14] God says,[d]
    "Because you are devoted to me,
    I'll rescue you.
  I'll protect you
    because you know my name.
[15] Whenever you cry out to me,
    I'll answer.
  I'll be with you in troubling times.
  I'll save you and glorify you.
[16] I'll fill you full with old age.
  I'll show you my salvation."

Psalm 92
A psalm.
A song for the Sabbath day.
[1] It is good to give thanks to the LORD,
    to sing praises to your name,
    Most High;
[2] to proclaim your loyal love
    in the morning,
    your faithfulness at nighttime
[3] with the ten-stringed harp,
    with the melody of the lyre
[4] because you've made me happy,
    LORD,
    by your acts.
  I sing with joy
    because of your handiwork.
[5] How awesome are your works, LORD!
  Your thoughts are so deep!

---

[c] Heb *Shaddai*   [d] Heb lacks *God says.*

⁶ Ignorant people don't know—
fools don't understand this:
⁷ though the wicked
spring up like grass
and all evildoers seem to blossom,
they do so
only to be destroyed forever.
⁸ But you, LORD, are exalted forever!

⁹ Look at your enemies, LORD!
Look at how your enemies die,
how all evildoers
are scattered abroad!
¹⁰ But you've made me
as strong as a wild ox.
I'm soaked in precious ointment.
¹¹ My eyes have seen
my enemies' defeat;
my ears have heard
the downfall of my evil foes.

¹² The righteous will spring up
like a palm tree.
They will grow strong
like a cedar of Lebanon.
¹³ Those who have been replanted
in the LORD's house
will spring up
in the courtyards of our God.
¹⁴ They will bear fruit
even when old and gray;
they will remain lush and fresh
¹⁵ in order to proclaim:
"The LORD is righteous.
He's my rock.
There's nothing unrighteous
in him."

Psalm 93

¹ The LORD rules!
He is robed in majesty—
the LORD is robed,
clothed with strength.

Yes, he set the world firmly in place;ᵉ
it won't be shaken.
² Your throne is set firm
for a very long time.
You are eternal!

³ LORD, the floods have raised up—
the floods have raised up
their voices;
the floods raise up a roar!
⁴ But mightier than the sound
of much water,
mightier than the sea's waves,
mighty on high is the LORD!
⁵ Your laws are so faithful.
Holiness decorates your house,
LORD, for all time.

Psalm 94

¹ LORD, avenging God—
avenging God, show yourself!
² Rise up, judge of the earth!
Pay back the arrogant
exactly what they deserve!
³ How long will the wicked—
oh, LORD!—
how long will the wicked win?
⁴ They spew arrogant words;
all the evildoers are bragging.
⁵ They crush your own people, LORD!
They abuse your
very own possession.
⁶ They kill widows and immigrants;
they murder orphans,
⁷ saying all the while,
"The LORD can't see it;
Jacob's God doesn't know
what's going on!"

⁸ You ignorant people
better learn quickly.
You fools—
when will you get some sense?

ᵉLXX, Vulg; MT *the world is set firmly in place*; cf Ps 96:10

⁹ The one who made the ear,
   can't he hear?
The one who formed the eye,
   can't he see?
¹⁰ The one who disciplines nations,
   can't he punish?
The one who teaches humans,
   doesn't he know?ᶠ
¹¹ The LORD does indeed
   know human thoughts,
   knows that they are nothing
   but a puff of air.

¹² The people you discipline, LORD,
   are truly happy—
   the ones you teach
   from your Instruction—
¹³ giving them relief
   from troubling times
   until a pit is dug for the wicked.
¹⁴ The LORD will not reject his people;
   he will not abandon
   his very own possession.
¹⁵ No, but justice will once again
   meet up with righteousness,
   and all whose heart is right
   will follow after.

¹⁶ Who will stand up for me
   against the wicked?
Who will help me against evildoers?
¹⁷ If the LORD hadn't helped me,
   Iᵍ would live instantly
   in total silence.
¹⁸ Whenever I feel my foot slipping,
   your faithful love steadies me, LORD.
¹⁹ When my anxieties multiply,
   your comforting calms me down.

²⁰ Can a wicked ruler be your ally;
   one who wreaks havoc
   by means of the law?

²¹ The wicked gang up
   against the lives of the righteous.
   They condemn innocent blood.
²² But the LORD is my fortress;
   my God is my rock of refuge.
²³ He will repay them
   for their wickedness,
   completely destroy them
   because of their evil.
   Yes, the LORD our God
   will completely destroy them.

Psalm 95

¹ Come, let's sing out loud to the LORD!
   Let's raise a joyful shout
   to the rock of our salvation!
² Let's come before him with thanks!
   Let's shout songs of joy to him!
³ The LORD is a great God,
   the great king over all other gods.
⁴ The earth's depths are in his hands;
   the mountain heights
   belong to him;
⁵ the sea, which he made, is his
   along with the dry ground,
   which his own hands formed.

⁶ Come, let's worship and bow down!
   Let's kneel before the LORD,
   our maker!
⁷ He is our God,
   and we are the people
   of his pasture,
   the sheep in his hands.

If only you would listen
   to his voice right now!
⁸ "Don't harden your hearts
   like you did at Meribah,
   like you did when you
   were at Massah,
   in the wilderness,

ᶠ Correction; MT *the one who teaches humans knowledge*   ᵍ Or *soul*; also in 94:19, 21

⁹ when your ancestors tested me
  and scrutinized me,
  even though they had already seen
  my acts.
¹⁰ For forty years I despised
  that generation;
  I said, 'These people have
  twisted hearts.
  They don't know my ways.'
¹¹ So in anger I swore:
  'They will never enter
  my place of rest!'"

Psalm 96

¹ Sing to the LORD a new song!
  Sing to the LORD, all the earth!
² Sing to the LORD! Bless his name!
  Share the news of his saving work
  every single day!
³ Declare God's glory
  among the nations;
  declare his wondrous works
  among all people
⁴ because the LORD is great
  and so worthy of praise.
  He is awesome beyond all other gods
⁵ because all the gods of the nations
  are just idols,
  but it is the LORD
  who created heaven!
⁶ Greatness and grandeur
  are in front of him;
  strength and beauty
  are in his sanctuary.

⁷ Give to the LORD,
  all families of the nations—
  give to the LORD glory and power!
⁸ Give to the LORD the glory
  due his name!
  Bring gifts!
  Enter his courtyards!

⁹ Bow down to the LORD
  in his holy splendor!
  Tremble before him, all the earth!

¹⁰ Tell the nations, "The LORD rules!
  Yes, he set the world
  firmly in place;ʰ
  it won't be shaken.
  He will judge all people fairly."
¹¹ Let heaven celebrate!
  Let the earth rejoice!
  Let the sea and
  everything in it roar!
¹² Let the countryside
  and everything in it celebrate!
  Then all the trees of the forest too
  will shout out joyfully
¹³ before the LORD
  because he is coming!
  He is coming to establish justice
  on the earth!
  He will establish justice
  in the world rightly.
  He will establish justice
  among all people fairly.

Psalm 97

¹ The LORD rules! Let the earth rejoice!
  Let all the islands celebrate!
² Clouds and thick darkness
  surround God.
  His throne is built
  on righteousness and justice.
³ Fire proceeds before him,
  burning up his enemies
  on every side.
⁴ His lightning lights up the world;
  the earth sees it and trembles!
⁵ The mountains melt like wax
  before the LORD,
  before the Lord
  of the whole world!

ʰLXX, Vulg; MT *the world is firmly established*; cf Ps 93:1

⁶ Heaven has proclaimed
   God's righteousness,
   and all nations have seen his glory.
⁷ All those who worship images,
   those who are proud of idols,
   are put to shame.
   All gods bow down to the Lord!
⁸ Zion has heard and celebrates,
   the towns[i] of Judah rejoice,
   because of your acts of justice, LORD,
⁹ because you, LORD,
   are the Most High
   over all the earth,
   because you are so superior
   to all other gods.

¹⁰ Those of you who love the LORD,
   hate evil!
   God guards the lives
   of his faithful ones,
   delivering them from
   the power of the wicked.
¹¹ Light is planted like seed
   for the righteous person;
   joy too for those
   whose heart is right.
¹² Rejoice in the LORD, righteous ones!
   Give thanks to his holy name!

Psalm 98
A psalm.

¹ Sing to the LORD a new song
   because he has done
   wonderful things!
   His own strong hand
   and his own holy arm
   have won the victory!
² The LORD has made his salvation
   widely known;
   he has revealed his righteousness
   in the eyes of all the nations.
³ God has remembered his loyal love

and faithfulness to the house
   of Israel;
   every corner of the earth has seen
   our God's salvation.

⁴ Shout triumphantly to the LORD,
   all the earth!
   Be happy!
   Rejoice out loud!
   Sing your praises!
⁵ Sing your praises to the LORD
   with the lyre—
   with the lyre
   and the sound of music.
⁶ With trumpets and a horn blast,
   shout triumphantly
   before the LORD, the king!
⁷ Let the sea and everything in it roar;
   the world and all
   its inhabitants too.
⁸ Let all the rivers clap their hands;
   let the mountains rejoice
   out loud altogether
   ⁹ before the LORD
   because he is coming
   to establish justice on the earth!
   He will establish justice
   in the world rightly;
   he will establish justice
   among all people fairly.

Psalm 99

¹ The LORD rules—
   the nations shake!
   He sits enthroned on
   the winged heavenly creatures—
   the earth quakes!
² The LORD is great in Zion;
   he is exalted over all the nations.
³ Let them thank your great
   and awesome name.
   He is holy!

---

[i] Or *daughters*

⁴Strong king[j] who loves justice,
   you are the one
      who established what is fair.
   You worked justice
      and righteousness in Jacob.
⁵Magnify the LORD our God!
   Bow low at his footstool!
   He is holy!

⁶Moses and Aaron were among
      his priests,
   Samuel too among those
      who called on his name.
They cried out to the LORD,
   and he himself answered them—
⁷he spoke to them
      from a pillar of cloud.
They kept the laws and the rules
   God gave to them.
⁸LORD our God, you answered them.
   To them you were a God
      who forgives
   but also the one who avenged
      their wrong deeds.
⁹Magnify the LORD our God!
   Bow low at his holy mountain
   because the LORD our God is holy!

Psalm 100
A psalm of thanks.

¹Shout triumphantly to the LORD,
   all the earth!
²Serve the LORD with celebration!
   Come before him
      with shouts of joy!
³Know that the LORD is God—
   he made us; we belong to him.[k]
   We are his people,
      the sheep of his own pasture.
⁴Enter his gates with thanks;
   enter his courtyards with praise!
   Thank him! Bless his name!

⁵Because the LORD is good,
   his loyal love lasts forever;
   his faithfulness lasts
      generation after generation.

Psalm 101
Of David. A psalm.

¹Oh, let me sing
   about faithful love and justice!
   I want to sing my praises to you,
      LORD!
²I want to study the way
   of integrity—
      how long before it gets here?
   I will walk with a heart of integrity
      in my own house.
³I won't set my eyes
   on anything worthless.
   I hate wrongdoing;
      none of that will stick to me.
⁴A corrupt heart will be far from me.
   I won't be familiar with evil.
⁵I will destroy anyone
   who secretly tells lies
      about a neighbor.
I can't stomach anyone
   who has proud eyes
      or an arrogant heart.
⁶My eyes focus on those
   who are faithful in the land,
   to have them close to me.
The person who walks without blame
   will work for me.
⁷But the person who acts deceitfully
   won't stay in my house.
The person who tells lies
   won't last for long before me.
⁸Every morning I will destroy
   all those who are wicked
      in the land
   in order to eliminate all evildoers
      from the LORD's city.

ʲCorrection; MT *A king's strength*   ᵏQere; Kethib *and not we ourselves*

Psalm 102

A prayer of an oppressed person,
when weak and pouring out grief
to the Lord.

¹ Lord, hear my prayer!
    Let my cry reach you!
² Don't hide your face from me
    in my time of trouble!
  Listen to me!
    Answer me quickly as I cry out!
³ Because my days disappear
    like smoke,
  my bones are burned up
    as if in an oven;
⁴ my heart is smashed
    like dried-up grass.
  I even forget to eat my food
⁵ because of my intense groans.
  My bones are protruding
    from my skin.
⁶ I'm like some wild owl—
    like some screech owl
    in the desert.
⁷ I lie awake all night.
  I'm all alone like a bird on a roof.
⁸ All day long my enemies
    make fun of me;
  those who mock me
    curse using my name!
⁹ I've been eating ashes
    instead of bread.
  I've been mixing tears
    into my drinks
¹⁰ because of your anger and wrath,
    because you picked me up
    and threw me away.
¹¹ My days are like a shadow soon gone.
  I'm dried up like dead grass.

¹² But you, Lord, rule forever!
    Your fame lasts
    from one generation to the next!
¹³ You will stand up—
    you'll have compassion on Zion

because it is time
    to have mercy on her—
  the time set for that has now come!
¹⁴ Your servants cherish Zion's stones;
    they show mercy even to her dirt.
¹⁵ The nations will honor
    the Lord's name;
  all the earth's rulers
    will honor your glory
¹⁶ because the Lord will rebuild Zion;
    he will be seen there in his glory.
¹⁷ God will turn
    to the prayer of the impoverished;
    he won't despise their prayers.

¹⁸ Let this be written down
    for the next generation
  so that people not yet created
    will praise the Lord:
¹⁹ The Lord looked down
    from his holy summit,
  surveyed the earth from heaven,
²⁰ to hear the prisoners' groans,
  to set free those condemned
    to death,
²¹ that the Lord's name
    may be declared in Zion
  and his praise
    declared in Jerusalem,
²² when all people
    are gathered together—
  all kingdoms—to serve the Lord.

²³ God broke my strength in midstride,
    cutting my days short.
²⁴ I said, "My God, don't take me away
    in the prime of life—
  your years go on
    from one generation to the next!
²⁵ You laid the earth's foundations
    long ago;
  the skies are your handiwork.
²⁶ These things will pass away,
    but you will last.

All of these things will wear out
    like clothing;
  you change them like clothes,
    and they pass on.
27 But you are the one!
  Your years never end!
28 Let your servants' children live safe;
  let your servants' descendants
    live secure in your presence."

Psalm 103
Of David.

1 Let my whole being[1] bless the LORD!
  Let everything inside me
    bless his holy name!
2 Let my whole being bless the LORD
  and never forget all his good deeds:
3 how God forgives all your sins,
  heals all your sickness,
4 saves your life from the pit,
  crowns you with faithful love
    and compassion,
5 and satisfies you
  with plenty of good things
  so that your youth
    is made fresh like an eagle's.

6 The LORD works righteousness;
  does justice for all
    who are oppressed.
7 God made his ways known to Moses;
  made his deeds known
    to the Israelites.
8 The LORD is compassionate
  and merciful,
  very patient,
    and full of faithful love.
9 God won't always play the judge;
  he won't be angry forever.
10 He doesn't deal with us
  according to our sin
  or repay us
    according to our wrongdoing,

11 because as high as heaven
  is above the earth,
  that's how large God's faithful love
    is for those who honor him.
12 As far as east is from west—
  that's how far God has removed
    our sin from us.
13 Like a parent feels compassion
  for their children—
  that's how the LORD
  feels compassion for those
    who honor him.
14 Because God knows how we're made,
  God remembers we're just dust.

15 The days of a human life
  are like grass:
  they bloom like a wildflower;
16 but when the wind blows through it,
  it's gone;
  even the ground where it stood
    doesn't remember it.
17 But the LORD's faithful love is from
  forever ago to forever from now
    for those who honor him.
  And God's righteousness reaches
    to the grandchildren
18 of those who keep his covenant
  and remember to keep
    his commands.
19 The LORD has established his throne
  in heaven,
  and his kingdom rules over all.

20 You divine messengers,
  bless the LORD!
  You who are mighty in power
  and keep his word,
  who obey everything he says,
    bless him!
21 All you heavenly forces,
  bless the LORD!

[1] Or *soul*; also in 103:2, 22

All you who serve him
and do his will,
bless him!
²² All God's creatures,
bless the LORD!
Everywhere, throughout
his kingdom,
let my whole being
bless the LORD!

Psalm 104

¹ Let my whole being[m] bless the LORD!
LORD my God,
how fantastic you are!
You are clothed in glory
and grandeur!
² You wear light like a robe;
you open the skies like a curtain.
³ You build your lofty house
on the waters;
you make the clouds your chariot,
going around on the wings
of the wind.
⁴ You make the winds your messengers;
you make fire
and flame your ministers.
⁵ You established the earth
on its foundations
so that it will never ever fall.
⁶ You covered it with the watery deep
like a piece of clothing;
the waters were higher
than the mountains!
⁷ But at your rebuke they ran away;
they fled in fear
at the sound of your thunder.
⁸ They flowed over the mountains,
streaming down the valleys
to the place you established
for them.
⁹ You set a boundary
they cannot cross

so they'll never again
cover the earth.

¹⁰ You put gushing springs
into dry riverbeds.
They flow between the mountains,
¹¹ providing water
for every wild animal—
the wild donkeys
quench their thirst.
¹² Overhead, the birds in the sky
make their home,
chirping loudly in the trees.
¹³ From your lofty house,
you water the mountains.
The earth is filled full
by the fruit of what you've done.
¹⁴ You make grass grow for cattle;
you make plants
for human farming
in order to get food
from the ground,
¹⁵ and wine,
which cheers people's hearts,
along with oil,
which makes the face shine,
and bread,
which sustains the human heart.
¹⁶ The LORD's trees are well watered—
the cedars of Lebanon,
which God planted,
¹⁷ where the birds make their nests,
where the stork has a home
in the cypresses.
¹⁸ The high mountains
belong to the mountain goats;
the ridges are the refuge of badgers.
¹⁹ God made the moon for the seasons,
and the sun too,
which knows when to set.
²⁰ You bring on the darkness
and it is night,
when every forest animal prowls.

[m] Or *soul*; also in 104:35

²¹The young lions roar for their prey,
seeking their food from God.
²²When the sun rises,
they gather together
and lie down in their dens.
²³Then people go off to their work,
to do their work until evening.

²⁴LORD, you have done so many things!
You made them all so wisely!
The earth is full of your creations!
²⁵And then there's the sea,
wide and deep,
with its countless creatures—
living things both small and large.
²⁶There go the ships on it,
and Leviathan, which you made,
plays in it!
²⁷All your creations wait for you
to give them their food on time.
²⁸When you give it to them,
they gather it up;
when you open your hand,
they are filled completely full!
²⁹But when you hide your face,
they are terrified;
when you take away their breath,
they die and return to dust.
³⁰When you let loose your breath,
they are created,
and you make the surface
of the ground brand-new again.

³¹Let the LORD's glory last forever!
Let the LORD rejoice
in all he has made!
³²He has only to look at the earth,
and it shakes.
God just touches the mountains,
and they erupt in smoke.

³³I will sing to the LORD
as long as I live;
I will sing praises to my God
while I'm still alive.

³⁴Let my praise be pleasing to him;
I'm rejoicing in the LORD!
³⁵Let sinners be wiped clean
from the earth;
let the wicked be no more.
But let my whole being
bless the LORD!
Praise the LORD!

Psalm 105

¹Give thanks to the LORD;
call upon his name;
make his deeds known
to all people!
²Sing to God;
sing praises to the Lord;
dwell on all his wondrous works!
³Give praise to God's holy name!
Let the hearts rejoice of all those
seeking the LORD!
⁴Pursue the LORD and his strength;
seek his face always!
⁵Remember the wondrous works
he has done,
all his marvelous works,
and the justice he declared—
⁶you who are the offspring
of Abraham, his servant,
and the children of Jacob,
his chosen ones.

⁷The LORD—he is our God.
His justice is everywhere
throughout the whole world.
⁸God remembers his covenant forever,
the word he commanded
to a thousand generations,
⁹which he made with Abraham,
the solemn pledge
he swore to Isaac.
¹⁰God set it up as binding law for Jacob,
as an eternal covenant for Israel,
¹¹promising, "I hereby give you
the land of Canaan
as your allotted inheritance."

¹² When they were few in number—
   insignificant, just immigrants—
¹³ wandering from nation to nation,
   from one kingdom to the next,
¹⁴ God didn't let anyone oppress them.
   God punished kings for their sake:
¹⁵ "Don't touch my anointed ones;
   don't harm my prophets!"

¹⁶ When God called for a famine
   in the land,
   destroying every source of food,
¹⁷ he sent a man ahead of them,
   who was sold as a slave:
   it was Joseph.
¹⁸ Joseph's feet hurt in his shackles;
   his neck was in an iron collar,
¹⁹ until what he predicted
   actually happened,
   until what the LORD had said
   proved him true.ⁿ
²⁰ The king sent for Joseph
   and set him free;
   the ruler of many people
   released him.
²¹ The king made Joseph master
   of his house and ruler
   over everything he owned,
²² to make sure his princes
   acted according to his will,
   and to teach wisdom to his advisors.
²³ That's how Israel came to Egypt,
   how Jacob became an immigrant
   in the land of Ham.

²⁴ God made his people very fruitful,
   more powerful than their enemies,
²⁵ whose hearts God changed
   so they hated his people
   and dealt shrewdly
   with his servants.

²⁶ God sent Moses his servant
   and the one he chose, Aaron.
²⁷ They put God's signs on Egypt,ᵒ
   his marvelous works
   on the land of Ham.
²⁸ God sent darkness,
   and it became dark,
   but the Egyptians
   rejected his word.
²⁹ God turned their waters into blood
   and killed their fish.
³⁰ God made their land
   swarm with frogsᵖ—
   even in the bedrooms
   of their king!
³¹ God spoke, and the insects came—
   gnats throughout
   their whole country!
³² God turned their rain into hail
   along with lightning flashes
   throughout their land.
³³ God destroyed their vines
   and their fig trees;
   shattered the trees
   of their countryside.
³⁴ God spoke, and the locusts came—
   countless grasshoppers came!
³⁵ They devoured all the plants
   in their land;
   they devoured the fruit
   of their soil.
³⁶ God struck down all the oldest sons
   throughout their land;
   struck down their very pride
   and joy.
³⁷ Then God brought Israel out,
   filled with silver and gold;
   not one of its tribes stumbled.
³⁸ Egypt celebrated when they left,
   because the dread of Israel
   had come upon them.

ⁿHeb uncertain ᵒCorrection; MT *they put on them the words of God's signs* ᵖCorrection;
DSS (11QPsᵃ) *their land swarmed with frogs*

³⁹ God spread out clouds as a covering;
   gave lightning to provide light
      at night.
⁴⁰ The people asked,
      and God brought quail;
   God filled them full
      with food from heaven.
⁴¹ God opened the rock
      and out gushed water—
   flowing like a river
      through the desert!
⁴² Because God remembered
      his holy promise
   to Abraham his servant,
⁴³ God brought his people
      out with rejoicing,
   his chosen ones with songs of joy.
⁴⁴ God gave them the lands
      of other nations;
   they inherited the wealth
      of many peoples—
   ⁴⁵ all so that they would keep
      his laws
   and observe his instructions.

Praise the LORD!

Psalm 106

¹ Praise the LORD!
   Give thanks to the LORD
      because he is good,
   because his faithful love
      endures forever.
² Who could possibly repeat
      all of the LORD's mighty acts
   or publicly recount all his praise?

³ The people who uphold justice,
      who always do what is right,
   are truly happy!
⁴ Remember me, LORD, with the favor
      you show your people.

Visit me with your saving help
   ⁵ so I can experience the good things
      your chosen ones experience,
   so I can rejoice
      in the joy of your nation,
   so I can praise along
      with your possession.

⁶ We have sinned—
      right along with our ancestors.
   We've done what is wrong.
   We've acted wickedly.
⁷ Our ancestors in Egypt
      didn't understand
      your wondrous works.
   They didn't remember
      how much faithful love you have.
   So they rebelled by the sea—
      at the Reed Sea.^q
⁸ But God saved them
      for the sake of his good name,
   to make known his mighty power.
⁹ God scolded the Reed Sea,
      and it dried right up;
   he led them through the deeps
      like they were a dry desert.
¹⁰ God saved them from hostile powers;
      he redeemed them
      from the power of the enemy.
¹¹ But the waters covered over
      their foes—
   not one of them survived!
¹² So our ancestors trusted
      God's words;
   they sang God's praise.

¹³ But how quickly they forgot
      what he had done!
   They wouldn't wait for his advice.
¹⁴ They were overcome with craving
      in the desert;
   they tested God in the wastelands.

^q Or *Red Sea*; also in 106:9, 22

¹⁵ God gave them what they asked for;
    he sent food^r
    to satisfy their appetites.

¹⁶ But then they were jealous of Moses
    in the camp,
    jealous too of Aaron,
    the LORD's holy one.
¹⁷ So the earth opened up,
    swallowing Dathan,
    and covering over Abiram's crowd.
¹⁸ Fire blazed throughout
    that whole group;
    flames burned up the wicked.

¹⁹ They made a calf at Horeb,
    bowing down to a metal idol.
²⁰ They traded their glorious God^s
    for an image of a bull that eats grass.
²¹ They forgot the God
    who saved them—
    the one who had done
    great things in Egypt,
²² wondrous works in the land of Ham,
    awesome deeds at the Reed Sea.
²³ So God determined
    that he would destroy them—
    except for the fact that Moses,
    his chosen one,
    stood in the way,
    right in front of him,
    and turned God's
    destructive anger away.

²⁴ But then they rejected the land
    that was so desirable.
    They didn't trust God's promise.
²⁵ They muttered in their tents
    and wouldn't listen
    to the LORD's voice.
²⁶ So God raised his hand against them,
    making them fall in the desert,

²⁷ scattering their offspring
    among the nations,
    casting them across many lands.

²⁸ They joined themselves to Baal-peor
    and ate sacrifices offered to the dead.
²⁹ They made God angry
    by what they did,
    so a plague broke out against them.
³⁰ Then Phinehas stood up and prayed,
    and the plague was contained.
³¹ That's why Phinehas
    is considered righteous,
    generation after generation, forever.

³² But they angered God
    at Meribah's waters,
    and things went badly for Moses
    because of them,
³³ because they made him bitter
    so that he spoke rashly
    with his lips.

³⁴ They didn't destroy the nations
    as the LORD had ordered
    them to do.
³⁵ Instead, they got mixed up
    with the nations,
    learning what they did
³⁶ and serving those false gods,
    which became a trap for them.
³⁷ They sacrificed their own
    sons and daughters to demons!
³⁸ They shed innocent blood,
    the blood of their own
    sons and daughters—
    the ones they sacrificed
    to Canaan's false gods—
    so the land was defiled
    by the bloodshed.
³⁹ They made themselves unclean
    by what they did;

^{r}LXX ^{s}Or *their Glory*

they prostituted themselves
by their actions.

40 So the LORD's anger burned
    against his people;
  he despised his own possession.
41 God handed them over
    to the nations;
  people who hated them
    ruled over them.
42 Their enemies oppressed them,
    and they were humbled
    under their power.
43 God delivered them
    numerous times,
  but they were determined
    to rebel,
  and so they were brought down
    by their own sin.
44 But God saw their distress
    when he heard their loud cries.
45 God remembered his covenant
    for their sake,
  and because of how much
    faithful love he has,
  God changed his mind.
46 God allowed them
    to receive compassion
    from all their captors.

47 LORD our God, save us!
    Gather us back together
  from among all the nations
  so we can give thanks
    to your holy name
  and rejoice in your praise!

48 Bless the LORD, the God of Israel,
    from forever ago
    to forever from now!
  And let all the people say, "Amen!"

Praise the LORD!

BOOK V
(Psalms 107–150)

Psalm 107

1 "Give thanks to the LORD
    because he is good,
    because his faithful love
    lasts forever!"
2 That's what those who are redeemed
    by the LORD say,
  the ones God redeemed
    from the power of their enemies,
3 the ones God gathered
    from various countries,
  from east and west, north and south.

4 Some of the redeemed
    had wandered into the desert,
    into the wasteland.
  They couldn't find their way
    to a city or town.
5 They were hungry and thirsty;
    their lives were slipping away.
6 So they cried out to the LORD
    in their distress,
  and God delivered them from
    their desperate circumstances.
7 God led them straight
    to human habitation.
8 Let them thank the LORD
    for his faithful love
  and his wondrous works
    for all people,
9 because God satisfied the one
    who was parched with thirst,
  and he filled up the hungry
    with good things!

10 Some of the redeemed
    had been sitting in darkness
    and deep gloom;
  they were prisoners
    suffering in chains

[11] because they had disobeyed
    God's instructions
    and rejected the Most High's plans.
[12] So God humbled them
    with hard work.
    They stumbled, and there was
    no one to help them.
[13] So they cried out to the LORD
    in their distress,
    and God saved them from
    their desperate circumstances.
[14] God brought them out
    from the darkness and deep gloom;
    he shattered their chains.
[15] Let them thank the LORD
    for his faithful love
    and his wondrous works
    for all people,
[16] because God has shattered
    bronze doors
    and split iron bars in two!

[17] Some of the redeemed were fools
    because of their sinful ways.
    They suffered because of
    their wickedness.
[18] They had absolutely no appetite
    for food;
    they had arrived at death's gates.
[19] So they cried out to the LORD
    in their distress,
    and God saved them from
    their desperate circumstances.
[20] God gave the order
    and healed them;
    he rescued them from their pit.
[21] Let them thank the LORD
    for his faithful love
    and his wondrous works
    for all people.
[22] Let them offer
    thanksgiving sacrifices
    and declare what God has done
    in songs of joy!

[23] Some of the redeemed had gone out
    on the ocean in ships,
    making their living
    on the high seas.
[24] They saw what the LORD had made;
    they saw his wondrous works
    in the depths of the sea.
[25] God spoke and stirred up a storm
    that brought the waves up high.
[26] The waves went as high as the sky;
    they crashed down to the depths.
    The sailors' courage melted
    at this terrible situation.
[27] They staggered and stumbled
    around like they were drunk.
    None of their skill was of any help.
[28] So they cried out to the LORD
    in their distress,
    and God brought them out safe from
    their desperate circumstances.
[29] God quieted the storm to a whisper;
    the sea's waves were hushed.
[30] So they rejoiced because the waves
    had calmed down;
    then God led them to the harbor
    they were hoping for.
[31] Let them thank the LORD
    for his faithful love
    and his wondrous works
    for all people.
[32] Let them exalt God
    in the congregation of the people
    and praise God
    in the assembly of the elders.

[33] God turns rivers into desert,
    watery springs into thirsty ground,
[34] fruitful land into unproductive dirt,
    when its inhabitants are wicked.
[35] But God can also turn the desert
    into watery pools,
    thirsty ground into watery springs,
[36] where he settles the hungry.
    They even build a city and live there!

³⁷ They plant fields and vineyards
   and obtain a fruitful harvest.
³⁸ God blesses them,
   and they become many.
   God won't even let
      their cattle diminish.
³⁹ But when they do diminish—
   when they're brought down
      by oppression, trouble,
      and grief—
⁴⁰ God pours contempt
      on their leaders,
   making them wander aimlessly
      in the wastelands.
⁴¹ But God raises the needy
      from their suffering;
   he makes their families
      as numerous as sheep!
⁴² Those who do right see it
      and celebrate,
   but every wicked person
      shuts their mouth.
⁴³ Whoever is wise will pay attention
      to these things,
   carefully considering
      the LORD's faithful love.

Psalm 108

A song. A psalm of David.
¹ My heart is unwavering, God.
   I will sing and make music—
   yes, with my whole being!
² Wake up, harp and lyre!
   I will wake the dawn itself!
³ I will give thanks to you, LORD,
      among all the peoples;
   I will make music to you
      among the nations,
⁴ because your faithful love
      is higher than heaven;
   your faithfulness reaches the clouds.

⁵ Exalt yourself, God,
      higher than heaven!
   Let your glory be over all the earth!
⁶ Save me by your power
      and answer me
   so that the people you love
      might be rescued.

⁷ God has spoken in his sanctuary:
   "I will celebrate
      as I divide up Shechem
   and portion out the Succoth Valley.
⁸ Gilead is mine, Manasseh is mine;
   Ephraim is my helmet,
      Judah is my scepter.
⁹ But Moab is my washbowl;
   I'll throw my shoe at Edom.
   I shout in triumph over Philistia!
¹⁰ I wish someone would bring me
      to a fortified city!
   I wish someone would lead me
      to Edom!"

¹¹ But you have rejected us, God,
      haven't you?
   You, God, no longer accompany
      our armies.
¹² Give us help against the enemy—
      human help is worthless.
¹³ With God we will triumph:
   God is the one who will trample
      our adversaries.

Psalm 109

To the leader. Of David. A psalm.
¹ God of my praise, don't keep quiet,
² because the mouths of wicked liars
      have opened up against me,
   talking about me
      with lying tongues.
³ Hateful words surround me;
   they attack me for no reason.

ᵗPs 108:1-5 parallels Ps 57:7-11; Ps 108:6-13 parallels Ps 60:5-12.

⁴ Instead of returning my love,
    they accuse me—
    but I am at prayer.
⁵ They repay me evil for good,
    hatred in return for my love.

⁶ "Appoint a wicked person to be
    against this person," they say,
    "an accuser to stand right
    next to him.
⁷ When the sentence is passed,
    let him be found guilty!
    let his prayer be found sinful!
⁸ Let his days be few;
    let someone else
    assume his position.
⁹ Let his children become orphans;
    let his wife turn into a widow.
¹⁰ Let his children wander aimlessly,
    begging,
    driven out of their ruined homes.
¹¹ Let a creditor seize
    everything he owns;
    let strangers plunder his wealth.
¹² Let no one extend faithful love to him;
    let no one have mercy
    on his orphans.
¹³ Let his descendants be eliminated;
    let their names be wiped out
    in just one generation!
¹⁴ Let his father's wrongdoing
    be remembered before the LORD;
    let his mother's sin
    never be wiped out.
¹⁵ Let them be before the LORD always,
    and let God eliminate
    the very memory of them
    from the land.
¹⁶ All because this person
    didn't remember to demonstrate
    faithful love,
    but chased after the poor
    and needy—
    even the brokenhearted—
    with deadly intent!

¹⁷ Since he loved to curse,
    let it come back on him!
    Since he didn't care much for blessing,
    let it be far away from him!
¹⁸ Since he wore curses like a coat,
    let them seep inside him like water,
    seep into his bones like oil!
¹⁹ Let them be like the clothes he wears,
    like a belt that is always
    around him."

²⁰ But let all that be the reward
    my accusers get from the LORD,
    the reward for those
    who speak evil against me!
²¹ But you, LORD, my Lord!—
    act on my behalf
    for the sake of your name;
    deliver me because
    your faithful love is so good;
²² because I am poor and needy,
    and my heart is broken.
²³ Like a lengthening shadow,
    I'm passing away;
    I'm shaken off, like some locust.
²⁴ My legs are weak from fasting;
    my body is skin and bones.
²⁵ I've become a joke to my accusers;
    when they see me,
    they just shake their heads.

²⁶ Help me, LORD my God!
    Save me according
    to your faithful love!
²⁷ And let them know
    that this is by your hand—
    that you have done it, LORD!
²⁸ Let them curse—but you, bless me!
    If they rise up,
    let them be disgraced,
    but let your servant celebrate!
²⁹ Let my accusers be dressed in shame;
    let them wear their disgrace
    like a coat.

³⁰ But I will give great thanks
to the LORD with my mouth;
among a great crowd
I will praise God!
³¹ Because God stands
right next to the needy,
to save them from any
who would condemn them.

Psalm 110
Of David. A psalm.

¹ What the LORD says to my master:
"Sit right beside me
until I make your enemies
a footstool for your feet!"

² May the LORD make
your mighty scepter
reach far from Zion!
Rule over your enemies!
³ Your people stand ready
on your day of battle.
"In holy grandeur,
from the dawn's womb, fight!ᵘ
Your youthful strength
is like the dew itself."
⁴ The LORD has sworn a solemn pledge
and won't change his mind:
"You are a priest forever
in line with Melchizedek."ᵛ
⁵ My master, by your strong hand,
God has crushed kings
on his day of wrath.ʷ

⁶ God brings the nations to justice,
piling the dead bodies,
crushing heads throughout
the earth.
⁷ God drinks from a stream
along the way,
then holds his head up high.ˣ

Psalm 111ʸ

א ¹ Praise the LORD!
I thank the LORD
with all my heart
ב in the company of those
who do right,
in the congregation.
ג ² The works of the LORD
are magnificent;
ד they are treasured
by all who desire them.
ה ³ God's deeds are majestic
and glorious.
ו God's righteousness
stands forever.
ז ⁴ God is famous
for his wondrous works.
ח The LORD is
full of mercy and compassion.
ט ⁵ God gives food
to those who honor him.
י God remembers
his covenant forever.
כ ⁶ God proclaimed his powerful deeds
to his people
ל and gave them what had belonged
to other nations.
מ ⁷ God's handiwork is honesty
and justice;
נ all God's rules are trustworthy—
ס ⁸ they are established
always and forever:
ע they are fulfilled
with truth and right doing.
פ ⁹ God sent redemption
for his people;
צ God commanded
that his covenant last forever.
ק Holy and awesome
is God's name!

ᵘCorrection; or *Go!*; MT *to you*   ᵛOr *a rightful king by my decree*   ʷOr *My Lord (God), because of your (the king's) strong hand, has crushed* or *The LORD is above your strong hand, crushing kings*   ˣHeb uncertain   ʸPs 111 is an alphabetic acrostic poem; see the note at Pss 9–10.

ר ¹⁰ Fear of the LORD
is where wisdom begins;

ש sure knowledge
is for all who keep God's laws.

ת God's praise lasts forever!

Psalm 112ᶻ

א ¹ Praise the LORD!
Those who honor the LORD,

ב who adore God's commandments,
are truly happy!

ג ² Their descendants will be strong
throughout the land.

ד The offspring of those
who do right will be blessed;

ה ³ wealth and riches
will be in their houses.

ו Their righteousness stands forever.

ז ⁴ They shine in the dark
for others who do right.

ח They are merciful, compassionate,
and righteous.

ט ⁵ Those who lend generously
are good people—
as are those who conduct
their affairs with justice.

כ ⁶ Yes, these sorts of people
will never be shaken;
the righteous
will be remembered forever!

מ ⁷ They won't be frightened
at bad news.

נ Their hearts are steady,
trusting in the LORD.

ס ⁸ Their hearts are firm;
they aren't afraid.

ע In the end, they will witness
their enemies' defeat.

פ ⁹ They give freely to those in need.
Their righteousness stands forever.

צ Their strength increases gloriously.

ק ¹⁰ The wicked see all this and fume;

ש they grind their teeth,
but disappear to nothing.

ת What the wicked want
to see happen comes to nothing!

Psalm 113

¹ Praise the LORD!
You who serve the LORD—praise!
Praise the LORD's name!

² Let the LORD's name be blessed
from now until forever from now!

³ From sunrise to sunset,
let the LORD's name be praised!

⁴ The LORD is high over all the nations;
God's glory is higher than the skies!

⁵ Who could possibly
compare to the LORD our God?
God rules from on high;

⁶ he has to come down
to even see heaven and earth!

⁷ God lifts up the poor from the dirt
and raises up the needy
from the garbage pile

⁸ to seat them with leaders—
with the leaders of his own people!

⁹ God nests the once barren woman
at home—
now a joyful mother with children!

Praise the LORD!

Psalm 114

¹ When Israel came out of Egypt—
when the house of Jacob came out
from a people who spoke
a different language—

² Judah was God's sanctuary;
Israel was God's territory.

³ The sea saw it happen and ran away;
the Jordan River retreated!

ᶻPs 112 is an alphabetic acrostic poem; see the note at Pss 9–10.

⁴ The mountains leaped away
   like rams;
   the hills leaped away like lambs!
⁵ Sea, why did you run away?
   Jordan, why did you retreat?
⁶ Mountains, why did you leap away
   like rams?
   Hills, why did you leap away
   like lambs?

⁷ Earth: Tremble before the Lord!
   Tremble before the God of Jacob,
⁸ the one who turned
      that rock into a pool of water,
      that flint stone into a spring
         of water!

Psalm 115

¹ Not to us, Lord, not to us—
   no, but to your own name give glory
   because of your loyal love
      and faithfulness!

² Why do the nations say,
   "Where's their God now?"
³ Our God is in heaven—
   he can do whatever he wants!
⁴ Their idols are just silver and gold—
   things made by human hands.
⁵ They have mouths,
   but they can't speak.
   They have eyes,
   but they can't see.
⁶ They have ears,
   but they can't hear.
   They have noses,
   but they can't smell.
⁷ They have hands,
   but they can't feel.
   They have feet,
   but they can't walk.
   They can't even make a noise
      in their throats!

⁸ Let the people who made these idols
   and all who trust in them
   become just like them!

⁹ But you, Israel, trust in the Lord!
   God is their help and shield.
¹⁰ Trust in the Lord, house of Aaron!
   God is their help and shield.
¹¹ You who honor the Lord,
   trust in the Lord!
   God is their help and shield.
¹² The Lord remembers us
   and will bless us:
   God will bless the house of Israel;
   God will bless the house of Aaron;
¹³ God will bless those
   who honor the Lord—
   from the smallest to the greatest.

¹⁴ May the Lord add to your numbers—
   both you and your children.
¹⁵ May you be blessed by the Lord,
   the maker of heaven and earth!
¹⁶ The highest heaven
   belongs to the Lord,
   but he gave the earth to all people.
¹⁷ The dead don't praise the Lord,
   nor do those
      who go down to silence.
¹⁸ But us? We will bless the Lord
   from now until forever from now!

Praise the Lord!

Psalm 116

¹ I love the Lord because he hears
   my requests for mercy.
² I'll call out to him as long as I live,
   because he listens closely to me.
³ Death's ropes bound me;
   the distress of the grave[a]
      found me—

ᵃHeb Sheol

I came face-to-face
with trouble and grief.
⁴ So I called on the LORD's name:
"LORD, please save me!"ᵇ

⁵ The LORD is merciful
and righteous;
our God is compassionate.
⁶ The LORD protects simple folk;
he saves me
whenever I am brought down.

⁷ I tell myself,
You can be at peace again,
because the LORD
has been good to you.
⁸ You, God, have delivered me
from death,
my eyes from tears,
and my foot from stumbling,
⁹ so I'll walk before the LORD
in the land of the living.
¹⁰ I have remained faithful,
even when I said,
"I am suffering so badly!"
¹¹ even when I said, out of fear,
"Everyone is a liar!"

¹² What can I give back to the LORD
for all the good things
he has done for me?
¹³ I'll lift up the cup of salvation.
I'll call on the LORD's name.
¹⁴ I'll keep the promises
I made to the LORD
in the presence of all God's people.
¹⁵ The death of the LORD's faithful
is a costly loss in his eyes.

¹⁶ Oh yes, LORD, I am definitely
your servant!
I am your servant and the son
of your female servant—

you've freed me from my chains.
¹⁷ So I'll offer a sacrifice
of thanksgiving to you,
and I'll call on the LORD's name.
¹⁸ I'll keep the promises I made
to the LORD
in the presence of all God's people,
¹⁹ in the courtyards
of the LORD's house,
which is in the
center of Jerusalem.

Praise the LORD!

Psalm 117

¹ Praise the LORD, all you nations!
Worship him, all you peoples!
² Because God's faithful love toward us
is strong,
the LORD's faithfulness
lasts forever!
Praise the LORD!

Psalm 118

¹ Give thanks to the LORD
because he is good,
because his faithful love
lasts forever.
² Let Israel say it:
"God's faithful love lasts forever!"
³ Let the house of Aaron say it:
"God's faithful love lasts forever!"
⁴ Let those who honor the LORD say it:
"God's faithful love lasts forever!"

⁵ In tight circumstances,
I cried out to the LORD.
The LORD answered me
with wide-open spaces.
⁶ The LORD is for me²—
I won't be afraid.
What can anyone do to me?

ᵇ Or *my soul*; also in 116:7-8   ᶜ LXX *with me* or *mine*; also in 118:7

⁷The LORD is for me—as my helper.
    I look in victory
        on those who hate me.
⁸It's far better to take refuge
        in the LORD
    than to trust any human.
⁹It's far better to take refuge
        in the LORD
    than to trust any human leader.

¹⁰All the nations surrounded me,
    but I cut them down[d]
        in the LORD's name.
¹¹Yes, they surrounded me
        on every single side,
    but I cut them down
        in the LORD's name.
¹²They surrounded me like bees,
    but they were extinguished
        like burning thorns.
    I cut them down
        in the LORD's name!
¹³I was pushed so hard[e] I nearly died,
    but the LORD helped me.
¹⁴The LORD was my strength
        and protection;
    he was my saving help!
¹⁵The sounds of joyful songs
        and deliverance
    are heard in the tents
        of the righteous:
    "The LORD's strong hand
        is victorious!
¹⁶The LORD's strong hand
        is ready to strike!
    The LORD's strong hand
        is victorious!"
¹⁷I won't die—no, I will live
    and declare what the LORD
        has done.

¹⁸Yes, the LORD definitely
        disciplined me,
    but he didn't hand me over
        to death.

¹⁹Open the gates of righteousness
        for me
    so I can come in
        and give thanks to the LORD!
²⁰This is the LORD's gate;
    those who are righteous
        enter through it.

²¹I thank you
    because you answered me,
    because you were my saving help.
²²The stone rejected by the builders
    is now the main foundation stone!
²³This has happened because
        of the LORD;
    it is astounding in our sight!
²⁴This is the day the LORD acted;
    we will rejoice and celebrate in it!

²⁵LORD, please save us!
    LORD, please let us succeed!

²⁶The one who enters
        in the LORD's name is blessed;
    we bless all of you
        from the LORD's house.
²⁷The LORD is God!
    He has shined a light on us!
    So lead the festival offering
        with ropes
    all the way to the horns
        of the altar.[f]
²⁸You are my God—
    I will give thanks to you!
    You are my God—
    I will lift you up high!

[d]Heb uncertain; LXX, Vulg *drove* or *warded off*; also in 118:11-12   [e]LXX, Vulg, Syr; MT *you pushed me*   [f]Heb uncertain

²⁹Give thanks to the LORD
    because he is good,
    because his faithful love
       lasts forever.

Psalm 119ᵍ

א ALEF

¹Those whose way is blameless—
    who walk in the LORD's
       Instruction—are truly happy!
²Those who guard God's laws
    are truly happy!
    They seek God
       with all their hearts.
³They don't even do anything wrong!
    They walk in God's ways.
⁴God, you have ordered
    that your decrees
    should be kept most carefully.
⁵How I wish my ways were strong
    when it comes
       to keeping your statutes!
⁶Then I wouldn't be ashamed
    when I examine
       all your commandments.
⁷I will give thanks to you
    with a heart that does right
    as I learn your righteous rules.
⁸I will keep your statutes.
    Please don't leave me all alone!

ב BET

⁹How can young people
    keep their paths pure?
    By guarding them
       according to what you've said.ʰ
¹⁰I have sought you with all my heart.
    Don't let me stray
       from any of your commandments!
¹¹I keep your word close, in my heart,
    so that I won't sin against you.

¹²You, LORD, are to be blessed!
    Teach me your statutes.
¹³I will declare out loud
    all the rules you have spoken.
¹⁴I rejoice in the content of your laws
    as if I were rejoicing
       over great wealth.
¹⁵I will think about your precepts
    and examine all your paths.
¹⁶I will delight in your statutes;
    I will not forget what you have said.

ג GIMEL

¹⁷Be good to your servant
    so I can go on living
    and keeping your word.
¹⁸Open my eyes so I can examine
    the wonders of your Instruction!
¹⁹I'm an immigrant in the land.
    Don't hide your commandments
       from me!
²⁰I'm worn out by longing
    every minute for your rules!
²¹You rebuke the arrogant,
    accursed people
    who stray from
       your commandments.
²²Take all their insults and contempt
    away from me
    because I've kept your laws!
²³Even if rulers gather and scheme
    against me,
    your servant will contemplate
       your statutes!
²⁴Yes, your laws are my joy—
    they are my most trusted advisors!

ד DALET

²⁵My life is stuck in the dirt.
    Now make me live again
    according to your promise!

ᵍPs 119 is an alphabetic acrostic poem (cf Pss 9–10) in Heb, with each line of Heb within the marked sections beginning with the same letter of the alphabet. ʰLXX

²⁶ I confessed my ways
    and you answered me.
    Now teach me your statutes!
²⁷ Help me understand
    what your precepts are about
    so I can contemplate
    your wondrous works!
²⁸ My spirit sags because of grief.
    Now raise me up
    according to your promise!
²⁹ Remove all false ways from me;
    show mercy to me
    by means of your Instruction.
³⁰ I've chosen the way of faithfulness;
    I'm set on your rules.
³¹ I'm holding tight to your laws, LORD.
    Please don't let me be put to shame.
³² I run the same path
    as your commandments
    because you give my heart insight.

ה HE

³³ LORD, teach me what your statutes
    are about,
    and I will guard every part of them.
³⁴ Help me understand
    so I can guard your Instruction
    and keep it with all my heart.
³⁵ Lead me on the trail
    of your commandments
    because that is what I want.
³⁶ Turn my heart to your laws,
    not to greedy gain.
³⁷ Turn my eyes away from looking
    at worthless things.
    Make me live by your way.
³⁸ Confirm your promise
    to your servant—
    the promise that is
    for all those who honor you.
³⁹ Remove the insults that I dread
    because your rules are good.
⁴⁰ Look how I desire your precepts!
    Make me live by your righteousness.

ו WAW

⁴¹ LORD, let your faithful love
    come to me—
    let your salvation come to me
    according to your promise—
⁴² so I can have a response
    for those who mock me
    because I have trusted
    in your word!
⁴³ Please don't take your true word
    out of my mouth,
    because I have waited
    for your rules.
⁴⁴ I will always keep your Instruction,
    always and forever!
⁴⁵ I will walk around
    in wide-open spaces,
    because I have pursued
    your precepts.
⁴⁶ I will talk about your laws
    before rulers with
    no shame whatsoever.
⁴⁷ I will rejoice in your commandments
    because I love them.
⁴⁸ I will lift up my hands
    to your commandments
    because I love them,
    and I will contemplate
    all your statutes.

ז ZAYIN

⁴⁹ Remember your promise
    to your servant,
    for which you made me wait.
⁵⁰ My comfort during my suffering
    is this:
    your word gives me new life.
⁵¹ The arrogant make fun of me
    to no end,
    but I haven't deviated
    from your Instruction.
⁵² When I remember
    your ancient rules,
    I'm comforted, LORD.

53 But I'm seized with anger
    because of the wicked—
    because of those who abandon
        your Instruction.
54 Your statutes have been
        my songs of praise
    wherever I lived as an immigrant.
55 LORD, I remember your name
        at nighttime,
    and I keep your Instruction.
56 This has been my practice
    because I guard your precepts.

ח KHET

57 The LORD is my possession.
    I promise to do what you have said.
58 I've sought your favor
        with all my heart;
    have mercy on me
        according to your word.
59 I've considered my ways and turned
    my feet back to your laws.
60 I hurry to keep
        your commandments—
    I never put it off!
61 Though the wicked
        have surrounded me
        with their ropes,
    I haven't forgotten
        your Instruction.
62 I get up in the middle of the night
    to give thanks to you
    because of your righteous rules.
63 I'm a friend to everyone
        who honors you
    and to all who keep your precepts.
64 LORD, the world is full
        of your faithful love!
    Teach me your statutes!

ט TET

65 You have treated your servant well,
    LORD, according to your promise.

66 Teach me knowledge and
        good judgment
    because I've put my trust
        in your commandments.
67 Before I suffered,
        I took the wrong way,
    but now I do what you say.
68 You are good and you do good.
    Teach me your statutes.
69 The arrogant cover me
        with their lies,
    but I guard your precepts
        with all my heart.
70 Their hearts are unfeeling,
        like blubber,
    but I rejoice in your Instruction.
71 My suffering was good for me,
    because through it
        I learned your statutes.
72 The Instruction you've given to me
        is better
    than thousands of pieces
        of gold and silver!

י YOD

73 Your hands have made me
    and set me in place.
    Help me understand so I can learn
        your commandments.
74 Then those who honor you
    will see me and be glad
    because I have waited
        for your promise.
75 LORD, I know that your rules
        are right
    and that you rightly
        made me suffer.
76 Please let your faithful love
        comfort me,
    according to what you've said
        to your servant.
77 Let your compassion come to me
    so I can live again,
    because your Instruction is my joy!

⁷⁸ But let the arrogant be ashamed
    because they oppressed me
        with lies—
    meanwhile, I will be contemplating
        your precepts!
⁷⁹ Let the people who honor you
        come back to me;
    let those who know your precepts
        return to me.
⁸⁰ Let my heart be blameless
        in your statutes
    so that I am not put to shame.

כ KAF

⁸¹ My whole being yearns
        for your saving help!
    I wait for your promise.
⁸² My eyes are worn out
        looking for your word.
    "When will you comfort me?" I ask,
⁸³ because I've become like a bottle
        dried up by smoke,
    though I haven't forgotten
        your statutes.
⁸⁴ How much more time
        does your servant have?
    When will you bring my oppressors
        to justice?
⁸⁵ The arrogant have dug pits for me—
    those people who act
        against your Instruction.
⁸⁶ All your commandments are true,
    but people harass me
        for no reason.
    Help me!
⁸⁷ They've almost wiped me
        off the face of the earth!
    Meanwhile, I haven't abandoned
        your precepts!
⁸⁸ Make me live again
        according to your faithful love
    so I can keep the law you've given!

ל LAMED

⁸⁹ Your word, LORD,
    stands firm in heaven forever!
⁹⁰ Your faithfulness extends
        from one generation to the next!
    You set the earth firmly in place,
        and it is still there.
⁹¹ Your rules endure to this day
        because everything serves you.
⁹² If your Instruction hadn't been
        my delight,
    I would have died
        because of my suffering.
⁹³ I will never forget your precepts
    because through them
        you gave me life again.
⁹⁴ I'm yours—save me
    because I've pursued your precepts!
⁹⁵ The wicked wait for me,
        wanting to kill me,
    but I'm studying your laws.
⁹⁶ I've seen that everything,
    no matter how perfect, has a limit,[i]
    but your commandment
        is boundless.

מ MEM

⁹⁷ I love your Instruction!
    I think about it constantly.
⁹⁸ Your commandment makes
        me wiser than my enemies
    because it is always with me.
⁹⁹ I have greater insight
        than all my teachers
    because I contemplate your laws.
¹⁰⁰ I have more understanding
        than the elders
    because I guard your precepts.
¹⁰¹ I haven't set my feet
        on any evil path
    so I can make sure
        to keep your word.

[i] Heb uncertain

102 I haven't deviated
from any of your rules
because you are the one
who has taught me.

103 Your word is so pleasing
to my taste buds—
it's sweeter than honey
in my mouth!

104 I'm studying your precepts—
that's why I hate every false path.

ℷ NUN

105 Your word is a lamp before my feet
and a light for my journey.

106 I have sworn, and I fully mean it:
I will keep your righteous rules.

107 I have been suffering so much—
LORD, make me live again
according to your promise.

108 Please, LORD, accept my
spontaneous gifts of praise.
Teach me your rules!

109 Though my life
is constantly in danger,
I won't forget your Instruction.

110 Though the wicked have set a trap
for me,
I won't stray from your precepts.

111 Your laws are my possession forever
because they are my heart's joy.

112 I have decided to keep
your statutes forever,
every last one.

○ SAMEK

113 I hate fickle people,
but I love your Instruction.

114 You are my shelter
and my shield—
I wait for your promise.

115 Get away from me, you evildoers;
I want to guard
my God's commandments!

116 Sustain me according to your word
so I can live!

Don't let me be put to shame
because of hope.

117 Support me so I can be saved
and so I can focus constantly
on your statutes.

118 You discard everyone who strays
from your statutes
because they are dishonest
and false.

119 You dispose of all the wicked people
on earth like waste—
that's why I love your laws.

120 My body shudders
because I fear you;
I'm in awe of your rules.

ν AYIN

121 I've done what is just and right.
Don't just hand me over
to my oppressors.

122 Guarantee good things
for your servant.
Please don't let the arrogant
oppress me.

123 My eyes are worn out
looking for your saving help—
looking for your word
that will set things right.

124 Act toward your servant
according to your faithful love.
Teach me your statutes!

125 I'm your servant!
Help me understand
so I can know your laws.

126 It is time for the LORD
to do something!
Your Instruction has been broken.

127 But I love your commandments
more than gold,
even more than pure gold.

128 That's why I walk straight
by every single one
of your precepts.
That's why I hate every false path.

 פ **PE**

¹²⁹Your laws are wonderful!
That's why I guard them.
¹³⁰Access to your words ʲgives light,
giving simple folk understanding.
¹³¹I open my mouth up wide, panting,
because I long for
your commandments.
¹³²Come back to me
and have mercy on me;
that's only right
for those who love your name.
¹³³Keep my steps steady by your word;
don't let any sin rule me.
¹³⁴Redeem me from the people
who oppress me
so I can keep your precepts.
¹³⁵Shine your face on your servant,
and teach me your statutes.
¹³⁶Rivers of tears stream from my eyes
because your Instruction
isn't being kept.

צ **TSADE**

¹³⁷LORD, you are righteous,
and your rules are right.
¹³⁸The laws you commanded
are righteous,
completely trustworthy.
¹³⁹Anger consumes me
because my enemies have forgotten
what you've said.
¹⁴⁰Your word has been tried and tested;
your servant loves your word!
¹⁴¹I'm insignificant and unpopular,
but I don't forget your precepts.
¹⁴²Your righteousness lasts forever!
Your Instruction is true!
¹⁴³Stress and strain have caught up
with me,
but your commandments
are my joy!

¹⁴⁴Your laws are righteous forever.
Help me understand so I can live!

ק **QOF**

¹⁴⁵I cry out with all my heart:
"LORD, answer me
so I can guard your statutes!"
¹⁴⁶I cry out to you, "Save me
so I can keep your laws!"
¹⁴⁷I meet the predawn light
and cry for help.
I wait for your promise.
¹⁴⁸My eyes encounter each hour
of the night
as I think about your word.
¹⁴⁹Listen to my voice,
according to your faithful love.
LORD, make me live again,
according to your justice.
¹⁵⁰The people who love to plot
wicked schemes are nearby,
but they are so far
from your Instruction!
¹⁵¹But you, LORD, are nearby too,
and all your commandments
are true.
¹⁵²Long ago I learned from your laws
that you had established
them forever.

ר **RESH**

¹⁵³Look at my suffering
and deliver me
because I haven't forgotten
your Instruction.
¹⁵⁴Argue my case and redeem me.
Make me live again by your word.
¹⁵⁵Salvation is far from the wicked
because they haven't pursued
your statutes.
¹⁵⁶You have so much compassion,
LORD—

ʲVulg, Sym

make me live again,
  according to your rules.
⁵⁷My oppressors and enemies
  are many,
  but I haven't turned away
    from your laws.
⁵⁸I look on the faithless,
  and I am disgusted
  because they haven't kept
    your word.
⁵⁹Look at how much
  I love your precepts.
  Make me live again, LORD,
    according to your faithful love!
⁶⁰The first thing to know
  about your word is that it is true
  and that all your righteous rules
    last forever.

ש SIN AND ש SHIN

¹⁶¹Rulers oppress me without cause,
  but my heart honors
    what you've said.
¹⁶²I'm overjoyed at your word,
  like someone who
    finds great treasure.
¹⁶³I hate, I absolutely despise,
  what is false,
  but I'm in love
    with your Instruction.
¹⁶⁴I praise you seven times a day
  for your righteous rules.
¹⁶⁵The people who love
  your Instruction enjoy peace—
  and lots of it.
  There's no stumbling for them!
¹⁶⁶LORD, I wait for your saving help.
  I do what you've commanded.
¹⁶⁷I keep your laws;
  I love them so much!
¹⁶⁸I keep your precepts and your laws

because all my ways are seen
  by you.

ת TAV

¹⁶⁹Let my cry reach you, LORD;
  help me understand
    according to what you've said.
¹⁷⁰Let my request for grace
  come before you;
  deliver me according
    to your promise!
¹⁷¹Let my lips overflow with praise
  because you've taught me
    your statutes.
¹⁷²Let my tongue declare your word,
  because all your commandments
    are righteous.
¹⁷³Let your power help me
  because I have chosen
    your precepts.
¹⁷⁴LORD, I long for your saving help!
  Your Instruction is my joy!
¹⁷⁵Let me live again so I can praise you!
  Let your rules help me!
¹⁷⁶I've wandered off like a sheep, lost.
  Find your servant
  because I haven't forgotten
    your commandments!

Psalm 120
*A pilgrimage song.*ᵏ
¹I cried out to the LORD
  when I was in trouble
    (and he answered me):
²"LORD, deliver me**ˡ** from lying lips
  and a dishonest tongue!"
³What more will be given to you,
  what more will be done to you,
  you dishonest tongue?
⁴Just this:ᵐ
  a warrior's sharpened arrows,

ᵏOr *song of ascents* or *song of going up* (that is, to Jerusalem); cf Ps 122:4. The heading is found in every psalm from Ps 120 to Ps 134. ˡOr *my soul*; also in 120:6 ᵐHeb lacks *this*.

coupled with burning coals
from a wood[n] fire!

5 Oh, I'm doomed
   because I have been an immigrant
      in Meshech,
   because I've made my home
      among Kedar's tents.
6 I've lived far too long
   with people who hate peace.
7 I'm for peace,
   but when I speak, they are for war.

Psalm 121
A pilgrimage song.

1 I raise my eyes toward the mountains.
   Where will my help come from?
2 My help comes from the LORD,
   the maker of heaven and earth.

3 God won't let your foot slip.
   Your protector won't fall asleep
      on the job.
4 No! Israel's protector
   never sleeps or rests!

5 The LORD is your protector;
   the LORD is your shade
      right beside you.
6 The sun won't strike you
   during the day;
   neither will the moon at night.

7 The LORD will protect you
   from all evil;
   God will protect your very life.[o]
8 The LORD will protect you
   on your journeys—
   whether going or coming—
   from now until forever from now.

Psalm 122
A pilgrimage song. Of David.

1 I rejoiced with those who said to me,
   "Let's go to the LORD's house!"

2 Now our feet are standing
   in your gates, Jerusalem!

3 Jerusalem is built like a city
   joined together in unity.
4 That is where the tribes go up—
   the LORD's tribes!
   It is the law for Israel
      to give thanks there
         to the LORD's name,
5 because the thrones of justice
   are there—
   the thrones of the house of David!

6 Pray that Jerusalem has peace:
   "Let those who love you have rest.
7 Let there be peace on your walls;
   let there be rest
      on your fortifications."
8 For the sake of my family and friends,
   I say, "Peace be with you, Jerusalem."
9 For the sake of
   the LORD our God's house
   I will pray for your good.

Psalm 123
A pilgrimage song.

1 I raise my eyes to you—
   you who rule heaven.
2 Just as the eyes of servants attend
   to their masters' hand,
   just as the eyes of a female servant
      attend to her mistress' hand—
   that's how our eyes
      attend to the LORD our God
   until he has mercy on us.

3 Have mercy on us, LORD!
   Have mercy
   because we've had
      more than enough shame.
4 We've had more than enough
   mockery from the self-confident,

more than enough shame
  from the proud.

Psalm 124
A pilgrimage song. Of David.
[1] If the LORD hadn't been for us—
  let Israel now repeat!—
[2] if the LORD hadn't been for us
  when those people attacked us,
[3] then they would have swallowed
  us up whole
  with their rage burning against us!
[4] Then the waters
  would have drowned us;
  the torrent
  would have come over our necks;[P]
[5] then the raging waters
  would have come over our necks!

[6] Bless the LORD
  because he didn't hand us over
  like food for our enemies' teeth!
[7] We escaped like a bird
  from the hunters' trap;
  the trap was broken so we escaped!
[8] Our help is in the name of the LORD,
  the maker of heaven and earth.

Psalm 125
A pilgrimage song.
[1] The people who trust in the LORD
  are like Mount Zion:
  never shaken, lasting forever.
[2] Mountains surround Jerusalem.
  That's how the LORD
  surrounds his people
  from now until forever from now!
[3] The wicked rod won't remain
  in the land given to the righteous
  so that they don't use their hands
  to do anything wrong.[P]

[P]Or *soul*; also in 124:5, 7   [q]Heb uncertain

[4] LORD, do good to people who are good,
  to people whose hearts are right.
[5] But as for those people who turn
  to their own twisted ways—
  may the LORD march them off
  with other evildoers!

Peace be on Israel!

Psalm 126
A pilgrimage song.
[1] When the LORD changed
  Zion's circumstances for the better,
  it was like we had been dreaming.
[2] Our mouths were suddenly filled
  with laughter;
  our tongues were filled
  with joyful shouts.
It was even said, at that time,
  among the nations,
  "The LORD has done great things
  for them!"
[3] Yes, the LORD has done great things
  for us,
  and we are overjoyed.

[4] LORD, change our circumstances
  for the better,
  like dry streams
  in the desert waste!
[5] Let those who plant with tears
  reap the harvest with joyful shouts.
[6] Let those who go out,
  crying and carrying their seed,
  come home with joyful shouts,
  carrying bales of grain!

Psalm 127
A pilgrimage song. Of Solomon.
[1] Unless it is the LORD
  who builds the house,
  the builders' work is pointless.

Unless it is the LORD
　who protects the city,
　the guard on duty is pointless.
[2] It is pointless that you get up early
　and stay up late,
　eating the bread of hard labor
　because God gives sleep
　　to those he loves.

[3] No doubt about it:
　children are a gift from the LORD;
　the fruit of the womb
　　is a divine reward.
[4] The children born
　when one is young
　are like arrows in the hand
　　of a warrior.
[5] The person who fills a quiver
　full with them is truly happy!
　They won't be ashamed
　when arguing with their enemies
　　in the gate.

Psalm 128
A pilgrimage song.
[1] Everyone who honors the LORD,
　who walks in God's ways,
　　is truly happy!

[2] You will definitely enjoy
　what you've worked hard for—
　you'll be happy;
　and things will go well for you.
[3] In your house, your wife will be
　like a vine full of fruit.
　All around your table,
　your children will be like
　　olive trees, freshly planted.
[4] That's how it goes for anyone
　who honors the LORD:
　they will be blessed!

[5] May the LORD bless you from Zion.
　May you experience

Jerusalem's goodness
　your whole life long.
[6] And may you see
　your grandchildren.

Peace be on Israel!

Psalm 129
A pilgrimage song.
[1] From youth, people have
　constantly attacked me—
　let Israel now repeat!—
[2] from youth people have
　constantly attacked me—
　but they haven't beaten me!
[3] They plowed my back like farmers;
　they made their furrows deep.
[4] But the LORD is righteous—
　God cut me free
　from the ropes of the wicked!

[5] Let everyone who hates Zion
　be ashamed, thoroughly frustrated.
[6] Let them be like grass on a roof
　that dies before it can be pulled up,
[7] which won't fill the reaper's hand
　or fill the harvester's arms.
[8] Let no one who passes by
　say to them:
　"May the LORD's blessing be on you!
　We bless you in the LORD's name!"

Psalm 130
A pilgrimage song.
[1] I cry out to you from the depths,
　LORD—
[2] my Lord, listen to my voice!
　Let your ears pay close attention
　to my request for mercy!
[3] If you kept track of sins, LORD—
　my Lord, who would
　　stand a chance?
[4] But forgiveness is with you—
　that's why you are honored.

⁵ I hope, LORD.
My whole being^r hopes,
    and I wait for God's promise.
⁶ My whole being waits for my Lord—
    more than the night watch
        waits for morning;
    yes, more than the night watch
        waits for morning!

⁷ Israel, wait for the LORD!
    Because faithful love
        is with the LORD;
    because great redemption
        is with our God!
⁸ He is the one who will redeem Israel
    from all its sin.

Psalm 131
A pilgrimage song. Of David.
¹ LORD, my heart isn't proud;
    my eyes aren't conceited.
    I don't get involved with things
        too great or wonderful for me.
² No. But I have calmed
    and quieted myself^s
    like a weaned child on its mother;
    I'm like the weaned child that is with me.

³ Israel, wait for the LORD—
    from now until forever from now!

Psalm 132
A pilgrimage song.
¹ LORD, remember David—
    all the ways he suffered
² and how he swore to the LORD,
    how he promised
        the strong one of Jacob:
³ "I won't enter my house,
    won't get into my bed.
⁴ I won't let my eyes close,

won't let my eyelids sleep,
⁵ until I find a place for the LORD,
    a dwelling place
        for the strong one of Jacob."

⁶ Yes, we heard about it in Ephrathah;
    we found it^t in the fields of Jaar.
⁷ Let's enter God's dwelling place;
    let's worship at the place
        God rests his feet!
⁸ Get up, LORD, go to your residence—
    you and your powerful
        covenant chest!
⁹ Let your priests be dressed
    in righteousness;
    let your faithful shout out
        with joy!
¹⁰ And for the sake
    of your servant David,
    do not reject your anointed one.

¹¹ The LORD swore to David
    a true promise that God
        won't take back:
    "I will put one of your own
        children on your throne.
¹² And if your children keep
    my covenant
        and the laws
        that I will teach them,
    then their children too
        will rule on your throne forever."
¹³ Because the LORD chose Zion;
    he wanted it for his home.
¹⁴ "This is my residence forever.
    I will live here
        because I wanted it for myself.^u
¹⁵ I will most certainly
    bless its food supply;
    I will fill its needy full of food!
¹⁶ I will dress its priests in salvation,

^rOr *soul*; also in 130:6 ^sOr *my soul* ^t*It may refer to the covenant chest (132:8b).* ^uHeb lacks *for myself.*

Psalm 132:17   **444**

and its faithful
will shout out loud with joy!
[17] It is there that I will make
David's strength thrive.[v]
I will prepare a lamp
for my anointed one there.
[18] I will dress his enemies in shame,
but the crown he wears
will shine."

Psalm 133

A pilgrimage song. Of David.
[1] Look at how good and pleasing it is
when families[w] live together
as one!
[2] It is like expensive oil
poured over the head,
running down onto the beard—
Aaron's beard!—
which extended over the collar
of his robes.
[3] It is like the dew on Mount Hermon
streaming down
onto the mountains of Zion,
because it is there that the LORD
has commanded the blessing:
everlasting life.

Psalm 134

A pilgrimage song.
[1] All you who serve the LORD:
bless the LORD right now!
All you who minister
in the LORD's house at night:
bless God!
[2] Lift up your hands
to the sanctuary
and bless the LORD!
[3] May the LORD,
the maker of heaven and earth,
bless you from Zion.

Psalm 135

[1] Praise the LORD!
Praise the LORD's name!
All you who serve the LORD,
praise God!
[2] All you who stand
in the LORD's house—
who stand in the courtyards
of our God's temple—
[3] praise the LORD,
because the LORD is good!
Sing praises to God's name
because it is beautiful!
[4] Because the LORD chose Jacob
as his own,
God chose Israel
as his treasured possession.

[5] Yes, I know for certain
that the LORD is great—
I know our Lord is greater
than all other gods.
[6] The LORD can do whatever he wants
in heaven or on earth,
in the seas and
in every ocean depth.
[7] God forms clouds at the far corners
of the earth.
God makes lightning for the rain.
God releases the wind
from its storeroom.
[8] God struck down
the Egyptians' oldest offspring—
both human and animal!
[9] God sent signs and wonders
into the very center of Egypt—
against Pharaoh
and all his servants.
[10] God struck down many nations
and killed mighty kings:
[11] Sihon the Amorite king,

---

[v]Or *make a horn sprout* [w]Or *brothers (and sisters)*; the term often encompasses extended
family relationships.

Og the king of Bashan,
and all the Canaanite kings.
¹² Then God handed their land
over as an inheritance—
as an inheritance to Israel,
his own people.

¹³ LORD, your name is forever!
LORD, your fame extends
from one generation to the next!
¹⁴ The LORD gives justice to his people
and has compassion
on those who serve him.

¹⁵ The nations' idols
are just silver and gold—
things made by human hands.
¹⁶ They have mouths,
but they can't speak.
They have eyes, but they can't see.
¹⁷ They have ears, but they can't listen.
No, there's no breath in their lungs!
¹⁸ Let the people who made these idols
and all who trust in them
become just like them!

¹⁹ House of Israel, bless the LORD!
House of Aaron, bless the LORD!
²⁰ House of Levi, bless the LORD!
You who honor the LORD,
bless the LORD!
²¹ Bless the LORD from Zion—
bless the one who lives in Jerusalem!

Praise the LORD!

Psalm 136

¹ Give thanks to the LORD
because he is good.
God's faithful love lasts forever!

² Give thanks to the God of all gods—
God's faithful love lasts forever.

³ Give thanks to the Lord
of all lords—
God's faithful love lasts forever.
⁴ Give thanks to the only one
who makes great wonders—
God's faithful love lasts forever.
⁵ Give thanks to the one
who made the skies with skill—
God's faithful love lasts forever.
⁶ Give thanks to the one
who shaped the earth
on the water—
God's faithful love lasts forever.
⁷ Give thanks to the one
who made the great lights—
God's faithful love lasts forever.
⁸ The sun to rule the day—
God's faithful love lasts forever.
⁹ The moon and the stars
to rule the night—
God's faithful love lasts forever!

¹⁰ Give thanks to the one
who struck down
the Egyptians' oldest offspring—
God's faithful love lasts forever.
¹¹ Give thanks to the one
who brought Israel out of there—
God's faithful love lasts forever.
¹² With a strong hand
and outstretched arm—
God's faithful love lasts forever!

¹³ Give thanks to the one
who split the Reed Seaˣ in two—
God's faithful love lasts forever.
¹⁴ Give thanks to the one
who brought Israel through—
God's faithful love lasts forever.
¹⁵ And tossed Pharaoh and his army
into the Reed Sea—
God's faithful love lasts forever!

ˣOr *Red Sea;* also in 136:15

16 Give thanks to the one
    who led his people
    through the desert—
        God's faithful love lasts forever.

17 Give thanks to the one
    who struck down great kings—
        God's faithful love lasts forever.

18 And killed powerful kings—
        God's faithful love lasts forever.

19 Sihon, the Amorite king—
        God's faithful love lasts forever.

20 Og, king of Bashan—
        God's faithful love lasts forever.

21 Handing their land over
    as an inheritance—
        God's faithful love lasts forever.

22 As an inheritance to Israel,
    his servant—
        God's faithful love lasts forever!

23 God remembered us
    when we were humiliated—
        God's faithful love lasts forever.

24 God rescued us from our enemies—
        God's faithful love lasts forever.

25 God is the one who provides
    food for all living things—
        God's faithful love lasts forever!

26 Give thanks to the God of heaven—
        God's faithful love lasts forever!

Psalm 137

1 Alongside Babylon's streams,
    there we sat down,
    crying because we
        remembered Zion.
2 We hung our lyres up
    in the trees there
3 because that's where
    our captors asked us to sing;

our tormentors requested
    songs of joy:
    "Sing us a song about Zion!"
        they said.
4 But how could we possibly sing
    the LORD's song on foreign soil?

5 Jerusalem! If I forget you,
    let my strong hand wither!
6 Let my tongue stick
    to the roof of my mouth
    if I don't remember you,
    if I don't make Jerusalem
        my greatest joy.

7 LORD, remember what
    the Edomites did
    on Jerusalem's dark day:
    "Rip it down, rip it down!
    All the way to its foundations!"
        they yelled.
8 Daughter Babylon, you destroyer,[y]
    a blessing on the one
    who pays you back
    the very deed you did to us!
9 A blessing on the one
    who seizes your children
    and smashes them against the rock!

Psalm 138
Of David.

1 I give thanks to you
    with all my heart, LORD.[z]
    I sing your praise
    before all other gods.
2 I bow toward your holy temple
    and thank your name
    for your loyal love and faithfulness
    because you have made
    your name and word
    greater than everything else.[a]

ySym, Tg, Syr; MT *the devastated* zLXX, Syr, Tg, DSS (11QPsª); MT lacks LORD. aCorrection;
Heb uncertain

³ On the day I cried out,
   you answered me.
   You encouraged me
      with inner strength.ᵇ

⁴ Let all the earth's rulers
      give thanks to you, LORD,
   when they hear what you say.
⁵ Let them sing about the LORD's ways
   because the LORD's glory is so great!
⁶ Even though the LORD is high,
      he can still see the lowly,
   but God keeps his distance
      from the arrogant.

⁷ Whenever I am in deep trouble,
      you make me live again;
   you send your power
      against my enemies' wrath;
   you save me with your strong hand.
⁸ The LORD will do all this for my sake.

   Your faithful love lasts forever, LORD!
      Don't let go of what your hands
      have made.

Psalm 139
For the music leader.
Of David. A song.
¹ LORD, you have examined me.
   You know me.
² You know when I sit down
      and when I stand up.
   Even from far away,
      you comprehend my plans.
³ You study my traveling and resting.
   You are thoroughly familiar
      with all my ways.
⁴ There isn't a word on my tongue,
   LORD,
      that you don't
      already know completely.

⁵ You surround me—front and back.
   You put your hand on me.
⁶ That kind of knowledge
      is too much for me;
   it's so high above me
      that I can't reach it.

⁷ Where could I go to get away
      from your spirit?
   Where could I go to escape
      your presence?
⁸ If I went up to heaven,
      you would be there.
   If I went down to the grave,ᶜ
      you would be there too!
⁹ If I could fly on the wings of dawn,
   stopping to rest only
      on the far side of the ocean—
¹⁰ even there your hand
      would guide me;
   even there your strong hand
      would hold me tight!
¹¹ If I said,
   "The darkness will definitely
   hide me;
      the light will become night
      around me,"
¹² even then the darkness
      isn't too dark for you!
   Nighttime would shine
      bright as day,
   because darkness is the same
      as light to you!

¹³ You are the one who created
      my innermost parts;
   you knit me together
      while I was still
      in my mother's womb.
¹⁴ I give thanks to you
   that I was marvelously set apart.
   Your works are wonderful—
      I know that very well.

ᵇHeb uncertain ᶜHeb *Sheol*

¹⁵ My bones weren't hidden from you
    when I was being put together
        in a secret place,
    when I was being woven together
        in the deep parts of the earth.
¹⁶ Your eyes saw my embryo,
    and on your scroll every day
        was written that was being
            formed for me,ᵈ
    before any one of them
        had yet happened.ᵉ

¹⁷ God, your plans are incomprehensible
        to me!
    Their total number is countless!
¹⁸ If I tried to count them—
        they outnumber grains of sand!
    If I came to the very end—
        I'd still be with you.ᶠ

¹⁹ If only, God,
        you would kill the wicked!
    If only murderers
        would get away from me—
²⁰ the people who talk about you,
        but only for wicked schemes;
    the people who are
        your enemies,
    who use your name as if
        it were of no significance.ᵍ
²¹ Don't I hate everyone
        who hates you?
    Don't I despise those
        who attack you?
²² Yes, I hate them—
        through and through!
    They've become my enemies too.

²³ Examine me, God! Look at my heart!
    Put me to the test!
        Know my anxious thoughts!

²⁴ Look to see if there
        is any idolatrous wayʰ in me,
    then lead me on the eternal path!

Psalm 140

For the music leader.
A psalm of David.

¹ Rescue me from evil people, LORD!
    Guard me from violent people
²   who plot evil things in their hearts,
    who pick fights every single day!
³ They sharpen their tongues
        like a snake's;
    spider poisonⁱ is on their lips.
                                    Selah

⁴ Protect me from the power
        of the wicked, LORD!
    Guard me from violent people
        who plot to trip me up!
⁵ Arrogant people have laid a trap
        for me with ropes.
    They've spread out a net
        alongside the road.
    They've set snares for me.   *Selah*

⁶ I tell the LORD, "You are my God!
    Listen to my request for mercy,
        LORD!"
⁷ My LORD God,
        my strong saving help—
    you've protected my head
        on the day of battle.
⁸ LORD, don't give the wicked
        what they want!
    Don't allow their plans to succeed,
        or they'll exalt themselves
            even more!ʲ   *Selah*

⁹ Let the heads of the people
        surrounding me

ᵈCorrection; Heb lacks *for me*. ᵉHeb uncertain ᶠCorrection ᵍHeb lacks *your name.*
ʰCorrection; cf Tg; LXX, Syr, Vulg *painful* or *wicked* or *hurtful way* ⁱLXX *snake poison*
ʲHeb uncertain

be covered with the trouble
their own lips caused!^{k}
¹⁰ Let burning coals fall on them!
Let them fall into deep pits
and never get out again!
¹¹ Let no slanderer be safe in the land.
Let calamity hunt down
violent people—and quickly!^{l}

¹² I know that the LORD
will take up the case of the poor
and will do what is right
for the needy.
¹³ Yes, the righteous will give thanks
to your name,
and those who do right
will live in your presence.

Psalm 141
A psalm of David.
¹ I cry out to you, LORD:
Come to me—quickly!
Listen to my voice
when I cry out to you!
² Let my prayer stand before you
like incense;
let my uplifted hands
be like the evening offering.

³ Set a guard over my mouth, LORD;
keep close watch over the door
that is my lips.
⁴ Don't let my heart turn aside
to evil things
so that I don't do wicked things
with evildoers,
so I don't taste their delicacies.

⁵ Instead, let the righteous
discipline me;

let the faithful correct me!
Let my head never reject
that kind of fine oil,
because my prayers are always
against the deeds of the wicked.^{m}
⁶ Their leaders will fall
from jagged cliffs,
but my words will be heard
because they are pleasing.^{n}
⁷ Our bones^o have been scattered
at the mouth of the grave,^{p}
just like when the ground
is broken up and plowed.^{q}

⁸ But my eyes are on you,
my LORD God.
I take refuge in you;
don't let me die!
⁹ Protect me from the trap
they've set for me;
protect me from the snares
of the evildoers.
¹⁰ Let the wicked fall into
their own nets—
all together!—
but let me make it
through safely.

Psalm 142
*A maskil^r of David, when he was
in the cave. A prayer.*
¹ I cry out loud for help from the LORD.
I beg out loud
for mercy from the LORD.
² I pour out my concerns
before God;
I announce my distress to him.

³ When my spirit is weak inside me,
you still know my way.

---

^{k}Heb uncertain ^{l}Heb uncertain ^{m}Heb uncertain ^{n}Heb uncertain ^{o}LXX manuscripts, Syr *their bones;* DSS (11QPsᵃ) *my bones* ^{p}Heb *Sheol* ^{q}Heb uncertain ^{r}Perhaps *instruction*

But they've hidden a trap for me
    in the path I'm taking.
⁴ Look right beside me: See?
    No one pays attention to me.
There's no escape for me.
    No one cares about my life.

⁵ I cry to you, LORD, for help.
    "You are my refuge," I say.
    "You are all I have
    in the land of the living."
⁶ Pay close attention
    to my shouting,
    because I've been brought down
    so low!
Deliver me from my oppressors
    because they're stronger than me.
⁷ Get me out of this prison
    so I can give thanks to your name.
Then the righteous
    will gather all around me
    because of your good deeds to me.

Psalm 143
A psalm of David.

¹ Listen to my prayer, LORD!
    Because of your faithfulness,
    hear my requests for mercy!
    Because of your righteousness,
    answer me!
² Please don't bring your servant
    to judgment,
    because no living thing
    is righteous before you.

³ The enemy is chasing me,ˢ
    crushing my life in the dirt,
    forcing me to live in the dark
    like those who've been
    dead forever.
⁴ My spirit is weak inside me—
    inside, my mind is numb.

⁵ I remember the days long past;
    I meditate on all your deeds;
    I contemplate your handiwork.
⁶ I stretch out my hands to you;
    my whole being is like dry dirt,
    thirsting for you.ᵗ   *Selah*

⁷ Answer me, LORD—and quickly!
    My breath is fading.
    Don't hide your face from me
    or I'll be like those going down
    to the pit!
⁸ Tell me all about your faithful love
    come morning time,
    because I trust you.
Show me the way I should go,
    because I offer my life up to you.
⁹ Deliver me from my enemies, LORD!
    I seek protection from you.ᵘ
¹⁰ Teach me to do what pleases you,
    because you are my God.
Guide me by your good spirit
    into good land.
¹¹ Make me live again, LORD,
    for your name's sake.
Bring me out of distress
    because of your righteousness.
¹² Wipe out my enemies
    because of your faithful love.
Destroy everyone who attacks me,
    because I am your servant.

Psalm 144
Of David.

¹ Bless the LORD, my rock,
    who taught my hands how to fight,
    who taught my fingers
    how to do battle!
² God is my loyal one, my fortress,
    my place of safety, my rescuer,
    my shield, in whom I take refuge,
    and the one who subdues
    people before me.

ˢOr *my soul*; also in 143:6, 8, 11-12 ᵗHeb lacks *thirsting*. ᵘHeb uncertain; MT *to you I have hidden*

³ What are human beings, LORD,
     that you know them at all?
   What are human beings
     that you even consider them?
⁴ Humans are like a puff of air;
     their days go by like a shadow.

⁵ LORD, part your skies and come down!
     Touch the mountains so they smoke!
⁶ Flash lightning and scatter the enemy!
     Shoot your arrows and defeat them!
⁷ Stretch out your hand from above!
     Rescue me and deliver me
      from deep water,
   from the power of strangers,
    ⁸ whose mouths speak lies,
     and whose strong hand is
      a strong hand of deception!

⁹ I will sing a new song to you, God.
     I will sing praises to you
      on a ten-stringed harp,
    ¹⁰ to you—the one
     who gives saving help to rulers,
     and who rescues his servant
      David from the evil sword.
¹¹ Rescue me and deliver me
     from the power of strangers,
    whose mouths speak lies,
     and whose strong hand
      is a strong hand of deception,
¹² so that^v our sons can grow up fully,
     in their youth, like plants;
   so that our daughters can be like
     pillars carved to decorate a palace;
¹³ so that our barns can be full,
     providing all kinds of food;
   so that our flocks can be
     in the thousands—
     even tens of thousands—
      in our fields;

¹⁴ so that our cattle can be loaded
     with calves;
   so that there won't be any breach
     in the walls,
   no exile, no outcries in our streets!

¹⁵ The people who have it like this
     are truly happy!
   The people whose God is the LORD
     are truly happy!

Psalm 145^w
Praise. Of David.

א   ¹ I will lift you up high, my God,
     the true king.
   I will bless your name
     forever and always.
ב   ² I will bless you every day.
   I will praise your name
     forever and always.
ג   ³ The LORD is great
     and so worthy of praise!
   God's greatness can't be grasped.
ד   ⁴ One generation will praise
     your works to the next one,
     proclaiming your mighty acts.
ה   ⁵ They will talk all about^x
     the glorious splendor
     of your majesty;
   I will contemplate
     your wondrous works.
ו   ⁶ They will speak of the power
     of your awesome deeds;
   I will declare
     your great accomplishments.
ז   ⁷ They will rave in celebration
     of your abundant goodness;
   they will shout joyfully
     about your righteousness:
ח   ⁸ "The LORD is merciful
     and compassionate,

---

^vHeb uncertain   ^wPs 145 is an alphabetic acrostic poem; see the note at Pss 9–10.   ^xLXX, Syr, DSS (11QPs^a); MT *and words of*

very patient,
and full of faithful love.

צ ⁹ The LORD is good to everyone
and everything;
God's compassion extends
to all his handiwork!"

ר ¹⁰ All that you have made
gives thanks to you, LORD;
all your faithful ones bless you!

כ ¹¹ They speak of the glory
of your kingdom;
they talk all about your power,

ל ¹² to inform all human beings
about God's power
and the majestic glory
of God's kingdom.

מ ¹³ Your kingdom is a kingship
that lasts forever;
your rule endures
for all generations.

נ   The LORD is trustworthy
in all that he says,
faithful in all that he does.ʸ

ס ¹⁴ The LORD supports all
who fall down,
straightens up all
who are bent low.

ע ¹⁵ All eyes look to you, hoping,
and you give them their food
right on time,

פ ¹⁶ opening your hand
and satisfying the desire
of every living thing.

צ ¹⁷ The LORD is righteous
in all his ways,
faithful in all his deeds.

ק ¹⁸ The LORD is close to everyone
who calls out to him,
to all who call out to him sincerely.

ר ¹⁹ God shows favor to those
who honor him,

listening to their cries for help
and saving them.

ש ²⁰ The LORD protects all who love him,
but he destroys
every wicked person.

ת ²¹ My mouth will proclaim
the LORD's praise,
and every living thing
will bless God's holy name
forever and always.

Psalm 146

¹ Praise the LORD!

Let my whole beingᶻ
praise the LORD!

² I will praise the LORD
with all my life;
I will sing praises to my God
as long as I live.

³ Don't trust leaders;
don't trust any human beings—
there's no saving help with them!

⁴ Their breath leaves them,
then they go back to the ground.
On that very same day,
their plans die too.

⁵ The person whose help
is the God of Jacob—
the person whose hope
rests on the LORD their God—
is truly happy!

⁶ God: the maker of heaven and earth,
the sea, and all that is in them.
God: who is faithful forever,
⁷ who gives justice to people
who are oppressed,
who gives bread to people
who are starving!

ʸLXX, DSS (11QPsᵃ), Syr; MT lacks these lines, but they correspond to the *nun* line in the alphabetic acrostic poem. ²Or *soul*

The LORD:
  who frees prisoners.
⁸ The LORD:
  who makes the blind see.
The LORD:
  who straightens up
    those who are bent low.
The LORD:
  who loves the righteous.
⁹ The LORD:
  who protects immigrants,
  who helps orphans and widows,
  but who makes the way
    of the wicked twist and turn!

¹⁰ The LORD will rule forever!
  Zion, your God will rule
    from one generation to the next!

Praise the LORD!

Psalm 147

¹ Praise the LORD!
  Because it is good to sing praise
    to our God!
  Because it is a pleasure
    to make beautiful praise!

² The LORD rebuilds Jerusalem,
    gathering up Israel's exiles.
³ God heals the brokenhearted
    and bandages their wounds.
⁴ God counts the stars by number,
    giving each one a name.
⁵ Our Lord is great and so strong!
    God's knowledge can't be grasped!
⁶ The LORD helps the poor,
  but throws the wicked down
    on the dirt!

⁷ Sing to the LORD with thanks;
    sing praises to our God
      with a lyre!
⁸ God covers the skies with clouds;

God makes rain for the earth;
    God makes the mountains
      sprout green grass.
⁹ God gives food to the animals—
    even to the baby ravens
      when they cry out.
¹⁰ God doesn't prize the strength
    of a horse;
  God doesn't treasure
    the legs of a runner.
¹¹ No. The LORD treasures the people
    who honor him,
  the people who wait
    for his faithful love.

¹² Worship the LORD, Jerusalem!
    Praise your God, Zion!
¹³ Because God secures the bars
    on your gates,
  God blesses the children
    you have there.
¹⁴ God establishes
    your borders peacefully.
  God fills you full
    with the very best wheat.

¹⁵ God issues his command
    to the earth—
  God's word speeds off fast!
¹⁶ God spreads snow like it was wool;
    God scatters frost like it was ashes;
¹⁷ God throws his hail down
    like crumbs—
  who can endure God's
    freezing cold?
¹⁸ Then God issues his word
    and melts it all away!
  God makes his winds blow;
    the water flows again.

¹⁹ God proclaims his word to Jacob;
    his statutes and rules to Israel.
²⁰ God hasn't done that
    with any other nation;

those nations have no knowledge
of God's rules.[a]

Praise the LORD!

Psalm 148

[1] Praise the LORD!

Praise the LORD from heaven!
Praise God on the heights!
[2] Praise God, all of you
who are his messengers!
Praise God, all of you
who comprise his heavenly forces!
[3] Sun and moon, praise God!
All of you bright stars, praise God!
[4] You highest heaven, praise God!
Do the same, you waters
that are above the sky!
[5] Let all of these praise
the LORD's name
because God gave the command
and they were created!
[6] God set them in place
always and forever.
God made a law
that will not be broken.

[7] Praise the LORD from the earth,
you sea monsters
and all you ocean depths!
[8] Do the same, fire and hail,
snow and smoke,
stormy wind that does
what God says!
[9] Do the same, you mountains,
every single hill,
fruit trees, and every single cedar!
[10] Do the same, you animals—
wild or tame—
you creatures that creep along
and you birds that fly!

[11] Do the same, you kings of the earth
and every single person,
you princes and every single ruler
on earth!
[12] Do the same, you young men—
young women too!—
you who are old together
with you who are young!

[13] Let all of these praise
the LORD's name
because only God's name
is high over all.
Only God's majesty
is over earth and heaven.
[14] God raised the strength[b]
of his people,
the praise of all his faithful ones—
that's the Israelites,
the people who are close to him.

Praise the LORD!

Psalm 149

[1] Praise the LORD!

Sing to the LORD a new song;
sing God's praise
in the assembly of the faithful!
[2] Let Israel celebrate its maker;
let Zion's children rejoice
in their king!
[3] Let them praise God's name
with dance;
let them sing God's praise
with the drum and lyre!
[4] Because the LORD is pleased
with his people,
God will beautify the poor
with saving help.

[5] Let the faithful celebrate
with glory;

---

[a]LXX, Tg, DSS (11QPsᵃ) *God hasn't let those nations know his rules.*   [b]Or *horn*

let them shout for joy
on their beds.^c

⁶ Let the high praises of God
be in their mouths
and a double-edged sword
in their hands,
⁷ to get revenge
against the nations
and punishment
on the peoples,
⁸ binding their rulers in chains
and their officials
in iron shackles,
⁹ achieving the justice
written against them.
That will be an honor
for all God's faithful people.

Praise the LORD!

Psalm 150

¹ Praise the LORD!

Praise God in his sanctuary!
Praise God in his fortress, the sky!
² Praise God in his mighty acts!
Praise God as suits
his incredible greatness!
³ Praise God with the blast
of the ram's horn!
Praise God with lute and lyre!
⁴ Praise God with drum and dance!
Praise God with strings and pipe!
⁵ Praise God with loud cymbals!
Praise God with clashing cymbals!
⁶ Let every living thing
praise the LORD!

Praise the LORD!

PROVERBS

Purpose of Proverbs

1 The proverbs of Solomon,
King David's son, from Israel:
² Their purpose is to teach wisdom
and discipline,
to help one understand
wise sayings.
³ They provide insightful instruction,
which is righteous, just,
and full of integrity.
⁴ They make the naive mature,
the young knowledgeable
and discreet.
⁵ The wise hear them
and grow in wisdom;
those with understanding
gain guidance.
⁶ They help one understand
proverbs and difficult sayings,

the words of the wise,
and their puzzles.
⁷ Wisdom begins with the fear
of the LORD,
but fools despise wisdom
and instruction.

Avoid evil associations

⁸ Listen, my son,
to your father's instruction;
don't neglect
your mother's teaching;
⁹ for they are a graceful wreath
on your head,
and beads for your neck.
¹⁰ My son, don't let sinners entice you.
Don't go ¹¹ when they say:
"Come with us.
Let's set up a deadly ambush.

^cHeb uncertain

Let's secretly wait for the innocent
just for fun.
¹² Let's swallow up the living
like the grave[a]—
whole, like those who go down
into the pit.
¹³ We'll find all sorts
of precious wealth;
we'll fill our houses with plunder.
¹⁴ Throw in your lot with us;
we'll share our money."
¹⁵ My son, don't go on the path
with them;
keep your feet from their way,
¹⁶ because their feet run to evil;
they hurry to spill blood.
¹⁷ It's useless to cast a net
in the sight of a bird.
¹⁸ But these sinners
set up a deadly ambush;
they lie in wait for their own lives.
¹⁹ These are the ways of all
who seek unjust gain;
it costs them their lives.

Listen to "Woman Wisdom"

²⁰ Wisdom shouts in the street;
in the public square
she raises her voice.
²¹ Above the noisy crowd,
she calls out.
At the entrances of the city gates,
she has her say:
²² "How long will you clueless people
love your naïveté,
mockers hold their mocking dear,
and fools hate knowledge?
²³ You should respond
when I correct you.
Look, I'll pour out my spirit on you.
I'll reveal my words to you.
²⁴ I invited you, but you rejected me;

I stretched out my hand to you,
but you paid no attention.
²⁵ You ignored all my advice,
and you didn't want me
to correct you.
²⁶ So I'll laugh at your disaster;
I'll make fun of you
when dread comes over you,
²⁷ when terror hits you
like a hurricane,
and your disaster comes in
like a tornado,
when distress and oppression
overcome you.
²⁸ Then they will call me,
but I won't answer;
they will seek me,
but won't find me
²⁹ because they hated knowledge
and didn't choose
the fear of the LORD.
³⁰ They didn't want my advice;
they rejected all my corrections.
³¹ They will eat from the fruit
of their way,
and they'll be full
of their own schemes.
³² The immature will die
because they turn away;
smugness will destroy fools.
³³ Those who obey me
will dwell securely,
untroubled by the dread of harm."

Benefits of wisdom

2 My son, accept my words
and store up my commands.
² Turn your ear toward wisdom,
and stretch your mind
toward understanding.
³ Call out for insight,
and cry aloud for understanding.

---

[a]Heb Sheol

⁴ Seek it like silver;
   search for it like hidden treasure.
⁵ Then you will understand
   the fear of the LORD,
   and discover the knowledge of God.
⁶ The LORD gives wisdom;
   from his mouth come knowledge
   and understanding.
⁷ He reserves ability for those
   with integrity.
   He is a shield for those
   who live a blameless life.
⁸ He protects the paths of justice
   and guards the way of those
   who are loyal to him.
⁹ Then you will understand
   righteousness and justice,
   as well as integrity,
   every good course.
¹⁰ Wisdom will enter your mind,
   and knowledge will fill you
   with delight.
¹¹ Discretion will guard you;
   understanding will protect you.
¹² Wisdom will rescue you
   from the evil path,
   from people who twist their words.
¹³ They forsake the way of integrity
   and go on obscure paths.
¹⁴ They enjoy doing evil,
   rejoicing in their twisted evil.
¹⁵ Their paths are confused;
   they get lost in their way.
¹⁶ Wisdom will rescue you
   from the mysterious woman,
   from the foreign woman
   with her slick words.
¹⁷ She leaves behind the partner
   of her youth;
   she even forgets her covenant
   with God.
¹⁸ Her house sinks down to death,

and her paths go down
   to the shadowy dead.
¹⁹ All those who go to her
   will never return;
   they will never again
   reach the ways of the living.
²⁰ So you should stay on the path
   of good people,
   guarding the road of the righteous.
²¹ Those who have integrity
   will dwell in the land;
   the innocent will remain in it.
²² But the wicked will be cut off
   from the land,
   and the treacherous
   will be ripped up.

Trust in the Lord

3 My son, don't forget my instruction.
   Let your heart guard my commands,
² because they will help you live
   a long time
   and provide you with well-being.
³ Don't let loyalty and faithfulness
   leave you.
   Bind them on your neck;
   write them on the tablet
   of your heart.
⁴ Then you will find favor
   and approval
   in the eyes of God and humanity.
⁵ Trust in the LORD
   with all your heart;
   don't rely on your own intelligence.
⁶ Know him in all your paths,
   and he will keep
   your ways straight.
⁷ Don't consider yourself wise.
   Fear the LORD and turn away
   from evil.
⁸ Then your body^b will be healthy
   and your bones strengthened.

^{b}Heb *navel*

⁹ Honor the LORD with your wealth
  and with the first of all your crops.
¹⁰ Then your barns will be filled
  with plenty,
  and your vats will burst with wine.
¹¹ Don't reject the instruction
  of the LORD, my son;
  don't despise his correction.
¹² The LORD loves those he corrects,
  just like a father who treats his son
  with favor.

Value of wisdom

¹³ Happy are those who find wisdom
  and those who gain understanding.
¹⁴ Her profit is better than silver,
  and her gain better than gold.
¹⁵ Her value exceeds pearls;
  all you desire
  can't compare with her.
¹⁶ In her right hand is a long life;
  in her left are wealth and honor.
¹⁷ Her ways are pleasant;
  all her paths are peaceful.
¹⁸ She is a tree of life
  to those who embrace her;
  those who hold her tight are happy.
¹⁹ The LORD laid the foundations
  of the earth with wisdom,
  establishing the heavens
  with understanding.
²⁰ With his knowledge,
  the watery depths burst open,
  and the skies drop dew.

Integrity of wisdom

²¹ My son, don't let them slip
  from your eyes;
  hold on to sound judgment
  and discretion.
²² They will be life for your whole being,
  and an ornament for your neck.
²³ Then you will walk safely
  on your path,

and your foot won't stumble.
²⁴ If you lie down,
  you won't be terrified.
  When you lie down,
  your sleep will be pleasant.
²⁵ Don't fear sudden terror
  or the ruin that comes
  to the wicked.
²⁶ The LORD will be your confidence;
  he will guard your feet
  from being snared.
²⁷ Don't withhold good
  from someone who deserves it,
  when it is in your power to do so.
²⁸ Don't say to your neighbor,
  "Go and come back;
  I'll give it to you tomorrow,"
  when you have it.
²⁹ Don't plan to harm your neighbor
  who trusts and lives near you.
³⁰ Don't accuse anyone
  without reason,
  when they haven't harmed you.
³¹ Don't envy violent people
  or choose any of their ways.
³² Devious people are detestable
  to the LORD,
  but the virtuous are his close friends.
³³ The LORD's curse is on
  the house of the wicked,
  but he blesses the home
  of the righteous.
³⁴ He mocks mockers,
  but he shows favor to the humble.
³⁵ The wise gain respect,
  but fools receive shame.

Love wisdom

4 Hear, children, fatherly instruction;
  pay attention to gain understanding.
² I'll teach you well.
  Don't abandon my instruction.
³ When I was a son to my father,
  tender and my mother's favorite,

⁴ he taught me and said to me:
"Let your heart hold on to my words:
Keep my commands and live.
⁵ Get wisdom; get understanding.
Don't forget and don't turn away
from my words.
⁶ Don't abandon her,
and she will guard you.
Love her, and she will protect you.
⁷ The beginning of wisdom:
Get wisdom!
Get understanding
before anything else.
⁸ Highly esteem her,
and she will exalt you.
She will honor you
if you embrace her.
⁹ She will place a graceful wreath
on your head;
she will give you a glorious crown."

Stay on the path of wisdom

¹⁰ Listen, my son,
and take in my speech,
then the years of your life
will be many.
¹¹ I teach you the path of wisdom.
I lead you in straight courses.
¹² When you walk,
you won't be hindered;
when you run, you won't stumble.
¹³ Hold on to instruction;
don't slack off;
protect it, for it is your life.
¹⁴ Don't go on the way of the wicked;
don't walk on the path
of evil people.
¹⁵ Avoid it! Don't turn onto it;
stay off of it and keep going!
¹⁶ They don't sleep unless they do evil;
they are robbed of sleep unless
they make someone stumble.
¹⁷ They eat the bread of evil,
and they drink the wine of violence.

¹⁸ The way of the righteous
is like morning light
that gets brighter and
brighter till it is full day.
¹⁹ The path of the wicked
is like deep darkness;
they don't know where
they will stumble.

Be careful about what you say

²⁰ My son, pay attention to my words.
Bend your ear to my speech.
²¹ Don't let them slip from your sight.
Guard them in your mind.
²² They are life to those who find them,
and healing for their entire body.
²³ More than anything you guard,
protect your mind,
for life flows from it.
²⁴ Have nothing to do
with a corrupt mouth;
keep devious lips far from you.
²⁵ Focus your eyes straight ahead;
keep your gaze on
what is in front of you.
²⁶ Watch your feet on the way,
and all your paths will be secure.
²⁷ Don't deviate a bit to the right
or the left;
turn your feet away from evil.

Avoid the mysterious woman

5 My son, pay attention
to my wisdom.
Bend your ear to what I know,
² so you might remain discreet,
and your lips
might guard knowledge.
³ The lips of a mysterious woman
drip honey,
and her tongue is smoother
than oil,
⁴ but in the end she is bitter as gall,
sharp as a double-edged sword.

⁵ Her feet go down to death;
  her steps lead to the grave.ᶜ
⁶ She doesn't stay on the way of life.
  Her paths wander,
  but she doesn't know it.

⁷ Now children, listen to me,
  and don't deviate
  from the words of my mouth.
⁸ Stay on a path that is far from her;
  don't approach the entrance
  to her house.
⁹ Otherwise, you will give
  your strength to others,
  your years to a cruel person.
¹⁰ Otherwise, strangers
  will sap your strength,
  and your hard work will end up
  in a foreigner's house.
¹¹ You will groan at the end
  when your body and flesh
  are exhausted,
¹² and you say,
  "How I hated instruction!
  How my heart despised correction!
¹³ I didn't listen to the voice
  of my instructor.
  I didn't obey my teacher.
¹⁴ I'm on the brink of utter ruin
  in the assembled community."

¹⁵ Drink water from your own cistern,
  gushing water from your own well.
¹⁶ Should your fountains
  flood outside,
  streams of water
  in the public squares?
¹⁷ They are yours alone,
  not for you as well as strangers.
¹⁸ May your spring be blessed.
  Rejoice in the wife of your youth.
¹⁹ She is a lovely deer, a graceful doe.

Let her breasts intoxicate you
  all the time;
  always be drunk on her love.

²⁰ Why, my son, should you lose
  your senses with
  a mysterious woman
  and embrace the breasts
  of a foreign female?

²¹ The LORD's eyes watch
  over every person's path,
  observing all their ways.
²² The wicked will be caught
  by their own evil acts,
  grabbed by the ropes
  of their own sin.
²³ Those without instruction will die,
  misled by their own stupidity.

Wise advice

6 My son, if you guarantee a loan
  for your neighbor
  or shake hands in agreement
  with a stranger,
² you will be trapped by your words;
  you will be caught by your words.
³ Do this, my son, to get out of it,
  for you have come under the control
  of your neighbor.
  So go, humble yourself,ᵈ
  and pester your neighbor.
⁴ Don't give sleep to your eyes
  or slumber to your eyelids.
⁵ Get yourself free like a gazelle
  from a hunter,
  like a bird from the hand
  of a fowler.
⁶ Go to the ant, you lazy person;
  observe its ways and grow wise.
⁷ The ant has no commander, officer,
  or ruler.

ᶜHeb *Sheol* ᵈHeb uncertain

⁸ Even so, it gets its food in summer;
   gathers its provisions at harvest.
⁹ How long, lazy person,
   will you lie down?
   When will you rise from your sleep?
¹⁰ A little sleep, a little slumber,
   a little folding of the arms
      to lie down—
¹¹ and poverty will come on you
   like a prowler,
      destitution like a warrior.
¹² Worthless people and guilty people
   go around with crooked talk.
¹³ They wink their eyes,
   gesture with their feet,
   and point with their fingers.
¹⁴ Their hearts are corrupt
   and determined to do evil;
   they create controversies
      all the time.
¹⁵ Therefore, sudden disaster
   will come upon them;
   they will be quickly broken
      beyond healing.
¹⁶ There are six things
   that the LORD hates,
   seven things detestable to him:
¹⁷ snobbish eyes,
   a lying tongue,
   hands that spill innocent blood,
¹⁸ a heart set on wicked plans,
   feet that run quickly to evil,
¹⁹ a false witness who breathes lies,
   and one who causes conflicts
      among relatives.

Danger of adultery

²⁰ My son, keep your father's command;
   don't abandon
      your mother's instruction.
²¹ Bind them on your heart
   for all time;
   fasten them around your neck.

²² When you walk around,
   they will lead you;
   when you lie down,
      they will protect you;
   when you awake,
      they will occupy your attention.
²³ The commandment is a lamp
   and instruction a light;
   corrective teaching is the path
      of life.
²⁴ They guard you from the evil woman,
   from the flattering tongue
      of the foreign woman.
²⁵ Don't desire her beauty in secret;
   don't let her take you in
      with her eyelashes.
²⁶ for a prostitute costs
   a loaf of bread,ᵉ
   but a married woman
      hunts for a man's very life.
²⁷ Can a man scoop fire into his lap
   and his clothes not get burned?
²⁸ If a man walks on hot coals,
   don't his feet get burned?
²⁹ So is the man who approaches
   his neighbor's wife;
   anyone who touches her
      will be punished.
³⁰ People don't despise a thief
   if he steals
   to fill his starving stomach.
³¹ But if he is caught,
   he must pay sevenfold;
   he must give all the riches
      of his house.
³² He who commits adultery
   is senseless.
   Doing so, he destroys himself.
³³ He is wounded and disgraced.
   His shame will never
      be wiped away.
³⁴ Jealousy makes a man rage;

ᵉ Heb uncertain

he'll show no mercy
on his day of revenge.
³⁵ He won't accept compensation;
he'll refuse even a large bribe.

Avoid loose women

7 My son, keep my words;
store up my commands within you.
² Keep my commands and live,
and my instruction
like the pupil of your eye.
³ Bind them on your fingers;
write them on the tablet
of your heart.
⁴ Say to wisdom, "You are my sister";
call understanding "friend,"
⁵ so she might guard you
against the mysterious woman,
from the foreign woman
who flatters you.

⁶ When from the window
of my house,
from behind the screen,
I gazed down,
⁷ I looked among
the naive young men
and noticed among the youth,
one who had no sense.
⁸ He was crossing the street
at her corner
and walked down the path
to her house
⁹ in the early evening,
at the onset of night and darkness.
¹⁰ All of a sudden a woman
approaches him,
dressed like a prostitute
and with a cunning mind.
¹¹ She is noisy and defiant;
her feet don't stay long
in her own house.

¹² She has one foot in the street,
one foot in the public square.
She lies in wait at every corner.
¹³ She grabs him and kisses him.
Her face is brazen
as she speaks to him:
¹⁴ "I've made a sacrifice of well-being;
today I fulfilled
my solemn promises.
¹⁵ So I've come out to meet you,
seeking you, and I have found you.
¹⁶ I've spread my bed
with luxurious covers,
with colored linens from Egypt.
¹⁷ I've sprinkled my bed with myrrh,
aloes, and cinnamon.
¹⁸ Come, let's drink deep of love
until morning;
let's savor our lovemaking.
¹⁹ For my husband isn't home;
he's gone far away.
²⁰ He took a pouch of money with him;
he won't come home till full moon."
²¹ She seduces him with all her talk.
She entices him with her flattery.
²² He goes headlong after her,
like an ox to the slaughter,
like a deer leaping into a trap,^f
²³ until an arrow pierces his liver,
like a bird hurrying to the snare,
not aware that it will cost him
his life.

²⁴ Now children, listen to me,
and pay attention to my speech.
²⁵ Don't turn your heart to her ways;
don't wander down her paths.
²⁶ She has caused many corpses to fall;
she has killed many people.
²⁷ Her house is a path to the grave,^g
going down to the chambers
of death.

---

^fHeb uncertain   ^gHeb *Sheol*

Wisdom's autobiography

8 Doesn't Wisdom cry out
and Understanding shout?
² Atop the heights along the path,
at the crossroads she takes her stand.
³ By the gate before the city,
at the entrances she shouts:

⁴ I cry out to you, people;
my voice goes out to all of humanity.
⁵ Understand skill, you who are naive.
Take this to heart, you fools.
⁶ Listen, for I speak things
that are correct;
from my lips comes what is right.
⁷ My mouth utters the truth;
my lips despise wickedness.
⁸ All the words of my mouth
are righteous;
nothing in them is twisted
or crooked.
⁹ All of them are straightforward
to those who understand,
and upright for the knowledgeable.
¹⁰ Take my instruction
rather than silver,
knowledge rather than choice gold.
¹¹ Wisdom is better than pearls;
nothing is more delightful than she.

¹² I, Wisdom, dwell with prudence;
I have found knowledge
and discretion.
¹³ To fear the LORD is to hate evil.
I hate pride and arrogance,
the path of evil and corrupt speech.
¹⁴ I have advice and ability,
as well as understanding
and strength.
¹⁵ By me kings rule,
and princes issue righteous decrees.
¹⁶ By me rulers govern,
and officials judge righteously.ʰ

¹⁷ I love those who love me;
those who seek me will find me.
¹⁸ Riches and honor are with me,
as well as enduring wealth
and righteousness.
¹⁹ My fruit is better than gold,
even fine gold;
my crops are better
than choice silver.
²⁰ I walk on the way of righteousness,
on the paths of justice,
²¹ to provide for those who love me
and to fill up their treasuries.

²² The LORD created me
at the beginning of his way,
before his deeds long in the past.
²³ I was formed in ancient times,
at the beginning,
before the earth was.
²⁴ When there were no watery depths,
I was brought forth,
when there were no springs
flowing with water.
²⁵ Before the mountains were settled,
before the hills,
I was brought forth;
²⁶ before Godⁱ made the earth
and the fields
or the first of the dry land.
²⁷ I was there when he established
the heavens,
when he marked out the horizon
on the deep sea,
²⁸ when he thickened
the clouds above,
when he secured the fountains
of the deep,
²⁹ when he set a limit for the sea,
so the water couldn't go beyond
his command,
when he marked out
the earth's foundations.

ʰHeb uncertain ⁱHeb lacks God.

³⁰ I was beside him
    as a master of crafts;[j]
    I was having fun,
    smiling before him all the time,
³¹ frolicking with his inhabited earth
    and delighting in the human race.

³² Now children, listen to me:
    Happy are those who keep
      to my ways!
³³ Listen to instruction, and be wise;
    don't avoid it.
³⁴ Happy are those who listen to me,
    watching daily at my doors,
    waiting at my doorposts;
³⁵ Those who find me find life;
    they gain favor from the LORD.
³⁶ Those who offend me
    injure themselves;
    all those who hate me love death.

"Woman Wisdom's" invitation

9 Wisdom built her house;
    she has carved out her seven pillars.
² She slaughtered her animals,
    mixed her wine,
    and set her table.
³ She sends out her female servants;
    she issues an invitation
    from the top of the city heights:
⁴ "Whoever is naive turn aside here,"
    she says to those who lack sense.
⁵ "Come, eat my food,
    and drink the wine I have mixed.
⁶ Abandon your simplistic ways
    and live;
    walk in the way of understanding."

Wise advice

⁷ Whoever instructs the cynic
    gets insulted;
    whoever corrects the wicked
    gets hurt.

⁸ Don't correct the impudent,
    or they will hate you;
    correct the wise,
    and they will love you.
⁹ Teach the wise,
    and they will become wiser;
    inform the righteous,
    and their learning will increase.
¹⁰ The beginning of wisdom
    is the fear of the LORD;
    the knowledge of the holy one
    is understanding.
¹¹ Through me your days will be many;
    years will be added to your life.
¹² If you are wise, it is to your benefit;
    if you are cynical,
    you will bear it all alone.

"Woman Folly's" invitation

¹³ Woman Folly is noisy;
    she's stupid and
    doesn't even know it.
¹⁴ She sits at the doorway of her house,
    on a seat at the city heights.
¹⁵ She invites those
    who pass by on the path,
    those going straight on their way.
¹⁶ "Whoever is naive, come in here,"
    she says to those who lack sense.
¹⁷ "Stolen water is sweet;
    food eaten in secret is pleasant."
¹⁸ But they don't know that the dead
    are there;
    her guests are in the depths
    of the grave.[k]

Proverbs of Solomon

10 The proverbs of Solomon:
    A wise child makes a father glad,
    but a foolish child
    brings sorrow to his mother.
² The treasure of the wicked
    won't profit them,

---

[j]Heb uncertain   [k]Heb *Sheol*

but righteousness rescues people
from death.

³ The LORD doesn't let
the righteous starve,
but he rejects the desires
of the wicked.

⁴ Laziness brings poverty;
hard work makes one rich.

⁵ A wise son harvests in the summer;
a disgraceful son
sleeps right through the harvest.

⁶ Blessings cover the head
of the righteous,
but the mouth of the wicked
conceals violence.

⁷ The memory of the righteous
is a blessing,
but the name of the wicked rots.

⁸ The skilled mind accepts commands,
but a foolish talker is ruined.

⁹ Those who walk in innocence
walk with confidence,
but those on crooked paths
will be found out.

¹⁰ Those who wink an eye bring trouble;
those who speak foolishly
are ruined.

¹¹ The mouth of the righteous
is a fountain of life,
but the mouth of the wicked
conceals violence.

¹² Hate stirs up conflict,
but love covers all offenses.

¹³ Wisdom is found on the lips
of those who have understanding,
but there is a rod for the back
of those with no sense.

¹⁴ The wise store up knowledge,
but the mouth of a fool
brings ruin.

¹⁵ The riches of the wealthy
are their strong city;
the ruin of the poor
is their poverty.

¹⁶ The wages of the righteous
lead to life;
the earnings of the wicked
lead to sin.

¹⁷ Those who heed instruction
are on the way to life,
but those who ignore correction
lose their way.

¹⁸ Lying lips conceal hate,
and those who spread slander
are fools.

¹⁹ With lots of words
comes wrongdoing,
but the wise restrain their lips.

²⁰ The tongue of the righteous
is choice silver,
but the heart of the wicked
lacks value.

²¹ The lips of the righteous
nourish many people,
but fools who lack sense will die.

²² The LORD's blessing
makes a person rich,
and no trouble is added to it.

²³ Fools enjoy vile deeds,
but those with understanding
take pleasure in wisdom.

²⁴ What the wicked dread
will come on them,
but what the righteous desire
will be given to them.

²⁵ After a whirlwind passes by,
the wicked are no more,
but the righteous
stand firm forever.

²⁶ Like vinegar to the teeth
and smoke to the eyes,
so are lazy people
to those who authorize them.

²⁷ The fear of the LORD
increases one's life,
but the years of the wicked
will be cut short.

²⁸ The expectations of the righteous
result in joy,

but the hopes of the wicked
will perish.
²⁹ The path of the LORD is a refuge
for the innocent
and ruin for those who do evil.
³⁰ The righteous will never be shaken,
but the wicked won't dwell
in the land.
³¹ The mouth of the righteous
flows with wisdom,
but the twisted tongue
will be cut off.
³² The lips of the wise
know what is acceptable,
but the mouth of the wicked
knows only what is perverse.

11 The LORD detests
dishonest scales,
but delights in an accurate weight.
² When pride comes, so does shame,
but wisdom brings humility.
³ Integrity guides the virtuous,
but dishonesty ruins
the treacherous.
⁴ Riches don't help in the day of wrath,
but righteousness rescues
from death.
⁵ The righteousness of the innocent
makes their path straight,
but the wicked fall
in their wickedness.
⁶ Those who do right
are saved by their righteousness,
but the untrustworthy
are caught by their own desires.
⁷ When the wicked die,
their hope perishes.
Yes, any hope based
on money perishes.
⁸ The righteous are saved
from distress,
and the wicked take their place.
⁹ The godless destroy their neighbors
by their words,

but the righteous are saved
by their knowledge.
¹⁰ When the righteous succeed,
a city rejoices;
when the wicked perish,
there are shouts of joy.
¹¹ A city is honored
by the blessing of the virtuous;
it is destroyed
by the words of the wicked.
¹² Whoever despises their neighbor
lacks sense;
a sensible person keeps quiet.
¹³ A slanderer walks around
revealing secrets,
but a trustworthy person
keeps a confidence.
¹⁴ Without guidance, a people will fall,
but there is victory
with many counselors.
¹⁵ Guaranteeing the debt of a stranger
brings big trouble,
but the one who refuses
to shake hands will be secure.
¹⁶ A gracious woman gains honor;
violent men gain only wealth.
¹⁷ Kind persons benefit themselves,
but cruel people harm themselves.
¹⁸ The wicked earn false wages,
but those who sow righteousness
receive a true reward.
¹⁹ The righteous are headed
toward life,
but those who pursue evil,
toward death.
²⁰ The LORD detests a crooked heart,
but he favors those
whose path is innocent.
²¹ The evil person will surely not
go unpunished,
but the children of the righteous
will escape.
²² Like a gold ring in a pig's nose
is a beautiful woman
who lacks discretion.

²³ The desires of the righteous
end up well,
but the expectations of the wicked
bring wrath.
²⁴ Those who give generously
receive more,
but those who are stingy with
what is appropriate
will grow needy.
²⁵ Generous persons will prosper;
those who refresh others
will themselves be refreshed.
²⁶ People curse those who hoard grain,
but they bless those[l] who sell it.
²⁷ Those who look for good find favor,
but those who seek evil—
it will come to them.
²⁸ Those who trust in their wealth
will wither,
but the righteous will thrive
like leafy trees.
²⁹ Those who trouble their family
will inherit the wind.
The fool will be servant to the wise.
³⁰ The fruit of the righteous
is a tree of life,
and the wise gather lives.[m]
³¹ If the righteous receive their due
on earth,
how much more the wicked
and sinners?

12 Those who love discipline
love knowledge,
and those who hate correction
are stupid.
² The LORD favors good people,
but he condemns schemers.
³ No one is established by wicked acts,
but the roots of the righteous
can't be disturbed.
⁴ A strong woman is a crown
to her husband,

but a disgraceful woman
is like rot in his bones.
⁵ The plans of the righteous are just,
but the guidance of the wicked
is deceptive.
⁶ The words of the wicked
are a deathtrap,
but the speech of those who do right
rescues them.
⁷ The wicked are destroyed
and are no more,
but the family of the righteous
will endure.
⁸ A person is praised for his insight,
but a warped mind
leads to contempt.
⁹ Better to be held in low regard
and have a servant
than to be conceited and lack food.
¹⁰ The righteous care about
their livestock's needs,
but even the compassion
of the wicked is cruel.
¹¹ Those who work their land
will have plenty to eat,
but those who engage
in empty pursuits have no sense.
¹² Desiring evil is a trap for the wicked,
but the root
of the righteous endures.[n]
¹³ The wicked are trapped
by the transgressions of their lips,
but the righteous escape
from distress.
¹⁴ From the fruit of their speech,
people are well satisfied;
their work results in reward.
¹⁵ Fools see their own way as right,
but the wise listen to advice.
¹⁶ Fools reveal their anger right away,
but the shrewd
hide their contempt.

---

[l]Or *the heads of those* [m]Or LXX, Syr *violence takes lives away* [n]Or *gives*

¹⁷ Those who state the truth
speak justly,
but a false witness deceives.
¹⁸ Some chatter on
like a stabbing sword,
but a wise tongue heals.
¹⁹ Truthful lips endure forever,
but a lying tongue
lasts only for a moment.
²⁰ Deceit is in the heart
of those who plan evil,
but there is joy
for those who advise peace.
²¹ No harm happens to the righteous,
but the wicked receive
their fill of trouble.
²² The LORD detests false lips;
he favors those who do what is true.
²³ The shrewd conceal their knowledge,
but the heart of fools
proclaims their stupidity.
²⁴ A hard worker is in charge,
while a lazy one will be sentenced
to hard labor.
²⁵ Anxiety leads to depression,
but a good word encourages.
²⁶ The righteous offer guidance
to their neighbors,ᵒ
but the path of the wicked
makes them wander.
²⁷ The lazy don't roastᵖ their prey,
but hard workers receive
precious riches.
²⁸ The way of the righteous
leads to life,
but the detestable�q path
leads to death.

13 A wise son listens toʳ
the discipline of his father,
but a mocker doesn't listen
to correction.

² People eat well from the fruit
of their words,
but the treacherous have
an appetite only for violence.
³ People who watch their mouths
guard their lives,
but those who open their lips
are ruined.
⁴ The lazy have strong desires
but receive nothing;
the appetite of the diligent
is satisfied.
⁵ The righteous hate false words,
but the wicked create
disgust and scorn.
⁶ Righteousness guards the innocent
on the path,
but wickedness misleads sinners.
⁷ Some pretend to be rich
but have nothing,
while others pretend to be poor,
but have great riches.
⁸ Wealth can ransom a person's life,
but the poor don't even
receive threats.
⁹ The light of the righteous rejoices,
but the lamp of the wicked
goes out.
¹⁰ The empty-headed cause conflict
out of pride;
those who take advice are wise.
¹¹ Riches gotten quicklyˢ will dwindle,
but those who acquire them
gradually become wealthy.
¹² Hope delayed makes the heart sick;
longing fulfilled is a tree of life.
¹³ Trouble will come on those
who despise a word,
but those who respect
the commandment
will be rewarded.

ᵒHeb uncertain ᵖHeb uncertain qLXX; MT *the path of the trail* ʳHeb lacks *listens to.* ˢLXX;
MT *from meaninglessness*

¹⁴ The teaching of the wise
   is a fountain of life,
   turning a person away
   from deathtraps.
¹⁵ Good insight brings favor,
   but the way of the faithless
   is their ruin.ᵗ
¹⁶ The prudent all act intelligently,
   but fools display their stupidity.
¹⁷ Wicked messengers fall
   into trouble,
   but a reliable one
   brings healing.
¹⁸ Poverty and shame come to those
   who don't care about instruction;
   honor belongs to those
   who heed correction.
¹⁹ A desire fulfilled is pleasant,
   but fools find deviating
   from evil disgusting.
²⁰ Walk with wise people
   and become wise;
   befriend fools and get in trouble.
²¹ Trouble pursues sinners,
   but good things reward
   the righteous.
²² Good people leave their
   grandchildren an inheritance,
   but the wealth of sinners
   is stored up for the righteous.
²³ A poor person's land
   might produce much food,
   but it is unjustly swept away.
²⁴ Those who withhold the rod
   hate their children,
   but the one who loves them
   applies discipline.
²⁵ The righteous eat their fill,
   but the wicked
   have empty stomachs.

14 A wise woman builds her house,
while a foolish woman

tears hers down
   with her own hands.
² Those who walk with integrity
   fear the LORD,
   but those who take a crooked path
   despise him.
³ Pride sprouts in the mouth of a fool,ᵘ
   but the lips of the wise protect them.
⁴ When there are no oxen,
   the stall is clean,
   but when there is a strong bull,
   there is abundant produce.
⁵ A truthful witness doesn't lie,
   but a false witness spews lies.
⁶ A mocker searches for wisdom
   and gets none,
   but knowledge comes quickly
   to the intelligent.
⁷ Stay away from fools,
   for you won't learn
   wise speech there.
⁸ By their wisdom the prudent
   understand their way,
   but the stupidity of fools
   deceives them.
⁹ Fools mock a compensation offering,
   but favor is with those who do right.
¹⁰ The heart knows its own distress;
   another person can't share its joy.
¹¹ The house of the wicked is destroyed,
   but the tent flourishes
   for those who do right.
¹² There is a path that may seem straight
   to someone,
   but in the end it is a path to death.
¹³ The heart feels pain even in laughter,
   and in the end, joy turns to sorrow.
¹⁴ Rebellious hearts receive satisfaction
   from their ways;
   the good receive the due reward
   for their deeds.
¹⁵ The naive believe anything,

ᵗLXX, Syr, Vulg; MT *endures*   ᵘHeb uncertain

but the prudent give thought
  to their steps.
16 The wise are careful and avoid evil,
  but fools become excited
  and overconfident.
17 Short-tempered people
  make stupid mistakes,
  and schemers are hated.
18 Stupidity is the lot of the naive,
  but the prudent are crowned
  with knowledge.
19 Evil people will bow down
  before the good;
  wicked people are at the gates
  of the righteous.
20 Even their neighbors hate the poor,
  but many love the wealthy.
21 Those who despise their neighbors
  are sinners,
  but happy are those
  who are kind to the needy.
22 Don't those who plan evil go astray?
  Those who plan good
  receive loyalty and faithfulness.
23 There is profit in hard work,
  but mere talk leads to poverty.
24 Wealth is the crown of the wise,
  and the folly of fools is folly.
25 A truthful witness saves lives,
  but a deceiver proclaims lies.
26 In the fear of the LORD
  is strong confidence
  and refuge for one's children.
27 The fear of the LORD is a fountain
  of life,
  turning people away
  from deathtraps.
28 A king's glory is a large population,
  but a dwindling people
  is a ruler's ruin.
29 Patience leads to
  abundant understanding,

but impatience leads to
  stupid mistakes.
30 A peaceful mind gives life
  to the body,
  but jealousy rots the bones.
31 Those who exploit the powerless
  anger their maker,
  while those who are kind
  to the poor honor God.
32 The wicked are thrown down
  by their own evil,
  but the righteous find refuge
  even in death.
33 Wisdom resides
  in an understanding heart,
  but it's not[v] known in fools.
34 Righteousness dignifies a nation,
  but sin disgraces a people.
35 The king favors
  an insightful servant,
  but is furious at a shameful one.

15 A sensitive answer
  turns back wrath,
  but an offensive word
  stirs up anger.
2 The tongue of the wise
  enhances knowledge,
  but the mouth of a fool
  gushes with stupidity.
3 The LORD's eyes are everywhere,
  keeping watch on
  evil and good people.
4 Wholesome speech is a tree of life,
  but dishonest talk
  breaks the spirit.
5 A fool doesn't like
  a father's instruction,
  but those who heed correction
  are mature.
6 Great treasure is in the house
  of the righteous,
  but the gain of the wicked
  brings trouble.

vLXX; MT lacks not.

⁷The lips of the wise
  spread knowledge,
  but the hearts of fools have none.
⁸The LORD detests the sacrifices
    of the wicked,
  but favors the prayers
    of those who do right.
⁹The LORD detests the path
    of the wicked,
  but loves those
    who pursue righteousness.
¹⁰Discipline is severe for those
    who abandon the way;
  those who hate correction will die.
¹¹The grave^w and the underworld^x
    lie open before the LORD;
  how much more the hearts
    of human beings!
¹²Mockers don't like those
    who correct them.
  They won't go to the wise.
¹³A joyful heart brightens one's face,
  but a troubled heart
    breaks the spirit.
¹⁴An understanding heart
    seeks knowledge;
  but fools feed on folly.
¹⁵All the days of the needy are hard,
  but a happy heart
    has a continual feast.
¹⁶Better a little with fear of the LORD
  than a great treasure with turmoil.
¹⁷Better a meal of greens with love
  than a plump calf with hate.
¹⁸Hotheads stir up conflict,
  but patient people
    calm down strife.
¹⁹The path of the lazy
    is like a hedge of thorns,
  but the way of those who do right
    is a clear road.
²⁰A wise child brings joy to a father,

but fools despise their mothers.
²¹Folly is joy to those who lack sense,
  but those with understanding
    walk straight ahead.
²²Plans fail with no counsel,
  but with many counselors
    they succeed.
²³To give an appropriate answer
    is a joy;
  how good is a word
    at the right time!
²⁴For those with insight,
    life is an upward path,
  avoiding the grave^y below.
²⁵The LORD snatches away
    the arrogant one's house,
  but he preserves
    the widow's boundaries.
²⁶The LORD detests evil plans,
  but gracious words are pure.
²⁷Those who acquire things unjustly
    gain trouble for their house,
  but those who hate bribes will live.
²⁸The righteous heart reflects
    before answering,
  but the wicked mouth
    blurts out evil.
²⁹The LORD is far from the wicked,
  but he listens to the prayers
    of the righteous.
³⁰Bright eyes give joy to the heart;
  good news strengthens the bones.
³¹The ear that listens
    to life-giving correction
  dwells among the wise.
³²Those who refuse discipline
    despise themselves,
  but those who listen to correction
    gain understanding.
³³The fear of the LORD
    is wise instruction,
  and humility comes before respect.

^wHeb Sheol ^xHeb Abaddon ^yHeb Sheol

16 To people belong the plans
of the heart,
but the answer of the tongue
comes from the LORD.

² All the ways of people
are pure in their eyes,
but the LORD tests the motives.

³ Commit your work to the LORD,
and your plans will succeed.

⁴ The LORD made everything
for a purpose,
even the wicked for an evil day.

⁵ The LORD detests all
who are arrogant;
they surely won't go unpunished.

⁶ Love and faithfulness reconcile guilt;
the fear of the LORD
turns away evil.

⁷ When people draw favor
from the LORD,
even their enemies are at peace
with them.

⁸ Better a little with righteousness
than great profits without justice.

⁹ People plan their path,
but the LORD secures their steps.

¹⁰ A king's speech is like an oracle;
in a judgment,
one can't go against his words.

¹¹ Honest balances and scales
are the LORD's;
all the weights in the bag
are his doing.

¹² Kings detest wicked deeds,
for their thrones are founded
on righteousness.

¹³ Kings favor those with righteous lips;
they love words of integrity.

¹⁴ The king's anger is a messenger
of death;
the wise will calm him.

¹⁵ There's life in the light
of the king's face.
His favor is like a cloud
that brings spring rain.

¹⁶ Acquiring wisdom
is much better than gold,
and acquiring understanding
is better than silver.

¹⁷ The road of those who do right
turns away from evil;
those who protect their path
guard their lives.

¹⁸ Pride comes before disaster,
and arrogance before a fall.

¹⁹ Better to be humble with the needy
than to divide plunder
with the proud.

²⁰ Those with insight find prosperity;
those who trust the LORD
are blessed.

²¹ The skilled mind
is called discerning,
and pleasant speech
enhances teaching.

²² One who has insight
is a fountain of life,
but the instruction of the foolish
is folly.

²³ The mind of the wise
makes their speech insightful
and enhances the teaching
of their lips.

²⁴ Pleasant words are flowing honey,
sweet to the taste
and healing to the bones.

²⁵ There is a path that may seem straight
to someone,
but in the end it is the path of death.

²⁶ The appetite of workers labors
for them,
for their hunger presses them on.

²⁷ Worthless people dig up trouble;
their lips are like a scorching fire.

²⁸ Destructive people produce conflict;
gossips alienate close friends.

²⁹ Violent people entice their neighbors
and walk them down a path
that isn't good.

³⁰ Those who wink their eye
plot destruction;
those who purse their lips plan evil.
³¹ Gray hair is a crown of glory;
it is found on the path
of righteousness.
³² Better to be patient than a warrior,
and better to have self-control
than to capture a city.
³³ The dice are cast into the lap;
all decisions are from the LORD.

17 Better a dry crust with quiet
than a house full of feasting
with quarrels.
² An insightful servant rules
over a disgraceful son
and will divide an inheritance
with the brothers.
³ A crucible is for silver
and a furnace for gold,
but the LORD tests the heart.
⁴ An evildoer pays attention
to guilty lips;
a liar listens
to a destructive tongue.
⁵ Those who mock the poor
insult their maker;
those who rejoice in disaster
won't go unpunished.
⁶ Grandchildren are the crown
of the elderly,
and the glory of children
is their parents.
⁷ Too much talking isn't right
for a fool;
even less so false speech
for an honorable person.
⁸ A bribe seems magical in the eyes
of those who give it,
granting success to all who use it.
⁹ One who seeks love
conceals an offense,
but one who repeats it
divides friends.

¹⁰ A rebuke goes deeper
to an understanding person
than a hundred lashes to a fool.
¹¹ Evil people seek only rebellion;
a cruel messenger
will be sent against them.
¹² Safer to meet a bear robbed
of her cubs
than fools in their folly.
¹³ Evil will never depart
from the house
of those who return evil for good.
¹⁴ The start of a quarrel is like
letting out water,
so drop the dispute
before it breaks out.
¹⁵ Judging the righteous wicked
and the wicked righteous—
the LORD detests both of these.
¹⁶ Why should a fool have money
to pay for wisdom?
He has no mind.
¹⁷ Friends love all the time,
and kinsfolk are born
for times of trouble.
¹⁸ One with no sense shakes hands
on a deal,
securing a loan for a friend.
¹⁹ Those who love an offense
love a quarrel;
those who build a high doorway
invite a collapse.
²⁰ Those with crooked hearts
won't prosper,
and those with twisted tongues
will fall into trouble.
²¹ Having a fool for a son brings grief;
there's no joy
for a scoundrel's father.
²² A joyful heart helps healing,
but a broken spirit
dries up the bones.
²³ The wicked take secret bribes
to twist the way of justice.

²⁴ Wisdom is right in front of those
     with understanding,
     but the eyes of fools
     are off to the edges of the earth.
²⁵ A foolish son is irritating
     to his father
     and bitter to her
     who gave birth to him.
²⁶ It isn't good to punish the righteous,
     to strike the honorable
     for their integrity.
²⁷ Wise are those who restrain
     their talking;
     people with understanding
     are coolheaded.
²⁸ Fools who keep quiet
     are deemed wise;
     those who shut their lips are smart.

18 Unfriendly people look out
     for themselves;
     they bicker with sensible people.
² Fools find no pleasure
     in understanding,
     but only in expressing
     their opinion.
³ When the wicked arrive,
     so does contempt;
     with shame comes insult.
⁴ The words of a person's mouth
     are deep waters,
     a bubbling stream,
     a fountain of wisdom.
⁵ Favoring the wicked isn't good;
     it denies justice to the righteous.
⁶ The lips of fools make accusations;
     their mouths elicit beatings.
⁷ The mouth of fools is their ruin;
     their lips are a trap for their lives.
⁸ The words of gossips
     are like choice snacks;
     they go down to the inmost parts.
⁹ Those who are lazy in their work
     are brothers to thugs.
¹⁰ The LORD's name is a strong tower;

the righteous run to it
     and find refuge.
¹¹ The riches of the wealthy
     are a strong city
     and like a high wall
     in their imagination.
¹² Pride comes before a disaster,
     but humility comes before respect.
¹³ Those who answer before they listen
     are foolish and disgraceful.
¹⁴ The human spirit sustains
     a sick person,
     but who can bear a broken spirit?
¹⁵ An understanding mind
     gains knowledge;
     the ear of the wise
     seeks knowledge.
¹⁶ A gift opens the way
     for access to important people.
¹⁷ The first person to testify
     seems innocent,
     until the other comes
     and cross-examines him.
¹⁸ The dice settle conflicts
     and keep strong opponents apart.
¹⁹ An offended ally
     is more formidable than a city;
     such quarreling
     is like the bars of a castle.
²⁰ The stomach is satisfied
     by the fruit of the mouth;
     one's lips can earn
     a satisfying income.
²¹ Death and life
     are in the power of the tongue;
     those who love it will eat its fruit.
²² He who finds a wife
     finds what is good,
     gaining favor from the LORD.
²³ The poor plead for help,
     but the wealthy answer harshly.
²⁴ There are persons for companionship,
     but then there are friends
     who are more loyal than family.

19

Better to be poor
and walk in innocence
than to have dishonest lips
and be a fool.

[2] Ignorant desire isn't good;
rushing feet make mistakes.

[3] People's own folly corrupts their way,
but their hearts rage
against the LORD.

[4] Riches increase one's friends,
but the poor lose their friends.

[5] A false witness won't go unpunished,
and a liar won't escape.

[6] Many seek favor from rulers;
everyone befriends a gift giver.

[7] All the relatives of the poor
hate them;
even more, their friends
stay far from them.
When they pursue them
with words, they aren't there.

[8] Those who acquire good sense
love themselves;
those who keep understanding
find success.

[9] False witnesses won't go unpunished,
and liars will perish.

[10] Luxury isn't fitting for a fool;
even less so for a servant
to rule over princes.

[11] Insightful people restrain their anger;
their glory is to ignore an offense.

[12] A raging king roars like a lion;
his favor is like the dew
on the grass.

[13] A foolish son is a disaster
to his father;
a contentious wife
is like constant dripping.

[14] House and riches are an inheritance
from one's ancestors,
but an insightful wife
is from the LORD.

[15] Laziness brings on deep sleep;

a slacker goes hungry.

[16] Those who keep the commandment
preserve their lives;
those who disregard their ways
will die.

[17] Those who are gracious to the poor
lend to the LORD,
and the Lord will fully repay them.

[18] Discipline your children while there
is hope,
but don't plan to kill them.

[19] Angry people must pay the penalty;
if you rescue them,
then you will have to do it again.

[20] Listen to advice
and accept instruction,
so you might grow wise
in the future.

[21] Many plans are in a person's mind,
but the LORD's purpose
will succeed.

[22] People long for trustworthiness;
it is better to be poor than a liar.

[23] The fear of the LORD leads to life;
then one rests content,
untouched by harm.

[24] Lazy people bury their hand
in the bowl;
they won't even
put it to their mouth.

[25] Strike someone who scoffs,
and a naive person
will become clever;
correct someone
with understanding,
and they will gain knowledge.

[26] Those who assault their father
and drive out their mother
are disgraceful children,
worthy of reproach.

[27] If, my child, you stop listening
to discipline,
you will wander away from words
of knowledge.

²⁸ A worthless witness mocks justice;
  the wicked mouth
    gulps down trouble.
²⁹ Punishments were made for mockers,
  and blows for the backs of fools.

20 Wine is a mocker;
    beer a carouser.
  Those it leads astray
    won't become wise.
² A king is as terrifying
  as a lion's growl.
  Those who anger him
    may lose their life.
³ It is honorable to back off
  from a fight,
  but fools jump right in.
⁴ The lazy don't plow during winter;
  at harvest they look
    but find nothing.
⁵ Advice comes from the deep waters
  of the heart;
  those with understanding
    can draw it out.
⁶ Many people will say
  that they are loyal,
  but who can find a reliable person?
⁷ The righteous live with integrity;
  happy are their children
    who come after them.
⁸ A king who sits
  on his judgment throne
  sifts out all evil with his eyes.
⁹ Who can say,
  "I'm innocent to the core;
  I'm cleansed from my sin"?
¹⁰ False weights and measures—
  the LORD detests them both.
¹¹ Even young people are known
  by their actions,
  whether their conduct is pure
    and upright.
¹² Ears to hear and eyes to see—
  the LORD made them both.
¹³ Don't love sleep or you will be poor;

stay alert and you will have
    plenty to eat.
¹⁴ The buyer says, "Bad, bad,"
  but then goes away and brags.
¹⁵ Much gold and many pearls exist,
  but wise speech
    is the most precious jewel.
¹⁶ Take the garment of the person
  who secures a loan for a stranger;
  take his pledge for a foreigner.
¹⁷ Stolen bread is sweet,
  but afterward the mouth is full
    of gravel.
¹⁸ Plans are firmed up by advice;
  wage wars with good guidance.
¹⁹ Gossips reveal secrets;
  don't associate with those
    who talk too much.
²⁰ Those who curse
  their father or mother—
  their lamp will be snuffed out
    when it becomes dark.
²¹ Inheritance gained quickly at first
  won't bless later on.
²² Don't say, "I'll repay the evildoer!"
  Wait for the LORD,
  and he will save you.
²³ The LORD detests false weights;
  deceptive scales aren't right.
²⁴ A person's steps are from the LORD;
  how then can people understand
    their path?
²⁵ It is a snare to say rashly, "It is holy,"
  and only reflect
    after making the promise.
²⁶ A wise king sifts out the wicked,
  and runs them over with a wheel.
²⁷ The breath of a person
  is the lamp of the LORD,
  searching all the inmost parts.
²⁸ Kindness and faithfulness
  protect the king;
  he supports his throne
    by kindness.

²⁹ Strength is the glory of young men;
  gray hair is the splendor of old age.

³⁰ Blows and bruises remove evil;
  beatings cleanse the inner parts.

21 The king's heart is like channels of
  water in the hand of the LORD;
  he directs it wherever he wants.

² Everyone's path is straight
  in their own eyes,
  but the LORD weighs the heart.

³ Acting with righteousness
  and justice
  is more valued by the LORD
  than sacrifice.

⁴ Prideful eyes, an arrogant heart, and
  the lamp of the wicked
  are all sinful.

⁵ The plans of the diligent
  end up in profit,
  but those who hurry
  end up with loss.

⁶ Those who gain treasure with lies
  are like a drifting fog,
  leading to death.

⁷ The violence of the wicked
  will sweep them away,
  for they refuse to act with justice.

⁸ The ways of some people
  are twisted and strange,
  but the behavior of those
  who do right is pure.

⁹ Better to live on the edge of a roof
  than with a contentious woman
  in a large house.

¹⁰ Wicked people desire evil;
  their neighbors receive
  no mercy from them.

¹¹ When a mocker is punished,
  the naive person gains wisdom;
  when insight comes to the wise,
  knowledge increases.

¹² The righteous one observes
  the house of the wicked,
  turning the wicked toward trouble.

¹³ Those who close their ears
  to the cries of the poor
  will themselves call out
  but receive no answer.

¹⁴ A secret gift calms anger,
  and a hidden bribe
  removes² furious wrath.

¹⁵ Acting justly is a joy to the righteous,
  but dreaded by those who do evil.

¹⁶ People who wander
  from the path of insight
  will rest in the company of the dead.

¹⁷ Those who love pleasure end up poor;
  lovers of wine and oil
  won't get rich.

¹⁸ The wicked are a ransom
  for the righteous;
  the treacherous will be punishedᵃ
  in the place of the virtuous.

¹⁹ Better to live in a wilderness
  than in a house with a contentious
  and angry woman.

²⁰ Precious treasure and oil
  stay in the home of the wise,
  but fools swallow them up.

²¹ Those who pursue righteousness
  and kindness
  will find life, righteousness,
  and honor.

²² A wise person fought
  a city of warriors
  and brought down the stronghold
  in which they felt safe.

²³ Those who guard their mouths
  and their tongues
  guard themselves from trouble.

²⁴ Incredibly proud—
  mockers are their name!
  Their conduct involves
  excessive pride.

²⁵ The desires of the lazy will kill them,

²Heb lacks *removes*. ªHeb lacks *will be punished*.

because their hands refuse
to do anything.
26 The lazy desire things constantly,
but the righteous give
without holding back.
27 The LORD detests
the sacrifices of the wicked,
especially when brought
with devious motives.
28 A lying witness will perish,
but one who listens
will testify successfully.
29 The wicked person appears brash,
but the virtuous
think about the path ahead.
30 No wisdom, understanding,
or advice
can stand up against the LORD.
31 A horse is made ready
for the day of battle,
but victory belongs to the LORD.

22 A good reputation
is better than much wealth;
high esteem
is better than silver and gold.
2 The rich and the poor
have this in common:
the LORD made them both.
3 Prudent people see trouble and hide,
while the simpleminded
go right to it and get punished.
4 The reward of humility
and the fear of the LORD
is wealth, honor, and life.
5 Thorns and nets are in the path
of the crooked;
those who guard their lives
keep their distance.
6 Train children in the way
they should go;
when they grow old,
they won't depart from it.
7 The wealthy rule over the poor;

a borrower is a slave to a lender.
8 Those who sow injustice
will harvest evil;
the rod of their fury
will come to an end.
9 Happy are generous people,
because they give some of their food
to the poor.
10 Remove the mocker
and conflict disappears;
judgment and shame also stop.
11 Those who love a pure heart—
their speech is gracious,
and the king is their friend.
12 The LORD's eyes protect knowledge,
but he frustrates the words
of the treacherous.
13 A lazy person says,
"There's a lion in the street!
I'll be killed in the town square!"
14 The mouth of a mysterious woman
is a deep pit;
those under the LORD's wrath
will fall in it.
15 Folly is bound up in a child's heart;
the rod of discipline removes it.
16 Oppressing the poor to get rich
and giving to the wealthy
lead only to poverty.

Thirty sayings of the wise

17 Turn your ear
and hear the words of the wise;
focus your mind on my knowledge.
18 It will be pleasant
if you keep the words in you,
if you have them ready
on your lips.
19 So that your trust will be in the LORD,
I'm teaching you today—yes, you.
20 Haven't I written for you
thirty[b] sayings
full of advice and knowledge?

[b] Heb uncertain

^{21}Their purpose is to teach you true,
   reliable words,
   so you can report back reliably
      to those who sent you.

^{22}Don't steal from the poor,
   because they are poor.
   Don't oppress the needy
      in the gate.
^{23}The LORD will take up their case
   and press the life out of those
      who oppress them.^{c}

^{24}Don't befriend people
   controlled by anger;
   don't associate with
      hot-tempered people;
^{25}otherwise, you will learn their ways
   and become trapped.

^{26}Don't shake hands
   to guarantee a loan.
^{27}If you can't repay,
   why should they be able
      to take your bed from you?

^{28}Don't remove
   an ancient boundary marker
   that your ancestors established.

^{29}Do you see people
   who work skillfully?
   They will work for kings
      but not work for lowly people.

23   When you sit down
      to dine with a ruler,
   carefully consider what is
      in front of you.
^{2}Place a knife at your throat
   to control your appetite.
^{3}Don't long for the ruler's delicacies;
   the food misleads.

^{4}Don't wear yourself out
   trying to get rich;
   be smart enough to stop.
^{5}When your eyes fly to wealth
   it is gone; it grows wings
   like an eagle and flies heavenward.

^{6}Don't eat food with stingy people;
   don't long for their delicacies,
^{7}because they are like a hair
   in the throat.^{d}
   They say to you, "Eat and drink!"
      but they don't mean it.
^{8}You will eat scraps
   and vomit them out.
   You will waste your pleasant words.
^{9}Don't speak in the ears of fools,
   for they will scorn
      your insightful words.

^{10}Don't remove an ancient
   boundary marker;
   don't invade the fields of orphans,
^{11}for their redeemer is strong.
   He will bring charges against you.

^{12}Bring your mind to instruction,
   your ear to knowledgeable sayings.

^{13}Don't withhold instruction
   from children;
   if you strike them with a rod,
      they won't die.
^{14}Strike them with a rod,
   and you will save their lives
      from the grave.^{e}

^{15}My child, if your heart is wise,
   then my heart too will be happy.
^{16}My inner being will rejoice
   when your lips speak
      with integrity.

---

^{c}Heb uncertain ^{d}LXX; Heb uncertain ^{e}Heb *Sheol*

¹⁷ Don't let your heart envy sinners,
    but fear the LORD constantly;
¹⁸ then you will have a future,
    and your hope won't be cut off.

¹⁹ Listen, my child, and be wise!
    Keep your mind straight
      on the path.
²⁰ Don't hang out with those
    who get drunk on wine
    or those who eat too much meat,
²¹ because drunks and gluttons
    will be impoverished;
    their stupor will clothe them in rags.

²² Listen to your father,
    who gave you life;
    don't despise your elderly mother.
²³ Buy truth and don't sell it;
    buy wisdom, instruction,
    and understanding.
²⁴ The father of the righteous
    will be very happy;
    the one who gives life to the wise
      will rejoice.
²⁵ Your father and your mother
    will rejoice;
    she who gave you birth
      will be happy.

²⁶ My child, give your mind to me
    and let your eyes keep to my path.
²⁷ A prostitute is a deep pit,
    and a foreign woman
      is a narrow well.
²⁸ Indeed, she ambushes like a robber
    and increases the number
      of the faithless.

²⁹ Who is suffering?
    Who is uneasy?
    Who has arguments?

Who has complaints?
    Who has unnecessary wounds?
    Who has glazed eyes?—
³⁰ those who linger over wine;
    those who go looking
      for mixed wine.
³¹ Don't look at wine when it is red,
    when it sparkles in the cup,
    going down smoothly.
³² In the end, it bites like a snake
    and poisons like a viper.
³³ Your eyes will see strange things,
    and your heart will speak
      distorted words.
³⁴ You will be like one who lies down
    while out on the sea[f]
    or one who lies on top of a mast.
³⁵ "Though hit, I feel no pain;
    though beaten up,
      I don't know anything about it.
    When I wake up,
      I'll look for wine again!"

24 Don't envy evil people,
    and don't long to be with them.
² Their hearts are focused
    on violence,
    and their lips speak of trouble.

³ By wisdom a house is built;
    by understanding it is established.
⁴ By knowledge rooms are filled
    with all precious
      and pleasant wealth.

⁵ A wise person is mightier
    than a strong one;[g]
    a knowledgeable person
    than a powerful one.
⁶ You should make war with guidance;
    victory comes
      with many counselors.

---

[f] Or *in the heart of the sea*   [g] LXX; MT *A wise man is strong.*

7 Wisdom is beyond foolish people.
  They don't open their mouths
    in the gate.
8 Those who plot evil
  will be called master schemers.
9 The scheming of fools is sin;
  people detest mockers.

10 If you show yourself weak
   on a day of distress,
   your strength is too small.
11 Rescue those being taken off
   to death;
   and from those staggering
     to the slaughter, don't hold back.
12 If you say,
   "Look, we didn't know about it,"
   the one who weighs hearts—
     doesn't he understand?
   The one who protects your life—
     he knows.
   He makes people pay
     for their actions.

13 My child, eat honey, for it is good.
   The honeycomb is sweet
     in your mouth.
14 Know that wisdom is like that
   for your whole being.
   If you find it, there is a future.
   Your hope won't be cut off.

15 Wicked one, don't wait secretly
   at the home of the righteous.
   Don't destroy their dwelling.
16 The righteous may fall seven times
   but still get up,
   but the wicked will stumble
     into trouble.

17 When your enemies fall, don't rejoice.
   When they stumble,
     don't let your heart be glad,
18 or the LORD will see it
   and be displeased,

and he will turn his anger
  from them.

19 Don't get fighting mad at evil people;
   don't be envious of the wicked.
20 Indeed, there is no future for the evil;
   the lamp of the wicked
     will be put out.

21 Fear the LORD, my child,
   as well as the king.
   Don't associate with those
     who are rebellious.
22 Disaster comes suddenly from them.
   Who can know the ruin
     that both can bring?

More sayings of the wise

23 These are also the sayings
   of the wise:

   Partiality in judgment isn't good.

24 Those who say to the guilty,
   "You are innocent"—
   the people will curse them.
   Nations will condemn them.
25 But it will go well for those
   who rebuke them.
   A rich blessing will come to them.
26 Those who speak honestly
   are like those who kiss on the lips.

27 Get your outside work done;
   make preparations in the field;
   then you can build your house.

28 Don't be a witness against
   your neighbor without reason;
   don't deceive with your lips.
29 Don't say, "I'll do to them
   what they did to me.
   I'll pay them back
     for their actions."

³⁰ I happened upon the field
    of a lazy person,
    by the vineyard of one
        with no sense.
³¹ Thorns grew all over it;
    weeds covered the ground,
    and the stone wall
        was falling down.
³² I observed this and took it to heart;
    I saw it and learned a lesson.
³³ "A little sleep, a little slumber,
    a little lying down
        with folded arms"—
³⁴ and poverty will come on you
    like a prowler,
    deprivation like a man
        with a shield.

More proverbs of Solomon

25 These are also proverbs of Solomon, copied by the men of Hezekiah, king of Judah:

² It is the glory of God
    to hide something
    and the glory of kings
        to discover something.
³ Like the high heavens
    and the depths of the earth,
    so the mind of a king
        is unsearchable.

⁴ Remove the dross from the silver,
    and a vessel will come out
        for the refiner.
⁵ Remove the wicked
    from the king's presence,
    and his throne will be established
        in righteousness.

⁶ Don't exalt yourself
    in the presence of the king,
    or stand in the place
        of important people,

⁷ because it is better
    that he say to you,
    "Come up here,"
    than to be demoted before a ruler.

What your eyes see,
⁸ don't be quick to quarrel over;
    what will you do in the future
    when your neighbor
        shames you?
⁹ Argue it out with your neighbor,
    and don't give away
        someone's secret.
¹⁰ Otherwise, the one who hears it
    will vilify you;
    the slander against you
        will never stop.

¹¹ Words spoken at the right time
    are like gold apples
        in a silver setting.
¹² Wise correction
    to an ear that listens
    is like a gold earring
        or jewelry of fine gold.

¹³ Like the coolness of snow
    on a harvest day
    are reliable messengers to those
        who send them;
    they restore the life
        of their master.
¹⁴ People who brag
    about a gift never given
    are like clouds and wind
        that produce no rain.
¹⁵ A commander can be persuaded
    with patience,
    and a tender tongue
        can break a bone.
¹⁶ If you find honey,
    eat just the right amount;
    otherwise, you'll get full
        and vomit it up.

¹⁷ Don't spend too much time
in your neighbor's house.
Otherwise, they'll get fed up
with you and hate you.

¹⁸ People who testify falsely
against their neighbors
are like a club, sword,
and sharpened arrow.

¹⁹ Trusting a treacherous person
at a difficult time
is like having a bad tooth
or a wobbly foot.

²⁰ Singing a song to a troubled heart
is like taking off a garment
on a cold day
or putting vinegar on a wound.^h

²¹ If your enemies are starving,
feed them some bread;
if they are thirsty,
give them water to drink.

²² By doing this, you will heap
burning coals on their heads,
and the LORD will reward you.

²³ The north wind stirs up rain,
and a person who plots quietly
provokes angry faces.

²⁴ Better to live on the edge of a roof
than to share a house
with a contentious woman.

²⁵ Good news from a distant land
is like cold water
for a weary person.

²⁶ A righteous person giving in
to the wicked
is like a contaminated spring
or a polluted fountain.

²⁷ Eating too much honey isn't good,
nor is it appropriate
to seek honor.

²⁸ A person without self-control
is like a breached city,
one with no walls.

26

Like snow in the summer
or rain at harvest,
so honor isn't appropriate
for a fool.

² Like a darting sparrow,
like a flying swallow,
so an undeserved curse
never arrives.

³ A whip for a horse,
a bridle for a donkey,
and a rod for the back of fools.

⁴ Don't answer fools
according to their folly,
or you will become
like them yourself.

⁵ Answer fools according to their folly,
or they will deem themselves wise.

⁶ Sending messages with a fool
is like cutting off one's feet
or drinking down violence.

⁷ As legs dangle
from a disabled person,
so does a proverb
in the mouth of fools.

⁸ Like tying a stone in a sling,
so is giving respect to a fool.

⁹ Like a thorny bush in the hand
of a drunk,
so is a proverb in the mouth of fools.

¹⁰ Like an archer who wounds
someone randomly,
so is one who hires a fool
or a passerby.

¹¹ Like a dog that returns to its vomit,
so a fool repeats foolish mistakes.

¹² Do you see people
who consider themselves wise?
There is more hope for a fool
than for them.

¹³ A lazy person says,
"There's a lion in the path!
A lion in the plazas!"

^hLXX; MT *vinegar on natron* (a detergent)

¹⁴ As a door turns on its hinge,
     so do lazy people in their beds.
¹⁵ Lazy people bury their hand
     into the bowl,
         too tired to return it to their mouth.
¹⁶ Lazy people think they are wiser
     than seven people
         who answer sensibly.

¹⁷ Like yanking the ears of a dog,
     so is one who passes by
         and gets involved in
         another person's fight.
¹⁸ Like a crazy person shooting
     deadly flaming arrows
         ¹⁹ are those who deceive their neighbor
         and say, "Hey, I was only joking!"
²⁰ Without wood a fire goes out;
     without gossips,
         conflict calms down.
²¹ Like adding charcoal to embers
     or wood to fire,
         quarrelsome people kindle strife.
²² The words of gossips
     are like choice snacks;
         they go down to the inmost parts.
²³ Smooth[i] lips and an evil heart
     are like silver coating on clay.
²⁴ Hateful people mislead
     with their lips,
         keeping their deception within.
²⁵ Though they speak graciously,
     don't believe them,
         for seven horrible things
         are in their heart.
²⁶ They may cover their hatred
     with trickery,
         but their evil will be revealed
         in public.
²⁷ Those who dig a pit will fall in it;
     those who roll a stone
         will have it turn back on them.

²⁸ A lying tongue hates those it crushes;
     a flattering mouth
         causes destruction.

27

Don't brag about tomorrow,
     for you don't know
         what a day will bring.
² Let another person praise you,
     and not your own mouth;
         a stranger, and not your own lips.
³ A stone is heavy
     and sand weighs much,
         but the nuisance of fools
         is heavier than both.
⁴ Wrath is cruel and anger is a flood,
     but who can withstand jealousy?
⁵ A public correction
     is better than hidden love.
⁶ Trustworthy are the bruises
     of a friend;
         excessive are the kisses
         of an enemy.
⁷ Someone who is full refuses honey,
     but anything bitter
         tastes sweet to a hungry person.
⁸ Like a bird wandering from its nest,
     so is one who wanders from home.
⁹ Oil and incense make the heart glad,
     and the sweetness of friends
         comes from their advice.[j]
¹⁰ Don't desert your friend
     or a friend of your family;
         don't go to your relative's house
         when disaster strikes.
     Better a neighbor nearby
         than a relative far away.
¹¹ Be wise, my child,
     and make my heart glad,
         so I can answer those who insult me.
¹² Prudent people see evil and hide;
     the simpleminded go right to it
         and get punished.

---

[i] LXX; Heb uncertain   [j] Heb uncertain

¹³ Take the garment of the person
   who secures a loan for a stranger;
   take his pledge for a foreigner.
¹⁴ Greeting a neighbor
   with a loud voice
   early in the morning
   will be viewed as a curse.
¹⁵ The constant dripping on a rainy day
   and a contentious woman are alike;
   ¹⁶ anyone who can control her
   can control the wind
   or pick up oil in his hand.
¹⁷ As iron sharpens iron,
   so one person sharpens
   a friend.
¹⁸ Those who tend a fig tree
   will eat its fruit,
   and those who look after
   their master will be honored.
¹⁹ As water reflects the face,
   so the heart reflects
   one person to another.
²⁰ The grave^k and the underworld^l
   are never satisfied;
   and people's eyes
   are never satisfied.
²¹ A crucible is for silver
   and a furnace for gold;
   so are people in the presence
   of someone who praises them.
²² Even if you grind fools in a mortar,
   even grinding them along
   with the grain,
   their folly won't be driven
   from them.
²³ Know your flock well;
   pay attention to your herds,
   ²⁴ for no treasure lasts forever,
   nor a crown
   generation after generation.
²⁵ When the grass goes away,
   new growth appears,

and the plants of the hills
   are gathered,
²⁶ then the lambs
   will provide your clothes,
   and the goats
   will be the price of your fields.
²⁷ There will be enough goat's milk
   for your food,
   for the food of your house,
   and to nourish your young women.

28

¹ The wicked run away even though
   no one pursues them,
   but the righteous
   are as confident as a lion.
² When a land rebels,
   there are many leaders;
   but a person with understanding
   brings order.
³ Poor people who oppress the needy
   are rain that washes away food.
⁴ Those who abandon Instruction
   praise the wicked,
   but those who follow Instruction
   battle them.
⁵ Evil people don't understand justice,
   but those who seek the LORD
   understand everything.
⁶ Better to be poor
   and walk in innocence
   than to be on crooked paths
   and wealthy.
⁷ Intelligent children
   follow Instruction,
   but those who befriend gluttons
   shame their parents.
⁸ Those who become rich
   through high interest rates
   gather money for those
   who are generous to the poor.
⁹ Those who turn their ears
   from hearing Instruction—
   even their prayers will be detested.

---

^k Heb Sheol ^l Heb Abaddon

¹⁰ Whoever misleads those
who do right onto an evil path
will fall into their own pit,
but the blameless
will inherit good things.
¹¹ Rich people think they are wise,
but an insightful poor person
sees through them.
¹² When the righteous rejoice,
there is great respect,
but people hide
when the wicked prosper.
¹³ Those who hide their sins
won't succeed,
but those who confess and
give them up will receive mercy.
¹⁴ Happy are those
who are continually fearful,
but those whose hearts are hard
fall into trouble.
¹⁵ A wicked ruler over the poor
is like a growling lion
or a prowling bear.
¹⁶ A prince without understanding
is a cruel oppressor,
but one who hates unjust gain
will live long.
¹⁷ If someone feels guilty about murder,
don't hold them back
from fleeing to the pit.
¹⁸ Those who walk in innocence
will be saved,
but those who go on twisted paths
will fall into the grave.
¹⁹ Those who work the land
will have plenty to eat,
but those with worthless pursuits
will have plenty of poverty.
²⁰ Reliable people
will have abundant blessings,
but those with get-rich-quick
schemes won't go unpunished.
²¹ Those who show favoritism
aren't good;

people do wrong
for a crust of bread.
²² The stingy try to get rich fast,
unaware that loss
will come to them.
²³ Those who correct someone will,
in the end, find more favor
than those with flattering tongues.
²⁴ Those who steal from their father
and mother,
and say, "It's not a crime,"
are friends of vandals.
²⁵ Greedy people stir up conflict,
but those who trust the LORD
become prosperous.
²⁶ Those who trust
in their own reasoning are fools,
but those who walk in wisdom
will be kept safe.
²⁷ Those who give to the poor
will lack nothing,
but those who turn a blind eye
will be greatly cursed.
²⁸ When the wicked rise up,
people hide,
but when they are destroyed,
the righteous multiply.

29 One who stays stubborn
after many corrections
will be suddenly broken,
beyond healing.
² When the righteous
become numerous,
the people rejoice,
but when the wicked dominate,
the people moan.
³ A man who loves wisdom
makes his father rejoice,
but one who spends time
with prostitutes destroys riches.
⁴ A king gives stability
to the land by justice,
but one who imposes heavy taxes
tears it down.

⁵ People who flatter their friends
spread out a net for their feet.
⁶ The wicked are snared
by their own sin;ᵐ
the righteous sing and rejoice.
⁷ The righteous know
the rights of the poor,
but the wicked don't understand.
⁸ Mockers set a city on fire,
but the wise turn back anger.
⁹ When the wise make a legal charge
against the foolish,
the fools shout, they laugh—
there is no calm.
¹⁰ Murderous people hate the innocent,
and they seek the lives
of the virtuous.
¹¹ Fools show all their anger,
but the wise hold it back.
¹² If a ruler listens to lies,
those who serve him will be wicked.
¹³ The poor and their oppressors
have a common bond—
the LORD gives light
to the eyes of both.
¹⁴ If a king judges the poor honestly,
his throne will be
established forever.
¹⁵ The rod and correction
lead to wisdom,
but children out of control
shame their mothers.
¹⁶ When the wicked become numerous,
so do crimes;
the righteous will see their downfall.
¹⁷ Instruct your children;
they will give you peace of mind
and bring delight into your life.
¹⁸ When there's no vision,
the people get out of control,
but whoever obeys instruction
is happy.

¹⁹ Servants aren't disciplined by words;
they might understand,
but they don't respond.
²⁰ Do you see people
who are quick to speak?
There is more hope for fools
than for them.
²¹ Pamper servants from a young age,
and later on there will be trouble.
²² Angry people stir up conflict;
hotheads cause much offense.
²³ Pride lays people low,
but those of humble spirit
gain honor.
²⁴ Those who share plunder
with thieves hate themselves;
even under oath, they don't testify.
²⁵ People are trapped
by their fear of others;
those who trust the LORD
are secure.
²⁶ Many seek access to the ruler,
but justice comes from the LORD.
²⁷ The unjust person is disgusting
to the righteous;
the straight path is disgusting
to the wicked.

Words of Agur

30 The words of Agur, Jakeh's son,
from Massa.
The man declares: I'm tired, God;
I'm tired, God, and I'm exhausted.
² Actually, I'm too stupid to be human,
a man without understanding.
³ I haven't learned wisdom,
nor do I have knowledge
of the holy one.

⁴ Who has gone up to heaven
and come down?
Who has gathered the wind
by the handful?

ᵐTg, Syr; MT *In the sin of an evil man is a snare*

Who has bound up the waters
in a garment?
Who has established all the ends
of the earth?
What is this person's name
and the name
of this person's child—
if you know it?

5 All God's words
are tried and true;
a shield for those
who take refuge in him.
6 Don't add to his words,
or he will correct you
and show you to be a liar.

7 Two things I ask of you;
don't keep them from me
before I die:
8 Fraud and lies—
keep far from me!
Don't give me
either poverty or wealth;
give me just the food I need.
9 Or I'll be full and deny you,
and say, "Who is the LORD?"
Or I'll be poor and steal,
and dishonor my God's name.

More sayings of the wise
10 Don't slander a servant to his master;
otherwise, the servant will curse you,
and you will be guilty.

11 There are those who curse
their father
and don't bless their mother.
12 There are those who think
they are clean,
but haven't washed off
their own excrement.

13 There are those—
how arrogant are their eyes;
how their eyebrows are raised!
14 There are those whose teeth
are swords;
their jaw is a butcher's knife,
ready to devour the needy
from the earth,
and the poor from humanity.

15 The leech has two daughters:
"Give, give!"
There are three things
that are never satisfied,
four that never say, "Enough!":
16 the grave[n] and a barren womb,
a land never filled with water,
and fire that doesn't say, "Enough!"

17 An eye that mocks a father
and rejects obedience to a mother,
may the ravens of the river valley
peck it out,
and the eagle's young eat it.

18 Three things are too wonderful
for me,
four that I can't figure out:
19 the way of an eagle in the sky,
the way of a snake on the rock,
the way of a ship
out on the open sea,
and the way of a man
with a young woman.

20 This is the way
of an adulterous woman:
she eats and wipes her mouth,
and she says,
"I've done nothing wrong!"

21 At three things the earth trembles,
at four it can't bear up:

[n]Heb Sheol

²² at a servant when he becomes king
and fools when they
are full of food;
²³ at a detested woman
when she gets married
and a female servant
when she replaces her mistress.

²⁴ Four things are among
the smallest on earth,
but they are extremely wise:
²⁵ Ants as creatures aren't strong,
but they store away their food
in the summer.
²⁶ Badgers as creatures
aren't powerful,
but they make their homes
in the rocks.
²⁷ Locusts don't have a king,
but they march together
in ranks.
²⁸ You can catch lizards in your hand,
but they are in kings' palaces.

²⁹ There are three things
that are excellent in their stride,
four that are excellent as they walk:
³⁰ a lion, a warrior among beasts,
which doesn't back down
at anything;
³¹ the strut of a rooster
or a male goat;
and a king with his army.

³² If you've been foolish and arrogant,
if you've been scheming,
put your hand to your mouth,
³³ because churning milk
makes curds,
squeezing the nose brings blood,
and stirring up anger
produces strife.

Words of King Lemuel

31 The words of King Lemuel
of Massa, which his mother
taught him:
² No, my son!
No, son of my womb!
No, son of my solemn promises!
³ Don't give your strength to women,
your ways to those
who wipe out kings.
⁴ It isn't for kings, Lemuel,
it isn't for kings to drink wine,
for rulers to craveᵒ strong drink.
⁵ Otherwise, they will drink
and forget the law,
and violate the rights of the needy.
⁶ Give strong drink
to those who are perishing
and wine to those
whose hearts are bitter.
⁷ Let them drink
and forget their poverty
and no longer remember their toil.
⁸ Speak out on behalf of the voiceless,
and for the rights of all
who are vulnerable.ᴾ
⁹ Speak out in order to judge
with righteousness
and to defend the needy
and the poor.

The competent wife

¹⁰ A competent wife,
how does one find her?
Her value is far above pearls.
¹¹ Her husband entrusts
his heart to her,
and with her
he will have all he needs.
¹² She brings him good and not trouble
all the days of her life.
¹³ She seeks out wool and flax;
she works joyfully with her hands.

ᵒOr where or or   ᴾOr all children who are passing away

¹⁴She is like a fleet
    of merchant ships,
    bringing food from a distance.
¹⁵She gets up while it is still night,
    providing food for her household,
    even some for her female servants.
¹⁶She surveys a field and acquires it;
    from her own resources,
    she plants a vineyard.
¹⁷She works energetically;
    her arms are powerful.
¹⁸She realizes that her trading
    is successful;
    she doesn't put out her lamp
    at night.
¹⁹She puts her hands to the spindle;
    her palms grasp the whorl.
²⁰She reaches out to the needy;
    she stretches out her hands
    to the poor.
²¹She doesn't fear for her household
    when it snows,
    because they are all dressed
    in warm�q clothes.
²²She makes bedspreads for herself;
    fine linen and purple
    are her clothing.

²³Her husband is known
    in the city gates
    when he sits with the elders
    of the land.
²⁴She makes garments and sells them;
    she supplies sashes to traders.
²⁵Strength and honor
    are her clothing;
    she is confident about the future.
²⁶Her mouth is full of wisdom;
    kindly teaching is on her tongue.
²⁷She is vigilant over the activities
    of her household;
    she doesn't eat
    the food of laziness.
²⁸Her children bless her;
    her husband praises her:
    ²⁹"Many women act competently,
    but you surpass them all!"
³⁰Charm is deceptive
    and beauty fleeting,
    but a woman who fears the LORD
    is to be praised.
³¹Let her share in the results
    of her work;
    let her deeds praise her
    in the city gates.

qLXX; MT *red*